D1413860

SIXTH EDITION

Measurement for Evaluation

IN Physical Education AND Exercise Science

Ted A. BAUMGARTNER University of Georgia

Andrew S. JACKSON University of Houston

Boston Burr Ridge, IL Dubuque, IA Madison, WI New York San Francisco St. Louis
Bangkok Bogotá Caracas Lisbon London Madrid
Mexico City Milan New Delhi Seoul Singapore Sydney Taipei Toronto

WCB/McGraw-Hill
A Division of The McGraw-Hill Companies

MEASUREMENT FOR EVALUATION IN PHYSICAL EDUCATION AND EXERCISE SCIENCE, SIXTH EDITION

This book is printed on acid-free paper.

3 4 5 6 7 8 9 0 QPF/QPF 9 3 2 1 0 9

ISBN 0-697-29484-6

Vice president and editorial director: *Kevin T. Kane*
Publisher: *Edward E. Bartell*
Executive editor: *Vicki Malinee*
Developmental editor: *Sarah Reed/Melissa Martin*
Senior marketing manager: *Pamela S. Cooper*
Senior project manager: *Kay J. Brimeyer*
Senior production supervisor: *Sandra Hahn*
Coordinator of freelance design: *Michelle D. Whitaker*
Supplement coordinator: *Rita Hingtgen*
Compositor: *Carlisle Communications Ltd.*
Typeface: *10/12 Times Roman*
Printer: *Quebecor Printing Book Group/Fairfield, PA*

Freelance interior designer: *Jeanne M. Rivera*
Freelance cover designer: *Christopher E. Reese*
Cover image: © *Steve Satushek/The Image Bank*

Library of Congress Cataloging-in-Publication Data

Baumgartner, Ted A.
Measurement for evaluation in physical education and exercise science / Ted A. Baumgartner, Andrew S. Jackson. — 6th ed.
p. cm.
Includes bibliographical references and index.
ISBN 0–697–29484–6
1. Physical fitness—Testing. 2. Physical education and training.
I. Jackson, Andrew S., 1936– . II. Title.
GV436.B33 1999
613.7—dc21 98-23747
CIP

www.mhhe.com

Brief Contents

PART 1 Introduction

PART 2 Quantitative Aspects of Measurement

PART 3 Performance Testing

PART 4 Cognitive and Affective Testing

Contents

Chapter 8
Evaluating Aerobic Fitness 240

Chapter 9
Evaluating Body Composition 279

Chapter 10
Evaluating Youth Fitness 321

Preface

In previous editions we responded to changes in the field by adding information for students seeking careers in areas other than teaching, expanding the application of microcomputers, and reorganizing the book. The result was a book that contained a solid foundation of the information needed by students in physical education or exercise science curriculums.

In preparing this sixth edition, the book was revised based on suggestions from successful professionals in the field and from our own expertise. We recognize that students using this text come from many backgrounds and with a great variety of interest areas (health, elementary or secondary physical education, fitness, adapted physical education, pre-physical therapy, athletic training, gerontology, exercise science, specialization areas, etc.). Sometimes we have roughly classified all students using the book as being in either physical education or exercise science. Thus, we have presented information that is important in most of the interest areas. Instructors should select from the information presented and supplement the book when necessary.

Changes to This Edition

Chapter 2, "The Use of Computers in Physical Education," from the fifth edition, has been deleted. Students taking this course noted that they are already very familiar with the information in this chapter. Information on computer applications that is still relevant to this text has been moved into appropriate chapters throughout the book.

Chapter 1, "Measurement and Evaluation in a Changing Society," has increased its focus on computer literacy for measurement and evaluation to include software, the World Wide Web, and computing power.

Chapter 2, "Statistical Tools in Evaluation," has been upgraded, with all computer analysis examples developed using the SPSS package of programs. Brief instructions for using the SPSS programs referenced are in the appendix.

Information on selecting a criterion score has been moved to Chapter 3, "Reliability and Objectivity," and its coverage expanded (more considerations are given for multiple trial data).

Chapter 5, "Evaluating Achievement," has been revised so that there is less emphasis on grading and more emphasis on setting evaluation standards. A section on authentic assessment has been added.

Chapter 6, "The Nature of Tests and Their Administration: With Applications to Individuals with Disabilities," includes new information on testing challenges for individuals with disabilities, selecting a method of performance measurement for individuals with disabilities, and more coverage for individuals in nonteaching roles.

Chapter 7, "Measuring Physical Abilities," includes new sections on back injuries in relation to the theory of basic abilities, pass-fail tests and continuously scored tests in relation to setting cut scores, absolute versus relative strength, male/female differences in absolute and relative strength, and the concept of strength testing and its link to rehabilitation (closed vs. open chain).

Chapter 8, "Evaluating Aerobic Fitness," includes a new discussion of the role of aerobic fitness in lifetime health, more information on nonexercise tests, and descriptions of new maximal distance run/walk tests (field tests) used to estimate aerobic fitness.

Chapter 9, "Evaluating Body Composition," includes a number of new graphs indicating the relationship between diseases/mortality and body composition.

Chapter 10, "Evaluating Youth Fitness," now includes a comparison of criterion-referenced standards and a historical view of youth fitness testing.

Chapter 11, "Aging and Adult Fitness," is an entirely new chapter with information devoted to our aging population. The chapter discusses evaluating adult fitness, the methods used to study fitness associated with aging, identifies the types of tests used to evaluate adult fitness, the general age-related decline in health-related fitness, and the computer programs available for use in adult fitness programs.

Chapter 12, "Evaluating Skill Achievement," has been shortened by removing old tests and tests seldom administered. The emphasis is now on developing tests.

Chapter 13, "Evaluating Knowledge," has been revised so that there is less emphasis on knowledge tests for teachers and more emphasis on knowledge testing for all people in physical education and exercise science. The section on questionnaires has been expanded.

Chapter 14, "Exercise Psychological Measurement" (new title), contains a new section on eating disorders that includes discussion of the nature of these diseases and of eating disorder scales.

Pedagogy

Key words. The key terms that are defined in every chapter are highlighted at the beginning of each chapter and boldfaced in the text. The definitions can also be found in the end-of-text glossary.

Objectives. The objectives at the opening of each chapter focus the students' attention on the key concepts that will be discussed in the chapter.

Formulas. Important formulas are now numbered throughout the text to provide easy and quick reference to those used frequently in the course and in students' professional lives.

Tables and figures. Many of the graphics have been updated in this edition to give students a visual representation of the concepts discussed in the text.

Summary. The end-of-chapter summaries provide a brief overview of what was discussed within the chapter.

Formative evaluation of objectives. This section at the close of each chapter helps to determine if the students have mastered the objectives set forth at the beginning of the chapter.

Additional learning activities. These activities provide students with a way to gain more experience with the concepts presented within the chapter.

Ancillaries

The sixth edition of *Measurement for Evaluation in Physical Education and Exercise Science* also features a solid ancillary package. Elements include:

1. *Instructor's Manual and Test Bank.* A complete Instructor's Manual features a course introduction, a list of changes to the new edition, a discussion of course format, and multiple-choice test questions for each chapter. This manual is free to adopters of the text.
2. *Computerized Test Bank.* Available to qualified adopters, a computerized test bank allows the instructor to select, edit, delete, or add questions, as well as construct and print tests and answer keys. It is available in IBM Windows or Macintosh formats.
3. *Student SPSS.* McGraw-Hill is very pleased to be able to offer this package with our text. This comprehensive statistics package can perform any of the procedures discussed in the text. Available with this book for a nominal fee is the CD-Rom version that is compatible with Windows 95 systems. More information on the specifics of this program is provided in the appendix. Feel free to contact your McGraw-Hill sales representative for further information regarding other versions of this software that may be available.

We have tried to present measurement in physical education and exercise science from a sound theoretical standpoint. We feel that physical educators and exercise scientists will be better able to apply the theory of measurement and evaluation if they first understand it. We hope that this book prepares students to cope with any problems of measurement and evaluation that they may encounter once they are on the job.

Acknowledgments

We would like to express our gratitude to the many people who reviewed previous editions of this book or manuscripts and offered excellent suggestions for improvements. They include professors Andrew Proctor, Stephen Langendorfer, Dale Mood, Antoinette Tiburzi, George McGlynn, Harry Duvall, Ronald Deitrick, Joy L. Hendrick, Emma S. Gibbons, Martin W. Johnson,

Lloyd L. Laubach, Marilyn A. Looney, Patricia Patterson, Robert Sonstroem, Alex Waigandt, and Charles W. Jackson.

In addition, we would like to extend a special thanks to the reviewers of this edition. Because of the extensive changes in the field of exercise science, these comments were especially useful. They are professors Kathleen M. Knutzen, Western Washington University; Mary Jo Campbell, University of New Mexico; Jane A. Beougher, Capital University; William G. Jennings, Saint Joseph College; James W. Coburn, California State University, Fullerton.

We would also like to thank Dr. Jessie Jones and Dr. Roberta Rikli from California State University, Fullerton for graciously sharing their pre-publication information of their LifeSpan project. We believe that their work will have a major impact on fitness testing of elderly.

Finally we would like to thank our wives for their patience and consideration during the preparation of the manuscript, as this always comes out of family time. Finally, we would like to express our thanks to former teachers, who contributed to our knowledge of measurement techniques, as well as to our former students, who forced us to bridge the gap between theory and practice.

T.A.B.
A.S.J.

To the Student

The major goal of this text is to help you apply the principles of measurement and evaluation to your job. Often evaluation is viewed as a necessary evil, not directly related to the real purpose of the job. This text was designed to help you learn how to use evaluation as an essential part of the total process.

We developed the text with two purposes in mind. First, we want to help you master the essential content, principles, and concepts needed to become an effective evaluator. We tried to provide the practical aspects, the "how" and the "why" of evaluation. We want this text to help you build a foundation based on theoretical concepts so that you can then apply these concepts in developing, using, and evaluating various tests.

Second, we designed the text to provide the practical skills and materials that you will need. We provide a wide assortment of tests, administrative instructions, and norms. We selected the tests, which provide the "how" of evaluation, either for their application to the job setting or for their value for teaching basic concepts discussed in the text.

A practical tool for you to use now and later is the computer. Practical computer applications are provided, by examples, with standard microcomputer programs. As mentioned in the preface, an excellent microcomputer program is available with the book (Student SPSS). Learn to use the computer and programs such as SPSS as a student while help is available, and it will be easier to use whatever computer support is available once you are on the job.

The approach we use in the text follows a teaching method that is basically an outgrowth of Benjamin Bloom's ideas on "mastery learning." The method stresses letting the student know what is to be learned, providing the material to accomplish the learning, and furnishing evaluation procedures to determine whether the learning has been achieved.

This approach, formative evaluation, is an essential feature of mastery learning. Psychologists maintain that feedback is one of the most important factors in learning. Formative evaluation is designed to provide that feedback. It enables you to diagnose weaknesses, and lets you know the content you have mastered, so that you can put more effort into problem areas.

Instructional objectives at the beginning of each chapter enable you to focus your attention on the concepts to be learned. The **text**—supplemented with class lectures, discussions, projects, and laboratory experiments—provides the information you need to help you achieve the objectives. The **evaluation of objectives** at the end of each chapter help you determine whether you have mastered the skills set forth.

The formative evaluation in this text offers two types of questions. The first, in **question/answer format,** is most appropriate for testing yourself on the statistics content. If you cannot calculate a statistic, you have not mastered the technique. The second type of question requires you to define, summarize, analyze, apply, or synthesize content. This is typical of an **essay-type** question, and is more appropriate for testing yourself on basic content, principles, and concepts.

A common complaint of students is that they dislike learning by rote. We hope that the techniques of instructional objectives and formative evaluation will help you to avoid that approach. The objectives and evaluation questions identify key points in a given chapter. Once you have read the chapter itself, you should be familiar with these points. Finally, we hope that by using this approach you will master important content rather than just isolated facts.

We are aware that each student studies differently. However, the following suggestions may help you achieve mastery learning:

1. Before reading a chapter, review the instructional objectives and formative evaluation questions for the chapter. This gives you an overview and directs your attention to the important content areas.
2. Read the chapter, underlining important content. Also underline material that you do not fully understand. After reading the entire chapter, return to the underlined parts to reinforce the important content and to try to grasp the material you do not fully understand.
3. Without referring to the text, answer the formative evaluation questions. After you have written your answers, go back to the material in the text and check your answers. Spend additional time on the questions that you did not answer correctly. If you do not feel comfortable with your answers to some questions, spend more time on these as well.
4. Practical learning activities are provided at the end of each chapter. Try them. We have found that these exercises help students gain further insight into the statistical or theoretical concepts being stressed. (Many of these suggested activities are enjoyable as well as helpful.)
5. When studying for summative exams, use the formative evaluation questions and your corrected answers as the basis for final review of the instructional objectives of each chapter. Examine the list of key words at the beginning of each chapter. They are a good second means for formative evaluation. If you find that you cannot think of a precise definition of a term, go back over the chapter until you find the term's definition.

We wish you good luck with your evaluating techniques.

T.A.B.
A.S.J.

PART ONE

1

Introduction

1

CHAPTER

Measurement and Evaluation in a Changing Society

Contents

Key Words

cardiovascular disease
coronary heart disease
criterion-referenced standard
database
digital
evaluation
floppy disk
formative evaluation
hard disk
health-related fitness
measurement
norm-referenced standard
norms
objective
personal computer (PC)
prevalence
random-access memory (RAM)
software
spreadsheet
subjective
summative evaluation

Objectives

The profession of physical education and exercise science is constantly changing. Graduates of physical education programs are becoming not only teachers and coaches but also exercise specialists, physical and occupational therapists, personal trainers, sport psychologists, and consultants. Some are even starting or entering private business. Many colleges and universities are expanding their degree programs to include sport management. The process of measurement and evaluation is an integral component of all these professional efforts.

While many factors influence kinesiology and physical education professional preparation programs, several contemporary social forces are especially salient. One major force pressuring our educational and public health institutions is demographic change. The American population is aging,[1] and the ethnic mix is changing. Our occupations are becoming more sedentary, and medical and public health officials have concluded that inactivity and obesity are major public health problems. Increasing numbers of elderly and minorities, combined with increasing numbers of obese and sedentary individuals, are adding pressure to health care systems. These forces have led to the development of public health programs that promote establishing and maintaining health through exercise and weight control. In September 1990, the U.S. Public Health Service published *Healthy People 2000: National Health Promotion and Disease Prevention Objectives,* and in 1996, the Surgeon General of the United States issued an important report on physical activity and health. This chapter reviews these historic public health initiatives and integrates them with K–12 physical education and adult fitness programming. These public health initiatives explain why many youth and adult programs have become health-related programs.

The final section of this chapter examines computer applications as they relate to measurement and evaluation. The dynamic nature of society and evolving computer technology are altering the type of measurement and evaluation skills needed by K–12 physical education teachers and exercise specialists. This chapter will help you understand the place of measurement and evaluation in our changing social and professional world.

After reading Chapter 1, you should be able to:

1. Define and differentiate between measurement and evaluation.
2. Define and differentiate between criterion- and norm-referenced standards.
3. Define and differentiate between formative and summative methods of evaluation.
4. Understand models of evaluation as they apply to teaching (K–12) and exercise science settings.
5. Describe the role of public health initiatives on physical education and exercise science.
6. Describe the influence of computer technology on our profession.

[1]A new chapter of this text, Chapter 11, has as its primary focus the evaluation of adult fitness, with emphasis on the elderly, the fastest growing segment of the American population.

Measurement and Evaluation

We tend to regard test results as a valid basis for decision making. They govern matters such as student promotions, college acceptances, and defining health-related levels of fitness. The terms *measurement* and *evaluation* are widely used, but often with little regard for their meanings. **Measurement** is the collection of information on which a decision is based; **evaluation** is the use of measurement in making decisions. This chapter clarifies these activities within the changing context of the fields of physical education, exercise science, and **health-related fitness** and introduces the procedures that have evolved to meet the challenges created by these dynamic fields.

Measurement and evaluation are interdependent concepts. Evaluation is a process that uses measurements, and the purpose of measurement is to collect information for evaluation. Tests are used to collect information. In the evaluation process, information is interpreted according to established standards so that decisions can be made. Clearly, the success of evaluation depends on the quality of the data collected. If test results are not consistent (or reliable) and truthful (or valid), accurate evaluation is impossible. The measurement process is the first step in evaluation; improved measurement leads to accurate evaluation. People are different. They vary in body size, shape, speed, strength, and many other respects. Measurement determines the degree to which an individual possesses a defined characteristic. It involves first defining the characteristic to be measured and then selecting the instrument with which to measure that characteristic (Ebel 1973). Stopwatches, tape measures, written tests, skill tests, attitude scales, skinfold calipers, treadmills, and cycle ergometers are common instruments used by physical education teachers and exercise specialists to obtain measurements.

Test scores vary between being **objective** or **subjective.** A test is objective when two or more people score the same test and assign similar scores. Tests that are most objective are those that have a defined scoring system and are administered by trained testers. A multiple-choice written test, a stopwatch, skinfold calipers, and an ECG heart rate tracing all have a defined scoring system. Testers need to be trained to secure objective measurements. For example, if percent body fat is to be measured by the skinfold method, the tester needs to be trained in the proper method of measuring a skinfold with a caliper. A subjective test lacks a standardized scoring system, which introduces a source of measurement error. We use objective measurements whenever possible because they are more reliable than subjective measurements.

Evaluation is a dynamic decision-making process that involves (1) collecting suitable data (measurement); (2) judging the value of these data according to some standard; and (3) making decisions based on these data. The function of evaluation is to facilitate rational decisions. For the teacher, this can be to facilitate student learning; for the exercise specialist, this could mean helping someone establish scientifically sound weight-reduction goals.

Functions of Measurement and Evaluation

Too often tests are administered with no definite purpose in mind. The ultimate purpose of testing is to enhance the decision-making process so that improvement can be made. There are six general purposes that facilitate this process. These are equally applicable to K–12 teachers and exercise specialists.

Placement. Tests can be used to place students in classes or groups according to their abilities. Adult fitness tests are used to determine current status so that an individualized program can be prescribed.

Diagnosis. Tests can be used to diagnose weaknesses. While placement usually involves the status of the individual relative to others, diagnosis is used to isolate specific deficiencies that make for low or an undesirable status. In K–12 settings, the test can identify areas where improvements need to be made. In an exercise or health setting, test results are used to diagnose a problem. For example, a treadmill stress test is a screening test for heart disease.

Evaluation of Achievement. The goal of testing is to determine whether important objectives have been reached. Placement, diagnosis, and the evaluation of achievement together form the basis of individualized instruction. In K–12 settings, this can be the achievement of instructional objectives. In exercise settings, this can be meeting important goals or showing progress—for example, documenting changes made during rehabilitation.

Prediction. Test results can be used to predict an individual's level of achievement in future activities. Prediction is like placement in that it seeks, from a measure of present status, information on future achievement; it differs from placement in helping students to select the activities they are most likely to master. For example, a student's performance in a physical education program may suggest a high probability of success in interschool athletics. An adult found to have a high aerobic capacity may decide to engage in road racing or become a triathlete.

Program Evaluation. Test results of participants can be used as one bit of evidence to evaluate the program. By plotting the results of a school district against national norms or comparing the yearly changes made within a school district, general comparisons can be made. Comparing the changes made in fitness between two tests provides evidence of the effectiveness of an adult fitness program.

Motivation. Test scores can be motivating. Achievement of important standards can encourage one to achieve higher levels of performance.

Formative and Summative Evaluation

Typically, **summative evaluation** involves the administration of tests at the conclusion of an instructional unit or training period. Motor-learning research shows that feedback is one of the most powerful variables in learning and testing during instruction, while formative evaluation enhances learning. Bloom and others (1971) postulate that to achieve mastery, evaluation needs to be continual.

Formative evaluation was developed initially for use in classroom settings. Formative evaluation begins during the early stages and continues throughout instruction. It involves dividing instruction into smaller units of learning and evaluating the student's mastery of these subunits during instruction. Its main purpose is "to determine the degree of mastery of a given learning task and to pinpoint the part of the task not mastered" (Bloom et al. 1971, p. 61). The strength of formative evaluation is that it provides feedback.

In contrast, summative evaluation takes place after instruction. It is used to decide whether broad objectives have been achieved. Summative evaluation is also useful in areas of learning when goals cannot be explicitly defined. The similarities and differences between formative and summative evaluation identified by Bloom are summarized in Table 1.1.

Table 1.1 Similarities and Differences between Formative and Summative Evaluation

	Formative	Summative
Purpose	Feedback to student and teacher on student progress throughout an instructional unit	Certification or grading at the end of a unit, semester, or course
Time	During instruction	At the end of a unit, semester, or course
Emphasis in Evaluation	Explicitly defined behaviors	Broader categories of behaviors or combinations of several specific behaviors
Standard	Criterion-referenced	Norm-referenced but can be criterion-referenced

Formative and summative evaluation and master learning were developed for use by classroom teachers (Bloom et al. 1971). However, the logic of the system can be applied to adult fitness programs. Helping adults set realistic fitness goals and using periodic testing to determine current status can be used to provide feedback that facilitates achievement. A key element of a successful self-supervised fitness program for NASA executives was periodic fitness testing (Owen et al. 1980). Measuring body weight daily is a behavioral strategy used for weight-reduction programs (deBakey et al. 1984). The fitness training program can become a major source of information for formative evaluation. To illustrate, increasing the intensity and/or duration of aerobic exercise is not only a sound instructional method of improving fitness, but it can provide formative evaluation. Chapter 11 contains an example of a computer-generated exercise prescription. Over the six-step program, exercise intensity has been increased from 65% to 75% of maximal aerobic capacity, and duration extended from 25 to 45 minutes. The increase in caloric expenditure can serve as a means of formative evaluation; it communicates to the participant that improvements in fitness are being achieved. A fitness test after training can serve as a summative evaluation.

You are encouraged to use the formative evaluation provided after each chapter. After you have read the chapter, attempt to answer the questions. If you cannot answer a question or if you feel unsure of your answer, this is an indication that you need additional work. The key element of formative evaluation is the feedback it provides; it communicates to the participant what yet needs to be achieved. For this course, your instructor probably will administer several major tests that will evaluate your ability to integrate and apply the readings. These would be an example of summative evaluation.

Standards for Evaluation

As previously explained, evaluation is the process of giving meaning to a measurement by judging it against some standard. The two most widely used types of standards are criterion- and norm-referenced. A **criterion-referenced standard** is used to find if someone has attained a specified level. A **norm-referenced standard** is used to judge an individual's performance in relation to the performances of other members of a well-defined group—for example, 11-year-old boys. Criterion-referenced standards are useful for setting performance standards for all, whereas norm-referenced standards are valuable for comparisons among individuals when the situation requires a degree of selectivity.

Criterion- and norm-referenced standards have application in a wide variety of settings. They are used extensively in K–12 educational settings, and there is a growing use of both standards in exercise and public health settings. Youth fitness tests tend to use norm-referenced standards, but the most popular health-related youth fitness test, the FITNESSGRAM® (see Chapter 10), uses sound criterion-referenced standards. The popular YMCA program (Golding, Meyers & Sinning 1989) presented in Chapter 11 evaluates adult fitness with norm-referenced standards, but there is a growing trend to use criterion-referenced standards. The criterion-referenced adult fitness standards are evolving from medical research (Blair et al. 1989, 1995) showing that the relationship between health and aerobic fitness is not linear. Once a level of aerobic fitness is achieved, becoming more fit has little influence on health. These criterion-referenced aerobic standards are provided in Chapter 10.

Norm-Referenced Standards

Norm-referenced standards are developed by testing a large number of people of a defined group. Descriptive statistics are then used to develop standards. A common norming method is to use percentile ranks. This type of norm reflects the percentage of the group that can be expected to score below a given value. For example, a 1-mile-run time of 11:31 for a boy 11 years of age is at the 25th percentile; only 25% ran slower, while 75% of the 11-year-old boys could be expected to exceed this time. Many fitness and motor performance tests with percentile rank norms for children in grades K–12 and adults are provided in this text.

Percentile rank norms are commonly used to evaluate health status. For example, percentile norms are used at the Cooper Medical Clinic, Dallas, Texas, to communicate adult fitness and health status to patients. Pollock and Wilmore (1990) have published the Cooper percentile rank norms. Procedures for developing percentile rank norms are fully presented in Chapter 2. Many examples of percentile rank norm-referenced standards are provided in the chapters that follow.

A major concern when using norm-referenced standards is the characteristics of the group on which the standards were developed. The **norm** does not always translate to the desirable. This can be illustrated by examining blood cholesterol norms from the Cooper Clinic (Pollock & Wilmore 1990). The average cholesterol of men ages 40–49 is 214 mg/dl, but this average is not considered a desirable level. A serum cholesterol of less than 200 mg/dl is considered a desirable level for health. The average of the Cooper norms is typical of the general American population, and this elevated average can be traced to a diet high in calories from fats and cholesterol-rich foods. In contrast, blood cholesterol values are much lower in vegetarians, who consume less fat and cholesterol. In this instance, average is not desirable because it has been shown that there is a powerful relationship between dietary high-fat, high-cholesterol animal products and risk of coronary heart disease mortality (Anderson, Castelli & Levy 1987; Castelli 1977; Wood et al. 1988).

When making norm-referenced evaluations, a useful method is to consider the norms developed on the groups being evaluated as well as other relevant groups. As an example, adult body composition standards are presented in Chapter 9. These were developed by examining normative data of adults and data published on many other groups including defined athletic groups.

Criterion-Referenced Standards

A criterion-referenced standard is a predetermined standard of performance that shows the individual has achieved a desired level of performance. Unlike with norm-referenced standards, the performance of the individual is not compared with that of other individuals, but rather just against the standard.

Many authors use the term "criterion-referenced" test, suggesting that the difference is not just with the standard, but also with the method used to develop the test (Glaser & Nitko 1971; Safrit 1989). Glaser and Nitko define a criterion-referenced test as one developed to provide measurements that are directly interpretable in terms of explicit performance standards, that is, criterion-referenced. While it is true that some tests used in education were constructed to be criterion-referenced tests, the more common practice is to apply a criterion-referenced standard to a norm-referenced test. For example, the mile run is a common item of a youth fitness test. The mile run previously was norm-referenced, but now, in the FITNESSGRAM® test (Cooper Institute 1992), it is criterion-referenced. In this instance, the test itself has not changed, only the type of standard used to evaluate youth aerobic fitness. All the health-related youth fitness tests (Chapter 10) use criterion-referenced standards.

Determining Accuracy of Criterion-Referenced Standards. Unlike a norm-referenced standard, which uses a continuous variable, a criterion-referenced standard is a dichotomy. Terms such as pass-fail, mastery-nonmastery, or positive-negative are used to describe the dichotomy. The validity of the criterion-referenced standard is examined by using a 2 × 2 contingency table. The accuracy of the criterion-referenced standard is analyzed by comparing the criterion-referenced standard and a criterion that represents the person's true state. This creates four possible options, which are illustrated in Figure 1.1.

A common method of determining the accuracy of a criterion-referenced test by estimating its reliability and validity is provided in Chapters 2 and 3 of this text. For a more complete discussion, see Safrit (1989) and Looney (1989). A method more

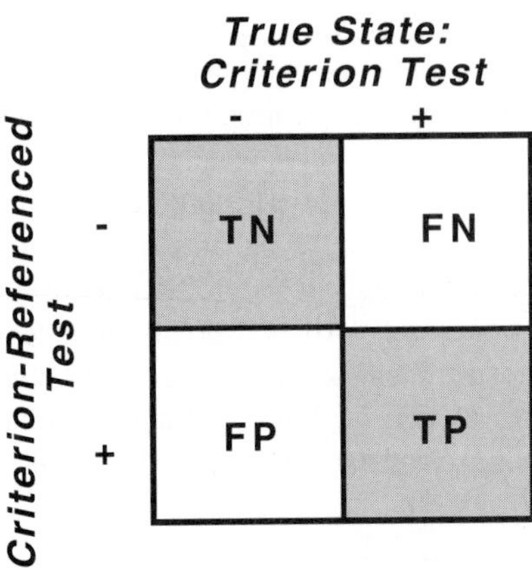

TN - True Negative -
The criterion-referenced test correctly indicates the failure to reach the criterion.

TP - True Positive -
The criterion-referenced test correctly indicates reaching the criterion.

FN - False Negative -
The criterion-referenced test incorrectly indicates the failure to reach the criterion.

FP - False Positive -
The criterion-referenced test incorrectly indicates reaching the criterion.

Figure 1.1
A 2 × 2 table is used to determine the accuracy of a criterion-referenced test. The criterion-referenced test can be wrong in two ways—false-negative and a false-positive evaluation. (Source: CSI Software Company, Houston, TX. Reprinted by permission.)

commonly used in exercise science and public health is to compute test sensitivity and specificity. Using the cells of the 2 × 2 table, sensitivity and specificity are computed by:

Sensitivity **(EQ 1.1)**

$$\text{Sensitivity} = \left(\frac{\text{TP}}{\text{TP} + \text{FN}}\right) \times 100$$

Specificity **(EQ 1.2)**

$$\text{Specificty} = \left(\frac{\text{TN}}{\text{FP} + \text{TN}}\right) \times 100$$

The sensitivity of a test is the proportion of true positive tests found by the criterion-referenced tests. To illustrate, if sensitivity were 80%, this would mean that the criterion-referenced test has the capacity to correctly identify the positive condition 80% of the time. Sensitivity is the probability that a criterion-referenced test will find a positive condition when it exists in the criterion test.

The specificity of a test is the proportion of true negative tests found by the criterion-referenced tests. For example, if the specificity of 2 test is found to be 85%, this means that a negative condition found by the criterion-referenced test will be correct 85% of the time. Specificity is the probability that the criterion-referenced test will correctly identify a negative condition when it exists.

Limitations of Criterion-Referenced Standards. A common and serious limitation of the criterion-referenced approach is that it is often not possible to find a criterion that explicitly defines mastery. Assume, for example, that a physical education teacher wants a criterion for mastering volleyball skills. Tests of mastery of complex motor skills are typically not readily available and the criterion is then arbitrarily set. There are, however, situations where criterion-referenced standards can be easily set. For example, skill activities such as beginning swimming and tumbling lend themselves to the criterion-referenced approach. The successful execution of these defined skills can be clearly determined and judged.

The lack of availability of a suitable criterion is an obvious problem, but a second major problem typically not recognized by educators is that the accuracy of a criterion-referenced test will vary with the population being tested. According to Bayes theorem, the accuracy of a criterion-referenced decision varies with the proportion of the population that exceeds the criterion (Snedecor & Cochran 1967). This problem has been studied extensively with medical tests and can be illustrated by examining the accuracy of an exercise stress test.

A stress test is an exercise test that examines the changes in the electrical activity of the heart from rest to exercise. Explicit criteria have been established (ACSM 1991; Ellestad 1980) to define a positive stress test—for example, presence of heart disease. The true coronary disease state is defined by the cardiac catheterization test, which involves passing a catheter into the coronary artery and then injecting dye into the artery. The flow of the dye is traced, with heart disease being defined as a coronary blood flow blockage of more than 70%. Since the catheterization test is dangerous, the exercise stress test is used first.

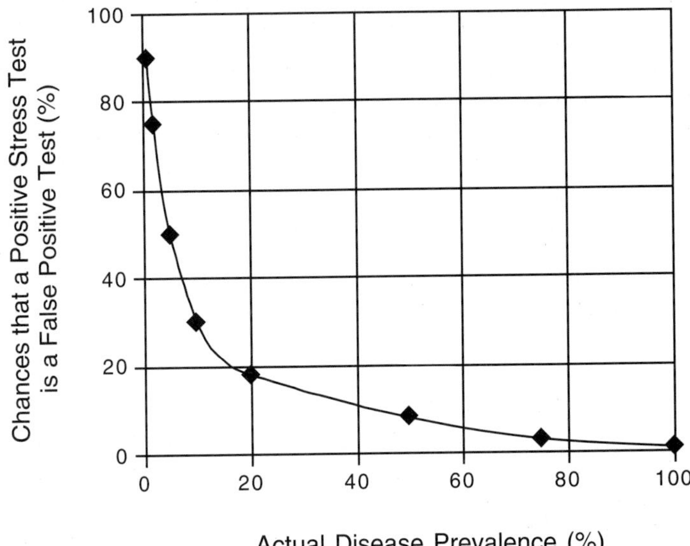

Figure 1.2
The accuracy of an exercise stress test increases as the disease prevalence increases in the population being tested. When the disease prevalence is very low, the chances are very high that a positive criterion-referenced test is a false-positive test, but if the disease prevalence is very high, a positive criterion-referenced test is likely to be a true positive test. (Graph developed from data published by Vecchio 1986). (Source: CSI Software Company, Houston, TX. Reprinted by permission.)

Researchers have discovered that the accuracy of the exercise stress test varies with disease prevalence in the group studied—that is, the percentage of patients who truly have coronary artery disease (Vecchio 1986). The problem is with false-positive tests: the stress test shows the person has heart disease, but the cardiac catheterization test shows the person is healthy. Vecchio reported that when the disease **prevalence** of the population was only 1%, nearly 85% of the positive stress tests were false-positive, whereas if the disease prevalence was high (75%), less than 2% of the tests were false-positive tests. This change in accuracy is illustrated in Figure 1.2.

The problem in accuracy difference of criterion-referenced tests has direct application to educational settings and American society in general. If the group being tested has a low percentage of individuals who truly exceed the criterion, a high proportion of the obtained positive tests will be false-positive. In an educational setting, many who have been judged to pass the criterion really did not. In other situations, the consequences of criterion-referenced decisions can be more serious. During the 1980s, some called for mass testing for drug usage and AIDS. Public health experts have rightfully challenged this approach. Since the prevalence of AIDS and drug usage in the general population is very low, the chances are high that a positive test would be false-positive. The human consequences of being labeled a drug user or having AIDS would be tragic.

Examples in Developing Health-Related Criterion-Referenced Standards

The health-related youth fitness tests (see Chapter 10) provide criterion-referenced standards, but the validity of the standards has not been determined because a criterion of true health-related fitness is presently not available. Then how were these standards developed? What may be most important in the development of criterion-referenced standards is the logic and data used to develop these standards. The Institute for Aerobics

Research, which is part of the Cooper Clinic in Dallas, Texas, published and administers the FITNESSGRAM® health-related youth fitness test and includes criterion-referenced norms (Cooper Institute 1992). Provided next is the logic and data used to establish the standards for the aerobic and body composition tests.

Aerobic Test. The aerobic test for FITNESSGRAM® is the 1-mile-run test. Different standards (see Chapter 10) were defined for boys and girls for different ages. The factors considered to establish the criterion-referenced standards were:

1. Published distance run norms show performance times vary by age.
2. Gender norms are needed because of male-female differences in $\dot{V}O_2$ Max. These differences can be traced to male-female differences in blood hemoglobin, body composition, and rates of growth and development.
3. Published data (Blair et al. 1989, 1995) with adults showed that low aerobic fitness increases the risk of all-cause mortality. Chapter 8 provides a discussion of these data.
4. Data (Buskirk & Hodgson 1987) clearly show that aerobic fitness declines with age, but the rate of decline is related to one's life-style. Recent data (Jackson et al. 1995, 1996) showed that rates of decline can be expected for different levels of physical activity and body composition. Chapter 11 provides a discussion of these trends.
5. Standard equations are available to convert running speed into level of $\dot{V}O_2$ Max (Cureton et al. 1995). These equations were used to convert 1-mile-run performance into $\dot{V}O_2$ Max estimates.

The FITNESSGRAM® criterion-referenced standards were derived by: (1) using the run performance $\dot{V}O_2$ Max estimates; (2) considering the expected loss in $\dot{V}O_2$ Max due to aging; and (3) considering the health promotion standards reported by Blair and associates (Blair et al. 1989). Cureton and Warren (1990) provide a more detailed analysis of this process.

Chapter 10 gives FITNESSGRAM® standards. Boys and girls that meet the FITNESSGRAM® aerobic fitness standard have a good chance of maintaining a $\dot{V}O_2$ Max at a healthy level if they control their weight and remain reasonably active during adulthood.

Body Composition. The FITNESSGRAM® uses two methods to evaluate body composition of children or youth. The preferred method involves estimating percent body fat from the sum of triceps and calf skinfolds. The second and easier method is with body mass index, or BMI.

1. Research has repeatedly shown that skinfolds and BMI are a valid index of body composition determined by the underwater weighing method (see Chapter 9). This is true for males and females, youths and adults.
2. The distributions of skinfolds and percent body fat of boys and girls differ.
3. Many Americans, especially young women, become overly concerned about being thin. Extreme thinness can cause health problems such as eating disorders (see Chapter 14) and can even be fatal.

4. The body composition distributions of both boys and girls are positively skewed (see Chapter 2 for a discussion on skewness), which suggests that a small defined proportion are seriously overweight.
5. The mortality rates associated with body weight for a given height are U-shaped (see Chapter 9). These data show that mortality is associated with being either very thin or very much overweight, but a somewhat wide range of normalcy exists between these two extremes.

The public health data, skewed skinfold fat distribution, and U-shaped weight and mortality relationship were used to define the criterion-referenced standard. The defined FITNESSGRAM® standards are consistent with public health BMI definitions of overweight (USDHHS 1990). Lohman (1992) provides an authoritative discussion of the methods to consider when defining obesity and overweight standards for children and adolescents.

Models of Evaluation

While the professional environments of a K–12 physical education teacher and an exercise specialist are very different, the evaluation processes used are quite similar. Illustrated next are evaluation models commonly used in K–12 educational and adult fitness settings. The main difference between the two models is test selection.

Educational Model

A primary purpose of teaching is to produce a measurable change in behavior. Figure 1.3 is an evaluation model appropriate for use in K–12 educational settings. It shows the evaluation process showing the relationship of objective, instructional, and testing. This dynamic model integrates measurement and evaluation with the instructional process. Each component of the model is briefly discussed next.

Objective. Preparation of the objective is the first step in the evaluation process because objectives determine what we will seek to achieve. The objective gives direction to instruction and defines what behaviors we want to change.

Pretest. With some type of pretest, we can answer three questions: (1) How much has already been learned? (2) What are the individual's current status and capabilities? (3) What type of activity should be prescribed to help achieve the objectives? Pretesting does not necessarily involve administering the same test that will be given after instruction; it can include any form of measurement that helps to answer these questions. For example, observing students swim a width of the pool can be an effective pretest.

Instruction. Sound instructional methods are needed to achieve the agreed-on objectives. Different instructional procedures may be needed to meet students' individual needs.

Measurement. This involves the selection or development of a test to gauge the achievement of the objectives. It is crucial that the test be designed to measure the behavior specified in the objectives. The objectives can be cognitive, affective, psychomotor, or fitness. These general types of tests are provided in this text. The key

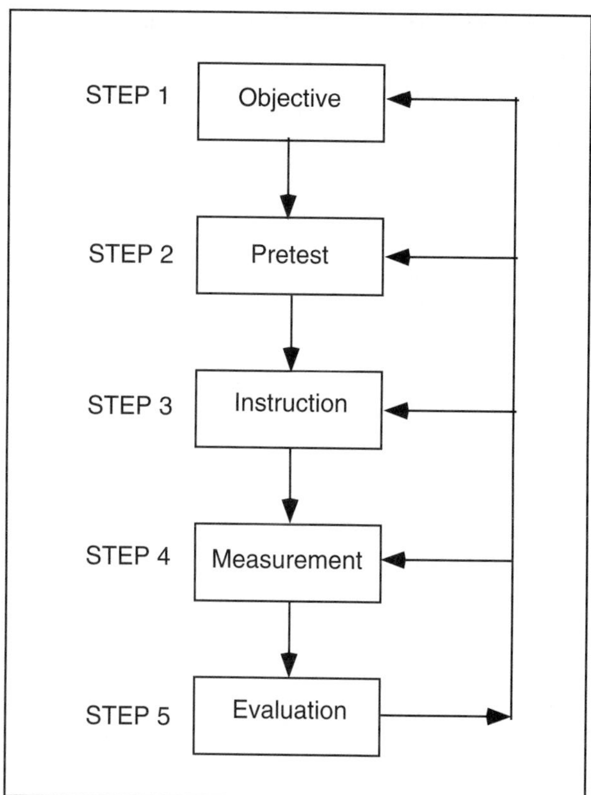

Figure 1.3
A systematic model of evaluation suitable for K–12 educational settings.

element is to select or develop a test that measures the objective. Often, teachers will need to develop their own tests because standardized tests are not consistent with instructional objectives. Content validity (see Chapter 4) is achieved when the test is congruent with the instructional objective. This is a common method used to establish test validity in educational settings.

Evaluation. Once the instructional phase has been completed and achievement has been measured, test results are judged (i.e., evaluated) to find whether the desired changes achieved the stated objective.

What happens if students do not achieve the desired objective? Figure 1.3 shows a feedback loop from evaluation back to each component of the model. Failure to achieve the stated objective may be due to any segment of the model. First, it may be discovered that the objectives are not appropriate and may need to be altered. The instruction may not have been suitable for the group, or the selected test may not have been appropriate for the instruction. The educational evaluation model is dynamic. The evaluation model provides information needed to alter any aspect of the educational process.

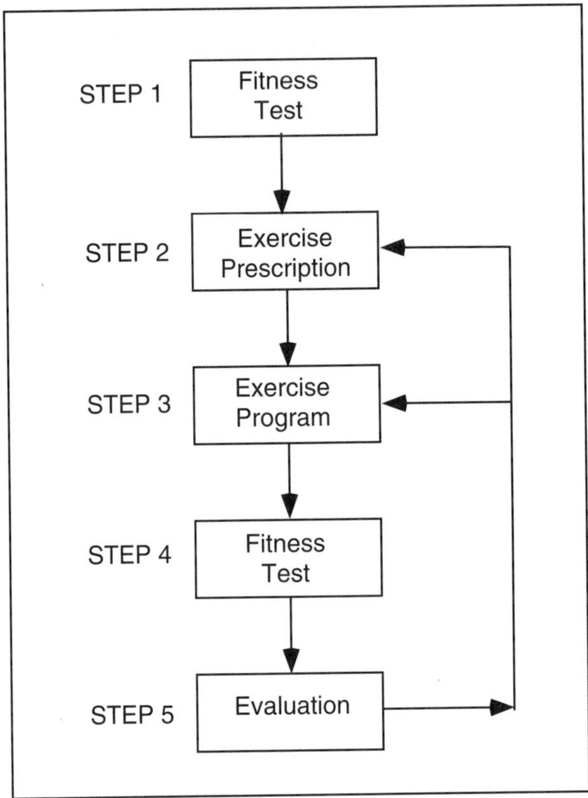

Figure 1.4
Evaluation model applied to adult fitness. (Source: CSI Software Company, Houston, TX. Reprinted by permission.)

Adult Fitness Evaluation Model

Similar to the teacher, the common goal of the exercise specialist is to produce changes in fitness. This may be in many different settings such as hospital, physical therapy clinic, fitness center, or personal trainer working with a client. Figure 1.4 shows how evaluation works in exercise settings.

Fitness Test. The first step in the development of an individualized fitness program is a fitness test. This may consist of more than one component. For some, medical clearance may be needed before the person can start a fitness program. The American College of Sports Medicine has published guidelines (ACSM 1991). Once a person is cleared to engage in an exercise program, he or she is given a fitness assessment. Chapters 7–9 provide comprehensive coverage of adult fitness tests.

Exercise Prescription. Once the person's fitness is known, the exercise prescription is developed. The purpose of the exercise prescription is to define the individual's fitness needs and develop the exercise parameters that are consistent with scientific research (ACSM 1990; ACSM 1991). For example, the goal may be to exercise aerobically at 70% of $\dot{V}O_2$ Max. In order to prescribe this level of aerobic exercise, the person's $\dot{V}O_2$ Max would need to be known. Chapter 11 provides a computer-generated example of this type of exercise prescription.

Exercise Program. Once the exercise parameters are known, the next step is to develop the person's exercise program. This is based on the initial fitness assessment, exercise prescription, and interests and goals of the person. A program for weight loss would be different from one designed to rehabilitate a knee or back.

Fitness Test. Once the program has been completed, a second fitness assessment is administered. The tests used will likely be the same as those used for the initial fitness assessment.

Evaluation. Once the training program has been completed and the fitness parameters of interest have been measured, test results are judged (i.e., evaluated) to find whether the desired changes have been made. Either norm- or criterion-referenced standards can be used to evaluate performance.

Like the educational model, the fitness evaluation model is dynamic. The model shows a loop from evaluation back to exercise prescription. Once changes in fitness are made, the exercise prescription parameters also change. To illustrate: a common guideline for aerobic exercise is a 70% of maximum aerobic capacity, or $\dot{V}O_2$ Max (ACSM 1991; Jackson & Ross 1997). If the initial exercise program increased the person's aerobic capacity, new exercise prescriptions would need to be prepared to maintain a suitable exercise intensity. Chapter 11 contains a computer-generated fitness assessment and exercise prescription that is consistent with this evaluation model.

Public Health Initiatives

Public health and medical scientists now agree that sedentary life-style and obesity are major public health problems. This is true not only for adults but also for youth. In 1992, the American Heart Association issued a medical and scientific position statement on exercise for health promotion (Fletcher et al. 1992). In September 1990, the U.S. Public Health Service published *Healthy People 2000: National Health Promotion and Disease Prevention Objectives* (USDHHS 1990). In 1996, the Surgeon General of the United States issued its historic report on physical activity and health (USDHHS 1996).

There are two basic approaches to health promotion. The first attempts to change the behavior of the individual. The second targets a group. The public health approach is designed to change the behavior of the group. This, for example, has been used to alter tobacco use. Smoking cessation programs experience little success in changing the behavior of smokers, but public health programs have been highly successful in lowering the number of people who become smokers. A public health approach has the greatest possible impact when the prevalence is high. The prevalence of sedentary lifestyle is high for both youth and adults. Provided next are overviews of two major public health initiatives: *Physical Activity and Health: A Report of the Surgeon General;* and the *Healthy People 2000: National Health Promotion and Disease Prevention Objectives.*

As these reports show, public health professionals have targeted K–12 physical education and adult fitness programs as target groups for health promotion.

Surgeon General's Report—Physical Activity and Health

Throughout history people have believed that physical activity is beneficial, but it was not until the 1950s that scientific evidence began to accumulate confirming this belief. Many public health reports have documented that sedentary life-style and obesity are major health problems for adults. Regular physical activity and exercise are critical elements of health promotion for older adults. Increased physical activity is associated with a reduced incidence of coronary heart disease, hypertension, noninsulin-dependent diabetes mellitus, colon cancer, depression, and anxiety. These are diseases prominent in older adult populations (Caspersen 1989). Much of adulthood obesity and physical inactivity has its roots in childhood. Unfortunately, youth fitness data show that children are becoming fatter and less aerobically fit (Morrow et al. 1984; NCYFS 1985), and less active (USDHHS 1996).

Physical activity is a complex behavior and its relationship with health is multifaceted. The American Heart Association in its Position Statement on exercise concludes that regular aerobic physical activity increases exercise capacity and plays a role in both primary and secondary prevention of **cardiovascular disease** (Fletcher et al. 1992). In 1996 The Surgeon General of the United States published the report *Physical Activity and Health* (USDHHS 1996). The report was written by leading medical, public health, and exercise scientists. The major purpose of the report was to summarize the existing literature on the role of physical activity in preventing disease and on the status of interventions to increase physical activity. This review led to eight major conclusions (USDHHS 1996, p. 4). These conclusions are given next.

1. People of all ages, both male and female, benefit from regular physical activity.
2. Significant health benefits can be obtained by a moderate amount of physical activity . . . on most, if not all, days of the week. Through a modest increase in daily activity, most Americans can improve their health and quality of life.
3. Additional health benefits can be gained through greater amounts of physical activity. People who can maintain a regular regimen of activity that is of longer duration or of more vigorous intensity are likely to derive greater benefit.
4. Physical activity reduces the risk of premature mortality in general, and of coronary heart disease, hypertension, colon cancer, and diabetes mellitus in particular. Physical activity also improves mental health and is important for the health of muscles, bones, and joints.
5. More than 60 percent of American adults are not regularly physically active. In fact, 25 percent of all adults are not active at all.
6. Nearly half of American youths 12–21 years of age are not vigorously active on a regular basis. Moreover, physical activity declines dramatically during adolescence.
7. Daily enrollment in physical education classes has declined among high school students from 42 percent in 1991 to 25 percent in 1995.
8. Research on understanding and promoting physical activity is at an early stage, but some interventions to promote physical activity through schools, worksites, and health care settings have been evaluated and found to be successful.

The publication of the Surgeon General's report gives a clear signal that sedentary life-style is a major health risk. Provided next is brief discussion of selected public health studies that helped establish that sedentary life-style is a major health risk. Provided first are studies that showed occupational physical activity was related to cardiovascular disease, the leading cause of death of Americans. Finally, the classic Harvard Alumni studies are briefly reviewed. They show the public health impact of a physically active life-style.

Occupation and Coronary Heart Disease. In the 1950s, medical scientists started to suspect that leading a sedentary life increases the risk of heart disease. The first approach used to study exercise and health was to compare sedentary individuals with those who were physically active. This is a common approach used in physiology, where many studies compare physically active athletes to nonathlete controls. One of the first methods used to study exercise and health was to study occupational groups that varied in physical activity. The approach was to compare heart disease rates of workers who held physically active and less active jobs. The general conclusion of these studies was that individuals who had the most physically demanding jobs suffered fewer fatal heart attacks than their sedentary counterparts. For example, conductors who walked up and down the stairs of double-decker buses in London had fewer heart attacks than the more sedentary bus drivers. In the United States, postal workers who walked and delivered the mail were found to have a lower incidence of heart disease than those who just stood and sorted it.

One of the classical studies of the role of occupational physical activity on heart disease was conducted by medical scientists from the University of Minnesota (Taylor et al. 1962). They studied more than 191,000 American railroad workers. Because of union rules and benefits, railroad workers had excellent medical records, which provided the data for the study. In addition, union rules discourage shifting from one occupation class to another. A 55-year-old person with 20 years of service was likely to have spent all 20 years at the same job.

The occupational groups studied were: (1) clerks, (2) switchmen, and (3) section men. The clerks represented men in jobs requiring little physical activity, while the work of the section men was the most physically demanding, and the work demands of the switchmen were moderate. Figure 1.5 presents the death rates ascribed to **coronary heart disease** for the age groups studied. The trends show the well-established influence of age on heart disease: older workers had a higher incidence of heart disease than younger workers. The data also showed that for each age group, the most physically active workers (i.e., section men) had the lowest heart disease rate, while the least physically active (clerks) had the highest rates. The switchmen were between the two extremes. These data suggested that exercise reduced the risk of heart disease.

The accepted method of quantifying physical activity is by caloric expenditure (ACSM 1991; Ross & Jackson 1990). Paffenbarger and associates (1977) studied the role of caloric expenditure on fatal heart attacks of San Francisco longshoremen. This was an ideal group to study because most workers stayed in the same job throughout their working lives, and the amount of energy expended to perform a job could be determined. The study included a 22-year history of more than 3,500 longshoremen. Workers were divided into three general categories based on the energy expenditure of their jobs. The job categories were:

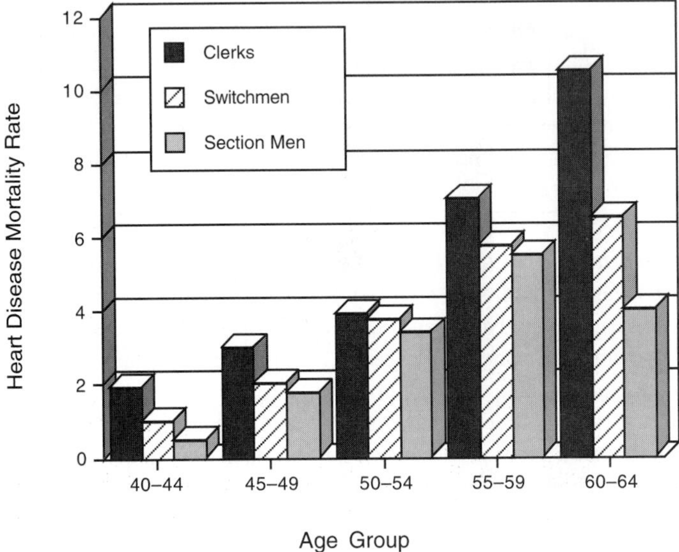

Figure 1.5
The relation between the specific job of railroad workers and death from heart disease. The heart disease death rate was related to the physical activity required by the occupation type. The clerks were most sedentary while the jobs of the section men were the most physically demanding. (Source: Jackson and Ross, R. M. *Understanding Exercise for Health and Fitness*, 1997. Reprinted by permission.)

- High—5.0 to 7.5 kilocalories per minute
- Intermediate—2.4 to 5.0 kilocalories per minute
- Light—1.5 to 2.0 kilocalories per minute

Figure 1.6 shows the fatal heart attack rates for major risk factors contrasted with the high- and low-energy output work groups. The data showed that for each of the heart disease risk factors, the longshoremen who expended the highest level of energy had the lowest rate of fatal heart attacks. Most impressive was the difference found between those active and inactive workers who had a history of diagnosed heart disease. The heart attack rate of the sedentary workers with a history of heart disease was about double the rate found for the physically active workers with previous heart problems. These data showed that it was not just occupation but energy expenditure that provided a margin of protection for these longshoremen.

The effect of caloric expenditure on heart disease was also documented in a study designed to examine the effects of nutrition on heart disease (Gordon et al. 1981). The diets of more than 16,000 men from three different populations were studied and related to coronary heart disease risk. To the surprise of the investigators, men who had a greater total caloric intake, or caloric intake per kilogram of body weight were less likely to develop coronary heart disease. Yes, that is correct: those who ate more had less heart disease. How can this be? These surprising results led the investigators to conclude that the inverse relation between caloric intake and coronary heart disease was due to differences in physical activity. It is well established that physically active individuals consume more calories than those who are sedentary. The dietary measure of caloric consumption was an index of the person's level of physical activity.

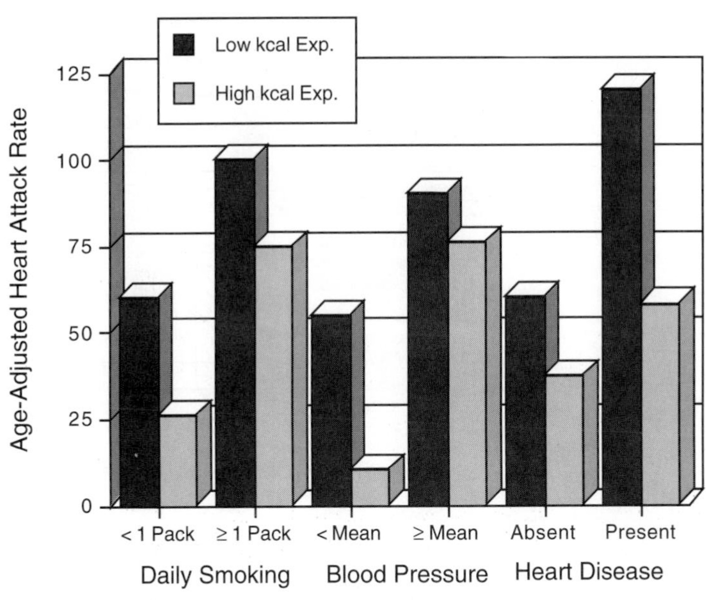

Figure 1.6
The number of fatal heart attacks suffered by San Francisco longshoremen contrasted by physical activity level and other known heart disease risk factors. These data show that for each risk factor, the high caloric expenditure jobs provided a margin of protection, and illustrate that low energy expenditure was an independent risk factor of heart disease. (Graph developed from data published by Paffenbarger, et al. 1977) (Source: CSI Software Company, Houston, TX. Reprinted by permission.)

Harvard Alumni Studies. The Harvard Alumni studies were surveys of the health and physical activity of nearly 17,000 Harvard alumni. Questionnaire data were used to quantify exercise expenditure in terms of caloric expenditure. The forms of physical activity included various types of sports, stair climbing, and walking. The researchers showed that caloric expenditure was related to the heart attack rate (Paffenbarger et al. 1984) and all-cause mortality (Paffenbarger et al. 1986).

Harvard alumni who consistently exercised during their lifetimes had lower heart attack and mortality rates than their sedentary classmates. Walking regularly, climbing stairs, and playing either light or vigorous sports provided a margin of health benefits. The total amount of energy expended through all forms of exercise was most highly related to heart disease and mortality rates. As total caloric expenditure increased, heart disease and mortality rates moved progressively lower. The highest rates were with alumni who expended less than 500 kilocalories per week. The heart disease and mortality rates dropped steadily with a caloric expenditure of about 2,000 kilocalories per week and then leveled off. Being a college athlete did not reduce risk unless the ex-athlete remained physically active after leaving college. The alumni at highest risk of a heart attack were those former athletes who led a post-college sedentary life-style (Paffenbarger et al. 1984).

The key conclusion of the Harvard Alumni studies was that physical activity was a major determinant of public health. This was examined by calculating what public health researchers call community-attributable risk, an estimate of the

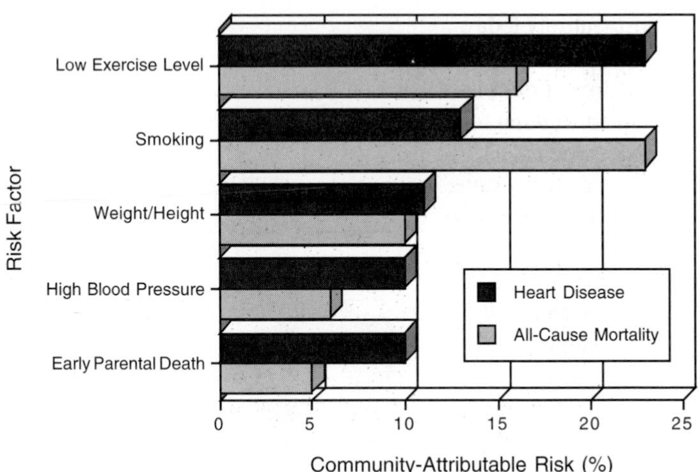

Figure 1.7
The community attributable risks of first heart attack and all-cause mortality of Harvard alumni. The risk estimates the percentage reduction in heart attacks and deaths that could be expected in the total group if the adverse characteristic was not present. Elimination of sedentary life-style and smoking would provide the greatest improvement of public health of Harvard alumni. (Graph published from published data Paffenbarger, Wing, and Hyde 1978; Paffenbarger et al. 1984). (Source: CSI Software Company, Houston, TX. Reprinted by permission.)

potential reduction of heart attacks in the population if the risk factor was not present. This calculation considers the prevalence of the risk factor in the population. Prevalence in this context refers to the percentage of people in the group who have the risk factor. The higher the prevalence, the greater the potential improvement in public health.

Figure 1.7 presents the community-attributable risk estimates for all the risk factors considered in the Harvard Alumni studies. Provided are community-attributable risk estimates for first heart attack and all-cause mortality. Eliminating sedentary life-style has the greatest potential public health effect for preventing a heart attack. If all alumni had been physically active, the heart attack rate of the Harvard Alumni could be expected to be reduced by nearly 25%. This effect is nearly twice as high as the effect of any other risk factor including family history.

Figure 1.7 also lists the community-attributable risk estimates for all-cause mortality. Elimination of smoking would have the greatest impact on the health of the alumni. Smoking is not only a primary risk factor of heart disease, but also the major cause of lung disease. By eliminating smoking, nearly 25% of the deaths could be prevented. The next most important adverse characteristic was sedentary life-style: about 16% fewer deaths would be expected if all alumni were physically active. Since these estimates are additive, the death rate could be cut by nearly 40% if all alumni were physically active nonsmokers. Of least importance was early parental death, which was defined by the death of one or both parents before the age of 65. While the importance of genetics is well understood, these data demonstrate the importance of life-style. Genetics cannot be changed, but life-style can.

Tobacco use, sedentary life-style, and obesity are widely prevalent health problems. Tobacco use is the most important single preventable cause of death of Americans. A conclusion made by public health scientists is that altering the American diet and increasing physical activity could have the same impact on public health as the elimination of tobacco use. These scientists concluded that "If tobacco use in this country stopped entirely today, an estimated 390,000 fewer Americans would die before their time each year. If all Americans reduced their consumption of foods high in fat to well below current levels and engaged in physical activity no more strenuous than sustained walking for 30 minutes a day, additional results of a similar magnitude could be expected" (USDHHS 1990, p. 1).

Exercising regularly extends life expectancy. Paffenbarger and associates (1986) estimated that at age 35, the physically active alumni could be expected to live about 2.5 years longer than their sedentary classmates. This may not sound like much. However, Paffenbarger[2] has made a rather startling comparison. If all forms of cancer deaths were eliminated (i.e., nobody died from cancer), the average increase in longevity would be just slightly *under* 2 years. In this context, regular forms of suitable exercise are potentially equally beneficial to public health as cancer prevention. The important role of physical activity on public health has been clearly established. Chapters 8 and 9 give additional research on the role of aerobic fitness and obesity in health.

Physical Activity and Fitness—*Healthy People 2000*

Healthy People 2000: National Health Promotion and Disease Prevention Objectives (USDHHS 1990) is a national strategy for significantly improving the health of Americans by the year 2000. It grew out of work initiated in 1979 with the publication of *Healthy People: The Surgeon General's Report on Health Promotion and Disease Prevention* (USDHHS 1979) and expanded with the publication in 1980 of *Promoting Health/Preventing Disease: Objectives for the Nation* (USDHHS 1980). This comprehensive public health study has three major goals:

- To increase the span of healthy life for Americans.
- To reduce health disparities among Americans.
- To achieve access to preventive services for all Americans.

Healthy People 2000 is a comprehensive national public health directive that established health promotion and disease prevention objectives. Physical activity and fitness is one of eight priority health promotion areas. An assumption of *Healthy People 2000* is that the high prevalence of sedentary life-style and overweight can be best attacked with a public health approach.

Healthy People 2000 lists objectives for eight major health promotion efforts, of which the first is Physical Activity and Fitness. The strong potential public health effect of physical activity and weight control can be traced to prevalence—a large proportion of Americans are sedentary and overweight. This was shown in the previous section with the Harvard Alumni data. The report lists twelve objectives for physical activity and fitness. These objectives are placed into three general classes: (1) Health Status Objectives; (2) Risk Reduction Objectives; (3) Services and Protection Objectives. The three classes of objectives provide public health goals for improvement in health status, exercise goals for reaching the health goals, and methods for implementing the exercise goals. These are listed next.

---

[2]Communication with Dr. R. Paffenbarger, Jr. at the Texas Chapter Meeting of the American College of Sports Medicine, Houston, Texas, December, 1985.

Table 1.2 Target Goals for Populations with the Most Serious Levels of Overweight Prevalence

Population	1976–80 Baseline	2000 Target
Low-Income Women (Age ≥ 20)	37%	25%
Black Women (Age ≥ 20)	44%	30%
Hispanic Women (Age ≥ 20)		
Mexican-American Women	39%	25%
Cuban Women	34%	25%
Puerto Rican Women	37%	25%
American Indians/Alaska Natives	29–75%§	30%
People with Disabilities	36%	25%
Women with High Blood Pressure	50%	41%
Men with High Blood Pressure	39%	35%

§ Estimates for different tribes

Health Status Objectives. These objectives focus on the medical problems that can be reduced through physical activity and physical fitness. There are two objectives.

1.1 Reduce coronary heart disease deaths to no more than 100 per 100,000 people.

1.2 Reduce overweight to a prevalence of no more than 20% among people aged 20 and older and no more than 15% among adolescents aged 12 through 19.

Coronary heart disease is the leading cause of death and disability in the United States. As previously presented, there is increasing evidence showing that physical activity can decrease the risk of coronary heart disease and that physically inactive people are almost twice as likely to develop coronary heart disease as those who exercise regularly (Paffenbarger et al. 1984; Powell et al. 1987).

The age-adjusted American coronary heart disease death rate in 1987 was 135 per 100,000. Reaching this goal by the year 2000 would amount to a 26% reduction in heart disease deaths. The heart disease death rate of black Americans is over 20% higher than the general rate. The *Healthy People 2000* report recommends that black Americans be targeted for special emphasis.

Objective 1.2 focuses on the high prevalence of overweight. The role of caloric expenditure and weight control are linked and firmly established (Skender et al. 1996). In 1980, the prevalence of overweight was 24% for men and 27% for women aged 20 through 74 years. The height and weight ratio body mass index (BMI) was used to define overweight. Chapter 9 gives the BMI standards used to define overweight.

Achieving objective 1.2 amounts to about a 25% reduction in the prevalence of overweight. The prevalence is much higher in several ethnic groups, and a reduction to 20% would be an unrealistic goal. Table 1.2 gives the 1976–87 prevalence rates and 2000 target goals for these groups. The racial and ethnic composition of the American population is changing. Between the years of 1990 and 2000, the proportion of whites will decline from 76% to 72%, while the proportion of Hispanic Americans will increase from 8% to 11.3% and of blacks from 12.4% to 13.1%. The remaining groups, including American Indians, Alaska Natives, Asians, and Pacific Islanders, will increase from 3.5% to 4.3% of the total American population (USDHHS 1990).

Risk Reduction Objectives. The *Healthy People 2000* report lists five objectives that concentrate on increasing exercise. These objectives are:

1.3 Increase to at least 30% the proportion of people aged 6 and older who engage regularly, preferably daily, in light to moderate physical activity for at least 30 minutes per day.

1.4 Increase to at least 20% the proportion of people aged 18 and older and at least 75% of children and adolescents aged 6 through 17 who engage in vigorous physical activity that promotes the development and maintenance of cardiorespiratory fitness 3 or more days per week or more than 20 minutes per occasion.

1.5 Reduce to no more than 15% the proportion of people aged 6 and older who engage in no leisure-time physical activity.

1.6 Increase to at least 40% the proportion of people aged 6 and older who regularly perform physical activities that enhance and maintain muscular strength, muscular endurance, and flexibility.

1.7 Increase to at least 50% the proportion of overweight people aged 12 and older who have adopted sound dietary practices combined with regular physical activity to attain an appropriate body weight.

Both light to moderate and vigorous exercise have health benefits. The primary benefit of light to moderate daily exercise is caloric expenditure. It is estimated that exercising at this level would involve a weekly caloric expenditure of about 1,000 kilocalories per week. Medical research (Leon 1989) suggests that caloric expenditure of this magnitude would not only help control weight, but reduce the risk of heart disease, especially for those who were originally sedentary.

Light to moderate daily exercise is beneficial to all, but due to the low exercise intensity, it is unlikely that this type of exercise will develop aerobic fitness. Regular vigorous exercise is needed to achieve and maintain higher levels of aerobic fitness that allow one to exercise at a high intensity for extended periods without undue stress. Sufficient aerobic fitness is needed to carry out physically demanding occupational tasks (e.g., firefighter) and demanding leisure pursuits. Not only does vigorous physical activity enhance aerobic fitness, it also contributes substantially to caloric expenditure and provides additional protection against coronary heart disease (Blair et al. 1989; Paffenbarger et al. 1984). Baseline data shows that only 12% of adults and 66% of youth aged 10–17 exercise to this degree. The goal is to increase this by over 60% for the population. A group with a high prevalence of inactivity is lower-income people aged 18 years and older.

Objective 1.7 is directed toward the high prevalence of overweight and the failure of overweight people to lose weight by just diet restriction. The success rate for weight-reduction programs that use just diet is dismal (Skender et al. 1996). Not only does physical activity burn calories, it alters percent body fat by increasing fat-free weight and decreasing fat weight, and raises metabolic rate (Ross & Jackson 1990; Wood et al. 1988). Overweight occurs because too few calories are expended and too many consumed. Sound weight-reduction programs focus not only on caloric restriction but on caloric expenditure.

In 1985, only 30% of overweight women and 25% of overweight men used this combined approach. This ambitious objective deserves special importance because it targets one of our major health problems. Achieving this objection will help reduce not only one of our major nutrition problems but also the risk of degenerative diseases associated with overweight.

Both occupational and leisure-time physical activity provide health benefits. Because of the changing nature of American occupations and laborsaving devices, the amount of physical activity engaged in at work and at home has declined. For many, leisure-time activities provide the only means of being active. About 24% of men and women aged 18 and older report no leisure-time physical activity and the prevalence of leisure-time sedentarism increases with age: 33% for people aged 45–64 years, and 43% for those over age 65. Another exercise objective is to increase leisure-time activity by over 40%, an objective that targets older people, people with disabilities, and lower-income people (USDHHS 1990). As shown in Chapter 11, the elderly are the fastest growing segment of American society.

Muscular strength, muscular endurance, and flexibility are components of health-related fitness. A suitable level of this type of fitness is needed to complete daily living and occupational tasks. Cady and associates (Cady et al. 1979) reported that the incidence of back injuries for firefighters was related to physical fitness. The reported injury rates were 7.1% for the least fit, 3.2% for the middle fit, and 0.8% for the most fit firefighters. It is estimated that lifting causes nearly 50% of the back injuries (Snook et al. 1978). It appears that the workers most likely to injure themselves lifting are those without sufficient strength to meet the work demands (Chaffin 1974; Chaffin et al. 1978; Keyserling et al. 1980a; Keyserling et al. 1980b; Snook et al. 1978). The logic is that if a job requires lifting a 100-pound object using the back, the individual with a capacity of 100 pounds is more prone to injury than one with a 200-pound lifting capacity (Ayoub 1982). Chapter 7 provides a discussion of pre-employment testing for physically demanding jobs.

Services and Protection Objectives. The *Healthy People 2000* services and protection objectives focus on methods for achieving the exercise and fitness objectives. These objectives are directed toward youth and adult physical education programming, expanding community exercise facilities, and increasing medical supervision and education of adult exercise programs. The five objectives are:

1.8 Increase to at least 50% the proportion of children and adolescents in 1st through 12th grade who participate in daily school physical education.

1.9 Increase to at least 50% the proportion of school physical education class time that students spend being physically active, preferably engaging in lifetime physical activities.

1.10 Increase the proportion of worksites offering employer-sponsored physical and fitness programs as follows:

Worksite Size	1985 Baseline	2000 Target
50–99 employees	14%	20%
100–249 employees	23%	35%
250–749 employees	32%	50%
≥750 employees	54%	80%

1.11 Increase community availability and accessibility of physical activity and fitness facilities. The 2000 Target is based on population and recommends adding the following: hiking, biking, and fitness trail miles; public swimming pool; and acres of park and recreation open space.

1.12 Increase to at least 50% the proportion of primary care providers who routinely assess and counsel their patients regarding the frequency, duration, type, and intensity of each patient's physical activity practices. Physicians provided exercise counseling for about 30% of sedentary patients in 1988.

School physical education is the targeted public health program for increasing physical activity and fitness of youth. In 1986, only 36% of students in 1st through 12th grade participated in daily physical education, and only 27% of class time involved some form of physical activity. These objectives call for an increase in the duration, frequency, and intensity of aerobic exercise. Lifetime activities are those activities that may be readily carried into adulthood because they generally need only one to two people. Some examples are swimming, bicycling, jogging, and racquet sports. Excluded are competitive team and group sports.

The final three services and protection objectives are designed to enhance the exercise and fitness of adults. These objectives call for an increase in adult exercise facilities and more medical supervision.

Computer Literacy for Measurement and Evaluation

Being computer literate is becoming important for all. Computer literacy is being able to use hardware and software to accomplish needed tasks. Provided in this section are the critical computer tasks for measurement and evaluation. These involve collecting, storing, analyzing, and presenting data.

Brief History

When we published the first edition of this text in the 1970s, all computer applications were with a mainframe computer. A mainframe computer has enormous capacity, allowing the storage of huge amounts of information and the ability to conduct complex data analyses. The only computing services available at colleges and universities in that era were mainframes. In the late 1980s and early 1990s this all changed with the development of micro or **personal computers (PC).** What could be done only on a mainframe in the 1970s is now easily done on a personal computer. In this section we provide a brief overview of the evolution of computer technology and the application of this technology to measurement and evaluation.

In the 1970s, there were few people who were computer literate. Today computer literacy has grown at an exponential rate. Moving from the mainframe to the personal computer is one major reason for the rise in computer literacy. While there are many different reasons for the growth in computer usage and literacy, our experience suggests that four are especially important. These relate to computing power, powerful software, user-friendly operating systems and the World Wide Web.

Computing Power

Computers are **digital** machines. All information in a digital computer is stored, transferred, or processed by a dual-state condition—a binary digit or bit (e.g., on/off, yes/no, or 0/1). Binary digits are used to quantify the capacity of a microcomputer. The speed of a computer is determined by its microprocessor. The microprocessor of the first PCs was an 8-bit, 4.77-MHz machine. An 8-bit machine simply means that a series of 8 binary digits is simultaneously moved with each clock click of the processor. MHz[3] is used to quantify the electronic speed at which a computer can operate. It is like a clock in that with each click a specified number of operations can be completed. A power of 4.77 MHz meant that 4.77 million operations could be completed per second. Thus, the processing power of the first machines was the capacity to process 8 bits of information 4.77 million times per second.

PCs soon moved to 16-, 32-, and finally today's 64-bit machines. Mainframe computers are 64-bit machines, the same as the PC you can buy at any store. What is the advantage of a 64-bit computer? Compared to an 8-bit computer, a 64-bit machine can move 8 times more digital bits with each operation. In addition to the increase in bit size, the clock speed of PCs dramatically increased. The speeds of common 1998 PCs are 350 MHz and increasing. A 350-MHz machine is about 73 times faster than the first 4.77-MHz machines. Today's 64-bit, 350-MHz machines can move 350 million 64-bits of information per second. In comparison to the 8-bit, 4.77-MHz machine, the 64-bit, 350-MHz PC is over 1,168 times faster.[4] Looking at it in another way, a computer operation that took 20 minutes to complete with one of the first PCs would be completed in about 1 second with what is available today.

The increase in computing speed is one major factor in defining the power of a computer. Another major factor is the increased size of computer memory. **Random-access memory (RAM)** allows for information to be "written in" or "read out" very rapidly. Information stored in RAM is stored on a temporary basis and will disappear when the computer is turned off. Since RAM is used to run a program, the size of the RAM is an indication of a PC's power. Think of RAM as your "work space." You can increase the power and speed of a PC by increasing RAM, which is possible by adding RAM chips to a computer. In the first computers, RAM was less than 1 MB. A common size of RAM for 1998 PCs is 32 MB, expandable to over 500 MB. It is a good idea to double the RAM on any new computer.

Another factor in the increased power of PCs is storage capacity. Microcomputer programs and data are stored on a disk. A disk can be a floppy or hard disk. A **floppy disk** can transfer information with a PC through a disk drive, while a **hard disk** is either part of the PC (internal disk) or connected to it. Both the floppy and hard disk function in the same manner: they store data and computer programs (also called applications) and allow the user to communicate with the machine. The major difference between a floppy and hard disk is storage capacity. The 3.5-inch floppy disk can store 1.4 megabytes (MB) of information. The first hard disks were about 20 MB. A 20 MB hard drive could store about 14 times more information than the 1.4 MB disk. The size of hard drives grew rapidly from 20 MB to 100 MB; present hard disk storage capacity is in the gigabytes.[5]

---

[3]MHz is the abbreviation for megahertz, which is the clock frequency. A hertz is the international unit of frequency and equals one cycle per second. Megahertz is one million hertz.

[4]The change in speed is the product of the increase in bit size and MHz, i.e., $[(64/4) \times 350/4.77)] = 16/73 = 1{,}168$.

[5]A gigabyte is 1,024 megabytes.

Powerful Software

The increase in speed, RAM, and memory has led to the development of more powerful computer **software,** the programs that enable a computer to operate. The history of computer technology reveals a general trend. Computer companies develop computers that exceed the capacity of the programs being written. Software developers then redesign their programs to take advantage of this additional capacity. This motivates computer companies to increase the capacity of their machines, and the process spirals. The result is the constant development of more powerful hardware and software. This process marked the evolution of mainframe computers and is being repeated with PCs.

This increase in power has led to the development of many new computer programs, or applications. The explosion in computer graphics is an excellent example. Graphic programs need large amounts of RAM and storage. The initial graphics programs allowed us to draw simple graphs and drawings. Contemporary movies and television advertisements are now being made with "high-end" computer graphics. The same expansion occurred in statistical computer programs. Statistical programs like SPSS and SAS were initially written for use on the mainframe. These huge, powerful statistical programs easily run on today's PC.

User-friendly PC Operating Systems

The development of user-friendly operating systems has dramatically expanded the number of computer users. The initial PC operating systems were somewhat difficult to use. A user had to have an understanding of computers in order to use the machine. The Macintosh computer changed this with the introduction of a graphic interface featuring icons and pull-down menus. The popularity and initial success of the Macintosh computer can be traced to its icon and pull-down menu operating system. The popularity of the Macintosh dramatically waned in the late 1990s with the introduction of Microsoft's Windows-95 operating system.[6] Windows-95 is an icon/pull-down menu operating system that is very similar to the Mac operating system.

The principle advantage of the icon/pull-down menu operating system is that it made the computer user-friendly. Before Windows-95, MS-DOS was the major operating system of the non-Macintosh computers. This system forced the user to learn commands, which often required reading complicated manuals. If you forgot the command, typed in the wrong command, or misspelled a word you could not accomplish a desired task. This was extremely frustrating and was a deterrent to many who wanted to learn how to use the computer. Now anyone can become computer literate. "Just click on an icon and something happens."

World Wide Web

Prior to the Web, the computer was commonly used to accomplish difficult, often scientific tasks. In order to be computer literate, a user not only had to understand the software, but also had to have the technical background related to the task. For example, the computer is especially useful for data analyses, or "number crunching." In order to analyze data, the user needs to understand not only statistical software but statistic applications. The World Wide Web has changed all this. There are now computer tasks that are useful for everyone. The Web can be used for complicated scientific tasks such as completing a computer literature search, but it also may be used for many tasks such as buying a new car, making an airline reservation, or communicating with someone by e-mail who is in another part of the world.

---

[6]Windows-98, an upgrade of Windows-95, is now on the market.

Microcomputer Programs—Software

A key to being computer literate is to find programs that serve your needs and master them. The programs that you use for your personal needs will differ from those used for measurement and evaluation. For example, you may use a program to write checks or pay your bills electronically. The computer software valuable to the K–12 teacher will differ from that used by the exercise scientist. Provided in this section is a brief discussion of programs useful in measurement and evaluation.

Statistics Programs. The most popular mainframe statistical programs such as SPSS and SAS are now available on PCs. Versions of these statistical programs are available for both Windows and Macintosh machines. A student version of SPSS can be obtained with this textbook.

A major advantage of PC statistical packages over the old mainframe versions is the ease with which data can be graphically presented. Figure 1.8 illustrates the professional quality of the graphic output from a statistical package. In Chapter 2, we show how to examine the shape of a distribution of scores with a histogram. This can be accomplished by first constructing a frequency distribution, then using that data to construct the histogram. When we speak of the shape of the curve, we are referring to the distribution's pattern. Shape is defined as skewed or normal. These concepts are given in Chapter 2. In discussing the table of normal curve, your professor may draw a "bell curve" on the board to represent a normal curve as it relates to the histogram data. Figure 1.8 illustrates this concept. Another example is a scattergram showing the relationship between two variables—age and aerobic fitness. A scattergram is very cumbersome to do by hand, but is easily done with a computer. Examples of a scattergram are provided in Chapters 8 and 9.

Scientific Graphic Programs. Many of the graphs presented in this book were completed on a standard, scientific graphic program (Macintosh Cricket Graph III)

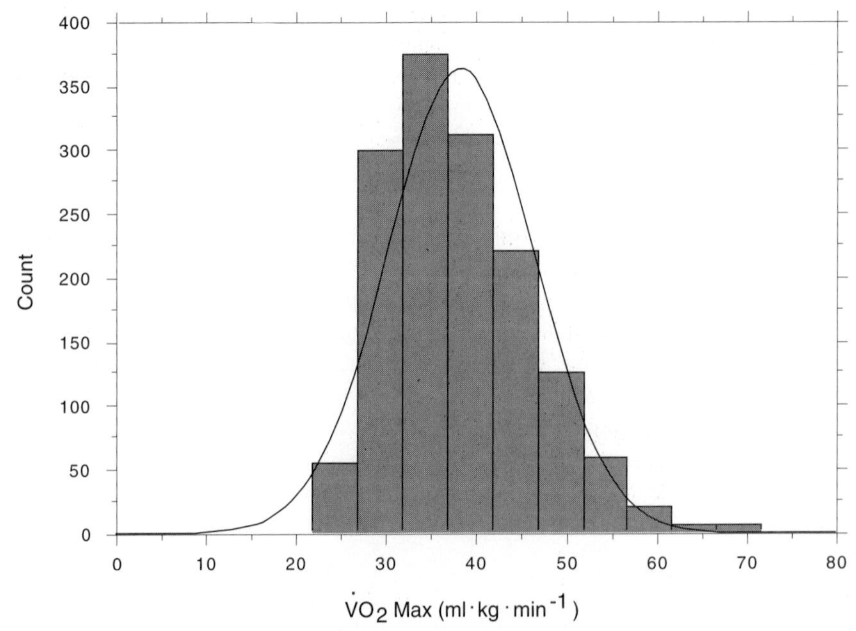

Figure 1.8
Histogram of the aerobic fitness of 1,604 men tested at the Cardio-pulmonary Laboratory at NASA/Johnson Space Center, Houston, Texas. The statistical program Statview (4.01) has the capacity not only to produce the histogram, but to superimpose a normal curve over the distribution. This provides a way to evaluate visually the shape of the distribution. These concepts are presented in Chapter 2.

and made in just a few minutes. Prior to the PC era, such graphs were made by an artist using graph paper, and it was an expensive, laborious task. In addition, graphic programs can be used with a laser printer, which results in crisp images and allows the printing of mathematically defined curves. These programs are especially valuable for presenting statistical data.

Database and/or Spreadsheet. Database and spreadsheet programs are developed primarily for use in business, but they have excellent applications for teachers, exercise specialists, and especially those who must make and administer budgets (e.g., sport managers). A database program is a file of computer data structured for general use. A **spreadsheet** program allows the user to work with numbers in rows and columns and to use equations to complete various calculations, but database programs also have this capacity. Many computers come with spreadsheet programs. For example, many computers will come with Microsoft Office. The popular spreadsheet program Microsoft Excel is one application of Microsoft Office.

Spreadsheets and database programs can be somewhat complicated to learn, but once learned you will discover many different data-based applications. This text includes many different equations used to compute fitness variables. To illustrate, equations are provided to estimate aerobic fitness (VO_2 Max) and percent body fat of both youth and adults. This can be very cumbersome to complete by hand, but is easily accomplished by a database or spreadsheet program. This is illustrated in the computer computation appendix of this book. All teachers are required to grade their students. This typically means recording and adding different tests together. While there are gradebook computer programs available, these tasks can also be done with a spreadsheet or database program. Learn how to use these programs—they are a valuable asset.

Evaluation of Youth Fitness. One of the more useful PC programs for K–12 physical education teachers is the software designed to evaluate youth fitness. The Chrysler-AAU (1992) and Prudential FITNESSGRAM® (1992) health-related fitness programs provide a PC program. The health-related fitness tests are fully presented in the youth fitness chapter (Chapter 10). These programs are very easy to use; either the teacher or student can enter fitness test results. The programs are designed to generate a variety of reports that provide summary results for groups such as students, parents, school boards, or evaluation teams. The FITNESSGRAM® program is illustrated in Chapter 10.

Adult Fitness and Health Promotion. The use of PC technology in adult fitness and the health promotion industry is accelerating. This trend was started in the late 1960s by Dr. Kenneth Cooper when the Institute for Aerobics Research developed a computer system for the quantification of exercise and the storing of adult fitness and medical test results (Cooper 1970). The use of commercial health and fitness software in corporate, medical, and private fitness facilities has become the norm. The output of a fitness and exercise prescription program is provided in Chapter 11. Besides general applications such as assigning lockers, the general capabilities of this commercial software[7] include the following:

---

[7]One of the leading commercial health and fitness software companies is CSI Software, 15425 North Frwy., Suite 180, Houston, TX 77090-6041. Information can be obtained from their Web site: WWW.csisoftwareusa.com.

1. **General fitness assessment.** The program has the capacity to compute $\dot{V}O_2$ Max and body composition by any method presented in this text. The program provides a graphic profile of the person's fitness, compares their fitness to normative standards, and on retests compares changes in fitness.
2. **Exercise prescriptions.** The fitness assessment parameters are used to develop an individualized exercise program.
3. **Exercise logging.** The program quantifies the energy expenditure of exercise from the frequency, duration, and intensity of exercise. The program stores these data and provides means to generate meaningful reports.
4. **Health-risk appraisal.** Using basic data, the program provides a health-risk appraisal including a cardiovascular risk profile.
5. **Dietary analysis.** The program provides a detailed analysis of one's diet from dietary recall data.

Scientific Instrumentation. Computers are now being interfaced with various types of research equipment to automate data collection and complete complex calculations; for example, the calculation of $\dot{V}O_2$ Max (see Chapter 8). Prior to the computer era, $\dot{V}O_2$ Max was very time-consuming to measure because expired gases had to be collected in a bag for analysis. Now this analysis can be done quickly and accurately with a computer (see Figure 1.9).

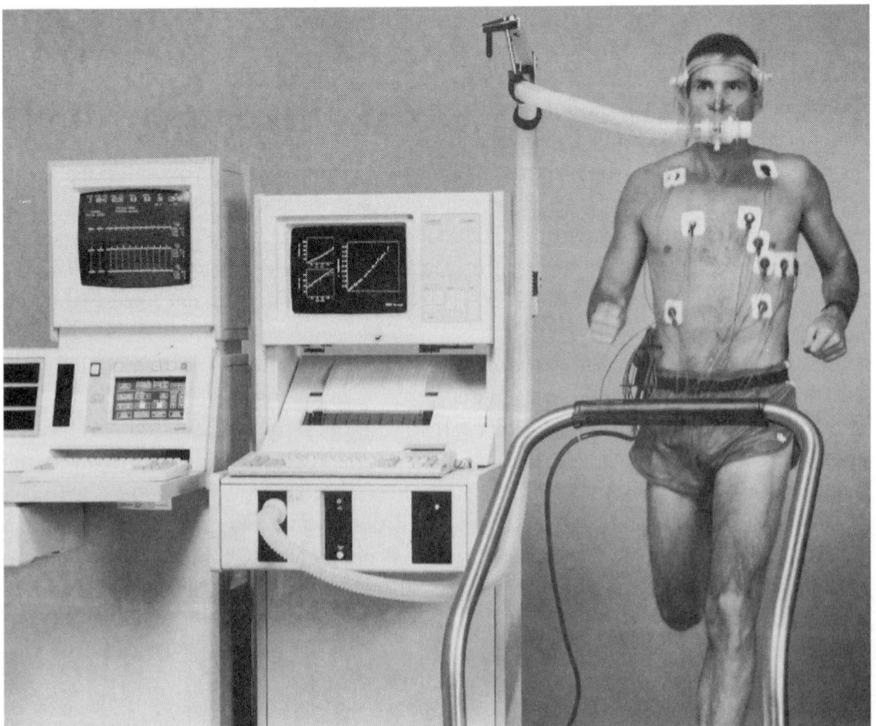

Figure 1.9
Maximal oxygen uptake ($\dot{V}O_2$ Max) can be easily measured with a computerized metabolic system. (Courtesy of Pat Bradley)

Summary

Measurement uses reliable and valid tests to secure the data essential to the evaluation process. Evaluation is a decision-making process with a goal for improved instruction. Tests can be used in six ways: (1) placing students in homogeneous groups to facilitate instruction; (2) diagnosing weaknesses; (3) determining whether important objectives have been reached; (4) predicting performance levels in future activities; (5) comparing a program with others like it; and (6) motivating participants. The evaluation models appropriate for K–12 physical education teachers are quite similar to those used to evaluate adult fitness.

Evaluation is a means of determining whether objectives are being reached, and of facilitating achievement. Formative evaluation clarifies what remains to be achieved; summative evaluation determines whether general objectives have been reached. Evaluation, then, is the feedback system by which the quality of the instructional or training process is monitored. Criterion-referenced standards specify the level of performance necessary to achieve specific instructional objectives; norm-referenced standards identify a level of achievement within a group of individuals.

Medical and public health scientists acknowledge that physical activity and fitness promote health. The importance of exercise for health has been documented with the publication of the *Physical Activity and Health: A Report of the Surgeon General.* This report shows that about 50% of youth are not vigorously active and that physical activity declines during adolescence. Daily enrollment in K–12 physical education programs is declining. The K–12 physical education programs provide one vehicle for increasing the activity levels of Americans. More than 60% of American adults are not active on a regular basis and 25% are not active at all. While activity levels of youth and adults are low, medical research shows that physical activity has a positive influence on health. Sedentary life-style increases the risk of premature mortality in general, and of coronary heart disease, high blood pressure, colon cancer, and diabetes mellitus. Significant health benefits can be obtained from a moderate amount of daily physical activity. The demographic trends in America are increasing the need for exercise and weight-control programs. Our population is getting older, minorities are growing, and jobs are becoming more sedentary in nature. Older Americans and those from low-income groups have a higher prevalence of inactivity and overweight than the total population. The *Healthy People 2000* public health study defines physical activity and fitness objectives to be reached by the year 2000. These objectives give direction to both K–12 physical education and adult fitness programs.

Computers may be classified as a mainframe computer, minicomputer, and microcomputer. The major difference in these computers is in their size and computing power. Microcomputers, or personal computers, are small, but powerful enough to meet the needs of teachers and exercise specialists. Computer literacy is a basic understanding of PCs and a working knowledge of the applications needed by someone in a profession. The general measurement and evaluation applications include graphics, databases, and statistics. Several programs are available to K–12 physical education teachers for the evaluation of youth health-related fitness. Programs designed to evaluate adult fitness and prescribe and evaluate exercise are available to the exercise specialist.

Formative Evaluation of Objectives

Objective 1 Define and differentiate between measurement and evaluation.

1. The terms *measurement* and *evaluation* often are used interchangeably. Define each term.

2. What are the key differences between measurement and evaluation?
3. Although measurement and evaluation are distinct functions, explain how they are related.

Objective 2 Define and differentiate between criterion- and norm-referenced standards.

1. What are the key differences between criterion- and norm-referenced standards?
2. Explain how a physical education teacher or exercise specialist could use both types of standards.
3. What is sensitivity and specificity?

Objective 3 Define and differentiate between formative and summative methods of evaluation.

1. Many believe that greater achievement is possible if both formative and summative evaluation are used. Briefly describe formative and summative evaluation.
2. What are the key differences between formative and summative evaluation? Why could you expect to stimulate greater achievement by using both formative and summative evaluation?

Objective 4 Understand models of evaluation as they apply to teaching (K–12) and exercise science settings.

1. What are the steps of the K–12 evaluation model?
2. What are the steps of the exercise science evaluation model?
3. What are the similarities and differences of these two evaluation models?

Objective 5 Describe the role of public health initiatives in physical education and exercise science.

1. What are the major conclusions of the Surgeon General's report on *Physical Activity and Health?*
2. What is community-attributable risk?
3. What are the three goals of *Healthy People 2000?*
4. List the three general categories of objectives of *Healthy People 2000.*
5. List the twelve physical activity and fitness objectives of *Healthy People 2000.* How do they affect physical educators and exercise scientists?

Objective 6 Describe the influence of computer technology on our profession.

1. What is computer literacy?
2. What are the programs that are most useful for measurement and evaluation?

Additional Learning Activities

1. Visit physical education classes and determine if students meet the activity standards recommended in the *Healthy People 2000* report.
2. Visit a public school physical education program and discover the type of fitness test it is using. Many will not be using a health-related fitness test. Does the evidence warrant its use?
3. Visit a facility that conducts an adult fitness program. Identify the types of tests that are administered and the type of program offered.
4. Visit a public school physical education program. Analyze the program and determine the student's level of physical activity.
5. Develop a unit of instruction showing how you could use both formative and summative evaluation procedures.
6. For the same unit of instruction, develop criterion-referenced standards for the tests. Explain your logic and sources of data used to establish the standards.
7. Check for commercial health and fitness software on the World Wide Web. The address of the CSI software company is: www.csisoftwareusa.com.

Bibliography

ACSM. 1990. The recommended quantity and quality of exercise for developing and maintaining cardiorespiratory and muscular fitness in healthy adults. *Medicine and Science in Sports and Exercise* 22: 265–274.

ACSM. 1991. *Guidelines for exercise testing and prescription.* 3rd ed. Vol. 4. Philadelphia: Lea and Febiger.

Anderson, K. V., W. P. Castelli, and D. Levy. 1987. Cholesterol and mortality: 30 years of follow-up from the Framingham study. *Journal of the American Medical Association* 257: 2176–2180.

Blair, S. N. et al. 1989. Physical fitness and all-cause mortality: A prospective study of healthy men and women. *Journal of the American Medical Association* 262: 2395–2401.

Blair, S. N. et al. 1995. Changes in physical fitness and all-cause mortality: A prospective study of healthy and unhealthy men. *Journal of the American Medical Association* 273(14): 1093–1098.

Bloom, B. S. et al. 1971. *Handbook on formative and summative evaluation of student learning.* New York: McGraw-Hill.

Buskirk, E. R. and J. L. Hodgson. 1987. Age and aerobic power: The rate of change in men and women. *Federation Proceedings* 46: 1824–1829.

Cady, L. D. et al. 1979. Back injuries in firefighters. *Journal of Occupational Medicine* 21: 269–272.

Caspersen, C. J. 1989. Physical activity epidemiology: Concepts, methods, and applications to exercise science. *Exercise and Sport Sciences Reviews* 17: 423–473.

Castelli, W. P. et al. 1977. HDL-cholesterol and other lipids in coronary heart disease. The cooperative lipoprotein phenotyping study. *Circulation* 55: 767–772.

Chaffin, D. B. 1974. Human strength capability and low-back pain. *Journal of Occupational Medicine* 16: 248–254.

Chaffin, D. B., G. D. Herrin, and W. M. Keyserling. 1978. Preemployment strength testing. *Journal of Occupational Medicine* 67: 403–408.

Cooper Institute. 1992. *The Prudential Fitnessgram®: Test administration manual.* Dallas: Cooper Institute for Aerobics Research.

Cureton, K. J. et al. 1995. A generalized equation for prediction of $\dot{V}O_2$ peak from 1-mile run/walk performance. *Medicine and Science in Sports and Exercise* 27(3): 445–451.

Cureton, K. J. and G. L. Warren. 1990. Criterion-referenced standards for youth health-related fitness tests: A tutorial. *Research Quarterly for Exercise and Sport* 61: 7–19.

deBakey, M. F. et al. 1984. *The living heart diet.* New York: Simon and Schuster.

Ebel, R. L. 1973. *Measuring educational achievement.* Englewood Cliffs, NJ: Prentice-Hall.

Ellestad, M. S. 1980. *Stress testing principles and practice.* 2nd ed. Philadelphia: F. A. Davis Co.

Fletcher, G. F. et al. 1992. Position statement: Statement on exercise: Benefits and recommendations for physical activity programs for all Americans. *Circulation* 86: 340–344.

Glaser, R. 1963. Instructional technology and the measurement of learning outcomes: Some questions. *American Psychologist* 27: 519–521.

Glaser, R. and A. J. Nitko. 1971. Measurement in learning and instruction. In R. L. Thorndike (Ed.) *Educational measurement.* pp. 625–670. Washington, DC: American Council on Education.

Golding, L. A., C. R. Meyers, and W. E. Sinning. 1989. *The Y's way to physical fitness.* 3rd ed. Chicago: National Board of YMCA.

Gordon, T. et al. 1981. Diet and its relation to coronary heart disease and death in three populations. *Circulation* 63: 500–515.

Jackson, A. S. and R. M. Ross. 1997. *Understanding exercise for health and fitness.* 3rd ed. Dubuque: Kendall/Hunt Publishing Co.

Jackson, A. S. et al. 1995. Changes in aerobic power of men ages 25–70 years. *Medicine and Science in Sports and Exercise* 27: 113–120.

Jackson, A. S. et al. 1996. Changes in aerobic power of women ages 20–64 years. *Medicine and Science in Sports and Exercise* 28: 884–891.

Katz, S. et al. 1983. Active life expectancy. *New England Journal of Medicine.* 309: 1218–1224.

Keyserling, W. et al. 1980a. Establishing an industrial strength testing program. *American Industrial Hygiene Association Journal* 41: 730–736.

Keyserling, W. M., G. D. Herrin, and D. B. Chaffin. 1980b. Isometric strength testing as a means of controlling medical incidents on strenuous jobs. *Journal of Occupational Medicine* 22: 332–336.

Leon, A. S. 1989. Effects of physical activity and fitness on health. In N.C.F.H. Statistics (Eds.). *Assessing physical fitness and physical activity in population-based surveys.* Hyattsville, MD: U.S. Department of Health and Human Services.

Lohman, T. G. 1992. *Advances in body composition assessment.* Champaign, IL: Human Kinetics.

Looney, M. A. 1989. Chapter 7. Criterion-referenced measurement: Reliability. In M. J. Safrit, and T. M. Woods (Eds.). *Measurement concepts in physical education and exercise science.* Champaign, IL: Human Kinetics.

Morrow, J. R. et al. 1984. *Texas youth fitness study.* Austin, TX: AAHPER.

NCYFS. 1985. Summary of findings from national children and youth fitness study. *JOPERD* 56: 43–90.

Owen, C. A. et al. 1980. Longitudinal evaluation of an exercise prescription intervention program with periodic ergometric testing: A ten-year appraisal. *Journal of Occupational Medicine* 22: 235–240.

Paffenbarger, R. S. et al. 1986. Physical activity, all-cause mortality, and longevity of college alumni. *New England Journal of Medicine* 314: 605–613.

Paffenbarger, R. S. et al. 1977. Work-energy level, personal characteristics, and fatal heart attack: A birth cohort effect. *American Journal of Epidemiology* 105: 200–213.

Paffenbarger, R. S., A. L. Wing, and R. T. Hyde. 1978. Physical activity as an index of heart attack risk in college alumni. *American Journal of Epidemiology* 108: 161–175.

Paffenbarger, R. S. Jr. et al. 1984. A natural history of athleticism and cardiovascular health. *Journal of American Medical Association.* 252: 491–495.

Pollock, M. L. and J. H. Wilmore. 1990. *Exercise in health and disease.* 2nd ed. Philadelphia: W. B. Saunders.

Powell, K. E. et al. 1989. Physical activity and chronic disease. *American Journal of Clinical Nutrition* 49: 999–1006.

Powell, K. E. et al. 1987. Physical activity and the incidence of coronary heart disease. *Annual Review of Public Health* 8: 253–287.

Ross, R. M. and A. S. Jackson. 1990. *Exercise concepts, calculations and computer applications.* Carmel, IN: Benchmark Press.

Safrit, M. J. 1989. Chapter 6. Criterion-referenced measurement. In M. J. Safrit, and T. M. Woods (Eds.). *Validity in measurement concepts in physical education and exercise science.* pp. 119–136. Champaign IL: Human Kinetics.

Skender, M. L. et al. 1996. Comparison of 2-year weight loss trends in behavioral treatments of obesity: Diet, exercise, and combination interventions. *Journal of the American Dietetic Association* 96: 342–246.

Snedecor, G. W. and W. G. Cochran. 1967. *Statistical methods.* Ames, IA: Iowa State University Press.

Snook, S. H., R. A. Campanelli, and J. W. Hart. 1978. A study of three preventive approaches to low-back injury. *Journal of Occupational Medicine* 20: 478–481.

Taylor, H. L. et al. 1962. Death rates among physically active and sedentary employees of the railroad industry. *American Journal of Public Health* 52: 1692–1707.

USDHHS (U.S. Department of Health and Human Services). 1979. *Healthy people: The surgeon general's report on health promotion and disease prevention.* Washington, DC: U.S. Department of Health and Human Services.

USDHHS (U.S. Department of Health and Human Services). 1980. *Promoting health/preventing disease: Objectives for the nation.* Washington, DC: U.S. Department of Health and Human Services.

USDHHS (U.S. Department of Health and Human Services). March 1988. *Health United States 1987.* Washington, DC: U.S. Department of Health and Human Services, DHHS Pub. No. (PHS) 88–1232.

USDHHS (U.S. Department of Health and Human Services). 1990. *Healthy People 2000: National health promotion and disease prevention objectives.* Washington, DC: U.S. Department of Health and Human Services.

USDHHS (U.S. Department of Health and Human Services). 1996. *Physical activity and health: A report of the surgeon general.* Washington DC: U.S. Department of Health and Human Services.

Vecchio, T. 1986. Predictive value of a single diagnostic test in unselected populations. *New England Journal of Medicine* 274: 1171–1177.

Wood, P. D. et al. 1988. Changes in plasma lipids and lipoproteins in overweight men during weight loss through dieting as compared with exercise. *New England Journal of Medicine* 319: 1173–1179.

PART TWO 2

Quantitative Aspects of Measurement

2

CHAPTER

Statistical Tools in Evaluation

Contents

Key Words

analysis of variance
bell-shaped curve
central tendency
coefficient of determination
continuous scores
correlation
correlation coefficient
cross-validation
curvilinear relationship
dependent variable
discrete scores
frequency polygon
independent variable
interval scores
leptokurtic curves
linear relationship
line of best fit
mean
median
mode
multiple correlation
multiple prediction (regression)
negatively skewed curve
nominal scores
normal curve
ordinal scores
percentile
percentile rank
platykurtic curves
positively skewed curve
prediction
range
rank order correlation coefficient
ratio scores
regression
regression line
simple frequency distribution
simple prediction (regression)
standard deviation
standard error of prediction
standard error of the mean
standard score
T-score
t-test
variability
variance
z-score

Objectives

This chapter presents statistical techniques that can be applied to evaluate a set of scores. Not all techniques are used on every set of scores, but you should be familiar with all of them in order to select the appropriate one for a given situation.

After reading Chapter 2 you should be able to:

1. Select the statistical technique that is correct for a given situation.
2. Calculate accurately with the formulas presented.
3. Interpret the statistical value selected or calculated.
4. Make decisions based on all available information about a given situation.
5. Utilize a computer to analyze data.

Introduction

Once test scores have been collected, they must be analyzed. You can use the techniques presented here to summarize the performance of a group and to interpret the scores of individuals within that group. Many of these techniques are used and discussed in later chapters.

You may find a good elementary statistics book such as Ferguson and Takane (1989), Kuzma (1998), Runyon and associates (1996), or Sanders (1995) helpful when studying the material in this chapter.

Elements of Score Analysis

There are many reasons why we analyze sets of test scores. For a large group, a simple list of scores has no meaning. Only by condensing the information and applying descriptive terms to it can we interpret the overall performance of a group, its improvement from year to year or since the beginning of a teaching or training unit, or its performance in comparison to other groups of like background.

Score analysis is also used to evaluate individual achievement. Once information on the overall performance of a group has been obtained, an individual's achievement can be evaluated in relation to it. Analysis also helps the instructor or therapist develop performance standards, either for evaluative purposes or simply to let individuals know how they are doing.

Type of Scores

Scores can be classified as either continuous or discrete. **Continuous scores,** as most are in physical education and exercise science, have a potentially infinite number of values because they can be measured with varying degrees of accuracy. Between any two values of a continuous score exist countless other values that may be expressed as fractions. For example, 100-yard dash scores are usually recorded to the nearest tenth of a second, but they could be recorded in hundredths or thousandths of a second if accurate timing equipment was available. The amount of weight a person can lift might be recorded in 5-, 1-, or ½-pound scores, depending on how precise a score is desired. **Discrete scores** are limited to a specific number of values and usually are not expressed as fractions. Scores on a throw or shot at a target numbered 5-4-3-2-1-0 are discrete because one can receive a score of only 5, 4, 3, 2, 1, or 0. A score of 4.5 or 1.67 is impossible.

Most continuous scores are rounded off to the nearest unit of measurement when they are recorded. For example, the score of a student who runs the 100-yard dash in 10.57 seconds is recorded as 10.6 because 10.57 is closer to 10.6 than to 10.5. Usually when a number is rounded off to the nearest unit of measurement, it is increased only when the number being dropped is 5 or more. Thus, 11.45 is rounded off to 11.5, while 11.44 is recorded as 11.4. A less common method is to round off to the last unit of measure, awarding the next higher score only when that score is actually accomplished. For example, an individual who lifts a weight 8 times but cannot complete the 9th lift receives a score of 8.

We can also classify scores as ratio, interval, ordinal, or nominal (Ferguson & Takane 1989). How scores are classified influences whether calculations may be done on them. **Ratio scores** have a common unit of measurement between each score and a true zero point so that statements about equality of ratios can be made. Length and weight are examples, since one measurement may be referred to as two or three times that of another. **Interval scores** have a common unit of measurement between each score but do not have a true zero point. (A score of 0 as a measure of distance is a true zero, indicating no distance. However, a score of 0 on a knowledge test is not a true zero because it does not indicate a total lack of knowledge; it simply means that the respondent answered none of the questions correctly.) Most physical performance scores are either ratio or interval. **Ordinal scores** do not have a common unit of measurement between each score, but there is an order in the scores that makes it possible to characterize one score as higher than another. Class ranks, for example, are ordinal: if 3 students receive push-up scores of 16, 10, and 8 respectively, the first is ranked 1, the next 2, and the last 3. Notice that the number of push-ups necessary to change the class ranks of the second and third students differs. Thus there is not a common unit of measurement between consecutive scores. **Nominal scores** cannot be rank ordered and are mutually exclusive. For example, individuals can be classified by sport preference, but we cannot say that one sport is better than another. Gender is another example.

Common Unit of Measure

Many scores are recorded in feet and inches or in minutes and seconds. To analyze scores, they must be recorded in a single unit of measurement, usually the smaller one. Thus distances and heights are recorded in inches rather than feet and inches, and times are recorded in seconds rather than minutes and seconds. Recording scores in the smaller unit of measure as they are collected is less time-consuming than converting them into that form later.

Calculators and Computers

The analysis of a set of test scores is conducted in three steps: (1) selecting the appropriate analysis technique, (2) calculating with the analysis technique, and (3) interpreting the result of the analysis technique. Using a calculator or computer to quickly and accurately accomplish step 2 reduces the drudgery of analyzing a set of scores.

Score analysis should be accurate and quick. Particularly when a set of scores is large, say 50 or more, calculators and computers should be used to ensure both accuracy and speed. Today calculators are relatively inexpensive. A calculator will serve you well as a student and in your career. Your calculator should have the four basic mathematical operations, plus square root and squaring keys, a memory, and some of the basic statistical values.

Calculators work well to a point, but when the number of scores is very large, the use of a calculator is time-consuming and the user tends to make more errors. Computers are very fast and accurate and are available in school districts and universities, agencies, and businesses. Provided with each statistical example in this chapter is an example of the microcomputer application. Sometimes the output from the microcomputer program will have more on it than has been discussed in this chapter. In these cases do not be concerned.

Throughout Chapter 2, we will reference computer programs from the SPSS package of statistical programs. There are many reasons for selecting the SPSS package. It provides all of the statistical values and graphs you will ever need as a teacher, exercise specialist, therapist, or researcher. The SPSS package is found in universities, secondary schools, businesses, industries, and agencies, and can be installed on a single computer or on all the computers in a computer lab. There are versions of SPSS for mainframe computers, and for personal computers using DOS, Windows, and Macintosh operating systems. Although the standard personal computer version of SPSS is expensive, the student version of SPSS is reasonably priced and it will meet almost all of your statistical needs as a student and as a professional on the job. All personal computer versions are similar; so if you learn one you can easily change to another version (e.g. change from student version to standard version). All of the personal computer versions have desired features such as being user-friendly and having menus, good prompts, online help and user manual. No one wants to have to enter a large set of data more than once. Another nice feature of SPSS is that data entered in the program can be used in another program (exported to another program), and data entered using another program can be imported into SPSS. A copy of the student version of SPSS for Windows 95 is available from the book publisher at a reduced and very reasonable price.

There are other packages of statistical computer programs very similar to SPSS. On many campuses SPSS or another good package of statistical computer programs will be installed on the computers to which you have access. In this case, use what is available and if it is SPSS there is no reason to purchase the student version of SPSS unless you need it to work on your computer at home and/or you think it is a good professional investment. If there is not a good package of statistical computer programs installed on your campus computers, then installing the student version of SPSS on the computers or having each student purchasing a copy of the student version of SPSS may be the solution.

The important thing is that what you learn to use as a student is either available or prepares you to use what is available when you become a professional. Learning to use a very expensive program and/or a mainframe computer while in college makes no sense if the program and/or a mainframe computer will not be available to you on the job. It is helpful to become computer proficient while in college where there are many people to help you learn how to use the computer and answer your questions when you have problems. Once you are working, you may have to solve all of the problems yourself. Few students, once they are on the job, will be able to do an adequate job of data analysis using the statistical techniques presented in this book without using the computer to handle the large amount of data.

When entering data to be computer analyzed, always save the data on disk so that if you have to reanalyze the data because of a mistake in the original analysis or need to conduct a different analysis, the data do not have to be reentered. Additional analysis on the data is quite common, and for large amounts of data it is inconvenient to reenter it. If the data are saved on disk, the data has to be saved as a file with a name. The computer program will ask the name of the data file to be analyzed.

Versions of the SPSS package of statistical programs have changed rapidly. As indicated at the beginning of Appendix A, this edition of the book was developed using version 6.1 of SPSS, but the student version for version 8.0 of SPSS is distributed with the book. The examples of printouts from SPSS programs presented in the book were developed using version 6.1, but printouts from later versions (e.g. 7.5, 8.0) are for all practical purposes the same.

Computer programs come with instruction manuals. The user must read the manual to learn how to use the program. There are a set of manuals for each version of SPSS. If there are few changes in SPSS from the older version to the newer version, the manuals for either version will be sufficient. Chapters 1 and 2 in the SPSS Base System manual (SPSS 1998a) are helpful in getting started using SPSS. A smaller manual than the base system manual, *SPSS 8.0 for Windows Brief Guide* (SPSS 1998c), is excellent. The Student version of SPSS (SPSS 1998d) sold commercially has an excellent manual, but it is not part of the student version distributed with this book. Throughout Chapters 3 and 4 in this book, programs in the SPSS package will be referenced. A few instructions on using each program are presented in Appendix A. More complete instructions are found in the manuals. Guides for using SPSS are available and quite helpful (Shin 1996; Pavkov & Pierce 1998).

Organizing and Graphing Test Scores

Simple Frequency Distribution

The 50 scores in Table 2.1 are not very useful in their present form. They become more meaningful if we know how many people received each score when we order the scores. To do this, we first find the lowest and highest scores in the table. Now we find the number of people who received each score between the lowest (46) and the highest (90) by making up a tally, as illustrated in Figure 2.1.

Notice that all possible scores between 40 and 99 appear on the chart. The first score in Table 2.1 is 66, so we make a mark in row 60 under column 6 (60 + 6 = 66). This mark indicates that one score of 66 has been tabulated. We continue through the table, making a mark in the appropriate row and column for each score.

Table 2.1 Standing Long Jump Scores for 50 Junior High-School Boys

66*	67	54	63	90
56	56	65	71	82
68	68	76	55	78
47	58	68	78	76
46	68	68	90	62
58	49	62	84	75
75	65	66	72	73
71	75	83	83	64
60	76	65	79	56
68	70	48	77	59

*66 inches

	0	1	2	3	4	5	6	7	8	9
40							/	/	/	/
50					/	/	///		//	/
60	/		//	/	/	///	//	/	~~////~~ /	
70	/	//	/	/		///	///	/	//	/
80			/	//	/					
90	//									

Figure 2.1
Ordering a set of scores.

Once the scores are ordered, it is easy to make up a simple frequency distribution of the results, as shown in the first two columns of Table 2.2. We list the scores in rank order with the best score first. In most cases, the higher scores are better scores, but this is not true of running events, numbers of errors or accidents, and so on. A **simple frequency distribution** of a running event would list the lower scores first.

From a simple frequency distribution we can determine the range of scores at a glance, as well as the most frequently received score and the number of people receiving each score. For example, from Table 2.2 we can see that the scores ranged from 90 down to 46, that the most frequently received score was 68, and that with one exception all scores had a frequency of 3 or less.

With a large number of scores, forming a simple frequency distribution is time-consuming without a computer. The computer allows you to enter the scores into the computer and to analyze them using any one of a number of programs. Most packages of statistical programs for mainframe and microcomputers have a frequency count program. The SPSS package has such a program. See Appendix A for brief instructions on using it. The output from the Frequencies program in SPSS for the data in Table 2.1 is presented in Table 2.2. The frequency count program in SPSS and many packages of statistical programs rank order the scores from smallest to largest (ascending order), which is opposite of the instructions in this book if a large score is better than a small score. So, Table 2.2 does not appear exactly like the printout from SPSS. The Frequencies program in SPSS does have an option for listing the scores in descending order which must be used if a small score is good. From Table 2.2 it can be seen that test scores were from 46

Table 2.2 Simple Frequency Distribution of Standing Long Jump Scores of 50 Junior High-School Boys in Table 2.1

Score	Freq.	Cum. F	Percent	Cum. %
90	2	50	4.00	100.00
84	1	48	2.00	96.00
83	2	47	4.00	94.00
82	1	45	2.00	90.00
79	1	44	2.00	88.00
78	2	43	4.00	86.00
77	1	41	2.00	82.00
76	3	40	6.00	80.00
75	3	37	6.00	74.00
73	1	34	2.00	68.00
72	1	33	2.00	66.00
71	2	32	4.00	64.00
70	1	30	2.00	60.00
68	6	29	12.00	58.00
67	1	23	2.00	46.00
66	2	22	4.00	44.00
65	3	20	6.00	40.00
64	1	17	2.00	34.00
63	1	16	2.00	32.00
62	2	15	4.00	30.00
60	1	13	2.00	26.00
59	1	12	2.00	24.00
58	2	11	4.00	22.00
56	3	9	6.00	18.00
55	1	6	2.00	12.00
54	1	5	2.00	10.00
49	1	4	2.00	8.00
48	1	3	2.00	6.00
47	1	2	2.00	4.00
46	1	1	2.00	2.00

to 90, and six people scored 68. Other useful information provided is the percent of the total group receiving each score (Percent column), the cumulative summing of the frequency column (Cum. F column, which is not provided by SPSS), and the percent column (Cum. % column) starting with the worst score and working upward to the best.

Grouping Scores for Graphing

We could present the information in Table 2.2 in the form of a graph. If there are many different scores, the graph is usually formed by grouping like scores together. A graph shows the general shape of a score distribution. In grouping a set of scores, we try to form about 15 groupings. To do this, divide the difference between the largest and smallest scores by 15 and round off the result to the nearest whole number if necessary (Interval size = [largest score − smallest score]/15). This number, the interval size, tells us how many scores to group together. Design the first grouping to contain the best score.

Problem 2.1. Group the 50 standing long jump scores listed in Table 2.2.

Solution. Before we can determine the actual groupings, we must determine the interval size.

Grouping	*Tally*	*Frequency*
89–91	//	2
86–88		0
83–85	///	3
80–82	/	1
77–79	////	4
74–76	~~////~~ /	6
71–73	////	4
68–70	~~////~~ //	7
65–67	~~////~~ /	6
62–64	////	4
59–61	//	2
56–58	~~////~~	5
53–55	//	2
50–52		0
47–49	///	3
44–46	/	1

Figure 2.2
Grouping of data in Table 2.2.

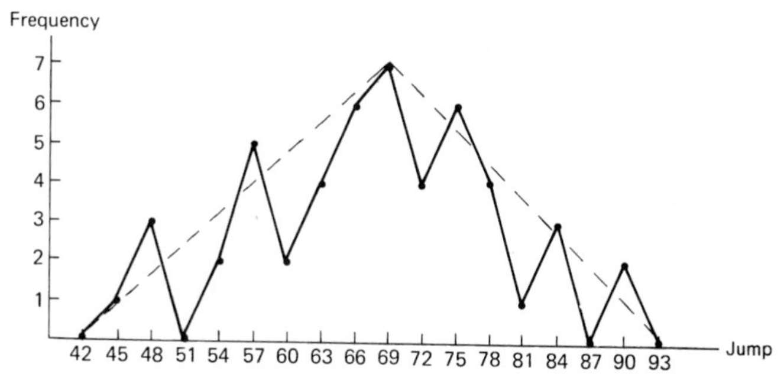

Figure 2.3
A graph of standing long jump scores recorded in inches.

Step 1
From the table we see that the largest score is 90 and the smallest is 46, giving us an interval size of 3:

$$\text{Interval size} = \frac{90 - 46}{15} = \frac{44}{15} = 2.9 = 3.$$

Step 2
The first grouping must contain 3 possible scores, including the score 90 (the best score). The first grouping of 89–91 was selected. Once the first grouping is established, it is easy to work up the rest as presented in Figure 2.2.

Figure 2.3 is a graph of the 50 scores. Test scores, in intervals of 3 (only midpoints are plotted), are listed along the horizontal axis, from low scores on the left to high scores on the right. The frequency is listed on the vertical axis, starting with 0 and increasing upward. We place a dot above each score to indicate its frequency. For example, the dot above score 66 is opposite the frequency value 6, indicating that 6

Figure 2.4
A normal curve.

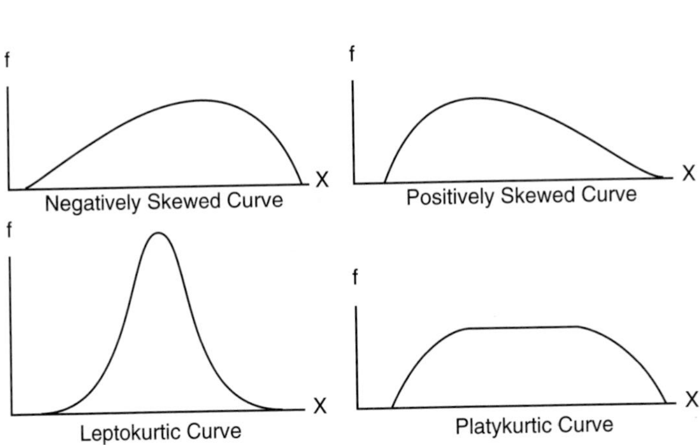

Figure 2.5
Negatively skewed, positively skewed, leptokurtic, and platykurtic curves.

students received scores in the grouping 65–67. By connecting the dots with straight lines, we complete the graph, forming an angled figure called a **frequency polygon.**

By smoothing out the frequency polygon, we create a curve that, by its shape, tells us the nature of the distribution. In Figure 2.3 the smoothing out is indicated by the broken line. If that line resembles the curve in Figure 2.4, the graph is called a **normal** or **bell-shaped curve.** The normal curve is discussed in detail later in the chapter.

When a smoothed graph has a long, low tail on the left, indicating that few students received low scores, it is called a **negatively skewed curve.** When the tail of the curve is on the right, the curve is called **positively skewed.** A curve is called **leptokurtic** when it is more sharply peaked than a normal curve and **platykurtic** when it is less sharply peaked (see Figure 2.5). Leptokurtic curves are characteristic of extremely homogeneous groups. Platykurtic curves are characteristic of heterogeneous groups.

A computer can be used to create a graph. An option of most microcomputer programs is any number of groupings and several different types of graphs. The data in Table 2.2 was analyzed using the Line Chart program in SPSS. See Appendix A for brief instructions on using it. The graph is presented in Figure 2.6. Another type of graph that is quite common is a *histogram.* Again, the frequencies for the intervals are plotted and bars are constructed at the height of the frequency running the full length of the interval. A histogram for the data in Table 2.2 is presented in Figure 2.7. This was generated by the Histogram program in SPSS with the option that a normal curve

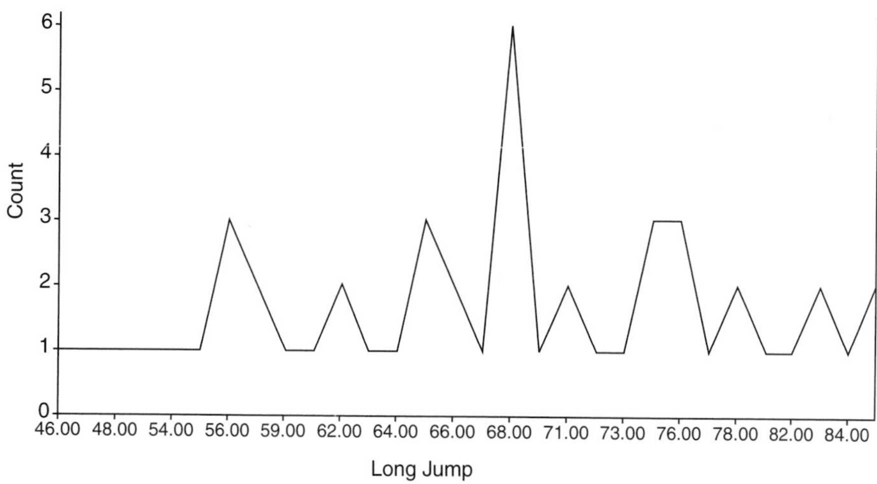

Figure 2.6
Computer-generated frequency polygon for the Table 2.2 data.

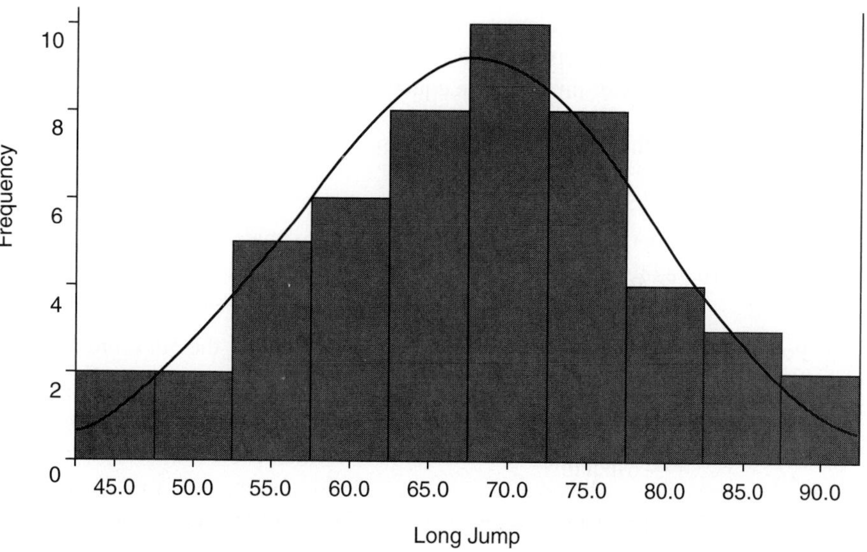

Figure 2.7
Computer-generated histogram for the Table 2.2 data with a normal curve superimposed.

be superimposed on the graph. Notice the intervals in Figures 2.2, 2.6, and 2.7 differ. This is because the microcomputer picked a different number of groupings.

Descriptive Values

Once a large set of scores has been collected, certain descriptive values can be calculated—values that summarize or condense the set of scores, giving it meaning. Descriptive values are used, not only to evaluate individual performance by the person who administered the test, but also to describe the group's performance or compare its performance with that of another group.

Measures of Central Tendency

One type of descriptive value is the measure of **central tendency,** which indicates those points at which scores tend to be concentrated. There are three measures of central tendency: the mode, the median, and the mean.

Mode. The **mode** is the score most frequently received. It is used with nominal data. In Table 2.2 the mode is 68: More students received a score of 68 than any other one score in the set. It is possible to have several modes if several scores tie for most frequent. The mode is not a stable measure because the addition or deletion of a single score can change its value considerably. In Table 2.2, if two of the students who scored 68 had scored 66, the mode would be 66 and 68. Unless the data is nominal or the most frequent score is desired (e.g., most frequent injury or disease), other measures of central tendency are more appropriate.

Median. The **median** is the middle score; half the scores fall above the median and half below. It cannot be calculated unless the scores are listed in order from best to worst. Where n is the number of scores in the set, we can calculate the position of the approximate median using the following formula:

$$\text{Position of approximate median} = \frac{n + 1}{2}$$

Notice that the formula calculates the median's position, or rank, in the listing—not the median itself. The approximate value, always a whole or half number, is that score in the position determined by the equation.

Problem 2.2. Find the approximate median score for the 9 numbers: 4, 3, 1, 4, 10, 7, 7, 8, and 6.

Solution. First, order the listing of scores. The approximate median score is the 5th score in the ordered listing, or the score 6.

$$\text{Position of approximate median} = \frac{9 + 1}{2} = \frac{10}{2} = 5\text{, or the 5th score}$$

10, 8, 7, 7, 6, 4, 4, 3, 1

↑ Median

Problem 2.3. Find the approximate median score for the 6 numbers: 1, 3, 4, 5, 6, and 10.

Solution. First, order the listing of scores. The approximate median score is that score that falls halfway between the 3rd and 4th scores in the ordered listing, or the score 4.5.

$$\text{Position of approximate median} = \frac{6 + 1}{2} = \frac{7}{2} = 3.5\text{, or the 3.5th score}$$

10, 6, 5, 4, 3, 1

↑ Median

The approximate value of the median is often used by teachers, exercise specialists, and other practitioners in preference to the exact value, which is harder to obtain and unnecessarily precise. Notice that the value of the median is affected only by the position, not the value, of each score. If, in Problem 2.2, the scores were 10, 8, 7, 6, 6, 3, 2, 1, and 0, the approximate median would still be 6. This characteristic of the median is sometimes a limitation.

When scores are listed in a simple frequency distribution, we can obtain either an approximate or an exact value of the median. The approximate value of the median for the scores in Table 2.2 falls halfway between the 25th and 26th scores, at a median score of 68. Notice that we count up the frequency column from the lowest score to the 25th and 26th scores received; we do not work in the score column until we have reached the approximate median value.

Researchers are likely to need an exact value of the median. When scores in a simple frequency distribution are listed from best to worst, we can calculate the exact value of the median.

The calculation of the median is a 3-step process:

Step 1
Order the scores in a simple frequency distribution, listing the best score first (see columns 1 and 2 of Table 2.2).

Step 2
Make a cumulative frequency (cf) column by adding the frequencies, starting with the worst score and working upward to the best (see column 3 of Table 2.2).

Step 3
Calculate the median using the following formula:

$$\text{Median} = \text{lrl} + \left(\frac{.5\text{n} - \text{cfb}}{\text{fw}}\right)(\text{UM})$$

where X is the score that contains the median score (the score below which at least half of the frequencies lie), lrl is the lower real limit (X − .5UM), n is the number of scores (the sum of the frequency column), cfb is the cumulative frequency below (the number of scores below X), fw is the frequency within (the frequency for X), and UM is the unit of measurement in which the scores are expressed.

Problem 2.4. Find the exact median score for the scores listed in Table 2.2.

Solution. Because the scores in Table 2.2 are presented in a simple frequency distribution, **Step 1** has been done.

Step 2
To make the cumulative frequency column (cf), we begin adding the frequencies from the worst score (46) up to the best score (90). Thus, the starting values are 1, 2(1 + 1), and 3(2 + 1) as seen in the chart below:

x	f	cf	x	f	cf
90	2	50	60	1	13
.	.	.	59	1	12
.	.	.	58	2	11
.	.	.	56	3	9
70	1	30	55	1	6
68	6	29	54	1	5
67	1	23	49	1	4
66	2	22	48	1	3
65	3	20	47	1	2
64	1	17	46	1	1
63	1	16			
62	2	15			

Step 3
Notice .5n = .5(50) = 25. Where X is 68 (looking at the cf column in Step 2, at least 25 scores are below 68), lrl is 67.5 (68 − .5), n is 50, cfb is 23, and UM is 1 (because the scores are recorded in whole numbers [inches], UM is 1), the exact median score is 67.83:

$$\text{Median} = 67.5 + \left(\frac{25 - 23}{6}\right)(1)$$

$$= 67.5 + \left(\frac{2}{6}\right)(1) = 67.5 + .33 = 67.83.$$

Notice how close this is to the approximate median score, 68.

When the scores in a simple frequency distribution are listed from lowest to highest, as they would be in a running event, we use a different formula to calculate the exact median score:

$$\text{Median} = \text{url} + \left(\frac{\text{cfb} - .5\text{n}}{\text{fw}}\right)(\text{UM})$$

where url is the upper real limit (X + .5UM).

Problem 2.5. Find the exact median score of the 100-yard dash times listed in the following frequency distribution.

x	f	cf
10.0	1	36
10.1	2	35
10.2	4	33
10.3	7	29
10.4	8	22
10.5	9	14
10.7	4	5
11.0	1	1

Solution. Since .5n = .5(36) = 18, X is 10.4, url is 10.45 (10.4 + .05), n is 36, cfb is 14, fw is 8, and UM is .1 (because the scores are in tenths of a second, UM is .1), the exact median score is 10.4:

$$\text{Median} = 10.45 + \left(\frac{14 - 18}{8}\right)(.1)$$

$$= 10.45 + \left(\frac{-4}{8}\right)(.1) = 10.45 + (-.5)(.1)$$

$$= 10.45 + (-.05) = 10.45 - .05 = 10.4.$$

Mean. The mean is ordinarily the most appropriate measure of central tendency with interval or ratio data. It is affected by both the value and the position of each score. The **mean** is the sum of the scores divided by the numL er of scores.

$$\overline{X} = \frac{\Sigma X}{n}$$

where $\overline{X}$ is the mean, ΣX is the sum of the score, and n is the number of scores.

Problem 2.6. Calculate the mean of the following scores: 2, 3, 6, 7, 1, 5, and 10.

Solution. Where ΣX is 34 and n is 7, the mean is 4.86:

$$\overline{X} = \frac{34}{7} = 4.857 = 4.86.$$

Notice that the scores need not be ordered from highest to lowest to calculate the mean. For example, the mean for the scores in Table 2.1 is 67.78, the sum of the randomly ordered scores divided by 50.

When the graph of the scores is a normal curve, the mode, median, and mean are equal. When the graph is positively skewed, the mean is larger than the median; when it is negatively skewed, the mean is less than the median. For example, the graph for the scores, 2, 3, 1, 4, 1, 8, and 10 is positively skewed, with the mean 4.14 and the median 3.

The mean is the most common measure of central tendency. But when scores are quite skewed or lack a common interval between consecutive scores (as do ordinal scores), the median is the best measure of central tendency. The mode is used only when the mean and median cannot be calculated (e.g., with nominal scores) or when the only information wanted is the most frequent score (e.g., most common uniform size, most frequent error).

Measures of Variability

A second type of descriptive value is the measure of **variability,** which describes the set of scores in terms of their spread or heterogeneity. For example, consider these sit-up scores for 2 groups:

Group 1	Group 2
9	5
5	6
1	4

For both groups the mean and median are 5. If you simply report that the mean and median for both groups are identical without showing the scores, another person could conclude that the two groups have equal or similar ability. This is not true: Group 2 is more homogeneous in performance than is Group 1. A measure of variability is the descriptive term that indicates this difference in the spread, or heterogeneity of a set of scores. There are two such measures: the range and the standard deviation.

Range. The range is the easiest measure of variability to obtain and the one that is used when the measure of central tendency is the mode or median. The **range** is the difference between the highest and lowest scores. For example, the range for the scores in Table 2.2 is 44 (90 − 46). The range is neither a precise nor stable measure because it depends on only two scores and is affected by a change in either of them. For example, the range of scores in Table 2.2 would have been 38 (84 − 46) if the students who scored 90 had been absent.

Standard Deviation. The **standard deviation** (symbolized s) is the measure of variability used with the mean. It indicates the amount that all the scores differ or deviate from the mean—the more the scores differ from the mean, the higher the standard deviation. The sum of the deviations of the scores from the mean is always 0. Provided are two types of formulas: (1) the definitional formula; and (2) a calculational formula. The definitional formula illustrates what the standard deviation is, but is more difficult to use. The calculational formula is easier to use if you have only a simple calculator to use. They will both be illustrated by example.

The definitional formula for the standard deviation is:

$$s = \sqrt{\frac{\Sigma(X - \overline{X})^2}{n}} \text{ (definitional formula)} \tag{2.1}$$

where s is the standard deviation, X is the scores, $\overline{X}$ is the mean, and n is the number of scores.

Some books, calculators, and computer programs will use the term n − 1 rather than n in the denominator of the standard deviation formula. The use of n is preferred in this chapter. Either can be used because the difference is minimal unless n is very small. If n − 1 is used, the formula for the standard deviation is:

$$s = \sqrt{\frac{\Sigma(X - \overline{X})^2}{n - 1}}. \tag{2.2}$$

If the group tested is viewed as the group of interest, it is considered the *population* and formula (2.1) is used. If the group tested is viewed as a representative part of the population, it is considered a *sample* and formula (2.2) is used. In other words, if the standard deviation calculated on sample data is to be used as an estimate of the population standard deviation, Formula 2.2 is used. Many introductory statistics books have a comprehensive discussion of this point.

Problem 2.7a. Compute the standard deviation using the definitional formulas for the following set of scores:

7, 2, 7, 6, 5, 6, 2.

Solution. The process is 4 steps: calculate the mean, subtract the mean from each score, square the differences, and determine s. After calculating the mean, we can combine Steps 2 and 3 by creating a table, working across the rows, and then totaling the columns. Finally s is calculated.

Step 1

$$\overline{X} = \frac{\Sigma X}{n} = \frac{35}{7} = 5$$

Steps 2–3

X	$(X - \overline{X})$	$(X - \overline{X})^2$
7	(7 − 5) 2	4
2	(2 − 5) −3	9
7	2	4
6	1	1
5	0	0
6	1	1
2	−3	9
Σ = 35	Σ = 0	Σ = 28

Step 4

$s = \sqrt{28/7} = \sqrt{4} = 2$ (by Formula 2.1) or

$s = \sqrt{28/(7 - 1)} = \sqrt{4.67} = 2.2$ (by Formula 2.2)

Since n is small, the difference in using n or n − 1 is somewhat large. Some calculators will calculate the standard deviation once the data is entered. These calculators provide the option of using n or n − 1. Microcomputer programs usually use n − 1.

The definitional formula is seldom used to calculate the standard deviation by hand because it is cumbersome when the mean is a fraction. Instead, the following formula is used to calculate s:

$$s = \sqrt{\frac{\Sigma X^2}{n} - \frac{(\Sigma X)^2}{n^2}} \text{ (calculational formula)} \tag{2.3}$$

where ΣX^2 is the sum of the squared scores, ΣX is the sum of the scores, and n is the number of scores. If n − 1 is used in the formula, it is

$$s = \sqrt{\frac{\Sigma X^2 - (\Sigma X)^2/n}{n - 1}} \tag{2.4}$$

Formula 2.3 will be used most often in this chapter.

Problem 2.7b. Compute the standard deviation using the computational formulas for the following set of scores: 7, 2, 7, 6, 5, 6, 2.

Solution. The process is 3 steps: calculate ΣX, calculate ΣX^2, and determine s. We can combine the first 2 steps by creating a table, working first across the rows and then totaling the columns:

X	X^2
7	49
2	4
7	49
6	36
5	25
6	36
2	4
Σ = 35	Σ = 203

Where ΣX is 35, ΣX^2 is 203, and n is 7, the standard deviation is 2:

$$s = \sqrt{\frac{203}{7} - \frac{35^2}{7^2}} = \sqrt{\frac{203}{7} - \frac{1225}{49}} = \sqrt{29 - 25} = \sqrt{4} = 2$$

or 2.2:

$$s = \sqrt{\frac{203 - 35^2/7}{7 - 1}} = \sqrt{\frac{203 - 1225/7}{6}} = \sqrt{\frac{203 - 175}{6}}$$

$$= \sqrt{4.67} = 2.2.$$

Notice that with this formula the scores are listed in a column and the square of each score is listed in a second column. The sums of these two columns are needed to calculate the standard deviation.

Table 2.3 Output from the Frequencies Program for the Data in Table 2.1

Variable	Cases	Mean	Median	Mode	Std. Dev.	Min.	Max.
Score	50	67.78	68.00	68.00	10.74	46	90

Remember that the standard deviation indicates the variability of a set of scores around the mean. The larger the standard deviation, the more heterogeneous the scores. The minimum value of s is 0.

The calculations in Problem 2.7 are easy because the number of scores is small and the number for which we needed the square root (4) is a perfect square. Unhappily, you will usually be working with between 50 and 300 scores and a number that is not a perfect square. You can speed up the calculations using a calculator. In fact, there are calculators that, by pushing the appropriate key, compute the mean and standard deviation once the data are entered. Remember, though, that if the number of scores is very large, you may find a computer more accurate and faster than a calculator.

Computer programs that calculate means and standard deviations are very common. The Descriptives program in the SPSS package provides these statistics and other optional statistics. The optional statistics in Frequencies provide the same statistics and in addition the median. See Appendix A for brief instructions on using either program. In calculating the standard deviation, both programs use $n - 1$ in the denominator. The output from Frequencies for the data in Table 2.1 is presented in Table 2.3. Computer programs that calculate the median are not numerous.

Variance. A third measure of variability that is commonly calculated is the **variance.** It is not used as a descriptive term like the range and standard deviation but rather as a useful statistic in certain high level statistical procedures like regression analysis or analysis of variance, which will be discussed later in this chapter. The variance is the square of the standard deviation. If, for example, the standard deviation is 5, the variance is 25 (5^2). The calculation of the variance is the same as for the standard deviation, except the square root step is eliminated.

Measuring Group Position

Percentile Ranks

After a test session, most individuals want to know how their performance compares with those of others in the group. Ranks can be calculated by assigning the individual who earned the best score the rank of 1, the individual who earned the next best score the rank of 2, and so on. But rank has little meaning unless the number of individuals in the group is known. A rank of 35 is quite good when there are 250 individuals in the group; it is very poor when there are 37. **Percentile ranks** that indicate the relative position of an individual in a group indicate the percentage of the group that scored below a given score.

The calculation of percentile ranks is a three-step process:

Step 1
Order the scores in a simple frequency distribution, listing the best score first (see Table 2.2).

Step 2
Make a cumulative frequency (cf) column, by adding the frequencies, starting with the worst score and working upward to the best.

Step 3
Calculate the percentile rank of a given score using the following formula:

$$PR_x = \left(cfb + \frac{fw}{2}\right)\left(\frac{100}{n}\right) \tag{2.5}$$

where PR_x is the percentile rank of score X, cfb is the number of scores below X (the entry in the cf column one level below X), fw is the frequency of X, and n is the number of scores (the sum of the frequency column).

Problem 2.8. Given the following scores and frequencies, determine the percentile rank for a score of 6:

x	f
10	1
6	4
5	10
4	6
3	3
0	1

Solution. Because the scores are presented in a simple frequency distribution, **Step 1** has been done.

Step 2
To make the cumulative frequency column, we begin adding the frequencies from the worst score (here, 0) up to the best score (10). Thus the entry in the cf column opposite score 3 would be 4 ($1 + 3 = 4$); and the entry opposite score 4 would be 10 ($4 + 6 = 10$). The final chart would look like this:

x	f	cf
10	1	25
6	4	24
5	10	20
4	6	10
3	3	4
0	1	1

Step 3
The percentile rank of score 6 where cfb is 20, fw is 4, and n is 25 is 88:

$$PR_6 = \left(20 + \frac{4}{2}\right)\left(\frac{100}{25}\right)$$

$$= (20 + 2)(4) = (22)(4) = 88.$$

Of the scores received, 88% are below 6.

In the percentile rank formula, the term $cfb + \frac{fw}{2}$ is the number of scores in theory below the score (x). This is based on the assumption that half the individuals who have received a given score actually scored below that score before rounding off. That is, when four people receive a score of 10, we assume that two of them originally had scores between 9.5 and 10.0.

Usually the percentile rank for each score in a set is calculated. Because the value of $\frac{100}{n}$ in the formula is seldom a whole number, computing PRs can be tedious without a calculator. Using a calculator, carry $\frac{100}{n}$ out to three digits to the right of the decimal point (thousandths), rounding off the PR to a whole number only after multiplying the cfb + $\frac{fw}{2}$ value by $\frac{100}{n}$. For example, if n in our set of scores in Problem 2.8 had been 26 rather than 25, the value of $\frac{100}{n}$ would have been 3.846 $\frac{100}{26}$ = 3.846 and the PR for score 6 would have been 85:

$$PR_6 = (22)(3.846) = 84.612 = 85.$$

Disadvantages. Percentile ranks are ordinal scores. There is no common unit of measurement between consecutive percentile rank values because they are position measures, totally depending on the scores of the group. We can see this clearly in the following PR column, the percentile ranks for the complete set of scores with which we have been working.

x	f	cf	PR
10	1	25	98
6	4	24	88
5	10	20	60
4	6	10	28
3	3	4	10
0	1	1	2

As the scores go up from 4 to 5 and from 5 to 6, notice that the percentile ranks rise at different rates: 32 and 28 respectively. For this reason, it is inappropriate to add, subtract, multiply, or divide percentile rank values.

Another disadvantage is that a small change in actual performance near the mean results in a disproportionate change in percentile rank; the opposite is true of changes at the extremes. We can see this in the columns above, where a change of 1 from X = 4 to X = 5 is a PR change of 32, while a score change of 4 from 6 to 10 is a PR change of only 10.

Percentiles

We often express test standards, or norms, in percentile ranks that are multiples of 5 (5, 10, 15, and so on). To develop these norms we must first determine the test score, or **percentile,** that corresponds to each rank. Here we have a percentile rank from which to calculate a test score (percentile). When the larger score is the better score, we use the following formula to calculate the test score that corresponds to a particular rank:

$$P = lrl + \left[\frac{\frac{(PR)\,(n)}{100} - cfb}{fw} \right] (UM) \qquad \textit{(2.6)}$$

where P is the test score (percentile) that corresponds to the percentile rank, X is the score that contains the percentile (the score below which the wanted percentage of frequencies fall), lrl is the lower real limit (X − .5UM), PR is the percentile rank,

Table 2.4 Sample Scores and Frequency Distribution

x	f	cf
21	2	52
18	3	50
15	3	47
14	4	44
13	4	40
11	10	36
10	7	26
9	4	19
8	6	15
7	5	9
6	2	4
5	1	2
1	1	1

n is the number of scores (sum of the frequency column), cfb is the number of scores below X, fw is the frequency for X, and UM is the unit of measurement in which the test scores are expressed.

Note: When the smaller score is the better score, the formula becomes

$$P = \text{url} + \left[\frac{\text{cfb} - \dfrac{(\text{PR})\,(\text{n})}{100}}{\text{fw}}\right](\text{UM}) \qquad \textit{(2.7)}$$

where url is the upper limit (X + .5UM). Note that the formulas for calculating the median are a special case of these formulas.

Problem 2.9. Given the scores and frequency distribution in Table 2.4, determine which score has a percentile rank of 45. (What is P for a PR of 45?)

Solution. Before we can solve the formula for P, we must determine the value of X that gives us terms lrl, cfb, and fw:

$$\frac{(\text{PR})(\text{n})}{100} = \frac{(45)(52)}{100} = \frac{2340}{100} = 23.4.$$

So X is the 23.4th score from the bottom. Looking at the cf column in Table 2.4, we see that score 10 contains the 23.4th score. Now we can solve for P. Where lrl is 9.5 (10 − .5), PR is 45, n is 52, cfb is 19, fw is 7, and UM is 1, P is 10:

$$P = 9.5 + \left[\frac{\dfrac{(45)(52)}{100} - 19}{7}\right](1)$$

$$= 9.5 + \left[\frac{\dfrac{2340}{100} - 19}{7}\right](1)$$

$$= 9.5 + \frac{23.4 - 19}{7}$$

$$= 9.5 + \frac{4.4}{7} = 9.5 + .63 = 10.13 = 10.$$

The score below which 45% of the scores fall is 10; it has a percentile rank of 45.

Using the Computer

With a large number of scores, percentile ranks and percentiles should be obtained by using the computer. Some packages of statistical programs have these programs. Percentiles can be obtained in the SPSS package by using the Frequencies program. See the SPSS manual or Appendix A for the procedures. SPSS does not have a percentile rank program. In the absence of a percentile rank program, one possibility is to use a frequency count program to get a simple frequency distribution, which would make the hand calculation of percentile ranks much easier. Another possibility is to use the computer to obtain a frequency count printout like the one in Table 2.2. If you are willing to modify the definition of a percentile rank, so that it is the percentage of the group that scored at or below a given score (rather than below), the Cum. % column values in Table 2.2 can be interpreted as percentile ranks. If you are not willing to modify the definition of a percentile rank, there are two ways the information in Table 2. 2 could be used to obtain percentile ranks. One, using columns two and three in Table 2.2, percentile ranks could quickly be calculated by hand using the formulas already presented. Two, percentile ranks could quickly be calculated by hand using columns four and five in Table 2.2 and the formula

$$PR_X = \text{Cum. \% below X} + \frac{\text{Percent for X}}{2}. \quad \textbf{(2.8)}$$

Problem 2.10. Using the information in Table 2.2, what is the percentile rank for the score 56?

Solution. The Cum. % below 56 is 12 and the Percent for 56 is 6.00, so

$$PR_{56} = \text{Cum. \% below 56} + \frac{\text{Percent for 56}}{2}$$

$$= 12 + \frac{6.00}{2} = 15.$$

Some frequency count computer programs (SPSS is one) treat a large score as being better than a small score, but list scores from smallest (worst) to largest (best) and calculate the cumulative frequency and cumulative percentage columns from smallest score to largest score (upside down to the way we have been doing it). In a situation like this you must think carefully and adjust formulas and/or procedures accordingly. For example, $PR_X = \text{Cum. \% above X} + \frac{\text{Percent for X}}{2}$.

Problem 2.11. Using the information provided here with a large score better than a small score, what is the percentile rank for the score 3?

Score	Freq.	Cum. F	Percent	Cum. %
1	1	1	5.0	5
3	4	5	20.0	25
4	12	17	60.0	85
5	3	20	15.0	100

Solution. The Cum. % above 3 is 5 and the Percent for 3 is 20, so

$$PR_3 = \text{Cum. \% above } 3 + \frac{\text{Percent for } 3}{2}$$

$$= 5 + \frac{20}{2} = 15.0$$

Computer programs usually treat a large score as being better than a small score. In situations where a small score is better than a large score (mile run, number of days injured, etc.), how do we obtain percentile ranks? If the computer program provides percentile ranks, subtract the percentile rank for each score from 100 to get the correct percentile rank. If you are using a computer printout like the one in Table 2.2, recalculate the cumulative frequency or cumulative percentage column by summing from the top (largest and worst score) to the bottom (smallest and best score) of the table before hand-calculating percentile ranks by the formula

$$PR_x = \left[\text{Cum. F above X} + \frac{\text{Freq. for X}}{2}\right]\left[\frac{100}{n}\right] \quad \text{or}$$

$$PR_x = \text{Cum. \% above X} + \frac{\text{Percent for X}}{2}$$

If you are using the SPSS frequency count program to obtain the information necessary for calculating percentile ranks by hand using the formula requiring frequencies and cumulative frequencies, do the following:

1. In the SPSS program select the option for printing the scores in ascending order (small to large).
2. Using the computer printout, make a cumulative frequency column summing the frequencies from the largest score up to the smallest score.
3. By hand, calculate the percentile ranks using the formula:

$$PR_x = \left[\text{Cum. F below X} + \frac{\text{Freq. for X}}{2}\right]\left[\frac{100}{n}\right]$$

Example Information Table: Columns 1–4 are from the SPSS printout and column five is the column you made

Score	Freq.	%	Cum. %	Cum. F
2	1	10	10	10
3	2	20	30	9
4	3	30	60	7
5	4	40	100	4

If you are using the SPSS frequency count program to obtain the information necessary for calculating percentile ranks by hand using percentages and cumulative percentages, do the following:

Table 2.5 Percentile Output in Units of Five for the Table 2.1 Data

Percentile	Value
95	86.70
90	82.90
85	78.35
80	76.80
75	76.00
70	75.00
65	72.15
60	70.60
55	68.00
50	68.00
45	66.95
40	65.40
35	64.85
30	62.30
25	59.75
20	58.00
15	56.00
10	54.10
5	47.55

Table 2.6 Percentile Ranks for the Table 2.2 Data

Score	Percentile Rank
90	98.00
84	95.00
83	92.00
82	89.00
79	87.00
.	.
.	.
.	.
54	9.00
49	7.00
48	5.00
47	3.00
46	1.00

1. In the SPSS program select the option for printing the scores in descending order (large to small).
2. By hand, calculate the percentile ranks using the formula:

$$PR_x = \text{Cum. \% above X} + \frac{\text{Percent for X}}{2}$$

Example Information Table: All columns are from the SPSS printout.

Score	Freq.	%	Cum. %
5	4	40	40
4	3	30	70
3	2	20	90
2	1	10	100

For the data in Table 2.1, the printout of percentiles in units of 5 is presented in Table 2.5, and the hand calculation of percentile ranks using the information in Table 2.2 is presented in Table 2.6. Percentile norms are commonly reported in units of 5. Notice in Table 2.5 that a score is calculated for each percentile, but in Table 2.6 a percentile rank is calculated for each score. Also, notice that in Table 2.5 the 50th percentile is the median score.

Standard Scores

Standard scores are used frequently to evaluate students at the end of a semester or to determine class ranks based on all the tests administered over a period of time. When each student has scores, for example, on sit-ups, sit-and-reach for flexibility, and mile run, how does the teacher determine which student's overall performance is best? A fitness specialist working in a health club or corporate fitness program could face the same problem. The three scores cannot be added together because the unit of measurement differs from test to test (executions, inches, seconds). We eliminate this problem by translating each test score into a standard score and summing the standard scores for each student or participant. The individual with the largest sum is the best overall.

z-Scores

A **z-score** indicates how many standard deviations above or below the mean a test score lies. We calculate z-scores with the following formula:

$$z = \frac{X - \overline{X}}{s}. \tag{2.9}$$

A person who scores at the mean receives a z-score of 0; a person who scores one-half a standard deviation below the mean receives a z-score of −.5. Thus, the mean z-score is 0, and the standard deviation for a distribution of z-scores is 1.

T-Scores

Because z-scores are usually fractional and can be negative, physical educators are more likely to use T-scores to combine different tests together. **T-scores** are usually rounded off to the nearest whole number and are rarely negative. The mean T-score is 50, and the standard deviation for a distribution of T-scores is 10. The formula for calculating T-scores is as follows:

$$T = \frac{10(X - \overline{X})}{s} + 50. \tag{2.10}$$

Note that the term $\frac{(X - \overline{X})}{s}$ in the T-score formula is the equation for determining the z-score. We could restate the T-score formula, then, as follows:

$$T = 10z + 50.$$

Problem 2.12. Given a mean of 87 and a standard deviation of 2.35, determine the T-score for a score of 90.

Solution. Where X is 90, $\overline{X}$ is 87, and s is 2.35, T is 63:

$$T = \frac{(10)(90 - 87)}{2.35} + 50 = \frac{(10)(3)}{2.35} + 50$$

$$= \frac{30}{2.35} + 50 = 12.76 + 50 = 62.76 = 63.$$

Notice that T-scores rise as performances rise above the mean. When smaller scores are better, T-scores must rise as performances fall below the mean. Thus, for speed events, we use the following formula to calculate T-scores:

$$T = \frac{10(\overline{X} - X)}{s} + 50. \tag{2.11}$$

The relationship among test scores, z-scores, and T-scores for a hypothetical test with mean 75 and standard deviation 8 is shown in Table 2.7. From the table we can see that a T-score of 50 is equivalent to a z-score of 0, or a test score equal to the test mean. Also a test score 2 standard deviations above the mean equals a T-score of 70.

T-scores are easy to interpret if we remember the mean T-score is 50 and the standard deviation for T-scores is 10. For example, a T-score of 65 is 1.5 standard deviations

Table 2.7 Relationship among Test Scores (Mean 75, Standard Deviation 8), z-Scores, and T-Scores

	Score Position						
	$\overline{X} - 3s$	$\overline{X} - 2s$	$\overline{X} - s$	$\overline{X}$	$\overline{X} + s$	$\overline{X} + 2s$	$\overline{X} + 3s$
Hypothetical Test Scores	51	59	67	75	83	91	99
z-Scores	−3	−2	−1	0	1	2	3
T-Scores	20	30	40	50	60	70	80

Table 2.8 T-Scores Calculated by Formula and Rounded to Whole Numbers

Student	Mile Run*	Pull-Up†	Sit-Up‡	Mile Run T	Pull-Up T	Sit-Up T	Sum T
1	407	0	43	64	43	52	159
2	511	4	45	51	64	54	169
3	478	2	50	55	54	60	169
4	525	1	51	49	48	61	158
5	480	4	53	55	64	64	183
6	440	8	51	60	85	61	206
7	519	1	39	50	48	47	145
8	488	2	43	54	54	52	160
9	510	0	30	51	43	37	131
10	456	3	47	58	59	57	174
11	603	1	38	40	48	46	134
12	495	0	40	53	43	48	144
13	435	1	45	60	48	54	162
14	588	1	29	42	48	36	126
15	630	0	29	37	43	36	116
16	638	0	42	36	43	51	130
17	511	0	40	51	43	48	142
18	721	0	28	26	43	35	104
19	482	0	52	55	43	62	160
20	630	0	30	37	43	37	117
21	360	1	54	69	48	65	182
22	540	0	30	48	43	37	128

*Mean 520.32; standard deviation 83.47.
†Mean 1.32; standard deviation 1.92.
‡Mean 41.32; standard deviation 8.59.

above the mean, a T-score of 40 is 1 standard deviation below the mean, and a T-score of 78 is 2.8 standard deviations above the mean.

The T-scores for 22 students with 3 test scores are listed in Table 2.8, Student 6 is the best overall student because the sum of that student's score (206) is the largest.

Methods of Determining T-Scores. Obviously, translating test scores to T-scores takes time and effort. Few physical education teachers, exercise specialists, or practitioners given 5 to 15 scores for each of a hundred or more individuals, have the time to calculate T-scores by hand. However, it would be unfortunate to bypass a good, easy technique for lack of time. There are two methods that allow us to obtain T-scores quickly: calculated conversion tables and computer analysis.

Calculated Conversion Tables. For most tests, each score will be obtained by several people. For example, we can see in Table 2.8 that 10 students did no pull-ups, 6 students did 1 pull-up, and so on. Once the T-score for a test score is determined, it is not necessary to recalculate the T-score every time that test score is repeated. Instead, we develop a test score–T-score conversion table. The method of development is either calculation by hand or by using the computer.

When the number of different scores is small, we can construct the test score–T-score conversion table by hand, calculating the T-score for each existing test score and expressing the T-score as a whole number. For example, from the pull-up scores in Table 2.8 we can develop this conversion table:

X	0	1	2	3	4	5	6	7	8
T	43	48	54	59	64	69	74	80	85

Using the Computer

When the number of different test scores is large, the computer method should be utilized. From the computer output, conversion tables can be developed.

Computer Analysis. The fastest and easiest way to calculate T-scores is through computer analysis. In fact, with a large amount of data it may be the only feasible method. The standard scores option in the SPSS Descriptive program calculates z-scores for each score of a person. The z-scores are calculated and attached to the data file as additional variables. To see the z-scores you must display or print the data file. The z-scores are not saved on the data disk, so if there is a future need for them, it would be best to save the file with the data and z-scores as a new file. In this way you will have one file with the data and a second file with the data and z-scores. Whether or not the z-scores are saved, after the z-scores are calculated, you probably want the computer to provide you with the sum of the z-scores. See Appendix A for how to do this using the transformation feature available in SPSS and in most computer packages of statistical programs. A computer program (TSCORE) that does many of these calculations easily and automatically is discussed in this section.

The TSCORE program is available for DOS, Windows 3.1, and Windows 95 operating systems (Seong & Baumgartner 1998). It is user-friendly, full of prompts, able to output to screen or printer, able to handle missing data for a subject, and able to import and export data. Data must be saved on a disk before it can be analyzed.

Table 2.9 lists the scores of 45 students on a fitness test. The scores were analyzed using the TSCORE program. The output of that program is shown in Table 2.10.

From Table 2.10 we can see each student's (No) T-scores listed for each test and the sum of each student's T-scores is listed as well. For example, the sum of Student 1's T-scores is 261.50. Mean and standard deviation are provided for each test. The printout also shows that for the 44 students who were measured on all 5 tests (Student 45 did not take all the tests), the mean and standard deviation for the sum of the T-scores were 249.75 and 33.78 respectively. Finally, at the bottom of Table 2.10 are percentile ranks for each test score, as well as a percentile rank for the sum of each student's T-scores. For example, Student 1 had a percentile rank of 48 on the sit-up test and an overall percentile rank of 60.

General database computer programs can also be used to calculate T-scores. These programs must be programmed to produce the desired results by using the T-score equation. The advantage of TSCORE is that it is designed to complete all the necessary calculations, whereas a database program is more difficult to use. The advantage of a database program is that it can be used for many different functions other than just T-scores.

Table 2.9 Scores of 45 Students on a Fitness Test

Student	Skinfold	Mile Run	Sit-and-Reach	Pull-Up	Sit-Up
1	27.00	407.00	38.00	0.00	43.00
2	24.00	511.00	45.00	4.00	45.00
3	22.00	478.00	22.00	2.00	50.00
4	24.00	525.00	38.00	1.00	51.00
5	23.00	480.00	40.00	4.00	53.00
6	16.00	440.00	41.00	8.00	51.00
7	31.00	519.00	39.00	1.00	39.00
8	33.00	488.00	34.00	2.00	43.00
9	28.00	510.00	40.00	0.00	30.00
10	27.00	456.00	39.00	3.00	47.00
11	28.00	603.00	37.00	1.00	38.00
12	39.00	495.00	31.00	0.00	40.00
13	24.00	435.00	37.00	1.00	45.00
14	22.00	588.00	36.00	1.00	29.00
15	25.00	630.00	34.00	0.00	29.00
16	38.00	638.00	28.00	0.00	42.00
17	43.00	511.00	35.00	0.00	40.00
18	37.00	721.00	28.00	0.00	28.00
19	22.00	482.00	37.00	0.00	52.00
20	25.00	630.00	37.00	0.00	30.00
21	28.00	360.00	36.00	1.00	54.00
22	28.00	540.00	31.00	0.00	30.00
23	30.00	507.00	28.00	2.00	40.00
24	22.00	454.00	33.00	2.00	58.00
25	22.00	472.00	37.00	2.00	54.00
26	34.00	588.00	35.00	1.00	56.00
27	18.00	588.00	28.00	1.00	42.00
28	37.00	524.00	22.00	0.00	48.00
29	38.00	713.00	21.00	0.00	37.00
30	19.00	440.00	28.00	3.00	42.00
31	28.00	417.00	25.00	0.00	30.00
32	40.00	720.00	28.00	0.00	47.00
33	19.00	525.00	21.00	2.00	30.00
34	21.00	400.00	17.00	1.00	25.00
35	20.00	390.00	27.00	5.00	53.00
36	17.00	375.00	33.00	13.00	52.00
37	30.00	390.00	26.00	2.00	49.00
38	18.00	385.00	25.00	4.00	49.00
39	23.00	390.00	34.00	5.00	51.00
40	14.00	342.00	30.00	13.00	45.00
41	42.00	384.00	10.00	1.00	36.00
42	15.00	510.00	31.00	3.00	35.00
43	40.00	592.00	24.00	0.00	43.00
44	19.00	500.00	35.00	5.00	63.00
45	22.00		32.00		47.00

Table 2.10 Sample Computer Printout of Data in Table 2.9

Raw Score Summary:

Score	*Mean*	*Std Dev*	*Missing*
Skin	26.71	7.77	
Mile	501.20	96.33	1
Reach	31.40	7.00	
Pullup	2.14	2.97	1
Situp	43.13	9.19	

Sum of (Weighted) T-Scores:

Mean:	249.75
Std Dev:	33.78
Missing:	1

Score Table:

1	Skin
2	Mile
3	Reach
4	Pullup
5	Situp

Weighting Table:

No	*Score*	*Weight*
1	Skin	1.00
2	Mile	1.00
3	Reach	1.00
4	Pullup	1.00
5	Situp	1.00

Table 2.10 *Continued*

	T-Scores:					
No	*SC00l*	*SC002*	*SC003*	*SC004*	*SC005*	*Sum*
1	49.63	59.78	59.42	42.82	49.85	261.50
2	53.49	48.98	69.42	56.27	52.03	280.19
3	56.06	52.41	36.58	49.54	57.47	252.06
4	53.49	47.53	59.42	46.18	58.56	265.18
5	54.78	52.20	62.28	56.27	60.74	286.26
6	63.79	56.35	63.71	69.72	58.56	312.13
7	44.48	48.15	60.85	46.18	45.50	245.17
8	41.90	51.37	53.71	49.54	49.85	246.38
9	48.34	49.09	62.28	42.82	35.71	238.24
10	49.63	54.69	60.85	52.90	54.21	272.28
11	48.34	39.43	58.00	46.18	44.41	236.36
12	34.18	50.64	49.43	42.82	46.59	223.66
13	53.49	56.87	58.00	46.18	52.03	266.57
14	56.06	40.99	56.57	46.18	34.62	234.43
15	52.20	36.63	53.71	42.82	34.62	219.98
16	35.47	35.80	45.14	42.82	48.77	208.00
17	29.03	48.98	55.14	42.82	46.59	222.56
18	36.75	27.18	45.14	42.82	33.53	185.43
19	56.06	51.99	58.00	42.82	59.65	268.52
20	52.20	36.63	58.00	42.82	35.71	225.36
21	48.34	64.66	56.57	46.18	61.82	277.57
22	48.34	45.97	49.43	42.82	35.71	222.27
23	45.77	49.40	45.14	49.54	46.59	236.44
24	56.06	54.90	52.28	49.54	66.18	278.97
25	56.06	53.03	58.00	49.54	61.82	278.46
26	40.62	40.99	55.14	46.18	64.00	246.93
27	61.21	40.99	45.14	46.18	48.77	242.30
28	36.75	47.63	36.58	42.82	55.30	219.08
29	35.47	28.01	35.15	42.82	43.33	184.77
30	59.93	56.35	45.14	52.90	48.77	263.10
31	48.34	58.74	40.86	42.82	35.71	226.47
32	32.89	27.29	45.14	42.82	54.21	202.35
33	59.93	47.53	35.15	49.54	35.71	227.86
34	57.35	60.51	29.44	46.18	30.27	223.74
35	58.64	61.54	43.72	59.63	60.74	284.26
36	62.50	63.10	52.28	86.53	59.65	324.06
37	45.77	61.54	42.29	49.54	56.38	255.52
38	61.21	62.06	40.86	56.27	56.38	276.79
39	54.78	61.54	53.71	59.63	58.56	288.22
40	66.36	66.53	48.00	86.53	52.03	319.45
41	30.32	62.17	19.44	46.18	42.24	200.34
42	65.08	49.09	49.43	52.90	41.15	257.65
43	32.89	40.57	39.43	42.82	49.85	205.57
44	59.93	50.13	55.14	59.63	71.62	296.44
45	56.06	−1.00	50.86	−1.00	54.21	−1.00

−1 indicates missing data
SC is a T-score

Table 2.10 *Continued*

			Percentile Ranks:			
No	*SC00I*	*SC002*	*SC003*	*SC004*	*SC005*	*Sum*
1	44	78	84	17	48	60
2	54	39	99	83	54	83
3	69	60	11	65	72	53
4	54	30	84	45	77	65
5	60	58	93	83	87	88
6	94	70	97	94	77	94
7	26	35	89	45	30	47
8	23	53	57	65	48	49
9	37	43	93	17	14	42
10	44	65	89	76	61	72
11	37	15	77	45	28	38
12	10	51	43	17	34	24
13	54	74	77	45	54	67
14	69	22	69	45	7	35
15	49	11	57	17	7	17
16	13	8	31	17	41	13
17	1	39	63	17	34	22
18	18	1	31	17	3	3
19	69	56	77	17	82	69
20	49	11	77	17	14	28
21	37	97	69	45	91	76
22	37	26	43	17	14	19
23	29	47	31	65	34	40
24	69	67	51	65	97	81
25	69	63	77	65	91	78
26	21	22	63	45	94	51
27	89	22	31	45	41	44
28	18	33	11	17	66	15
29	13	6	7	17	26	1
30	83	70	31	76	41	63
31	37	76	18	17	14	31
32	7	3	31	17	61	8
33	83	30	7	65	14	33
34	77	81	3	45	1	26
35	79	85	23	90	87	85
36	92	94	51	98	82	99
37	29	85	21	65	69	56
38	89	90	18	83	69	74
39	60	85	57	90	77	90
40	99	99	39	98	54	97
41	3	92	1	45	23	6
42	97	43	43	76	21	58
43	7	17	14	17	48	10
44	83	49	63	90	99	92
45	69	−1	48	−1	61	−1

The Normal Curve

Earlier in this chapter we discussed the normal curve as a model for the graph of a set of scores. Here we discuss the normal curve and its role in making probability statements.

Characteristics

The **normal curve** is a mathematically defined, smooth, bilaterally symmetrical curve, centered around a point that is simultaneously the mode, median, and mean (see Figure 2.8). Because the center point is both mode and median, it is the most frequent score and that score below which half the scores fall. The normal curve, by mathematical definition, has a mean of 0 and a standard deviation of 1. Thus, the normal curve is the graph of an infinite number of z-scores (see Figure 2.9).

Probability

When you flip a coin, the probability of it coming up heads is $\frac{1}{2}$: There are 2 possible outcomes, and heads represents only 1 of those outcomes—the event or outcome desired. The statement is written $P(H) = \frac{1}{2}$. In general, the probability of an event is the number of possible outcomes that satisfy the event, divided by the total number of possible outcomes.

For example, when you flip two coins, what is the probability of their both coming up tails (TT)? You have 4 possible outcomes: both heads (HH), both tails (TT), the first coin heads and the second tails (HT), and vice versa (TH). The wanted outcome, event TT, is 1 of the 4 possible outcomes, so the probability of TT occurring is $\frac{1}{4}$:

$$P(TT) = \frac{1}{4}.$$

To use the normal curve (see Figure 2.9) to make probability statements, think of the area under the curve as 100 equal portions. If there are 100 possible outcomes under the normal curve, then 50 of these outcomes lie on each side of the mean. Because the curve is symmetrical, the number of outcomes between 0 and -1 equals the number of outcomes between 0 and 1.

Problem 2.13. What is the probability of a z equal to or greater than ($\geq$) 0?

Solution. To begin, we must determine the percentage of the area under the curve that lies to the right of 0. From our definition we know that half of the possible outcomes lie to each side of 0 (the midpoint). Any of the 50 outcomes that lie to the right of 0 would satisfy $z > 0$. Thus, the probability of $z > 0$ is $\frac{1}{2}$:

$$P(z \geq 0) = \frac{50}{100} = \frac{1}{2}.$$

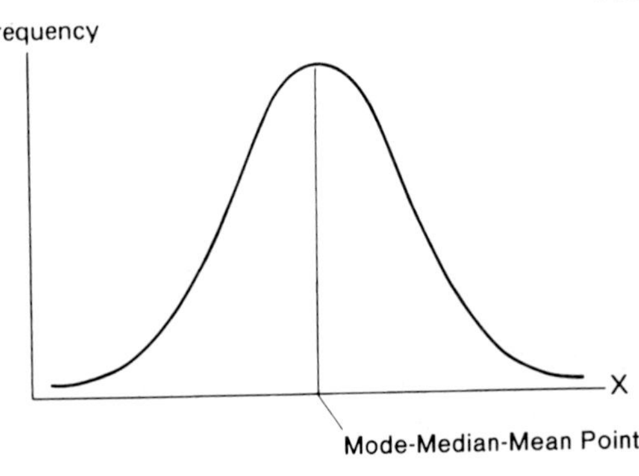

Figure 2.8
Normal curve for test scores.

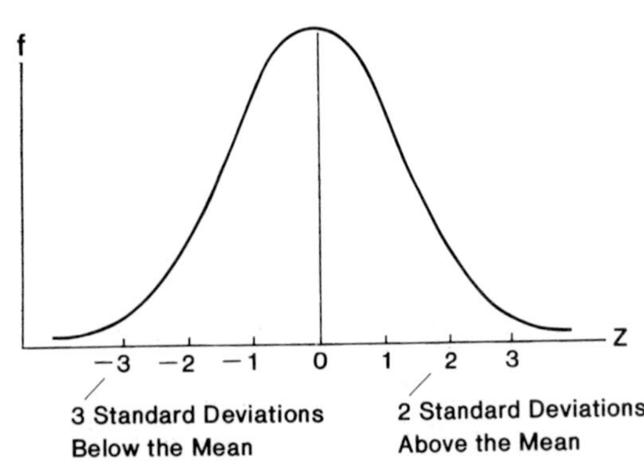

Figure 2.9
Normal curve for Z-scores.

Table 2.11 Percentage of Total Area under the Normal Curve between the Mean and Ordinate Points at Any Given Standard Deviation Distance from the Mean

z	.00	.01	.02	.03	.04	.05	.06	.07	.08	.09
0.0	00.00	00.40	00.80	01.20	01.60	01.99	02.39	02.79	03.19	03.59
0.1	03.98	04.38	04.78	05.17	05.57	05.96	06.36	06.75	07.14	07.53
0.2	07.93	08.32	08.71	09.10	09.48	09.87	10.26	10.64	11.03	11.41
0.3	11.79	12.17	12.55	12.95	13.31	13.68	14.06	14.43	14.80	15.17
0.4	15.54	15.91	16.28	16.64	17.00	17.36	17.72	18.08	18.44	18.79
0.5	19.15	19.50	19.85	20.19	20.54	20.88	21.23	21.57	21.90	22.24
0.6	22.57	22.91	23.24	23.57	23.89	24.22	24.54	24.86	25.17	25.49
0.7	25.80	26.11	26.42	26.73	27.04	27.34	27.64	27.94	28.23	28.52
0.8	28.81	29.10	29.39	29.67	29.95	30.23	30.51	30.78	31.06	31.33
0.9	31.59	31.86	32.12	32.38	32.64	32.90	33.15	33.40	33.65	33.89
1.0	34.13	34.38	34.61	34.85	35.08	35.31	35.54	35.77	35.99	36.21
1.1	36.43	36.65	36.86	37.08	37.29	37.49	37.70	37.90	38.10	38.30
1.2	38.49	38.69	38.88	39.07	39.25	39.44	39.62	39.80	39.97	40.15
1.3	40.32	40.49	40.66	40.82	40.99	41.15	41.31	41.47	41.62	41.77
1.4	41.92	42.07	42.22	42.36	42.51	42.65	42.79	42.92	43.06	43.19
1.5	43.32	43.45	43.57	43.70	43.83	43.94	44.06	44.18	44.29	44.41
1.6	44.52	44.63	44.74	44.84	44.95	45.05	45.15	45.25	45.35	45.45
1.7	45.54	45.64	45.73	45.82	45.91	45.99	46.08	46.16	46.25	46.33
1.8	46.41	46.49	46.56	46.64	46.71	46.78	46.86	46.93	46.99	47.06
1.9	47.13	47.19	47.26	47.32	47.38	47.44	47.50	47.56	47.61	47.67
2.0	47.72	47.78	47.83	47.88	47.93	47.98	48.03	48.08	48.12	48.17
2.1	48.21	48.26	48.30	48.34	48.38	48.42	48.46	48.50	48.54	48.57
2.2	48.61	48.64	48.68	48.71	48.75	48.78	48.81	48.84	48.87	48.90
2.3	48.93	48.96	48.98	49.01	49.04	49.06	49.09	49.11	49.13	49.16
2.4	49.18	49.20	49.22	49.25	49.27	49.29	49.31	49.32	49.34	49.36
2.5	49.38	49.40	49.41	49.43	49.45	49.46	49.48	49.49	49.51	49.52
2.6	49.53	49.55	49.56	49.57	49.59	49.60	49.61	49.62	49.63	49.64
2.7	49.65	49.66	49.67	49.68	49.69	49.70	49.71	49.72	49.73	49.74
2.8	49.74	49.75	49.76	49.77	49.77	49.78	49.79	49.79	49.80	49.81
2.9	49.81	49.82	49.82	49.83	49.84	49.84	49.85	49.85	49.86	49.86
3.0	49.87									
3.5	49.98									
4.0	49.997									
5.0	49.99997									

From Lindquist, E. F., *A First Course in Statistics* (Boston: Houghton Mifflin, 1942), p. 242. By permission.

This problem is simple because we have the answers to it by definition. To answer most probability statements about the normal curve, we have to use a special table, which appears here as Table 2.11. The table allows us to determine the percentage of a given area under the curve, and thus the basis for determining the probability of z falling within that area. The values along the left side and top of the table are z values, or standard deviation distances from the mean. The values in the body of the table indicate the percentage of the area under the curve between a given z-score and the mean z-score, 0.

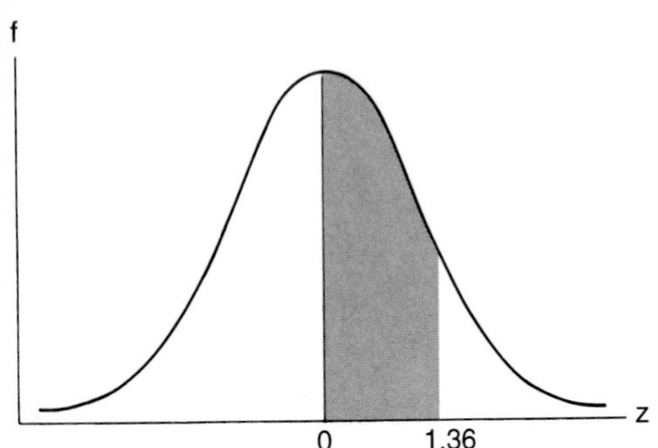

Figure 2.10
Normal curve graph for Problem 2.14.

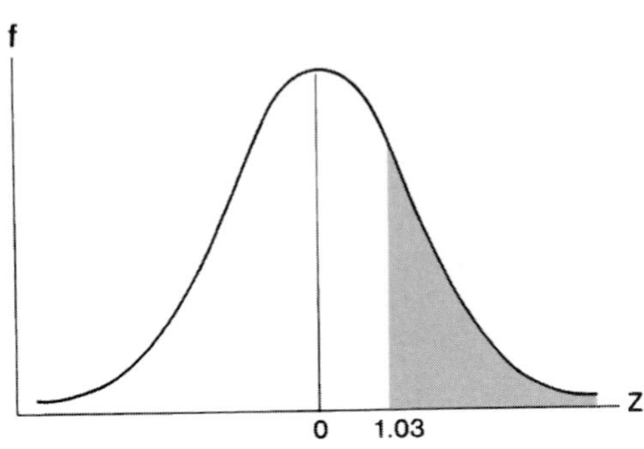

Figure 2.11
Normal curve graph for Problem 2.15.

Problem 2.14. What percentage of the area under the normal curve lies between 0 ($z = 0$) and 1.36($z = 1.36$)?

Solution. Because

$$1.36 = 1.30 + .06$$

we read down the left side of the table to 1.3 and across the row to column .06. The value listed there, 41.31, is that percentage of the area under the normal curve that lies between 0 and 1.36 (see Figure 2.10).

Once we know the possible outcomes that satisfy an event, we can determine the probability of that event happening. The probability that z falls between 0 and 1.36 on the normal curve is the satisfactory outcomes (41.31) divided by the possible outcomes (100), or .41:

$$\text{P(z between 0 and 1.36)} = \frac{41.31}{100} = .4131 = .41.$$

Because the normal curve is symmetrical, the values in Table 2.11 hold true for equivalent distances from the mean to the left of it. That is, the percentage of the area under the normal curve between 0 and -1.36 is still 41.31, and the probability that z falls somewhere between 0 and -1.36 is still .41.

Although the table lists percentages only from the mean, we can extrapolate from it, remembering that 50% of all possible outcomes lie to each side of the mean. To solve any probability statement, make sure the statement is in terms of z, draw a normal curve graph as was done for Problem 2.12, and remember that the normal curve tables provide the percent of the area under the normal curve between 0 and the z-score you used in the normal curve table. Thus, the percentage read from the table may not be the answer to the probability statement.

Problem 2.15. What is the probability that z is equal to or greater than 1.03?

Solution. First we determine the overall area between 0 and 1.03. Reading down the left side of Table 2.11 to 1.0 and across to column .03, we see that 34.85% of the total area to the right of the mean lies between 0 and 1.03 (see Figure 2.11). Because we know that the possible outcomes to the right (or left for that matter) of 0 represent $\frac{50}{100}$, we can subtract the amount we know, $\frac{34.85}{100}$, from $\frac{50}{100}$. The result is our answer. The probability that z is equal to or greater than 1.03 is .15.

$$P(z \geq 1.03) = \frac{50}{100} - \frac{34.85}{100}$$

$$= .50 - .3485 = .1515 = .15.$$

Often the probability statement requires a translation from test score X to the equivalent z, or vice versa, as we can see in the following problems.

Problem 2.16. A teacher always administers 100-point tests and always gives As to scores of 93 and above. On the last test the mean was 72 and the standard deviation was 9. Assuming test scores are normally distributed, what was the probability of receiving an A on that test?

Solution. This is the same as asking what percentage of the class probably received As: What is the probability that a score X was greater than or equal to 93? Before we can solve the probability statement, then, we must change score 93 to a z-score. Where X is greater than or equal to 93, $\overline{X}$ is 72, and s is 9, the z-score must be greater than or equal to 2.33:

$$z \geq \frac{93 - 72}{9} \geq \frac{21}{9} \geq 2.33.$$

Now, using Figure 2.12 and Table 2.11, it is easy to determine the probability. At the intersection of z row 2.3 and column .03, we see that the percentage under the normal curve between 0 and 2.33 is 49.01. By subtracting that amount from the percentage of possible outcomes above 0, we see that the probability that z is greater than or equal to 2.33 is .01.

$$P(z \geq 2.33) = \frac{50}{100} - \frac{49.01}{100} = \frac{.99}{100} = .0099 = .01.$$

Problem 2.17. To develop some performance standards, a teacher decides to use the normal curve to determine that score above which 7% of the scores should fall. That is, what is the z-score above which 7% of the area under the normal curve falls (see Figure 2.13)?

$$P(z \geq ?) = \frac{7}{100}$$

Solution. We know that 43% of the area under the curve lies between 0 and the unknown z-score. If we scan Table 2.11, we see that percentage 43.06 is closest to 43%. Because 43.06 is at the intersection of z row 1.4 and column .08, the unknown z-score (the z-score above which 7% of the area falls) is 1.48. Thus, the teacher would use the following formula to calculate X:

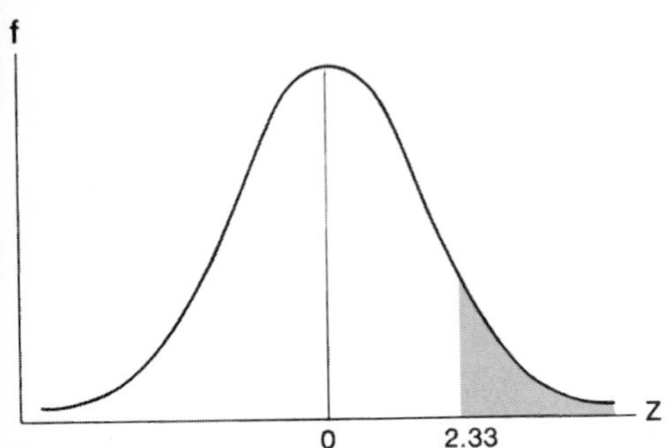

Figure 2.12
Normal curve graph for Problem 2.16.

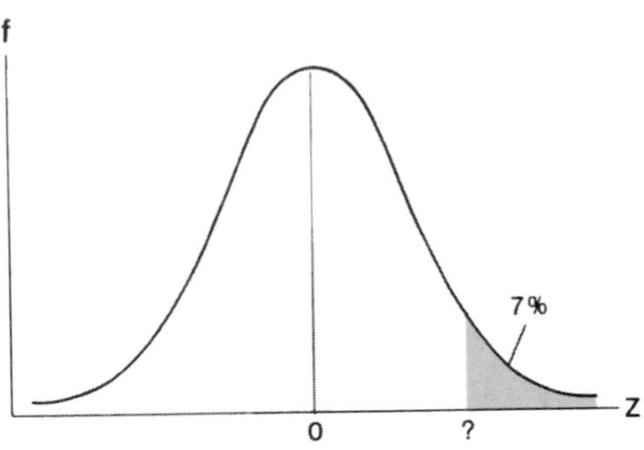

Figure 2.13
Normal curve graph for Problem 2.17.

$$X = \overline{X} + z(s)$$

$$X = \overline{X} + 1.48(s)$$

and if $\overline{X} = 31.25$, $s = 5.0$ then

$$X = 31.25 + 1.48(5.0) = 31.25 + 7.4 = 38.65$$

Determining Relationships between Scores

There are many situations in which the physical education teacher, exercise specialist or physical therapist, would like to know the relationship between scores on two different tests. For example, if speed and the performance of a sport skill were found to be related, the physical education teacher might try to improve the speed of poor performers. Or, if weight and strength scores were found to be related, the exercise specialist or physical therapist might want to use a different evaluation standard for each weight classification. Knowing the relationship between scores can also lead to greater efficiency in a measurement program. For example, if there are seven tests in a physical fitness battery and two of them are highly related, the battery could be reduced to six tests with no loss of information. We use two different techniques to determine score relationships: a graphing technique and a mathematical technique called correlation.

The Graphing Technique

The graphing technique is quicker than the mathematical technique but not as precise. It requires that each individual have a score on each of the two measures. To graph a relationship, we develop a coordinate system according to those values of one measure listed along the horizontal axis and those of the other measure listed along the vertical axis. We plot a point for each individual above his score on the horizontal axis and opposite his score on the vertical axis, as shown in Figure 2.14. The graph obtained is called a "scattergram."

The point plotted for Person A is at the intersection of push-up score 15 and pull-up score 10, the scores the person received on the two tests. The straight line—the **line of best fit** *or the* **regression line**—represents the trend in the data, in this case that individuals with large push-up scores have large pull-up scores, and vice versa. When large scores on one measure are associated with large scores on the other measure, the relationship is *positive.* When large scores on one measure are associated with small scores on the other measure, as shown in Figure 2.15, the relationship is *negative.*

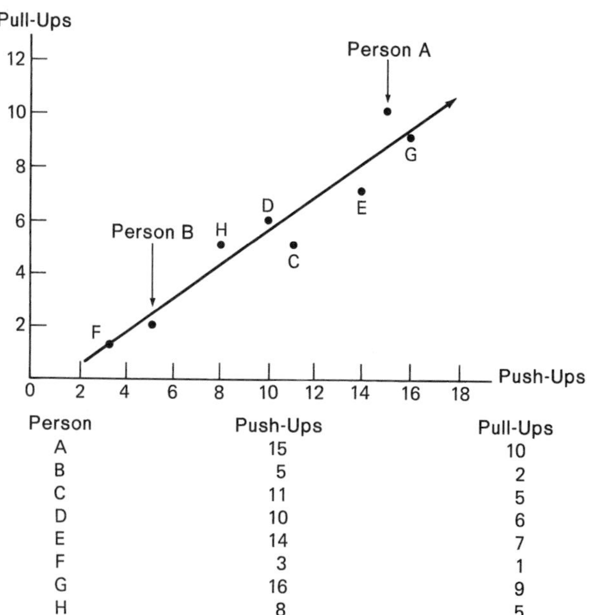

Person	Push-Ups	Pull-Ups
A	15	10
B	5	2
C	11	5
D	10	6
E	14	7
F	3	1
G	16	9
H	8	5

Figure 2.14
Graph of a positive relationship.

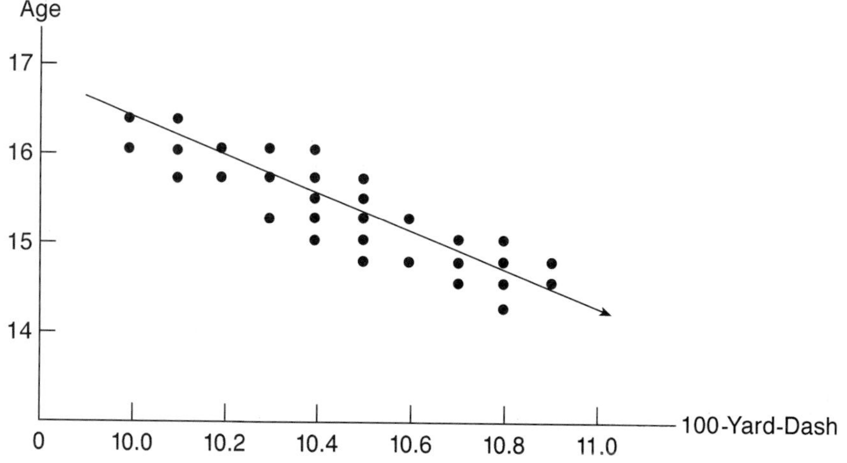

Figure 2.15
Graph of a negative relationship.

The closer all the plotted points are to the trend line, the higher or larger the relationship. The maximum relationship occurs when all plotted points are on the trend line. When the plotted points resemble a circle, making it impossible to draw a trend line, there is no linear relationship between the two measures being graphed. We can see this in the graph for Figure 2.16.

Microcomputer programs have scattergram graphic programs that facilitate plotting data. In SPSS this program is called Scatterplot. See Appendix A for brief instructions on using it. An example of a computer-generated scattergram using the sit-up and pull-up scores from Table 2.9 is presented in Figure 2.17.

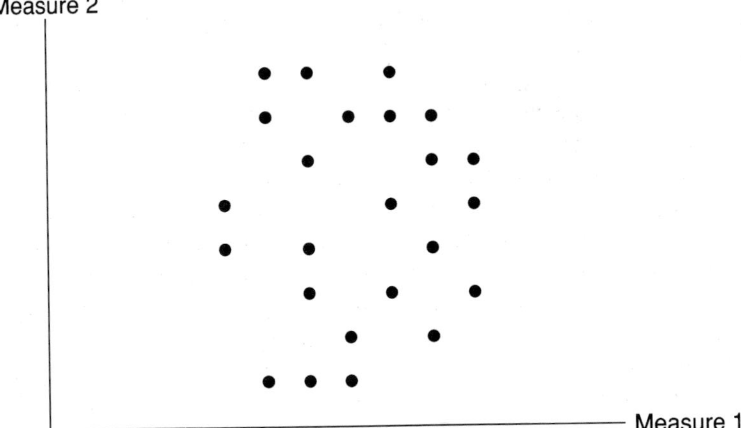

Figure 2.16
Graph of no relationship.

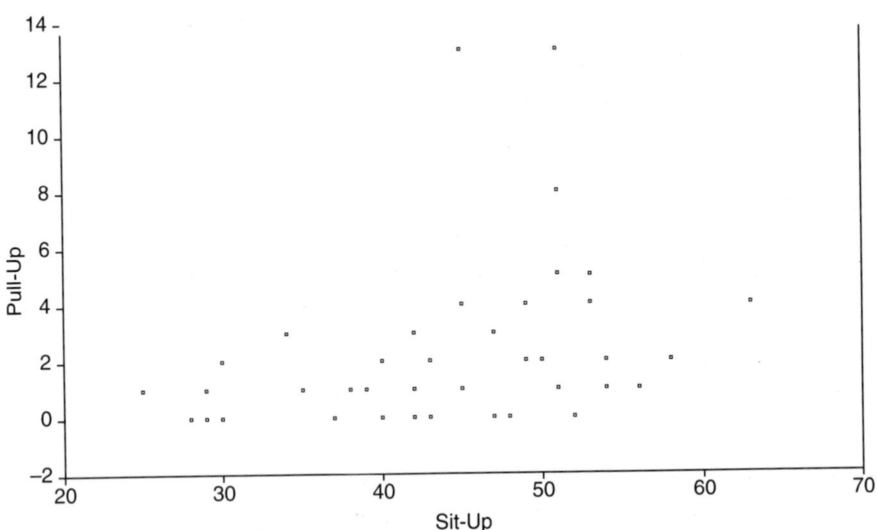

Figure 2.17
Computer-generated scattergram using the Table 2.9 data.

The Correlation Technique

Correlation is a mathematical technique for determining the relationship between two sets of scores. The formula was developed by Karl Pearson to determine the degree of relationship between two sets of measures (called X measures and Y measures):

$$r = \frac{n\Sigma XY - (\Sigma X)(\Sigma Y)}{\sqrt{[n\Sigma X^2 - (\Sigma X)^2]\,[n\Sigma Y^2 - (\Sigma Y)^2]}}$$

where r is the Pearson product-moment correlation coefficient, n is the number of individuals, ΣXY is the sum of each individual's X times Y value, ΣX is the sum of the scores for one set of measures, ΣY is the sum of the scores for the other set of measures, ΣX^2 is the sum of the squared X scores, and ΣY^2 is the sum of the squared Y scores.

Table 2.12 Scores for Correlation Calculation

Individual	Pull-Up (X)	Push-Up (Y)	XY	X^2	Y^2
A	10	15	150	100	225
B	2	5	10	4	25
C	5	11	55	25	121
D	6	10	60	36	100
E	7	14	98	49	196
F	1	3	3	1	9
G	9	16	144	81	256
H	5	8	40	25	64
n = 8	$\Sigma X = 45$	$\Sigma Y = 82$	$\Sigma XY = 560$	$\Sigma X^2 = 321$	$\Sigma Y^2 = 996$

Problem 2.18. Using the scores in Table 2.12, determine the correlation between the pull-up scores (X) and the push-up scores (Y).

Solution. Where n is 8 (the number of individuals), ΣXY is 560 (the sum of column XY), ΣX is 45 (the sum of column X), ΣY is 82 (the sum of column Y), ΣX^2 is 321 (the sum of column X^2), and ΣY^2 is 996 (the sum of column Y^2), the correlation coefficient r is 0.96:

$$r = \frac{(8)(560) - (45)(82)}{\sqrt{[(8)(321) - 45^2][(8)(996) - 82^2]}}$$

$$= \frac{4480 - 3690}{\sqrt{(2568 - 2025)(7968 - 6724)}} = \frac{790}{\sqrt{(543)(1244)}}$$

$$= \frac{790}{\sqrt{675492}} = \frac{790}{821.88} = .96.$$

Correlation coefficients have two characteristics, direction and strength. Direction of the relationship is indicated by whether the correlation coefficient is positive or negative, as indicated under the graphing technique. Strength of the relationship is indicated by how close the r is to 1, the maximum value possible. A correlation of 1 ($r = 1$) shows a perfect positive relationship, indicating that an increase in scores on one measure is accompanied by an increase in scores on the second measure. A perfect negative relationship ($r = -1$) indicates that an increase in scores on one measure is accompanied by a decrease in scores on the second. (Notice that a correlation of -1 is just as strong as a correlation of 1.) Perfect relationships are rare, but any such relationship that does exist is exactly described by mathematical formula. An example of a perfect positive and a perfect negative relationship is shown in Table 2.13. When the correlation coefficient is 0 ($r = 0$), there is no linear relationship between the two sets of scores.

Because the relationship between two sets of scores is seldom perfect, the majority of correlation coefficients are factions (.93, $-.85$, and the like). The closer the correlation coefficient is to 1 or -1, the stronger the relationship. When the relationship is not perfect, the scores on one measure only tend to change with the scores on

Table 2.13 Examples of Perfect Relationships

Individual	Height	Weight	Individual	100-Yard Dash	Pull-Up
A	60	130	A	10.6	14
B	52	122	B	10.6	14
C	75	145	C	11.2	8
D	66	136	D	11.7	3
E	70	140	E	10.5	15
	r = 1			r = −1	
Exact formula: weight = height + 70			Exact formula: dash = 12 − .1 (pull-up)		

Table 2.14 Example of an Imperfect Correlation

Individual	Height (Inches)	Weight (Pounds)
A	60	130
B	52	125
C	75	145
D	66	136
E	70	150
	r = .91	

the other measure. Look, for example, at Table 2.14. The correlation between height and weight is not perfect: Individual C, whose height is 75 inches, is not heavier than Individual E, whose height is only 70 inches.

When the scores for the two sets of scores are ranks, a correlation coefficient called *rho* or *Spearman's rho* or the **rank order correlation coefficient** may be calculated. The formula is just a simplification of the Pearson correlation formula. Since the same value will be obtained by applying the Pearson correlation formula to the two sets of ranks (provided no tied ranks exist), the formula is not presented, but it is commonly included in microcomputer statistical programs.

Interpreting the Correlation Coefficient. A high correlation between two measures does not usually indicate a cause- and effect-relationship. The perfect height and weight relationship in Table 2.13, for example, does not indicate that an increase in weight causes an increase in height. Also, the degree of relationship between two sets of measures does not increase at the same rate as does the correlation coefficient. The true indicator of the degree of relationship is the **coefficient of determination**—the amount of variability in one measure that is explained by the other measure. The coefficient of determination is the square of the correlation coefficient (r^2). For example, the square of the correlation coefficient in Table 2.14 is .83 ($.91^2$), which means that 83% of the variability in height scores is due to the individuals having different weight scores.

Thus when one correlation coefficient is twice as large as another, the larger coefficient really explains four times the amount of variation that the smaller coefficient explains. For example, when the r between agility and balance is .80 and the r between strength and power is .40, the r^2 for agility and balance is $.80^2$, or 64%, and the r^2 for strength and power is $.40^2$, or 16%.

Remember, when you interpret a correlation coefficient, there are no absolute standards for labeling a given r "good" or "poor"; only the relationship you want or expect determines the quality of a given r. For example, if you or others had obtained a correlation coefficient of .67 between leg strength and standing long jump scores for males, you might expect a similar correlation coefficient in comparing leg strength and long jump scores for females. If the relationship between the females' scores were only .45, you might label that correlation coefficient "poor" because you expected it to be as high as that of the males.

There are two reasons why correlation coefficients can be negative: (1) opposite scoring scales and (2) true negative relationships. When a measure on which a small score is a better score is correlated with a measure on which a larger score is a better score, the correlation coefficient probably will be negative. Consider, for example, the relationship between scores on a speed event like the time it takes to run one mile and a nonspeed event like the number of sit-ups executed in one minute. Usually individuals best on the sit-up test are the best runners, but the correlation is negative because the scoring scales are reversed. Two measures can be negatively related as well. We would expect, for example, a negative correlation between body weight and measures involving support or motion of the body (pull-ups) or between number of risk factors (smoking, drinking, obesity, etc.) and physical health.

The Question of Accuracy. In calculating r, we assume that the relationship between the two sets of scores is basically linear. A **linear relationship** is shown graphically by a straight line, as is the trend line in Figure 2.14. However, a relationship between two sets of scores can be represented by a curved line, a **curvilinear relationship.** A curvilinear relationship between two measures is best described by a curved line. If a relationship is truly curvilinear, the correlation coefficient will underestimate the relationship. For example, r could equal 0 even when a definite curvilinear relationship exists. More concerning curvilinear relationships is presented later in the regression section of this chapter.

Although we need not assume when calculating r that the graph of each of the two sets of scores is a normal curve, we do assume that the two graphs resemble each other. If they are dissimilar, the correlation coefficient will underestimate the relationship between the scores. Considerable differences in the two graphs are occasionally found, usually when the number of people tested is small. For this reason, the correlation coefficient ideally should be calculated with the scores of several hundred people.

Other factors also affect the correlation coefficient. One is the reliability of the scores; low reliability reduces the correlation coefficient (see Chapter 3). Another factor is the range in the scores; the correlation coefficient will be smaller for a homogeneous group than for a heterogeneous group. Ferguson and Takane (1989) suggest that generally the range in scores increases as the size of the group tested increases. Certainly small groups exhibit a greater tendency than large groups to be either more homogeneous or more heterogeneous than is typical for the group measured and the test administered. This is another reason to calculate the correlation coefficient only when the group tested is large. Ferguson and Takane (1989) cover this subject in greater detail.

The calculation of the correlation coefficient in Problem 2.18 was easy because the number of scores was small and the values of the scores were small. Usually you will be working with between 25 and 500 scores that may be three- or four-digit numbers.

Table 2.15 Correlations Among All the Variables for the Data in Table 2.9

Label	Skin	Mile	Reach	Pullup	Situp
Skin	1.00	0.45	−0.26	−0.59	−0.20
Mile	0.45	1.00	0.02	−0.52	−0.35
Reach	−0.26	0.02	1.00	0.14	0.28
Pullup	−0.59	−0.52	0.14	1.00	0.40
Situp	−0.20	−0.35	0.28	0.40	1.00

In this case the use of a calculator to speed up the calculations is essential. Many calculators have a correlation key, so only the X and Y scores have to be entered into the calculator and it does the rest.

When the group tested is large or when the physical education teacher and exercise specialist want the correlation between all possible pairings of more than two tests (pull-up and sit-up, pull-up and mile run, sit-up and mile run), using a computer is the most efficient way to obtain the correlation coefficients. Computer programs that calculate correlation coefficients are commonly found in packages of statistical programs for microcomputers. In the SPSS package, the correlation program will calculate the correlation between two variables or among all variables at one time. For example, the correlation between pull-up and push-up scores in Table 2.12 or among all the variables in Table 2.9 could be calculated. See Appendix A for brief instructions on using it.

A common printout format is presented in Table 2.15 for the data in Table 2.9. In Table 2.15 the correlation between any two tests is found by finding the value listed in the cell formed by the row and column of the two tests. For example, the correlation between pull-up and sit-up is .40.

Prediction-Regression Analysis

The terms *correlation, regression,* and *prediction* are so closely related in statistics that they are often used interchangeably. **Correlation** refers to the relationship between two variables. When two variables are correlated, it becomes possible to make a prediction. **Regression** is the statistical model used to predict performance on one variable from another. An example is the prediction of percent body fat from skinfold measurements. This is illustrated in Chapter 9.

Teachers, coaches, exercise specialists, and researchers have long been interested in predicting scores that are either difficult or impossible to obtain at a given moment. **Prediction** is estimating a person's score on one measure based on the person's score on one or more other measures. Although prediction is often imprecise, it is occasionally useful to develop a prediction formula.

Simple Prediction

Simple prediction is predicting an unknown score Y′ for an individual by using that person's performance X on a known measure. To develop a **simple prediction,** or regression formula, a large number (at least $n = 50$, with $n > 100$ even better) of people must be measured and a score on the **independent,** or predictor, **variable** X and the **dependent,** or criterion, **variable** Y obtained for each.

$$Y' = \left[r \left(\frac{s_y}{s_x} \right) \right] (X - \overline{X}) + \overline{Y} \qquad (2.12)$$

where Y′ is the predicted Y score for an individual, r is the correlation between X and Y scores, s_y is the standard deviation for the Y scores, s_x is the standard deviation for the X scores, X is the individual's known score on measure X, $\overline{X}$ is the mean for the X scores, and $\overline{Y}$ is the mean for the Y scores. Once the formula is developed for any given relationship, only the predictor variable X is needed to predict the performance of an individual on measure Y. Two indexes of the accuracy of a simple prediction equation are r and r^2.

Problem 2.19. A coach found the correlation coefficient between physical fitness and athletic ability to be .88. The mean of the physical fitness test is 12; its standard deviation is 5.15. The mean of the athletic ability test is 9; its standard deviation is 4.30. What is the predicted athletic ability score for an athlete with a physical fitness score of 14?

Solution. Where r is .88, s_y is 4.30, s_x is 5.15, X is 14, $\overline{X}$ is 12, and $\overline{Y}$ is 9, the athlete's predicted athlete ability score, Y′, is 10.46:

$$Y' = \left[(.88) \left(\frac{4.30}{5.15} \right) \right] (14 - 12) + 9$$

$$= (.73)\,(2) + 9 = 1.46 + 9 = 10.46.$$

Prediction being a correlational technique, there is a *line of best fit* or *regression line* that can be generated (see graphing technique pp. 73–74). In case of simple prediction, this is the regression line for the graph of the X variable on the horizontal axis and the Y variable on the vertical axis.

The general form of the simple prediction equation is

$$Y' = bX + c$$

where b is a constant and termed the slope of the regression line. The slope is the rate at which Y changes with change on X. The constant, c, is called the Y-intercept and is the point at which the line crosses the vertical axis. It is the value of Y that corresponds to an X of 0. To obtain the slope and Y-intercept, all values except X are put into the prediction formula and then the formula is reduced to simplest form. For the values used in Problem 2.19:

$$Y' = \left[(.88) \left(\frac{4.30}{5.15} \right) \right] (X - 12) + 9$$

$$= (.73)(X - 12) + 9 = .73X - 8.76 + 9$$

$$= .73X + .24, \text{ so } b = .73 \text{ and } c = .24.$$

Thus

$$Y' = .73(X) + .24$$

Sometimes calculators and computer programs report the simple prediction equation in terms of slope and Y-intercept. If a calculator or computer is programmed to obtain the simple prediction equation, only the X and Y scores have to be entered.

The Standard Error of Prediction. An individual's predicted score, Y′, will not equal the actual score, Y, unless the correlation coefficient used in the formula is perfect—a rare event. Thus, for each individual there is an error of prediction. We estimate the standard deviation of this error, the **standard error of prediction,** using the following formula:

$$\text{estimated } s_{y \cdot x} = s_y\sqrt{1 - r^2}$$

where $s_{y \cdot x}$ is the standard error of score Y predicted from score X, s_y is the standard deviation for the Y scores calculated with formula 4 on page 53, and r^2 is the square of the correlation coefficient (the coefficient of determination) for the X and Y scores. (Notice that the larger the coefficient, the smaller the standard error.) This estimate of $s_{y \cdot x}$ is sufficiently accurate if the number of individuals tested (n) is large (at least $n = 50$, with $n > 100$ even better). The exact formula for $s_{y \cdot x}$ can be found in many statistics and advanced measurement books (Kachigan 1991; Safrit & Wood 1989, p. 190). Actually multiplying the estimated $s_{y \cdot x}$ by $(n - 2) / (n - 1)$ yields the exact value. Computer programs that provide the standard error of prediction should provide the exact value. The standard error of prediction is another index of the accuracy of a simple prediction equation.

The standard error of prediction is not a good index of the error associated with a single prediction. When a Y′ is calculated from the X-score of a certain person, the error in it will be smaller when X is near $\overline{X}$ than when X is far from $\overline{X}$. Thus, the formula for the standard error of prediction for a Y′ based on a certain X-score is

$$s'_{y \cdot x} = s_{y \cdot x}\sqrt{1 + \frac{1}{n} + \frac{(X - \overline{X})^2}{(n - 1)(s_x^2)}}$$

where $(X - \overline{X})$ is the difference between the certain X-score and the mean X-score. Using this formula, confidence limits (boundaries) for the Y-score of a person can be calculated. For example, the probability is .68 that the Y-score of a person falls between $Y' \pm s'_{y \cdot x}$.

Problem 2.20. What is the standard error of prediction and .68 confidence limits for the Y-score predicted in Problem 2.19?

Solution.

Where $n = 5$, $\overline{X} = 12$, $s_x = 5.15$, $\overline{Y} = 9$, $s_y = 4.30$, $r = .88$, Y' for X of $14 = 10.46$:

A. $$\text{estimated } s_{y \cdot x} = s_y\sqrt{1 - r^2} = 4.30\sqrt{1 - (.88)^2}$$
$$= 4.30\sqrt{.23} = (4.30)(.48) = 2.06$$

B. $$\text{exact } s_{y \cdot x} = \left(\frac{n - 2}{n - 1}\right)(\text{estimated } s_{y \cdot x}) = \left(\frac{5 - 2}{5 - 1}\right)(2.06)$$
$$= (.75)(2.06) = 1.55$$

C. $s'_{y \cdot x}$ for X of 14 $= s_{y \cdot x}\sqrt{1 + \frac{1}{n} + \frac{(X - \bar{X})^2}{(n - 1)(s_x^2)}} = 1.55\sqrt{1 + \frac{1}{5} + \frac{(14 - 12)^2}{(5 - 1)(5.15)^2}}$

$= 1.55\sqrt{1 + \frac{1}{5} + \frac{4}{(4)(26.52)}} = 1.55\sqrt{1 + .2 + .04} = 1.55\sqrt{1.24}$

$= (1.55)(1.11) = 1.72$

D. .68 confidence limits for the Y-score of person with X-score of 14 is

$Y' \pm s'_{y \cdot x} = 10.46 \pm 1.72$

The probability is .68 that the Y-score of a person with an X-score of 14 falls between 8.74 (10.46 − 1.72) and 12.18 (10.46 + 1.72).

If the prediction formula and standard error seem acceptable, the physical education teacher or exercise specialist should try to prove the prediction formula on a second group of individuals similar to the first. This process is called **cross-validation.** If the formula works satisfactorily for the second group, it can be used with confidence to predict score Y for any individual who resembles the individuals used to form and cross-validate the equation. If the formula does not work well for the second group, it is unique to the group used to form the equation and has little value in predicting performance.

Multiple Prediction

A prediction formula using a single measure X is usually not very accurate for predicting a person's score on measure Y. *Multiple correlation-regression* techniques allow us to predict score Y using several X scores. For example, a **multiple prediction** formula has been developed to predict arm strength in pounds (Y′) using both the number of pull-ups (X_1) and pounds of body weight (X_2):

$$Y' = 3.42(X_1) + 1.77(X_2) - 46.$$

A multiple regression equation will have one intercept and several bs, one for each independent variable. The general form of two and three predictor multiple regression equations are

$$Y' = b_1X_1 + b_2X_2 + c$$

$$Y' = b_1X_1 + b_2X_2 + b_3X_3 + c.$$

The *multiple correlation coefficient R* is one index of the accuracy of a multiple prediction equation. The minimum and maximum values of R are 0 and 1 respectively. The percentage of variance in the Y scores explained by the multiple prediction equation is R^2. A second index of the accuracy of a multiple prediction equation is the standard error of prediction. Multiple prediction formulas and **multiple correlations** are presented in later chapters of this book (see Chapter 10, Evaluating Body Composition). More comprehensive coverage of multiple regression can be found in Cohen and Cohen (1983), Ferguson and Takane (1989), Pedhazur (1982), and Safrit and Wood (1989).

Nonlinear Regression. The regression models discussed to this point assume a linear relationship. With some data, this is not the case. For example, when relating

Table 2.16 Output from Multiple Regression Using the Data in Table 2.9

Dependent Variable:		**Mile**
R = .45081		R-Square = .20323
Variable	*B*	*Beta*
Skin	5.55149	.45081
Constant	352.32371	
Dependent Variable:		**Mile**
R = .54770		R-Square = .29997
Variable	*B*	*Beta*
Skin	2.71712	.22064
Pull	−12.53334	−.38694
Constant	455.11206	

age and strength, the relation is linear for the ages of 10 through 17 because the person is growing and gaining muscle mass, but for ages 18 through 65 the relationship would be nonlinear. As one starts to reach middle age, aging is associated with a loss of lean body weight, which results in a loss of strength. As explained in the correlation section, if the relationship is not linear, the linear correlation will be lower than the true correlation. Microcomputer programs have what is termed a "polynomial regression" program to compute the curvilinear correlation. Polynomial regression analysis is beyond the scope of this text.

Using the Computer

The simple prediction and multiple prediction equations are both time-consuming and complicated, especially when the number of people being tested is large. (It is suggested that prediction equations be developed using the scores of several hundred people.) Computer programs that do either simple or multiple prediction are commonly available for both the mainframe and microcomputer.

In the SPSS package, a prediction equation can be obtained by selecting Regression. In this option both a simple and multiple prediction equation can be obtained. See Appendix A for brief instructions for using it. The variables to be used must be identified, and then the dependent variable (Y) and the predictor (independent) variables (Xs) must be identified.

Using the data in Table 2.9 with Y equal to the mile run, and X equal to the skinfold, a simple prediction equation was obtained (see Table 2.16). The prediction equation is $Y' = 5.55149(\text{Skin}) + 352.32371$. The R (.45081) and the R-Square (.20323) values for the prediction equation suggest that it is not very accurate. In an effort to obtain a more accurate prediction equation, a multiple prediction equation with Y equal to the mile run, X_1 equal to the skinfold, and X_2 equal to the pull-up was obtained (see Table 2.16). The prediction equation is $Y' = 2.71712(\text{Skin}) - 12.53334(\text{Pull}) + 455.11206$. The R (.54770) and R-Square (.29997) values for the prediction equation suggest that it is not very accurate and not much better than the simple prediction equation. In a multiple prediction equation, a high correlation between the Y-score and each X-score but a low correlation among the X-scores is desirable. Note in Table 2.15 that all three variables used in the multiple prediction equation correlated about the same amount (.45 − .59) with each other.

Reliability of the Mean

Throughout this chapter we have placed considerable emphasis on the usefulness of the mean in describing the performance of a group. The mean is not constant: It can vary from day to day among the same individuals in a retest or from year to year if a new but similar group of individuals is tested. The performance of a group of individuals changes from day to day, even if ability has not changed, simply because people have good days and bad days. And the mean performances of different groups of individuals are seldom identical, even when the subjects are apparently equal in ability. If we can expect little variation in the mean, it is a highly reliable indicator of group ability; if we can expect considerable variation, it is not very reliable. We call the estimated variability of the mean the **standard error of the mean.** It is found using the following formula:

$$S_{\bar{x}} = \frac{s}{\sqrt{n}}$$

where $s_{\bar{x}}$ is the standard error of the mean, s is the standard deviation for the scores $(s = \sqrt{(\Sigma X^2 - (\Sigma X)^2/n)/(n - 1)})$, and n is the number of individuals in the group.

Statistics books show that when many groups—all members of the same larger group, or population—are tested, the graph of the means is normal, centered around the population mean. The standard error is the standard deviation of the group means. The standard error can be used with the normal curve in the same manner as can be standard deviation; that is, 68% of the group means will be within one standard error of the population mean.

Problem 2.21. The mean for an agility test performed by 81 senior citizens is 12.5; the standard deviation is .81. Determine the standard error of the mean.

Solution. Where s is .81 and n is 81, the standard error of mean 12.5 is .09:

$$s_{\bar{x}} = \frac{.81}{\sqrt{81}} = \frac{.81}{9} = .09.$$

If 12.5 is the population mean, 68% of the means for groups belonging to this population (senior citizens) will fall between 12.41 (12.5 − .09) and 12.59 (12.5 + .09). Thus any senior citizen groups with agility test means between 12.41 and 12.59 are probably similar in ability. In fact, if the group with mean 12.5 is tested on another day, the probability is 68% that its mean performance will fall between 12.41 and 12.59.

Additional Statistical Techniques

The statistical techniques presented to this point are those commonly used in measurement situations. There are times when the goal is to determine if various groups are different, that is, males versus females, or various groups of athletes. Researchers commonly use **t-tests** (not to be confused with T-scores) and Analysis of Variance (ANOVA) to determine if there is a large enough difference between two or more groups in mean performance to conclude that the groups are not equal in average performance. A detailed discussion of t-tests and ANOVA is beyond the scope of this book, but a brief introduction into the logic is presented. If you wish a more detailed coverage of t-tests and ANOVA, an excellent nonmathematical discussion occurs in Baumgartner and Strong (1998) and Huck and Cormier (1996). A more complete coverage of t-tests and ANOVA can be found in any introductory level statistics book. The presentation by Ferguson and Takane (1989) is easy to follow. Microcomputer packages of statistical programs include t-test and ANOVA.

Background to Statistical Tests

Often researchers are interested in the characteristics of a large group. For example, what is the mean percent body fat for the 40,000 males who work for a particular industry, or which of three fitness training techniques is best for the 40,000 workers? To answer the first question, a researcher might measure all 40,000 males for percent body fat and then calculate the mean. This would be very time-consuming and expensive, and likely impossible. Instead of testing all of the large group of interest, called the *population,* the researcher tests some part of the population, called a *sample.* The mean for the sample is calculated, and then the researcher assumes the sample and population mean are equal. In other words, if the sample mean is 17, the researcher infers that the population mean is 17. In the earlier example of which fitness training technique is best, the researchers would obtain three samples and use a different fitness training technique on each sample. After the training technique had been used for a length of time (e.g., 6 weeks or longer) the researcher would test all the participants and determine if the mean performance of the groups was equal. Whatever the outcome, the researcher would infer the sample finding to the population.

In order to make this inference, the sample should be representative of the population and randomly selected. For a sample to be representative it must be taken from an identified population and it must be sufficiently large (i.e., 30 or more) so that all different abilities in the population are represented. Random selection of participants guarantees that all members of the population have an equal chance of being selected. In a research setting, this is done with a special table called a table of random numbers, but in a practical setting it might be accomplished by placing each person's name on a piece of paper, putting all the pieces of paper in a container, drawing out 50 pieces of paper, and designating the people drawn as the sample.

A researcher starts out with a statement concerning what he or she thinks may be the case at the population level. This statement is called the *null hypothesis.* For example, 18% is the mean percent body fat for adult males, or the three fitness training techniques are equally effective so the means of the three groups are equal. Usually the mean or means obtained from the sample(s) will not equal the values in the null hypothesis. Then the question is whether the difference between what was hypothesized at the population level and found at the sample level is large enough to suggest that the null hypothesis is false or whether the difference is due to sampling error. *Sampling error* is due to the sample not being 100% representative of the population. For example, if the mean percent body fat was hypothesized to be 18 but was 17 in the sample, is the hypothesis false or is this difference due to sampling error? If all three samples do not have the same mean after receiving their respective training technique, does this indicate that the hypothesis is false? To be able to make an objective decision, a statistical test is conducted. This statistical test is much like the probability statements earlier in this chapter. Based on the statistical test, the probability of the sample finding occurring if the null hypothesis is true can be determined. If the probability is quite small, the null hypothesis is rejected and the difference is considered to be real. Otherwise it is accepted and the difference is considered to be due to sampling error. Thus, a researcher must select some probability level that warrants rejection of the null hypothesis. This probability level is called the *alpha level,* and it is usually specified as .05 or .01. What most researchers do is look in the appropriate statistical table to find the value of the statistical test needed to reject the null hypothesis at the alpha level selected. Many microcomputer programs provide a probability level (p) for the value of the statistical test. In this case the researcher rejects the null hypothesis if the p-value is less than or equal to the alpha level. All of this will become clearer with the examples provided, each with a different research design and statistical test.

t-Test for One Group

Step 1
The researcher's null hypothesis was that the mean percent body fat for the population was 18, so the hypothesized population mean (μ) is 18 ($H_0{:}\mu = 18$). As alternatives to this hypothesis, the researcher thought it possible that the mean could be less than 18 ($H_1{:}\mu < 18$) or greater than 18 ($H_2{:}\mu > 18$).

Step 2
An alpha level of .05 was selected.

Step 3
Knowing that a t-test would be the statistical test and the sample size would be 41, the researcher went to the t-tables and found that to reject the null hypothesis at alpha level .05 the value of the t-test would have to be at least ± 2.021. This step is not needed if a microcomputer program is used because p-values are calculated.

Step 4
The researcher randomly selected 41 men from the population as the sample, measured their percent body fat, calculated the mean and standard deviation for the body fat measurements, and calculated the t-test.

$\overline{X} = 16.50 \qquad s^1 = 2.50 \qquad n = 41$

$$t = \frac{\overline{X} - \mu}{s/\sqrt{n}} = \frac{16.50 - 18}{2.50/\sqrt{41}} = \frac{-1.50}{2.50/6.40}$$

$$= \frac{-1.50}{.39} = -3.85.$$

Step 5
Since the calculated value of t (-3.85) at Step 4 is less than the tabled value of t (-2.021) at Step 3, the research concludes that the difference between the null hypothesis valued (18) at Step 1 and the sample value (16.50) at Step 4 is real and not due to sample error. Thus, the researcher rejects the null hypothesis and accepts the most likely alternate hypothesis, which in this case is H_1, the population mean is less than 18, since the sample mean was less than 18.

---

[1]Note: In this case $s = \sqrt{\dfrac{\Sigma X^2 - \dfrac{(\Sigma X)^2}{n}}{n - 1}}$

Table 2.17 Scores for Three Groups on a Sit-and-Reach Test

Group A	Group B	Group C
12	7	13
15	10	14
10	11	10
11	8	9
9	9	12
14	10	11
12	12	11
13	9	15

Now a few points of information about what was presented in the five-step example. At Step 3 when the researcher went to the t-tables (the tables in Ferguson & Takane were used) to identify the t-value needed for rejecting the null hypothesis, he had to line up a value called *degrees of freedom* and the alpha level to find the t-value. The degrees of freedom for this t-test is $(n - 1)$ where n is the sample size. Since there were two alternate hypotheses, the researcher used the alpha level under a *two-tailed test.* For a two-tailed test this value is always interpreted as both plus and minus. If there had been only one alternate hypothesis, the alpha level under *one-tailed test* would have been used and the value read from the table would have been interpreted as either plus or minus, depending on whether the alternate hypothesis was greater than (table value plus) or less than (table value minus). The table value is sometimes called the *critical value* or *critical region.* At Step 5 if the value of the statistical test at Step 4 is equal to or greater than the table value at Step 3, the difference and the statistical test are called *significant* (the difference is considered to be real), and the null hypothesis is rejected. If the value of the statistical test at Step 4 is not equal to or greater than the table value at Step 3, the difference and statistical test are called *nonsignificant* (the difference is considered to be due to sampling error), and the null hypothesis is accepted.

This t-test is useful in any measurement situation where the mean performance of a group is being compared to an expected mean or a standard or norm expressed as a mean. Does the mean of the group really differ from the expected mean?

Now, this t-test we just studied is one of three t-tests available, and the other two t-tests are not as easy to calculate by hand. Fortunately most computer packages of statistical programs contain all three t-tests. In SPSS the t-test for one group is called One Sample t-test. See Appendix A for brief instructions on using it. The computer will ask for the null hypothesis value.

Presented in Table 2.17 are the scores of three groups on a sit-and-reach test. The scores of Group A were analyzed using the One Sample t-test program to test the null hypothesis that the population mean equals $10(H_0{:}\mu = 10)$. The output of this program is presented in Table 2.18. Notice in Table 2.18 that the computer provides a two-tailed significance value (.025 in our example) so that looking up a table value is not necessary.

Halfing the two-tailed significance value provided by the computer yields the one-tailed significance value (.0125) if it is needed. In either case, if the significance value is less than or equal to the alpha level selected, the value of the statistical test

Table 2.18 Output of the One-Sample t-Test of Group A in Table 2.17

Number of Cases	8
Mean	12.00
Test Value	10.00
Difference	2.00
Standard Deviation	2.00
t-value	2.83
Degrees of Freedom	7
Two-Tailed Significance	.025

is significant and the null hypothesis (H_0) is rejected. Otherwise the null hypothesis is accepted.

t-Test for Two Independent Groups

In the situation of a t-test for two independent groups, either two samples are drawn from the same population and each sample is administered a different treatment or a sample is drawn from each of two populations. In the first case, two samples of size 75 each were drawn from a population of female college freshmen. Each sample received a different fitness program (treatment). Then a fitness test was administered to all the participants in both samples. After the treatments were administered, each sample represented a different population. In the second case, samples of size 40 were drawn from populations of last year's participants in a fitness program and this year's participants in the same fitness program. Then a fitness test was administered to all people in both samples. In either case, in the end the two samples represent different populations, and the question is whether there is a difference between the two samples in mean performance as an indication of whether there is a difference at the population level.

This t-test is useful in any measurement situation where the mean performances of two groups are being compared. For example, is the mean for a group in a fitness program last year equal to the mean for a group in the same fitness program this year, or are two groups in different fitness programs equal in mean performance?

Step 1: $H_0: \mu_1 - \mu_2 = 0$ (hypothesis that population means are equal)

$H_1: \mu_1 - \mu_2 > 0$
$H_2: \mu_1 - \mu_2 < 0$

Step 2: Alpha = .05

Step 3: Find t-test table value with degrees of freedom equal $(n_1 + n_2 - 2)$ where n_1 is the sample size for Group 1 and n_2 is for Group 2.

Step 4: Conduct the study, collect the data, and calculate the t-test.

Step 5: Compare the calculated t at Step 4 to the table value t at Step 3 and draw a conclusion to accept or reject H_0.

The Independent Samples t-test in SPSS does this t-test. See Appendix A for brief instructions on using it. The data of Groups A and B in Table 2.17 are used for an example analysis with this program. If a data file containing the data of the two groups

Table 2.19 Output of the t-Test for Independent Samples for Groups A and B in Table 2.17

Item	Group A	Group B
Number of Cases	8	8
Mean	12.00	9.50
Standard Deviation	2.00	1.60
t-value	2.76	
Degrees of Freedom	14	
Two-Tailed Significance	0.015	

is developed, each person must have a variable identifying group membership and a second variable that is his score. For example, the researcher might tell the computer that each person has two scores called *group* and *score.* The researcher is using group to indicate the group membership and score to indicate the score of the person. Thus, all participants in group A will have a group score of 1 (always use numbers rather than letters), and all participants in group B will have a group score of 2. The results of the analysis are presented in Table 2.19, where one can see that there is a significant difference between the two groups in favor of Group A. The two-tailed significance (.015) is less than .05, indicating significance. (The computer program only provides a two-tailed p-value.) (The one-tailed p-value would be .0075, which is also significant at .05.) With 14 degrees of freedom (8 + 8 − 2) and alpha .05, the two-tailed tabled t-value is 2.145, which also indicates significance. In either case, significance indicates that the null hypothesis (H_0) is rejected.

t-Test for Two Dependent Groups

One example of a t-test for two dependent groups is a group of people who are measured on two different occasions, usually the beginning and end of the treatment condition. In this case there is some degree of correlation or dependency between the two columns of scores. This t-test is useful in any measurement situation where you want to determine whether the mean performance of a group changed over time or as the result of an instructional/training program.

Suppose eight people were selected and initially (I) measured for number of mistakes when juggling a ball. Then the people were taught to juggle and finally (F) retested. Let us say that in Table 2.17 the Group A scores are the initial scores and the Group B scores are the retest. To determine if the people improved in juggling ability as a result of the juggling instruction, a t-test for dependent groups is conducted.

Step 1: $H_0{:}\mu_I - \mu_F = 0$

$H_1{:}\mu_I - \mu_F < 0$

Step 2: Alpha = .05

Step 3: Find t-test table value with degrees of freedom equal n − 1, where n is the number of people. In this example the degrees of freedom is seven (8 − 1), and the tabled t-value is −1.895 for alpha equals .05 and a one-tailed test.

Step 4: Conduct the study and calculate the t-test.

Table 2.20 Output of the t-Test for Dependent Measures Treating the A and B Groups Data in Table 2.17 as Repeated Measures

Item	Score 1		Score 2
Number of Pairs		*8*	
Mean	12.00		9.50
Std. Dev.	2.00		1.60
Difference in Means		−2.50	
t-value		−2.89	
Degrees of Freedom		7	
Two-Tailed Significance		.028	

The Paired-Samples t-test in SPSS was used to analyze the example data. See Appendix A for brief instructions on using it. The data had to be entered in pairs, so the initial and final scores for Person 1 (12,7) were entered, followed by the initial and final scores for Person 2 (15,10), and so on. The printout of this analysis is presented in Table 2.20.

> **Step 5:** Since the probability in Table 2.20 is less than the .05 alpha level selected, the difference between the initial and final means is significant, and the null hypothesis is rejected. Notice that the calculated t exceeds the tabled t and the same conclusion would be drawn.

One-Way ANOVA

There are many research situations where there are more than two independent groups. This is just an extension of the two independent group situations already discussed. In these situations the statistical analysis is a one-way **analysis of variance** (one-way ANOVA). Actually one-way ANOVA can be used with two or more independent groups, so it could be used rather than the t-test for two independent groups. The null hypothesis being tested is that the populations represented by the groups (samples) are equal in mean performance. The one alternate hypothesis is that the population means are not equal. One-way ANOVA is presented in Chapter 3 of this book, but with an application to measurement rather than research. However, the calculations are similar or the same with both applications.

One-Way ANOVA in SPSS will do the analysis. See Appendix A for brief instructions on using it. As in the t-test for two independent groups, when the data are entered there must be a variable identifying group membership and a variable that is the score of a person. One-Way ANOVA was applied to the data in Table 2.17. The output from One-Way ANOVA for the data in Table 2.17 is presented in Table 2.21.

The statistical test in ANOVA is an F-ratio. From Table 2.21 it can be seen that the probability of the F of 4.45 is .0244. Since this probability is less than an alpha level of .05, a researcher would conclude that there is a significant difference among the means and accept the alternate hypothesis.

Table 2.21 Output from One-Way ANOVA for the Data in Table 2.17

Source	DF	Sum of Sq.	Mean Sq.	F-Ratio	F Prob.
Between Groups	2	31.75	15.88	4.45	0.0244
Within Groups	21	74.88	3.57		
Total	23	106.63			

Group	Count	Mean	Std. Dev.
A	8	12.00	2.00
B	8	9.50	1.60
C	8	11.88	2.03

Table 2.22 Output of the Repeated Measures ANOVA on the Data in Table 2.17, Treating the Three Groups as Repeated Measures

Trial	Mean	Std. Dev.	Cases
A	12.00	2.00	8
B	9.50	1.60	8
C	11.88	2.03	8

Source	Sum of Sq.	DF	Mean Sq.	F	Prob.
Between People	32.63	7	4.66		
Within People	74.00	16	4.63		
Between Measures	31.75	2	15.88	5.26	.020
Residual	42.25	14	3.02		
Total	106.63	23	4.64		

Two-Way ANOVA, Repeated Measures

This is just an extension of the t-test for two dependent groups, with people repeatedly measured. In this case each person is measured on two or more occasions. Thus, if there are only two measures for each person, this ANOVA design is an alternative to the t-test for two dependent groups, but if there are more than two measures for each person, this ANOVA design must be used. The null hypothesis being tested is that at the population level the means for the repeated measures are equal. The alternate hypothesis is that the means are not equal. This ANOVA design is presented in Chapter 3 of this book, but with an application to measurement rather than research. However, the calculations are similar or the same with both applications. Using Reliability Analysis, which is in the Professional Statistics enhancement (SPSS 1998b) to the SPSS Base system, with the F-test option, a repeated measures ANOVA can be obtained. (Reliability Analysis is available with the standard but not the student version of SPSS.) See Appendix A for brief instructions on using it. A repeated measures ANOVA was conducted on the data in Table 2.17 as if the first score in each group was the score of Person 1 who was tested under treatments A, B, and C (12,7,13), the second score in each group was the scores of Person 2 (15,10,14), and so on. By selecting the option for item (treatment) means, the treatment means were obtained. The output from Reliability Analysis is presented in Table 2.22. The things of interest in Table 2.22 are the between people, between measures, and residual sources plus the F of 5.26, which is significant at the .05 level since the probability is .02. Thus, the alternate hypothesis is accepted and the researcher concludes that the treatment means differ.

Summary

You should be sufficiently familiar with each of the techniques presented in this chapter to determine when it should be used, to calculate its value, and to interpret the results. Among the techniques discussed, means and standard deviations are most widely used. T-scores, a very useful measure, are being used more frequently every year. The concept of correlation is crucial to the determination of reliability and validity, as will be discussed in Chapters 3 and 4. Also, you will find that percentile-rank norms accompany most physical performance tests.

Some understanding of the additional statistical techniques presented will certainly be helpful in reading the research literature. Good ability to use the microcomputer is an essential outcome of this chapter.

Formative Evaluation of Objectives

Objective 1 Select the statistical technique that is correct for a given situation.

1. The situations listed below are common to most physical education teachers and exercise specialists. In each case, determine what statistical value(s) is(are) needed.
   a. Determining the typical group performance.
   b. Determining which of two groups is the more heterogeneous in performance.
   c. Determining whether a group has improved in performance during a 6-week training unit.
   d. Determining what percentage of the class scores fall below 70 on a 100-point knowledge test.
   e. Determining on which of four fitness tests an individual performed best in reference to the mean performance of his or her peers.
   f. Determining whether a certain test discriminates against heavy individuals.
   g. Determining whether a performance standard for a test is realistic in regard to the mean and standard deviation of the test.
   h. Determining the typical group performance if the scores are ordinal or the distribution of scores are skewed.
2. One reason for calculating various statistical values is to help in describing group performance. What statistics must be calculated to adequately describe the performance of a group?

Objective 2 Calculate accurately with the formulas presented.

1. The ability to calculate accurately using the formulas presented in the text is vital. To check your ability to work with the formulas, use the following scores to calculate.
   a. The three measure of central tendency and the standard deviation for the 50 scores.
   b. The mean and standard deviation for each column of scores.

c. The percentile rank for scores 66 and 82.

84	82	95	92	83
80	58	82	81	60
79	87	71	90	69
82	75	70	89	85
69	79	80	74	69
84	81	71	90	87
66	79	52	92	72
70	86	87	77	87
90	89	69	68	83
85	92	76	74	89

2. There are many reasons why physical education teachers and exercise specialists use T-scores. You should not only realize when T-scores are needed, but you should also be able to calculate them.
   a. Determine the T-score when X is 60 for a 2-minute sit-up test with mean 42 and standard deviation 8.
   b. Determine the T-score when X is 11.3 for a 100-yard dash with mean 11.6 and standard deviation .55.
   c. Use the information below to determine which individual did best overall when both tests are considered.

	100-yard dash	**600-yard run**
Tom	10.50	2 minutes
Bill	11.10	1 minute, 35 seconds
Mean	10.74	2 minutes
Standard Deviation	1.12	20 seconds

3. It is possible to solve probability statements using the normal curve, and there are several advantages to doing so. Consider the following probability statements, and solve them using the normal curve.
   a. $P(0 < z < 1.5)$
   b. $P(-.78 < z < 0)$
   c. $P(z < -1.34)$
   d. $P(X > \overline{X} + 2s)$
   e. $P(.5 < z < 1.5)$
   f. $P(z < .53)$
   g. $P(X > 15, \text{ if } \overline{X} = 11 \text{ and } s = 2.5)$
   h. $P(z < ?) = (10/100)$

4. The median is sometimes used instead of the mean. Use the counting method to determine the median for each set of the following scores.
   a. 1,13,12,1,8,4,5,10,2,5,6,8,9
   b. 7,13,2,1,1,9,12,5,6,11,4,10
   c. 5,1,4,8,14,7,1,2,5

5. Correlation coefficients have many uses in physical education as you will see in the next chapter. A correlation coefficient should be calculated using the scores of a large number of people, but to give you practice, the following are scores of a few people. Calculate the correlation coefficient for the two sets of scores.

Person	Long Jump	Dash
A	67	5.2
B	68	5.4
C	57	6.1
D	60	5.5
E	71	5.1

Objective 3 Interpret the statistical value selected or calculated.

1. In addition to being able to calculate with the formulas presented in the chapter, you should be able to interpret the statistical values you have selected or calculated. For each situation below, indicate how you might explain or describe the statistical value to a group with which you typically work.
   a. Mean 11.67 and standard deviation 2.39 for a pull-up test
   b. Percentile rank 83 for a 100-yard dash score of 11.9
   c. T-score 61 for the test described in (a)
2. In the next chapter, correlation coefficients are used and referenced extensively. It is essential, then, that you understand both the term and its interpretation. In your own words, summarize what a correlation coefficient is and how to interpret either a positive or negative value.

Objective 4 Make decisions based on all available information about a given situation.

1. The text presents several methods for calculating T-scores for the entire class. Identify which formulas you would use if a calculator was to be used.

Objective 5 Utilize the microcomputer to analyze data.

1. Use the microcomputer to analyze several of the sets of scores in this chapter and check your answers against those in the chapter.

Additional Learning Activities

1. Using the techniques presented for finding T-scores for the entire class, determine the T-score for each score in a set of scores.
2. Select three units you would teach during a semester and decide which tests you would administer after each unit. Now decide which statistical techniques you would apply to the scores collected during the semester.

Bibliography

Baumgartner, T. A. and C. H. Strong. 1998. *Conducting and reading research in health and human performance.* 2nd ed. Dubuque, IA: WCB/McGraw-Hill.

Cohen, J. and P. Cohen. (1983). *Applied multivariate analysis/linear regression.* 2nd ed. Hillsdale, NJ: Erlbaum.

Ferguson, G. A. and Y. Takane. 1989. *Statistical analysis in psychology and education.* 6th ed. New York: McGraw-Hill.

Huck, S. W. and W. H. Cormier. 1996. *Reading statistics and research.* 2d ed. Reading, PA: Addison-Wesley.

Kachigan, S. K. 1991. *Multivariate statistical analysis.* 2d ed. New York: Radius.

Kuzma, J. W. 1998. *Basic statistics for the health sciences.* 3rd ed. Mountain View, CA: Mayfield.

Pavkov, T. and K. Pierce. (1998). *Ready, Set, Go! A Student Guide to SPSS for Windows 7.5.* Mountain View, CA.: Mayfield.

Pedhazur, E. J. 1982. *Multiple regression in behavioral research: Explanation and prediction.* 2nd ed. New York: Holt, Rinehart and Winston.

Seong, J. and T. Baumgartner. 1998. *TSCORE.* University of Georgia.

Runyon, R. P. et al. 1996. *Fundamentals of behavioral statistics.* 8th ed. New York: McGraw-Hill.

Safrit, M. J. and T. M. Wood. 1989. *Measurement concepts in physical education and exercise science.* Champaign, IL: Human Kinetics Publishers.

Sanders, D. H. 1995. *Statistics: A first course.* 5th ed. New York: McGraw-Hill.

Shin, K. 1996. *SPSS guide for DOS version 5.0 and Windows versions 6.0 and 6.1.2.* 2nd ed. Chicago: Irwin.

SPSS. (1998a). *SPSS Base 8.0 User's Guide.* Chicago: SPSS Inc.

SPSS. (1998b). *SPSS Professional Statistics 8.0.* Chicago: SPSS Inc.

SPSS. (1998c). *SPSS 8.0 for Windows Brief Guide.* Chicago: SPSS Inc.

SPSS. (1998d). *SPSS 8.0 for Windows Student Version.* Upper Saddle River, NJ: Prentice-Hall.

CHAPTER 3

Reliability and Objectivity

Contents

Key Words

analysis of variance
criterion score
internal-consistency reliability coefficient
intraclass correlation coefficient
kappa coefficient
objectivity
proportion of agreement coefficient
reliability
stability reliability coefficient
standard error of measurement
test-retest method

Objectives

This chapter discusses the methods used to estimate reliability and objectivity, and the factors that influence both of these values.

Many physical performance tests can be given several times in the same day. When there are multiple trials of a test, the test administrator must decide how many to administer and what trial(s) to use as the criterion score.

After reading Chapter 3 you should be able to:

1. Define and differentiate between reliability and objectivity for norm-referenced tests and outline the methods used to estimate these values.
2. Identify those factors that influence reliability and objectivity for norm-referenced tests.
3. Identify those factors that influence reliability for criterion-referenced tests.
4. Select a reliable criterion score based on measurement theory.

Introduction

There are certain characteristics essential to a measurement; without them, little faith can be put in the measurement and little use made of it. Measurement theory, the discussion of these characteristics, is covered in detail in this chapter and is referred to throughout the book.

The most important characteristic of a measurement is validity. A test or measuring instrument is valid if it measures what it is supposed to measure. Validity is discussed in greater detail in Chapter 4.

The second most important quality of a measurement is **reliability.** A reliable test or instrument measures whatever it measures consistently. That is, if an individual whose ability has not changed is measured twice with a perfectly reliable measuring device, the two scores will be identical. For a test to be valid it must be reliable.

Another important characteristic of a measurement is objectivity. **Objectivity** is sometimes called rater reliability because it is defined in terms of the agreement of competent judges about the value of a measurement. Thus, if two judges scoring the same individual on the same test cannot agree on a score, the test lacks objectivity and neither score is really reliable nor valid. A lack of objectivity, then, reduces both reliability and validity.

The majority of this chapter deals with reliability and objectivity for norm-referenced tests. Since criterion-referenced tests are becoming quite common, reliability for criterion-referenced tests is presented in the last section of the chapter.

Reliability Theory

We can better understand reliability for norm-referenced tests if we understand the mathematical theory at its foundation. Reliability can be explained in terms of "observed scores," "true scores," and "error scores." Reliability theory assumes that any measurement on a continuous scale contains an inherent component of error, the measurement error. Any one or more of the following factors can be a source of measurement error:

1. lack of agreement among scorers (i.e., objectivity);
2. lack of consistent performance by the individual tested;
3. failure of an instrument to measure consistently; and
4. failure of the tester to follow standardized testing procedures.

Assume that we are about to measure the heights of five people, all 68 inches tall. If we report any scores other than 68, an error of measurement has occurred. Thus, the variance for the reported heights is a good indicator of the amount of measurement error. As discussed in Chapter 2, a population is all the people who have a specified set of characteristics; a sample is a subgroup of a population. The variance is the square of the standard deviation and is symbolized as σ^2 for the variance of a population of s^2 as the variance of a sample. If all reported scores are 68, the measurement error is not serious and the variance is zero. However, if the five people are not all the same height, the variance for the reported heights may be due either to a true difference in height or to an error of measurement. In either case, the variance cannot be used as an indicator of measurement error.

In theory, the observed (recorded) score X is the sum of the true score t and an error of measurement score e:

$$X = t + e.$$

For example, if an individual who is 70.25 inches tall (t) has a recorded height of 70.5 (X), the error of measurement (e) is .25:

$$70.5 = 70.25 + .25.$$

If that individual is measured again and the recorded score is 69.5, the error of measurement equals $-.75$.

$$69.5 = 70.25 + -.75$$

The variance for a set of observed scores equals the variance of the true scores plus the variance of the error scores:

$$\sigma_x^2 = \sigma_t^2 + \sigma_e^2$$

where σ_x^2 is the variance of the observed scores, σ_t^2 is the variance of the true scores, and σ_e^2 is the variance of the error scores.

Reliability, then, is the ratio of the true-score variance to the observed-score variance:

$$\text{Reliability} = \frac{\sigma_t^2}{\sigma_x^2} = \frac{\sigma_x^2 - \sigma_e^2}{\sigma_x^2} = 1 - \frac{\sigma_e^2}{\sigma_x^2}.$$

We can see from this formula that, when no measurement error exists—that is, when σ_e^2 equals 0—the reliability is 1. As measurement error increases, σ_e^2 increases and reliability decreases. Thus, reliability is an indicator of the amount of measurement error in a set of scores.

Reliability depends on two basic factors:

1. reducing the variation attributable to measurement error; and
2. detecting individual differences (i.e., variation of the true scores) within the group measured.

The reliability of an instrument, then, must be viewed in terms of its measurement error (error variance) and its power to discriminate among different levels of ability within the group measured (true-score variance).

Types of Reliability

The reliability of physical performance measures has traditionally been estimated by one of two methods: the test-retest (stability) or internal-consistency method. Because each yields a different reliability coefficient, it is important to use the most appropriate method for a given measuring instrument. It is also important to notice the methods others have used to calculate their reliability coefficients. Remember too that a test may be reliable for one group of individuals and not for another. For example, a test that is highly reliable for college students may be only moderately reliable for high school students or participants in a fitness program.

An issue involved in the calculation of a reliability coefficient is whether the reliability coefficient should indicate *stability* or *internal consistency.*

Stability Reliability

When individual scores change little from one day to the next, they are stable. When scores remain stable, we consider them reliable. We use the test-retest method to obtain the **stability reliability coefficient.** With this method, each person is measured with the same test or instrument on several (usually 2) different days. The correlation between these two sets of scores is the stability reliability coefficient. The closer this coefficient is to positive one (+1), the more stable and reliable the scores.

Three factors can contribute to a low stability reliability coefficient:

1. the people tested may perform differently;
2. the measuring instrument may operate or be applied differently; and
3. the person administering the measurement may change.

Lack of sleep, minor injuries, and anxiety all tend to lower one's level of performance. Also, if the instrument is not consistent from day to day—for example, if measuring devices get out of calibration or malfunction—or if the procedures used to collect the measures change, the stability reliability decreases. Finally, if the way in which the administrator scores the people tested or perceives their performance changes, reliability decreases.

As a rule of thumb, test-retest scores are collected 1 to 3 days apart. However, for a maximum-effort test, we advise retesting 7 days later because fatigue and soreness can affect test scores. If the interval between measurement is too long, scores may change because of increased maturation or practice, factors that are generally not considered sources of measurement error.

Some people object to the **test-retest method** because of the time required to administer a measuring instrument at least twice. Also, only the Day-1 scores are used as performance measures; subsequent scores are used solely to determine reliability. Yet the method is probably the most appropriate of the procedures for determining the reliability of physical performance measures. Without test-retest consistency, we lack a true indicator, not only of each participant's ability, but of the faith we can place in the measure.

To save time, it is acceptable to calculate the test-retest reliability coefficient by retesting only some of the individuals originally tested. The typical procedure is to administer the test to all people on Day 1, and then to pick thirty to sixty people at random to be retested. (Draw names from a hat or use any procedure that gives all people an equal chance of being selected.) The test-retest reliability is then calculated using the scores of the randomly selected people.

Most physical measures are stable from day to day, exhibiting test-retest reliability coefficients between .80 and .95. There are others, however, that are not particularly stable from day to day. Baumgartner (1969b) found that scores may not be stable if people have not had prior experience and/or practice with the test prior to being measured. Of course, the reliability of a test or instrument depends on the type of measure, the age and gender of the people, the abilities of the administrator, and other factors, making it impossible to specify a universal minimum acceptable reliability. Each test administrator must base his or her minimum acceptable reliability on the degree of reliability necessary and that which other people have obtained with similar individuals.

Internal-Consistency Reliability

Many people use an internal-consistency coefficient as an estimate of the reliability of their measures. The advantage of this coefficient is that all measures are collected in a single day. Internal consistency refers to a consistent rate of scoring by the individuals being tested throughout a test or, when multiple trials are administered, from trial to trial.

Multiple trials are commonly administered when measuring physical ability. Examples are multiple measures of the skinfold at a site, multiple measures of the strength of a muscle or muscle group using electronic isometric equipment, and multiple trials of a physical performance test.

To obtain an **internal-consistency reliability coefficient,** the evaluator must give at least two trials of the test within a single day. Changes in the scores of the people being tested from trial to trial indicate a lack of test reliability. The correlation among the trial scores is the internal-consistency reliability coefficient. Obviously this technique should not be used with a maximum-performance test (e.g., the mile run) when fatigue would certainly affect the second trial scores.

Stability versus Internal Consistency

The internal-consistency reliability coefficient is not comparable to the stability reliability coefficient. The former is not affected by day-to-day changes in performance, a major source of measurement error in the latter. An internal-consistency coefficient is almost always higher than its corresponding stability reliability coefficient. In fact, internal-consistency coefficients between .85 and .99 are not uncommon for motor-performance tests.

Education, psychology, and other disciplines that rely heavily on paper-and-pencil tests seldom, if ever, use the test-retest method, using instead the internal consistency method. Remember that the stability coefficient assumes that true ability has not changed from one day to the next, an assumption often unjustifiable with paper-and-pencil tests because cognitive learning usually does occur between administrations. Psychomotor learning is less apt to vary in a 1- or 2-day span, making the stability coefficient a better indicator of the reliability of physical performance data.

Estimating Reliability—Intraclass Correlation

As we have noted, an observed score (X) is theoretically composed of a true score (t) and an error score (e). Furthermore, the variance of the observed scores (σ_x^2) equals the variance of the true scores (σ_t^2) plus the variance of the error scores (σ_e^2). Reliability equals the true-score variance divided by the observed-score variance. Just as observed-score variance can be divided into several parts, the total variability (s^2) for a set of scores can be divided into several parts. To divide, or petition the variance, we use the technique of **analysis of variance** (ANOVA). We can then use these parts of the total variance to calculate an intraclass reliability coefficient.

Intraclass R from One-Way Analysis of Variance

To calculate an intraclass correlation coefficient, R, as an estimate of reliability, each person tested in a physical education class, activity or fitness program, or therapy program must have at least two scores. Here we replace the reliability formula

$$\text{Reliability} = \frac{\sigma_t^2}{\sigma_x^2}$$

with

$$R = \frac{MS_A - MS_W}{MS_A}$$

where R is the **intraclass correlation coefficient** (the reliability of the mean test score for each person), MS_A is the mean square among people, and MS_W is the mean square within people. To obtain the two mean squares, a one-way analysis of variance was applied to the data. In other words, the term $MS_A - MS_W$ is an estimate of σ_t^2 ; and the term MS_A is an estimate of σ_x^2 . A mean square value is a variance just like the variance s^2 discussed in Chapter 2.

To calculate MS_A and MS_W, we must first define six values from the sets of scores:

1. the sum of squares total, SS_T (used to check our calculations)
2. the degrees of freedom total, df_T (used to check our calculations)
3. the sum of squares among people, SS_A
4. the sum of squares within people, SS_W
5. the degrees of freedom among people, df_A
6. the degrees of freedom within people, df_W

$$SS_T = \Sigma X^2 - \frac{(\Sigma X)^2}{nk} \qquad SS_A = \frac{\Sigma T_i^2}{k} - \frac{(\Sigma X)^2}{nk} \qquad SS_W = \Sigma X^2 - \frac{\Sigma T_i^2}{k}$$

$$df_T = nk - 1 \qquad df_A = n - 1 \qquad df_W = n(k - 1)$$

where ΣX^2 is the sum of the squared scores, ΣX is the sum of the scores of all people; n is the number of people; k is the number of scores for each person, and T_i is the sum of the scores for person i. With these values in hand, it is a simple matter to calculate the mean square among people,

$$MS_A = \frac{SS_A}{df_A} = \frac{SS_A}{n - 1}$$

and the mean square within people,

$$MS_W = \frac{SS_W}{df_W} = \frac{SS_W}{n(k - 1)}.$$

Problem 3.1. Using one-way analysis of variance, calculate R for the data in Table 3.1.

Solution. To solve for R, we use a 9-step procedure:

Table 3.1 One-Way ANOVA Data

Person	Day 1	Day 2
A	9	9
B	1	2
C	8	7

Step 1
Obtain the sum of the scores, T, for each person:

Person	Day 1	Day 2	T
A	9	9	18
B	1	2	3
C	8	7	15

Step 2
Obtain the sum of the scores; ΣX, and the sum of the squared scores, ΣX^2:

$$\Sigma X = 9 + 9 + 1 + 2 + 8 + 7^* = 36$$

$$\Sigma X^2 = 9^2 + 9^2 + 1^2 + 2^2 + 8^2 + 7^2 = 81 + 81 + 1 + 4 + 64 + 49 = 280$$

Step 3
Calculate the 3 sum-of-squares values:

$$SS_T = \Sigma X^2 - \frac{(\Sigma X)^2}{nk} = 280 - \frac{36^2}{(3)(2)} = 280 - \frac{1296}{6} = 280 - 216 = 64$$

$$SS_A = \frac{\Sigma T_i^2}{k} - \frac{(\Sigma X)^2}{nk} = \frac{18^2 + 3^2 + 15^2}{2} - \frac{36^2}{(3)(2)}$$

$$= \frac{324 + 9 + 225}{2} - \frac{1296}{6} = \frac{558}{2} - 216 = 279 - 216 = 63$$

$$SS_W = \Sigma X^2 - \frac{\Sigma T_i^2}{k} = 280 - \frac{18^2 + 3^2 + 15^2}{2}$$

$$= 280 - \frac{324 + 9 + 225}{2} = 280 - \frac{558}{2} = 280 - 279 = 1$$

Step 4
Check your calculations. The sum of squares among people (SS_A) plus the sum of squares within people (SS_W) should equal the sum of squares total (SS_T):

$$63 + 1 = 64$$

(If your figures here were incorrect, you would go back and recalculate.)

*You could total the T column for this value as well: (18 + 3 + 15 = 36).

Step 5
Calculate the 3 degrees of freedom values:

$$df_T = nk - 1 = (3)(2) - 1 = 5$$

$$df_A = n - 1 = 3 - 1 = 2$$

$$df_W = n(k - 1) = 3(2 - 1) = 3$$

Step 6
Check your calculations. The degrees of freedom among people (df_A) plus the degrees of freedom within people (df_W) should equal the degrees of freedom total (df_T):

$$2 + 3 = 5.$$

Step 7
Calculate MS_A and MS_W. Where SS_A is 63, n is 3, SS_W is 1, and k is 2, the mean square among people, MS_A, is 31.50 and the mean square within people, MS_W, is .33:

$$MS_A = \frac{63}{3 - 1} = \frac{63}{2} = 31.50$$

$$MS_W = \frac{1}{(3)(2 - 1)} = \frac{1}{3} = .33.$$

Step 8
Place all your values in an ANOVA summary table to make sure nothing has been left out and everything is correct.

Source	df	SS	MS
Among people	df_A	SS_A	MS_A
Within people	df_W	SS_W	MS_W
Total	df_T		

Source	df	SS	MS
Among people	2	63	31.50
Within people	3	1	.33
Total	5	64	

Step 9
Now we can calculate R. Where MS_A is 31.50 and MS_W is .33, the intraclass reliability coefficient R is .99:

$$R = \frac{31.50 - .33}{31.50} = \frac{31.17}{31.50} = .99.$$

R indicates the reliability of the sum or mean test score for each person. When R equals 0 there is no reliability; when R equals 1 there is maximum reliability. Whenever multiple trials are administered on one day or a test is administered on at least two days, we can use R to estimate the reliability of the mean score. If the person's scores change from trial to trial or from day to day, R will be lower.

With the availability of calculators and computers, the calculation of R is quite easy. A simple or one-way analysis-of-variance computer program provides the mean squares needed to calculate R. These computer programs are easily found for any computer. In the SPSS package of statistical programs, the One-Way ANOVA program will do a one-way analysis of variance (see Additional Statistical Techniques in

Table 3.2 Sample ANOVA Summary Table for n People and k Trials

Source	DF	SS	MS
Among people	$n - 1$	SS_P	MS_P
Among trials	$k - 1$	SS_t	MS_t
Interaction	$(n - 1)(k - 1)$	SS_I	MS_I
Total	$nk - 1$	SS_T	

Chapter 2). If a computer program is used, notice that each person is treated as a group. This may be a problem since the number of people often exceeds the maximum number of groups allowed by a computer program. Further, the data input organization for a one-way ANOVA is not compatible with the data input organization required by other statistical techniques if additional statistical analyses are applied to the data. To avoid these two problems, use a repeated measures ANOVA program for the data analysis (see Computer Use section later in this chapter).

This reliability coefficient using a one-way ANOVA is only one of many intraclass reliability coefficients. It is the simplest to determine because it requires the least calculation and decision making. Slightly more advanced procedures may yield a more precise criterion score. Baumgartner (1969a) describes a selection procedure that yields a criterion score minimally influenced by learning or fatigue and the intraclass reliability for that score. Feldt and McKee (1958) present a way to estimate reliability using the intraclass method when multiple trials are administered on each of several days. Safrit and Wood (1989) have several strong chapters on reliability.

Intraclass R from Two-Way Analysis of Variance

Suppose that k scores were collected for each of n people. These scores could have been collected over k trials or k days. For discussion purposes, we will refer to the k scores as trials. If a two-way analysis of variance were applied to the k scores of these n people, a summary table could be developed as shown in Table 3.2.

For two-way ANOVA, the following formulas are used to calculate the various sums of squares:

$$\text{Sum of squares total } (SS_T) = \Sigma X^2 - \frac{(\Sigma X)^2}{nk}$$

$$\text{Sum of squares among people } (SS_P) = \frac{\Sigma(T_i)^2}{k} - \frac{(\Sigma X)^2}{nk}$$

$$\text{Sum of squares among trials } (SS_t) = \frac{\Sigma(T_j)^2}{n} - \frac{(\Sigma X)^2}{nk}$$

$$\text{Sum of squares interaction } (SS_I) = \Sigma X^2 + \frac{(\Sigma X)^2}{nk} - \frac{\Sigma(T_i)^2}{k} - \frac{\Sigma(T_j)^2}{n}$$

$$df_T = nk - 1,\ df_P = n - 1,\ df_t = k - 1,\ df_I = (n - 1)(k - 1)$$

where ΣX^2 is the sum of the squared scores, ΣX is the sum of the scores of all people, n is the number of people, k is the number of scores for each person, T_i is the sum of the scores for Person i, and T_j is the sum of the scores for Trial j.

Table 3.3 Two-Way ANOVA Data for 3-Trial Test Administered on 1 Day

Person	Trial 1	Trial 2	Trial 3
A	5	6	7
B	3	3	4
C	4	4	5
D	7	6	6
E	6	7	5

Problem 3.2. Using the two-way analysis of variance formulas, develop a summary table of the data in Table 3.3.

Solution. These first 4 steps in the procedure are similar to those used in one-way ANOVA.

Step 1
Step up a table to calculate the sum of scores for each person (T_i) and for each trial (T_j):

Person	Trial 1	Trial 2	Trial 3	T_i
A	5	6	7	18
B	3	3	4	10
C	4	4	5	13
D	7	6	6	19
E	6	7	5	18
T_j	25	26	27	78

Step 2
Calculate the values needed to determine the sums of squares:

$$\Sigma X^2, \Sigma X, \frac{\Sigma(T_i)^2}{k}, \text{ and } \frac{\Sigma(T_j)^2}{n}.$$

$$\Sigma X^2 = 5^2 + 6^2 + 7^2 + \ldots + 6^2 + 7^2 + 5^2$$
$$= 25 + 36 + 49 + \ldots + 36 + 49 + 25 = 432$$

$$\Sigma X = 5 + 6 + 7 + \ldots + 6 + 7 + 5^* = 78$$

$$\frac{\Sigma(T_i)^2}{k} = \frac{18^2 + 10^2 + 13^2 + 19^2 + 18^2}{3} = \frac{324 + 100 + 169 + 361 + 324}{3}$$

$$= \frac{1278}{3} = 426$$

$$\frac{\Sigma(T_j)^2}{n} = \frac{25^2 + 26^2 + 27^2}{5} = \frac{625 + 676 + 729}{5} = \frac{2030}{5} = 406.$$

*Here too, the sum of the T_j column could be used.

Step 3

Where ΣX^2 is 432, ΣX is 78, n is 5, k is 3, $\frac{\Sigma(T_i)^2}{k}$ is 426,

and $\frac{\Sigma(T_j)^2}{n}$ is 406, SS_T, SS_S, and SS_t, and SS_I are as follows:

$$SS_T = 432 - \frac{78^2}{(5)(3)} = 432 - \frac{6084}{15} = 432 = 405.6 = 26.4$$

$$SS_P = 426 - 405.6 = 20.4$$

$$SS_t = 406 - 405.6 = .4$$

$$SS_I = 432 + 405.6 - 426 - 406 = 837.6 - 832 = 5.6.$$

Step 4

Check your calculations. The sum of the sum of squares among people, the sum of squares among trials, and the sum of squares interaction should equal the sum of squares total:

$$20.4 + .4 + 5.6 = 26.4$$

Step 5

Following the procedure in Table 3.2, the summary table for the data in Table 3.3 would look like this:

Source	DF	SS	MS
Among people	4	20.4	5.10
Among trials	2	.4	.20
Interaction	8	5.6	.70
Total	14	26.4	

Compare Means. Once the summary table has been developed, we need to determine whether the trial means seem to be different. One way to do this is to visually compare the trial means. For the data used in Problem 3.2, the trial means are 5.0, 5.2, and 5.4; so there does not seem to be a true difference among the trial means. There is nothing wrong with using the visual comparison of the means (and this is what most practitioners will do), but it is approximate. Researchers and people who want to be very precise in making a decision concerning whether the trial means differ will determine whether the trial means differ significantly using the F-test formula $F = MS_t / MS_I$. For example, the F from the summary table in Problem 3.2 is .29 ($F = .20/.70 = .29$).

If the F is significant, there is real, or true, difference among the trial means. If the F is nonsignificant, the difference between trial means is not considered a true difference, but rather a chance one. (To review significance versus nonsignificance, see Additional Statistical Techniques in Chapter 2.)

For example, using the summary table in Problem 3.2, the F-table value for 2 and 8 degrees of freedom is 4.46 at the 0.5 level and 8.65 at the .01 level. Because the calculated F for the data in the problem is .29, the difference among trial means is nonsignificant. If F-tables are not available, you might arbitrarily decide that if the calculated F is 5.0 or larger it is significant.

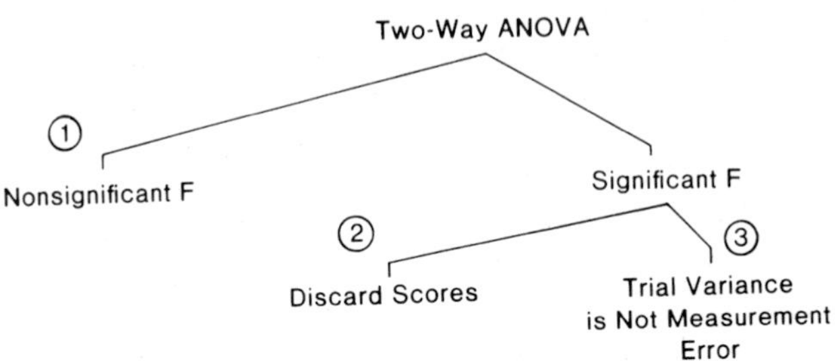

Figure 3.1
Two-way ANOVA decision process.

After the F-test, there are three potential ways the analysis can progress, as shown in Figure 3.1.

Nonsignificant F. If there is a nonsignificant F, indicating no difference among the trial means, the reliability of the criterion score, which is the sum or mean of a person's trial scores, is as follows:

$$R = \frac{MS_P - MS_W}{MS_S} \tag{3.1}$$

where

$$MS_W = \frac{SS_t + SS_I}{df_t + df_I}$$

Using the data in Problem 3.2, where MS_W is $.6\left(\frac{.4 + 5.6}{2 + 8}\right)$, R is .88:

$$R = \frac{5.10 - .6}{5.10} = \frac{4.50}{5.10} = .882 = .88.$$

Notice that Formula 3.1 is the same as the Formula for R presented with a one-way ANOVA since SS_S in a two-way ANOVA is the same as SS_A in a one-way ANOVA. Applying the one-way ANOVA formulas to the data in Table 3.3 we obtain the following:

$$MS_A = \frac{20.4}{5 - 1} = 5.1 \qquad MS_W = \frac{6}{(5)(3 - 1)} = .6 \qquad R = \frac{5.1 - .6}{5.1} = .88$$

Significant F. The other alternative ways for the analysis to go are possible when the F is significant, indicating a difference among the trial means. With the first technique (number 2 in Figure 3.1), which can be used when each person is tested several times in one day or on several days, the scores from trials whose means are lower than or not approximately equal to the means of the other trials are discarded (Baumgartner 1969a). A second two-way analysis of variance is then conducted on the retained scores, and another F-test is calculated. If the recalculated F is nonsignificant, Formula 3.1 is used to estimate the reliability of the **criterion score,** the sum or mean of each person's retained trial scores. For example, suppose the data for a 6-trial test were as presented in Figure 3.2. Trials 1, 2, and 6 would be discarded, and another two-way ANOVA would be conducted using the scores from Trials 3, 4, and 5.

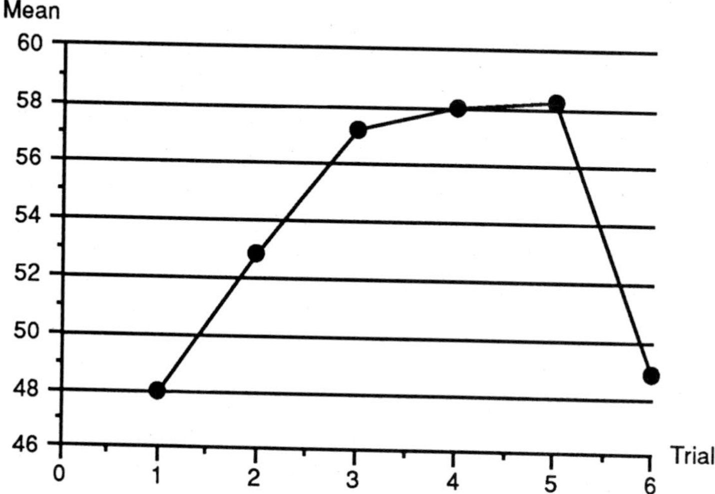

Figure 3.2
Graph of the means for a six-trial test.

The purpose of this technique (number 2 in Figure 3.1) is to find a measurement schedule free of trial differences and yielding the largest possible criterion score for most people. This criterion score is usually very reliable. Baumgartner and Jackson (1970) used this technique. Trial-to-trial variance is random after finding a nonsignificant F, so trial-to-trial variance is considered a measurement error in Formula 3.1. Interaction is also considered a measurement error.

The last alternative (number 3 in Figure 3.1) does not consider a trial-to-trial variance as measurement error. This technique is often used when it is known that people will improve from trial to trial. Also, this technique is often used when estimating objectivity (judges replace trials) and all judges are not expected to use the same standards. The formula for estimating the reliability of the criterion score (the sum or mean of all trials) is as follows:

$$R = \frac{MS_P - MS_I}{MS_P}. \tag{3.2}$$

For the data in Problem 3.2, using Formula 3.2, R is .86:

$$R = \frac{5.10 - .70}{5.10} = \frac{4.40}{5.10} = .86.$$

Measurement error is supposed to be random. Significant difference among the trial means indicates a lack of randomness. Thus, when significant difference is found, one could argue that the variance for trials should not be combined with the sum of squares interaction to form the mean square within Formula 3.1. Statistically this position is defensible. However, one could counter that every source of variance not attributable to students is error-score variance. In keeping with this philosophy, you can either conduct a one-way analysis of variance with the test scores or, as Baumgartner (1969a) advocates, discard scores until no significant difference among trial means is found in the data and then use Formula 3.1.

Of the three potential data analyses shown in Figure 3.1, it seems that most people are using alternatives 2 and 3. Only when people must do the data analysis by hand is a one-way ANOVA initially applied to the data.

Table 3.4 Two-Way ANOVA for the Data in Table 3.3 Using the SPSS Reliability Analysis Program

Source	Sum of Sq.	DF	Mean Sq.	F.	Prob.
Between People	20.40	4	5.10		
Within People	6.00	10	0.60		
Between Measures	0.40	2	0.20	.29	0.7588
Residual	5.60	8	0.70		
Total	26.40	14	1.89		

Item	Mean	Std. Dev.	Cases
Trial 1	5.00	1.58	5
Trial 2	5.20	1.64	5
Trial 3	5.40	1.14	5

Computer Use. Most people use the computer to apply a two-way ANOVA to their data. Two-way ANOVA computer programs that will handle repeated measures on each person are commonly available for computers. Some two-way ANOVA programs cannot be used in this situation because they will not handle repeated measures on each person and/or expect the people to be in two or more groups. Unless the amount of data is small, all physical education and exercise science specialists should use the computer to do a two-way ANOVA on their data. The advantage of a two-way ANOVA over a one-way ANOVA is that the computer will give you the mean for each trial, a significance test for difference among trial means is possible, and the R can still be calculated as if a one-way ANOVA was used (Formula 3.1) or by using the two-way ANOVA information (Formula 3.2).

In the standard version of the SPSS package of computer programs, the Reliability Analysis program provides an option to the two-way ANOVA for the analysis of repeated measures on each person. Reliability Analysis is not in the SPSS Base system, but is in an add-on enhancement option called SPSS Professional Statistics. Professional Statistics is not available for the Student SPSS version. A brief introduction to Reliability Analysis is provided in Appendix A. When entering the data in Table 3.3 there must be three variables (Trial 1, Trial 2, Trial 3).

When analyzing the data using Reliability Analysis, trials 1, 2, and 3 must be identified as the variables, and the option to print the item (trial) means should be selected. The output from the analysis of the data in Table 3.3 is presented in Table 3.4.

In Table 3.4 the "between" and "within people" are the sources if a one-way ANOVA is applied to the data. The "between people," "between measures," and "residual" are the sources if a two-way ANOVA is applied to the data. Note that within people from the one-way ANOVA is composed of between measures and residual from the two-way ANOVA. In terms of the terminology used up to this point and in Table 3.2, between measures and residual in Table 3.4 are among trials and interaction respectively. Since the probability (Prob.) for between measures (.7588) is larger than .05, there is not a significant difference among the trial means (see F-Test p. 105), which has implications as to how R is calculated. There is sufficient information in Table 3.4 to calculate R no matter the formula that is selected.

Coefficient Alpha

Coefficient alpha is often used to determine the reliability of dichotomous data (see chapter 13). When the data are ordinal, we may use the coefficient alpha to determine reliability (Ferguson & Takane 1989; Nunnally and Bernstein 1994). In fact, with ordinal or interval data the coefficient alpha is the same as the intraclass R $\left[R = \frac{(MS_P - MS_I)}{MS_P}\right]$ just discussed. Coefficient alpha is an estimate of the reliability of a criterion score that is the sum of the trial scores in one day. There is no reason why the coefficient could not be applied to multiple-day or multiple-judge data to estimate stability reliability or objectivity. We determine coefficient alpha using the following formula:

$$r_\alpha = \left(\frac{k}{k-1}\right)\left(\frac{s_x^2 - s_j^2}{s_x^2}\right) \tag{3.3}$$

where r_α is coefficient alpha, k is the number of trials, s_x^2 is the variance for the criterion scores, and s_j^2 is the sum of the variances for the trials.

Problem 3.3. Calculate coefficient alpha for the data in Table 3.3.

Solution. Here too, the procedure, involves multiple steps.

Step 1
The simplest way to do this is to set up a table like the one below:

Person	TRIAL 1 X_1	TRIAL 2 X_2	TRIAL 3 X_3	TOTAL X
A	5	6	7	18
B	3	3	4	10
C	4	4	5	13
D	7	6	6	19
E	6	7	5	18
	25	26	27	78

Step 2
Have the computer calculate the variance for X_1, X_2, X_3, and X. Using the formula

$$s^2 = \frac{\Sigma X^2}{n} - \frac{(\Sigma X)^2}{n^2} \qquad \left[\frac{\Sigma(X - \bar{X})^2}{n}\right]$$

the variances are

$s_1^2 = 2;$ $s_2^2 = 2.16;$ $s_3^2 = 1.04;$ $s_x^2 = 12.24.$

If the computer calculates with the formula $s^2 = \frac{(\Sigma X^2 - (\Sigma X)^2/n)}{(n-1)} \left[\frac{\Sigma(X - \bar{X})^2}{n-1}\right]$, the variances above will be different, but the value of r_α will not be affected. Each variance has the same denominator (n or n − 1), and these values appear in both the numerator and denominator of the $(s_x^2 - s_j^2) / (s_x^2)$ section of the coefficient alpha formula. Thus, the values cancel out (e.g., the expression [5/6 − 3/6][5/6] reduces to [5 − 3]/[5]) and has no effect on coefficient alpha.

Step 3

Now we can calculate r_a. Where k is 3, s_x^2 is 12.24, and s_j^2 is 5.2 (the sum of s_1^2, s_2^2, and s_3^2: 2 + 2.16 + 1.04), the coefficient alpha r is .86:

$$r_\alpha = \left(\frac{3}{3-1}\right)\left(\frac{12.24 - 5.2}{12.24}\right) = \left(\frac{3}{2}\right)\left(\frac{7.04}{12.24}\right) = \frac{21.12}{24.48} = .86.$$

Notice R = .86 with Formula 3.2.

Besides providing the needed variances, the computer can also provide the correlations for the trial scores with the sum of the trial scores, which could be useful in deciding which trials to sum as the criterion score. Only trials that correlate positively at a reasonably high value with the sum of the trial scores should be retained. Normally, with motor performance tests, each trial is correlated with the sum of all trials.

The SPSS program, Reliability Analysis, just discussed, calculates coefficient alpha. Coefficient alpha might be calculated by hand, as was done in Problem 3.3, when a repeated measures ANOVA computer program is not available to provide the values needed to calculate an intraclass R. With a large amount of data (persons tested and/or trials), it would be easier to just enter the trial scores and let the computer calculate the criterion score (sum of the trial scores) before calculating the variances. In Problem 3.3 this would require entering the three trial scores for each person, having the computer calculate TOTAL, and finally having the computer calculate the four variances needed to calculate coefficient alpha. The sum of the trial scores can be obtained once the trial scores are entered by using the Transformation program in the SPSS package or any other package of statistical analysis programs. You must indicate to the computer program the name of the variable that is to be the sum of the trial scores (e.g., TOTAL in Problem 3.3) and indicate how the sum of the trial scores is to be formed (e.g., in Problem 3.3, X = X1 + X2 + X3). This procedure is outlined in Appendix A.

Single Score

All the formulas for calculating the intraclass reliability coefficient thus far have been for the mean or sum of all trials or days. Sometimes it is necessary to estimate the reliability of a single trial or day. Two formulas are used to calculate the reliability of a single score when there are k trials or days; the decision of which to use rests on the analysis procedure. If the procedures leading to Formula 3.1 were used, we calculate R with the following equation:

$$R = \frac{MS_P - MS_W}{MS_P + (k/k' - 1)(MS_W)}. \quad \textbf{(3.4)}$$

If the procedures leading to Formula 3.2 were used, we use this formula instead:

$$R = \frac{MS_P - MS_I}{(MS_P + (k/k' - 1)(MS_I)} \quad \textbf{(3.5)}$$

where k is the number of trials administered and k′ is the number of trials for which R is estimated.

Several authors present these formulas for estimating or predicting what R would be if the number of trials was increased or decreased.

We can easily see this in a test-retest situation. For example, suppose people were tested on each of 2 days, and the test administrator wants to estimate the reliability of a score collected on one of those days. In this case, using Formula 3.4, the R is:

$$R = \frac{MS_P - MS_W}{MS_P + (2/1 - 1)(MS_W)} = \frac{MS_P - MS_W}{MS_P + MS_W}.$$

Problem 3.4. Calculating R for a single score, using the data in Table 3.1.

Step 1
From Step 7 in Problem 3.1, the $MS_A = 31.5$ and $MS_W = .33$.

Step 2
Calculate R

$$R = \frac{31.5 - .33}{31.5 + .33} = \frac{31.37}{31.83} = .98.$$

R indicates the reliability of a test score collected on 1 day.

Intraclass R in Summary

Occasionally, an intraclass correlation coefficient will be lower than wanted even though the test seemed reliable (individual scores changed little from trial to trial or day to day). This happens when the sum of squares among people is small, indicating a group homogeneous in ability. In a situation like this, you must understand why the coefficient is low. Or you can try to increase test sensitivity or ability to discriminate among individuals in terms of ability. Remember, though, that you cannot accept something as reliable if the reliability coefficient is low.

Occasionally people want to test intraclass correlation coefficients as to value at the population level, whether two coefficients are equal, or develop confidence limits for a coefficient. Feldt (1990) and Alsawalmeh and Feldt (1992) address these needs.

Selecting a Criterion Score

Mean Score versus Best Score

A **criterion score** is the measure used to indicate a person's ability. Unless a test has perfect reliability it is a better indicator when it is developed from more than one trial. Multiple-trial tests are common in physical education with skinfold, flexibility, jumping, throwing, and short running—tests whose performance is not adversely affected by fatigue. Multiple trials with skinfold, flexibility and isometric strength tests are common in exercise science. For a multiple-trial test, the criterion score can be either the person's best score or mean score. The best score is the optimal score a person receives on any one trial; the mean score is the mean of all the person's trial scores.

Much research has been done on the selection of a criterion score (Baumgartner 1974; Berger & Sweney 1965; Disch 1975; Henry 1967; Hetherington 1973; Johnson & Meeter 1977; Whitley & Smith 1963). The choice of best or mean score should be based on the amount of time available to obtain the criterion score and the use to be made of it. It is a much slower process to calculate a mean score than to list a best score for each person. This is probably why standardized instructions for most multiple-trial tests suggest using the best score. Certainly when the criterion score is to be used as an indicator of maximum possible performance, the best score should be used. However, the best score from several trials may not be typical, in that it is unlikely to be achieved again for a long time and may be inflated by measurement error. Reliability of a criterion score increases as the number of measures it is based on increases. Thus, the most reliable criterion score and the best indicator of true ability (typical performance), may be the mean score. In theory, the sum of the errors of measurement is 0 when all of an individual's trial scores are added together. Because in most situations one wants an indication of status or typical performance, the mean score may be the preferred criterion score for a multiple-trial test. When scores are not stable, as may be true for individuals with disabilities, the mean of the scores collected on several days may well be the only indicator of true ability.

More Considerations

Darracott (1995) believes that for multiple-trial physical performance tests where maximal ability rather than typical ability is desired, and the equipment and scoring procedure are highly accurate (which could be the case with many physiological measurements taken in a laboratory setting), the best score is the best indicator of a person's true ability and it is likely lower trial scores are due to negative measurement error. Particularly for physiological tests with highly accurate scoring procedures and/or equipment, a person can't score better than his or her physiological capacity. The multiple-trial field-based fitness tests that Darracott analyzed were not physiological capacity type tests, but still the distribution of the trial scores of most of the people were negatively skewed (see chapter 2) rather than normally distributed. Thus, the best trial score or maybe median trial score of a person would seem to be a better criterion score than the mean of the trial scores of a person. Darracott found that the test-retest reliability (stability reliability) for criterion scores that were the mean trial score and the best trial score were very similar for the several field-based tests she examined.

Further, she found that the trend in the multiple-trial data of individuals did not follow the trend in the multiple-trial data of the group. For example, even though for a four-trial test the mean score for the group was best on trials 2 and 3, with the mean score on trials 1 and 4 much worse, in each trial there were some people who received their best score and some people who received their worst score. This suggests that decisions as to which trial(s) to use in determining the criterion score should be based on individual performance rather than group mean performance. Thus, in the previous four trial test example, rather than the criterion score being the mean of the scores of trials 2 and 3, it should be the mean of an individual's two best scores. It was suggested at the beginning of this section that the criterion score be based on more than one trial. Also, if the best score of multiple-trial scores is the criterion score, (1) it still follows the suggestion of being based on multiple trials, and (2) it is not the same trial for each person.

Summary

Based on all that has been presented concerning estimating reliability, intraclass correlation, and selecting a criterion score, an individual's criterion score for multiple-trial data could be determined in any of the following ways, depending on the situation and what the test administrator believes is most appropriate: (1) mean of all the trial scores, (2) best score of all the trial scores, (3) mean of selected trial scores based on the trials on which the group scored best, or (4) mean of selected trial scores based on the trials on which the individual scored best. In terms of the fourth method (based on the data Darracott [1995] used in her study), if four to six trials are administered, there seems to be a tendency for a person to have one trial score that is markedly worse than the rest of the trial scores. Thus, the worst trial score could be discarded and the mean of the remaining trial scores could be the criterion score. It is interesting to note here that discarding the worst trial score for a person makes the distribution of the remaining trial scores for the person considerably more like a normal distribution (researchers would call the trial score discarded an "outlier").

In the next chapter you will learn that for a score to be valid it must be reliable, but reliability does not guarantee validity. Thus, with multiple-trial data the method used to determine the criterion score must be selected by considering what is the most reliable and valid criterion score and not simply what is the most reliable score.

Spearman-Brown Prophecy Formula

This equation is used to estimate the reliability of a test when its length is increased. It assumes that the additional length (or new trial), although as difficult as the original, is neither mentally nor physically tiring. This formula estimates the reliability of a criterion score, which is the mean or sum of the trial scores.

$$r_{k,k} = \frac{k(r_{1,1})}{1 + (k - 1)(r_{1,1})}$$

where $r_{k,k}$ is the estimated reliability of a test increased in length k times, k is the number of times the test is increased in length, and $r_{1,1}$ is the reliability of the present test.

Problem 3.5. The reliability of a 6-trial test was found to be .94. Determine the reliability if 18 trials were administered.

Solution. Where k is 3 and $r_{1,1}$ is .94, the estimated reliability of a criterion score based on 18 trials is .98:

$$r_{k,k} = \frac{(3)(.94)}{1 + (3 - 1)(.94)} = \frac{2.82}{1 + (2)(.94)} = \frac{2.82}{1 + 1.88} = \frac{2.82}{2.88} = .979 = .98.$$

Baumgartner (1968) investigated the accuracy with which the Spearman-Brown prophecy formula predicts reliability. He compared the predicted reliability coefficients to the reliability coefficients actually obtained when the number of trials of a test was increased. He found that the formula's accuracy increased as the value of k in the formula decreased, concluding, then, that the reliability coefficient predicted by the Spearman-Brown formula is the maximum reliability that can be expected.

Standard Error of Measurement

It is sometimes useful to be able to estimate the measurement error in each test score. If each person is administered multiple trials of a test, a standard deviation for the trial scores could be calculated for each person, and this standard deviation is the measurement error for the individual. If each person is administered only one trial, the average amount of measurement error in the test scores is estimated for the whole group by calculating the standard error of measurement by the following formula:

$$s_e = s_x\sqrt{1 - r_{x,x}}$$

where s_e is the standard error of measurement, s_x is the standard deviation for the test scores, and $r_{x,x}$ is the reliability coefficient for the test scores.

Since the variance of all measurements contains some measurement error, the **standard error of measurement** of a test score reflects the degree one may expect a test score to vary due to measurement error.

Problem 3.6. A written test has a standard deviation of 5 and a reliability coefficient of .91. Determine the standard error of measurement for the test.

Solution. Where s_x is 5 and $r_{x,x}$ is .91, the standard error of measurement s_e is 1.5:

$$s_e = 5\sqrt{1 - .91} = 5\sqrt{.09} = (5)(.3) = 1.5.$$

The standard error acts like a test score's standard deviation and can be interpreted in much the same way using the normal curve. From the normal curve table (Table 2.12, page 75), we know that approximately 68% of the scores lie within 1 standard deviation of the mean, which in this case is the test score. If a person who scored 73 on the test in Problem 3.6 were to take the test 100 times and his or her ability did not change, we would expect the person's scores to fall between 71.5 (73 − 1.5) and 74.5 (73 + 1.5) 68 times out of 100. The standard error, then, specifies the limits within which we can expect scores to vary due to measurement error. In fact, there is a growing tendency to report a confidence band—the score, plus and minus the standard error—with test scores. For more lengthy discussion, see Ferguson and Takane (1989) or any other statistics text that includes a chapter on measurement theory. Crocker and Algina (1986) and Nunnally and Bernstein (1994) are excellent sources on measurement theory.

Be aware that the standard error of measurement is based on the scores of a group and all members of the group will not follow the scoring pattern of the group. Darracott (1995) found that the standard deviation for the multiple-trial scores of most individuals is larger than the standard error of measurement.

Factors Affecting Reliability

Many factors can affect test reliability. Among them are scoring accuracy, the number of test trials, test difficulty, instructions, and the testing environment, as well as the person's familiarity with the test and present performance level. The range of talent and the use of a reliability coefficient also can affect reliability. The reliability coefficient is larger for scores from a long test than those from a short one, and for a group with a broad range of abilities than for one with a narrow range of abilities.

Table 3.5 shows a categorization proposed by Zuidema (1969) of the factors that influence test reliability. We can expect an acceptable degree of reliability when

1. the people are heterogeneous in ability, motivated to do well, ready to be tested, and informed about the nature of the test;
2. the test discriminates among ability groups, and is long enough or repeated sufficiently for each person to show his or her best performance;
3. the testing environment and organization are favorable to good performance; and
4. the person administering the test is competent.

The reliability coefficient should be calculated using the scores of a large group (at least 100 people), since it is relatively easy to obtain extremely high or low correlation coefficients with a small group.

Objectivity

Objectivity, or rater reliability, is an important characteristic of a test or measuring instrument. For a measurement to be valid and reliable, it must have objectivity. We can define objectivity as the close agreement between the scores assigned to each person

Table 3.5 Factors Influencing Test Reliability

Category of Factors	Illustrative Sources of Imperfect Reliability
Characteristics of the performers	Range of talent; motivation; good day vs. bad day; learning; forgetting; fatigue
Characteristics of the test	Length; difficulty; discriminative power; trial homogeneity; number of performers
Characteristics of the testing situation	Instructions; environment; class organization; class management; warm-up opportunity
Characteristics of the measurement process	Nature of measurement instrument; selection of scoring unit; precision; errors in measurement; number of trials; recording errors
Characteristics of the evaluator(s)	Competences; confidence in test; concentration on task; familiarity with instrument; motivation; number of evaluators
Characteristics of the mode of statistical estimation	Breakdown of observed score variance into true score and error score variance, with retest design: error source is variation within individuals between days. Does not include within-day variance. With split-trial design: variation within individuals between trials. Does not include between-day variance or variance between grouped trials.

by two or more judges. Judges in this case could be judges in gymnastics or scorers of a sit-up test.

Factors Affecting Objectivity

Objectivity depends on two related factors: (1) the clarity of the scoring system and (2) the degree to which the judge can assign scores accurately. Certain tests have clearly defined methods of scoring: a mile run is scored with a stopwatch; and a sit-up is scored in executions. In this type of test the rater can easily determine the person's scores. In contrast, an essay test or a dance performance does not offer a well-defined scoring system, relying on the rater's judgment in the assignment of points.

The second factor is more obvious. If a judge does not know how to assign a score, he or she cannot do it accurately. For example, a scorer who is unfamiliar with stopwatches will probably not assign an accurate score on a timed speed event. Of course, it is a simple matter to train a scorer in the use of scoring equipment and scoring procedures.

A high degree of objectivity is essential when two or more people are administering a test. For example, say that a group of fifty people is divided into two groups and each group is tested by a different person. If a high degree of objectivity is lacking because the two scorers of the test use different administrative procedures and/or scoring standards, a person's score is dependent on the identity of the scorer. If one scorer is more lenient than the other, the people tested by that scorer have an advantage.

A high degree of objectivity is also needed when one person scores on several occasions. For example, a scorer may measure one-third of a group on each of 3 days, or the entire group at the beginning and end of a teaching or training unit. Certainly, in the first case, it is essential that the same administrative procedures and scoring standards be used each day. This is true in the second case as well, where any variation in a person's scores should represent changed performance, not changed procedures or standards.

Estimation

To determine the degree of objectivity in a physical performance test, two or more judges score each person as he or she is tested. Then we calculate an intraclass correlation coefficient on the basis of judges' scores of each person.

To calculate the objectivity coefficient, we think of the judges as trials, inserting their individual scores into the trial terms of our reliability formulas. If all judges are supposed to be using the same standards, we could consider a difference among judges to be measurement error and would calculate objectivity using the one-way ANOVA formula

$$R = \frac{MS_A - MS_W}{MS_A}$$

If all judges are not expected to use the same standards, we would calculate objectivity using either the alpha coefficient or the appropriate intraclass R formula (see Formula 3.2). Very seldom, if ever, would we discard the data of judges as was suggested by Baumgartner (1969a) with multiple trials.

Reliability of Criterion-Referenced Tests

Criterion-referenced standards and the setting of criterion-referenced standards were discussed in Chapter 1. Based on a criterion-referenced standard, a person is classified as either proficient or nonproficient, either pass or fail. For example, in a Red Cross certification course a person either meets the minimum requirements and is certified or does not meet the minimum requirements and is not certified. As mentioned in Chapter 1, the criterion-referenced standard for an adult fitness course could be the ability to jog continuously for 30 minutes. Based on this standard a person is classified as either proficient or nonproficient. A very nice characteristic of a criterion-referenced standard is that there is no predetermined quota as to how many people are classified as proficient.

Criterion-referenced reliability is defined differently than norm-referenced reliability. In the criterion-referenced case, reliability is defined as consistency of classification. Thus, if a criterion-referenced test is reliable, a person will be classified the same on each of two occasions. This could be trial-to-trial within a day or day-to-day.

To estimate the reliability of a criterion-referenced test, form a double classification table as presented in Table 3.6. In the A-box is the number of people who passed on both days and in the D-box is the number of people who failed on both days. Notice the B-box and C-box are the numbers of people who were not classified the same on both occasions. Obviously larger numbers in the A-box and D-box and smaller numbers in the B-box and C-box are desirable because reliability is consistency of classification on both occasions. All packages of statistical computer programs have a crosstabulation program which will provide the double classification table (see Table 3.6) needed to estimate the reliability of a criterion-referenced test.

The most popular way to estimate reliability from this double classification table is to calculate the **proportion of agreement coefficient** (P) where

Table 3.6 Table for Estimating Reliability of a Criterion-Referenced Test

		Day 2	
		Pass	*Fail*
Day 1	*Pass*	A	B
	Fail	C	D

Table 3.7 Data for Determining the Reliability of a Criterion-Referenced Test

		TRIAL 2	
		Pass	*Fail*
TRIAL 1	*Pass*	84	21
	Fail	5	40

$$P = \frac{A + D}{A + B + C + D}.$$

Problem 3.7. Determine the proportion of agreement (P) for a criterion-referenced test using the data in Table 3.7.

Solution. Where the sum of the A-box and D-box is 124 and the sum of the four boxes is 150, P = .83:

$$P = \frac{84 + 40}{84 + 21 + 5 + 40} = \frac{124}{150} = .827 = .83.$$

The proportion of agreement (P) does not allow for the fact that some same classifications on both occasions may have happened totally by chance. The **kappa coefficient** (k) corrects for chance agreements. The formula for kappa is

$$k = \frac{Pa - Pc}{1 - Pc},$$

where Pa = proportion of agreement

Pc = proportion of agreement expected by chance

$$= \frac{(A + B)(A + C) + (C + D)(B + D)}{(A + B + C + D)^2} \text{ in a } 2 \times 2 \text{ double classification table.}$$

Problem 3.8. Determine the kappa coefficient (k) for a criterion-referenced test using the data in Table 3.7.

Solution. To solve for k, we use a 3-step procedure:

Step 1
Calculate Pa

$$\text{Pa} = \frac{\text{A} + \text{D}}{\text{A} + \text{B} + \text{C} + \text{D}} = \frac{84 + 40}{84 + 21 + 5 + 40} = \frac{124}{150} = .827 = .83$$

Step 2
Calculate Pc

$$\text{Pc} = \frac{(\text{A} + \text{B})(\text{A} + \text{C}) + (\text{C} + \text{D})(\text{B} + \text{D})}{(\text{A} + \text{B} + \text{C} + \text{D})^2}$$

$$= \frac{(105)(89) + (45)(61)}{(84 + 21 + 5 + 40)^2} = \frac{9345 + 2745}{150^2} = \frac{12090}{22500} = .537 = .54$$

Step 3
Calculate kappa

$$\text{k} = \frac{\text{Pa} - \text{Pc}}{1 - \text{Pc}} = \frac{.83 - .54}{1 - .54} = \frac{.29}{.46} = .63$$

Notice that for the data in Table 3.7 there is a definite difference between the proportion of agreement (P) and coefficient kappa (k). A more extensive discussion of both coefficients is presented by Looney (Safrit & Wood 1989).

Since **P** can be affected by classifications by chance, values of **P** less than .50 are interpreted as unacceptable. Thus, values of **P** need to be closer to 1.0 than .50 to be quite acceptable. Values of *k* also should be closer to 1.0 than 0.00 to be quite acceptable.

Summary

There are three characteristics essential to a sound measuring instrument: reliability, objectivity, and validity. Reliability and objectivity were the focus of this chapter. A test has reliability when it consistently measures what it is supposed to measure. There are two types of reliability for mean-referenced tests: stability and internal consistency.

Objectivity, the second vital characteristic of a sound instrument, is the degree to which different judges agree in their scoring of each individual in a group. A fair test is one in which qualified judges rate individuals similarly and/or offer the same conditions of testing to all individuals equally.

Reliability of criterion-referenced tests was also discussed. The definition of reliability and techniques for estimating reliability differ from those for norm-referenced tests.

Formative Evaluation of Objectives

Objective 1 Define and differentiate between reliability and objectivity for norm-referenced tests and outline the methods used to estimate these values.

1. Two important characteristics of all measurements are that they be reliable and objective. Describe the basic nature of each of these characteristics.
2. In theory, reliability is the ratio of the true-story variance to the observed-score variance. Observed-score variance consists of both error-score variance and true-score variance. Describe these basic sources of variance and the combination that yields the highest estimate of reliability.

3. Two basic methods are used to estimate the reliability of a measuring instrument: stability, reliability and internal-consistency reliability. Briefly describe each method and the procedure it uses to estimate reliability.
4. The standard error of measurement is an estimate of the amount of measurement error in the test score. List the formula for the standard error of measurement and describe the characteristics of the statistic.
5. Objectivity, or rater reliability, is achieved when the scores of two or more different judges closely agree. The correlation between the scores is an objectivity coefficient. Summarize the procedures that yield high objectivity.

Objective 2 Identify those factors that influence reliability and objectivity for norm-referenced tests.

1. Acceptable reliability is essential for all measurements. Many factors affect the reliability of a measurement, and some of these are listed below. Identify the conditions under which the highest reliability can be expected for the following factors:
   a. People tested
   b. Test length
   c. Testing environment
   d. Test administrator
2. According to measurement theory, if a test is lengthened, its reliability is increased. If the reliability of a standing long-jump test composed of 2 jumps is found to be .83, how reliable might the test be if 6 jumps were scored?
3. A physical performance test administrator can improve test objectivity in several ways. Summarize them.

Objective 3 Identify those factors that influence reliability for criterion-referenced tests.

1. Acceptable reliability is essential for all measurements. Many factors affect the reliability of a measurement, and some of these are listed below. Identify how each of these factors affect the estimated reliability coefficient obtained:
   a. Reliability coefficient calculated
   b. Chance
   c. Composition of the group

Objective 4 Select a reliable criterion score based on measurement theory.

1. Many psychomotor tests involve several trials. What can a person do to make sure that the criterion score is as reliable as possible?

Additional Learning Activities

1. Many tests suggest 2 or 3 trials within a day. The number may have been arbitrarily selected so that the tests can be given quickly. Administer a multiple-trial test with more trials than recommended. By looking at the trial means, determine when the performance of the group reaches its maximum and becomes consistent.

2. There are many tests commonly used in testing programs (runs, jumps, maximum effort). Administer one of these tests and determine the reliability of it.
3. Construct a new physical performance test. Administer the test and decide how to calculate its reliability and objectivity.

Bibliography

Alsawalmeh, Y. M. and L. S. Feldt. 1992. Test of the hypothesis that the intraclass reliability coefficient is the same for two measurement procedures. *Applied Psychological Measurement 16(2):*195–205.

Baumgartner, T. A. 1968. The application of the Spearman-Brown prophecy formula when applied to physical performance tests. *Research Quarterly 39:*847–56.

———. 1969a. Estimating reliability when all test trials are administered on the same day. *Research Quarterly, 40:*222–25.

———. 1969b. Stability of physical performance test scores. *Research Quarterly, 40:*257–61.

———. 1974. Criterion score for multiple trial measures. *Research Quarterly 45:*193–98.

Baumgartner, T. A. and A. S. Jackson. 1970. Measurement schedules for tests of motor performance. *Research Quarterly 41:*10–17.

Berger, R. A. and A. B. Sweney. 1965. Variance and correlation coefficients. *Research Quarterly* 36: 368–70.

Crocker, L. and J. Algina. 1986. *Introduction to classical and modern test theory.* New York: Holt, Rinehart and Winston.

Darracott, S. H. 1995. Individual differences in variability and pattern of performance as a consideration in the selection of a representative score from multiple trial physical performance data. Ph.D. Dissertation, University of Georgia, Athens, GA.

Disch, J. 1975. Considerations for establishing a reliable and valid criterion measure for a multiple trial motor performance test. In T. A. Baumgartner, (Ed.) *Proceedings of the C.I.C. symposium on measurement and evaluation in physical education.* Indiana University.

Feldt, L. S. 1990. The sampling theory for the intraclass reliability coefficient. *Applied Measurement in Education 3:*361–67.

Feldt, L. S. and M. E. McKee. 1958. Estimating the reliability of skill tests. *Research Quarterly 29:* 279–93.

Ferguson, G. A. and Y. Takane. 1989. *Statistical analysis in psychology and education.* 6th ed. New York: McGraw-Hill.

Henry, F. M. 1967. Best versus average individual score. *Research Quarterly 38:* 317–20.

Hetherington, R. 1973. Within subject variation, measurement error, and selection of a criterion score. *Research Quarterly* 44: 113–17.

Johnson, R. and D. Meeter. 1977. Estimation of maximum physical performance. *Research Quarterly* 48: 74–84.

Nunnally, J. C. and I. H. Bernstein. 1994, 1978. *Psychometric theory.* 3rd ed. New York: McGraw-Hill.

Safrit, M. J. and T. M. Wood. 1989. *Measurement concepts in physical education and exercise science.* Champaign, IL: Human Kinetics.

Whitley, J. D. and L. E. Smith. 1963. Larger correlations obtained by using average rather than best strength scores. *Research Quarterly* 34: 248–49.

Zuidema, M. A. 1969. A brief on reliability theory: Theoretical concepts, influencing factors, and empirical estimates of the reliability of measurements especially applied to physical performance tests. Mimeographed. Bloomington, IN: University of Indiana.

CHAPTER 4

Validity

Contents

Key Words

concurrent validity
construct validity
criterion score
decision validity
domain-referenced validity
logical validity
predictive validity
validity

Objectives

This chapter discusses the methods used to estimate validity for norm-referenced tests, the relationship between reliability and validity, and the factors that influence validity.

Many physical performance tests can be given several times in the same day. When there are multiple trials of a test, the test administrator must decide how many to administer and what trial(s) to use as the criterion score.

Finally, the methods used to estimate validity for criterion-referenced tests are discussed. After reading Chapter 4 you should be able to:

1. Define validity, and outline the methods used to estimate it.
2. Describe the influence of test reliability on test validity.
3. Identify those factors that influence validity.
4. Select a valid criterion score based on measurement theory.

Introduction

There are certain characteristics essential to a measurement; without them, little faith can be put in the measurement and little use made of it. Two of these characteristics, reliability and objectivity, were discussed in Chapter 3. A third important characteristic of a measurement is **validity.** The American Psychological Association (1985) indicates that validity is the most important.

A test or measuring instrument is valid if it measures what it is supposed to measure. For example, pull-ups are a valid measure of arm and shoulder girdle strength and endurance because strength and endurance of the arm and shoulder girdle muscles are necessary to do a pull-up; pull-ups are not a valid measure of arm speed because the number of pull-ups one can execute is not influenced by arm speed. For a measure to be valid it must be reliable, but a reliable test may not be valid. Obviously for a test or instrument to measure what it is supposed to measure, it must first measure consistently. For example, the mile-run test is reliable and is a valid measure of aerobic capacity; however, it is not a valid measure of running speed. Thus, for a test, first objectivity, then reliability, and finally validity are determined.

Recognize that validity of a test or measuring instrument is in terms of the intended use of the data. The pull-up mentioned in the previous paragraph is an example. If the data from a test or measuring instrument are invalid in terms of their intended use, the data are useless. Any decisions made about subjects based on the invalid data probably will be in error.

Only an overview of validity is presented in this chapter. A more comprehensive coverage of validity is available in sources like Safrit and Wood (1989), Nunnally and Bernstein (1994), and Crocker and Algina (1986).

Validity for Norm-Referenced Tests

Validity may be discussed in terms of norm-referenced or criterion-referenced tests. A review of these two types of tests (see Chapter 1) might be helpful. Traditionally validity has been discussed in terms of norm-referenced tests, so first we will discuss validity from this standpoint.

When a test measures what it purports to measure, it is a valid test. To have validity, then, a test must be both relevant and reliable—relevant to the trait being tested and reliable as a measurement of that trait. Figure 4.1 shows the interrelationship between validity, relevance, and reliability.

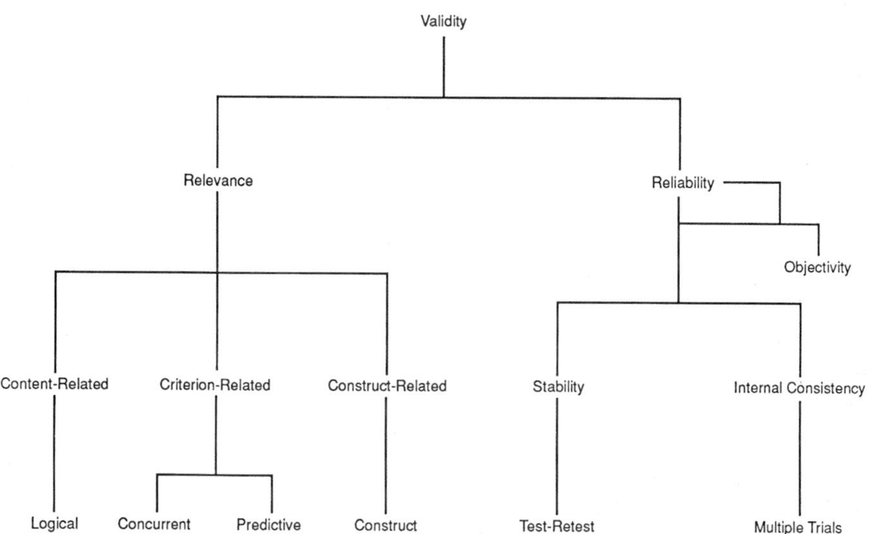

Figure 4.1
Relationship of relevance and reliability to validity.

In Figure 4.1 it can be seen that validity has two major components, relevance and reliability, with objectivity (sometimes called rater reliability) a component of reliability. As we demonstrated in Chapter 3, there are two general types of reliability: stability estimated by the test-retest method, and internal consistency estimated by the multiple-trials-within-a-day method. As we will find in this chapter, there are three basic types of relevance with definite estimation methods leading to what is called logical validity, concurrent validity, predictive validity, and construct validity.

Types and Estimation

A test's degree of validity should indicate to the user the degree to which that test is capable of achieving certain aims (APA 1985). These aims, and the four types of validity that parallel these aims, are logical, concurrent, predictive, and construct validity.

Validity can be estimated either logically or statistically. Recently the trend in education and psychology has been away from the statistical approach, while exercise science depends more on the statistical approach. This does not necessarily mean that physical education and exercise science should follow suit. Education and psychology work predominantly with paper-and-pencil tests, while physical education and exercise science work predominantly with physical performance tests. The test method for estimating validity must be chosen in terms of the situation, not the trend.

An overview of the commonly used validity approaches and basic issues involved in establishing validity are presented. A more comprehensive coverage of validity is presented in Safrit and Wood (1989).

Logical Validity. A measuring instrument has **logical validity** to the extent that it measures the capacities about which conclusions are to be drawn. Logical validity is established by examining the capacities to be measured and determining whether the instrument is, in fact, measuring them. For example, the 50-yard dash and 100-yard dash are obviously valid tests of running speed because they measure the speed a person can run. A written test has logical validity (often called content validity) when its questions are reliable, based on the material taught, and sample the stated educational objectives of the unit. For a complicated, multicomponent skill such as team sports, clearly defined objectives provide the only means of determining the degree of logical validity.

It is certainly true that logical validity has been both successfully used and badly misused at times. The American Psychological Association (1985) suggests that, ideally, several different types of validity evidence (content-related, criterion-related, construct-related) be provided with a test, but one solid piece of evidence is better than several weak pieces of evidence. If possible, logical validity should be used in conjunction with other validity evidence.

Logical validity seems to have been used quite successfully with physical fitness tests and fitness test batteries. For example, sit-ups are a valid measure of abdominal strength and endurance because abdominal strength and endurance are required to do a sit-up. A second example, the items in the health-related physical fitness tests were logically selected based on what the biggest health problems in the United States are today. However, Jackson and Baker (1986) did not find the sit-and-reach test a valid measure of hamstring and lower back flexibility.

Logical validity seems to have been less successfully used with complex sports skill tests. Claims of logical validity for certain sports skill tests and sports skill test batteries have been occasionally questioned. The wall volley in volleyball is one example. Another is a comprehensive skills test battery constructed of the basic components of softball, basketball, or volleyball ability.

Logical validity, then, rests solely on subjective decision making, which has led to criticism of this type of validity. However, this validity is not the only one to rest on subjective decision; concurrent validity is often determined by using the subjective decisions of an expert judge or judges.

Concurrent Validity. **Concurrent validity** is a measure of a test's correlation to some specified criterion. This is a traditional procedure for establishing the validity of a test. It involves calculating the Pearson product-moment correlation coefficient or some other similar type of correlation between scores on the test and those achieved on a criterion measure. The resulting correlation coefficient—the validity coefficient—is an estimate of the validity of the test. When the validity coefficient is close to 1, the instrument is measuring similarly to the criterion measure and is valid; when the coefficient is close to 0, the instrument has little validity.

A crucial step in establishing the concurrent validity of a test is the choice of a suitable criterion measure. Expert ratings and tournament standings are commonly used for sports skills tests. Predetermined criteria such as VO_2 Max and body composition are commonly used criteria in exercise science.

Expert Ratings. One criterion measure is the subjective rating of one or more experts. Because one judge may overlook certain factors in a person's performance or may have certain biases that affect his or her ratings, the sum of several qualified judges' ratings is a more reliable criterion measure. Obviously, high objectivity among judges is vital.

Subjective ratings usually take the form of either group ranks or a point scale. Using group ranks, the people in the group are ordered from best to worst on the basis of performance. Using a point scale, the people in the group are scored individually on a numbered point scale, as they would be in a gymnastics meet. Group ranks become unworkable as the size of the group increases. Further, a point scale system is preferable, since it does not require that one person be ranked best and another worst. One usually obtains higher validity with a scoring system than with group ranks, provided the scoring system is well defined so that high objectivity is possible.

Expert ratings have been commonly used to estimate the validity of skill tests. A skill test has certain advantages over tests that must be judged by experts. Providing the judges are qualified, they furnish a valid index of skill performance. However, in practice it is hard to find even one expert, let alone several, who have the time to subjectively evaluate a class of students. Then, too, skill tests are usually easier to administer and less time-consuming than are subjective evaluations.

Tournament Standings. A second method of estimating the validity of an instrument is to correlate the scores from the instrument (using the Pearson product-moment correlation coefficient or some other appropriate correlation coefficient) with the tournament standings of the students being measured. The method assumes that tournament standing is a good indicator of overall ability in the tested skill, usually an individual or dual activity like tennis or badminton. Many teachers are eager to find an instrument that is a valid indicator of skill. Such an instrument makes it unnecessary to conduct round-robin tournaments to evaluate the skill level of the students.

Predetermined Criteria. The final method uses a known valid, accepted instrument, which yields a quantitative score as the criterion measure. The validity of a test is then estimated by determining the Pearson product-moment correlation coefficient between scores from the test and scores from the accepted instrument. The method is usually used in developing a test that is quicker and/or easier to administer than is the accepted instrument.

Ideally the criterion measure is one that everyone recognizes as the "gold standard" (the ultimate or best standard). If there is not a gold standard, and often there isn't, one of the acceptable criterion measures available has to be selected. All people may not agree which criterion measure to use, and the criterion measure selected influences the value of the validity coefficient. This is why it is difficult to conduct a validation of a test, and the validity coefficient may not be high.

For example, the predetermined criteria method has been used to validate the use of skinfolds to measure body composition. A valid, accepted measure of percentage body fat can be obtained by weighing a subject under water; a person with a high percentage of body fat weighs less under water because fat tissue is less dense than muscle and bone. Skinfold measurements are easy to obtain and correlate highly (r is at least .80) with the percentage of fat determined by the more complicated underwater weighing method. Further, they can be used on people fearful of being weighed under water. By obtaining selected skinfold measurements, we can estimate the person's percent body fat using a regression equation. In fact, multiple correlation and regression equations (see Chapter 2) are often used to establish concurrent validity. In these situations, Y is the criterion score (dependent variable), and the several scores used to estimate Y are the X-scores (independent variables). In the earlier example, Y would be the underwater weight, and the X-scores would be the skinfold measures.

Predictive Validity. Predictive validity, like concurrent validity, is determined by using a criterion measure. **Predictive validity** represents the value of a measure for predicting performance on another measure (criterion). This may be either predicting a criterion with a regression equation (see Chapter 2) or predicting a criterion that will not be immediately available. An example of the first situation is predicting percent body fat by using skinfold measures. An example of the second situation follows.

Consider, for example, the question of predicting academic success in college. A student's performance on one measure such as a high school grade point average, determined before entering college, is correlated with a criterion measure of success in college, usually the student's college grade point average. The correlation between the two measures indicates the predictive validity of the measure obtained before entering college.

For example, to determine the validity of high school grade point average for predicting college grade point average, the following steps would be used:

1. for college graduates, obtain from their records the college and high school grade point average; and
2. calculate the correlation between the two measures—the predictive validity coefficient.

If the predictive validity coefficient is sufficiently high and the standard error of prediction (see Chapter 2) sufficiently low, high school grade point average is a valid predictor of college grade point average. In this case the college admissions officer would develop a simple prediction equation (see Chapter 2) to predict college grade point averages for students applying for admission to the college.

Again, multiple correlation and regression equations could be used to establish predictive validity. You could determine how valid a combination of high school grade point average (X_1) and a standardized test score (like ACT or SAT) (X_2) are in predicting college grade point average (Y). As a second example, you could determine how valid a combination of present fitness level (X_1), health history (X_2), and previous activity level (X_3) is in predicting how long a person would continue in an adult fitness program (Y).

Construct Validity. Logical validity, concurrent validity, and predictive validity are established methods for examining test validity; **construct validity** is a comparatively new and more complex validation procedure. It was first introduced in 1954 by the American Psychological Association and has been used extensively in psychological testing since then. Today the method is being used more and more in testing in physical education, exercise science, and related fields.

Construct validity is used with abstract rather than concrete tests (Nunnally & Bernstein 1994). An abstract test measures something that is not directly observable. Attitudes toward physical activity are abstract human traits that are neither readily apparent nor easily understood by an untrained professional. The number of basketball free throws made out of 100 tries, on the other hand, is a concrete test of skill.

Construct validity is based on the scientific method. First, there is a hunch that a test or tests can measure some abstract trait. Second, a theory is developed to explain both the construct and the tests that measure it. Finally, various statistical procedures are applied to confirm or reject the theory. An excellent example of this process is shown in the validation of distance run tests by Disch, Frankiewicz, and Jackson (1975).

Construct validity is determined by judging the extent to which theoretical and statistical information supports assumed constructs. The procedure gives physical education teachers and exercise specialists a way to evaluate their tests. For example, consider a swimming test administered to intermediate and varsity swimmers. Because the varsity swimmers are known to be better swimmers, we can demonstrate construct validity whenever the mean score of the varsity swimmers is superior to that of the intermediate swimmers. Probably a statistical test of the significance of the difference between the two means at alpha equal .01 should be conducted (see Additional Statistical Techniques in Chapter 2) to make sure the two swimming groups really do differ.

A second example of this approach is the comparison of the performance of a group before and after instruction or training. This involves testing a group for initial ability, applying some instructional or training technique for multiple weeks, and then retesting the group for final ability. Since the group should have improved in ability as a result of the instruction or training, we can demonstrate construct validity if the final test mean is significantly better than the initial test mean (see the repeated measures t-test in Chapter 2).

Scientists may not consider this a scientifically "true" example of the construct validation process; however, it does demonstrate that the process can be applied in physical education and exercise science. Whenever a superior performer does not achieve a score comparable to those of previously administered tests, the teacher must be alert to the possibility that the test lacks either reliability or validity.

Factor analysis is a statistical procedure that can be used to identify constructs and the valid tests of isolated constructs. In this context the isolated factor of the analysis is an abstract construct. Factor analysis has often been used to identify the basic components of fitness or a sport skill (see Chapters 7 and 12).

Factor analysis assumes that tests that correlate with each other measure the same basic factor, and that tests that do not correlate measure different factors. A factor, then, is simply a group of intercorrelations among tests that cluster together. The nature of factor analysis can best be demonstrated with data from an actual study (Disch et al. 1975) that was designed to identify the factors common to running tests. It was believed that endurance and speed were constructs common to these tests, and that the importance of endurance increased as distance increased. To prove this theory, ten tests were administered to college men. Among them were sprints of 50 and 100 yards, seven runs varying in distance from 1/2 mile to 2 miles, and the 12-minute run for distance.

Factor analysis determines the number of basic factors, or clusters, in a group of tests, and the degree to which each test measures each basic factor. Table 4.1 shows the final stage of the factor analysis of the intercorrelations of the ten tests, which indicates that two basic factors (I: endurance; II: speed) are represented in this group of tests. The values, called *factor loadings,* listed under columns I and II can be interpreted as the correlation between the test and the basic factors. The 50- and 100-yard dashes are highly correlated with Factor II, speed; the distance runs are highly correlated with Factor I, endurance, and there is a tendency for a higher correlation as the distance increases. The negative correlations for the 12-minute run are due to the method of scoring: a high score is a good score on the 12-minute run, whereas a low score is better on the other tests. As can be seen in Table 4.1, the 50- and 100-yard dashes measure running speed. As the runs become longer, speed becomes less important and endurance more important.

Factor analysis is useful, not only for isolating the abstract being measured, but also for selecting valid tests of the construct. By examining the factor loadings of all

Table 4.1 Rotated Factor Loadings of Running Tests

Distance of Run	Factors I	Factors II
1. 50 yards	.18	.86
2. 100 yards	.17	.88
3. ½ mile	.76	.46
4. ¾ mile	.74	.53
5. 1 mile	.84	.38
6. 1¼ miles	.88	.33
7. 1½ miles	.73	.27
8. 1¾ miles	.94	.23
9. 2 miles	.87	.10
10. 12-minute run	−.91	−.01

tests, a pattern that identifies the construct should become apparent. Once the pattern is apparent, the best test or combination of tests can be selected to measure the construct. In the running tests example, the 50-yard dash and the 12-minute run could be used to measure the speed and endurance factors. Because of the nature of endurance tests, only one test would be selected: however, a more reliable measurement of a construct would be obtained by selecting several measures of the same construct.

Factors Affecting Validity

Selected Criterion Measure. The magnitude of a validity coefficient can be affected by several factors, among them the criterion measure selected. We have suggested several possible criterion measures (expert ratings, tournament standards, predetermined criteria) to use in estimating the validity of a test. It is reasonable to expect that each measure, when correlated with the same set of test scores, would yield a different validity coefficient. This is particularly true for a test of multicomponent skills.

Characteristics of the Individuals Tested. Characteristics of the individuals tested also play a part in determining validity. A test that is valid for 6-year-old children may not be valid for 15-year-olds; a test valid for males may not be valid for females; a test that is valid for beginners may not be valid for advanced performers. We can assume that a test is valid only for individuals similar in age, gender, and experience to those on whom the test was validated. In fact, it is a good idea to determine validity for yourself the first time you use a test, even for like groups, because the individuals you are measuring cannot be exactly like those originally used to validate the test.

Reliability. As we have said, a test must be reliable to be valid. The validity coefficient is directly related to the reliability of both the test and the criterion measure. The maximum validity coefficient possible between two tests can be estimated by:

$$r_{x,y} = \sqrt{(r_{x,x})\,(r_{y,y})}$$

where $r_{x,y}$ is the correlation between Tests X and Y, $r_{x,x}$ is the reliability coefficient for Test X, and $r_{y,y}$ is the reliability coefficient for Test Y (Ferguson & Takane 1989). For example, if the reliability of both Tests X and Y is .90, the maximum validity coefficient possible would be .90:

$$r_{x,y} = \sqrt{(.90)\,(.90)} = \sqrt{.81} = .90.$$

If the reliability of Test X is .90 and that of Test Y is only .40, the maximum validity coefficient is much lower, only .60:

$$r_{x,y} = \sqrt{(.90\,(.40)} = \sqrt{.36} = .60.$$

Objectivity. Objectivity was defined as the agreement of two or more competent judges or scorers about the value of a measurement. Note that some people call objectivity "rater reliability." If two judges or raters scoring the same individual on the same test cannot agree on a score, the test lacks objectivity and the score of neither judge is valid. Thus, a lack of objectivity reduces the validity of a test much the way a lack of reliability does.

Lengthened Tests. We know that the validity of a test is influenced by its reliability. We know, from the Spearman-Brown formula, that reliability increases as the number of test trials or the length of the test increases. Further, the more measures you obtain for each individual, the more valid an indication you have of his or her true ability. For example, a dribbling test and a shooting test are better indications of basketball-playing ability than just a shooting test, but four measures of basketball-playing ability are preferable to just two. The same thing could be said for skinfold measures in terms of the number of measures taken at each site and the number of sites. Since reliability and validity are related, increasing the length of a test not only increases reliability, but also test validity.

Size of the Validity Coefficient. What is an acceptable validity coefficient when determining concurrent or predictive validity? The American Psychological Association (1985) does not address the issue. Safrit (1986) suggests that if a test is being used as a substitute for a more sophisticated test, coefficients of .90 and larger are desirable, but values exceeding .80 are acceptable. This recommendation seems to be for concurrent validity with a Pearson correlation coefficient. For predictive validity, she suggests that in some situations tests with values of .50 or .60 may be acceptable. When a predictive test is needed and/or high predictive validity is not required in a situation, a test with predictive validity of .50 or .60 is better than nothing and, thus, acceptable.

It seems the acceptable value of the validity coefficient must be dependent on many things, such as whether it is concurrent or predictive validity, whether it is a Pearson correlation coefficient or a multiple correlation coefficient, how good the criterion is, how high a validity coefficient is needed or expected based on what others have obtained in similar situations, how small a standard error (see Chapter 2) is needed, and how much variance must be explained. The fact that the square of the correlation coefficient indicates the amount of variance common to both tests and, thus, the degree to which the two tests measure the same thing should not be overlooked. A review of interpreting correlation coefficients in Chapter 2 might be worthwhile. It is interesting to note the variety of concurrent validity values for distance run tests reported in Chapter 12, since many of the values failed the .80 criteria suggested earlier.

Validity of a Criterion Score

Selecting the Criterion Score

A **criterion score** is the measure used to indicate a person's ability. Unless a test has perfect reliability it is a better indicator when it is developed from more than one trial. Multiple-trial tests are common in physical education with skinfold, flexibility, jumping, throwing, and short running—tests whose performance is not adversely affected by fatigue. Multiple trials with skinfold, flexibility and isometric strength tests are common in exercise science. In Chapter 3 the selection of the criterion score when multiple trials of the test are administered is discussed in detail. A review of this information might be helpful. Remember that reliability is essential for validity but reliability does not guarantee validity. Thus, the criterion score must be selected considering both reliability and validity. Since 1990 a few test developers have found that for multiple-trial sport skills test the best score and the mean score are similar in reliability; so they have used the best score because it is quicker and easier to obtain. This is a concern if the best score is much less valid than some other criterion score.

The Role of Preparation

Preparation is an important determinant of the validity of a criterion score. A criterion score is a better indicator of true ability if individuals are measured only after they fully understand how to take a test. For example, suppose your instructor announces one day that he or she is going to measure your aerobic capacity by having you run a mile for time. If you have never done any distance running, you would not know how to pace yourself, how to run in a relaxed manner, how to avoid being boxed in by other runners, or how to run near the inside curve. Your score that day will not be a true indication of your aerobic capacity. If you were tested again the next day, your score would improve, not because your aerobic capacity had improved, but because you would have learned how to approach the test. And on a third day you might do better still.

Research indicates that people often need a day of practice before physical performance testing to familiarize themselves with a test, even if they have had experience with it (Baumgartner 1969; Erickson et al. 1946). This practice allows a period of relearning and reinforcement necessary because skill retention is never perfect. Studies also show that a mean trial score for a multiple-trial test will be higher if several practice trials (called practice warm-up trials) are administered just before the test (Baumgartner & Jackson 1970).

Validity for Criterion-Referenced Tests

Generally, the definition of validity for a norm-referenced test applies to a criterion-referenced test. The techniques for validating a criterion-referenced test are different than the techniques for validating a norm-referenced test. Remember, a criterion-referenced test is used to classify people as either proficient or nonproficient, either pass or fail.

One technique for validating a criterion-referenced test is called **domain-referenced validity.** The term *domain* refers to the criterion ability or behavior the test is supposed to measure. Thus, the criterion-referenced test is logically validated by showing that the test measures the criterion ability or behavior. This technique is basically the same as the logical validity technique discussed earlier in the chapter.

Another technique for validating a criterion-referenced test is called **decision validity.** This deals with accuracy of the test in classifying people as either proficient or nonproficient. Essential to this technique is the ability to classify people as either proficient or nonproficient, independent of the test. This is often very difficult to do, but

Table 4.2 Table for Determining the Validity of a Criterion-Referenced Test

		Actual Classification	
		Proficient	Nonproficient
Test Classification	Proficient	A	B
	Nonproficient	C	D

Table 4.3 Data for Determining the Validity of a Criterion-Referenced Test

		Actual Classification	
		Proficient	Nonproficient
Test Classification	Proficient	40	5
	Nonproficient	10	20

for the moment let us say that we had the ability to do it. So, independent of the test and also as a result of the test, we have classified people as either proficient or non-proficient. These classifications enable us to generate a double-entry classification table as shown in Table 4.2. All packages of statistical computer programs have a cross-tabulation program that will provide a table like Table 4.2.

From this double-entry classification table, the classification of outcome probabilities (C) can be calculated as an estimate of test validity.

$$C = \frac{A + D}{A + B + C + D}$$

Problem 4.1. Calculate C for the data in Table 4.3.

Solution. Where the sum of the A-Box and D-Box is 60 and the sum of the four boxes is 75, C = .80.

$$C = \frac{40 + 20}{40 + 5 + 10 + 20} = \frac{60}{75} = .80$$

If C equals 0.50 it indicates that the classification by the test was no better than chance. For this reason a value of C closer to 1.0 than 0.50 is most desirable.

Another estimate of test validity that can be calculated from a double-entry classification table is phi (ϕ).

$$\phi = \frac{(AD) - (BC)}{\sqrt{(A + B)(C + D)(A + C)(B + D)}}$$

Problem 4.2. Calculate ϕ for the data in Table 4.3.

Solution.

$$\phi = \frac{(40)(20) - (5)(10)}{\sqrt{(40 + 5)(10 + 20)(40 + 10)(5 + 20)}}$$

$$= \frac{800 - 50}{\sqrt{1687500}} = \frac{750}{1299.04} = .58$$

Phi values can range from −1.0 to 1.0, so phi coefficients can be interpreted like any other correlation coefficient. However, because phi is the correlation between two dichotomous variables, high values of phi should not be expected (see Chapter 2 on correlation coefficients).

Let us come back to the problem of classifying people as either proficient or nonproficient, independent of the test (the actual classification in the double-entry table). In some instructional situations the proficient classification could be people who had received instruction, and the nonproficient classification could be people who had not received instruction. Also, in an instructional situation the nonproficient could be the classification of people before they received instruction, and the proficient could be the classification of the same people after receiving instruction. In some exercise science situations, an accepted standard or laboratory measure may exist that can be used for classifying people in terms of actual group membership.

Ideally the validity of criterion-referenced standards for youth health-related fitness tests would be determined by the test classification in the double-entry table being the subject's classification as a youth (fit or unfit) and the actual classification in the double-entry table being the subject's classification (fit or unfit) as an adult. Unfortunately, little if any data like this exists.

An excellent discussion of validity of criterion-referenced tests can be found in Safrit and Wood (1989). This source contains other information related to the validity issue, such as setting the cutoff score for proficiency on the criterion-referenced test. An excellent tutorial on standards setting is presented by Cureton and Warren (1990). Safrit and Looney (1992) should be read for their comments on the standards setting procedures of Cureton and Warren.

A discussion of many validity, reliability, and performance standards issues in reference to fitness tests for children is presented by Safrit (1990). She concludes that much has been done but much more remains to be done in terms of the goodness of fitness tests for children.

Summary

There are three characteristics essential to a sound measuring instrument: reliability, objectivity, and validity. Validity for norm-referenced tests may be of four different types: content, concurrent, predictive, and construct. Content validity is a logically determined measure—the test must measure the stated instructional objectives. Both concurrent and predictive validity gauge a person's test scores against an established criterion to determine that the test does correlate to the established criterion (concurrent validity) or does predict performance (predictive validity). Construct validity, which may be established through factor analysis, is the measure used with abstract rather than concrete tests.

Another major issue in testing is the selection of a criterion score, which can be either the person's best or mean score. A knowledge of how the criterion score is used is essential to intelligent selection and ultimately to the validity of the instrument itself.

Finally, when using criterion-referenced tests, the validity of these tests must be estimated. Two methods for estimating validity were presented.

Formative Evaluation of Objectives

Objective 1 Define validity, and outline the methods used to estimate it.

1. Important characteristics of all measurements are that they be reliable, objective, and valid. Describe the basic nature of validity.
2. Four types of norm-referenced test validity indicate the degree to which a test is capable of achieving certain aims: content validity, concurrent validity, predictive validity, and construct validity. Briefly describe these aims of testing and the four types of validity that parallel them.
3. Some authors refer to concurrent and predictive validity as criterion-related validity because validity is determined by the correlation between a test and criterion measure. Summarize the criterion measures especially suitable for physical education.
4. Briefly describe the two methods of estimating the validity of criterion-referenced tests.

Objective 2 Describe the influence of test reliability on test validity.

1. A basic principle of measurement theory is that a test must first be reliable to be valid. Why is this so?
2. What effect does objectivity have on test validity?

Objective 3 Identify those factors that influence validity.

1. It is well established that test reliability is an essential factor of test validity. What other factors affect test validity?

Objective 4 Select a valid criterion score based on measurement theory.

1. Many psychomotor tests involve several trials. What can a person do to make sure that the criterion score is as valid as possible?

Additional Learning Activities

1. There are many tests commonly used in testing programs (runs, lifts, throws). Administer one of these tests and determine the validity of it.
2. Construct a new sport-skill test. Administer the test and decide how to calculate its validity.

Bibliography

American Psychological Association. 1985. *Standards for educational and psychological tests.* Washington, DC: APA.

Baumgartner, T. A. 1969. Stability of physical performance test scores. *Research Quarterly 40:*257–61.

Baumgartner, T. A. and A. S. Jackson. 1970. Measurement schedules for tests of motor performance. *Research Quarterly 41:*10–17.

Crocker, L. and J. Algina. 1986. *Introduction to classical and modern test theory.* New York: Holt, Rinehart, and Winston.

Cureton, K. J. and G. L. Warren. 1990. Criterion-referenced standards for youth health-related fitness tests: A tutorial. *Research Quarterly for Exercise and Sport 61:*7–19.

Disch, J. R., R. J. Frankiewicz and A. Jackson. 1975. Construct validation of distance run tests. *Research Quarterly 46:*169–76.

Erickson, L. et al. 1946. The energy cost of horizontal and grade walking on the motor drive treadmill. *American Journal of Physiology 145:*391–401.

Ferguson, G. A. and Y. Takane. 1989. *Statistical analysis in psychology and education.* 6th ed. New York: McGraw-Hill.

Jackson, A. W. and A. B. Baker. 1986. The relationship of the sit-and-reach test to criterion measures of hamstring and back flexibility in young females. *Research Quarterly for Exercise and Sport 57:*183–86.

Nunnally, J. C. and I. R. Berstein. 1994. *Psychometric theory.* 3rd ed. New York: McGraw-Hill.

Safrit, M. J. *Introduction to measurement in physical education and exercise science.* St. Louis: Mosby Year Book, Inc.

———. 1990. The validity and reliability of fitness tests for children: A review. *Pediatric Exercise Science 2:*9–28.

Safrit, M. J. and M. L. Looney. 1992. Should the punishment fit the crime? A measurement dilemma. *Research Quarterly for Exercise and Sport 63:*124–27.

Safrit, M. J. and T. M. Wood. 1989. *Measurement concepts in physical education and exercise science.* Champaign, IL: Human Kinetics.

CHAPTER 5

Evaluating Achievement

Contents

Key Words

authentic assessment
final grades
natural breaks
program evaluation
rank order
teacher's standards

Objectives

In this chapter we discuss the differences between formative and summative evaluation and the standards used with each method. The attributes, issues, and techniques of evaluation show that the process is a complicated and often emotional one. There is no universal agreement among physical education teachers and exercise scientists as to which attributes are important or which evaluation system works best. Each issue, each technique, has its supporters; and each has its advantages and disadvantages as well. Recently, authentic assessment has been a popular topic in education, so we include a discussion of what it is and how it is conducted. Finally, we arrive at program evaluation—which should also be part of every teacher's and exercise scientist's measurement program.

After reading Chapter 5 you should be able to:

1. Define and compare the terms evaluation and measurement.
2. Select the components for inclusion in an evaluation program and determine evaluation standards using several methods.
3. Identify ways to make an evaluation system as quick and efficient as possible.
4. Identify why and how to do authentic assessment.
5. Outline the procedures used for evaluating programs.

Introduction

Much of what is presented in this chapter is from the standpoint of grading, which is certainly the responsibility of a teacher, but seldom the responsibility of an exercise scientist, such as an exercise specialist, physical therapist, athletic trainer, or program instructor. However, grading is actually just evaluating the participants in a program that happens to be an educational one. Exercise scientists must evaluate the participants in their programs. Thus, think of grading as individual evaluations, and it applies to teachers and exercise scientists. Adults, just like children, want to know how they compare to others or to a standard, even though grades are not assigned. Much of the process and philosophical issues discussed in terms of grading have implications for exercise scientists in their evaluation program.

A teacher's primary function is to promote desirable changes in students. The same thing can be said of any exercise scientist in regard to the program participants. The type of change deemed important by the teacher and exercise scientist depends on two factors: the stated instructional or program objectives and the procedures used to evaluate their achievement. If the instructional or program process is to be meaningful, it is essential that (1) the stated objectives be relevant, (2) the instruction or program be designed to achieve the objectives efficiently, and (3) the evaluation procedures reliably and validly assess student or participant achievement.

We administer tests primarily to facilitate the achievement of instructional and program objectives. As noted in Chapter 1, in education tests can be used for placement, diagnosis, evaluation of learning, prediction, program evaluation, and motivation. Similar uses exist in exercise science programs. Every teacher must formally or informally evaluate every student, and each exercise scientist must evaluate each participant in the program. The evaluation of student or program participant achievement is tantamount to the evaluation of the instructional or program process, and so it is a vital part of that process. A student's or program participant's failure to achieve important objectives can indicate that the program itself has failed and needs revision.

Student evaluation is not a popular issue with some teachers and prospective teachers, primarily because they think of it as synonymous with grading. But, evaluation is more than grading. In fact, it need not result in the assignment of grades. This does not mean that grading itself is not necessary. Grading continues to be an integral part of the educational system and thus one of the teacher's responsibilities. A teacher who passes all students without regard to their level of achievement is ignoring a professional responsibility. Grading is too often a system of rewards and punishments, reflecting the teacher's frustrations and biases rather than a reliable, valid measure of student achievement. Most, if not all, of what has been expressed in this paragraph applies to evaluation situations in exercise science. The exercise specialist, therapist, or program instructor having to evaluate participants in a program and telling them they are not adequate makes neither the exercise scientist nor the participants feel good about evaluation.

Evaluation

Evaluation often follows measurement, taking the form of a judgment about the quality of a performance. Suppose, for example, that each participant in a class or exercise program ran a mile, and their scores were recorded by the teacher or exercise specialist. When the person classified these measurements "excellent," "good," or "A", "B", "C," he or she was making an evaluation.

Evaluation can be subjective: The judge uses no set standards for each classification and/or evaluates during the performance without recording any measurements. The objectivity of evaluation increases when it is based on defined standards. Three common standards are (1) required levels of performance based on the exercise scientist's or teacher's experience and/or convictions; (2) the ranked performances of the rest of the group; and (3) existing standards, called norms.

Types of Evaluation

Formative evaluation, as noted in Chapter 1, occurs during instruction or the exercise science program to inform the participant and the teacher or exercise scientist of the participant's status. This information allows the teacher or exercise scientist to judge the effectiveness of the unit in progress and to make future plans. Participants are motivated by knowing the extent to which they are meeting the stated objectives. Thus, formative evaluation is both continuous throughout the teaching unit or program and related to the program's objectives.

Summative evaluation is the final measurement of participant performance at the end of the teaching unit or program. It is often used to assign grades in teaching. This type of evaluation is likely to involve comparisons among students rather than comparisons with a single level of achievement. In an exercise science program the summative evaluation is more likely to be a comparison of the participant's score to a performance goal set earlier or to an ideal standard, but the evaluation may result in the participant being allowed to discontinue the program or being required to continue the program.

Standards for Evaluation

Criterion-Referenced Standards. Criterion-referenced standards represent the level of achievement that nearly all participants should be able to reach given proper instruction and ample practice. These standards are valuable to the participant because they specify the expected level of performance and valuable to the teacher or exercise scientist because they clearly define participant status in relation to the standard.

Criterion-referenced standards must be used with explicit objectives—objectives that ordinarily must be accomplished before broader objectives can be achieved. Thus, criterion-referenced standards can be used in formative evaluation to diagnose weaknesses and to determine when participants are ready to progress.

For example, the American Red Cross has developed a hierarchy of swimming skills that reflect criterion-referenced standards:

Beginner Skills

1. Breath holding—10 seconds
2. Rhythmic breathing—10 seconds
3. Prone glide
4. Back glide and recovery
5. Prone glide with kick
6. Back glide with kick
7. Beginner stroke or crawl stroke—15 yards
8. Combined stroke on back—15 yards

Swimming Skills

1. Sidestroke
2. Back crawl
3. Breaststroke
4. Crawl stroke
5. Surface dives—pike, tuck
6. Feet-first surface dive

Obviously these standards must be met if the participant is to achieve a wanted level of competence in swimming. The inability to meet a specified standard indicates that additional instruction or learning activities are needed. On both the beginner and swimming skills' levels, summative evaluation would focus on combinations of these skills: at the swimming skills' level, for example, the distance a person can swim in 10 minutes using the breaststroke, sidestroke, crawl, and backstroke.

For an instructional unit on physical fitness, the criterion-referenced standards for 9th-grade boys might be a run of 1½ miles in 12 minutes, 35 bent-knee sit-ups in 2 minutes, and 3 pull-ups. Thus, criterion-referenced standards tend to be pass-fail. In this case, performance on all 3 tests (the sum of the T-scores) could be used to summatively evaluate the broader objective of total fitness.

In some programs there is a move to mastery of program content as the desired outcome. Thus, the evaluation of a participant is in terms of the number of desired outcomes achieved and not in comparison to his/her peers. This is basically a competency based criterion-referenced standard situation. In the earlier swimming skills example, each student could be evaluated on how many of the standards were achieved. Passing the course is dependent on reaching a certain outcome if the outcomes are rank ordered or mastering a certain number of outcomes if there is no ordering of outcomes.

Many different procedures are used to develop criterion-referenced standards. One method involves the following steps:

Step 1
Identify the specific behaviors that must be achieved to accomplish a broad objective.

Step 2
Develop clearly defined objectives that correspond to the specific behaviors.

Step 3
Develop standards that give evidence of successful achievement of the objective. These standards may be based on logic, expert opinion, research literature, and/or an analysis of test scores.

Step 4

Try the system and evaluate the standards. Determine whether the standards must be altered and do so if necessary.

The standards set in Step 3 often are arbitrary. If the mastery standard is set too high, it is likely to be obtained by only a few participants; and there will be little positive reinforcement for mastery for very many participants. On the other hand, if the mastery level is too low, then a large number of participants may have the illusion that they have mastered the objective when in fact they have fallen short.

Because physical education teachers and exercise scientists use a variety of testing instruments that apply different units of measurement, the importance to them of evaluating and readjusting criterion-referenced standards is evident.

Norm-Referenced Standards. Norm-referenced standards, those that compare the performances of peers, are useful for determining the degree to which participants have achieved a broad objective. In developing norm-referenced standards, levels of performance that discriminate among ability groups are specified; that is, the standards are set so that some participants are classified "high ability" and some "low ability."

The traditional grading system (A,B,C,D,F) is based on norm-referenced standards. Grading and the development of norm-referenced standards are so important that much of this chapter is devoted to these two topics.

Grading

As indicated in the introduction to this chapter, grading is the responsibility of teachers and seldom exercise scientists. However, much of the grading process and many of the issues discussed in terms of grading have implications for evaluation in all types of programs. The improvement of grading practices has been an educational issue for over fifty years. The grading process is twofold: (1) the selection of the measurements—either subjective or objective—that form the basis of the grade and (2) the actual calculation. Both steps can be undertaken in many different ways. As described in the systematic model of evaluation (see Chapter 1), the instructional process begins with the instructional objectives and culminates with evaluation. The instructional objectives, then, are the basis on which the factors used to grade students are selected, and the test must be suited to their nature and content. Clearly, using only a written test to grade students in a unit on physical fitness would be illogical and unfair.

Not only must grades be based on important instructional objectives, but the testing instruments must be both reliable and valid. If a test has no reliability, the scores by definition are due entirely to measurement error. Using such a test to calculate a student's grade is much like flipping a coin. Validity is a function of the instructional objectives: A test can be very reliable but unrelated to the objectives of the unit. Thus, when selecting testing instruments for grading, the teacher must ask: (1) What are the instructional objectives? (2) Were the students taught in accordance with these objectives? (3) Does the test reliably and validly measure the achievement of these objectives?

Issues

The relative merits of various attributes for grading have received much attention in professional books and journals. Any suggested attributes should be judged by three criteria:

1. Is it a major objective of the physical education program?
2. Do all students have identical opportunities to demonstrate their ability relative to the attribute?
3. Can the attribute be reliably and validly measured?

A teacher's philosophy on certain issues directly influences the grading system. There is no one correct approach to most of these issues, but you should consider them before developing a grading system. Remember that teachers communicate their values in their grading procedures.

If grades are assigned, it is only fair to explain to the students at the start of the course how grades will be determined. Thus, the teacher should plan the grading system before the course begins. Planning usually works, not only to lessen student complaints about assigned grades, but also to make it easier and faster to assign grades.

Grades should be based on a sufficient amount of evidence to be valid and reliable. One trial where multiple trials of a test were possible or one comprehensive exam at the end of the course is not likely to be sufficient evidence. The worst objective testing situation we can envision for a tests and measurement course is one test at the end of the course composed of one true-false question. If the student answers the question correctly, the student receives a high grade; if not, the student receives a low grade.

The distribution of grades in summative evaluation is a controversial issue. Should physical educators, like teachers of classroom subjects, use A-B-C-D-F grades? Note that a teacher grading A through F is equivalent to an exercise specialist evaluating participants in a fitness program as excellent, above average, average, below average, or poor. Low grades tend to discourage students from continuing with a given subject once basic requirements are fulfilled. In science programs, for example, the grades D and F are assigned to discourage low-ability students from continuing to take science courses. This means that by the senior year in high school only a select group of students is still in the program. (Of course, because only the better students continue to take courses, a smaller percentage of low grades should be given in advanced courses. For example, more As and Bs should be assigned in a senior-level course than in a junior-level course.) Physical education programs are not developed along these discriminatory lines. In an effort to encourage all students—despite their ability—to continue in the program, many physical educators assign only grades A, B, and C. The equivalence to an A-B-C grading system for an exercise specialist might be classifying participants in a fitness program as above average, average, or below average but better still would be classifying participants as excellent, above average, or average.

Another consideration that relates to the distribution of grades is whether the general quality of the class, or differences among classes, should affect the assignment or distribution of grades. With ability-grouped classes, it seems unfair to assign grades A through F in each class because every student in a high-ability class would probably have received a C or better if ability grouping were not used. On the other hand, grading A through C in a high-ability class, B through D in a middle-ability class, and C through F in a low-ability class is unfair because it makes no allowance for the misclassification of students. A high-ability student could loaf and still receive a C, while a middle-ability overachiever could never earn an A.

A philosophy endorsed by many experienced teachers and most measurement specialists is that the grade a student receives should not depend on (1) the semester or year in which the class is taken; (2) the instructor (if several instructors teach the course); or (3) the other students in the course. Thus, standards should not change from semester to semester or year to year unless the course itself has been changed or upgraded. For example, if 65 sit-ups represent an A for 7th graders this semester, the same should apply next semester. Likewise, if 65 sit-ups represents an A from one instructor, the same should be true for all instructors. Inherent in this philosophy is the principle that all students should be evaluated by the same standards. Two examples may clarify this point:

1. An instructor teaches five ungrouped 11th-grade classes, which are combined for grading purposes. The top 20% of the combined group receive As, the next 30% receive Bs, and the remaining students receive Cs. If grades had been allotted in the same percentages but assigned by classes, a student's grade would depend on those of the other students in the class. Thus, it would be possible for two students with identical scores to receive different grades if one were in a class with many good performers and the other in a class with many poor performers.
2. An instructor teaches three ability-grouped classes of 8th graders and two ability-grouped classes of 9th graders. The 8th-grade classes are composed of high, middle, and low achievers; the 9th-grade class, of low and middle achievers. Because of the age difference, higher grading standards are applied to the 9th graders than to the eighth graders, but the grading standards for each grade are applied consistently to all classes in that grade.

The teacher must decide whether a grade represents only achievement or student effort as well. The teacher must also decide what type of student achievement (fitness, skill, knowledge) should be considered and how each should be weighted in the grade.

Usually school policy governs certain issues, among them the type of grade assigned (A-B-C-D-F or pass-fail), although the teacher may have a choice. Letter grades are by far the most prevalent, but pass-fail grading is gaining popularity. This system reduces the competitive pressure of letter grading and encourages students to explore new subject areas. However, the system also provides less information about student ability.

If pass-fail grades are assigned, the teacher must decide whether, in reality, anyone will fail. It seems that in many classes, if students attend class regularly, they will not receive a failing grade. Also, the teacher must decide how much information is needed on each student to assign a grade of pass or fail. Possibly less information on each student is needed with a pass-fail system than with a letter-grade system. Finally, the teacher must decide on the standard for a passing grade. Is passing equivalent to a C or a D in a letter grade system?

Methods

Of the four methods that will be discussed, no single method of assigning grades is best for all situations or all teachers. Ordinarily, each method yields a unique distribution of grades. For example, a student who is on the borderline between an A and a B may receive an A with one grading method and a B with another. Thus, it is vital that the teacher understand the advantages and disadvantages of each grading method in order to select the one best suited to the situation. Also, these methods are not restricted to assigning grades. The exercise specialist can use these methods for classifying participants in a program. As suggested earlier in this chapter, a teacher grading A, B, C, D, F is equivalent to an exercise scientist classifying participants in a program as excellent, above average, average, below average, poor.

There are two ways to use several of the following methods. One way is to use the methods on the scores of a group to evaluate individual members of the group. The second way is to use the methods on the scores of a group to develop performance standards (norms) to be used on people who will be participating in the program in the future. Teachers have many participants (students) in a group (class) and often use these methods in both ways. Exercise scientists may have many participants in a group (e.g., a fitness program), but a physical therapist or athletic trainer may be working with one person at a time; so the group is considered to be all people who have received therapy over several months or years. Thus, the physical therapist or athletic trainer will be establishing standards for future participants.

Further, recognize that these methods can be used for assigning two or more grades or classifications. Usually two grades or classifications are a criterion-referenced evaluation, but using data analysis to set criterion-referenced standards is an acceptable technique. Normally these methods are used to develop norm-referenced standards with three or more grades or classifications.

Natural Breaks. When scores are ordered by rank, gaps usually occur in their distribution. The teacher may make each such break a cutoff point between letter grades as shown in Table 5.1. This is a norm-referenced standard.

The other methods to be discussed require that the teacher decide what letter grades are possible (e.g., A to F, or A to C) and usually what percentage of the students should receive each letter grade. This is not required with the **natural breaks** method. In theory, if there were no breaks in the distribution of scores, all students would receive the same grade. For the teacher who does not believe in specifying the possible grades and percentages for these grades, this is a useful method. Thus, the method has some characteristics of a criterion-referenced standard.

Although used by some teachers, this method is the poorest of the four listed here if it is used on the scores of the group to be graded. It provides no semester-to-semester consistency and makes each student's grade dependent on the performance of other students in the class. If, in another year, the breaks in the distribution occur in different places, the cutoff points between letter grades change, as is evident between semesters in Table 5.1. Natural breaks may not be as poor a method if used for developing norms (discussed later in this section) or developing pass-fail standards. For example, in Table 5.1 the passing standard might be a score greater than 65 for the first-semester data and a score greater than 73 for the second-semester data.

Teacher's Standard. Some teachers base grades on their own perceptions of what is fair and appropriate, without analyzing any data. For example, a teacher's standard for a 100-point knowledge test might be A, 93–100; B, 88–92; C, 79–87; D, 70–78; F, 0–69. If the teacher uses the same standard year after year, the grades will be consistent. Furthermore, a student's grade does not depend on the performance of other students in the class: Each student who scores 93 points or more receives an A. This is a fine method if the teacher's standards are realistic in terms of the students' abilities and if measurements are quite reliable and valid. First-year teachers, and teachers working with students younger than they are familiar with, tend to misuse this method by setting their standards too high.

Table 5.1 Two Sets of Grades Assigned by Natural Breaks

First Semester			Second Semester		
x	f		x	f	
98	1		92	1	
95	1	A	91	2	
93	2		90	1	
92	3		89	2	A
			88	2	
88	4		87	3	
87	5				
85	7	B	82	6	
84	7		80	8	
83	6		79	7	B
			78	11	
77	8				
76	14	C	73	12	
75	10		72	11	
72	5		71	14	C
			70	6	
65	2	D	68	1	
60	1				

The **teacher's standards** are norm-referenced, but the procedure used to develop them is very similar to that of criterion-referenced standards, in that standards are set by the teacher with no thought as to what percentage of the class receives a given grade. In theory, the entire class could receive As or Fs.

If the teacher's standards were used in a pass-fail or competent-incompetent system, the standards would be criterion-referenced. Again, in theory the entire class could be judged competent. Many teachers have difficulty selecting the standard for competence; there are no guidelines. The teacher must choose a standard that he or she believes is fair. This standard often becomes one of minimum competence. For example, the teacher might decide that hitting one out of five shots from the free-throw line in basketball or doing one sit-up is minimum competence.

One way minimum competence might be determined is by deciding what grade in a letter system corresponds to competent or pass. The letter grade D is defined as a low pass or minimum competence by some educators; it is defined as a "charity grade" by others who would assign a competent grade with a C or higher. In most colleges, the instructor does not know which students are taking a graded class on a pass-fail basis. He or she assigns a letter grade to each student, which is converted to a pass in the records office for letter grades of D or better.

Rank Order. **Rank order** is a straightforward, norm-referenced method of grading. The teacher decides what letter grades will be assigned and what percentage of the class should receive each letter grade; the scores are then ordered, and grades are assigned.

For example, assume there are 50 students in a class, and the teacher decides to assign grades as follows: As to 20% of the class, or 10 students [(.20)(50)]; Bs to 30% of the class, or 15 students [(.30)(50)]; Cs to 40% of the class, or 20 students [(.40)(50)]; and Ds to 10% of the class, or 5 students [(.10)(50)]. Now look at the scores and

Table 5.2 Rank-Ordered Scores

X	f		X	f		X	f		X	f	
78	1		64	4		60	8		51	2	
70	2	A	62	5	B	59	6	C	48	1	D
66	4		61	5		58	5		41	1	
65	4					57	2				

frequency distribution in Table 5.2. In the table, the first 10 scores were supposed to be As, but a choice had to be made between 7 or 11 As. It was decided to use 11 because that number was closer to the wanted number of As. To make up for the extra A, only 14 Bs were given. Then a choice had to be made between 19 or 21 Cs. The reasons for giving 21 rather than 19 Cs are twofold: (1) it is preferable to give the higher grade in borderline cases, and (2) a distinct natural break occurs below score 57.

Among the advantages of the rank-order method are that it is quick and easy to use and that it makes a student's grade dependent on his or her rank-order position rather than the instructor's feelings about the student. The system also allows grades to be distributed as wanted.

A disadvantage of the method if it is applied to the scores of the group being evaluated is that a student's grade depends on the performance of other students in the class. A student with average ability will receive a higher grade in a class with low-ability students than in a class with high-ability students. Another disadvantage is that no allowance is made for the quality of the class: A certain proportion of students must get high grades and a certain proportion must get low grades. For large, heterogeneous classes, in which all levels of ability are represented, this is probably not a bad method; however, it is not recommended for small or ability-grouped classes unless the teacher adjusts the percentages in light of the quality of each class. Teachers who use the rank-order method obtain grade standards that vary from semester to semester and year to year, depending on the quality of their class.

Norms. Norms are performance standards based on the analysis of data, not on a subjective standard chosen by a teacher. If norm-referenced standards are being used, norms are the best type of standard. Norms are developed by gathering scores for a large number of individuals of similar age, gender, ability, and other characteristics to the subjects with whom the norms will be used. These data are statistically analyzed, and performance standards are then constructed on the basis of the analysis. Norms have many advantages over other types of standards. First, they are unaffected by the performance of the group or the class being evaluated. For example, if it is considered excellent to run the mile in 10 minutes, all the students in the class can excel if they can run the mile within that time. Another advantage is that new performance standards need not be developed each year; once norms are developed, they usually can be used for 2 to 5 years. Also, because the same standards are used to evaluate several different groups or classes of students, the grades have a high degree of consistency—a given grade indicates the same degree of ability for each group.

There are many sources for norms. (Examples are given in Chapters 7 through 11.) Statewide tests often provide norms for that state; local norms for an entire school system are not uncommon; and teachers can develop norms using the scores of former students. Although norms should be developed using the scores of students similar to those on whom the norms will be used, this is unlikely to be true of national and state norms. Teacher-developed norms are probably fairest to the students.

Norms are often used by exercise specialists to interpret the performance of adults in their fitness and rehabilitation programs. The performance score of a participant must be evaluated by comparing it to the performance of a reference group before the score has any meaning. The norms based on this reference group reflect the expected performance for each participant. This is not to suggest that the same norms are used on all participants. Norms are usually gender and age specific and often health-status specific.

The first step in developing norms is the administration of the same test each year under the same conditions as much as is possible for 2 to 5 years, until several hundred scores have been collected. These scores are then analyzed and used to develop norms that can be employed for the next 2 to 5 years. At the end of this time, several hundred more test scores have been collected, and the test is renormed. The advantages of this procedure are numerous. Because the norms are based on recent student performances, they are applicable to students currently in the class. When combined, scores collected in different years tend to cancel out any differences among years in terms of the quality of the students, and thus represent typical performance. (Norms developed on the scores of students from a single year are not representative if the students are not typical.) Because students and conditions change, norms should be revised every few years. And if major changes are made in the curriculum, norms may need to be revised.

Depending on the needs of the teacher, percentile-rank norms, T-score norms (see Chapter 2), or letter-grade norms may be constructed. Probably because they are easier to explain to students and parents, percentile-rank norms are used more often than T-score norms. In deciding on a type of norm, determine how the norms will be used and then choose the type that best meets your needs. Percentile-rank norms are easily understood and indicate how a student's performance ranks relative to his or her peers. However, they should not be added together to obtain a composite score based on several measures. If you will eventually need a composite score, choose T-score norms. If students understand T-scores, they can determine their approximate class ranks for a single test. Examples of percentile-rank and T-score norms are shown in Tables 5.3 and 5.4.

For grading purposes, letter-grade norms must be developed. The teacher's task is to determine the test scores that constitute each letter grade to be assigned. For example, the letter-grade norms for a one-minute sit-up test for boys might be A, 59–70; B, 47–58; C, 35–46; D, 20–34; F, 0–19 using the percentile-rank norms in Table 5.3. These letter-grade norms are developed based on the decision to, over multiple years, assign basically 10% As, 30% Bs, 45% Cs, 15% Ds, and 0% Fs to students evaluated with these standards. The A-grade standard is obtained by observing in Table 5.3 that a score of 59 for boys corresponds to the 90th percentile, so 10% of the scores are 59 or larger. The minimum score to obtain a grade of B is determined by going to the 60th percentile in Table 5.3. This method of developing letter-grade norms is similar to the rank-order method discussed earlier. However, these letter-grade norms could have been developed using any of the other methods previously discussed. No matter what method is used, this grading standard is used each time the one-minute sit-up test is administered. Ideally these letter-grade norms are developed on the basis of an analysis of the one-minute sit-up scores of students who have taken the test in the past.

Table 5.3 Sample Percentile-Rank Norms for a One-Minute Sit-Up Test

Percentile	Boys	Girls	Percentile	Boys	Girls
100th	70	60	45th	44	33
95th	61	54	40th	43	32
90th	59	52	35th	41	31
85th	56	49	30th	40	30
80th	54	45	25th	38	29
75th	51	42	20th	36	28
70th	50	40	15th	35	27
65th	48	39	10th	30	23
60th	47	36	5th	28	20
55th	46	35	0	20	15
50th	45	33			

Table 5.4 Sample T-Score Norms for a Distance Run

T-Score	6-Lap Run	T-Score	6-Lap Run
80	287	48	458
78	297	46	468
76	308	44	479
74	319	42	490
72	330	40	500
70	340	38	511
68	351	36	522
66	362	34	532
64	372	32	543
62	383	30	554
60	394	28	564
58	404	26	575
56	415	24	586
54	426	22	597
52	436	20	607
50	447		

A second example of the use of norms involves a physical fitness test with seven items. For each of the seven items, local T-score norms have been developed. When the test is administered, T-scores do not have to be calculated but can be assigned by using the norms. The sum of the T-scores for the seven items in the test is the student's fitness score. Letter-grade norms corresponding to these fitness scores have been developed:

A, 420→; B, 385–419; C, 315–384; D, 245–314; F, ←244.

Notice that any of the grading methods discussed here can be used to develop letter-grade norms. The teacher's standard is sometimes used, but the rank-order method is more common.

Final Grades

At the end of a grading period a final grade must be assigned on the basis of all the information available on each student. For the exercise scientist, a classification based on all the information available is equivalent to a final grade. There are many approaches to the assignment of this grade, some very simple, others more complex. The information available, the manner in which it is recorded, and the commitment of the teacher to fairly assign grades influence both the approach chosen and the time required for the procedure.

It is definitely to the teacher's advantage to adopt a simple, quick method of assigning final grades. Some teachers spend countless hours determining grades at the end of each grading period. To be fair to the students and to have a workable system, the teacher should choose a grading system before the course begins. Preplanning allows the teacher to announce the system at the beginning of the course, telling the students on what they will be measured and what standards they must meet. Preplanning is also to the teacher's advantage, allowing many time-consuming problems to be eliminated in advance.

The three common methods of assigning **final grades** are (1) the sum of the letter grades, (2) a point system, and (3) the sum of the T-scores.

Sum of the Letter Grades. This method is used when test scores reflect different units of measure that cannot be summed. The scores on each test are translated into letter grades using one or more of the methods just discussed, and the letter grades, in turn, are translated into points. The sum of these points is used to assign each student a final grade.

Many teachers believe this method is quicker than translating test scores into T-scores, but it is probably at best only slightly faster than calculating T-scores by hand as described in Chapter 2.

If this method is selected, a plus-and-minus system should be used when assigning letter grades to each measure. If an A-B-C-D-F system is used for a given test, only 5 scores are possible (A is 4, B is 3, C is 2, D is 1, F is 0); a plus-and-minus system allows 15 possible scores (A+ is 14, A is 13, A− is 12, and so on, including F+ and F− values). (The final grades do not have to include pluses and minuses, which are seldom recorded on transcripts.)

To compute the final grade using the plus-and-minus system, we convert the student's letter grade on each test to points, add the points, and divide the sum by the total number of tests. This point value, the mean of the student's scores, is then converted back to a letter grade. For example, in Table 5.5, the student's scores on five tests are changed from letter grades to points and then added. The total, 45, is then divided by the number of tests. The student's mean grade in points, 9, is then converted back into a letter grade, B−.

This process has several drawbacks. In the first place, it is a waste of time to calculate the mean. By multiplying each of the plus-and-minus values by the number of grades per student, we can express the final grade standards in terms of total points—A+ is 70 [(5)(14)], A is 65 [(5)(13)], and so on. In the second place, no allowance is made in the final grade for the regression effect—the tendency for individuals who score exceptionally high or low on one measure to score closer to the mean performance of the group on a second. Thus, a student who earns an A or an F on one test is likelier on the next to earn a grade closer to C than to repeat the first performance. The regression effect phenomenon always exists and must be allowed for in assigning

Table 5.5 Sample Grades and Points for Calculating a Final Grade

Test	Grade	Points
Sit-ups	B+	11
Pull-ups	B	10
Distance run	C+	8
Volleyball	C−	6
Tumbling	B	10
		45

Table 5.6 Sample Grades and Points for the Best Student in the Class

Test	Grade	Points
Sit-ups	A	13
Pull-ups	A−	12
Distance run	A−	12
Volleyball	B+	11
Tumbling	B+	11
		Sum = 59

final grades. Thus, it would be unusual for a student to receive an A on each of five tests, although a superior student sometimes does. It is much more common to find the best student in the class receiving grades like those in Table 5.6.

Now, according to our standards, a student needs 60 points [(12)(5)] to receive an A− in the course. If the teacher makes no allowance for the regression effect, the best student in the class (grades shown in Table 5.6) will receive a B+, and no one in the class will get an A. In fact, if no allowance is made for the regression effect, very few final grades will be high or low; most students will receive grades in the middle of the possible range.

To allow for the regression effect, the teacher might decide to give the student with 59 points an A− because the student's total is closer to an A− than a B+. Another procedure is to lower the standards when assigning final grades. For example, the teacher might decide that any student who earns at least 3 As and 2 Bs will receive an A in the course. This means that 58 points are needed to earn an A when the final grade is based on five tests and an A+ is 14 points.

If such an arbitrary adjustment is made, it must be done for each letter grade. In the bottom half of the grading system, the adjustment must be up rather than down to allow for individuals below the mean regressing up toward the mean. But you must be careful in making arbitrary adjustments. If upward adjustments are made in the bottom half of the grading system, it is possible for a student to receive a final grade lower than any grade received on a test.

Rather than make arbitrary adjustments in the total number of points needed for each final grade, it might be better to calculate the total points earned by each student and use the rank-order, or norms method to assign final grades.

All tests need not be given equal weight in calculating a student's total points. If, using the grades in Table 5.6, the instructor wants 30% of a student's final grade to represent fitness (10% each for scores on sit-ups, pull-ups, and the distance run) and the other two grades to represent 35% each, the following procedure can be used:

$$\text{Final grade} = .10\,(\text{sit-ups} + \text{pull-ups} + \text{distance run}) + .35\,(\text{volleyball} + \text{tumbling})$$
$$= (.10)(13 + 12 + 12) + (.35)(11 + 11)$$
$$= (.10)(37) + (.35)(22) = 3.7 + 7.7 = 11.4\ (\text{B+ or A}-)$$

The calculation of final grades with unequally weighted tests is very common, but it can also be time-consuming when there are a large number of tests and/or students to grade. To save time, the teacher can use a calculator or computer.

Problem 5.1. At the end of a tennis unit you have assigned the following weights to the 6 grades that will make up the final grade: rally test, 20%; serve test, 20%; improvement, 5%; daily work, 10%; game observation, 5%; final exam, 40%. A student's scores on the items were C, B, A+, C+, C+, and C, respectively.

Solution. When using a calculator, the points from each multiplication can be summed in memory as the multiplications take place. Using 14 is an A+, 13 is A, and so on, the calculation is as follows:

Step 1
Rally test, 20% of C is .20 times 7 is 1.4.

Step 2
Put 1.4 in the calculator memory.

Step 3
Serve test, 20% of B is .20 times 10 is 2.

Step 4
Add 2 to the calculator memory. (There is now 3.4 [1.4 + 2] in memory.)

The process would continue for each grade and its weight, with the final 3 steps as follows:

Step 11
Final exam, 40% of C is .40 times 7 is 2.8.

Step 12
Add 2.8 to the calculator memory.

Step 13
Display the sum in memory, which is 8.10 and a C+.

The calculation of final grades with unequally weighted tests using the microcomputer would involve having a program with the letter-grade point values and test weightings already entered into the program so all that would have to be entered for each student would be the letter grades. Then the computer would do the calculations much like in Problem 5.1 and provide an answer. Grading programs like this are presently available commercially or can be easily written or developed on a spreadsheet program.

Table 5.7 Sample Point System for an Activity Course

I. Physical ability			70 points
A. Fitness		24 points	
1. sit-ups	8 points		
2. pull-ups	8 points		
3. distance run	8 points		
B. Volleyball		24 points	
1. serving test	8 points		
2. set or spike test	8 points		
3. game play	8 points		
C. Tumbling		22 points	
1. 11 stunts	2 points each		
II. Knowledge			20 points
40 questions	½ point each		
III. Subjective			10 points
Instructor's assessment of effort, improvement, attitude, attendance, and the like.			

Point Systems. Point systems are often used by classroom teachers so that all test scores are in the same unit of measure and can be easily combined. In physical education activity classes, point systems require a great deal of planning and the development of norms. A sample point system is shown in Table 5.7. To construct this system, the total number of points was chosen, points were allotted to the various activities, and standards were developed for each activity—that is, how many sit-ups earn 8 points, 7 points, and so on.

An instructor using the point system in Table 5.7 would have 3 fitness scores, 3 volleyball scores, a tumbling score, a knowledge score, and a subjective score in the record book. Thus, 9 scores must be summed before assigning a final grade, a procedure made easier if certain scores are combined before the calculation of final grades. For example, at the end of the fitness unit, the 3 fitness scores could be combined to form a single score. If the same thing is done at the end of the volleyball unit, only 5 scores have to be summed to calculate the final grade.

Sum of the T-Scores. When the units of measurement on a series of tests differ, some teachers translate the test scores into letter grades and the letter grades into points, and then sum the points. Another alternative is to change the test scores to T-scores and sum the T-scores, as discussed in Chapter 2. Obviously it is possible to weight each test differently in summing the T-scores by using the procedures outlined for weighting letter-grade points.

Other Evaluation Techniques

Some standards setting and evaluation situations that commonly occur have not yet been addressed. These situations are not like the grading situations just discussed. They tend to occur in exercise science.

Situation 1. The best five people receive a scholarship, raise, promotion, award/recognition, or job. This is a rank-order situation where the five best people in the present group are rewarded (passed) and the rest of the group get nothing (failed).

The important thing in this situation is that the decision is made without personal bias and is based on valid data or information.

Situation 2. The number of people who can be awarded or recognized is not limited. This is a typical criterion-referenced situation. The important thing is that the criterion-referenced standard is as good as possible. Ideally, this standard is like the "gold standard" discussed in Chapter 4. However, it is more likely that there is no gold standard; so several experts will have to set the standard. In many situations the only expert is you; so you must set the standard based on everything you can find in the literature, obtain by talking to people, draw upon based on your training and experience, and so on. The standard can even be set by data analysis. For example, if you believe that 10% of the group do not deserve to be recognized, rewarded, considered proficient, and so on, collect data on the group or a norming group, analyze the data, and set the standard at the score below which 10% (PR = 10) of the group scored (see sections on Rank Order and Norms grading). No matter how the standard is set, as indicated earlier in this chapter, the standard can be changed at a later time if a better standard is determined.

Situation 3. The physical therapist or athletic trainer must set a standard for releasing people from the therapy program. This is probably a criterion-referenced situation. The standard could be based on the minimum strength or ability needed to function in daily life. With injuries, the standard could be based on the difference between the injured and noninjured limb, or the difference between the injured limb at the beginning and end of the therapy program, or the difference between the limb before injury and after injury in terms of strength, flexibility, ability, and so on.

Authentic Assessment*

Since the early 1990s, authentic assessment has been a popular topic in education. Resulting from dissatisfaction with traditional testing methods and the need for accountability within education, **authentic assessment** is an attempt to evaluate students in a real-life or more "authentic" setting. Authentic assessment is one kind of alternative or nontraditional assessment. Another kind of alternative assessment is performance assessment. Many times in physical education, students are placed in a contrived setting for evaluation. For example, some skills tests place the student in situations that do not resemble those in which the skill would actually be used. How often in tennis are players responding to balls thrown to them rather than hit to them? Does hitting volleyball forearm passes against a wall as many times as possible in 30 seconds demonstrate an ability to use the forearm pass in a game? Are these authentic situations? Would it be more authentic to evaluate ability in an actual game?

Characteristics of Authentic Assessments

Lund (1997) has identified the following six characteristics that are present in most authentic assessments.

1. **Authentic assessments present challenges that are representative of real life.** How many times in a real-life situation are students going to be asked to take a multiple-choice test about tennis rules? Wouldn't it be more meaningful

*Appreciation is extended to Dr. A. Barry Joyner, Georgia Southern University, Statesboro, GA, for the material presented in this section.

for the assessment to mirror what the students will do in real life? Assessing them within a game where they apply the rules, strategies, and skills needed may be more appropriate.

2. **Authentic assessments require students to demonstrate higher level thinking.** Authentic assessments allow the students the opportunity to apply the concepts they have learned. After testing the students for their knowledge of the rules and strategies, authentic assessment could be used to determine if the students understand how to apply them in a real-life situation.
3. **Students know the standards for assessment from the beginning.** Authentic assessment involves setting up scoring rubrics or standards that serve as the criteria for the assessment. By knowing the criteria in advance, students will constantly be receiving feedback about their progress (Lund 1994). This is not unique to authentic assessment. Many physical educators routinely do this with skill and fitness testing.
4. **Authentic assessments are part of the curriculum.** When using more authentic assessments, teachers essentially teach to the test (Lund 1994). Although some may consider this undesirable, a goal of testing should be that the test matches the real-life situation.
5. **Students often present the culmination of the authentic assessment publicly.** This may help to stimulate pride in their work and show to the students that the material has meaning. The presentations might be at a PTA meeting, for other classes or other schools, or for the class itself.
6. **There is an emphasis on process and not just product.** *How* students arrive at the correct answer is just as important as the answer. By focusing solely on the product, students could be rewarded for using poor technique. In a basketball game, a student could have terrible technique but could score a lot of points because he or she is taller than everyone else.

Types of Authentic Assessments

In 1995, NASPE published *Moving into the Future: National Standards for Physical Education,* in which various alternative assessment options are discussed. Examples include student projects, student logs, student journals, peer observation, self-assessment, group projects, portfolios, event tasks, as well as teacher observation. Portfolios, or collections of student work, have received much recent attention. According to Kirk (1997), portfolios are a valuable means of combining the learning and assessment processes. NASPE (1995) includes hints for the development and use of portfolios. One suggestion is that the portfolio not include all examples of student work; the teacher specifies a certain number of pieces, and the student selects the pieces to include, submitting a cover letter explaining why those pieces were chosen. A scoring rubric should be included, outlining the goals the teacher would like the student to meet without limiting the creativity of the student. Kirk (1997) has developed sample portfolio tasks and a sample rubric for use in evaluating portfolios. Having the students include all possible information would make grading the portfolios impractical. Also, in some situations, physical educators may have too many students to make grading portfolios feasible.

Event tasks are those the students could complete in one class period, are written so that more than one possible solution can be presented, and are tasks that sim-

Table 5.8 Sample Scoring Rubric and Form for Tennis Playing Ability

5—Excellent	Demonstrates mastery of tennis skills and ability to consistently execute all strokes with little or no conscious effort, resulting in few unforced errors. Extensive knowledge base. Anticipates opponents' shots and employs effective strategy specific to the task or situation.
4—Good	Demonstrates competency and ability to perform basic tennis skills without making many errors. Complete understanding of rules and strategies of tennis. Usually selects appropriate strategy and shot for situation and generally displays consistent performance.
3—Satisfactory	Displays basic understanding of tennis and is able to perform fundamental skills adequately to be able to play game. Performance is frequently inconsistent, resulting in numerous errors being made. Understands basic strategies, but lacks ability to effectively employ.
2—Fair	Demonstrates inability to perform more than basic skills. Has difficulty in executing even the basic skills, making frequent errors, some critical, during performance. Generally inconsistent performance with only a minimal understanding of strategies and rules.
1—Poor	Rarely, if ever, performs skills well enough to be able to play a meaningful game of tennis. Demonstrates little understanding of tennis and is unable to execute skills without making significant and frequent errors. Makes little attempt to adjust performance.

Source: Hensley, L. D. (September, 1997). Authentic skills assessment in physical education. *Journal of Physical Education, Recreation, and Dance.* Used with permission of AAHPERD.

ulate a real-world experience (NASPE 1995). A good example of an event task comes from Whelan (1997) as a culmination to an outdoor adventure unit. A group of students were given a compass and directions; using orienteering skills, the students had to determine the correct place to pitch their tents. Students must find their way from a beginning point to a predetermined finishing point and pitch their tents within a certain distance of that point. After successfully setting up the tent, the students had to build a fire and make the teacher a cup of hot chocolate without getting ashes in it. These tasks were to be completed within the class period.

Teacher observations are common in any physical education setting. However, to use them as an alternative assessment, the teacher needs to standardize the observation. Checklists, anecdotal records, rating scales, and rubrics are some of the tools teachers can use to evaluate students through observation. Hensley (1997) developed a scoring rubric for tennis playing ability (see Table 5.8). Based on observations, the teacher would use this rubric to evaluate the ability of each student to play tennis. Table 5.9 has a generic scoring rubric developed by Hensley (1997) that could be applied to other activities. More information about using checklists and rating scales can be found in Chapter 12, Evaluating Skill Achievement.

Measurement Concerns with Authentic Assessments

Although authentic assessment seems attractive as a better way to evaluate students in physical education, it is not without potential problems. Within physical education, little attention has been paid to the psychometric properties (validity, reliability, and objectivity) of these assessments. Also, the question of how teachers can use authentic assessments for grading in physical education needs to addressed.

Table 5.9 Generic Scoring Rubric for Holistic Assessment of Sport Skills

5—Excellent	Demonstrates mastery of specific sports skills and ability to consistently perform with little or no conscious effort; resulting in few errors. Extensive knowledge base and understanding of sports or activity. Employs effective strategy specific to the task or situation.
4—Good	Demonstrates competency and ability to perform basic skills without making many errors. Complete understanding of rules and strategies of the specific sport or activity. Usually selects appropriate strategy and skill for situation and generally displays consistent performance.
3—Satisfactory	Displays basic knowledge of sport or activity and ability to perform fundamental skills adequately to be able to play game. Performance is frequently inconsistent, resulting in numerous errors being made. Understands basic strategies, but lacks ability to effectively employ.
2—Fair	Demonstrates inability to perform more than basic skills. Has difficulty in executing even the basic skills, making frequent errors, some critical, during performance. Generally inconsistent performance with only a minimal understanding of strategies and rules.
1—Poor	Rarely, if ever, performs skills well enough to be able to play a meaningful game. Demonstrates little understanding of sport or activity and is unable to execute skills without making significant and frequent errors. Makes little attempt to adjust performance.

Source: Hensley, L. D. (September, 1997). Authentic skills assessment in physical education. *Journal of Physical Education, Recreation, and Dance.* Used with permission of AAHPERD.

Concern has been expressed about the quality (i.e., validity, reliability, and objectivity) of authentic assessments. Some authors have conveyed the idea that unless the assessments are used for high stakes accountability, the quality of the assessments may not be as great a concern (Lund 1994). Grading would seem to involve high stakes accountability. Many teachers currently use teacher-made tests without regard for reliability and validity; therefore, many may use authentic assessments the same way. However, ignoring validity and reliability in one situation does not justify ignoring it in another situation.

The validity of authentic assessments can be defined as the accuracy of the interpretation of the assessment results. According to Safrit and Wood (1995), validation of authentic assessments has typically been demonstrated through a logical approach or face validity. In other words, does the assessment "look" like it is measuring the desired behavior. However, face validity is not enough evidence to say that an assessment is valid and would not be acceptable for high stakes accountability (Burger & Burger 1994).

Elliot (1995) discusses three concerns when considering the validity of authentic assessment. The first deals with how well the test relates to other measures. This is synonymous with concurrent validity. An authentic assessment of volleyball skill should be highly correlated with another measure of volleyball skill. A second concern is the ability of the assessment to predict future performance, or predictive validity. For example, can an authentic assessment dealing with fitness predict future fitness behaviors? The third issue concerns the assessment covering the content domain. Does the assessment cover all areas of the activity? If you are concerned with overall softball skill, is the assessment reflective of all the components of this domain?

Baker, O'Neill, and Linn (1993) identified several characteristics that valid authentic assessments possess. These include: having meaning for both students and teachers, serving as motivation for performance, evaluating attributes that are important to both the teachers and students, requiring demonstration of complex cognition, exemplifying current standards of content quality, minimizing the effects of irrelevant skills, and possessing explicit standards for rating or judgment.

The reliability and objectivity of the authentic assessment are dependent on the scoring rubric developed. A detailed rubric and practice scoring with that rubric can enhance reliability and objectivity by increasing the chances that the scores a teacher assigns the students one day will be similar to the scores that would be assigned on another day or by another teacher (see Chapter 3 for a review of reliability and objectivity). One issue that needs to be addressed within the scope of reliability of authentic assessments is the combination of the tasks. Reliability has usually been established for a single task that was independent of other tasks. With authentic assessments, teachers are usually concerned with a combination of tasks in a real-world setting where various single tasks are part of a set of tasks necessary to achieve a goal. Repeated evidence demonstrating that this combination of tasks is present would help increase the reliability of the assessment.

According to Frisbie (1988), reliability of teacher-made knowledge tests, including alternative assessments, is usually lower than reliability of standardized tests. Frisbie goes on to state that tests with low reliability can be acceptable if they are combined with other information for evaluation and that teachers should be more concerned with the reliability of the combination of all information rather than individual assessments. If the teacher has only a small number of items on which to evaluate, these must be of high quality. For example, if a teacher is basing a grade solely on two skill tests, these need to have high reliability and validity. However, if a teacher were to base a grade on two skill tests, two written tests, and two event tasks, the reliability and validity of this combination of items would be of more concern.

A grade in physical education should reflect whether or not the student has met the objectives of the program. If an objective is for the student to develop skill in a particular activity, teacher observation, event tasks, and student performance logs could be used. To determine if students are meeting cognitive objectives, teacher observation, portfolios, event tasks, group projects, and other authentic assessments could be used. Many different authentic assessments could be used to determine if effective objectives are being achieved. The use of authentic assessment should not mean the complete elimination of traditional means of evaluation. There may be times when a written test or skill test is appropriate and should be utilized. Also, when used in conjunction with authentic assessment, more traditional assessments may help to improve the reliability and validity of the final grade given.

Many physical education teachers lament the amount of time needed to grade their students using skill tests or fitness tests. It is unclear if the use of authentic assessments would result in more or less time spent on grading. Most physical educators spend at least part of each skill unit allowing the students to play the game. By making observations during this time, with a valid, reliable, and objective rating scale, the teacher could grade most, if not all, students in one class period. On the other hand, if a physical educator has 40 students in a class and six classes a day, is it feasible to use portfolios for grading those students? This would seem to work better for classroom teachers who have only 25–30 students in a class. In physical education, the number of students may deter the use of portfolios, which could be more time-consuming than traditional methods.

Examples of Authentic Assessment

Some examples of authentic and other alternative assessments are available. Two excellent examples can be found in *Moving into the Future: National Standards for Physical Education* by NASPE (1995). The first example is a fitness unit involving student assessment of the fitness levels of teachers and staff members at the school, development of individualized exercise programs, instruction for individuals on how to perform the activities, and monitoring of their progress (NASPE 1995). Students develop a portfolio of materials gathered throughout the project and are given feedback continually. A scoring rubric is developed and distributed prior to the assignment so that students know what criteria they must meet to succeed. The second example is an event task for gymnastics where the students have to develop a routine to perform at a half-time show for local basketball teams. The routine would be based on the gymnastics skills learned in class, and a scoring rubric has been included for evaluation. This event task could be easily adapted for dance and other activities.

Smith (1997) advocates using a portfolio card for authentic assessment. He points out some of the drawbacks of portfolios previously mentioned and suggests using a portfolio card to document student achievement for each grade level. He has included an example portfolio card and scoring rubric and relates the assessment to national outcomes. This would seem to be a useful way to document student performance and could be adapted to fit different situations.

Other examples of alternative assessment are available at the PE Central Web Page (http://www.chre.vt.edu/~/pe.central/) on the Internet. Alternative assessments for golf, tennis, motor skills, and fitness are available there. Also available are links to other pages containing assessments.

Program Evaluation

Program evaluation has focused on physical characteristics of the program. Score cards have been used to determine whether the environment—the facilities, professional staff, curriculum, equipment, and supplies—meets specified criteria. Evaluation specialists, however, view the environment as one of the least important factors in evaluating a program: A program may have excellent facilities and equipment, trained faculty, and so forth, and still produce few of the program objectives.

The success of an instructional program depends less on its physical characteristics than on the manner in which they are used in the instructional process. Thus, student performance offers the most valid index of the success of a program. The most crucial question is: Are students achieving important instructional objectives? If they are not, there is a need for change.

Similar statements can be made about an adult fitness program. The best facilities, staff, and program on paper cannot guarantee a successful program. Obviously a serious lack of these three essential attributes will be detrimental to a program. However, the most important indication of the success of an adult fitness program is whether participants are benefiting from the program and program objectives are being met. Both formative and summative procedures can be used to judge program effectiveness.

Data Collection for Program Evaluation

Some data must be available in order to do program evaluation. This data may be the result of testing or good daily record keeping. For the teacher it is primarily a result of testing. Much of the data for the exercise scientist may be the result of good record keeping. In both cases some forethought and planning must occur so that data is collected and available to do the program evaluation. The teacher commonly tests students at the beginning and end of a teaching unit or school year. The exercise specialist should be doing some fitness testing, but, in addition, the exercise specialist should be keeping daily records in terms of important outcomes on each participant such as attendance, amount of exercise, intensity of exercise, estimated calories burned, weight, resting and exercise heart rate, and so on. Without periodic testing and good record keeping, it is impossible to document improvement in program participants. With many participants in a program and considerable information collected daily, record keeping is a significant problem. Before starting an exercise program, considerable thought needs to be done as to how to store and retrieve this data with a computer. It is not uncommon for a staff person to enter the data daily or the participant to enter the data at the end of a session. Computer programs are available to provide a detailed evaluation of the use of a fitness facility (see Figure 5.1).

Barrow, McGee, and Tritschler (1989) have a chapter on program evaluation. They present an excellent discussion of program evaluation issues and several instruments for evaluating physical education, intramural, and athletic programs.

Formative Evaluation

Evaluation is the process of judging performance with reference to an established standard. The qualities and levels of performance that an adult fitness program is designed to produce are reflected in its stated instructional objectives and criterion-

MEMBER MANAGEMENT SYSTEM GENERAL STATISTICS
Report for Director
Dates: 7/1/98 through 7/31/98

	Male	**Female**	**Composite**
Number of Active Members	227	292	519
Number of New Members	87	117	204
Number of Memberships Expired	8	7	15
Number of Members Who Quit	26	63	89
Number of Members Who Checked In	174	218	392
Number of Members Who Logged	157	199	356
Number of Fitness Profiles	118	144	262
Number of Health-Life Assessments	1	0	1
Number of Sessions at the Facility	4542	4756	9298
Number of Activities Logged	12965	10896	23861
Total Calories Burned (X 1000)	3672.4	1820.7	5493.1
Average Calories Burned/Session	619	302	459
Average Calories Burned/Activity	283	167	230
Average Aerobic Minutes/Session	18	16	17
Average Aerobic Minutes/Activity	8	8	8
Average Aerobic Points/Session	9	4	6
Average Aerobic Points/Activity	4	2	3

Figure 5.1
Output of a computer program to evaluate the use of a fitness facility.

Table 5.10 Percentage of Adult Fitness Program Participants Who Achieved the Criterion-Referenced Standards for Three Fitness Tests

Test	1996	1997	1998
Two-arm curl	80	79	83
Bent-knee sit-up	90	93	91
1-Mile run	40	75	84

referenced standards. Let us assume that some of a program's instructional objectives are the development of (1) muscular strength and endurance of the arms, (2) muscular strength and endurance of the abdominal muscles, and (3) cardiorespiratory endurance. The tests and criterion-referenced standards are 3 two-arm barbell curls with 25 pounds, 25 bent-knee sit-ups, and a run of 1 mile in 10 minutes.

The formative evaluation of a program is the determination of the extent to which the stated standards are being achieved. The program developers may establish as a criterion that 80% of all participants should achieve these goals. Progress toward the goal is easily determined by calculating the percentage of participants who achieved the criterion-referenced standard for each fitness test. For example, assume that the percentage of participants who achieved these criterion-referenced standards is as listed in Table 5.10.

The program goal of 80% achievement was not reached in 1996 with the 1-mile run, which indicates that the instructional program failed in this aspect. The exercise specialist must analyze this failure and make an instructional decision. Several interpretations are possible. First, more aerobic conditioning activities may be needed. Second, it may be that the 10-minute criterion is an unrealistic standard for participants; perhaps the time should be changed to 12 minutes. Third, the value of the instructional objective may be questioned, and the objective retained or dropped.

The success of formative program evaluation depends directly on the selection of important, well-defined instructional objectives and the establishment of realistic standards. The failure to achieve a stated standard is thus a reliable indication that something is wrong. The value of formative program evaluation is that it signals that something is wrong while action can still be taken. In this sense, evaluation is a continuous process.

Summative Evaluation in Schools

The success of an instructional program is reflected in the degree of achievement of its broad objectives. Such success can usually be judged by comparing student performance to some norm. For this type of evaluation, published national, statewide, or local norms can serve as the basis for comparison.

It is common to compare a school's performance with national or statewide norms. For example, the mean performance of students from a given school or district might be compared to the norms that accompany a nationally distributed fitness test battery to determine whether the mean is above or below the 50th percentile (P_{50} = Median = Mean in normal curve) (see Chapter 2). Although this procedure does stimulate interest, it also has several disadvantages. First, tests with national or statewide norms may not reflect the true objectives of the school district. For example, if the general objectives of a school were directed primarily toward motor-skill

Table 5.11 Summative Evaluation of Weight Training

Test	Norm Sample		Fall 1998 Sample	
	Mean	*Standard Deviation*	*Mean*	*Standard Deviation*
1. Dips	17.30	6.65	19.40	6.91
2. Sit-ups	24.71	8.17	25.09	7.70
3. Lat pull	27.33	9.47	34.09	12.70
4. Arm curl	23.45	9.89	28.02	9.77
5. Bench press	17.85	8.34	23.39	8.69

development, the national norms for a fitness test would not validly apply. A second disadvantage arises from the geographic and environmental factors that affect performance. Often, the testing conditions used by a school district are not similar to those used to develop national norms.

Local norms offer the most realistic basis for summative program evaluation. Although it is quite likely that all schools in a given system will be above the national norms, several of them may score considerably lower than others, indicating a need for program improvement.

Table 5.11 presents the means and standard deviations for an instructional unit on weight training. The local norm sample represents the performance of over 500 students; the fall 1998 sample represents the performance of a group of students being compared to the established norms. As you can see, the average performance of the fall 1998 group exceeded that of the norm group, indicating that the program is functioning properly in light of these objectives. If a school's means are considerably lower than the local norms, action can be taken to identify and correct the difficulty. If the means become progressively larger over succeeding years, this may be objective evidence that the program is improving.

Summative Evaluation in Adult Fitness

The success of an adult fitness program can usually be judged by comparing participant performance to some norm. For this type of evaluation, published national standards or local standards can serve as the basis for comparison. Standards have been developed for body composition (see Chapter 9) and aerobic fitness (see Chapter 8).

A useful way to judge the quality of an adult fitness program is to evaluate the number who continue to exercise on a regular basis. The dropout rate of many poor programs is extremely high. Another method that is being used relates to caloric expenditure (see Figure 5.1). At many computerized fitness centers, participants log their exercise into a computer, and these data can be used for program evaluation. As shown in Chapter 1, caloric expenditure is related to health.

Program Improvement

Evaluation is a decision-making process that works toward program improvement. The adoption of appropriate standards is essential for program evaluation and improvement. Formative evaluation leads to higher-level achievement of objectives, evaluated summatively. Furthermore, the use of criterion- and norm-referenced standards helps the students or fitness program participants to determine expected levels of performance. People tend to strive to exceed standards. The use of explicit, realistic, and improvement standards, then, is necessary, not only for program evaluation, but also for motivation. A primary objective of program developers should be improved participant performance over time.

Summary

The method and rationale for student or program participant evaluation should be determined by the objectives and content of the course or program. It is crucial that evaluation be based on reliable, valid information and that the process be carefully planned and explained to the participants in the program.

Before evaluating a class, the teacher must decide whether formative or summative evaluation is wanted. For summative evaluation, one of the grading methods described in the chapter—or a combination of several—can be used. We cannot stress enough the importance of deciding in advance how final grades will be determined.

Regular measurement and analysis of scores are essential to the ongoing process of evaluating the physical education and exercise science program.

Formative Evaluation of Objectives

Objective 1 Define and compare the terms *evaluation* and *measurement.*

1. In discussing the broad topic of evaluation the terms *measurement, grading,* and *summative* and *formative evaluation* often are mentioned. In your own words, discuss how these terms are related to the broad topic of evaluation.
2. Many people feel strongly that grades should be eliminated. Is it possible that they are frustrated with the faculty techniques used to assign grades rather than the idea of grades? Explain your answer.

Objective 2 Select the components for inclusion in an evaluation program and determine evaluation standards using several methods.

1. There are certain attributes commonly used for determining grades in physical education. Also, as suggested in the text, grading programs themselves have desired characteristics. There are several different methods that can be used to assign grades. Considering these three points, outline the grading procedure you would like to use as a teacher.
2. Whatever method you select for assigning grades, it is important that you apply it accurately. Below are three situations to give you practice in using the various grading methods discussed in the text.
   a. Using the rank-order method, assign letter grades for the first-semester scores in Table 5.1, assuming As, 20%; Bs, 30%; Cs, 45%; and Ds, 5%.
   b. Using the percentages in part (a) and the norms in Table 5.3, what are the scores for an A, B, C, and D for girls on the one-minute sit-up test?
   c. Using a plus-and-minus grading system with A+ = 14, A = 13, and so on, what final grade would you assign a student based on the tests and percentages below?

Test	Percentage of Final Grade	Student's Grade
1	15%	C−
2	25%	B−
3	35%	B
4	25%	B+

Objective 3 Identify ways to make an evaluation system as quick and efficient as possible.

1. A common reason for not using an extensive evaluation system in physical education is lack of time. It is true that physical educators have large classes and that it does take time to combine scores from different tests and to grade knowledge tests; but with good planning, the time involved in administering an evaluation system could be minimized. List at least five ways to make an evaluation system as quick and efficient to administer as possible.
2. A common reason for not using an extensive evaluation/record-keeping system in adult fitness is lack of time. It is true that fitness specialists often have a large number of participants and testing/record keeping is time-consuming, but with good planning more could be done. List at least five ways to make an evaluation/record-keeping system efficient.
3. Which three procedures in question 1 do you think would be easiest to implement? Defend your choices.
4. Which three procedures in question 2 do you think would be easiest to implement? Defend your choices.

Objective 4 Identify why and how to do authentic assessment.

1. How are authentic assessment and traditional testing/evaluation methods similar and different?
2. How could authentic assessment be used in a noneducational setting?

Objective 5 Outline the procedures used for evaluating programs.

1. Evaluation of the instructional program is an important part of the total measurement. In your own words, indicate the importance of both formative and summative evaluation.

Additional Learning Activities

1. Interview faculty members at your school and in the local school system. Determine what attributes they consider in their grading systems, what methods they use for assigning grades, and what grading system (A-B-C-D-F, pass-fail) they use.
2. Interview fitness specialists about their evaluation/record-keeping system or survey the literature as to what is being done in some big adult-fitness programs.

Bibliography

Barrow, H. M., R. McGee and K. A. Tritschler. 1989. *Practical measurement in physical education and sport.* 4th ed. Philadelphia: Lee and Febiger.

Baker, E. L., H. F. O'Neill JR. and R. L. Linn. 1993. Policy and validity prospects for performance-based assessments. *American Psychologist* 48:1210–1218.

Burger, S. E. and D. L. Burger. 1994. Determining the validity of performance-based assessment. *Educational Measurement: Issues and Practice* 13:9–15.

Elliot, S. N. 1995. *Creating meaningful performance assessments* (Report No. EDO-EC-94-2). Reston, VA: Council for Exceptional Children. (ERIC Document Reproduction Service No. ED 375 566).

Frisbie, D. A. 1988. Reliability of scores from teacher-made tests. *Educational Measurement: Issues and Practices* 79(1):25–35.

Hensley, L. D. September, 1997. Authentic skills assessment in physical education. *Journal of Physical Education, Recreation, and Dance* 68(7):19–24.

Kirk, M. F. September, 1997. Using portfolios to enhance student learning and assessment. *Journal of Physical Education, Recreation, and Dance* 68(7):29–33.

Lund, J. 1994. Authentic assessment: Have we finally found user friendly assessment? *Proceedings of the World Congress for the Association Internationale des Ecoles Superieures d'Education Physique.*

Lund, J. January 1997. What is authentic assessment? *Measurement News* 2:3. NASPE (National Association for Sport and Physical Education). 1995. *Moving into the future: National standards for physical education.* Reston, VA: National Association for Sport and Physical Education.

Safrit, M. J. and T. M. Wood. 1995. *Introduction to measurement in physical education and exercise science.* 3d ed. New York: Mosby.

Smith, T. K. April 1997. Authentic assessment: Using a portfolio card in physical education. *Journal of Physical Education, Recreation, and Dance* 68(4):46–52.

Whelan, J. March 1997. Authentic adventure. Paper presented at the meeting of the American Alliance for Health, Physical Education, Recreation, and Dance, St. Louis, MO.

PART THREE 3

Performance Testing

6

CHAPTER

The Nature of Tests and Their Administration: With Applications to Individuals with Disabilities

Contents

Key Words

individual with disabilities
mass testability
posttest procedures
pretest planning
useful scores

Objectives

In the first part of this chapter we will discuss those attributes that make up a sound measuring instrument. These include not only reliability, objectivity, and validity, but also other content-related, person-related, and administration-related characteristics.

Pretest procedures, giving the test, and posttest procedures are also important aspects of testing. Pretest planning, in particular, is the key to a successful measurement procedure, providing the basis for all testing decisions and processes.

Finally, issues and problems associated with testing individuals with disabilities will be discussed. Realizing the problems in testing individuals with disabilities is vital.

After reading Chapter 6 you should be able to:

1. Identify the important characteristics of a test.
2. Plan the administration of a test.
3. Identify problems in measuring individuals with disabilities.

Introduction

Many existing measurement programs are neither effective nor efficient, while others produce invalid scores because the teacher, researcher, or exercise scientist (fitness specialist, physical therapist, athletic trainer, or program specialist) has been careless in selecting tests or in planning testing procedures. The first level of planning in a good measurement program focuses on the selection or construction of a test. The second level involves the administration of the test.

Teachers almost always test a group of students at the same time, with all students going through the test at the same time (the entire group running the mile for time), half the group going through the test while the other half of the group watch or assist in administering the test (half the group do the sit-up test and the other half hold the feet of those being tested and count the number of sit-ups executed), or one student going through the test while the rest of the group watch (the instructor takes skinfold measures). Sometimes researchers and exercise specialists test people in a group, but they are just as likely to test one person at a time, with one person coming to be tested every 30 to 60 minutes. Testing one person at a time is a clinical model common to adult fitness, athletic training, physical therapy, and cardiac rehabilitation programs. Some of the topics discussed in this chapter may not apply to situations where one person is tested at a time. However, many topics apply to all measurement situations.

Test Characteristics

Knowing the important characteristics of a test allows the teacher, researcher, or exercise scientist to construct effective, efficient instruments, and to recognize essential features in tests constructed by others. The characteristics themselves concern the test content, the individuals tested, and the administrative procedures, and, above all, reliability, objectivity, and validity.

Reliability, Objectivity, and Validity

The three most important characteristics of a test are reliability, objectivity, and validity (see Chapters 3 and 4). If a test does not fulfill these requirements, you need not consider it further. Yet there are no rigid standards for acceptable levels of these characteristics. Acceptability is determined by both the testing situation itself and the values others have obtained in their measurement programs. This is not to say that no standards exist. In general, the stability reliability of most physical measures is between .85 and .93. Objectivity coefficients of between .85 and .93 are also usually reported.

Published validity coefficients are .80 or higher for a well-constructed, properly administered physical performance test. Remember, though, that a validity coefficient depends greatly on the criterion and population used and that when construct validity is used there may be no coefficient at all. All of these values are dependent on the test and the age, sex, experience level, and so on of the group tested. All tests are not equally good, and the very young and very old tend to be less consistent in their test performance. Norm-referenced and criterion-referenced tests differ in terms of these values.

Content-Related Attributes

These characteristics relate to the nature of the test content—what it measures and how it does so.

Important Attributes. Typically, no more than 10% of the class or program time should involve testing. To meet this goal, only the most important skills and abilities should be measured. These skills and abilities are those listed in the educational objectives for the unit, or are the important componenets of a program.

Discrimination. A test should discriminate among different ability groups throughout the total range of ability. Ideally, there should be many different scores, and the distribution of the scores should be basically normal or at least not markedly skewed. Also, it is important to select a test difficult enough so that nobody receives a perfect score, but easy enough so that nobody receives a zero. Consider the problem of two individuals receiving the minimum or maximum score. Although two individuals who receive a zero on a pull-up test are both weak, they are probably not equal in strength per pound of body weight. Remember, however, that the fact that nobody receives a perfect score or a zero is no guarantee that a test discriminates satisfactorily; conversely, the fact that someone does receive a perfect score or a zero is no guarantee that the test is a poor one.

Resemblance to the Activity. A test, particularly a sport-skill test, must require the student to use good form, follow the rules of the activity, and perform acts characteristic of the activity. For example, a badminton short-serve test that does not require the serve to be low over the net is not requiring good form. And a basketball test that asks a student to run with the ball rather than dribble it is neither following the rules of the game nor demanding a performance characteristic of it. The validity of a test is questionable if the test does not resemble the activity.

Specificity. When a test measures a single attribute, it is possible to determine from it why a person is performing poorly; when a test measures an attribute that has several components, it is more difficult to determine why a person is performing at a given level. For example, consider a basketball test of 10 shots at the basket. If the test asks the student to stand 3 feet away from the basket to shoot and the student misses all 10 shots, it is easy to determine that the student is a poor shot. If, however, the student were standing 40 feet away from the basket and missed the 10 shots, it would be difficult to determine whether the student simply shoots poorly or lacks strength. Likewise, strength tests and flexibility tests should be as specific as possible.

Sometimes it is not possible to measure a single attribute; at other times your reason for testing is to measure how well a person combines several attributes. In either case, the test should be as specific as possible for whatever is being measured.

Unrelated Measures. Often an attribute has several components; so you will measure it using a battery composed of several tests. The measures in a battery should be unrelated—that is, the correlation between the tests should be low—both to save testing time and to be fair to the individuals being tested. Of course, all tests in a battery should correlate highly with the criterion used to determine validity.

When two tests are highly correlated, they are probably measuring the same ability. This wastes time and also gives the measured ability double weight in the battery, a practice unfair to individuals weak in the ability. If two tests in a battery are highly correlated, keep the better of the two and drop the other.

Student and Participant Concerns

Appropriateness to Student and Participants. Performance is influenced by the person's maturity, gender, and experience. For example, older students and boys generally score better on strength tests (push-ups, distance jumps) than do younger students and girls. The strength tests are usually valid and reliable for a variety of ages and both genders, but performance standards should be based on age and gender. Skill tests, on the other hand, are not universally applicable: They must apply to the age, gender, skill level, strength, and other capacities of the students. Again, skill tests that are valid and reliable with junior high students may not be valid and reliable with elementary or high school students; and tests that are valid and reliable with females may not be valid and reliable with males.

Performance is also influenced by the age and disabilities of the person. Physical performance tests (fitness tests in particular) for high school and college students are often not appropriate for adults over 30 years old and seldom appropriate for adults older than age 60 or preschool children. Individuals with disabilities often do not score as well as individuals without disabilities on most physical performance tests. Strength and skill tests for individuals without disabilities are usually not acceptable for individuals with disabilities.

Individual Scores. A person's test scores should not be affected by another person's performance. That is, a test should not require several individuals to interact and then score individuals on the basis of that interaction. For example, consider a basketball lay-up shot test in which Student 1 runs toward the basket and Student 2 throws the ball to him to make the shot. If Student 2 makes a poor or late throw, even the best student is going to look bad.

Enjoyable. When individuals enjoy taking a test and understand why they are being tested, they are motivated to do well, and their scores ordinarily represent their maximum capacity. To be enjoyable, a test should be interesting and challenging, within reason. People are more likely to enjoy a test when they have a reasonable chance to achieve an acceptable score. Testing comfort is also an aspect of enjoyment. Although certain aerobic capacity tests and other maximum-effort tests can be uncomfortable, avoid any test so painful that few people can do it well.

Safety. Obviously, you should not use tests that endanger the people being tested. Examine each test's procedures to see whether individuals might overextend themselves or make mistakes that could cause injury. The use of spotters in gymnastic tests, soft nonbreakable marking devices for obstacle runs or marking testing areas, and nonslip surfaces and large areas for running and throwing events is always necessary. The

ACSM (1986) offers guidelines for administering maximal stress tests. This is summarized in Chapter 10.

Confidentiality and Privacy of Testing. Many students and participants in fitness or rehabilitation programs would prefer that others did not know how well or poorly they score on a test. Often students are embarrassed when they receive a test score that is considerably better or worse than their peers. Participants in fitness and rehabilitation programs have similar feelings or just do not think that their score should be known by others. All people conducting measurement programs need to be sensitive to this issue. Testing one person at a time rather than in a group may be the only way to satisfy this concern.

Motivation to Score at Maximum Potential. Students tend to try hard on tests because their grade is affected. Generally, people who are in certification programs or whose job, salary, insurance premium, and so on are affected by their score try hard on tests. But, what motivates people not in these situations to try hard on tests? Poor effort by the person being tested makes scores not valid and not reliable. The tester must motivate participants to do well and constantly watch for lack of effort by participants. Exercise specialists doing testing in therapy programs need to be particularly aware of participant effort.

Administrative Concerns

Mass Testability. When there is a large number of people to test in a short period of time, **mass testability** can be a vital test characteristic. The longer it takes to administer each test, the fewer tests are likely to be administered. With large groups it is essential that people be measured quickly, either successively or simultaneously. A test can be mass testable when a participant performs every 10 to 15 seconds. A sit-up test can be mass testable when half the group is tested while the other half helps with the administration. Remember too that short tests or tests that keep most of the participants active at once help prevent the discipline problems that often result from student inactivity and reduce dissatisfaction of participants in research or fitness programs.

The teacher, researcher, or exercise scientist can become so concerned about mass testing that the validity and reliability of the data suffer. With careful thought and planning this need not be true.

Minimal Practice. People must be familiar with a test and be allowed to practice before testing. Familiarity, either from previous testing, from the program or class, or from practice sessions prior to the testing day, lessens both explanation and practice time. Even when a test is unfamiliar, if it is easy to understand that little time need be spent to explain it. Avoid tests that require elaborate directions or considerable practice.

In research or rehabilitation fitness testing and strength testing situations where participants are tested on treadmill and isokinetic equipment with no previous experience on the equipment and with minimum explanation and practice trials of the test, are valid and reliable scores obtained? The equipment may have the potential to provide very valid and precise scores, but if poor administrative techniques are used when testing with the equipment, the scores obtained will not be valid.

Minimal Equipment and Personnel. For teachers, tests that require a lot of equipment and/or administrative personnel are often impractical. Equipment is usually expensive to purchase and maintain and can be time-consuming to assemble. In the same way, when several people are needed to administer a test, time must be spent finding and training them. Even when you plan to use members of the class or program, you must expect to spend time training them.

Insufficient training of all test administrators contributes to lack of test objectivity (see Chapter 3). In some labs and rehabilitation programs where participants will be tested at regular intervals over a period of time to determine if they are improving, the same person, rather than different people, tests a participant each time to maximize the chances that improvement in the scores of the participant is really an improvement and not due to lack of objectivity.

Ease of Preparation. Select tests that are easy to set up over ones that take more time, provided the first does the job well. Tests that use complex equipment or several pieces of equipment placed at specific spots or that require a large number of boundary or dimension marks on floors and walls are usually neither easily nor quickly set up.

Adequate Directions. When you construct a test, you must develop a set of directions for it. When you use a test constructed by others, you must make sure that complete directions accompany it. Directions should specify how the test is set up, the preparation of individuals to be tested, and administration and scoring procedures.

Norms. When the norms provided with a test are both recent and appropriate, they can save the time necessary to develop local norms or at least offer temporary standards until local norms can be developed. Unhappily, those norms may be so old that they are no longer suitable, or they may be based on a group of different gender, age, or experience and so are not appropriate to the individuals being tested.

Useful Scores. A test should yield **useful scores.** These are scores that can be used at once or inserted into a formula with little effort. Most physical measures can be used immediately after a measurement session. If scores must be placed in a formula before they can be used, the formula should be sufficiently simple so that calculations can be done quickly. For example,

$$Y = 2X + 5,$$

where Y is the calculated score and X is the score collected, is a simple enough formula that a test requiring it could be considered. However, a test that requires the calculation:

$$Y = .6754\sqrt{X} + .2156X^2 - 3.14 \text{ or}$$

$$Y = .4521X_1 + .3334X_2 + 1.2$$

would be very time-consuming if a Y score had to be calculated by hand for each of several hundred people. With computer support, the computer program would have the formula for Y in it, and only the X score(s) for each person would have to be input to the computer. Computer support like this is quite common and should be used more often.

Administration

The key to good testing is the planning before the test is given and then the follow-up to that planning during and after the administration.

Pretest Procedures

We plan before giving a test to be sure that our preparation is adequate and that the actual administration will proceed smoothly. **Pretest planning** is all of the preparation that occurs before test administration. It involves a number of tasks: knowing the test, developing test procedures, developing directions, preparing the individuals to be tested, planning warm-up and test trials, securing equipment and preparing the test facility, making scoring sheets, estimating time needed, and giving the test.

Knowing the Test. Whenever you plan to administer a test for the first time, read the directions or test manual several times, thinking about the test as you read. This is the only way to avoid overlooking small details about procedures, dimensions, and the like.

Developing Test Procedures. Once you are familiar with the test, start to develop procedures for administering it. These include selecting the most efficient testing procedure, deciding whether to test all the individuals together or in groups, and determining whether one person will do all the testing or pairs of individuals will test each other.

If you plan to administer several tests on the same day, order them so that fatigue is minimized. Do not give consecutive tests that tire the same muscle groups. Also, plan to administer very fatiguing events, such as distance runs or other maximum exertion tests, last.

The next step is the identification of exact scoring requirements and units of measurement. For example, in a sit-up test, you would require the person to start in a supine position with both shoulder blades on the floor, then to sit up with hands interlaced behind the head, to lean forward until both elbows touch the thighs, and to return to the starting position, all to score one sit-up. Here too, when necessary, the unit of measurement with which you will score must be selected. For example, do you want to express distance in feet or inches or both; time in minutes or seconds or both? To obtain a score that can immediately be analyzed mathematically, only one unit of measurement—usually the smaller one—is used.

At this point you should also decide what to do if an individual makes a mistake during the test. By anticipating possible situations and rulings, you will be able to deal fairly with all individuals. For example, what do you do if an individual fails to go all the way down to the floor on a sit-up? Whether you disregard the mistake, warn the individual and count the sit-up, or discount it, you must follow the same policy for all individuals.

Finally, safety procedures are essential. Always plan to use spotters in tests where people can get injured or when testing the elderly. Consider your marking devices as well. In obstacle runs they should be soft, unbreakable, and tall enough so that participants cannot step over them. Use marking cones instead of chairs or soda bottles when marking testing areas or obstacle courses. Think too about the testing area. Hold running events in a large enough area so that participants do not run into obstacles. Plan for organization of participants waiting to be tested so that participants do not run into them.

If you have never administered a specific test before, try one or two practice administrations before the actual test. This is a good way not only to see what changes and additions to the procedures must be made, but also to train administrative personnel.

Developing Directions. After you have determined procedures, it is necessary to develop exact directions. It is perfectly acceptable to read these directions to a group before administering the test to them. The directions should be easy to understand and should specify the following:

1. Administration procedures
2. Instructions on performance
3. Scoring procedure and the policy on incorrect performance
4. Hints on techniques to improve scores

Preparing the Students or Program Participants. Announce the test well in advance so that people can practice if they think it will improve their scores. When the class or group is unfamiliar with a test, spend some time before the day of the test explaining it and the techniques that will improve test scores, and supervising pretest practice.

Even when people have had exposure to a test, they may need some time to relearn the necessary techniques. Girardi (1971) familiarized a group of high school boys with a jump-and-reach test and a 12-minute-run test, and then tested them. Eight weeks later, he retested the students without review, and found that a number of them, particularly the poorly skilled, had forgotten the necessary techniques.

With the exception of a few research situations (e.g., learning research), people should know well in advance that they are going to be tested, what the test is, and what it involves. This allows the person to be psychologically and physiologically ready to be tested and score up to his or her potential. This is vital when important things like grades, admission to or release from programs, or health-fitness ratings are involved.

Planning Warm-Up and Test Trials. We saw in Chapter 3 that reliability improves with pretest warm-up. The amount and nature of this warm-up must be planned. Ideally, warm-up should be specific to the skill being tested (i.e, practice rather than calisthenics). It has been shown too that supervised warm-up, in which the tester tells the individuals what to do and ensures that all individuals receive the same amount of practice, is better than unsupervised warm-up. In some situations it is acceptable to administer multiple trials of a test and to consider the first few trials as warm-up, making each individual's score the sum or mean of the latter test trials.

Securing Equipment and Preparing the Testing Facility. You should have all equipment on hand and the facility prepared before the day of the test. Having all equipment available and all boundary lines and other markings positioned correctly when the people arrive to be tested saves time and avoids the problems that inevitably arise when people are kept waiting while the test is set up.

Making Scoring Sheets. At some point before the test, locate or prepare either a master scoring sheet for the entire group or individual scorecards. Enter each person's name on the sheets or cards before they arrive to be tested.

There are many advantages to using individual scorecards over a master score sheet. Scorecards allow people to rotate among testing stations and to quickly record scores when they have tested one another. Even when one person is testing and recording the scores of the entire group, time can be saved by gathering the scorecards in order after the individuals are in line to be tested rather than having the individuals get in line in the same order they are listed on the scoring sheet.

Estimating the Time Needed. When a test will not take an entire class or program period, or when half the group will be tested on each day, you must plan some activity to fill the extra time or to occupy the rest of the group. If testing will occur during an agency or corporate fitness program, similar planning is necessary. Estimating the time needed to administer a test both minimizes confusion and maximizes the use of available time.

Giving the Test

If you have planned properly, the testing should go smoothly. Although your primary concern on the day of the test is the administration of the test itself, you should also be concerned with participant preparation, motivation, and safety. If, after you have administered the test, you can say, "The participants were prepared and the test was administered in a way that I would have liked if I were being tested," the testing session was undoubtedly a success.

Preparation. The participants should already know what the test is and why it is being given; so your first concern is the warm-up or practice. Next, explain the test instructions and procedures, even demonstrating the test for them if possible. Ask for questions both before and after the demonstration. When the skill or procedures are particularly complicated, let the participants run through a practice trial of the test.

Motivation. Give all participants the same degree of motivation and encouragement. Although we all tend to encourage poor performers and compliment superior ones, in fairness all or none of the participants should receive a comment. Whenever possible, indicate his or her score to a participant immediately after the test trial. This can motivate participants to perform better on a second or third trial. However, the reporting of the score should not embarrass the participant.

Safety. During a testing session, watch for safety problems. Participants often perform unsafely when they are not following instructions. Try to anticipate these or other unsafe situations.

Posttest Procedures

The rationale for testing is to collect information about the participants and, in education, about the instructional program. Only after the test is given can the information be used. Surprisingly, many teachers and exercise scientists fail to do enough, or even any, posttest analysis. The sooner the results of tests are returned to the participants, the more meaningful they will be in the evaluation process. **Posttest procedures** include the analyzing, reporting, and recording of test scores.

Analyzing Test Scores. Shortly after a test, the scores must be analyzed using the appropriate techniques from Chapter 2. This often requires entering the data into the computer, so analysis, record keeping, and/or data retrieval is possible. Analysis serves to reveal characteristics that could influence the teaching procedures or program conduct and to provide information for the group tested and prepare the data for grading or other evaluation purposes. People are usually interested in their scores, their relative standings in the group or class, and their degree of improvement or decline since the last test. Reporting test results to participants is an effective motivational device.

Recording Test Results. The recording of test results is usually nothing more than placing the scoring sheets and your analysis of them in an appropriate file. The information makes possible comparisons between classes or groups within and between years, program evaluation over years, as well as the development of norms. Notice that these are group or class standards rather than individual standards, based solely on the scores and your analysis. Often it is not even necessary to identify the scores, particularly in situations where a permanent record card for each student or program participant is kept. It is from this card, that follows the student from grade to grade or the program participant from year to year, that you can trace individual improvement over time.

Measuring Individuals with Disabilities*

Administering tests to individuals with disabilities can be especially difficult and requires special attention. An individual may be considered an **individual with disabilities** when special program or testing considerations must be extended to this individual due to limited ability to perform certain activities. Impairment and handicap are terms often used in place of disability, but individuals with disabilities is the accepted term at this time.

Most of the issues and problems associated with testing individuals with disabilities are beyond the scope of this test. However, some of them are discussed here. *Physical Best and Individuals with Disabilities* (Seaman 1995) is a source to consult for alternative fitness test items and ways of including individuals with disabilities in regular programs.

Background

At one time individuals with disabilities tended to be sent to special schools and/or placed in special classes. This may have had some advantages. The teachers who taught these classes were trained to work with individuals with disabilities. All members of the class were approximately similar in terms of their disability and performance level. The classes were small so that individual testing was feasible even if it was time consuming and often required special teacher expertise and equipment. However, there were also many disadvantages to special schools and/or special classes.

Public Law 94–142 (U.S. Congress 1975) and its reauthorization (1990, 1997) mandated that individuals with disabilities should be placed in an environment that affords the individual maximum opportunity for development and function but at the same time accommodates the individual's disabilities. This meant regular education where possible. Greater discussion of PL 94–142 and its subsequent reauthorizations can be found in adapted physical education books such as Eichstaedt and Lavay (1992) and Auxter, Pyfer, and Huettig (1993). One of the outcomes of this law is that many individuals with disabilities are no longer attending special schools or classes. Rather, they are included in regular physical education classes. "Inclusion: Physical Education

---

*Appreciation is extended to Dr. Janet A. Seaman, American Association for Active Lifestyles and Fitness, for suggesting many improvements to this section.

for All" was the feature section of the January 1994 *Journal of Physical Education, Recreation, and Dance.* Researchers have found that approximately 93% of all students with disabilities are being served in regular classes. By law these students must be receiving appropriate activities, be tested with appropriate tests, and be evaluated with appropriate standards. Specifically, the law states that "tests must be validated for the purpose for which they are intended." This means a test must measure motor performance and not the student's intelligence, language comprehension, and so on as is often the case if the student doesn't understand the test directions or grasp the meaning of words or concepts used during administration of the test.

There have been many positive outcomes of federal legislation, but inclusion of individuals with disabilities in regular physical education classes has caused teachers some testing problems. Many physical education teachers are not properly trained to work with individuals with disabilities nor recognize their unique problems. Measurement problems arise because tests and standards traditionally used in physical education programs are not appropriate for some individuals with disabilities. One would not expect a student with one arm to do pull-ups. With large classes, limited equipment, and limited expertise on the part of the teacher, individual testing with special equipment becomes difficult if not impossible.

There may be differences among individuals with disabilities in terms of their ability to understand test directions and do the test. The differences can be as great as the differences among preschool, college, and older adults in the ability to do some physical tasks. Individuals with disabilities may have single or multiple disabilities and therefore present multiple challenges in the testing situation. Teachers and exercise scientists must recognize these differences.

Problems in Measuring Individuals with Disabilities

There are some problems to recognize when measuring individuals with disabilities. Recognize that these problems exist and plan how to cope with them so that valid and reliable data are obtained.

Attributes of Individuals with Disabilities. Individuals with disabilities may be classified by a variety of methods. Presented in Table 6.1 is a brief description of the classifications approved in the 1997 amendments of IDEA, PL 105–17. Each of these disabilities has degrees of severity and functional ability. Thus, two individuals with the same disabilities may not be the same. People with sight and/or hearing problems tend to have problems in performing motor tasks, but there is a difference between having some sight or hearing and none.

A challenge in developing a testing program for individuals with disabilities or testing them is the need for a test battery for each possible combination of disabling conditions. This is similar to the problem of accounting for age and gender when testing individuals without disabilities.

Another challenge in testing individuals with disabilities is finding norm-referenced standards. For many disabilities, adequate age and gender norms do not exist. Norms for individuals without disabilities and individuals with disabilities on the same test are not usually available but are needed to determine if individuals with disabilities should be placed in regular or special programs. For example, an individual with disabilities could be at the 99th percentile in terms of his or her peers with disabilities, which might suggest that he or she could be moved into a regular physical education program, but only at the 1st percentile when compared to peers without disabilities.

Table 6.1 Classifications of Individuals with Disabilities

Classification	Description
Mentally retarded	Low IQ; mildly retarded 55–69; moderately retarded 40–54; etc.
Orthopedically impaired	Neurologically impaired; musculoskeletal conditions; postural deviations; trauma-caused physical impairments
Serious emotional disturbance	Autism; depression; mental illness; schizophrenia
Multihandicapped and severely handicapped	Two or more handicapping conditions varying in severity; severely handicapped are in special programs
Speech- and/or language-disabled	Difficulty in communicating thoughts or forming or sequencing sounds
Other health-impaired	Examples are asthma, cardiovascular disorders, diabetes, epilepsy, obesity
Deaf/hard of hearing	Little or no hearing
Blind/visually handicapped	Little or no sight
Deaf-blind	Combination of both hearing and sight impairments
Specific learning-disabled	Learning problems not due to mental retardation or emotional disturbance
Developmental delay	Children aged 3 through 9, who are experiencing developmental delays

Adapted from: "Summary of the Individuals with Disabilities Education Act (IDEA)," council for Exceptional Children web page, http://www.ccc.sped.org

Individuals with disabilities may be similar to individuals without disabilities who are chronologically younger. Many individuals with disabilities have a short attention span and problems with complicated directions. Often they cannot reliably test each other, even if the test lends itself to it, because they don't count accurately or are not good judges of properly executed performances.

Additional testing challenges for testing individuals with disabilities include:

- vast heterogeneity among students' needs and performance levels
- wide differences in ability from individuals without disabilities, making the reliable and valid use of common tests questionable
- lack of experience with test performances, thus eroding the reliability and validity of common tests when used with individuals with disabilities

Oververbalizing or not clearly verbalizing what is expected from an individual with disabilities can lead to testing problems and lack of valid and reliable data. For example, tell a child with a language disability to "run as fast as you can" and you probably will not get a valid response. The child is language disabled, not deaf, so you will get a response. However, because the child can not relate to the meaning of "as fast as you can," the response may not be a true indication of how fast the child can really run. This disability requires that there be a beginning and an end to a task and that the child not be required to draw relationships like "as fast as you can."

Limitations of Tests. Often individuals with disabilities do not stay on task and are not likely to give maximum exertion (as are young individuals without disabilities) because they may not understand why or how to give it, or do not understand the test protocol. For these reasons many field-based physical fitness batteries for individuals with disabilities do not have a valid item for aerobic capacity. The aerobic capacity tests commonly used with individuals with disabilities are distance run, step test, arm cranking, and wheelchair push. Each test has varying degrees of validity and applicability for an individual with disabilities. Certainly no single test could be used on all individuals with disabilities.

The most common aerobic capacity test is a distance run for time (6, 9, or 12 minutes) or distance (600, 880, or 1760 yards). Pizarro (1982) reported that 14- to 18-year-old individuals with mild and moderate mental retardation did not identify well with abstract concepts like run for time. Fifty percent of his individuals with mental retardation failed to complete the 9-minute run, and 70% of his individuals either quit running, walked, or completed less than 1000 yards. So, he substituted the 880-yard run, with individuals running from the starting line 440 yards out to a marker and then back to the starting line. He used this very goal-oriented task because the individuals had trouble staying on task when running around a track or for longer distances. He still found the 880-yard run questionable for individuals with mild mental retardation and not appropriate for individuals with moderate mental retardation because they walked too much. A distance run for time maintains students' dignity better because everyone finishes at the same time.

Exercise physiologists probably would say the 880-yard run is too short a distance to measure aerobic capacity and would recommend a run of at least a mile. The distance used should be dependent on the characteristics and abilities of the individual with disabilities being tested. The distance must be long enough to tax the cardiorespiratory system but not so long that extraneous factors like attention span and motivation influence the individual's performance and reduce test validity. Heart-rate monitors that are worn can be used to determine if a person is reaching an aerobic level of exercise. One of the issues here, as it affects the valid measurement of nearly any attribute, is practice and cognition. Unless the individual knows how to do the task and understands what is asked of him or her, it will be very difficult to get a valid measure. Sometimes this takes months of training, not just 3 trials. Just as with any short-term task, you need to be sure you are measuring aerobic capacity and not learning, cognition, or language acquisition.

The 6-minute run has been used with individuals with disabilities. Further, Disch, Frankiewicz, and Jackson (1975) found the 6-minute run to be a cardiorespiratory test rather than a speed test. The goal of selecting a single performance test that validly measures aerobic capacity for individuals with a variety of disabilities is a challenge. It is imperative that the performance demands the level of intensity within the range determined to be appropriate for the individual participant. For individuals who have all their faculties to move—that is, arms, legs, age-appropriate cognition—a single method of measurement is possible to obtain. For individuals with disabilities, who are variably limited in cognitive, language, or physical abilities, a single method of measurement is not possible to select. Current trends dictate that functional capacity be used to determine the aerobic range of activity either through the use of target heart rate (THR), rating of perceived exertion (RPE), and/or estimated energy expenditure defined in METs or oxygen consumption. Regardless of which performance measure is selected, the use of electronic monitoring devices noted above would be helpful in assuring that the students are reaching an acceptable level of exertion to qualify as a measure of aerobic capacity. The half-mile run has been used if a child is under 8 years of age.

Finding tests appropriate for individuals with disabilities is not easy. Many tests presented in adapted physical education books are designed to test one individual at a time and often require special equipment and teacher expertise. These tests seldom will be appropriate for mass testing. Other tests are nothing more than tests for individuals without disabilities with norms for individuals with disabilities. The validity and reliability of these tests for individuals with disabilities must be determined and then maybe norms for the individuals developed. If these tests prove to be valid and reliable, then they can be used to measure an individual's progress or improvement even if norms are not developed.

Forbus (1990) investigated the suitability and reliability of the Physical Best fitness test items with individuals with learning disabilities (LD), individuals with mild mental retardation (MiMR), individuals with moderate mental retardation (MoMR), and individuals without disabilities (ND). (The Physical Best test has been discontinued, but the items were nearly identical to those in FITNESSGRAM®.) Individuals were 11 to 15 years old. There were 25 males and 25 females from each of the four groups. Significant differences in mean score were found among all groups on each item of the Physical Best test. All of the reliability coefficients were at least .80 except for the pull-up and sit-and-reach tests for females in the MoMR and MiMR groups and the sit-up test for the LD group. Forbus concluded that the sit-and-reach test and the skinfolds test are suitable for all four groups. The sit-up test is not suitable for children with MoMR. The pull-up test is not suitable for children with MoMR, MiMR, and LD. The 1-mile-run/walk test is not suitable for children with MoMR and MiMR. Overall, he concluded that the Physical Best test should not be used with individuals with mental retardation. Alternative tests or modifications should be used when assessing the health-related physical fitness of individuals with mental retardation.

The health and physical fitness test in the Kansas Adapted/Special Physical Education Test Manual (Johnson & Lavay 1988) is one example of what seems to be a good test for many individuals with disabilities. Means and reliability coefficients for individuals 5–21 years of age can be found in Appendix D of Eichstaedt and Lavay (1992). In developing the manual, Johnson and Lavay used the concept of the non-classification approach to testing students. The test manual may be used with the majority of individuals with disabilities in school systems, regardless of their disability. Validity and reliability of test items were addressed.

The health and physical fitness items in the Kansas test are sit-ups as an indication of abdominal strength and endurance, sit-and-reach as an indication of lower back and hamstring flexibility, isometric push-ups (children under 13 years of age) or bench pressing a 35-pound barbell (children 13 years of age or older) as an indication of upper body strength and endurance, and aerobic movement as an indication of cardiovascular endurance. In the last test item the students may jog, march, walk with vigorous arm movement, propel themselves in a wheelchair or other appliance, ride an exercise bike, or move in any way to elevate the heart rate to 140–180 beats per minute for 12 minutes. The score of a student is the number of minutes this rate can be maintained (not to exceed 12 minutes) after 6 minutes of warm-up.

Several nationally distributed fitness tests for youth discussed in chapter 10 (FITNESSGRAM®, Chrysler Fund-AAU) have addressed testing individuals with disabilities. Modifications of these tests may be appropriate for many individuals with disabilities. Many of the alternative items in FITNESSGRAM® are very good because they require no modifications to test individuals with disabilities.

Summary

Whether you develop your own test or select a preconstructed test, which is certainly easier, you will require certain attributes in the instrument. It is these characteristics that make the measurement procedure both efficient and meaningful.

Although the successful administration of a test depends on many factors, the key to success is good planning in the pretest stage and attention to the details of that planning during and after the testing procedure.

Both physical educators and exercise scientists will be responsible for testing individuals with disabilities. In order to obtain reliable and valid scores, the tests and test procedures must be carefully selected.

Formative Evaluation of Objectives

Objective 1 Identify the important characteristics of a test.

1. The text discusses many important attributes of a test. In addition to reliability, objectivity, and validity, what are several of these attributes?
2. Certain characteristics listed in the text relate to the individuals taking the tests, while others act simply to make the procedure more efficient. What are the subject-related attributes?

Objective 2 Plan the administration of a test.

1. The success of a testing program depends on how well the pretest planning is carried out. What type of planning and procedures would you use to administer the following tests?
   a. A timed bent-knee sit-up test
   b. A pull-up test
   c. A 1-mile-run test or some other cardiovascular test

Objective 3 Identify problems in measuring individuals with disabilities.

1. What are five problems in measuring individuals with disabilities no matter what the disability?

Additional Learning Activities

1. From the material in this book and other physical education measurement tests, develop a summary of test characteristics and a checklist of pretest planning procedures.
2. Select a test with which you are unfamiliar and administer it to individuals with and without disabilities following the pretest, administrative, and posttest procedures outlined in the text.

Bibliography

ACSM. 1986. *Guidelines for exercise testing and prescription.* 3d ed. Philadelphia, PA: Lea & Febiger.

Auxter, D., J. Pyfer and C. Huettig. 1993. *Principles and methods of adapted physical education and recreation.* St. Louis, MO: Mosby-Year Book.

Disch, J., R. Frankiewicz and A. Jackson. 1975. Construct validation of distance run tests. *Research Quarterly* 46:169–176.

Eichstaedt, C. B. and B. W. Lavay. 1992. *Physical activity for individuals with mental retardation.* Champaign, IL: Human Kinetics.

Forbus, W. R., III. 1990. The suitability and reliability of the Physical Best fitness test with selected special populations. Ed. D. dissertation, University of Georgia, Athens, GA.

Girardi, G. 1971. A comparison of isokinetic exercises with isometric and isotonic exercises in the development of strength and endurance. P.E.D. dissertation, Indiana University.

Johnson, R. E. and B. Lavay. 1988. *Kansas adapted/special physical education test manual: Health related fitness and psychomotor testing.* Topeka, KS: Kansas State Department of Education.

Pizarro, D. C. 1982. Health-related fitness of mainstreamed emr/tmr children. Ed. D. dissertation, University of Georgia, Athens, GA.

Seaman, J. A. (Ed.) 1995. *Physical best and individuals with disabilities: A handbook for inclusion in fitness programs.* Reston, VA: AAHPERD.

U.S. 94th Congress. 1975. Public Law 94–142. Washington, DC: Authors.

7

CHAPTER

Measuring Physical Abilities

Contents

Key Words

absolute endurance
agility
balance
basic physical ability
classification index
closed kinetic chain
flexibility
general motor ability
isokinetic strength
isometric strength
isotonic strength
kinesthesis
motor educability
motor skill
muscular endurance
muscular power
muscular strength
open kinetic chain
power
speed

Objectives

Physical educators have long accepted the idea of generality—a general test can be used to predict an individual's capacity to perform a wide range of athletic or motor skills. The **Classification Index** derived from age, height and weight, general motor ability, and motor educability tests was used to measure generality, but it has not proven to be valid. The theory of basic physical abilities does provide a sound model for testing generality. The theory provides the foundation for many different testing programs, the most prominent being adult and youth fitness, testing athletes, and preemployment testing programs for physically demanding jobs. Chapters 10 and 11 cover youth and adult fitness testing, while athletic and preemployment testing is in this chapter. Back injuries are a major problem of industrial workers. One causal factor of industrial back problems is the lack of physical ability to do the work task. This chapter provides data on the role of strength in the risk of back injuries. Finally, this chapter provides common physical ability tests and normative data.

After reading Chapter 7 you should be able to:

1. Describe the tests that historically have been used to measure generality.
2. Apply the theory of basic physical abilities to the evaluation of athletes.
3. Identify the methods to develop preemployment tests for physically demanding jobs and the types of tests that compose preemployment batteries.
4. Understand the influence of physical abilities on the risk of back injuries.
5. Identify basic physical abilities and tests that validly measure each ability.

History of Generality Testing

The assumption of the concept of generality is that the performance of many different motor tasks can be predicted from a single or limited number of tests. The principle of generality can be traced to the work of Sargent (1921), who first reported a test of generality. The Sargent Physical Test of Man simply measures the height of a vertical jump, on the assumption that a single test is sufficient to measure motor ability. This assumption paralleled the concept of generality once accepted by psychologists, who felt that a g-factor, or general factor of intelligence, was adequate to represent human intellectual ability. While the intellectual g-factor is important, we now understand that there are several different intellectual factors.

The purpose of generality tests was to provide a method by which it would be possible to predict an individual's performance on a wide range of motor activities from a simple test battery. Several types of tests have been used by physical educators to measure generality, but their validity has not been established. Table 7.1 provides a brief overview of these tests.

In the late 1950s, Franklin Henry (1956, 1958) advanced the memory-drum theory of neuromotor reaction, claiming that motor ability is specific to a task rather than general to many tasks. In other words, a student's performance on one **motor skill** is of little or no value in predicting performance on a different task. By his theory, Henry claims that there is no such thing as **general motor ability;** rather, each individual possesses many specific motor abilities. A student who scores well on a general motor test is gifted with several specific abilities, whereas a student who scores poorly has only a few neural patterns stored on his or her memory drum. The theory of specificity casts doubt on the validity of general motor ability and **motor educability** tests and is largely responsible for the demise of these tests.

Table 7.1 A Historical Overview of Generality Tests Used in Physical Education

Generality Test	Type of Tests	Comments
Age-height-weight classification index (McCloy 1932)	Age, height, and weight	The classification index was a multiple regression equation that provided an index of maturity. Most tests are normed on the basis of age and gender. The index does not add any additional information.
Motor educability (McCloy & Young 1954)	Consisted of several gymnastic "stunt-like" tasks	The tests supposedly measured the ability to learn motor skills easily and well. The validity was never established. Motor educability tests have not been shown to correlate with the capacity to learn motor skills.
Motor ability (Barrow 1954; Scott 1939)	Jumping, throwing tests, running tests (speed and agility)	Purported to measure acquired and innate ability to perform motor skills. Lost support with the development of Henry's memory-drum theory.

Certainly, physical education teachers and exercise specialists must acknowledge the theory of specificity; however, complete acceptance of the theory would signal the need to measure all the specifics that enter the complex domain of motor skills. In fact, the practice of using physical abilities tests is on the rise. Testing programs for athletes are becoming common practice at public school, college, and professional levels. Physical abilities tests are now used to screen applicants for physically demanding jobs such as a firefighter or coal miner. Physical abilities tests not only provide a means to evaluate athletic potential and a job applicant's capacity to meet the demands of physically demanding work tasks, but also identify those most at risk of injury when performing physically demanding work.

Theory of Basic Abilities

The theory of **basic physical abilities** described by Edwin Fleishman (1964) is especially useful for generality testing because individual performance of a specific motor skill is explained in terms of a relatively small number of psychomotor abilities. His theory is based on research conducted for the U.S. Air Force, in which tests of psychomotor abilities were found valid for predicting the subsequent performance of various air crew members (Fleishman 1956).

Fleishman, a leading industrial/organizational psychologist, distinguishes between psychomotor skills and psychomotor abilities, but considers both essential and complementary. A psychomotor skill is one's level of proficiency on a specific task or limited group of tasks. Dribbling a basketball, catching a softball, swimming the sidestroke, and playing the piano are examples of very different psychomotor skills. Learning a psychomotor skill involves acquiring the sequence of responses that results in a coordinated performance of the task. A psychomotor ability is a more general trait that may be common to many psychomotor tasks. For example, being able to run fast enhances one's ability to excel in several different specific motor skills athletic events, such as playing football, performing the running long jump, or playing basketball.

Fleishman describes the relationship between basic physical abilities and motor skills as follows:

> The assumption is that the skills involved in complex activities can be described in terms of the more basic physical abilities. For example, the level of performance a man can attain on a turret lathe may depend on his basic physical abilities of manual dexterity and motor coordination. However, these same basic physical abilities may be important to proficiency in other skills as well. Thus, manual dexterity is needed in assembling electrical components, and motor coordination is needed to fly an airplane. Implicit in the previous analysis is the relation between abilities and learning. Thus, individuals with high manual dexterity may more readily learn the specific skill of lathe operation. (1964)

Basic physical abilities are measured with many types of tests, and individuals differ in the extent to which they possess an ability (e.g., some people run faster than others). An individual with many highly developed basic physical abilities can become proficient at a wide variety of specific motor skills. For example, the "all-around" athlete is a person who has many highly developed basic physical abilities important to many different sports. Then, too, certain basic physical abilities are more generalized than others. For example, in our culture, verbal abilities are important in a greater variety of tasks than are many other abilities. Certainly speed, jumping ability, and muscular strength are important basic physical abilities related to athletic success. Both the rate of learning and the final level of skill achieved depend on an individual's level of achievement in the more basic physical abilities.

The development of basic physical abilities is a product of both genetic and environmental influences, with the genetic factor the limiting condition. Consider, for example, muscular strength. By participating in weight-training programs, we can greatly influence the development of muscular strength; but the limit of that development (the maximum strength) depends on our genetics. Basic physical abilities develop during childhood and adolescence, reaching a fairly stable level in adulthood.

Because an ability is a lasting, stable pattern of behavior, individual differences in basic physical abilities make it possible to predict the subsequent performance of specific skills. For example, the SAT measures verbal and quantitative abilities. Using a student's score on the quantitative ability section would be predictive of success in programs such as engineering, where math skills are very important, but not predictive of success in nonmathematical majors such as English. In this same way, running speed is an important factor in the running long jump; on the basis of a student's speed, we could judge better how well he or she will do on the long jump. Former Olympic champion long jumper Carl Lewis was in a class of his own due to his world-class sprinting speed. He won medals in both the long jump and 100-meter dash.

Basic abilities are identified with the statistical method called factor analysis. This involves administering several different tests to a large sample of subjects. Typically, some tests are highly correlated with each other, but not correlated with others. Factor analysis identifies the groups of tests that are correlated with each other, and it is assumed that each test measures a common trait termed a factor.[1] In psychology, the factor is termed a "construct." The tests associated with the factor have construct validity—that is, the test is significantly correlated with the factor or construct. According to the theory, a basic ability is a construct. Numerous factor analysis studies have been published that identify basic motor performance abilities (Baumgartner & Zuidema 1972; Bernauer & Bonanno 1975; Considine et al. 1976; Cousins 1955; Cumbee 1954; Disch, Frankiewicz, & Jackson 1975; Fleishman 1964; Harris 1969; Ismail, Falls, & MacLeod 1965; Jackson 1971; Jackson & Frankiewicz 1975; Jackson & Pollock 1976; Larson 1941; Liba 1967; McCloy 1956; Meyers et al. 1984; Safrit 1966; Zuidema & Baumgartner 1974). The interested reader is directed to these sources for detailed coverage of this technique. Table 7.2 provides summary of these basic abilities.

Basic physical abilities tests have at least two important applications: first, for evaluating athletes, and second, for use as preemployment tests in physically demanding jobs. Additionally, strength, and endurance are believed to be associated with the risk of low-back injury. These topics are presented next.

Application 1—Testing Athletes

The testing of athletes has become an accepted procedure. Before the 1976 Olympics, sport scientists studied the psychological, physiological, biomechanical, and medical characteristics of twenty world-class distance runners (Pollock et al. 1978). Prior to the unification of Germany, the East German Olympic team, which had been very successful in Olympic competition, conducted an extensive testing program for its athletes. Several years before its 1978 Super Bowl victory, the Dallas Cowboys team had developed a scientific program for evaluating and training its football players. Today, all major university and professional football teams hire a full-time strength coach who is responsible for testing and training athletes. The United States Olympic Committee developed a central facility for testing athletes in Colorado Springs, Colorado. This facility is fully staffed with exercise scientists who provide comprehensive testing of athletes. These data are given to the athlete and coach and used to improve training and performance.

The important concern is to find the physical abilities that are most relevant to the demands placed on an athlete. The more specific the test, the more valid it will be. At the U.S. Olympic testing site, for example, different exercise modes are used to measure aerobic capacity ($\dot{V}O_2$ Max). For distance runners, a treadmill-running protocol is followed; in contrast, specially devised cycle ergometer protocols are used to evaluate cyclists. The physical ability tests that are most appropriate for evaluating athletes are:

- Aerobic capacity or $\dot{V}O_2$ Max (see Chapter 8)
- Body composition, either percent body fat or weight partitioned into fat weight and fat-free weight (see Chapter 9)
- Muscular strength
- Power
- Running speed, typically 40- or 50-yard dash

---

[1]The interested reader is directed to a body composition factor analysis study (Jackson & Pollock 1976) that provides a clear analysis that demonstrates this statistical methodology.

Table 7.2 Summary of Basic Gross Motor Basic Abilities

Basic Ability	Description
Strength, Power, and Endurance Abilities	
Muscular strength	The maximum force that a muscle group can exert over a brief period. Isometric, isotonic, and isokinetic tests are used to measure strength.
Muscular power	Power is the rate that work is performed. Ergometers are used to measure arm and leg power.
Endurance Abilities	
Muscular endurance	The ability to persist in physical activity or to resist muscular fatigue. Pull-ups and sit-ups are common tests used to measure endurance.
Cardiorespiratory endurance	The capacity to perform exhausting work. This is also termed maximal oxygen uptake, aerobic fitness, and VO_2 Max (see Chapter 8).
Basic Movement Patterns	
Running speed	Capacity to move rapidly. Measured by short runs, 10 to 60 yards in length.
Running agility	The ability to change the direction of the body or body parts rapidly. Measured by standard tests such as the shuttle run.
Jumping ability	The ability to expend maximum energy in one explosive act, projecting the body through space. Traditionally measured with the standing long jump and vertical jump.
Throwing ability	The capacity to throw a relatively light ball (baseball, softball, etc.) overarm for distance.
Neuromuscular Abilities	
Flexibility	The range of movement about a joint. Flexibility tends to be task specific, there being many different types of flexibility. Someone flexible at one joint may not be flexible in others.
Balance	The ability to maintain body position. Traditionally measured with static and dynamic balance tests.
Kinesthetic perception	The ability to perceive the body's position in space and the relationship of its parts. This important ability is very difficult to measure reliably.

- Vertical or standing long jump
- Agility run test that duplicates the athlete's movement patterns

We would suggest following six steps when developing a battery for evaluating athletes:

1. Consider the sport and the basic qualities it demands of the athlete. For example, jumping ability would be especially important for volleyball and basketball players, and VO_2 Max for endurance athletes, such as long-distance runners.

Table 7.3 Percentile-Rank Norms for High School and College Female Volleyball Players

	High School Players				College Players				
Percentile	*Height*	*Vertical Jump*	*20-Yard Dash*	*Basketball Throw*	*Height*	*Vertical Jump*	*20-Yard Dash*	*Basketball Throw*	*%Fat*
99	74.0	22.0	2.87	70.8	77.0	24.0	2.83	82.3	11.2
95	71.0	18.5	3.04	64.5	72.0	20.5	3.00	68.5	12.3
90	70.0	17.8	3.12	60.0	71.0	19.8	3.07	66.8	12.6
85	69.0	16.5	3.17	57.0	70.0	19.0	3.12	64.0	13.2
80	68.0	16.0	3.20	55.0	69.5	18.5	3.16	61.2	13.5
75	67.5	15.7	3.23	52.8	69.0	18.0	3.17	59.4	14.0
70	67.0	15.3	3.26	51.5	68.5	17.5	3.20	58.3	14.4
65	66.5	15.0	3.28	50.5	68.5	17.0	3.27	57.6	14.6
60	66.0	14.5	3.32	49.0	68.0	16.8	3.30	56.6	15.1
55	65.5	14.2	3.34	48.4	67.5	16.5	3.33	56.1	15.5
50	65.5	14.0	3.37	47.2	67.5	16.0	3.37	55.0	16.0
45	65.5	13.7	3.42	46.0	67.0	15.8	3.40	53.9	16.5
40	65.0	13.5	3.46	44.5	67.0	15.5	3.42	52.3	17.5
35	65.0	13.3	3.47	43.5	66.0	15.0	3.44	51.1	18.2
30	64.0	13.0	3.50	42.0	66.0	14.7	3.50	51.0	18.8
25	64.0	12.5	3.53	40.8	65.5	14.0	3.53	50.1	20.5
20	63.0	12.3	3.57	39.2	65.0	13.5	3.60	48.7	21.5
15	62.5	12.0	3.60	37.8	64.0	12.7	3.67	46.6	22.9
10	62.0	11.5	3.67	36.4	63.5	11.5	3.73	45.8	26.0
5	61.5	11.0	3.80	33.5	62.5	10.5	3.83	41.2	31.3

*Percent body fat was not determined for high school players. See Chapter 11 for methods and norms appropriate for high school girls.
Source: Data used with the permission of Dr. James G. Disch, Associate Professor of Physical Education, Rice University, Houston, TX.

2. Select tests that measure these defined traits. The tests may be found in Chapters 7 through 11.
3. Administer the tests to as many athletes as possible.
4. From their scores, develop percentile-rank norms using the procedures furnished in Chapter 2.
5. Use these norms to evaluate your athletes. The criterion for comparison here also can be earlier data on outstanding athletes, allowing you to evaluate your athletes with both the norm and outstanding players.
6. Reevaluate your selection of tests to be sure you are measuring the abilities most relevant to the sport. You should see a tendency for the best athletes to achieve the highest scores.

Provided in Tables 7.3 and 7.4 are sample test batteries used for college football players and female volleyball players. A profile for an athlete can be obtained by simply plotting his or her score on the table. In this way an athlete's strengths and weaknesses become apparent. The performance expectations of defined groups of football players are different, so profiles for defined subgroups of players are also provided on the team norms. The subgroup profile is the mean of all players in that subgroup. The subgroups shown in Table 7.4 are backs and linemen. Thus, an athlete's profile can be

Table 7.4 Percentile-Rank Norms for University Football Players

Percentile	0–5 Yards	20–40 Yards	0–40 Yards	%Fat	Bench Press	
99	0.985	1.933	4.412	4.1	422	
95	1.029	1.995	4.626	6.5	389	
90	1.052	2.028	4.737	7.7	376	
85	1.067	2.049	4.812	8.7	360	
80	1.080	2.067	4.903	9.2	350	LINEMEN
75	1.091	2.083	4.926	9.8	342	
70	1.101	2.096	4.973	10.3	335	
65	1.109	2.108	5.013	10.7	329	
60	1.118	2.121	5.057	11.3	322	
55	1.126	2.131	5.094	11.6	316	
50	1.134	2.143	5.134	12.0	310	
45	1.142	2.155	5.174	12.3	304	
40	1.150	2.166	5.212	12.7	298	
35	1.159	2.178	5.255	13.2	291	
30	1.167	2.190	5.295	13.6	285	BACKS
25	1.177	2.203	5.342	14.1	278	
20	1.188	2.219	5.394	14.6	270	
15	1.201	2.237	5.456	15.1	260	
10	1.216	2.258	5.531	15.9	244	
5	1.239	2.291	5.642	16.9	231	
1	1.283	2.353	5.856	18.8	198	

Source: Data used with the permission of William F. Yeoman, former Head Football Coach, University of Houston, Houston, TX.

compared to the entire team and any subgroup. The University of Houston players who have gone on to play professional football have all been faster, stronger, and leaner than the average for their respective subgroup. This lends credence to the system.

Percentile-rank norms allow us to plot the athletes' test scores individually in a profile that we can then examine to determine whether an athlete shows a performance level compatible to that needed for a given sport. The profile is more than an evaluative technique that shows variation from the general trend; it provides empirical evidence for designing a training program as well. For example, assume that a profile shows an athlete with a higher level of body fat than average. With this information, the coach can initiate an individualized diet and exercise program for the athlete. The profile provides both the coach and the athlete with an objective means of designing an individualized training program and motivating the athlete. Plotting retests can be used to gauge progress. And finally, the profile may give a coach insight into an athlete's potential.

Application 2—Preemployment Testing

Employers have always used some method to select an employee among potential job applicants. Much of the early preemployment testing focused on cognitive abilities, but with the rise in women seeking jobs that were once male dominated, the need for preemployment physical abilities tests increased. Most major fire and police departments require applicants to pass a physical ability test. Other occupations that use preemployment tests are telephone craft workers who climb poles, steel workers, coal miners, chemical plant workers, electrical transmission lineworkers, military personnel, oil field production workers, and freight handlers. You are directed to other sources for a more complete discussion (Hogan 1991; Jackson 1994).

There are at least three reasons physical ability tests are used as a condition for employment. First, a legal issue: equal employment opportunity legislation resulted in greater numbers of females and handicapped individuals seeking employment in occupations requiring high levels of physical ability. Second, risk of injury: there was evidence suggesting that physically unfit workers had higher incidences of low-back injuries. Third, inadequacy of medical examinations: preemployment medical evaluations used alone are inadequate for personnel selection for a physically demanding job (Campion 1983). With the passage of the Americans with Disabilities Act (July 26, 1992), medical examinations cannot be given until an offer of employment is made. Any medically disqualifying condition must be shown to be job-related. One possible consequence of ADA is that validated physical ability tests will play a greater role in employee selection.

Legal Issues. Preemployment tests face potential legal review because physical ability[2] tests are likely to have an adverse impact against females and ethnic groups such as Asians and Hispanics (Hogan 1991). Public safety jobs (firefighters, police officers, and correctional officers) have been the target of sex discrimination litigation, and they have not fared well. You are directed to other sources for a review of legal issues (Arvey & Faley 1988; Arvey et al. 1992; Hogan & Quigley 1986).

In the 1960s and 1970s, height and weight standards were a condition of employment of most public safety workers. Since women and some ethnic groups (e.g., Asians and Hispanics) are shorter and lighter, a lower proportion of them met the standard. Arvey and Faley (1988) reported that in 1973, nearly all the nation's large police departments had a minimum height requirement. The average requirement was 68 inches. More than 90% of the women but only 45% of the males failed the 68-inch height requirement. The rational used to defend the standard was that size was related to physical strength, and the effectiveness of an officer's job performance depended upon strength. The United States Supreme Court ruled that if strength is a real job requirement, then a direct measure of strength should have been adopted. The height and weight standards of public safety jobs are being replaced with physical ability tests.

Preemployment Test Methodology. If hiring practices produce adverse impact such as was the case with a height requirement, federal law requires that a validation study must support the selection method. The steps involved in a validation study are (1) complete a task analysis; (2) validate the selected tests; and (3) establish cut scores. Each is briefly reviewed next.

Broadly defined, a job analysis is the collection and analysis of any type of job-related information by any method for any purpose (Gael 1988). The objective of a job analysis is to find measures of work behavior(s) or performance that are used for the job and find the extent that they represent critical or important job duties, work behaviors, or work outcomes (EEOC 1978). Task analyses of physically demanding jobs often follow one or more of the following approaches.

---

[2]Some governmental literature uses the term "physical agility." The term *physical ability* will be used in this document.

Psychophysical Methods. This method involves developing a scale that can be used to rate the frequency and intensity of physical demands required by various work tasks. The scale is administered to several employees who are engaged in these work tasks. This provides data by which work tasks can be compared. In a recent study, employees rated the task of lifting boxes that weigh over 60 pounds to shoulder height more demanding than lifting them to waist height.

Biomechanical Methods. The types of data collected include heights, weights of the objects lifted or transported, and forces needed to complete work tasks such as opening and closing valves, or pushing and pulling objects. Biomechanical models provide a means of evaluating the stresses placed on the spine by the tasks of materials handling and lifting (NIOSH 1981; Waters et al. 1993).

Physiological Methods. Work tasks such as climbing stairs and fighting fires have a significant aerobic endurance component. Physiological methods document the cardiovascular response of these work tasks. For example, heart rate response when working provides an index of a work task's level of physical demands.

Validation Methods. The failure to conduct a valid task analysis is a major reason preemployment physical ability tests have been ruled by the courts to be illegal (Arvey & Faley 1988; Hogan & Quigley 1986). The task analysis becomes the framework for developing and validating a preemployment test. Validating a preemployment test involves determining the accuracy with which a test or other selection device measures the important work behaviors identified with the job analysis. There are three validation strategies that can be followed.

Criterion-Related Validity. A criterion-related validity study has data showing that the preemployment test is predictive of, or significantly correlated with, important elements of job performance. The concurrent approach uses current employees and relates tests to current job performance. In the predictive approach, test data are obtained on people prior to hire and compared with performance data obtained at a later date (EEOC 1978).

Content Validity. This is a rational process that involves gathering evidence that shows a logical relationship between the preemployment test and important duties or job behaviors. A content validity study needs to present data showing that the content of the selection procedure represents important aspects of performance on the job for which the candidates are to be evaluated (EEOC 1978). To illustrate, a typing test is a content-valid test to hire a person for jobs involving typing, but not content valid for something like shoveling coal.

Construct Validity. This approach is more theoretical than content validity because it is necessary to establish that a construct is required for job success and that the selection device measures the same construct. The data from a construct validation study should show that the preemployment test measures the degree to which candidates have identifiable characteristics that are important for successful job performance (EEOC 1978).

Figure 7.1
Common work-sample tests included in police officer and firefighter preemployment tests (Arvey and Faley 1988). The content validity of the test is judged to the extent that the test can be shown it is job-related.

POLICE OFFICERS

- Scaling a wall, usually 6 feet in height
- Long jumping a set distance
- Crawling through openings at ground level
- Running a set distance, usually a quarter mile
- Dragging a heavy object a set distance
- Running a course consisting of various obstacles

FIRE FIGHTERS

- Climbing a ladder
- Pushing and pulling a ceiling hook
- Dragging a dummy a set distance or time period
- Running up stairs carrying hose bundles

Types of Employment Tests. There are two general types of preemployment tests: (1) work-sample tests; and (2) physical ability tests. The advantage of work-sample tests is that they simulate the actual working conditions and are more likely to have content validity. Lifting and carrying boxes a specified distance is an example of a materials handling work-sample test. Arvey (1992) reported that many police and firefighter physical ability tests consist of some combination of job sample tests. Figure 7.1 lists work-sample tests commonly included in these public safety preemployment tests.

While work-sample tests have the advantage of appearing to be valid, Ayoub (1982) maintains that they have at least two limitations. The first is safety. Applicants seeking employment are likely to be highly motivated to pass the work-sample test. A highly motivated applicant that lacks the physical capacity to perform the task is likely to increase the risk of injury (Chaffin 1974; Chaffin, Herrin, & Keyserling 1978; Keyserling et al. 1980a; Keyserling et al. 1980b; Snook, Campanelli, & Hart 1978). Outdoor telephone craft jobs require employees to climb telephone poles, and accident data showed that this was a dangerous task (Reilly, Zedeck, & Tenopyr 1979). Using a pole climbing test to screen applicants would have content validity but likely would be too dangerous for untrained or physically unfit employees.

A second limitation of job simulation tests is they do not give any information about the applicant's maximum work capacity (Ayoub 1982). A work-sample test is often scored by pass or fail—for example, lifting a 95-pound jackhammer and carrying it a specified distance. Some can easily complete the test, while others may just pass and be working at their maximum. If it can be assumed that there is a linear relationship between job performance and the preemployment test performance, applicants with the highest test scores can be expected to be the more productive workers. Testing for maximum capacity not only identifies the potentially most productive workers, but also defines a level of reserve that may reduce the risk of musculoskeletal injury.

Physical ability tests are the second type of items used for preemployment tests. The most common include tests of strength, body composition, and aerobic fitness. Strength tests are the most common item used. A common strategy has been

Table 7.5 Correlations between the Sum of Isometric Strength* and Simulated Work-Sample Tests

Reference Work	Sample Test	Type of Test	r_{xy}
Jackson et al. 1991	Shoveling coal	Dynamic, endurance	0.71
Jackson et al. 1991	50-pound bag carry	Dynamic, endurance	0.63
Jackson & Osburn 1983	70-pound block carry	Dynamic, endurance	0.87
Jackson & Osburn 1983	One-arm push force	Isokinetic, peak torque	0.91
Jackson 1986	Push force	Static, max force	0.86
Jackson et al. 1993	Push force	Static, max force	0.78
Jackson 1986	Pull force	Static, max force	0.78
Jackson et al. 1993	Pull force	Static, max force	0.67
Laughery & Jackson 1984	Lifting force	Static, max force	0.93
Jackson et al. 1992	Valve-turning	Dynamic, endurance	0.83
Jackson et al. 1993	Box transport	Dynamic, endurance	0.76
Jackson et al. 1993	Moving document bags	Dynamic, endurance	0.70
Jackson et al. 1998	Valve cracking	Static, max force	0.91

*Isometric strength tests provided in this chapter.

to relate strength performance to criteria of job success (Reilly, Zedeck, & Tenopyr 1979; Jackson et al. 1998) or work-sample tests (Jackson, Osborn, & Laughery 1984; Jackson, Osborn, & Laughery 1991; Jackson et al. 1990b; Jackson et al. 1992; Jackson et al. 1993; Jackson et al. 1991; Reilly et al. 1979). Table 7.5 lists the correlations we have found between isometric strength tests and work-sample test performance. The isometric strength tests are presented in the later section of this chapter. The correlations in Table 7.5 show that isometric strength tests validly estimate an applicant's potential to perform a variety of work tasks. Interestingly, the isometric strength tests are highly correlated with several different types of tasks—not just those involving maximum force output, but also dynamic tasks performed either to exhaustion or at a "comfortable rate" set by the person being tested. A "blue-ribbon" panel suggested that fat-free weight be used to select military personnel for heavy lifting tasks (Marriott & Grumstrup-Scott 1992). Fat-free weight and strength are highly correlated.

Setting Cut Scores. After completing the validation study, the next, difficult step is to set a cut score. The cut score is the test score that an applicant must obtain to be considered for the job. The Uniform Guidelines merely specify that cut scores should be reasonable and consistent with normal expectations of acceptable proficiency within the work force (EEOC 1978). The cut score should be based on a rational process and valid selection system that is flexible and meets the needs of the organization. Based on legal, historical, and professional guidelines, Cascio and associates (1988) offer several recommendations.

- The cut score should be based upon the results of the job analysis. The validity and job-relatedness of the testing procedure are crucial.
- The cut score should be sufficiently high to ensure minimally accepted job performance.
- The performance level associated with a cut score should be consistent with the normal expectations of acceptable proficiency within the work force.

The strategies used to set cut scores evolved largely from preemployment studies using psychological paper and pencil tests. However, in physical testing, the discipline of work physiology is also used. This involves matching the worker to the physiological demands of the task. Maximum oxygen uptake and strength are the physiological variables used to evaluate a worker's capacity to meet the demands of the job.

A current, important research focus is to define the energy cost needed to fight fires. This research effort can be attributed to litigation leveled at the validity of firefighter preemployment tests and the use of age to terminate employment. Several investigators (Barnard & Duncan 1975; Davis & Dotson 1978; Lemon & Hermiston 1977; Manning & Griggs 1983; O'Connell et al. 1986; Sothmann et al. 1992) published data showing that fire suppression work tasks have a substantial aerobic component. In an excellent study, Sothmann and associates (1990) showed that the minimum $\dot{V}O_2$ Max required to meet the demands of fire fighting is 33.5 ml/kg/min. Firefighters below this level were not able to meet basic demands of fire suppression work.

Using a $\dot{V}O_2$ Max of 33.5 ml/kg/min provides a physiologically sound basis of setting a cut score for firefighters. Strength is a major determinate of physical capacity to perform physically demanding industrial tasks (Hogan 1991; Jackson 1994). Common work simulation strength tests involve testing one's capacity to complete a lift (e.g., lift 75 pounds from floor to knuckle height) and measuring one's maximum force generation capacity (generating force to move an object). Table 7.5 shows that isometric strength is correlated with these work simulation tasks. This provides a means of determining if an applicant has sufficient strength to meet the demands of the work task. Provided next are two examples that use regression analysis to define equations that can be used to define the level of strength required by the work task.

Pass-Fail Tests. Lifting and transporting objects (e.g., valves, boxes) is a common physically demanding work task. If a 75-pound load must be lifted and transported, a worker must have sufficient strength to complete the task. The results of the studies summarized in Table 7.5 show that strength is highly correlated with many industrial work-sample tasks. In a recent study (Jackson et al. 1998), the task analysis documented that a physically demanding task was to lift a valve that weighed 75 pounds from the floor and place it on the back of truck. This is a basic floor to knuckle height lift. A work-sample test was developed to simulate the lifting task. The work-sample test involved lifting weights that became progressively heavier until the person's physical limit was reached (i.e., they could not lift the weight). As the load got heavier, a higher percentage of individuals were not able to lift the weight. Figure 7.2 shows the method used to identify the chances that workers were able to complete various lift weights by level of isometric strength. The method, logic regression analysis (Hosmer & Lemeshow 1989), provides the probability that a person with a given level of strength would be able to lift the weight. For example, nearly 90% of individuals with 200 pounds of strength would be able to lift a 60-pound load, but only about 30% would be able to lift 90 pounds. The data in Figure 7.2 shows that lift capacity demanded by a job is a function of strength. The graphs provided an empirical basis of defining the level of strength required by the job. This provides the basis for developing a physiologically acceptable cut score.

Continuously Scored Tests. A task analysis showed that cracking industrial valves was a physically demanding task required by oil field production workers (Jack-

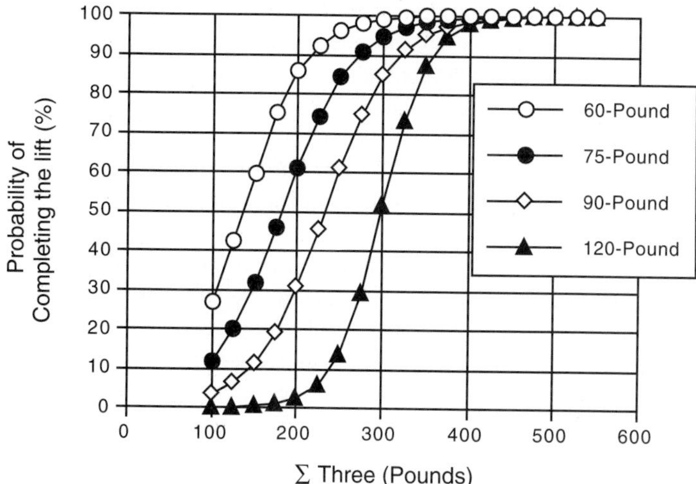

Figure 7.2
Probability curves that define the level of strength needed to lift weights from floor to knuckle height. Logistic regression analysis provides a method to quantify the relationship between dichotomous and continuously scaled variables (Hosmer & Lemeshow 1989). The curves define the level of strength needed to lift the weight. These data document the expected: (1) stronger individuals are more likely to be able to complete the lift; and (2) higher levels of strength are required to lift heavier loads. (Source: CSI Software Company, Houston, TX. Reprinted by permission.)

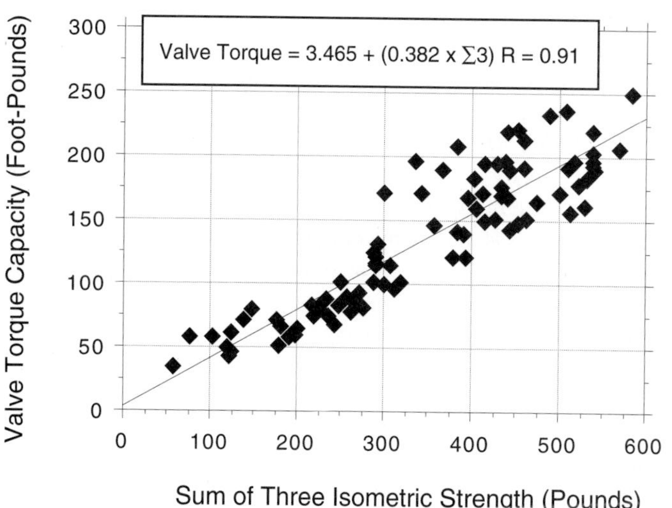

Figure 7.3
Scattergram and simple linear regression equation that defines the relationship between isometric strength and the capacity to generate valve-cracking torque. The torque required to crack oil field valves was measured with an electronic load cell. The regression equation defines the level of strength required to generate the torque required to crack valves that range in difficulty. (Source: CSI Software Company, Houston, TX. Reprinted by permission.)

son 1998). One phase of the task analysis was to go into the oil fields and measure the torque required to crack valves. Work-sample tests were developed to simulate the positions assumed by workers when cracking valves on the job. An electronic torque wrench was used to assess the torque production capacity of both workers and students. Isometric strength was found to be highly correlated ($r = 0.91$) with torque production capacity. Figure 7.3 is a regression plot between the sum of isometric strength and the capacity to generate valve cracking torque (Jackson et al. 1998). Regression equations define the level of strength needed to generate sufficient torque to crack valves. The regression equation can be used to define the level of strength demanded by the work task. To illustrate, Figure 7.3 shows that the maximum valve-cracking capacity of someone with a strength score of 400 pounds is about 150 foot-pounds of torque. If the forces required to perform a task are known, the regression equation can be used to select applicants who have the physical capacity to meet the demands of the task. To illustrate, if 150 foot-pounds is the level of valve-cracking torque demanded by the job, 400 pounds of isometric strength would be a valid cut score.

Application 3—Back Injuries

There is evidence that an individual's level of physical fitness is related to the risk of low-back injury. The youth and adult fitness health-related fitness batteries (Chapters 10 and 11) include test items designed to build strong, flexible backs with the hope of reducing the risk of low-back injuries. Plowman (1992) published a comprehensive review of the research relating fitness and low-back pain. While the medical research is not overwhelming, her review supports the continued use of sit-up and flexibility tests in health-related fitness batteries.

The most convincing research relating physical fitness and back injuries comes from the discipline of ergonomics, the scientific study of work. One conclusion of ergonomic research is the need to match the fitness of the worker with the demands of the job (Chaffin 1974; Chaffin, Andres, & Garg 1983; Chaffin, Herrin, & Keyserling 1978; Chaffin & Park 1973; Herrin, Chaffin, & Mach 1974; Keyserling et al. 1980a; Keyserling et al. 1980b; Snook, Campanelli, & Hart 1978). A goal of preemployment testing is to select workers capable of doing the work without injuring themselves. Reduction of low-back injuries is a primary objective of preemployment testing for physically demanding jobs.

Methods of Reducing Industrial Back Injuries. Back injuries sustained by workers are not only costly to the employee in terms of their health, well-being, and life-style, but also to the employer in terms of workmen compensation and health care costs. The economic costs absorbed by American industry is in the billions of dollars. About 50% of industrial back injuries are caused by lifting (Snook, Campanelli, & Hart 1978). Other major causes are twisting, bending, pushing, and pulling heavy objects. The ergonomic approaches to reducing the risk of industrial back injuries are:

- Redesigning the job
- Education, teaching how to lift "correctly"
- Matching the worker to the job design (i.e., preemployment testing)

The goal of job redesign is to engineer the stress out of the task. This is very effective, but it may not be possible or realistic to redesign the job.[3] The educational approach is to teach workers the "correct way to lift." Teaching people the correct way to lift has not proven to be effective (Dehlin, Hendenrud, & Horal 1976). The "correct" lifting technique taught is the bent-leg position pictured in many different

---

[3] As an example, one of the physically demanding tasks required of gas company construction workers is to transport and use heavy jackhammers. The weight of a steel jackhammer is about 95 pounds. In an effort to reduce the risk, an aluminum jackhammer was developed. While the aluminum jackhammer was much lighter and reduced stress, it could not generate the force required to break concrete, its primary function.

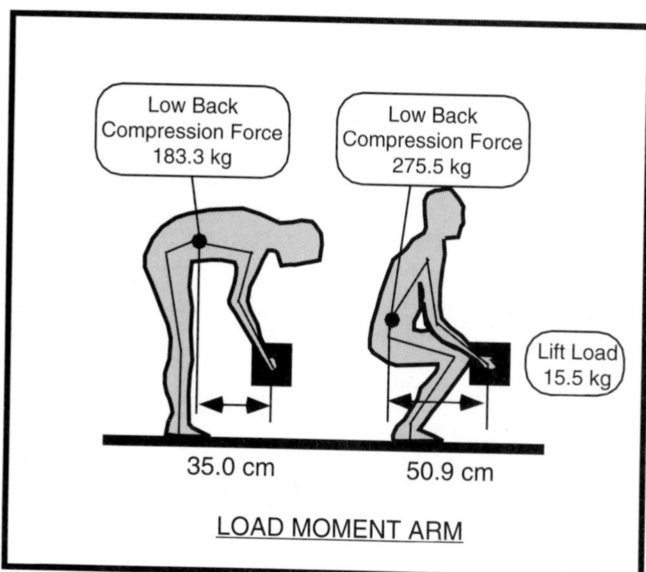

Figure 7.4
Do we know the "best way to lift?" The figure shows the biomechanical low-back stress associated with lifting from the stooped and "classic" bent-leg posture believed to be the "correct" way to lift. Compared to the straight-leg lift, the bent-leg posture increases low-back compression forces because the bending position forces the lifter to hold the load farther away from his low back. This increases the load-moment arm, the distance between the load and low back, and is one of the major sources of stress. Drawn to scale from data published by Park and Chaffin (1974). (Source: Jackson and Ross, R. M. *Understanding Exercise for Health and Fitness,* 1997. Reprinted by permission.)

texts. Biomechanical research by industrial engineers suggests that the classic bent-knee lifting position taught as the "correct" way to lift *may not* be the safest way and even may be more dangerous than lifting with straight legs (Park & Chaffin 1974). Figure 7.4 illustrates this. Lifting with bent legs increases the distance between the lift load and the low back. This distance is the "load-moment arm" and is a major source of stress placed on the low back. Higher levels of stress and low-back compression force increase the risk of back injury (NIOSH 1981; Waters et al. 1993). Quite simply, we may not know what is the "best" or "correct" way to lift.

Psychophysical Ratings and Back Injuries. A key causal factor of low-back injury is the worker's level of physical ability in relation to the lift load. Snook and associates (1978) published the classic epidemiologic study that showed a worker was three times more susceptible to low-back injury if he or she lifted loads that were not acceptable to the industrial population. An acceptable load was psychophysically defined by industrial workers who selected lift weights they could handle "without straining themselves." Snook and associates reported that lifting injuries could be reduced by 67% if workers lifted only loads that could be handled without undue strain (i.e., within the lifter's physical ability). This psychophysical research is a key element of ergonomic equations (NIOSH 1981; Hidalgo et al. 1997; Waters et al. 1993) designed to define acceptable lift loads for workers. The message from this research is clear and simple, if the lift feels "too heavy," do not attempt it, you are more likely to hurt your back.

Snook's psychophysical research is the basis of the publication of "safe" lift loads for industrial workers (Snook & Ciriello 1991). The major factors that affect "safe lift loads" not only include the weight of the load lifted, but also the type of lift, rate of work or number of lifts per minute, and whether one is male or female. The interested

Table 7.6 Correlations between Psychophysical Lift Difficulty and the Sum of Four Isometric Strength Tests

Lift Weight	r_{xy}*	r_{xy}**
30	−0.49	−0.52
45	−0.59	−0.55
60	−0.66	−0.62
75	−0.76	−0.65
85	−0.73	−0.52

Sources: *Jackson 1998; **Jackson et al. 1997

reader is directed to the original study (Snook & Ciriello 1991) for a comprehensive index of acceptable weights for male and female industrial populations.

Worker Strength and Back Injuries. The initial focus of psychophysically defined "safe lift loads" was for male and female industrial populations, not the individual. Industrial populations are extremely variable in strength. While some may be physically able to lift a load within a margin of safety, others are not. This has motivated researchers (Chin, Bishu & Halbeck 1995; Hidalgo et al. 1997; Jackson et al., 1997; Karwowski, 1996; Resnik, 1995) to define acceptable work loads for individuals. This work involves having the lifter rate lift difficulty with Borg's psychophysical rating scales (Borg 1998; Borg 1982; Borg & Ottoson 1986). Chapter 14 provides Borg's psychophysical scales. Research conducted (Jackson et al. 1997; Jackson et al. 1998) at the University of Houston showed that psychophysical lift difficulty was related to strength. Table 7.6 provides the correlations between isometric strength and lift loads ranging from 30 to 85 pounds. The isometric strength tests are described in a later section of the chapter. These data show that psychophysical lift difficulty for these lift loads is correlated with isometric strength level. As one would expect, these lifts are more difficult for weaker individuals. Figure 7.5 graphically illustrates this with floor to knuckle height lift loads ranging from 55 to 85 pounds. Individuals with the lowest levels of strength rate the lifts to be most difficult. There is a growing view that lifts with Borg CR-10 ratings greater than 5 (Heavy) may be unacceptable (Hidalgo et al. 1997; Karwowski 1996). The 55- to 85-pound lifts shown in Figure 7.5 would be too heavy for someone with 200 pounds of isometric strength, but within acceptable levels for individuals with 600 pounds or more of isometric strength.

Ergonomic research (Keyserling et al., 1980; Keyserling, Herrin, & Chaffin 1980) showed that workers with strength capacities below that demanded by the work task were at a higher risk of back injury than those with sufficient strength. Figure 7.6 shows the results of this study. While Keyserling and associates did not use psychophysical methods in their research, they examined work tasks in relation to the worker's maximum isometric strength capacity. These data show that the risk of injury increased as the worker approached their maximum strength capacity. Borg's psychophysical rating scale measures a person's relative intensity—that is, a percentage

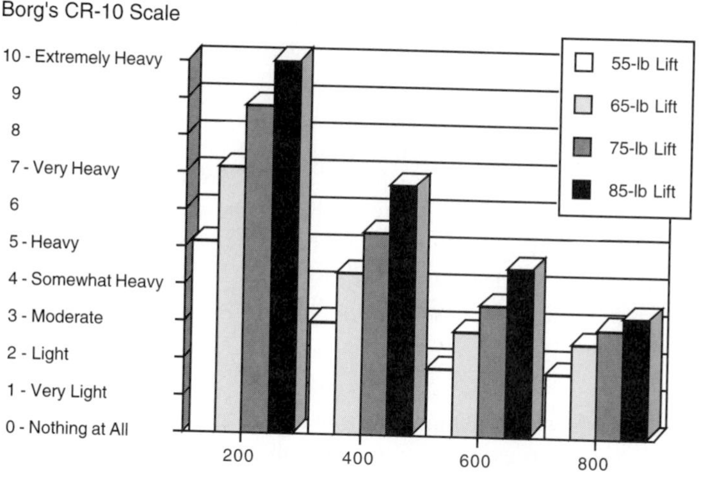

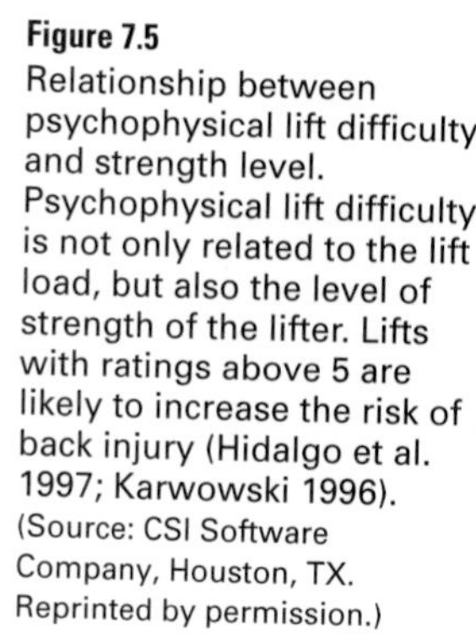
Figure 7.5
Relationship between psychophysical lift difficulty and strength level. Psychophysical lift difficulty is not only related to the lift load, but also the level of strength of the lifter. Lifts with ratings above 5 are likely to increase the risk of back injury (Hidalgo et al. 1997; Karwowski 1996). (Source: CSI Software Company, Houston, TX. Reprinted by permission.)

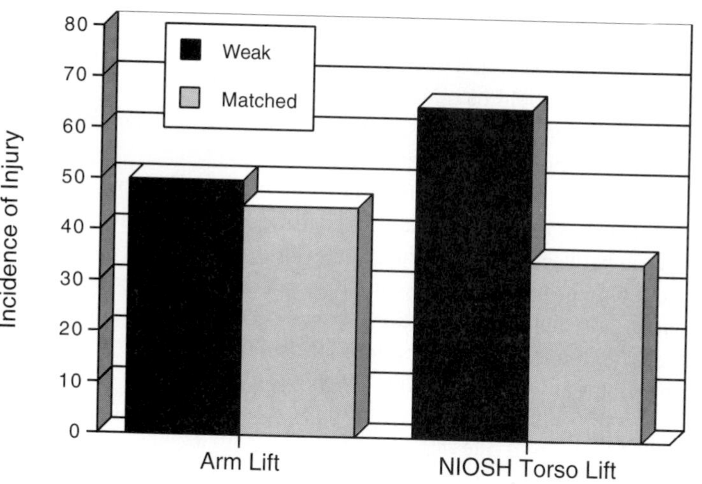

Figure 7.6
The incidence of musculoskeletal injuries was significantly related to isometric arm and back-lift strength. Workers who have less strength than demanded by the work task (i.e., weak) were more likely to incur a musculoskeletal injury during the 2-year follow-up than those who had sufficient strength (i.e., matched). Isometric arm and back-lift tests were used to match workers to the lift tasks. (Source: Jackson and Ross, R. M. *Understanding Exercise for Health and Fitness*, 1997. Reprinted by permission.)

of their maximum capacity. Resnik (1995) reported that the CR-10 scale was linearly related ($R^2 = 0.86$) with relative lift load defined as a percentage of the subject's maximum strength. Formula 7.1 defines this relationship.

Relative Strength and CR-10 Rating *(7.1)*

$$\%\text{Max Strength} = 10 \times \text{CR-10 Rating}$$

To illustrate, a Borg CR-10 rating of 7 would indicate that the subject was lifting a load that was 70% of their maximum. A stronger person would be expected to rate the same lift at a lower rating.

The fitness ability associated with low-back injury is strength. The link is not with absolute strength, but rather with strength in relation to the physical requirement of the task. The closer the lift demands are to 100% of the individual's maximum strength capacity (CR-10 rating of 10), the higher the risk of injury. This is an important issue of preemployment testing. To reduce the risk of back injury, workers need to be matched to the demands of the task. For example, a 75-pound lift may be within the "safe lift range" for one person, but be too difficult and potentially dangerous for someone with less strength.

Muscular Strength

Muscular strength is the maximum force that a muscle group can exert over a brief period. The test methods used to measure muscular strength are discussed in the next section of this chapter. Discussed next are three issues in general strength testing.

Absolute versus Relative Strength

Muscular strength may be evaluated in absolute or relative terms. Absolute strength is the maximum amount of force measured by the strength test. Absolute strength is correlated with body weight, or more correctly, fat-free weight, the body's force-producing component. Scaling a strength test in absolute terms is appropriate when the evaluation decision is related to determining the individual's maximum force generation capacity. This would be relevant when, for example, testing athletes or applicants for physically demanding tasks. In these environments, the goal is to determine an individual's maximum force generation capacity.

Relative strength is expressed in terms of an individual's body weight. Relative strength is more relevant when evaluating the fitness of the individual. There is a positive correlation between body weight and absolute strength; the goal of representing strength in relative terms is to express it independent of body weight. In this context, independent means that the correlation between the relative strength measure and weight is zero. A common method is to express strength performance as a ratio of body weight (Gettman 1993). Formula 7.2 shows this.

Relative Strength—Strength/Weight Ratio *(7.2)*

$$\text{Relative Strength Ratio} = \left(\frac{\text{Measured Strength}}{\text{Body Weight}}\right)$$

The relative strength ratio is very easy to use, but it does overcorrect for weight. To illustrate, we (Jackson et al. 1998) found that the correlation between the sum of isometric strength and weight for men was high, 0.61. When expressed as strength per pound of body weight, the correlation was −.17. The relative strength ratio (Formula 7.2) is slightly biased against heavier individuals.

A second method uses simple linear regression analysis (Chapter 2) to eliminate the influence of body weight. The first step is to estimate the average level of strength for a given body weight. The average strength value would be estimated with a simple linear regression equation (Chapter 2) that uses strength as the dependent variable and body weight as the independent variable. Subtracting the measured strength score from the estimated strength score provides a residual strength score, a score that has the influence of weight removed. Formula 7.3 shows this.

Relative Strength—Residual Strength Score **(7.3)**

$$\text{Residual Strength Score} = \text{Measured Strength} - \text{Average Strength for Body Weight}$$

The residual strength score can be a positive or negative value and represents the degree to which the person is stronger or weaker than others of that body weight. To illustrate, assume that the average arm strength for a 160-pound man is 76 pounds. Further assume that two men were tested and the measured arm strength of the men was 95 pounds and 71 pounds. Their residual strength scores (Formula 7.3) would be:

Man 1: Residual Strength Score $= 95 - 76 = 19$ pounds

Man 2: Residual Strength Score $= 71 - 76 = -5$ pounds

One man would be 19 pounds stronger than the average 160-pound man, while the other man would be 5 pounds weaker than the average 160-pound man. A residual strength score of 0 would indicate that the person has average strength for their weight.

The limitation of the residual strength method is that it is somewhat complicated, but it can be easily accomplished with a computer.[4] The correlation between weight and the residual strength score is 0, the desired goal of expressing strength in relative terms. The standard error of estimate (SEE) is the standard deviation of the residual strength score distribution. Using the estimated score, standard error of estimate, and normal curve (Chapter 2), it becomes possible to develop normative tables for evaluating a person's strength in relation to their body weight. This is illustrated in the isometric section of this chapter.

Male/Female Differences

Men and women differ in both absolute and relative strength. Much of this difference can be attributed to differences in body weight and body composition. Chapter 9 shows that men not only are heavier than women, but their average percent body fat is about 6–7% lower. The differences in body weight and percent body fat produce even larger differences in fat-free weight, which is the primary source of strength differences between males and females.

When strength is expressed in absolute terms, the average strength differences are substantial. A common view is that the average upper-body strength of women is about 50% to 60% that of men, but the difference in leg strength is less. Women reportedly have about 70% of the leg strength of men (Laubach 1976; McArdle, Katch, & Katch 1991). Analysis of the NIOSH (1977) leg strength data of male and female industrial workers does not show this. Figure 7.7 shows the difference between males and females in absolute isometric strength using the NIOSH data and two other samples from the University of Houston preemployment studies. These three databases show that the average arm and torso strength of women ranged from 49% to 57% that of men. This is consistent with published data (Laubach 1976; McArdle, Katch, &

[4]The computer computation example in appendix B illustrates the method with isometric strength tests.

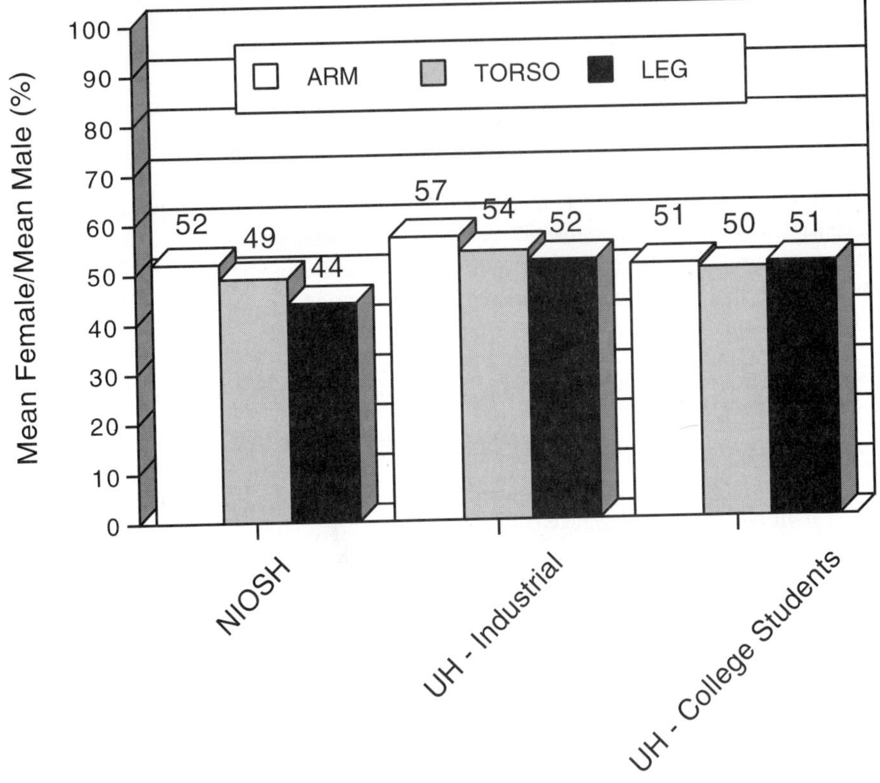

Figure 7.7
The comparison of male and female strength by body location for three different samples. Women tended to have about half the strength of men.
(Source: CSI Software Company, Houston, TX. Reprinted by permission.)

Katch 1991). Surprisingly, the greatest male/female difference in the NIOSH sample was leg strength—the industrial women's leg strength was only 44% that of the men. In the two samples from the University of Houston studies, the percentage was higher, about 50%. These data document the well-defined sexual difference in absolute strength, but show that the difference in upper body and lower body strength of men and women is similar.

Data presented in the strength testing sections of this chapter show that there are also male/female differences in relative strength. This is mainly due to the differences in percent body fat. A higher proportion of women's body weight is fat weight, the weight's nonforce production component. This results in a lower strength per pound of body weight.

Closed versus Open Kinetic Chain

Strength testing is closely linked with rehabilitation. The concept of "kinetic chain" is central to rehabilitation and muscle testing (Lephart 1996; Snyder-Mackler 1996). A kinetic chain can be either *open* or *closed.* An **open kinetic chain** is when the end of the limb segment is free in space. In contrast, a **closed kinetic chain** is when the end segment or joint meets with external resistance that prevents or restrains free motion. In a closed kinetic chain, movement at one joint produces movement at the other joints in the chain or system. Whereas, in a open kinetic setting, the distal limb segment can move freely.

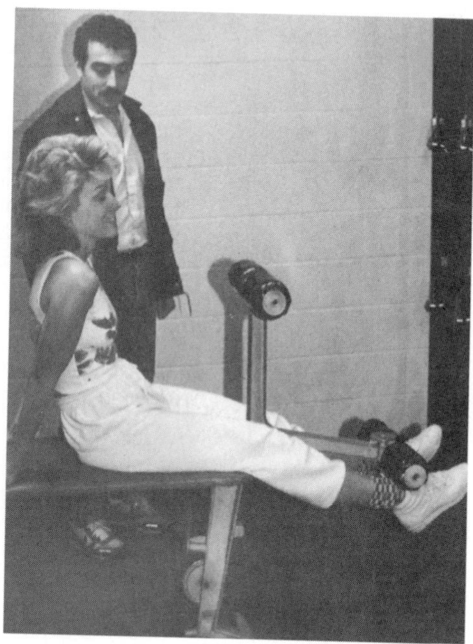

Figure 7.8
Examples of closed and open kinetic chain leg strength tests. The leg press test is a closed kinetic chain test while the leg extension test is an open kinetic chain test.

The concept of open and closed kinetic chains can be illustrated with common leg strength tests. Figure 7.8 shows isotonic leg press and leg extension 1-RM tests. The leg press test is an example of a closed kinetic chain test. The distal segment of the chain (i.e., feet) meets significant resistance to prevent movement. Movement is produced at all joints in the chain: the ankles, knees, and hips. In contrast, the leg extension test is an open kinetic chain test. In this test, the distal segment (i.e., feet) is able to move freely. The only movement is at the knee joint. The current trend in rehabilitation of muscle injuries is a closed kinetic chain, treating the entire limb rather than an individual joint or muscle. This is one major reason for the current trend to use closed kinetic strength testing.

Strength Testing Methods

Muscular strength is the maximum amount of force that a muscle group can exert. Muscle contractions can be either dynamic or static. Static contractions do not involve movement and are called isometric. Dynamic contractions involve movement: either concentric, in which the muscle shortens, or eccentric, in which the muscle lengthens. The dynamic forms include isotonic and isokinetic. Isotonic involves moving a weight against gravity. Lifting the weight uses a concentric contraction, while lowering the weight uses an eccentric contraction. Isokinetic involves muscle contractions at a fixed speed. Strength testing may involve either an open or closed kinetic chain. Table 7.7 provides an overview of the strengths and weaknesses of strength testing methods.

Table 7.7 A Comparison of Strength Testing Methods

Method	Strengths	Weaknesses
Isometric	1. Moderately inexpensive. 2. Can be used to test a variety of different muscle groups. 3. Closed kinetic chain. 4. Strong research base for preemployment testing. 5. Normative data are available. 6. Takes very little time to test a subject. 7. Easy to learn how to administer the tests.	1. Only one joint angle is tested. 2. Does not provide a torque strength curve. 3. Cannot measure dynamic contractions.
Isotonic	1. Very inexpensive. 2. Many different types of equipment can be used. 3. Closed kinetic chain. 4. Tests often duplicate strength development program. 5. Takes very little time to test a subject. 6. Easy to learn how to administer the tests.	1. Never measure "true maximum." 2. Cannot obtain a strength curve. 3. Risk of injury if free weights are used. 4. Different types of equipment affect the score; need equipment specific norms. 5. Can be difficult to find 1-RM.
Isokinetic	1. Can obtain strength curves for many different speeds. 2. Can obtain both eccentric and concentric contractions. 3. Data can be expressed in many different ways. 4. Valuable for rehabilitation process.	1. Very expensive equipment. 2. Not closed kinetic chain. 3. Velocity of movement affects torque output; need norms for various speeds.

Isometric Strength

Isometric strength testing has historically been popular. The equipment is relatively inexpensive. A principle advantage of isometric tests is their flexibility. If a position can be standardized, it is possible to measure isometric strength. Isometric tests have been developed to measure single muscle groups (e.g., elbow flexion or elbow extension) or a combination of muscle groups, such as closed kinetic leg strength.

Isometric strength is the maximum force that a muscle group can exert without movement. Tests of isometric strength are easy to perform as they require only a single, maximal contraction. In the early days of testing, mechanical devices such as tensiometers and spring dynamometers measured the force applied during an isometric contraction. Electronic load cells are now replacing these mechanical devices, which were somewhat inaccurate and difficult to calibrate. Professional standards for equipment and isometric test methods are published (Chaffin 1975; NIOSH 1977). Figure 7.9 shows a commercially available unit.

Isometric testing is a flexible method of evaluating strength. All one needs is to create the equipment to standardize the subject's test position, and place a load cell in such a position that it will record force (e.g., hand grip and cable-chain units). Some expensive back testing equipment uses elaborate chairs to standardize test positions

Figure 7.9
An electronic load cell is used to measure the force applied during an isometric strength test. Shown is the load cell that is attached to the platform. A chain-handle unit is used to standardize isometric test position. (Photograph courtesy of Lafayette Instrument Company, Lafayette, IN. Used with permission.)

and isolate muscle groups. These systems use load cells to measure strength at several different angles. Provided next are standard isometric strength tests.

***Isometric Strength Test Battery*[5].** Provided in this section are isometric strength tests that measure major muscle groups. These are common tests that have been used in preemployment test settings (Jackson 1996; NIOSH 1977), but also used for general fitness testing (Jackson et al. 1997).

Tests. Arm, Shoulder, Torso, and Leg Strength.

Objective. To measure the maximal force of arm, shoulder, torso, and leg muscle groups using a closed kinetic chain.

Validity. Isometric tests have been recognized as a valid method for measuring strength. The isometric strength tests are highly correlated with simulated work tasks of physically demanding occupations (Jackson 1996). Table 7.5 shows these validity coefficients.

Reliability. The reliability estimates exceed 0.94 for each test.

Equipment. The tests are administered on equipment manufactured by Lafayette Instrument Company, Lafayette, IN (Model 32528). The test equipment consists of a platform with a chain apparatus, and a load cell and digital recorder. The equipment was developed for preemployment testing for physically demanding jobs for the Shell Oil Company, Houston, TX. The equipment is now widely used in medical and rehabilitative settings.

Procedures. Once the subject is in the test position, the tester pushes the "start" button. A "beep" will sound and 3 seconds later a second "beep" will be heard. The subject is instructed to exert force on this first "beep" and stop on the second "beep." The equipment allows you to set the length of the trial. A 3-second trial is used, during which

[5] For a comprehensive manual for isometric strength testing, contact Lafayette Instrument Company, P.O. Box 5729, Lafayette, IN 47903. Phone (800) 428-7545.

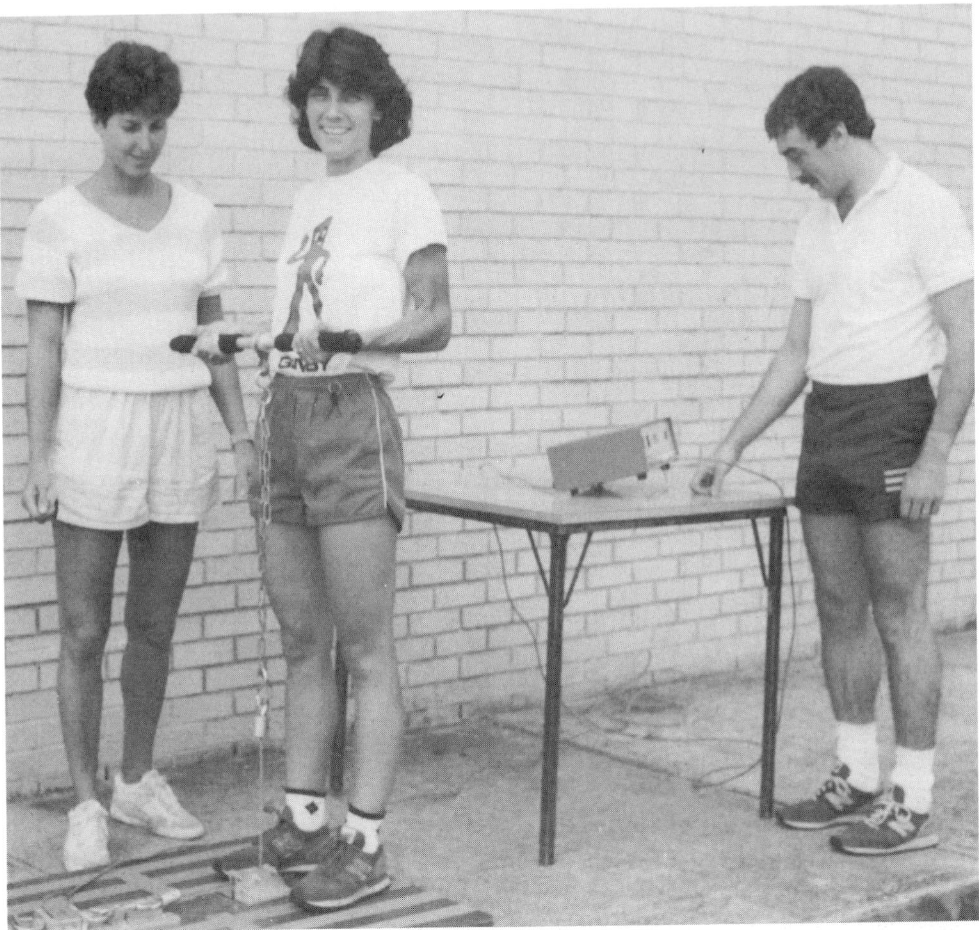

Figure 7.10
Arm strength test. (Photograph courtesy of Lafayette Instrument Company, Lafayette, IN. Used with permission.)

force is recorded only for the last 2 seconds. Typically, subjects will jerk at the start of the trial. By not measuring this first second, the jerk is not reflected in the strength score, which is the average force exerted during the final two seconds. A warm-up trial at 50% effort is administered first, followed by two trials for score. External forms of motivation are to be strictly avoided. Do not encourage the subject when he/she is exerting force. Do not give the subject his/her score after completing a trial.

1. *Arm Lift* (NIOSH 1978). The arm-lift apparatus is used to measure lifting strength. The load cell is attached and equipment is adjusted so the elbows are at 90° flexion. The cable should be at a right angle to the base. The legs should be straight, and the subject is not allowed to lean back. Maximal lifting force is exerted in this position (see Figure 7.10).
2. *Shoulder Lift.* The bar setting used for the arm-lift test is used for the shoulder lift. To assume the correct position, the subject moves forward until the bar touches her/his body. The cable should be at a right angle to the base. With the palms facing the rear, the subject grabs the bar so that the inside of the hands

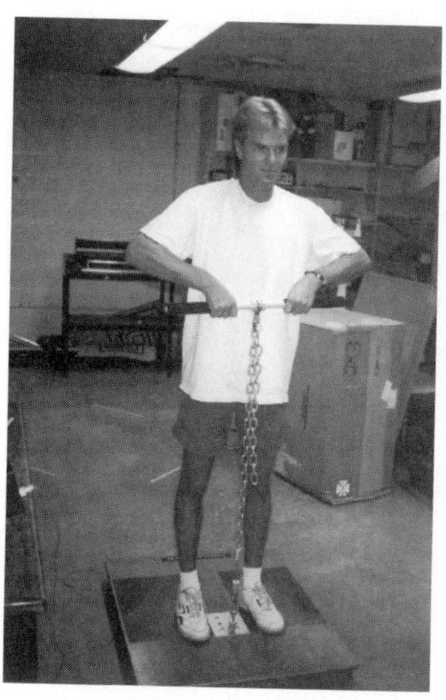

Figure 7.11
Shoulder strength test. (Photograph courtesy of Lafayette Instrument Company, Lafayette, IN. Used with permission.)

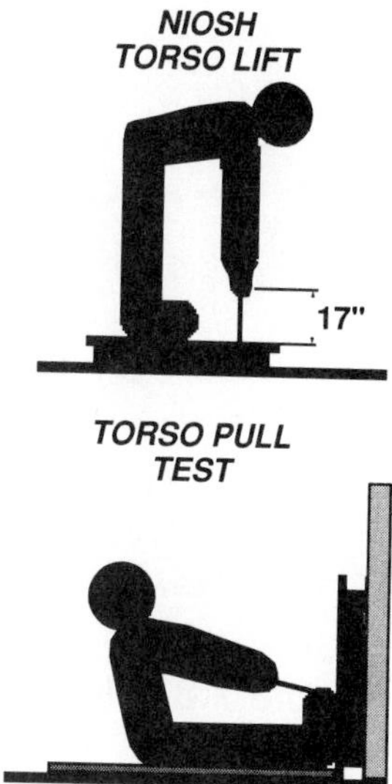

Figure 7.12
The test positions for the NIOSH torso lift and the torso pull tests. (Source: CSI Software Company, Houston, TX. Reprinted by permission.)

are on the inside of the black handle. In this position the elbows are pointing out, away from the body. This test measures the lifting strength of the shoulders. The subject is not allowed to lean back or use his/her legs (e.g., bending the knees and generating force with the legs). The force is correctly exerted by lifting up with the shoulders while the elbows point outward (see Figure 7.11). These muscle groups are commonly used for lifting tasks.

3. *Torso Strength.* The Torso lift test is recommended for preemployment testing (NIOSH, 1977). Figure 7.12 illustrates the NIOSH test position. It has been our experience that many are hesitant to be tested in this position. Our research led us to develop the torso pull test, also shown in Figure 7.12. With a sample of 246 industrial workers and 204 students, we found a high correlation ($r = 0.91$) between the two tests. We recommend that the torso pull test be used. The test procedure is described next.

The platform-chain apparatus is placed against the wall with the chain at its lowest point. The bar is set 17 inches from the base of the platform. The subject sits on a mat and places his or her feet against the platform. The subject uses a reverse grip (palms facing the floor) and keeps the legs straight. The force is correctly exerted by leaning and pulling back. Provided next is a regression equation that can be used to estimate the NIOSH torso lift strength from that of the torso pull.

Conversion to NIOSH Torso Lift Strength *(7.4)*

$$\text{NIOSH Torso Lift} = (0.973 \times \text{Torso Pull}) - 18.188$$

4. *Leg-Lift Test* (NIOSH 1977). Figure 7.13 show the leg-lift test position. The following procedures are used to get the subject into the test position to test leg strength. First, the platform is placed on the floor and the lift bar is attached to a chain link that places the bar 17 inches from the base of the platform. The same chain setting is used for all subjects. This is the same setting used for the torso test. The subject stands on the platform with their feet spread a

Figure 7.13
Leg strength test.
(Photograph courtesy of D. M. Jackson. Used with permission.)

Table 7.8 Means, Standard Deviations, and Sample Sizes for Isometric Strength Tests Administered to Male and Female Industrial Workers

Strength Test	Males			Females		
	Mean	SD	N	Mean	SD	N
Arm lift	86.3	16.8	195	49.1	11.8	55
Shoulder lift	118.7	22.6	195	66.8	17.3	55
Torso pull	222.6	57.3	195	119.6	38.9	55
Leg strength	229.7	50.7	195	118.9	38.3	55

comfortable distance. The bar is rotated 90° so the ends of the bar face the front and back of the platform. The subject grips the bar with the palms facing each other. The hands are as close to the center of the bar as possible. In this position the bar is between the legs with the arms as close to the body as possible.[6] The subject bends their knees, keeping the arms as close to the body as possible. The head is in such a position that forces the subject to look straight ahead, not down. In the test position, force is exerted by exerting force with the legs. The subject should not jerk, rather apply force in a consistent, forceful manner.

Scoring. The average of two trials is used for score. Tables 7.8 and 7.9 give the means, standard deviations, and sample sizes for college students and industrial workers by sex.

Norms. The descriptive statistics in Tables 7.8 and 7.9 provide absolute strength norms for industrial workers and college students. Table 7.10 provides regression equations with functions to estimate strength from body weight. These formulas serve as the basis for the relative strength percentile rank norms (Tables 7.11 and 7.12).

---

[6]Figure 7.4 shows the importance of keeping the load as close to the back as possible in order to minimize low-back compression forces.

Table 7.9 Means, Standard Deviations, and Sample Sizes for Isometric Strength Tests Administered to Male and Female College Students

Strength Test	Males			Females		
	Mean	SD	N	Mean	SD	N
Arm lift	74.1	17.4	133	37.9	11.6	249
Shoulder lift	105.1	26.3	133	53.3	17.3	249
Torso pull	222.2	60.0	133	109.5	38.3	249
Leg strength	203.3	58.8	133	103.6	37.0	249

Table 7.10 Regression Equation to Develop Relative Isometric Strength Norms

Test	Gender	Equation*	R	SEE
Arm lift	Female	$Y' = (0.18 \times Wt) + 15.34$	0.37	11.4
Arm lift	Male	$Y' = (0.20 \times Wt) + 44.35$	0.42	16.4
Shoulder lift	Female	$Y' = (0.20 \times Wt) + 28.62$	0.28	17.2
Shoulder lift	Male	$Y' = (0.32 \times Wt) + 54.77$	0.48	22.0
Torso pull	Female	$Y' = (0.46 \times Wt) + 49.84$	0.30	36.6
Torso pull	Male	$Y' = (0.61 \times Wt) + 112.25$	0.38	53.6
Leg strength	Female	$Y' = (0.40 \times Wt) + 54.40$	0.27	35.6
Leg strength	Male	$Y' = (0.70 \times Wt) + 90.14$	0.47	48.4

*The term Y′ is the average strength for a given body weight (Wt).

Table 7.11 Relative Percentile Rank* Isometric Strength Norms for Women for Four Strength Tests

Weight in Pounds	Arm Lift			Shoulder Lift			Torso Pull			Leg Lift		
	25	50	75	25	50	75	25	50	75	25	50	75
90	24	32	39	35	47	58	67	91	116	67	90	114
100	26	33	41	37	49	60	71	96	120	71	94	118
110	28	35	43	39	51	62	76	100	125	75	98	122
120	29	37	45	41	53	64	81	105	130	79	102	126
130	31	39	46	43	55	66	85	110	134	83	106	130
140	33	41	48	45	57	68	90	114	139	87	110	134
150	35	42	50	47	59	70	94	119	143	91	114	138
160	37	44	52	49	61	72	99	123	148	95	118	142
170	38	46	54	51	63	74	104	128	153	99	122	146
180	40	48	55	53	65	76	108	133	157	103	126	150
190	42	50	57	55	67	78	113	137	162	107	130	154
200	44	51	59	57	69	80	117	142	166	111	134	158

*The 50th percentile is the estimated strength score (Y′) from the weight regression equation. The 25th percentile is $Y' - (0.67 \times SEE)$ and the 75th percentile is $Y' + (0.67 \times SEE)$.

Table 7.12 Relative Percentile Rank* Isometric Strength Norms for Men for Four Strength Tests

Weight in Pounds	Arm Lift			Shoulder Lift			Torso Pull			Leg Lift		
	25	50	75	25	50	75	25	50	75	25	50	75
120	57	68	79	78	93	108	150	185	221	142	174	207
130	59	70	81	82	96	111	156	192	227	149	181	214
140	61	72	83	85	100	114	162	198	234	156	188	221
150	63	74	85	88	103	118	168	204	240	163	195	228
160	65	76	87	91	106	121	174	210	246	170	202	235
170	67	78	89	94	109	124	180	216	252	177	209	242
180	69	80	91	98	112	127	186	222	258	184	216	249
190	71	82	93	101	116	130	192	228	264	191	223	256
200	73	84	95	104	119	134	198	234	270	198	230	263
210	75	86	97	107	122	137	204	240	276	205	237	270
220	77	88	99	110	125	140	211	246	282	212	244	277
230	79	90	101	114	128	143	217	253	288	219	251	284
240	81	92	103	117	132	146	223	259	295	226	258	291
250	83	94	105	120	135	150	229	265	301	233	265	298

*The 50th percentile is the estimated strength score (Y′) from the weight regression equation. The 25th percentile is Y′ − (0.67 × SEE) and the 75th percentile is Y′ + (0.67 × SEE).

Isometric Grip Strength. The grip strength is a common isometric test. Equipment used to measure grip strength includes a electronic load cell, dynamometer, and JAMAR hydraulic unit.

Test. Grip Strength

Objective. To measure the maximal grip strength.

Validity. Grip strength is a standard test used to measure strength.

Reliability. The reliability estimates exceed 0.90 for each test.

Equipment. The electronic load cell unit manufactured by Lafayette Instrument Company, Lafayette, IN (Model 32528) and JAMAR hydraulic unit are recommended.

Procedures. The procedures for using the electronic load cell and Jamar unit differ.

Load Cell Procedures. The grip strength is tested with the load cell attached to the grip apparatus. The subject is seated at a table with the free hand on the table. The apparatus is gripped with the palm up. Maximal force is exerted in this position (see Figure 7.14).

JAMAR Procedures. The JAMAR hand dynamometer utilizes a hydraulic gauge with a peak-hold needle to record the highest strength effort. The following procedures need to be followed to measure grip strength with the JAMAR unit.

1. The JAMAR displays grip force in pounds and kilograms. Grip strength is measured in pounds.

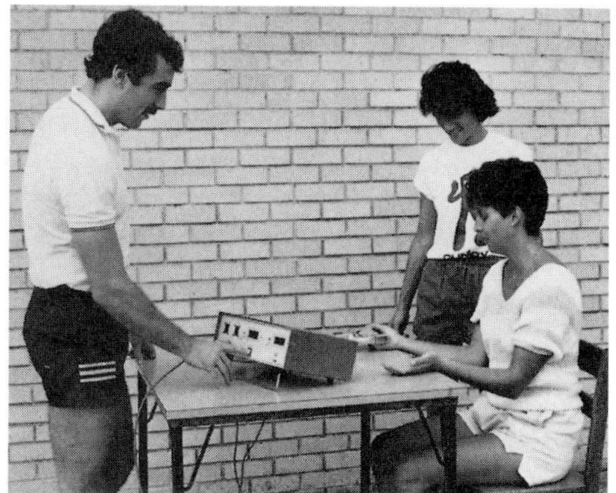

Figure 7.14
Lafayette isometric strength unit showing the grip strength test position.
(Photograph courtesy of Lafayette Instrument Company, Lafayette, IN. Used with permission.)

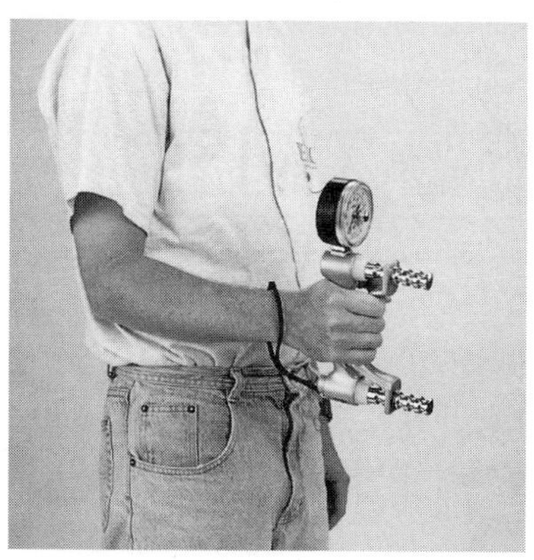

Figure 7.15
Test position for the grip strength test using the JAMAR hand dynamometer.
(Photograph courtesy of Lafayette Instrument Company, Lafayette, IN. Used with permission.)

2. The maximum grip strength is recorded by a special peak-hold needle. After each test trial, reset the needle to "0."
3. The adjustable handle allows for five settings; typically, settings 2 or 3 are used, depending upon hand size.
4. The subject stands comfortably with the shoulder adducted and neutrally rotated. The elbow is flexed to 90° and the forearm and wrist are in neutral position. The subject's right and left grip are tested. Figure 7.15 shows the test position. In the test position, force is exerted by gripping the handle with a single, forceful effort.

Scoring. The average of two trials is used for score. Table 7.13 lists the absolute grip strength norms for college students and occupational groups contrasted by sex.

Sum of Isometric Strength Tests. Table 7.14 provides the correlations among the arm, shoulder, torso, and leg isometric strength tests. The correlations among the four tests are high, ranging from 0.82 to 0.92. The high correlations support the practice of summing the tests for one measure of total strength. The University of Houston preemployment studies have used the sum of all four tests (ΣFour) or the sum of arm, shoulder, and torso (ΣThree). Either sum may be used; the correlation between them is 0.99.

Table 7.13 Means, Standard Deviations, and Sample Sizes for Grip Strength Administered to College Students and Different Groups of Industrial Workers

Sample	Women			Men		
	Mean	SD	N	Mean	SD	N
College students	64.1	15.5	207	99.4	27.0	193
Construction workers	80.2	23.3	18	111.1	23.3	234
Gas service workers	70.8	19.0	34	108.8	23.3	212
Police cadets	71.5	16.2 1	7	113.8	25.2	161
Coal miners	*			124.8	17.5	96
Refinery workers	76.8	12.8 1	4	118.1	23.3	75

*Not measured.

Table 7.14 Correlations Among Isometric Strength Tests ΣThree and ΣFour (n = 632)

Test	Arm	Shoulder	Torso	Leg	ΣThree	ΣFour
Arm lift	1.00					
Shoulder lift	0.92	1.00				
Torso pull	0.82	0.80	1.00			
Leg strength	0.85	0.86	0.85	1.00		
ΣThree*	0.93	0.93	0.96	0.90	1.00	
ΣFour**	0.92	0.92	0.95	0.96	0.99	1.00

*Sum of arm, shoulder and torso.
**Sum of all four tests.

Table 7.15 Absolute ΣThree and ΣFour Isometric Strength Norms for Men and Women*

Strength Test	Mean	SD	Percentile				
			10	25	50	75	90
Men (n = 328)							
ΣThree	417.0	87.0	302	361	414	479	536
ΣFour	635.9	134.0	466	542	632	740	809
Women (n = 304							
ΣThree**	207.0	61.7	135	165	201	245	284
ΣFour***	313.3	92.4	202	251	305	371	430

*Data from industrial workers and college students.
**Sum of arm, shoulder and torso.
***Sum of all four tests.

Tables 7.15 and 7.16 provides the male and female absolute strength norms for the ΣThree and ΣFour isometric strength tests. Tables 7.16 and 7.17 provide the relative male and female norms for the two sums.

Table 7.16 Relative Percentile Rank Isometric Strength Norms for Men for the Sum of Three and Four Strength Tests

Weight in Pounds	Sum of Three*			Sum of Four**		
	25	50	75	25	50	75
120	205	347	489	447	523	600
130	217	358	500	465	542	618
140	228	370	511	484	560	637
150	239	381	523	502	579	655
160	251	392	534	520	597	673
170	262	403	545	539	615	692
180	273	415	556	557	634	710
190	284	426	568	576	652	729
200	296	437	579	594	671	747
210	307	449	590	612	689	765
220	318	460	602	631	707	784
230	330	471	613	649	726	802
240	341	483	624	668	744	821
250	352	494	636	686	763	839

Estimated ΣThree = (1.13 × Wt) + 211.38; R = 0.48; SEE = 211.4
Estimated ΣFour = (1.84 × Wt) + 302.51; R = 0.51; SEE = 114.1
*Sum of arm, shoulder, and torso in Table 7.14
**Sum of all four tests in Table 7.14

Table 7.17 Relative Percentile Rank Isometric Strength Norms for Women for the Sum of Three and Four Strength Tests

Weight in Pounds	Sum of Three*			Sum of Four**		
	25	50	75	25	50	75
90	132	170	209	202	260	318
100	140	179	217	214	272	330
110	149	187	226	227	285	343
120	157	196	234	239	297	355
130	166	204	243	252	310	368
140	174	213	251	264	322	380
150	183	221	260	277	335	393
160	191	230	268	289	347	405
170	200	238	277	302	360	418
180	208	247	285	314	372	430
190	217	255	294	327	385	443
200	225	264	302	339	397	455

Estimated ΣThree = (0.85 × Wt) + 93.80; R = 0.34; SEE = 57.7
Estimated ΣFour = (1.25 × Wt) + 147.20; R = 0.33; SEE = 86.5
*Sum of arm, shoulder, and torso in Table 7.14
**Sum of all four tests in Table 7.14

Isotonic Strength Testing

Isotonic strength is measured by determining the maximal force that a muscle group can exert with a single contraction. An isotonic strength test measures the maximum weight that can be lifted with a single repetition. This is the one-repetition maximum test (1-RM). Free weights or progressive resistance equipment is used to measure 1-RM strength. The most difficult part of the test is to find the subject's maximal load. Several different weights will need to be tried to find the proper 1-RM weight. Morrow and associates (1995) recommend the following steps when measuring 1-RM strength.

1. Have the subject warm up with stretching and light lifting.
2. Have the subject perform a lift below the estimated maximum. A pretest session is extremely useful for novice subjects.
3. To prevent fatigue, have the subject rest at least 2 minutes between lifts.
4. Increase the weight by a small increment, 5 or 10 pounds, depending on the exercise and weight increments available.
5. Continue the process until the subject fails an attempt.
6. The last weight successfully completed is the 1-RM weight.

Isotonic 1-RM Strength Tests. This test can be administered with standard barbells, but we recommend strength development machines common to most facilities (e.g., Universal gym). Because equipment varies in design, 1-RM tests need to be specific to the muscle group tested. The maximal weight lifted will be higher for progressive resistance equipment (e.g., Nautilus) because the resistance changes during the exercise. Because of these differences, it is desirable to establish equipment specific norms.

Tests. Bench Press and Leg Press

Objective. To measure a closed kinetic chain 1-RM strength.

Validity. Construct validity of muscular strength of the arms.

Equipment. These isotonic tests are especially applicable in facilities that have strength development machines. Provided next are examples for Universal Gym equipment. The test can be used with other weight-training machines. Besides serving as a teaching station for weight-training instruction, this type of equipment is excellent for measuring arm strength. Free weights also can be used, with proper spotting.

Procedures. Follow the recommended procedure for finding the person's 1-RM. While it is possible to measure 1-RM many different ways (e.g., curls, lat pull, leg extension, etc.), the bench and leg press tests have become standards and are presented next.

1. *Bench Press.* The student can assume any width grasp outside the shoulders. Feet must be on the floor, the back straight. After each repetition the weights must be brought back to touch the weights beneath them. Figure 7.16 shows the test position.
2. *Leg Press.* The subject sits in the provided chair, fully extends the legs, and executes a maximal repetition. The starting position is shown in Figure 7.8. The seat should be adjusted to standardize the knee angle at approximately 120°.

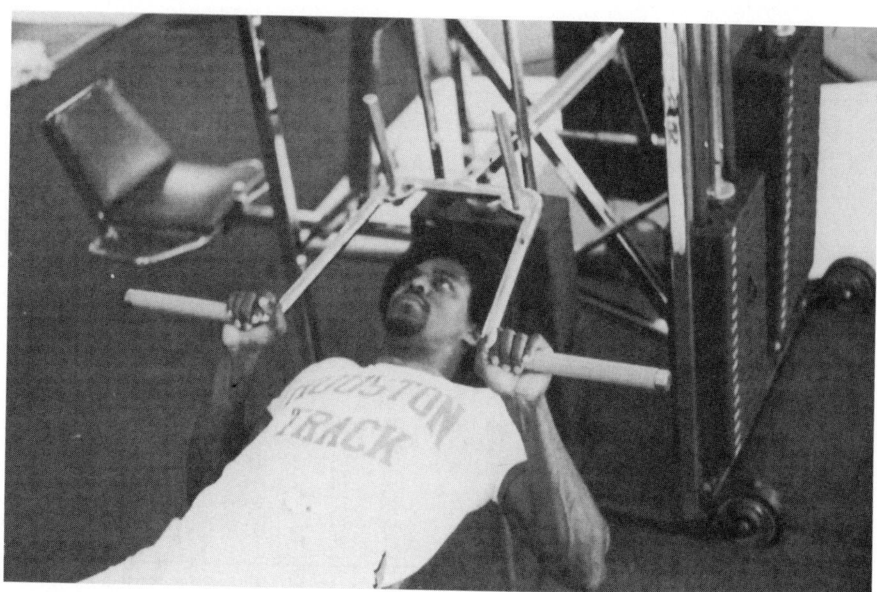

Figure 7.16
Isotonic 1-RM bench press test position.

Table 7.18 Relative Strength/Weight Ratio, Isotonic 1-RM Standards for Men

Age Group	Evaluation Standard				
	Excellent	**Good**	**Average**	**Fair**	**Poor**
1-RM Bench Press					
20–29	>1.25	1.17–1.25	0.97–1.16	0.88–0.96	<0.88
30–39	>1.07	1.01–1.07	0.86–1.00	0.79–0.85	<0.79
40–49	>0.96	0.91–0.96	0.78–0.90	0.72–0.77	<0.72
50–59	>0.85	0.81–0.85	0.70–0.80	0.65–0.69	<0.65
≥60	>0.77	0.74–0.77	0.64–0.73	0.60–0.63	<0.60
1-RM Upper Leg Press					
20–29	>2.07	2.00–2.07	1.83–1.99	1.65–1.82	<1.65
30–39	>1.87	1.80–1.87	1.63–1.79	1.55–1.62	<1.55
40–49	>1.75	1.70–1.75	1.56–1.69	1.50–1.55	<1.50
50–59	>1.65	1.60–1.65	1.46–1.59	1.40–1.45	<1.40
≥60	>1.55	1.50–1.55	1.37–1.49	1.31–1.36	<1.31

Standards for The Institute for Aerobic Research, Dallas, Texas. Used with permission.

Scoring. A student's score is the maximal weight lifted.

Norms. Because of differences in equipment and test procedures, it is recommended that situation-specific norms be developed. Tables 7.18 and 7.19 provide relative strength/weight ratio norms for the bench press and leg press 1-RM tests for men and women (Gettman 1993).

Table 7.19 Relative Strength/Weight Ratio, Isotonic 1-RM Standards for Women

Age Group	Evaluation Standard				
	Excellent	Good	Average	Fair	Poor
1-RM Bench Press					
20–29	>0.77	0.72–0.77	0.59–0.71	0.53–0.58	<0.53
30–39	>0.65	0.62–0.65	0.53–0.61	0.49–0.52	<0.49
40–49	>0.60	0.57–0.60	0.48–0.56	0.44–0.47	<0.44
50–59	>0.53	0.51–0.53	0.43–0.50	0.40–0.42	<0.40
≥60	>0.54	0.51–0.54	0.41–0.50	0.37–0.40	<0.37
1-RM Upper Leg Press					
20–29	>1.62	1.54–1.62	1.35–1.53	1.26–1.34	<1.26
30–39	>1.41	1.35–1.41	1.20–1.34	1.13–1.19	<1.13
40–49	>1.31	1.26–1.31	1.12–1.25	1.06–1.11	<1.06
50–59	>1.25	1.13–1.25	0.99–1.12	0.86–0.98	<0.86
≥60	>1.14	1.08–1.14	0.92–1.07	0.85–0.91	<0.85

Standards for the The Institute for Aerobic Research, Dallas, Texas. Used with permission.

Isotonic Absolute Endurance. Muscular strength and absolute endurance are highly correlated. In an **absolute endurance** test, a weight load is repeatedly lifted until exhaustion is reached, and the same weight is used for all subjects tested. DeVries (1980) reported that the correlations between strength and absolute endurance tests are high (at least 0.90). The reason for the high relation between strength and absolute endurance is that subjects are lifting at different percentages of maximal strength. For example, assume the maximal bench-press strengths of two people are 120 and 150 pounds. If the weight load for the test is 110 pounds, the weaker person would be lifting at 92% of maximal, while the stronger person would be lifting at 73% of maximal strength. The stronger person would complete more repetitions before becoming exhausted.

The YMCA adult fitness test uses an absolute endurance bench-press test (Golding, Meyers, & Sinning 1989). A constant weight of 35 pounds is used for testing women, and 80 pounds is used for men. The test is to complete as many repetitions as possible to exhaustion. The test and norms are provided in Chapter 11.

Isokinetic Strength Testing

Tests of **isokinetic strength** measure torque through a defined range-of-motion while keeping the speed of movement constant. The equipment used to measure isokinetic strength uses a load cell interfaced with a computer. The computer unit controls the speed of movement and measures torque. This yields the muscle group's torque curve for the selected constant velocity. Both muscle strength and the velocity of movement affect the shape and magnitude of the curve (Figure 7.17). As the muscle contracts at a faster rate, it cannot generate as much torque, so a lower curve is obtained. Test results from different test centers are not comparable unless the sites use the same equipment and the same test velocity.

Figure 7.18 shows isokinetic equipment, and Figure 7.19 shows a sample computer generated report of an isokinetic test. The isokinetic torque curve provides ther-

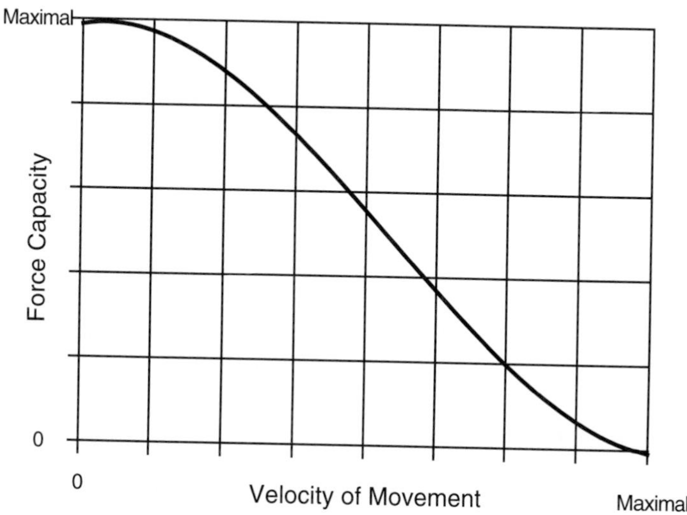

Figure 7.17
Isokinetic torque is affected by the velocity of movement. As the speed of movement increases, the amount of force produced by the muscle decreases. Peak force is produced when there is no movement, this is an isometric contraction. (Source: Jackson and Ross, R. M. *Understanding Exercise for Health and Fitness,* 1997. Reprinted by permission.)

apists with the capacity to evaluate the muscle group's symmetry. The equipment has the capacity to conduct both eccentric and concentric contractions and compute various ratios of interest—for example, agonist/antagonist, concentric/eccentric, or different tests.

Isokinetic equipment is expensive and so is generally used only at well-equipped testing centers such as NASA, the U.S. Olympic Center, and modern sports medicine and physical therapy facilities. At the time this chapter was being written, isokinetic testing was losing favor. There are several reasons for this. A major factor is the cost of the equipment and change in our health care systems. Managed health care corporations have dramatically reduced the amount of money they will pay for strength evaluations. Another reason is that isokinetic tests are largely open kinetic chains whereas the current rehabilitation philosophy is to use a closed kinetic chain. When isokinetic testing was at its peak in popularity, there were three major isokinetic test units on the market: Cybex, Biodex, and KinCom. Biodex purchased the KinCom unit and stopped its production. Cybex had been sold to another company, and the future availability of Cybex isokinetic equipment is now in question.

Correlations Among Types of Strength Tests

Strength tests involve dynamic and static contractions. When scored in absolute terms, these two kinds of strength tests are highly correlated. Table 7.5 shows that isometric strength tests are highly correlated with many different types of work-sample strength tests that involve dynamic and static contractions. As previously discussed, the correlations between 1-RM isotonic strength tests and absolute endurance tests are high—typically over 0.90 (deVries 1980). Isometric and isotonic 1-RM tests were found to be highly correlated (Russell et al. 1993). Using samples of high school and college students, the correlations between the sum of grip, torso, and arm isometric strength and 1-RM bench press was 0.80 and 0.83, respectively. The correlations between the sum of isometric strength and 1-RM leg strength was slightly lower, 0.73 and 0.74.

(a)

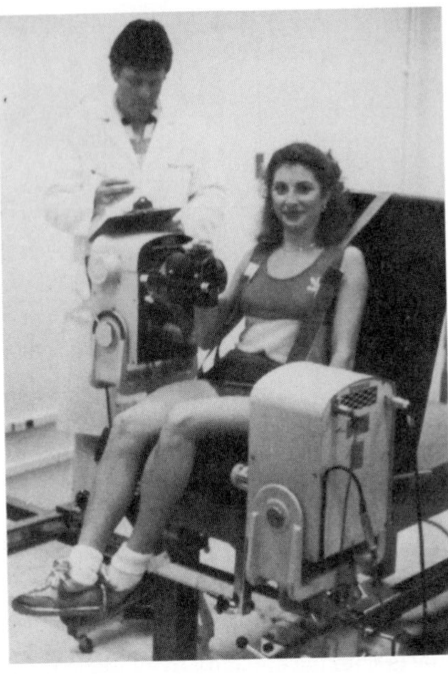

(b)

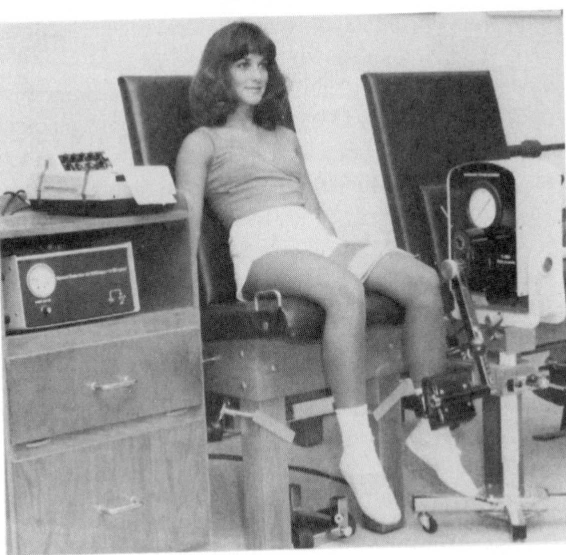

(c)

Figure 7.18
Biodex equipment for testing isokinetic strength. (Photos courtesy of Biodex Corp.)

Muscular Power. **Muscular power** has traditionally been defined as maximum force released in the shortest possible time. The vertical jump, standing long jump, and shot put have been the recommended measures of power (McCloy 1932), but jumping tests are not highly correlated with mechanically measured power (Barlow 1970; Considine 1970; Glencross 1966; Gray 1962). **Power** is the rate that work (product of force and distance) is performed and is defined by Formula 7.5.

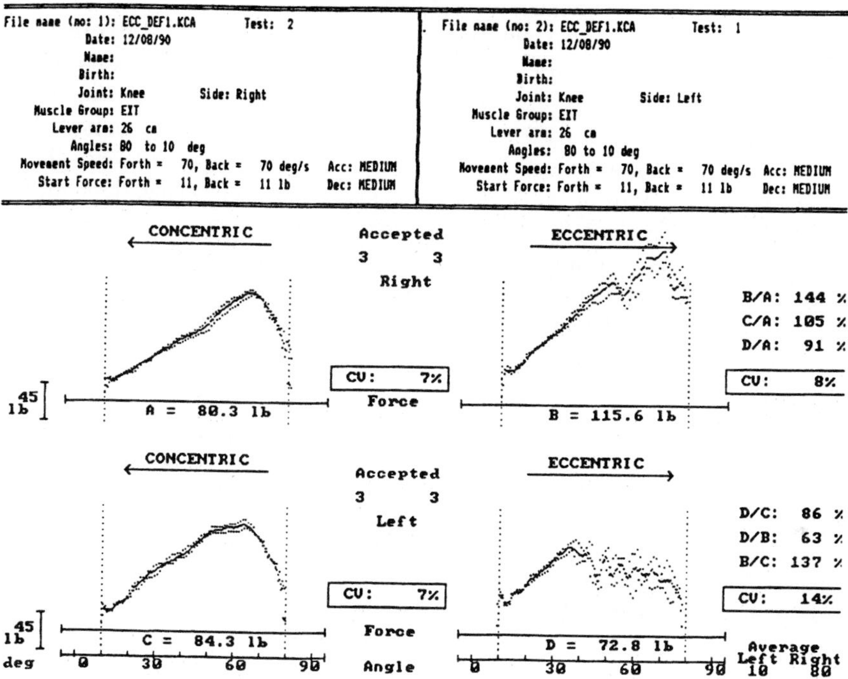

Comparative Report: Showing the Min., Max. and Average curves accepted which allows you to review the consistency of the patient's efforts and the control of the force produced. Note, in this example, the lack of eccentric control on the left and the reproducibility of this condition.

Figure 7.19
Sample computer generated output of an isokinetic test.

Definition of Power **(7.5)**

$$\text{Power} = \left(\frac{\text{Force} \times \text{Distance}}{\text{Time}}\right) = \left(\frac{\text{Work}}{\text{Time}}\right)$$

Margaria and his associates (1966) were the first to publish a leg-power test. The test involved running up a flight of stairs. By knowing the subject's weight and the height of the stairs, work was computed from the product of these two parameters. Power was computed by dividing the product of the two variables by the time required to run up the stairs. The trend in power testing has been to move away from the Margaria running test and use cycle and arm ergometers. An all-out cycling power test was first described in 1973 and called the Katch test (McArdle, Katch, & Katch 1991).

This test was refined at the Department of Research and Sport Medicine at the Wingate (Israel) Institute, and is now known as the Wingate anaerobic power test (Bar-Or 1987). This has become the test of choice for measuring power. The Wingate power test involves cycling as fast as possible for 30 seconds at a set resistance.

The Monarch cycle ergometer is one of the most popular testing ergometers. A distance of 6 meters is traveled with each revolution of the flywheel. This ergometer varies flywheel resistance with a weight load. The unit of measurement of the weight load is kiloponds (kp).[7] Thus, the amount of work performed for each revolution of the flywheel with a resistance of 1 kp would be 6 kilopond meters or 6 kpm. Increasing resistance to 2 kp increases the work to 12 kpm for each revolution. Power is the ratio of work and time. Power, expressed as kilopond meters per minute, (kpm/min) is computed by dividing work by the time required to complete the work.

The time for the Wingate test is constant, 30 seconds (0.5 minutes). For a given kp (kilopond) resistance, differences in Wingate power are a function of the total number of revolutions completed in 30 seconds. Assuming a Monarch cycle ergometer, the formula to measure power is:

Wingate Power Equation **(7.6)**

$$\text{Power (kpm/min)} = \left(\frac{6 \times \text{kp} \times \text{R}}{0.5}\right)$$

where 6 is the distance traveled with each revolution of the flywheel, kp is the ergometer resistance, and R is the total number of revolutions completed in 0.5 minutes (30 sec). Power tests are often expressed in watts. The conversion from kpm/min is:

Power Expressed in Watts **(7.7)**

$$\text{Power in Watts} = \left(\frac{\text{Power in kpm/min}}{6.12}\right)$$

Provided next are the tests procedures for the Wingate anarobic power tests.

Test. Wingate Power Test (Bar-Or 1987).

Objective. To measure anaerobic leg power.

Validity. By definition, the test measures leg power.

Reliability. Test-retest reliabilities between 0.89 and 0.98 have been reported for the test.

Equipment. The equipment needed is a calibrated cycle ergometer with the capacity to measure the number of flywheel revolutions completed in 30 seconds. A computerized system[8] has been developed that measures the number of revolutions with a photoelectric system that records the revolutions from reflective tape placed on the flywheel. The computer system also make all calculations. Figure 7.20 shows the test equipment.

---

[7] A kilopond is equal to 2.2 pounds or a kilogram. Both kilopond and kilograms are used in the literature.

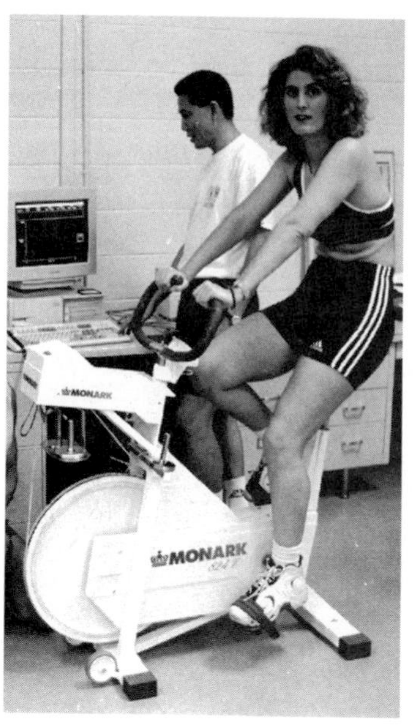

(A)

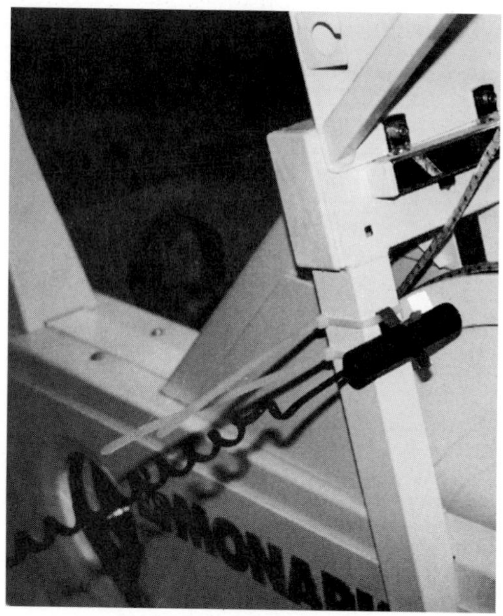

(B)

Figure 7.20
Test equipment used for the Wingate power test. One photograph shows the subjects test position (A) and the second (B) shows the photo cell and reflective tape on the ergometer flywheel that records the number of revolutions. (Photograph courtesy of D. M. Jackson. Used with permission.)

Procedures. The seat height of the ergometer is set for the subject's best comfort. It is recommended that toe clips be used. A warm-up is recommended. One common warm-up protocol is have the subject pedal at a low rate at the setting to be used in the test. The warm-up consists of pedaling for about 3 minutes, including two or three all-out 5-second bursts. The subject rests prior to being tested. Test administration involves making choices on resistance setting and starting method. These are discussed next.

Resistance Setting. The recommended setting is based on a proportion of body weight. The resistance settings (kp) for a Monarch ergometer are:

$$\text{Children} = 0.075 \times \text{Body Weight in kg}$$

$$\text{Adult Women} = 0.086 \times \text{Body Weight in kg}$$

$$\text{Adult Men} = 0.087 \times \text{Body Weight in kg}$$

$$\text{Athletes} = 0.10 \times \text{Body Weight in kg}$$

Starting Method. Once the resistance setting is determined, the start method must be selected. The three common start methods are:

1. *Still Start.* The ergometer is set at the predetermined resistance and the subject starts pedaling as fast as possible on the command of "Go." The test ends after 30 seconds of all-out cycling.
2. *Gradual Start.* The person starts pedaling at a moderate resistance. The resistance is increased as pedaling rate increases. The test starts when the set resistance is reached.

---

[8]The computerized equipment is available from: Sports Medicine Industries, Inc., 1806 Danielle Drive, St. Cloud, MN 56301 (320) 252-8577.

Table 7.20 Normative Data for the Wingate Power Test

Percentile	Average Power for 30 Seconds				Peak Power			
	Men (n = 60)		Women (n = 69)		Men (n = 60)		Women (n = 69)	
	Watts	Watts/kg	Watts	Watts/kg	Watts	Watts/kg	Watts	Watts/kg
90	662	8.24	470	7.31	822	10.89	560	9.02
75	604	7.96	413	6.93	768	10.20	518	8.53
50	565	7.44	381	6.39	689	9.22	449	7.65
25	521	6.79	347	5.94	646	8.34	396	6.77
10	471	5.98	306	5.25	570	7.06	353	5.98
Mean	563	7.28	381	6.35	700	9.18	454	7.61
SD	66	0.88	56	0.73	95	1.43	81	1.24

*From Maud 1989

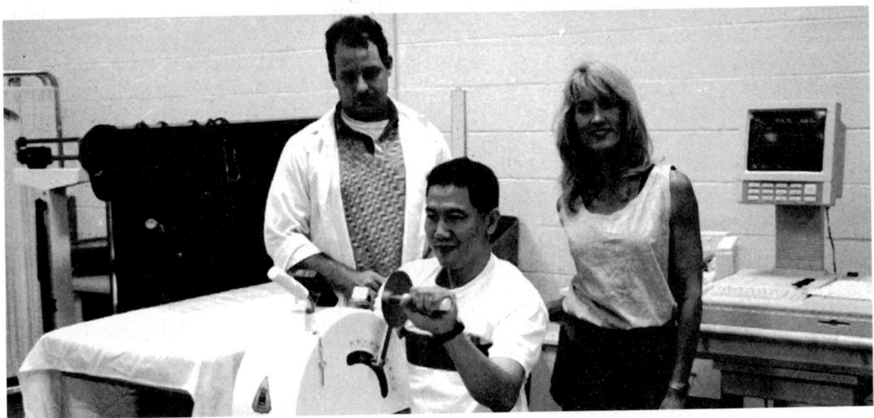

Figure 7.21
Test equipment used for the arm power test. (Photograph courtesy of D. M. Jackson. Used with permission.)

3. *All Out Start.* The ergometer resistance is set at 0 kp. At the start command, the subject starts to pedal at maximum velocity and the resistance is increased to the predetermined setting. The 30-second test starts when the setting is reached.

Scoring. Power output is determined from the resistance setting and the distance the flywheel traveled in 30 seconds. The test can be scored in absolute or relative terms. Absolute power output is in total watts, and relative power is watts per kilogram of body weight. With computer-controlled equipment, power output can be computed as the average for the 30 seconds or peak power achieved during the 30-second effort. Table 7.20 provides normative data for men and women (Maud & Scultz 1989).

While the Wingate power test has typically measured leg power, the same principles can be used to measure arm power. Figure 7.21 shows the test position with an arm ergometer. The same test principles used for leg-power tests are applied to the arm-power test. We have used an arm-power test to measure the anaerobic work capacity of coal miners (Laughery et al. 1985).

Muscular Endurance

Muscular endurance is the ability to persist in physical activity or to resist muscular fatigue. Endurance tests can measure absolute endurance where the weight load moved to exhaustion is the same for all subjects tested, or measure relative endurance where the weight moved varies among the subjects tested. The muscular endurance abilities described here involve moving or maintaining one's own body weight to exhaustion. Since body weights among subjects will vary, these are tests of relative endurance. Three basic endurance abilities have been identified: (1) muscular endurance of the arms and shoulder girdle, (2) muscular endurance of the abdominal muscles, and (3) cardiorespiratory endurance. Tests used to measure these endurance abilities are included in motor fitness and health-related fitness tests (see Chapters 9 and 10).

Arm and Shoulder Girdle Endurance Tests

Tests of arm and shoulder girdle endurance require the subject to move or support the body weight against the pull of gravity and may involve either isometric or isotonic contractions of the muscles executed to exhaustion. It has been claimed that tests of this ability measure both strength and endurance. Dynamic strength, arm and shoulder girdle strength, and muscular endurance are the terms used by physical educators to describe this ability. There is a negative correlation between body weight and this basic physical ability, and the correlation is even higher between percent of body fat and this basic ability.

The tests most often recommended for motor fitness or physical fitness batteries are pull-ups or chin-ups, and the flexed-arm hang. The AAHPERD Youth Fitness Test (1976) includes pull-ups for boys and the flexed-arm hang for girls. On both tests, the student is required to use the forward grip, palms facing away from the body. These tests can also be administered with the reverse grip, palms facing the body. Testing procedures for the AAHPERD pull-up and flexed-arm hang tests are provided in Chapter 9. Provided with the test instructions are norms.

When preparing to measure this ability, it is important to select a test of appropriate difficulty for the group being tested. There is a tendency for these test distributions to be positively skewed. Many students (e.g., junior high girls) have difficulty maintaining or moving their body weight against gravity. A high proportion of students, especially girls, cannot complete a single pull-up. This has led to the development of modified pull-up tests. Described next are two modified pull-up tests.

Youth Fitness Modified Pull-Up Test. The Prudential FITNESSGRAM® (1992) and AAHPERD Physical Best Tests (1989) youth fitness tests provide an optional test. For this test, the student lies down on his/her back with the shoulders directly under a bar that has been set 1 to 2 inches above the child's reach. The student grasps the bar with an overhand grip (palms away from the body). From this "down" position with the arms and legs straight, buttocks off the floor, and only the heels touching the floor, the student pulls until the chin reaches an elastic band placed on the pull-up equipment. The band is set 7 inches below the pull-up bar. Table 7.21 gives the optimal criterion-referenced standards for school-aged males and females.

Baumgartner Modified Pull-Up Test. The Baumgartner modified pull-up test can also be used for training (Baumgartner & Wood 1984). The equipment can be supported on either a floor stand or a wall bracket. The student lies down on the scooter and grasps the pull-up bar at the top end of the equipment with an overhanded grip, hands about

Table 7.21 Optimal Criterion-Referenced Standards for the Modified Pull-Up and Curl-Up Tests for Boys and Girls, Ages 5 to 17+

Age	Boys		Girls	
	Curl-Ups	*Modified Pull-Ups*	*Curl-Ups*	*Modified Pull-Ups*
5	7	10	7	10
6	7	10	7	10
7	9	14	9	14
8	11	20	11	20
9	11	24	11	22
10	15	24	13	26
11	17	28	13	29
12	20	36	13	32
13	22	40	13	32
14	25	45	13	32
15	27	47	13	35
16	30	47	13	35
17	30	47	13	35
17+	30	47	13	35

Standards from the Prudential FITNESSGRAM® test 1992.

shoulder-width apart (Figure 7.22). The student then assumes a straight-arm hanging position, pulls up the inclined board until the chin is over the bar, and returns to a straight-arm hanging position. This action is repeated as often as possible. The test is scored by the number of completed repetitions. Norms for most ages 6 through college and both sexes are reported by Baumgartner and associates (1984) and Jackson and associates (1982). Almost without exception, scores range from 3 to 50.

Measuring Abdominal Muscle Endurance

Tests of abdominal muscle endurance require the subject to use the abdominal muscles to move or maintain the body's upper extremity to exhaustion; they may require either isometric or isotonic contractions of these muscles. Tests that measure this ability have been called measures of abdominal muscle strength or endurance. These tests are fully covered in the youth and adult fitness chapters.

Measuring Cardiorespiratory Endurance

Cardiorespiratory endurance is another term for aerobic fitness or $\dot{V}O_2$ Max. This topic is fully discussed in Chapter 8.

Basic Movement Patterns

The importance of basic movement patterns—running, jumping, and throwing—is recognized by physical educators, and tests of these abilities are included in published general motor ability and motor fitness batteries. These abilities are especially important for evaluating athletes.

Measuring Running Speed

Tests of running **speed** require the subject to run at maximum speed in a straight path. The basic physical ability is measured by the elapsed time required to run a specified distance (usually 10 to 60 yards) or the distance the student can run during a specified time period (usually 4 to 8 seconds). This basic physical ability is

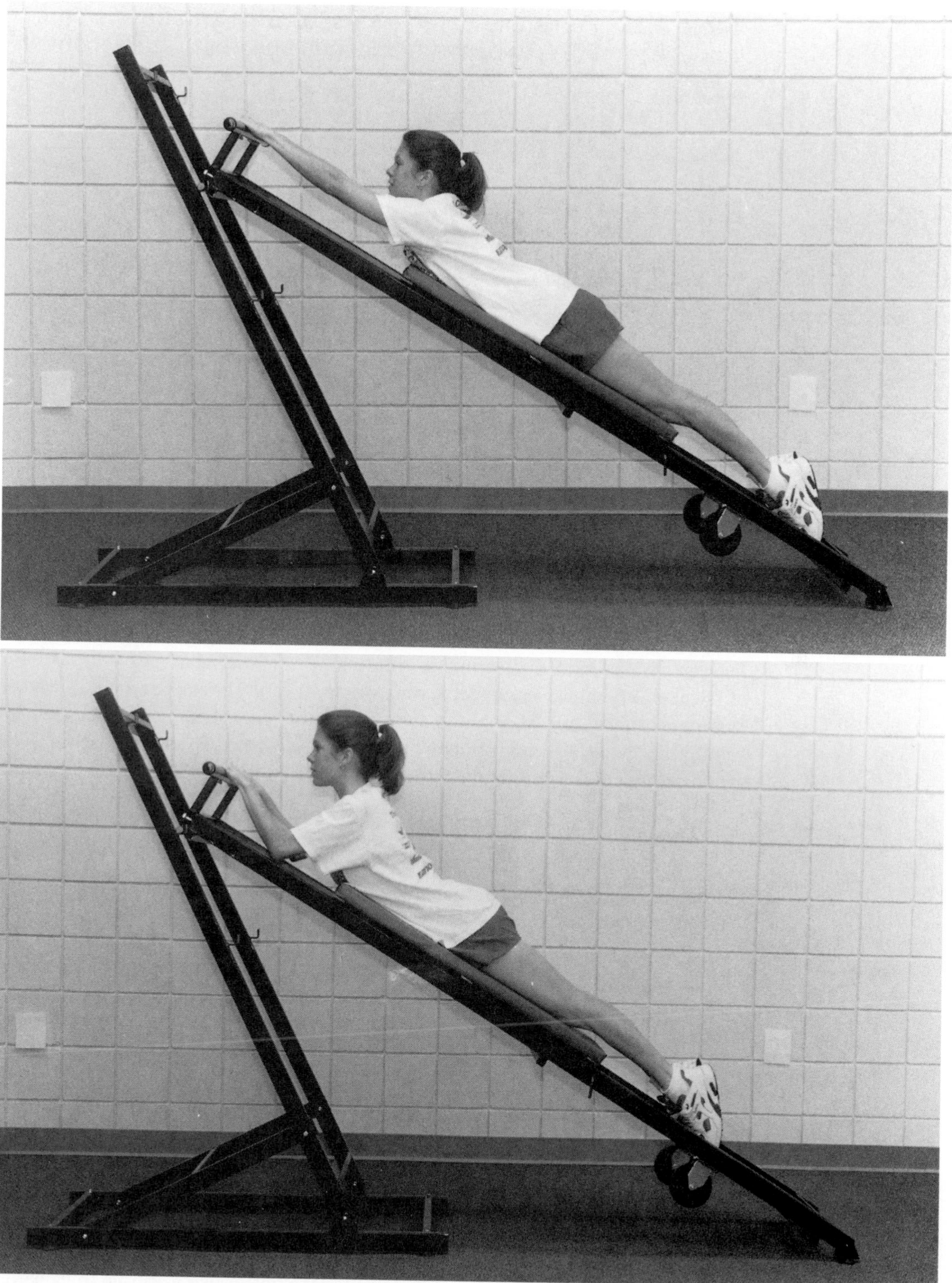

Figure 7.22 Baumgartner modified pull-up test. (Equipment pictures from Flaghouse, Hasbrouck Heights, NJ)

Table 7.22 Percentile-Rank Norms for Girls and Boys on the 50-Yard Dash (in Seconds and Tenths of Seconds)

Percentile	Age							
	9–10	*11*	*12*	*13*	*14*	*15*	*16*	*17+*
Girls								
95	7.4	7.3	7.0	6.9	6.8	6.9	7.0	6.8
75	8.0	7.9	7.6	7.4	7.3	7.4	7.5	7.4
50	8.6	8.3	8.1	8.0	7.8	7.8	7.9	7.9
25	9.1	9.0	8.7	8.5	8.3	8.2	8.3	8.4
5	10.3	10.0	10.0	10.0	9.6	9.2	9.3	9.5
Boys								
95	7.3	7.1	6.8	6.5	6.2	6.0	6.0	5.9
75	7.8	7.6	7.4	7.0	6.8	6.5	6.5	6.3
50	8.2	8.0	7.8	7.5	7.2	6.9	6.7	6.6
25	8.9	8.6	8.3	8.0	7.7	7.3	7.0	7.0
5	9.9	9.5	9.5	9.0	8.8	8.0	7.7	7.9

Source: Adapted from Youth Fitness Test Manual (Washington, DC: AAHPER, 1976), pp. 42 and 50. Used by permission.

normally represented on motor ability and motor fitness test batteries by a sprinting test ranging from 40 to 60 yards in length. Several investigators (Fleishman 1964; Jackson 1971) report that sprints as short as 20 yards reliably measure this basic physical ability; however, longer sprints, 40 or 50 yards, are more reliable (Jackson & Baumgartner 1969). Most motor ability or motor fitness batteries recommend 50-yard sprints, while 40-yard sprints are universally accepted by football coaches. Testing procedures and norms for the 50-yard dash (AAHPERD 1976) are provided next.

Test. 50-Yard Dash (AAHPER 1976)

Equipment. A stopwatch accurate to one-tenth second per runner, or a stopwatch accurate to a tenth of a second with a split timer, and a test course of suitable length to ensure safe stopping after the sprint.

Procedure. Have two students run at the same time for competition. The students assume a starting position behind the starting line. The starter uses the commands "Are you ready?" and "Go!" On "Go," the starter makes a downward sweep of the arm, giving a visual signal to the timer to start the watch. The timer, standing at the finish line, stops the watch when the runner crosses the line.

Scoring. The student's score is the elapsed time between the starter's signal and the instant the pupil crosses the finish line. Scores are recorded to the nearest tenth of a second. Selected AAHPERD norms for girls and boys are listed in Table 7.22.

Other Considerations. Allow students to take one or two warm-up trials before they are timed for score.

Measuring Running Agility

Agility is the ability to change the direction of the body or body parts rapidly. This ability is measured with running tests that require the subject to turn or start and stop. Such tests appear in most published general motor ability and motor fitness batteries. Running speed tends to be related to agility.

Research indicates that the tests used to measure running agility present a common measurement problem: students learn to perform these tests with practice (Baumgartner & Jackson 1970). It was found that when five trials were administered, the best scores for the group were achieved on Trials 4 and 5. These tests are time-consuming, so it would not normally be feasible to allow five trials, but you should give students an opportunity to practice before the test or while other students are being tested. Proper traction is another problem posed by these tests. It is essential that students wear proper shoes and that the test be administered on a suitable surface; a tile floor or a dirty floor may be too slippery.

Many tests of running agility have been published. The shuttle run requires the subject to run back and forth between two parallel lines. A second type of running agility test requires the student to run a test course that calls for constant turning. These two tests are provided to illustrate agility running tests. What would be more appropriate in the athletic setting is to study the types of agility movements made by the athlete and then develop sport-specific agility tests.

Test. Shuttle Run (AAHPER 1976)

Equipment. Floor space sufficiently large to allow acceptable traction, stopwatches accurate to a tenth of a second, and two wooden blocks (2 × 2 × 4) per test station.

Procedure. The test course is composed of two parallel lines placed on the floor 30 feet apart. The student starts from behind the first line and, after the starting command, runs to the second line, picks up one wooden block, runs back to the first line, and places the wooden block behind the line. The student then runs back and picks up the second block, carrying it back across the first line.

Scoring. The score is the elapsed time accurate to the nearest tenth of a second. Each student is allowed two trials and the best score is selected. The watch is started on the signal "Go," and stopped when the second block is carried across the line. Students who fall or slip significantly should be given another trial. Norms for boys and girls are listed in Table 7.23.

Other Considerations. This test is time-consuming because the trials must be administered individually. You can save time by setting up several test courses and having enough scorers. Efficiency can also be improved when two students run the course at the same time, in which case the tester needs two stopwatches or one with a split timer.

Test. Zigzag Run (Texas Fitness Test 1973)

Objective. To run a test course that requires turning as fast and efficiently as possible.

Validity. Construct validity of running agility.

Table 7.23 Percentile-Rank Norms for Boys and Girls on the Shuttle Run (in Seconds and Tenths)

Percentile	Age							
	9–10	*11*	*12*	*13*	*14*	*15*	*16*	*17+*
Boys								
95	10.0	9.7	9.6	9.3	8.9	8.9	8.6	8.6
75	10.6	10.4	10.2	10.0	9.6	9.4	9.3	9.2
50	11.2	10.9	10.7	10.4	10.1	9.9	9.9	9.8
25	12.0	11.5	11.4	11.0	10.7	10.4	10.5	10.4
5	13.1	12.9	12.4	12.4	11.9	11.7	11.9	11.7
Girls								
95	10.2	10.0	9.9	9.9	9.7	9.9	10.0	9.6
75	11.1	10.8	10.8	10.5	10.3	10.4	10.6	10.4
50	11.8	11.5	11.4	11.2	11.0	11.0	11.2	11.1
25	12.5	12.1	12.0	12.0	12.0	11.8	12.0	12.0
5	14.3	14.0	13.3	13.2	13.1	13.3	13.7	14.0

Source: Adapted from Youth Fitness Test Manual (Washington, DC: AAHPER, 1976), Used by permission.

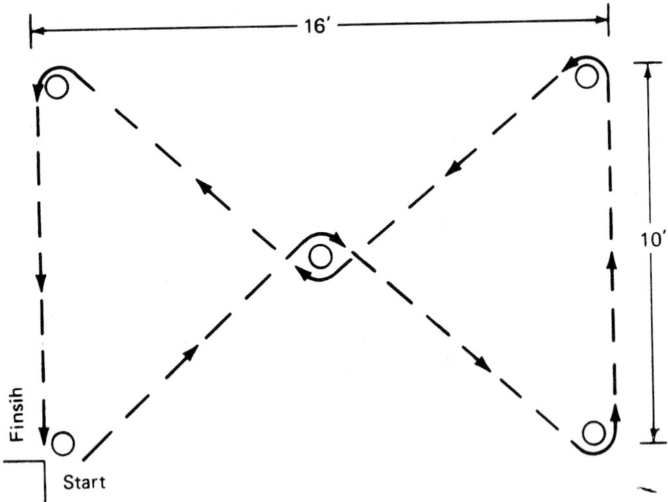

Figure 7.23
Test course for zigzag run.

Equipment. A test course of appropriate size, a stopwatch accurate to a tenth of a second, and five markers to outline the test course (see Figure 7.23). Although the instructions for several agility tests recommend the use of chairs, volleyball standards, or wooden clubs for outlining the test course, we strongly recommend that you not use these objects because of possible injury to students. Rubber pylons are ideal for safely outlining the course.

Procedure. At the signal, the student begins from behind the starting line and runs the outlined course one time as fast as possible.

Scoring. The student's score is the elapsed time accurate to the nearest tenth of a second. Give three trials. The first should be at three-quarter speed to familiarize the student with the procedure and to serve as a specific warm-up. The score is the mean of the last two trials.

Other Considerations. This is an example of an agility run test that involves turning rather than starting and stopping. By studying movements required by various athletes, these tests could be altered to reflect the movements required by the athlete and be more relevant for testing athletes.

Measuring Jumping Ability

Jumping tests measure the ability to expend maximum energy in one explosive act, projecting the body through space. The vertical jump, chalk jump, Sargent jump, and standing long jump (the easiest to administer) are the most frequently used tests of the ability.

Jumping tests have been described as tests of power (McCloy & Young 1954) and of explosive strength (Fleishman 1964). Although physical educators generally refer to these tests as measures of power, research has reported low correlations between jumping tests and mechanical measures of power (Barlow 1970; Considine 1970).

The need for leg strength in jumping is self-evident; body weight, however, is negatively correlated with jumping ability. The negative relation can be largely traced to body fatness. More force or greater muscular strength is needed to propel a heavier individual through space. Jumping ability, then, depends on individual differences in leg strength and body composition. If two individuals can generate the same amount of force, all other things being equal, the leanest person would jump highest.

The standing long jump is very easy to administer and is a common test of motor fitness batteries. The vertical jump is used by many coaches to test athletes.

Test. Standing Long Jump (AAHPER 1976)

Equipment. A tape measure at least 10 feet long and masking tape. You can construct the test station by attaching the tape measure to the floor with the starting line at 0 inches. We have found the gym floor to be a suitable surface, although mats can also be used.

Procedure. The student should straddle the tape measure, with feet parallel, about a shoulder-width apart, and toes behind the starting line. From this position, the student should squat and then jump horizontally as far as possible. The student should land straddling the tape measure.

Scoring. The recommended procedure is to administer three trials and award the student the best of the three trials. The test is scored in feet and inches to the nearest inch. Norms for boys and girls are listed in Table 7.24.

Other Considerations. Because the test must be administered individually, it is suggested that several test stations be used. It is important that students be allowed to practice the specific test because a learning effect has been shown to exist.

Test. Vertical Jump (Texas Test 1973)

Table 7.24 Percentile-Rank Norms for Boys and Girls on the Standing Long Jump (in Feet and Inches)

Percentile	Age							
	9–10	*11*	*12*	*13*	*14*	*15*	*16*	*17+*
Boys								
95	6′0″	6′2″	6′6″	7′1″	7′6″	8′0″	8′2″	8′5″
75	5′4″	5′7″	5′11″	6′3″	6′8″	7′2″	7′6″	7′9″
50	4′11″	5′2″	5′5″	5′9″	6′2″	6′8″	7′0″	7′2″
25	4′6″	4′8″	5′0″	5′2″	5′6″	6′1″	6′6″	6′6″
5	3′10″	4′0″	4′2″	4′4″	4′8″	5′2″	5′5″	5′3″
Girls								
95	5′10″	6′0″	6′2″	6′5″	6′8″	6′7″	6′6″	6′9″
75	5′2″	5′4″	5′6″	5′9″	5′11″	5′10″	5′9″	6′0″
50	4′8″	4′11″	5′0″	5′3″	5′4″	5′5″	5′3″	5′5″
25	4′1″	4′4″	4′6″	4′9″	4′10″	4′11″	4′9″	4′11″
5	3′5″	3′8″	3′10″	4′0″	4′0″	4′2″	4′0″	4′1″

Source: Adapted from Youth Fitness Test Manual (Washington, DC: AAHPER, 1976). Used by permission.

Objective. Using a double-foot takeoff, to jump vertically as high as possible with maximum effort.

Validity. Construct validity of jumping ability.

Equipment. A smooth wall of sufficient height, a yardstick, and chalk.

Procedure. Secure the student's standing height by having him or her stand with heels together on the floor and the side of his or her dominant hand holding a piece of chalk, next to the wall. From this position the student reaches upward as high as possible and marks on the wall. To execute the jump, the student squats next to the wall, jumps as high as possible, and marks the wall. Once in the starting position, the student should not walk in or step into the jump.

Scoring. The height of the jump is the measured distance between the standing and jumping heights. Measurements accurate to the last inch are precise enough for reliable results. Give three trials, the first at three-quarter speed to familiarize the student with the procedure and to serve as a specific warm-up. The score is the mean of the last two trials to the nearest half-inch.

Other Considerations. The vertical jump is more relevant for testing athletes such as volleyball and basketball players because jumping is an important part of the game. We are not aware of good normative data for this test. You are encouraged to develop norms relevant for your group.

Measuring Throwing Ability

Tests of throwing ability require the subject to throw a relatively light ball (baseball, softball, or basketball) overarm for distance. These tests have been reported to measure arm and shoulder girdle strength and/or coordination. Eckert (1965) reports a high correlation between muscular strength and speed of movement when the mass of the ball is high relative to the strength of the muscle groups involved. Obviously strength is necessary to throw a ball for distance; however, the weight of the ball relative to the strength of the thrower must be considered. For example, if young and relatively weak children are required to throw a basketball, muscular arm strength or power may be the dominant factor measured; if a Little League baseball is used, throwing ability is more likely to be measured. Given adequate strength, the basic physical ability measured is the execution of a coordinated overarm pattern with maximal speed.

Orthopedic surgeons have questioned the advisability of having children throw with maximal effort. "Little League elbow" is a common injury among preteen athletes. The softball throw for distance, once an item in the AAHPERD Youth Fitness battery, was dropped with the 1975 revision. For any throw for distance, it is recommended that the students be conditioned and warmed up before testing. Do not allow the students who complain of sore arms to take the test.

Test. Basketball Throw for Distance (Disch et al. 1977)

Objective. To throw a basketball as far as possible.

Validity and Reliability. The test has been shown to discriminate among levels of performance of female volleyball players. The intraclass reliability estimates with samples of females have ranged from 0.85 to 0.97.

Equipment. Two basketballs and a 100-foot tape measure.

Procedure. The throws are made with both feet parallel to the restraining line. The subject may not take a step to throw, but may follow through by stepping over the line after the throw, minimizing the action of the lower body. In this way the throw more closely represents the overarm pattern used when spiking or serving a volleyball. Each subject is awarded five throws.

Scoring. The student's score is the distance thrown to the nearest half-foot. This test was shown to have a warm-up effect; thus, the best score achieved is the recommended score.

Norms. Norms for female volleyball players are listed in Table 7.3.

Flexibility

Flexibility is the range of movement about a joint. Individual differences in flexibility depend on physiological characteristics that influence the extensibility of the muscles and ligaments surrounding a joint. Physical educators agree that certain levels and types of flexibility are wanted, but the degree of flexibility desired is yet to be determined.

Leighton (1955) has published the most comprehensive battery of flexibility tests using a specially developed instrument, the Leighton Flexometer, to measure the flexibility of a joint. Physical therapists use a protractorlike instrument called a goniometer to measure joint flexibility; in research laboratories, electronic and slow-motion

Figure 7.24
A type of flexibility.

photographic methods are used to measure flexibility. Although these are reliable methods for measuring flexibility, the investment of time and money prohibit their use out of the laboratory setting.

Flexibility is often regarded as a single general factor or ability. Clarke (1967) represents flexibility as a component of general motor ability. Harris (1969) conducted a factor analysis study to determine whether flexibility is a single general factor. Two types of flexibility tests were used in her study: (1) tests that measure the movement of a limb involving only one joint action; and (2) composite measures of movements that require more than one joint or more than one type of action within a single joint. The analysis revealed many intercorrelations to be near zero, which implies specificity rather than generality. A factor analysis of these data revealed thirteen different factors of flexibility. Harris concluded, then, that there is no evidence that flexibility is a single general factor.

Harris' finding indicates that we must think in terms of several types of flexibilities. We can easily recognize the importance of different types of flexibility in different motor skills. Figure 7.24 shows the types of flexibility needed by the modern dancer and the football punter. These specific types of flexibility are developed over time with special stretching exercises and practice in the given skill. The specificity of flexibility, then, means that we cannot use a single test to measure the various types of flexibility necessary to the execution of different motor skills.

Fleishman (1964) has identified a factor, called dynamic flexibility, involving the ability to change direction with the body parts rapidly and efficiently. Physical educators (McCloy & Young 1954) call this factor "agility that does not involve running." The squat thrust test is reported to measure the factor and is included in some motor fitness batteries as a measure of agility. Harris (1969) identified the same factor. The tests used to measure the factor are difficult to standardize and thus tend to lack reliability and are of questionable value. Fleishman (1964) offers a full description and norms for this test.

Kraus and Raab (1961) maintain that a degree of flexibility in the back and hamstring muscle groups is essential for the prevention of lower back disorders. Kraus and Hirschland (1954) have published a battery of minimum muscular fitness tests, the Kraus-Weber Tests, developed in a posture clinic for the diagnosis and treatment of patients with low-back pain. When these ten tests were administered to several thousand European and American school children, the American failure rate was considerably higher than the European rate. The test, scored on a pass-fail basis, is described next.

The subject stands erect in stockings or bare feet, hands at the sides, feet together. The test is for the subject to lean down slowly and touch the floor with the fingertips and hold the position for three seconds. The knees should be held straight and bouncing is not permitted. The value of flexibility for a healthy lower back is recognized by physicians, physical therapists, and physical educators. It is for this reason that the sit-and-reach test is a recommended test of health-related youth fitness tests reviewed in the next chapter. Test procedures and norms for these tests are provided in Chapter 9.

Balance

Balance is the ability to maintain body position, which is obviously essential to the successful execution of motor skills. Two general types of balance are commonly recognized: Static balance is the ability to maintain total body equilibrium while standing in one spot; and dynamic balance is the ability to maintain equilibrium while moving from one point to another. These two types of balance were first reported by Bass (1939), who stated that static balance depends on the ability to coordinate stimuli from: the three semicircular canals; the proprioceptive receptors located in the muscles, tendons, and joints; and visual perception. Dynamic balance depends on similar but more complex stimuli.

Singer (1968) argued against the assumption that there are only two general types of balance, claiming instead that different motor skills require different types of balance. The balance needed by the tennis player differs from that needed by the swimmer. Furthermore, he points out that different tests of balance do not correlate highly with each other. Fleishman (1964) suggests the existence of several factors in balance. He reported two factors in static balance, one measured with the eyes closed and the other with the eyes open. Because dynamic balance is more complex, it is likely to be composed of several more factors.

Due to the specificity of balance, the value of balance tests in the instructional process is yet to be determined. Balance tasks are often used by researchers of motor learning because significant improvements can be noted in a relatively short time. This learning effect, inherent in balance tests, indicates that they are not reliable in terms of stability. Thus, the tests do not offer stable measurements for purposes of placement, diagnosis, or prediction. By contrast, many gymnastic and tumbling stunts, including the headstand, involve learning a specific type of balance. Because the performance of balance stunts is an instructional objective of a tumbling or gymnastics unit, the value of measuring these specific types of balance is easily defended. Described next are common tests of static balance (eyes open or shut) and a test of dynamic balance commonly used to study skill acquisition.

Static Balance

The static balance test was first recommended by Bass (1939), and the test was revised by Fleishman (1964). Wooden sticks (1″ × 1″ > 12″) are taped to the floor. At the word "Ready," the subject places the supporting foot lengthwise on the stick. At the command "Go," the subject raises the free foot and holds this position as long as possible for a maximum of 60 seconds. The test is terminated if (1) either foot touches the floor; or (2) balance is maintained for 60 seconds. The subject is given three practice trials, and the subject's score is the sum of six trials of the test. Fleishman (1964) administered the test with the eyes open and closed and found they measured different factors.

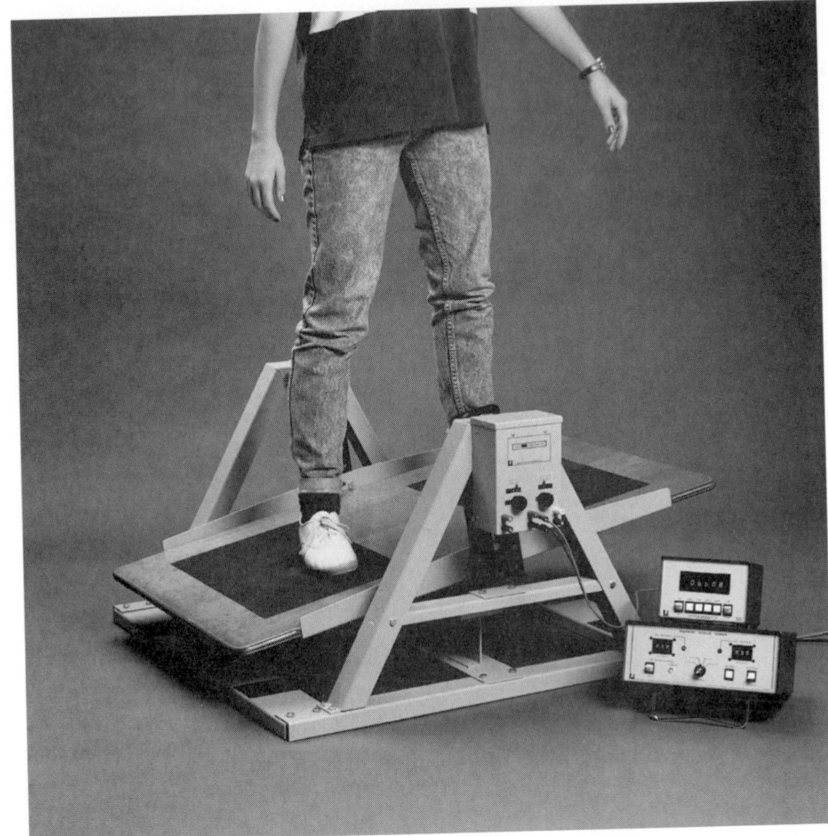

Figure 7.25
The stability platform is a laboratory task designed to measure dynamic balance. The apparatus uses electronic equipment to measure the time the subject can maintain balance. (Photo courtesy of Lafayette Instrument Company, Lafayette, IN.)

Dynamic Balance

Dynamic balance can be measured with a stability platform (Figure 7.25). The objective is to keep the balancing platform as level as possible during a regulated time period. Electronic clocks and interval timers are used to measure the subject's capacity to maintain balance for a given time period, often 30 seconds in duration. You are directed to another source (Rudisill & Jackson 1992) for a description of the equipment and task.[9]

Kinesthetic Perception

Kinesthesis, or kinesthetic perception, is the ability to perceive the body's position in space and the relationship of its parts (Singer 1968). The proprioceptors, highly developed sense organs located in the muscles, tendons, and joints, compose a highly sensitive system of kinesthetic perception. They provide the brain with information about what the parts of the body are doing when executing a skill.

The need for and importance of kinesthesis for skill learning is universally acknowledged, and several physical educators (Roloff 1953; Scott 1955; Wiebe 1954; Young 1954) have tried to develop kinesthesis tests. These tests tend to have

[9]Lafayette Instrument Company manufactures the electronic equipment and stability platform and distributes the lab manual (Rudisill & Jackson 1992) that describes this dynamic balance test. For information, call (800) 428–7545.

very low reliabilities, and their value for general testing is questionable. Kinesthesis is central to the execution of motor skill, but it cannot be measured with accuracy.

Fine Psychomotor Abilities

Fine motor abilities are those that do not involve total body movement. Some more common abilities are simple and complex forms of hand-eye coordination, reaction time, and movement time. Common methods of measuring these psychomotor abilities in the laboratory are described in another source (Rudisill & Jackson 1992). Fine psychomotor abilities are often used to study psychomotor skill acquisition.

Summary

Physical educators have traditionally accepted the notion of generality and believe that a test or group of tests is predictive of a wide range of motor skills. The theory of specificity of motor-skill acquisition was largely responsible for showing that motor ability and motor educability tests lacked validity. The theory of basic physical abilities does provide a theoretically sound base for generality testing. This theory is especially useful for testing athletes, for preemployment testing for physically demanding jobs, and for estimating a worker's capacity to be able to complete physically demanding work tasks. Adequate levels of physical ability are important for reducing the risk of back injuries associated with lifting.

Researchers have identified three basic motor performance abilities—muscular strength, muscular power, and endurance—and three basic movement patterns—running, jumping, and throwing. Several different tests are available to measure each ability. Although tests can be used for general evaluation, they are especially useful for identifying students with athletic potential.

The assessment of flexibility, balance, and kinesthesis is a difficult problem. Flexibility is not a general factor; rather it is task-specific, and different types are needed to perform different motor tasks. There were thought to be two basic types of balance: dynamic and static. However, research suggests that several additional types of balance also exist. Kinesthesis is the ability to perceive the body's position in space and the relationship of its parts. The reliability of kinesthetic tests tends to be low, making this trait difficult to measure.

Objective 1 Describe the tests that historically have been used to measure generality.

1. Summarize the traditional procedures used to measure the generality of motor performance.
2. Describe the differences between motor educability and general motor ability.
3. What effect did Henry's memory-drum theory have on the generality concept?
4. The terms *ability* and *skill* are often used interchangeably. Describe the essential difference between the two.
5. Could a basic ability be considered a measure of generality?

Objective 2 Apply the theory of basic physical abilities to the evaluation of athletes.

1. In evaluating different groups of athletes (e.g., gymnasts and basketball players), would you test the same basic abilities?
2. Outline the steps a teacher or coach could follow to develop a test for athletes.

Objective 3 Identify the methods to develop preemployment tests for physically demanding jobs and the types of tests that make up preemployment batteries.

1. What are the steps used to develop a preemployment physical test?
2. What kinds of tests are used for a preemployment test?
3. What types of physical ability tests are most often used for preemployment testing?

Objective 4 Understand the relation of physical ability to the risk of back injuries.

1. What are the primary reasons workers suffer low-back problems?
2. What is the relationship between psychophysical ratings of lift difficulty and the risk of injury?
3. What is the relationship between strength and lift difficulty?

Objective 5 Identify basic physical abilities and tests that validly measure each ability.

1. The text provides a system for classifying basic abilities and describes tests that measure each ability. Summarize the general characteristics of each basic ability and list one test that measures each.
2. Develop a five-item motor performance battery that includes tests of different basic abilities. Use tests that are feasible for mass testing.

Additional Learning Activities

1. Summarize the research supporting the specificity of motor-skill learning. Pay close attention to the procedures used by the researcher to conclude specificity or generality.
2. Select a sport and identify the basic abilities demanded by it. Using Fleishman's theory of basic abilities, develop a test battery that could be used to evaluate athletes.
3. Examine the effect of lift weight on psychophysical ratings of the lift. Put different weight loads (e.g., 25 to 95 pounds) in several different boxes. Starting with the lightest load, have a person lift the box and place it on a table. After completing the lift, have the person rate the lift difficulty with Borg's CR-10 scale. Move on to the next heaviest box and repeat the task until all boxes have been lifted and rated. Do not let the person know the weight in each box until he or she has completed the lifts. You can use this data to help the person determine their acceptable lift weight.
4. A test can be made more reliable, valid, and feasible for mass use by improving the procedures used to administer it. For example, some have constructed inexpensive devices to measure balance, vertical jumping, and push-ups. Try to develop equipment that would improve the testing of some basic ability.
5. Are absolute endurance and 1-RM really highly correlated? If you have access to weight-lifting equipment, devise tests that measure both. Administer the tests to a group of students and determine if the 1-RM score is correlated with the absolute endurance score.

6. Gain testing experience by using some of the tests listed in this chapter and administer the tests to a group of students. Determine how reliable your testing methods are.

Bibliography

AAHPER. 1976. *Youth fitness test manual.* Washington, DC: AAHPER.

———. 1980. *Health related physical fitness manual.* Washington, DC: AAHPERD.

———. 1989. *Physical best: Instructor's guide.* Reston, VA: AAHPERD.

American Health and Fitness Foundation. 1986. *FYT program manual.* Austin, TX.

Arvey, R. D. and R. H. Faley. 1988. *Fairness in selecting employees.* 2d ed. Reading, MA: Addison-Wesley.

Arvey, R. D., S. M. Nutting, and T. E. Landon. 1992. Validation strategies for physical ability testing in police and fire settings. *Public Personnel Management* 21:301–312.

Ayoub, M. A. 1982. Control of manual lifting hazards: II. Job redesign. *Journal of Occupational Medicine* 24:676–688.

Barlow, D. A. 1970. Relation between power and selected variables in the vertical jump. In J. M. Cooper (Ed.). *Selected topics on biomechanics* (pp. 233–241). Chicago, IL: Athletic Institute.

Barnard, R. and H. W. Duncan. 1975. Heart rate and ECG responses of firefighters. *Journal of Occupational Medicine* 17:247–250.

Bar-Or, O. 1987. The Wingate anaerobic test: An update on methodology, reliability and validity. *Sports Medicine* 4:381–394.

Bass, R. I. 1939. An analysis of the components of tests of semicircular canal function and static and dynamic balance. *Research Quarterly* 2:33–52.

Baumgartner, T. A. et al. 1984. Equipment improvements and additional norms for the modified pull-up test. *Research Quarterly for Exercise and Sport* 55:64–68.

Baumgartner, T. A. and A. S. Jackson. 1970. Measurement schedules for tests of motor performance. *Research Quarterly* 41:10–14.

Baumgartner, T. A. and S. Wood. 1984. Development of shoulder-girdle strength-endurance in elementary children. *Research Quarterly for Exercise and Sport* 55:169–171.

Baumgartner, T. A. and M. A. Zuidema. 1972. Factor analysis of physical fitness tests. *Research Quarterly* 43:443–450.

Bernauer, E. M. and J. Bonanno. 1975. Development of physical profiles for specific jobs. *Journal of Occupational Medicine* 17:22–33.

Borg, G. *Borg's Perceived Exertion and Pain Scaling Method.* Champaign: Human Kinetics. 1998.

Borg, G. 1977. Physical work and effort. *Proceedings of the First International Symposium.* Wenner-Gren Center, Stockholm, Sweden. Oxford, England: Pergamon Press.

———. 1982. A category scale with ratio properties for intermodal and interindividual comparisons. In Geissler, H. G. and P. Petzold (Eds.). *Psychophysical Judgment and the Process of Perception.* Berlin: VEB Deutscher Verlag der Wissenschaften.

Borg, G. and D. Ottoson. 1986. *The perception of exertion and physical work.* Stockholm: The Wenner-Gren Center.

Campion, M. A. 1983. Personnel selection for physically demanding jobs: Review and recommendations. *Personnel Psychology* 36:527–550.

Carpenter, A. 1942. The measurements of general motor capacity and general motor ability in the first three grades. *Research Quarterly* 13:444–446.

Cascio, W. F., R. A. Alexander, and G. V. Barrett. 1988. Setting cutoff scores: Legal, psychometric, and professional issues and guidelines. *Personnel Psychology* 41:1–24.

———. 1974. Human strength capability and low-back pain. *Journal of Occupational Medicine* 16:248–254.

Chaffin, D. B. 1975. Ergonomics guide for the assessment of human static strength. *American Industrial Hygiene Association Journal* 36:505–511.

Chaffin, D. B., R. O. Andres, and A. Garg. 1983. Volitional postures during maximal push/pull exertions in the sagittal plane. *Human Factors* 25:541–550.

Chaffin, D. B., G. D. Herrin, and W. M. Keyserling. 1978. Preemployment strength testing. *Journal of Occupational Medicine.* 67:403–408.

Chaffin, D. B. and K. S. Park. 1973. A longitudinal study of low-back pain as associated with occupational weight lifting factors. *American Industrial Hygiene Association Journal* 34:513–525.

Chin, A., R. R. Bishu, and S. Halbeck, 1995. Psychophysical measures of exertion. Are they muscle group dependent. *Proceedings of the Human Factors Society* 39:694–698.

Clarke, H. H. 1967. *Application of measurement to health and physical education.* 4th ed. Englewood Cliffs, NJ: Prentice-Hall.

Considine, W. J. 1970. A validity analysis of selected leg power tests utilizing a force platform. In J. M. Cooper, (Ed.). *Selected topics on biomechanics* (pp. 243–50). Chicago, IL: Athletic Institute.

Considine, W. et al. 1976. Developing a physical performance test battery for screening Chicago fire fighting applicants. *Public Personnel Management* 5:7–14.

Cousins, G. F. 1955. A factor analysis of selected wartime fitness tests. *Research Quarterly* 26:277–288.

Cumbee, F. 1954. A factorial analysis of motor coordination. *Research Quarterly* 25:412–420.

Davis, P. and C. Dotson. 1978. Heart rate responses to fire fighting activities. *Ambulatory Electrocardiology* 1:15–18.

Dehlin, O., B. Hendenrud, and J. Horal. 1976. Back symptoms in nursing aids in a geriatic hospital. *Scandinavian Journal of Rehabilitative Medicine* 8:47–53.

de Vries, H. A. 1980. *Physiology of exercise for physical education and athletics.* Dubuque, IA: Wm. C. Brown.

Disch, J., R. Frankiewicz, and A. S. Jackson. 1975. Construct validation of distance run tests. *Research Quarterly* 46:169–176.

Disch, J. G. et al. 1977. The construction and analysis of a test related to volleyball playing capacity in females. Mimeographed. Houston, TX: Rice University.

Eckert, H. M. 1965. A concept of force-energy in human movement. *Journal of American Physical Therapy Association* 45:13–18.

EEOC. 1978. Uniform guidelines on employment selection procedures. *Federal Register 43* (38289 28309).

Fleishman, E. A. 1956. Psychomotor selection tests: Research and application in the U.S. Air Force. *Personnel Psychology* 9:449–467.

Fleishman, E. A. 1964. *The structure and measurement of physical fitness.* Englewood Cliffs, NJ: Prentice-Hall.

Gael, S. 1988. *The job analysis handbook for business, industry, and government.* Vol. I. New York: John Wiley & Sons.

Gettman, L. R. 1993. Chapter 19. Fitness testing. In *Resource Manual for Guidelines for Exercise Testing and Prescription.* Philadelphia: Lea & Febiger.

Glencross, D. J. 1966. The nature of the vertical jump test and the standing broad jump test. *Research Quarterly* 37:353–359.

Golding, L. A., C. R. Meyers, and W. E. Sinning. 1989. *The Y's way to physical fitness.* 3d ed. Chicago, IL: National Board of YMCA.

Gray, R. K. 1962. Relationship between leg speed and leg power. *Research Quarterly* 33:395–400.

Harris, M. 1969. A factor analytic study of flexibility. *Research Quarterly* 40:62–70.

Henry, F. M. 1956. Coordination and motor learning. In *59th Annual Proceedings College Physical Education Association* 59:68–75.

Henry, F. M. 1958. Specificity vs. generality in learning motor skills. In *61st Annual Proceedings College Physical Education Association* 61:126–128.

Herrin, G. D., D. B. Chaffin, and R. S. Mach. 1974. *Criteria for research on the hazards of manual materials handling.* U.S. Government Printing Office. Washington, DC: NIOSH.

Hidalgo, J., et al. 1997. A comprehensive lifting model: Beyond the NIOSH lifting equation. *Ergonomics* 40(9):916–927.

Hogan, J. and A. M. Quigley. 1986. Physical standard for employment and courts. *American Psychologist* 41:1193–1217.

Hogan, J. C. 1991. Chapter 11. Physical abilities. In M. D. Dunette, and L. M. Hough (Eds.). *Handbook of industrial and organizational psychology.* 2d ed. Vol. 2 (pp. 743–831). Palo Alto, CA: Consulting Psychologist Press.

Hosmer, D. W. and S. Lemeshow. 1989. *Applied logistic regression.* New York: John Wiley & Sons.

Ismail, A., H. Falls, and D. MacLeod. 1965. Development of a criterion for physical fitness tests from factor analysis results. *Journal of Applied Physiology* 20:991–999.

Jackson, A. S. 1971. Factor analysis of selected muscular strength and motor performance test. *Research Quarterly* 42:164–172.

———. (1986). *Validity of isometric strength tests for predicting work performance in offshore drilling and producing environments. Houston: Shell Oil Company, 1986.* Houston: Shell Oil Company.

———. 1994. Chapter 3. Preemployment physical evaluation. *Exercise and Sport Science Review* 22:53–90.

———. 1996. *Physical work capacity pre-employment evaluation system.* Lafayette, IN: Lafayette Instrument Co.

Jackson, A. S. et al. 1990a. Prediction of functional aerobic capacity without exercise testing. *Medicine and Science in Sports* 22:863–870.

Jackson, A. S. et al. 1990b. Validation of physical strength tests for the Texas City plant of Union Carbide Corporation. Center for Applied Psychological Services, Rice University, Houston, TX.

Jackson, A. S. et al. 1991. Strength demands of chemical plant work tasks. *Proceedings of the Human Factors Society 35th Annual Meeting* 1:758–762.

Jackson, A. S. et al. 1992. Validity of isometric strength tests for predicting the capacity to crack, open and close industrial valves. *Proceedings of the Human Factors Society 36th Annual Meeting* 1:688–691.

Jackson, A. S. et al. 1993. Validation of physical strength tests for the Federal Express Corporation. Center of Applied Psychological Services, Rice University, Houston, TX.

Jackson, A. S. et al. 1997. Role of physical work capacity and load weight on psychophysical lift ratings. *International Journal of Industrial Ergonomics* 20:181–190.

Jackson, A. S. et al. 1998. Revalidation of methods for pre-employment assessment of physical abilities at Shell Western Exploration and Production, Inc., and CalResources LLC. Houston, TX: Departments of HHP and Psychology, University of Houston, and Department of Psychology, Rice University.

Jackson, A. S. and T. A. Baumgartner. 1969. Measurement schedules of sprint running. *Research Quarterly* 40:708–711.

Jackson, A. S. and R. J. Frankiewicz. 1975. Factorial expressions of muscular strength. *Research Quarterly* 46:206–217.

Jackson, A. S. and M. L. Pollock. 1976. Factor analysis and multivariate scaling of anthropometric variables for the assessment of body composition. *Medicine and Science in Sports* 8:196–203.

Jackson, A. S., H. G. Osburn, and K. R. Laughery. 1984. Validity of isometric strength tests for predicting performance in physically demanding jobs. *Proceedings of the Human Factors Society 28th Annual Meeting* 28:452–454.

Jackson, A. S., H. G. Osburn, and K. R. Laughery. 1991. Validity of isometric strength tests for predicting endurance work tasks of coal miners. *Proceedings of the Human Factors Society 35th Annual Meeting* 1:763–767.

Jackson, A. S. and R. M. Ross. 1997. *Understanding exercise for health and fitness.* 3d ed. Dubuque, IA: Kendall/Hunt.

Jackson, Allen et al. 1982. Baumgartner's modified pull-up test for male and female elementary school-aged children. *Research Quarterly for Exercise and Sport* 53:163–164.

Karwowski, W. 1996. Maximum safe weight of lift: A new paradigm for setting design limits in manual lifting tasks based on the psychophysical approach. *Proceedings of the Human Factors Society,* 40:614–618.

Keyserling, W. et al. 1980a. Establishing an industrial strength testing program. *American Industrial Hygiene Association Journal* 41:730–736.

Keyserling, W. M. et al. 1980b. Isometric strength testing as a means of controlling medical incidents on strenuous jobs. *Journal of Occupational Medicine* 22:332–336.

Kishino, N. D. et al. 1985. Quantification of lumbar function: Part 4: Isometric and isokinetic lifting simulation in normal subjects and low-back dysfunction patients. *Spine* 10:921–927.

Kraus, H. and R. P. Hirschland. 1954. Minimum muscular fitness test in school children. *Research Quarterly* 25:177–188.

Kraus, H. and W. Raab. 1961. *Hypokinetic disease.* Springfield, IL: Thomas.

Larson, L. A. 1941. A factor analysis of motor ability variables and tests for college men. *Research Quarterly* 12:499–517.

Laubach, L. L. 1976. Comparative muscular strength on men and women: A review of the literature. *Aviation, Space, and Environmental Medicine* 47:534–542.

Laughery, K. R., & Jackson, A. S. (1984). *Pre-employment physical test development for roustabout jobs on offshore production facilities.* Lafayette, Louisiana: Kerr-McGee Corp.

Laughery, K. R. et al. 1985. Physical abilities and performance tests for coal miner jobs. Houston, TX: Center of Applied Psychological Sciences, Rice University.

Leighton, J. 1955. An instrument and technique for the measurement of range of joint motion. *Archives of Physical Medicine* 36:571–578.

Lemon, P. W. R. and R. T. Hermiston. 1977. The human energy cost of firefighting. *Journal of Occupational Medicine* 19:558–562.

Lephart, S. M. and T. J. Henry. 1996. The physiological basis for open and closed kinetic chain rehabilitation for the upper extremity. *Journal of Sport Rehabilitation* 5(1):71–87.

Liba, M. R. 1967. Factor analysis of strength variables. *Research Quarterly 38:*649–662.

Manning, J. and T. Griggs. 1983. Heart rates in fire fighters using light and heavy breathing equipment: Similar near-maximal exertion in response to multiple work load conditions. *Journal of Occupational Medicine* 25:215–218.

Margaria, R. et al. 1966. Measurement of muscular power (anaerobic) in man. *Journal of Applied Physiology* 21:1662–1664.

Marriott, B. M. and J. Grumstrup-Scott. Eds. 1992. *Body composition and physical performance: Application for the military services.* Washington, DC: National Academy Press.

Maud, P. J. and B. B. Scultz. 1989. Norms for the Wingate anaerobic test with comparison to another similar test. *Research Quarterly for Exercise and Sport* 60(2):144–150.

McArdle, W. D., F. I. Katch, and V. L. Katch. 1991. *Exercise physiology: Energy, nutrition, and human performance.* 3d ed. Philadelphia: Lea & Febiger.

McCloy, C. H. 1932. *The measurement of athletic power.* New York: Barnes.

McCloy, C. H. 1956. A factor analysis of tests of endurance. *Research Quarterly* 27:213–216.

McCloy, C. H. and N. D. Young. 1954. *Test and measurements in health and physical education.* New York: Appleton-Century-Crofts.

Meyers, D. C. et al. 1984. Factor analysis of strength, cardiovascular endurance, flexibility, and body composition measures (Tech. Rep. R83-9). Bethesda, MD: Advanced Research Resources Organization.

Morrow, J. R., Jr. et al. 1995. *Measurement and evaluation in human performance.* Champaign, IL: Human Kinetics.

NIOSH. 1977. *Preemployment strength testing.* Washington, DC: U.S. Department of Health and Human Services.

NIOSH. 1981. *Work practices guide for manual lifting.* Washington, DC: U.S. Department of Health and Human Services.

O'Connell, E. et al. 1986. Energy costs of simulated stair climbing as a job-related task in fire fighting. *Journal of Occupational Medicine* 28:282–284.

Park, K. and D. B. Chaffin. 1974. Biomechanical evaluation of two methods of manual load lifting. *AIIE Transactions* 6 (2)22–26.

Plowman, S. A. 1992. Chapter 8. Physical activity, physical fitness, and low back pain. In Holloszy, J. O. (Ed.). *Exercise and Sport Sciences Reviews.* Baltimore, MD: Williams & Wilkins.

Pollock, M. L. et al. 1978. Characteristics of elite class distance runners. *Annals of New York Academy of Sciences* 301:278–410.

Prudential FITNESSGRAM Test Administration Manual. 1992. Dallas: The Cooper Institute for Aerobic Research.

Reilly, R. R., S. Zedeck, and M. L. Tenopyr. 1979. Validity and fairness of physical ability tests for predicting craft jobs. *Journal of Applied Psychology* 64:267–274.

Resnik, M. L. 1995. The generalizability of psychophysical ratings in predicting the perception of lift difficulty. *Proceedings of the Human Factors Society* 39:679–682.

Roloff, L. L. 1953. Kinesthesis in relation to the learning of selected motor skills. *Research Quarterly* 24:210–217.

Rudisill, M. E. and A. S. Jackson. 1992. *Theory and application of motor learning.* Onalaska, TX: MacJR Publishing Company.

Russell, J. A. et al. 1993. Can isometric strength measures be used to predict isotonic strength? *Research Quarterly for Exercise and Sport* 64:A–45.

Safrit, M. J. 1966. *The structure of gross motor skill patterns.* Washington, DC: U.S. Department of Health, Education, and Welfare. Office of Education Cooperative Research Project No. S 397.

Sargent, D. A. 1921. The physical test of man. *American Physical Education Review* 26:188–194.

SAS. 1989. *JMP User's Guide: Version 2 of JMP.* Cary, NC: SAS Institute.

Scott, M. G. 1955. Test of kinesthesis. *Research Quarterly* 26:324–341.

Singer, R. N. 1968. *Motor learning and human performance.* New York: Macmillan.

Snook, S. H., R. A. Campanelli, and J. W. Hart. 1978. A study of three preventive approaches to low-back injury. *Journal of Occupational Medicine* 20:478–481.

Snook, S. H. and V. M. Ciriello. 1991. The design of manual handling tasks: Revised tables of maximum acceptable weights and forces. *Ergonomics* 34:1197–1213.

Snyder-Mackler, L. 1996. Scientific rationale and physiological basis for the use of closed kinetic chain exercise in the lower extremity. *Journal of Sport Rehabilitation* 5(1):2–12.

Sothmann, M. S. et al. 1990. Advancing age and the cardiorespiratory stress of fire suppression: Determining a minimum standard for aerobic fitness. *Human Performance* 3:217–236.

Sothmann, M. S. et al. 1992. Heart rate response of firefighters to actual emergencies. *Journal of Occupational Medicine* 34:797–800.

Start, K. B. et al. 1966. A factorial investigation of power, speed, isometric strength, and anthropometric measures in the lower limb. *Research Quarterly* 37:553–558.

Texas Governor's Commission on Physical Fitness. 1973. *Physical fitness-motor ability test.* Austin, TX.

Waters, T. R. et al. 1993. Revised NIOSH equation for the design and evaluation of manual lifting tasks. *Ergonomics* 7:749–766.

Wiebe, V. R. 1954. A study of test of kinesthesis. *Research Quarterly* 25:222–227.

Wilmore, J. H. 1976. *Athletic training and physical fitness.* Boston, MA: Allyn and Bacon.

Young, O. G. 1954. A study of kinesthesis in relation to selected movements. *Research Quarterly* 16:277–287.

Zuidema, M. A. and T. A. Baumgartner. 1974. Second factor analysis of physical fitness tests. *Research Quarterly* 45:247–256.

8

CHAPTER

Evaluating Aerobic Fitness

Contents

Key Words

aerobic fitness
cycle ergometer
distance-run tests
maximal exercise test
METs
multi-stage exercise test
oxygen uptake
power output
rating of perceived exertion
single-stage exercise test
submaximal exercise test
$\dot{V}O_2$ Max

Objectives

Aerobic fitness, like body composition, is a major component of both adult and youth fitness. Epidemiological research has documented that low aerobic fitness is associated with an increased risk of mortality. While the same laboratory tests can be used to measure both adult and youth aerobic fitness, the field tests used often differ. Chapter 10 covers the methods for measuring the health-related fitness of school children. While treadmill and cycle ergometer tests can be used to evaluate youth aerobic fitness, distance-run tests are more likely to be used. In contrast, distance-run tests can be used to evaluate adult aerobic fitness, but a variety of aerobic fitness tests are available for adults. Evaluating the aerobic fitness of adults is likely to take place in a variety of places, including medical or university laboratories, YMCAs, and private or corporate fitness centers. This testing is most likely to be done by an exercise specialist. The purpose of this chapter is to outline the tests used to measure aerobic fitness. This involves integrating measurement theory with exercise physiology.

After reading Chapter 8, you should be able to:

1. Identify the role of aerobic fitness in health.
2. Differentiate between a stress test and fitness evaluation.
3. Define the methods used to measure VO_2 Max from (a) maximal tests; (b) submaximal tests; (c) walking and running field tests; and (d) nonexercise models.
4. Define the levels of aerobic fitness needed for health promotion and physically demanding exercise.
5. Identify maximal and submaximal treadmill protocols.
6. Identify cycle ergometer submaximal protocols.

Introduction

Aerobic fitness is, to a large extent, dependent on and limited by the body's ability to deliver oxygen to the working muscles. The lungs, heart, blood, circulatory system, and working muscles are all factors in determining one's aerobic fitness. The public health reports (U.S. Public Health Service 1990, 1996), reviewed in Chapter 1, place special importance on aerobic exercise and fitness for health promotion. Aerobic exercise is the most efficient form of exercise for developing aerobic fitness and expending sufficient amounts of energy (i.e., calories). Caloric expenditure is not only important for weight control and reducing the prevalence of overweight; it also provides a margin of protection from heart disease. In this chapter we briefly review the role of aerobic fitness in health. We review the difference between a fitness evaluation and the medical stress test and the medical criteria that exercise specialists need to consider when testing adults. Finally, the laboratory and field methods that are available to measure and evaluate adult and youth aerobic fitness are fully presented.

Essential Definitions

The maximal volume of oxygen one can consume during exhausting exercise (**VO_2 Max**) is considered the best index of aerobic fitness (Åstrand & Rodahl 1970, 1986; ACSM 1991). It is best measured by slowly and systematically increasing the intensity of exercise until exhaustion is reached. Computer-controlled metabolic carts have the capacity to measure the volume of oxygen used during the entire test. Provided next are definitions of terms used in this chapter.

Oxygen Uptake

Oxygen uptake ($\dot{V}O_2$) is the volume of oxygen used under given conditions. This may be at rest, during submaximal exercise, or during maximal exercise (i.e., $\dot{V}O_2$ Max). Oxygen uptake is expressed in two general ways: first, by the total volume used for a standard length of time. This is expressed in milliliters (ml) or liters (L)[1] of oxygen per minute (min^{-1}). The total volume of oxygen used is a function of one's muscle mass. The more muscle mass, the greater volume of oxygen consumed. To control for size difference, $\dot{V}O_2$ expressed in milliliters is divided by body weight and expressed by milliliters of oxygen used per kilogram of body weight per minute ($ml \cdot kg^{-1} \cdot min^{-1}$). Provided next is the general formula to quantify $\dot{V}O_2$ per kilogram of body weight at either maximal or submaximal levels.

Expressing $\dot{V}O_2$ per Kilogram of Body Weight **(8.1)**

$$\dot{V}O_2(ml \cdot kg^{-1} \cdot min^{-1}) = \left(\frac{\dot{V}O_2\ L \cdot min^{-1} \times 1000}{\text{Weight in kg}}\right)$$

Computation Example. Assume a 65-kilogram person exercises on a cycle ergometer at a $\dot{V}O_2$ of 1.5 $L \cdot min^{-1}$. Their $\dot{V}O_2$ expressed as $ml \cdot kg^{-1} \cdot min^{-1}$ (Formula 8.1) would be

$$\dot{V}O_2\ (ml \cdot kg^{-1} \cdot min^{-1}) = \left(\frac{1.5 \times 1000}{65}\right) = \left(\frac{1500}{65}\right) = 23.1$$

Oxygen consumption is also expressed in **METs.** A MET is a $\dot{V}O_2$ of 3.5 $ml \cdot kg^{-1} \cdot min^{-1}$, the amount of oxygen used at rest. The unit of METs quantifies oxygen uptake in multiples above resting. The formula for METs is

Converting $\dot{V}O_2$ Max ($ml \cdot kg^{-1} \cdot min^{-1}$) to METs **(8.2)**

$$\text{METs} = \left(\frac{\dot{V}O_2\ (ml \cdot kg^{-1} \cdot min^{-1})}{3.5}\right)$$

Calculation Example. Assume that the $\dot{V}O_2$ used to jog 6 miles per hour is 35 $ml \cdot kg^{-1} \cdot min^{-1}$. Using Formula 8.2, this is 10 METs, or 10 times above the resting state.

$$\text{METs} = \left(\frac{35}{3.5}\right) = 10$$

While $\dot{V}O_2$ can be expressed in any of these methods, aerobic fitness is expressed as $ml \cdot kg^{-1} \cdot min^{-1}$. Standards for evaluating aerobic fitness are presented in another section of this chapter.

$\dot{V}O_2$ Max versus $\dot{V}O_2$ Peak

Maximal oxygen uptake ($\dot{V}O_2$ Max) is the maximum volume of oxygen a subject uses during exhausting exercise (Mitchell & Blomqvist 1971; Mitchell, Sproule, & Chapman 1958; Rowell, Taylor, & Wang 1964). In the laboratory, the test involves gradually increasing power output and measuring expired gases (Figure 8.1). $\dot{V}O_2$ Max is that point at which the increased power output does not produce an increase in oxygen uptake (Noakes 1988). Figure 8.2 shows computer-generated graphs of two

[1] A liter equals 1000 milliliters.

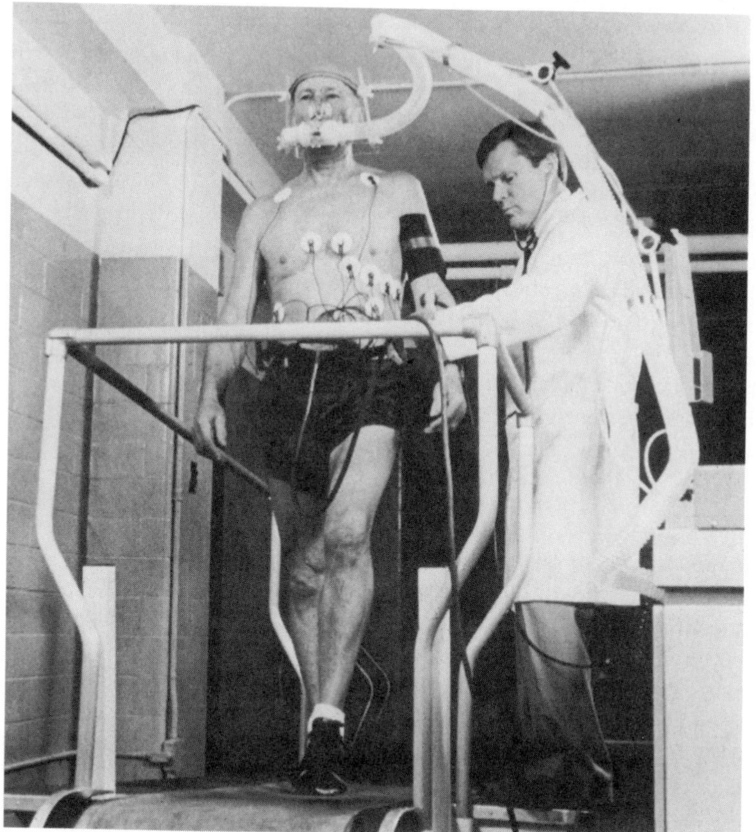

Figure 8.1
Dr. Michael Pollock monitoring an exercise test designed to measure $\dot{V}O_2$ Max by analyzing expired gases. Electrodes placed on the chest provide a means of monitoring the heart's rhythm and produce an electrocardiogram (EKG). $\dot{V}O_2$ Max is a fitness evaluation, while the EKG is a medical test to help diagnose heart disease.

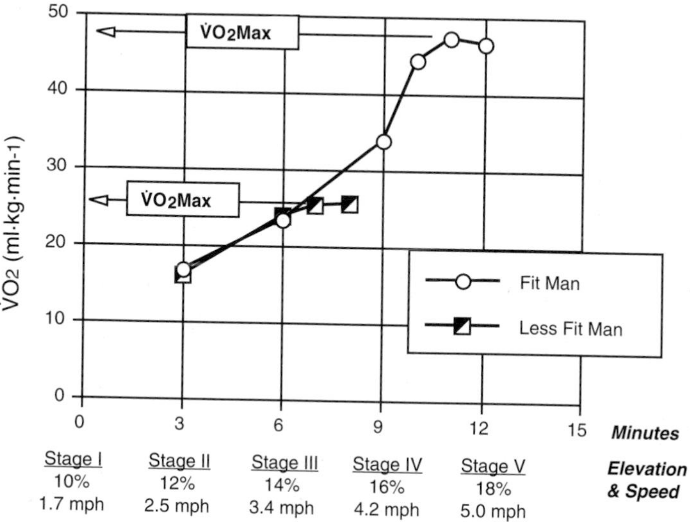

Figure 8.2
Oxygen uptake tests of an active and sedentary man. The fit man has the following characteristics: engages in aerobic exercise 5 days per week, age 46, 13.5% fat, and $\dot{V}O_2$ Max of 47.2. The less fit man is sedentary, younger (age 38), has a higher percent body fat (31%), and lower above $\dot{V}O_2$ Max (25.5 ml/kg/min). (Source: CSI Software Company, Houston, TX. Reprinted by permission.)

$\dot{V}O_2$ Max tests. The graphs show that as power output increased (increased speed and elevation), $\dot{V}O_2$ steadily increased and then flattened out during the last two minutes of the test when each person reached $\dot{V}O_2$ Max.

While Figure 8.2 presents the "textbook" definition of $\dot{V}O_2$ Max, many question the notion that the person reaches "true $\dot{V}O_2$ Max." In many instances a graphic representation is not available, and when it is, many subjects do not reach a plateau (Noakes 1988). A common procedure (Ross & Jackson 1990) is to use other criteria, which often include the following: (1) voluntary exhaustion; (2) a respiratory exchange ratio ≥ 1.0 or ≥ 1.1; and (3) an exercise heart $\geq 90\%$ of age-predicted maximum exercise heart rate.

The question of whether a person reaches true $\dot{V}O_2$ Max is somewhat controversial. This has led to the common practice of using the term "$\dot{V}O_2$ Peak," or the peak level reached. This appears to be more of an academic issue than a practical one. We will use $\dot{V}O_2$ Max in this text.

Aerobic Fitness

Aerobic fitness depends on several factors: efficient lungs, heart, and blood vessels; the quality and quantity of blood (red blood count, volume); and the cellular components that help the body use oxygen during exercise. Because an individual's ability to use oxygen during exhaustive work depends on these factors, maximal oxygen uptake, or $\dot{V}O_2$ Max, the maximal rate at which oxygen can be used, is an accepted test of aerobic fitness and an indicator of subsequent exercise capacity (ACSM 1990; ACSM 1991). Åstrand and Rodahl (1970) consider it to be the best index of physical fitness:

> During prolonged heavy physical work, the individual's performance capacity depends largely upon his ability to take up, transport, and deliver oxygen to working muscle. Subsequently, the maximal oxygen uptake is probably the best laboratory measure of a person's physical fitness, providing the definition of physical fitness is restricted to the capacity of the individual for prolonged heavy work. (Åstrand & Rodahl 1970, p. 314)

Aerobic fitness can be measured by several different tests, which can be categorized and contrasted in various ways. These include:

- Laboratory tests or field tests
- Maximal or submaximal tests
- Tests that do not involve exercise—that is, nonexercise tests

Laboratory tests are those that use specialized equipment. This can include gas analysis equipment, electronic heart-rate monitors, and equipment for regulating power output. Cycle ergometers and treadmills are used for this purpose. Field tests are those used for mass testing and may be either a maximal or submaximal test. For example, distance-run tests are maximal tests but are used in field settings to test large number of subjects. This chapter discusses these different test methods.

Aerobic Fitness and Health

A classic study from the Institute for Aerobics Research in Dallas, Texas, showed that low aerobic fitness was associated with higher mortality rates (Blair et al. 1989). The participants of the study were healthy people who were free of diseases such as high blood pressure or diabetes. After a maximal treadmill test, the participants were followed for several years. Figure 8.3 provides a graphic summary of the study. The

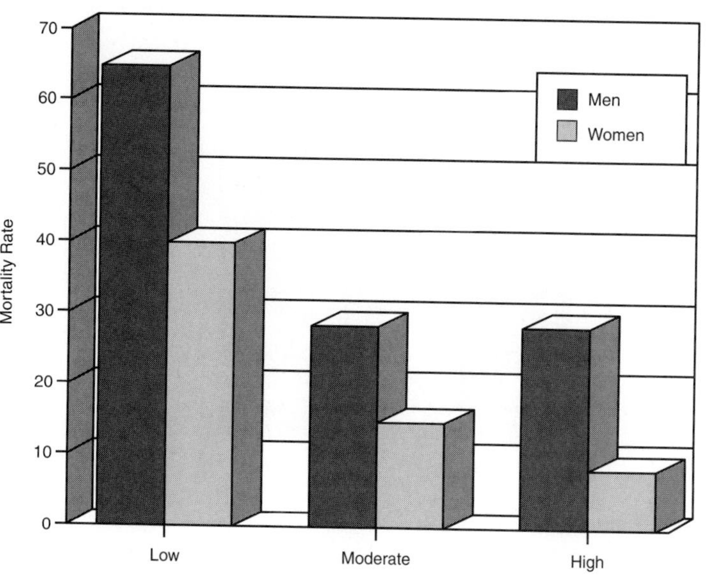

Figure 8.3
The participants in the lowest aerobic fitness group had the highest death rates. The mortality rate of the moderate and highly fit group was about the same. The high mortality rate occurs mainly in the low fitness group. Graph made from published data (Blair et al. 1989). (Source: Jackson and Ross, R.M. *Understanding Exercise for Health and Fitness,* 1997. Reprinted by permission.)

greatest drop in death rate was between the lowest and moderate fitness groups. The death rates of the moderate and high fitness groups were similar. This study shows the beneficial effect on mortality of a moderate level of aerobic fitness. For good health, it is not critical to be an elite athlete; rather, it is essential to be moderately fit, not a "couch potato." The "low fit" group comprised the 20% of the men and women with the lowest aerobic fitness for their age group.

In a second study, the researchers discovered that changes in fitness were related to changes in mortality risk (Blair et al. 1995). Those who improved their aerobic fitness by moving from the low to the moderate or high categories reduced their future risk of death. Moderate fitness levels can be attained for most people who engage in regular aerobic exercise, by doing the equivalent of walking about three miles a day.

Evaluating Aerobic Fitness

Aerobic fitness assesses the physical working capacity of athletes and individuals engaged in fitness programs. There is a growing trend to include aerobic fitness as part of a medical examination.[2] The standards used for athletes would not be suitable for evaluating the fitness level of nonathletic adults. Provided in Figure 8.4 are average oxygen uptake values for elite runners and average men and women. High-level endurance athletes (e.g., cross-country skiers and long-distance runners) have the highest aerobic fitness, nearly double the typical person. As a group, women have an aerobic fitness about 20% lower than a man of a similar age. This is primarily due to hormonal differences that cause women to have a lower concentration of hemoglobin in their blood and a higher percentage of body fat.

[2]Direct measurement of VO_2 Max during a stress test is part of a NASA/Johnson Space Center employee's medical examination.

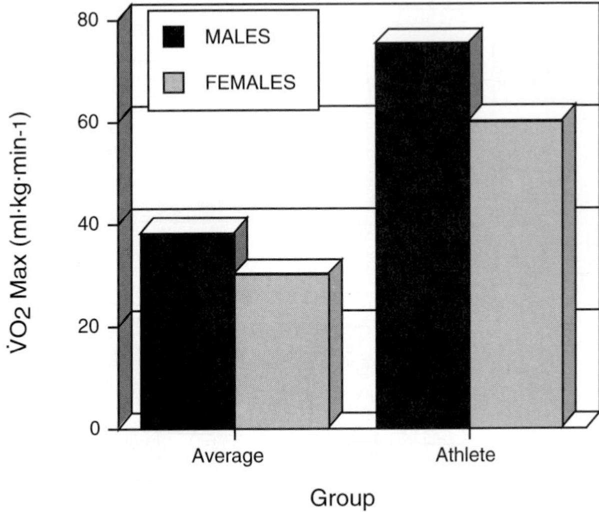

Figure 8.4
Average aerobic fitness of elite endurance athletes and normal adults. The aerobic fitness of the average man and woman is about 50% that of highly trained endurance athletes, and a woman's aerobic fitness is about 80% of a man's.
(Source: Jackson and Ross, R.M. *Understanding Exercise for Health and Fitness,* 1997. Reprinted by permission.)

Most of us have neither the ability nor the motivation to become world-class endurance athletes, but a suitable level of cardiorespiratory endurance is needed for health and fitness. Aerobic fitness is age-dependent, steadily increasing during childhood and reaching a peak at about age 25, after which it slowly declines (Buskirk & Hodgson 1987). The aerobic fitness of women is about 80% of men. This can be traced to gender differences in percent body fat and blood hemoglobin. Table 8.1 lists the aerobic fitness standards by age and sex recommended by the American College of Sports Medicine (Gettman 1993).

While the norms given in Table 8.1 describe the aerobic fitness of adults, the levels are not suitable for adult health promotion. The research published by Blair and associates (Blair et al. 1989) gives the first scientific data defining the level of aerobic fitness needed for health. They showed that the aerobic fitness health promotion threshold was 32 $ml \cdot kg^{-1} \cdot min^{-1}$ for women and 35 $ml \cdot kg^{-1} \cdot min^{-1}$ for men (Figure 8.5). The mortality rate of men and women with the lowest level of aerobic fitness was four times higher than the rate of those who exceeded these levels. However, there was no added advantage in terms of mortality to have fitness levels beyond these threshold levels. Aerobic fitness declines with age, and the levels of 35 or 32 $ml \cdot kg^{-1} \cdot min^{-1}$ were for men and women at age 45. Table 8.2 lists aerobic fitness suitable for health promotion, accounting for the age-related decline in aerobic fitness. Given is the value needed to have an aerobic capacity of 35 or 32 $ml \cdot kg^{-1} \cdot min^{-1}$ at age 45, assuming one maintains one's current level of exercise and percent body fat. Research shows that changing exercise habits and percent body fat dramatically affect the rate that aerobic fitness changes with age (Jackson et al. 1995; Jackson et al. 1996).

Fitness Evaluation or Stress Test?

It is important to make a distinction between a fitness evaluation and a stress test. A fitness evaluation evaluates just aerobic fitness. A stress test provides both medical and fitness data. A stress test is a medical procedure administered under the supervi-

Table 8.1 American College of Sports Medicine Standards for $\dot{V}O_2$ Max ($ml \cdot kg^{-1} \cdot min^{-1}$)*

Standard	Age in Years				
	20–29	30–39	40–49	50–59	≥60
Men					
Excellent	≥52	≥49	≥47	≥43	≥41
Good	49–51	46–48	44–46	40–42	38–40
Average	42–48	39–45	37–43	33–39	31–37
Fair	39–41	36–38	34–36	30–32	28–30
Poor	≤38	≤35	≤33	≤29	≤27
Women					
Excellent	≥43	≥40	≥38	≥34	≥34
Good	40–42	37–39	35–37	31–33	31–33
Average	33–39	31–36	29–34	25–30	25–30
Fair	30–32	28–30	26–28	22–24	22–24
Poor	≤29	≤27	≤25	≤21	≤21

*From Gettman 1993

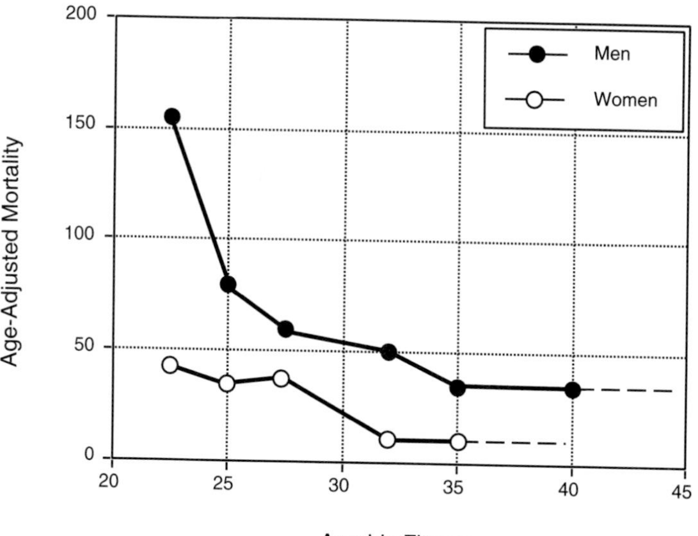

Figure 8.5
Curves of the relationship between aerobic fitness and health show that the curves level off at 32 $ml \cdot kg^{-1} \cdot min^{-1}$ for women and 35 $ml \cdot kg^{-1} \cdot min^{-1}$ for men. These values define the threshold level of fitness needed for health promotion (i.e., reduced mortality) for 45-year-old men and women. Graph made from published data (Blair et al. 1989). (Source: Jackson and Ross, R.M. *Understanding Exercise for Health and Fitness,* 1997. Reprinted by permission.)

sion of a physician. The primary objective of a stress test is to "stress the heart." The goal is to see if there is any evidence of myocardial ischemia or restricted blood flow to the myocardium or heart muscle. Electrocardiographic (EKG), cardiovascular (e.g., blood pressure and heart rate), and physical symptoms (e.g., shortness of breath or chest pain) are monitored during the test. The objective of a stress test is to identify

Table 8.2 Age-Adjusted Adult Aerobic Fitness Standards for Health Promotion* above $\dot{V}O_2$ Max ($ml \cdot kg^{-1} \cdot min^{-1}$)

Age Group	Men	Women
45 and under	35	32
50	34	31
55	32	29
60	31	28
65 and over	30	27

*Standards developed from data (Jackson et al. 1995; Jackson et al. 1996) and personal communication with S. Blair, September 30, 1993.

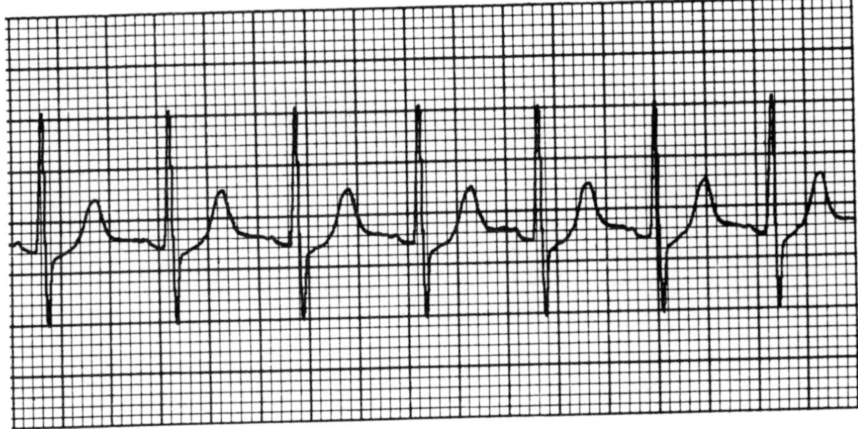

Figure 8.6
Sample of a computerized twelve-lead exercise EKG during peak exercise. These twelve-leads give the cardiologist a view of the heart's electrical activity from twelve different "windows." The figure shows the computer-smoothed twelve EKG tracings and the rhythm strip (bottom continuous tracing) in which the electric artifacts are still present. A physician uses these data to decide if a patient may have coronary heart disease. Figure 8.1 shows the twelve-lead EKG electrode placement. (Source: CSI Software Company, Houston, TX. Reprinted by permission.)

patients who may have cardiovascular disease, particularly coronary heart disease. Healthy individuals do not get myocardial ischemia when exercising at a maximal level. The pattern of the exercise EKG (Figure 8.6) provides this important information. A stress test and fitness evaluation are both typically administered on a motor-driven treadmill or cycle ergometer.

Who should have a stress test? Useful criteria have been developed to decide if an individual should have a medically supervised stress test prior to starting an exercise program. The best advice can be obtained from your physician, but the following are general guidelines.

1. Sedentary men over the age of 35 and postmenopausal sedentary women should have a stress test prior to starting an exercise program.
2. Any individual who has chest pains or a history of heart disease.
3. Any individual of any age who has significant cardiovascular disease risk factors should consider having a stress test and a medical evaluation prior to beginning an exercise program. These risk factors include:

PHYSICAL ACTIVITY READINESS QUESTIONNAIRE (PAR–Q)

- Has your doctor ever said you have heart trouble?
- Do you frequently suffer from pains in your chest?
- Do you often feel faint or have spells of severe dizziness?
- Has a doctor ever told you that you have a bone or joint problem, such as arthritis, that has been aggravated by exercise or might be made worse with exercise?
- Is there a good physical reason not mentioned here why you should not follow an activity program even if you wanted to?
- Are you over age 65 and unaccustomed to vigorous exercise?

Figure 8.7 The Physical Activity Readiness Questionnaire (PAR-Q) (ACSM 1991). If a person answers "yes" to any of the following questions, vigorous exercise or exercise testing should be postponed and medical clearance sought.

- A strong family history of cardiovascular disease, particularly occurring at an early age.
- A history of high blood pressure.
- A history of elevated cholesterol, particularly with a relatively low HDL fraction.
- A history of diabetes.
- A smoker, particularly if sedentary or with other cardiovascular risk factors.
- An abnormal resting EKG.

The Physical Activity Readiness Questionnaire (PAR-Q) is a screening method that has been used extensively in Canada to determine if individuals should not exercise or should take an exercise test (ACSM 1991). Almost all individuals for whom it might be dangerous to start a moderate exercise program or take an exercise test can be identified with the PAR-Q. Answering "Yes" to any of the six questions would disqualify a person from taking any form of an exercise test without medical supervision. Figure 8.7 gives the PAR-Q.

Laboratory Aerobic Fitness Tests

Aerobic fitness can be measured in the laboratory with either a maximal or submaximal test. At maximal exercise, VO_2 can be either measured directly from expired gases or estimated from power output. For submaximal tests, the heart-rate response to a given level of treadmill and cycle ergometer power output is used to estimate aerobic fitness. Laboratory tests, as used in this text, involve using a standard method of regulating power output. Provided next is a discussion of quantifying power output.

Regulating Power Output

Åstrand and Rodahl (1986) report a linear increase in oxygen uptake with a linear increase in **power output.** As the power output increases, the exercising muscle requires more oxygen. You can easily see this when you walk up a hill; as the hill gets steeper (increased power output), your heart rate and breathing rates increase (increased oxygen uptake) as your body needs and uses more oxygen. Cycle ergometers, treadmills, and bench stepping[3] are common methods used to regulate power output. Changing steady state jogging and walking speed is another method of changing power output. The methods of calculating cycle ergometer and treadmill power output are provided next.

Cycle Ergometer. Power output on a **cycle ergometer** is changed by increasing the resistance placed on the flywheel, altering the pedaling rate, or a combination of both. Kilopond (kp)[4] is the unit used to quantify the resistance. A kilopond (kp) is the amount of resistance placed on the cycle ergometer flywheel. The number of revolutions completed per minute (rpm) is the second factor used to calculate cycle ergometer power output. Each revolution of the flywheel represents a distance traveled. The Monarch cycle ergometer is one of the most popular testing ergometers. Work in kiloponds is regulated with a calibrated weight. Power output of a cycle ergometer is expressed in kilopond meters of work per minute (kmp/min) and is computed from resistance (kp), distance traveled (D), and speed of movement (rpm). The basic formula is:

Cycle Ergometer Power Output (kpm/min) **(8.3)**

$$\text{kpm/min} = \text{kp} \times \text{D} \times \text{rpm}$$

Other units used to quantify cycle ergometer power output are watts and $\dot{V}O_2$ (ml/min). One watt is equal to 6.12 kpm/min (Åstrand & Rodahl 1970). $\dot{V}O_2$ (ml/min) increases at a linear rate of 2 ml/min with each increase in power output (kpm/min) above rest. Resting $\dot{V}O_2$ is estimated to be 300 ml/min (Ross 1989). These formulas are:

Cycle Ergometer Power Output—Watts **(8.4)**

$$\text{Watts} = \left(\frac{\text{kpm/min}}{6.12}\right)$$

Cycle Ergometer Power Output—$\dot{V}O_2$ (ml/min) **(8.5)**

$$\dot{V}O_2\ (\text{ml}\cdot\text{min}^{-1}) = (2 \times \text{kpm/min}) + 300$$

Calculation Example. Assume a person is tested on a Monarch cycle ergometer. The distance traveled with each revolution is 6 meters. If the pedal rate is 50 revolutions per minute at a setting of 3 kp, the power output in kpm/min, watts, and $\dot{V}O_2$ ($\text{ml}\cdot\text{kg}^{-1}\cdot\text{min}^{-1}$) would be:

$$\text{kpm/min} = 3 \times 6 \times 50 = 900$$

$$\text{Watts} = \left(\frac{900}{6.12}\right) = 147.06$$

$$\dot{V}O_2\ (\text{ml}\cdot\text{min}^{-1}) = (2 \times 900) + 300 = 2100$$

---

[3] We do not consider bench stepping a suitable laboratory method of regulating power output. Step tests are sometimes used with adults. We present step tests in Chapter 11.

[4] A kilopond is equal to 2.2 pounds or a kilogram. Both terms have been used. For consistency the term kilopond will be used in this book.

Table 8.3 Cycle Ergometer Power Output Estimates for Common Kilopond (kp)-Resistance Settings, Pedaling at a Rate of 50 Revolutions per Minute

Scale Setting (kp)	kpm (1 min)	$\dot{V}O_2$ (ml·min^{-1})	$\dot{V}O_2$ (ml·kg^{-1}·min^{-1}) for Selected Body Weights			
			50 kg	60 kg	70 kg	80 kg
0.5	150	600	12.0	10.0	8.6	7.5
1.0	300	900	18.0	15.0	12.9	11.2
1.5	450	1200	24.0	20.0	17.1	15.0
2.0	600	1500	30.0	25.0	21.4	18.8
2.5	750	1800	36.0	30.0	25.7	22.5
3.0	900	2100	42.0	35.0	30.0	26.2
3.5	1050	2400	48.0	40.0	34.3	30.0
4.0	1200	2700	54.0	45.0	38.6	33.8
4.5	1350	3000	60.0	50.0	42.9	37.5
5.0	1500	3300	66.0	55.0	47.1	41.2
5.5	1650	3600	72.0	60.0	51.4	45.0
6.0	1800	3900	78.0	65.0	55.7	48.8
6.5	1950	4200	84.0	70.0	60.0	52.5
7.0	2100	4500	90.0	75.0	64.3	56.2

The most common method is to have the subject pedal at a constant rate, usually 50 revolutions per minute, and power output is increased by placing more resistance on the flywheel. The power output for common cycle ergometer pedaling rates is provided in Table 8.3.

Treadmill. The power output of a treadmill is regulated by changing treadmill speed, elevation, or a combination of both. Different methods are used for maximal and submaximal tests. For a maximal test, $\dot{V}O_2$ Max is estimated from the maximum time of a treadmill protocol. These maximal treadmill equations are presented in the next section of this chapter.

Standard equations (ACSM 1991; Ross & Jackson 1990) have been published to convert treadmill speed and elevation into submaximal $\dot{V}O_2$ (ml·kg^{-1}·min^{-1}). The accuracy of walking equations was evaluated with a large sample of men (Ross & Jackson 1986). While both equations were reasonably accurate, it was shown that the total work (TW) equation is more accurate than the ACSM equation (1991). The TW equation is based on the concept that a constant amount of oxygen (262.5 ml·kg^{-1}) is used to walk 1 mile. An additional constant volume of oxygen, 21 ml·kg^{-1}, is needed for each percent elevation per mile. The total work formula is

Total Work Treadmill Equation **(8.6)**

$$\dot{V}O_2\ (\text{ml}\cdot\text{kg}^{-1}\cdot\text{min}^{-1}) = [262.5 + (21 \times \%)] \times \left(\frac{\text{mph}}{60}\right)$$

where % is the elevation and mph is treadmill speed in miles per hour. Table 8.4 gives submaximal treadmill protocols suitable for submaximal testing.

Table 8.4 Submaximal Treadmill Test Protocols and the Estimated Power Output for the Last Minute of Each Stage

				Power Output	
Stage	**Minutes**	**mph**	**% Grade**	**$\dot{V}O_2$ (ml·kg^{-1}·min^{-1})**	**METs**
Bruce Protocol					
I	1–3	1.7	10	13.4	3.82
II	4–6	2.5	12	21.4	6.12
III	7–9	3.4	14	31.5	9.01
Ross Submaximal Protocol—Women					
I	1–3	3.4	0	14.9	4.25
II	4–6	3.4	3	18.4	5.27
III	7–9	3.4	6	22.0	6.29
IV	10–12	3.4	9	25.6	7.31
V	13–15	3.4	12	29.2	8.33
Ross Submaximal Protocol—Men					
I	1–3	3.4	0	14.9	4.25
II	4–6	3.4	4	19.6	5.61
III	7–9	3.4	8	24.4	6.97
IV	10–12	3.4	12	29.2	8.33
V	13–15	3.4	16	33.9	9.09

Calculation Example. Assume we test a subject on the treadmill at two levels: first, 3.3 mph at 0% elevation; and second, 3.1 mph at 15% elevation. The treadmill power output expressed as $\dot{V}O_2$ (ml/kg/min) is

$$\dot{V}O_2\ (\text{ml}\cdot\text{kg}^{-1}\cdot\text{min}^{-1}) = [262.5 + (21 \times 0)] \times \left(\frac{3.3}{60}\right) = 262.5 \times 0.055 = 14.\ 4$$

$$\dot{V}O_2\ (\text{ml}\cdot\text{kg}^{-1}\cdot\text{min}^{-1}) = [262.5 + (21 \times 5)] \times \left(\frac{3.1}{60}\right) = 577.5 \times 0.052 = 30.\ 0$$

Maximal Aerobic Fitness Laboratory Tests

The objective of a **maximal exercise test** is to increase systematically exercise intensity until the subject reaches exhaustion. The most accurate method is to measure oxygen uptake by indirect calorimetry, that is, to measure expired gases during the exercise test (Figure 8.1). The second method is to estimate $\dot{V}O_2$ Max from maximum power output.

Indirect Calorimetry

Maximal oxygen uptake is most accurately determined by measuring expired gases during maximal exercise. This method is conceptually simple but the most difficult to use and requires trained technicians with expensive equipment. The objective is to increase power output at a linear rate (e.g., increase treadmill elevation 4% or increase cycle ergometer resistance by 150 kmp/min every 3 minutes) until the individual reaches exhaustion. Expired gases are collected during all stages of exercise. The volume of oxygen used at this exhausting level is $\dot{V}O_2$ Max (see Figure 8.2). The parameters needed to compute $\dot{V}O_2$ Max are oxygen and carbon dioxide concentrations of room and expired air and volume of air expired per minute. Standard methods are available for calculating O_2 consumption (Consolazio, Johnson, & Pecora 1963; Jones & Campbell 1982).

The direct measurement of $\dot{V}O_2$ Max is expensive in terms of needed equipment and personnel and, for these reasons, is typically done in a research setting. Yet, with the advancement in microcomputer technology, several commercial systems are now available to speed these measurements. For example, at NASA/Johnson Space Center in Houston, astronauts' aerobic fitness is measured yearly and is even measured in space. Many colleges and universities now have the capacity to evaluate $\dot{V}O_2$ Max by indirect calorimetry.

Maximum Treadmill Tests

A maximal treadmill test is performed to voluntary exhaustion. The potential for a cardiac problem during a maximal test is low, about 1 per 10,000 tests. Even with this low risk, caution needs to be exercised when testing adults, especially those at risk of cardiovascular disease. Typically, exercise heart rate and blood pressure are monitored during a maximal effort. When true maximum heart rate is not known, exercise heart rate may not give a true reading of the individual's level of exertion. Borg's **rating of perceived exertion** scale (RPE) is often used when administering exercise tests to gain additional insight into the level of exertion (Borg 1977; Pollock, Jackson, & Foster 1986). During the test, the subject is asked to rate exercise intensity during the last 15 seconds of each minute of the test. These psychophysical ratings are useful for determining when the subject is reaching his/her maximum level. Chapter 14 gives the RPE scales and test directions.

Aerobic fitness can be measured from maximal treadmill or cycle ergometer exercise. Many people are not accustomed to riding a cycle ergometer and find it difficult to reach their maximum; their legs fatigue prior to reaching maximal exercise. So, maximum tests are more often administered on a treadmill. Power output systematically increases by time in a treadmill protocol. The elapsed time to reach exhaustion is an index of maximum work capacity (Figure 8.2). Provided in Figure 8.8 is a graphic representation of the speed and elevation for the two most common treadmill protocols. About 71% of all tests given in the United States follow the Bruce protocol and about 10% use the Balke (Pollock, Wilmore, & Fox 1984).

Several valid regression equations have been published that estimate $\dot{V}O_2$ Max (ml/kg/min) from maximal treadmill time (Bruce, Kusumi, & Hosmer 1973; Foster et al. 1984; Pollock et al. 1976). Since each treadmill protocol increases power output at different rates, unique equations are needed for each protocol. The reported correlations between $\dot{V}O_2$ Max measured directly and maximal treadmill exercise is high, ranging from 0.88 to 0.97. The standard error of prediction is about 3 ml/kg/min. Provided next are regression equations to estimate $\dot{V}O_2$ Max (ml/kg/min) from treadmill time in minutes (T) for the Balke and Bruce treadmill protocols.

Balke Treadmill Test (R = 0.88) ***(8.7)***

$$\dot{V}O_2 \text{ Max (ml/kg/min)} = 14.99 + (1.44 \times T)$$

Bruce Treadmill Test, Healthy Subjects (R = 0.97) ***(8.8)***

$$\dot{V}O_2 \text{ Max (ml/kg/min)} = 17.50 - (0.30 \times T) + (0.297 \times T^2) - (0.0077 \times T^3)$$

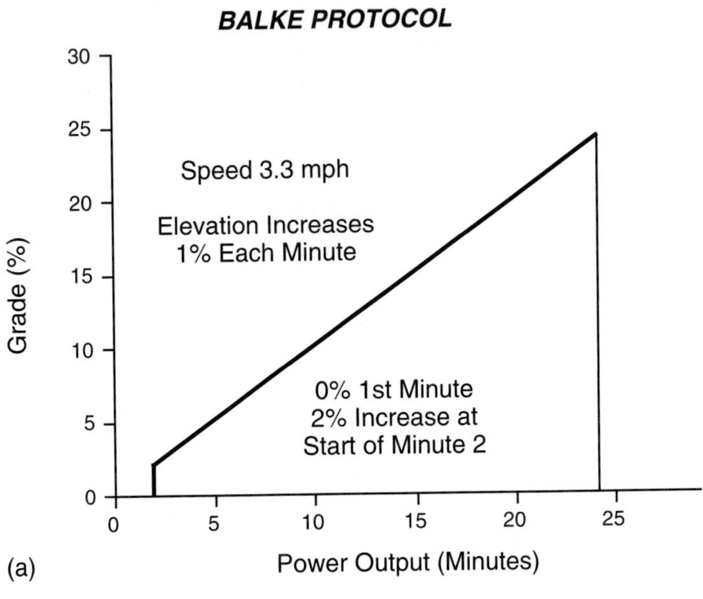

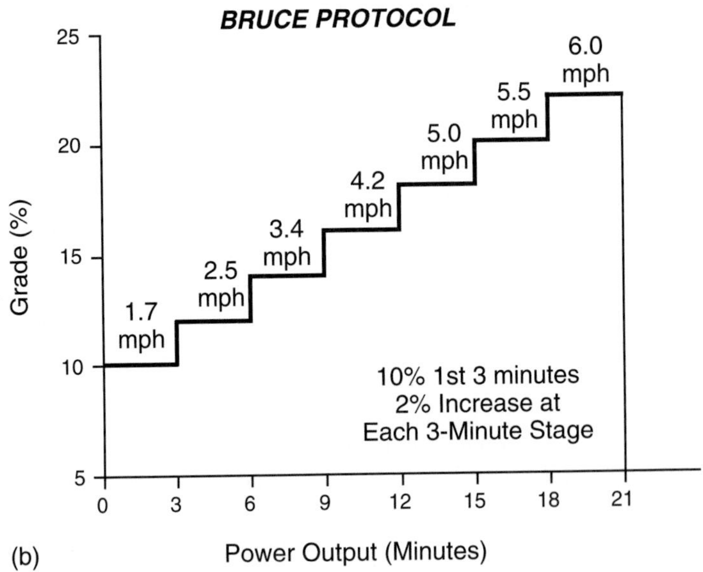

Figure 8.8
The (a) Balke and (b) Bruce treadmill protocols are most often used to measure $\dot{V}O_2$ Max. (Source: CSI Software Company, Houston, TX. Reprinted by permission.)

The Bruce protocol is a nonlinear equation that was developed on both healthy subjects and cardiac patients (Foster et al. 1984). Equation 8.8 is for individuals who are free from coronary heart disease. The $\dot{V}O_2$ Max of heart patients is 4.2 ml/kg/min lower than that of healthy patients for each maximum treadmill time. Figure 8.9 graphically shows $\dot{V}O_2$ Max from treadmill time for the Balke and Bruce protocols. The figure shows that it is important to use the correct equation for elapsed treadmill time.

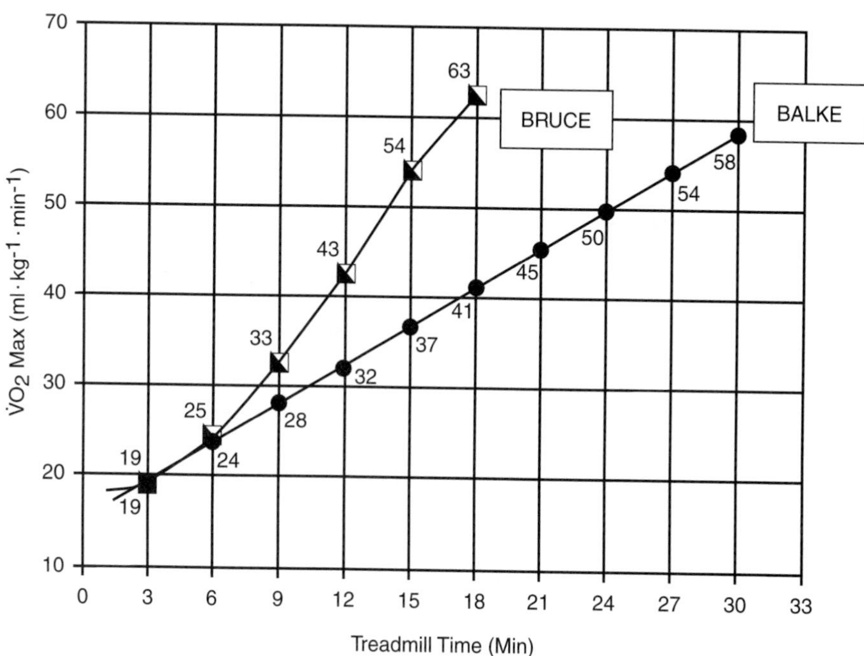

Figure 8.9
Estimated $\dot{V}O_2$ Max (ml/kg/min) from treadmill time for the Balke and Bruce maximum protocols.
(Source: CSI Software Company, Houston, TX. Reprinted by permission.)

After the first three minutes of treadmill performance, the $\dot{V}O_2$ Max for treadmill time on the Bruce protocol is higher than the corresponding time for the Balke.

Calculation Examples. Provided below are the $\dot{V}O_2$ Max estimates for treadmill time of 12 minutes and 35 seconds (12.58 minutes). The same maximum treadmill time was used to demonstrate the difference in the equations.

Balke Treadmill Test

$\dot{V}O_2$ Max (ml/kg/min) $= 14.99 + (1.44 \times 12.58)$

$= 14.99 + 18.12 = 33.1$ ml/kg/min

Bruce Treadmill Test, Healthy Subjects

$\dot{V}O_2$ Max (ml/kg/min) $= 17.50 - (0.30 \times 12.58) + (0.297 \times 12.58^2) - (0.0077 \times 12.58^3)$

$= 17.50 - (0.30 \times 12.58) + (0.297 \times 12.58 \times 12.58) - (0.0077 \times 12.58 \times 12.58 \times 12.58)$

$= 17.50 - 3.774 + 47.002 - 15.330 = 45.4$ ml/kg/min

Submaximal Aerobic Fitness Laboratory Tests

Exercising to $\dot{V}O_2$ Max is physically exhausting, time-consuming, and requires medical supervision when testing high-risk subjects. Laboratory submaximal tests provide a less accurate, but safer method of estimating aerobic fitness. The measurement objective of **submaximal exercise tests** is to define the slope of the individual's heart-rate response to exercise and use the slope to estimate $\dot{V}O_2$ Max from submaximal

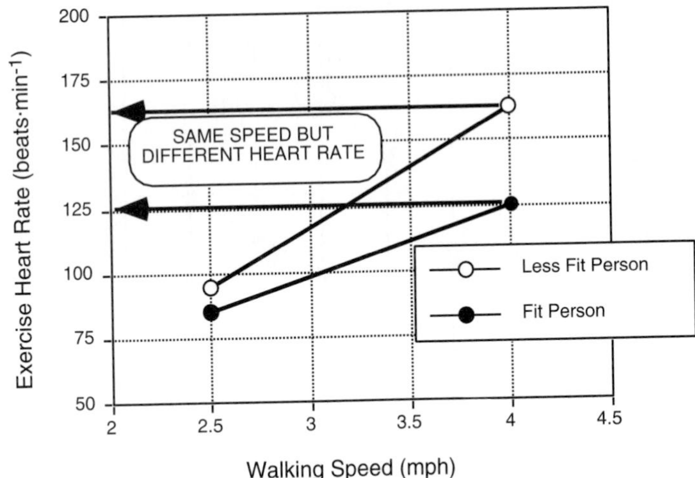

Figure 8.10 Exercise heart rate increases at a linear rate with exercise intensity, which in this example is walking speed. The exercise heart rate for the less fit person will be higher at any walking speed than the more fit person. Certain drugs may affect this relationship. (Source: Jackson and Ross, R.M. *Understanding Exercise for Health and Fitness,* 1997. Reprinted by permission.)

parameters. Three exercise physiological principles (Figure 8.10) are the foundation of submaximal tests. These are:

1. Heart-rate (i.e., pulse-rate) increases in direct proportion to the oxygen used during aerobic exercise.
2. $\dot{V}O_2$ Max is reached at maximum heart rate.
3. A less fit person will have a higher heart rate at any submaximal level than someone who is more aerobically fit.

Oxygen uptake ($\dot{V}O_2$) at any level of exercise is the product of cardiac output and the difference in the oxygen content of the arterial and venous blood. Cardiac output is the product of stroke volume (i.e., volume of blood pumped with each heart beat) and heart rate. Stroke volume increases early in exercise, stabilizing at about 45% of $\dot{V}O_2$ Max (see Figure 8.11). The testing goal of estimating $\dot{V}O_2$ Max from submaximal power output is to measure heart rate, between 45% and 70% ($\approx$ 115 to 150 beats·min^{-1}) of person's $\dot{V}O_2$ Max. Below 45% of $\dot{V}O_2$ Max, stroke volume has not leveled off, whereas, at about 70% $\dot{V}O_2$ Max, exercise is likely shifting from aerobic to anaerobic. Submaximal tests are based on a submaximal aerobic power output.

Single- and multi-stage models can be used to estimate $\dot{V}O_2$ Max from submaximal power output and exercise heart rate. These are presented in the next sections.

Multi-Stage Model. The **multi-stage exercise test** model requires that heart rate and power output be measured at two or more submaximal levels (Golding, Meyers, & Sinning 1989). These data points are then used to project to maximal heart rate, which is used to estimate aerobic fitness. The multi-stage model is the procedure used for the YMCA Adult Fitness Test (Golding, Meyers, & Sinning 1989). The YMCA test uses a cycle ergometer following the protocol shown in Figure 8.12 to regulate power output for each 3-minute stage. The goal of the test is to obtain at least two submaximal heart rates between 115 and 150 beats/min. $\dot{V}O_2$ Max is estimated by plotting the linear increase in exercise heart rate associated

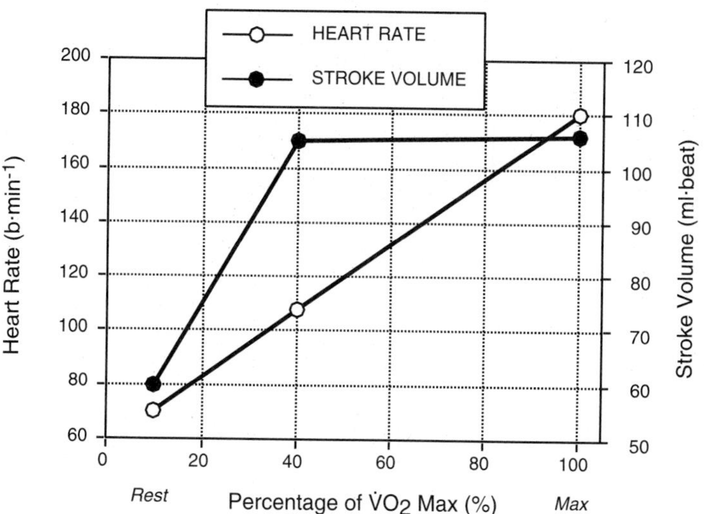

Figure 8.11
Cardiac output is the product of stroke volume and heart rate. Stroke volume reaches maximum at about 40% $\dot{V}O_2$ max. The increase in cardiac output after about 40% of maximum is due to an increase in heart rate. (Source: CSI Software Company, Houston, TX. Reprinted by permission.)

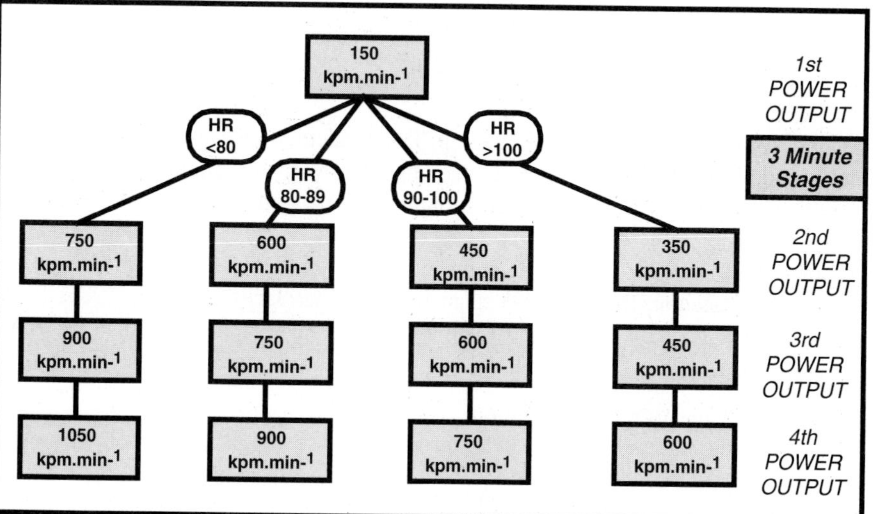

Figure 8.12
Cycle ergometer protocol used for the YMCA Adult Fitness Test (Golding et al. 1989). The test starts at a low power output, and the heart rate response to the first stage determines the next power output. Each stage is 3 minutes in length. (Source: CSI Software Company, Houston, Tx. Reprinted by permission.)

with increases in power output. Connecting the two points defines the linear power output heart-rate slope. Using the defined slope, the line is extended to maximum heart rate.[5] $\dot{V}O_2$ Max is estimated by dropping the line down to the power output scale.

The YMCA test manual gives graphs for making these determinations with just a cycle ergometer where power output is expressed in kmp/min. We have added a power output scale expressed as $\dot{V}O_2$ (ml/kg/min) to Figure 8.13, allowing the use of

[5]Since maximal heart rate is typically not known, it is estimated by 220 − Age.

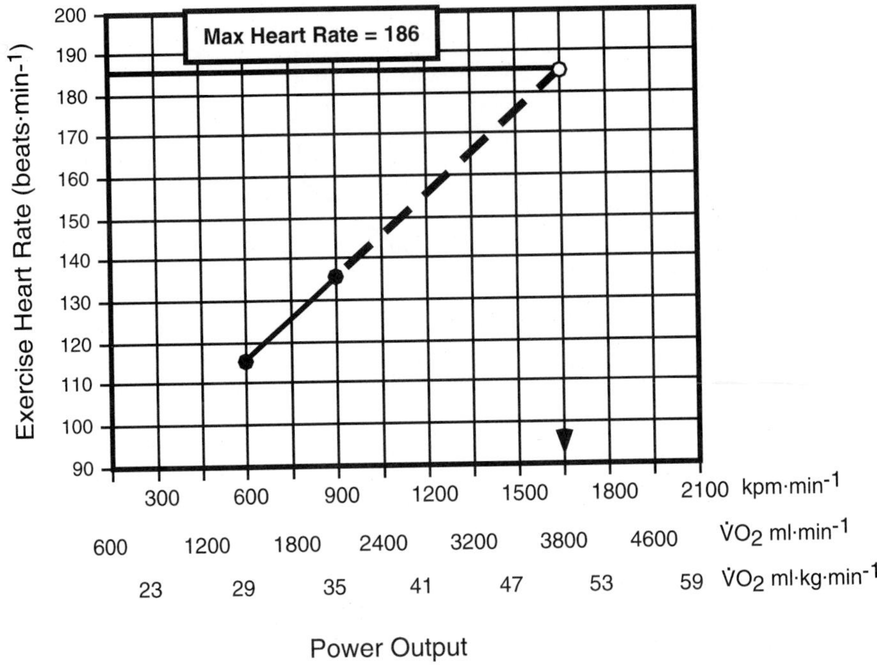

Figure 8.13 Illustration of estimating $\dot{V}O_2$ Max with the multi-stage model following the methods used for the YMCA test. (Golding et al. 1989) (Source: CSI Software Company, Houston, TX. Reprinted by permission.)

the graphic method with treadmill testing. These calculations can be somewhat difficult to do by hand, but can be easily accomplished with a computer. These are presented in the computer calculation section that is an appendix of this text.

Single-Stage Model. The **single-stage exercise test** model is both simpler to use and slightly more accurate than the multi-stage model (Mahar, Jackson, & Ross 1985). It was initially popularized by the Åstrand-Ryhming nomogram (Åstrand & Rodahl 1970; Åstrand & Rodahl 1986; Åstrand & Rhyming 1954). The single-stage formula is

Single-Stage $\dot{V}O_2$ Max Equation **(8.9)**

$$\dot{V}O_2\ \text{Max} = \dot{V}O_2\ \text{SM} \times \left(\frac{220 - \text{Age} - \text{k}}{\text{SM HR} - \text{k}}\right)$$

where $\dot{V}O_2$ SM is the $\dot{V}O_2$ at submaximal exercise, maximum heart rate is estimated from 220 − Age, SM HR is submaximal heart rate at $\dot{V}O_2$ SM, and k is the constant of 61 for males and 73 for females.

Either the cycle ergometer or treadmill can be used to regulate power output. The procedures (Åstrand and Rodahl 1977) recommended for a cycle ergometer protocol are listed next.

1. The pedaling position should be comfortable for the subject. When administering cycle ergometer tests, first adjust the seat height on the ergometer so that the knee is almost straight on the downward stroke.
2. A suitable pedaling rate is 50 revolutions per minute. A metronome is commonly used to standardize this pedaling rate.

3. The recommended starting loads are: women, 450 to 600 kpm/min; and men, 600 to 900 kpm/min.
4. The goal is to reach a steady state heart rate between 130 and 150 beats·min^{-1}. If after 6 minutes the heart rate is between 130 and 150 beats·min^{-1}, the test is ended.
5. If after 6 minutes exercise heart rate is below 130 beats·min^{-1}, add 300 kpm/min and continue the test for an additional 4 to 6 minutes.
6. Heart rate is measured during the final 15 seconds of each minute.

Table 8.4 provides submaximal treadmill protocols. Electronic equipment needs to be used to measure exercise heart rate for treadmill tests. The movement produced by walking on a treadmill makes it very difficult to measure heart rate by palpitation. Because of differences in fitness, individuals will vary in their heart-rate response to the power output. The submaximal heart rate at any stage should not exceed 150 to 155 beats·min^{-1}. The following guidelines are offered to ensure that submaximal exercise is achieved.

- **Bruce Protocol.** Do not go to the next stage if the subject's heart rate exceeds 135 beats·min^{-1}. For most healthy adults, a heart rate between 135 and 150 will be reached in the first 6 minutes at the treadmill test.
- **Ross Submaximal Protocol.** Do not go to Stage II if the heart rate exceeds 140 at Stage I; such a person is very unfit. Stages IV and V should be used only for individuals under age 50. Never go to the next stage if the heart rate exceeds 145 beats·min^{-1}.

The Ross modification of the Balke protocol is better than the modified Bruce for the multi-stage model because power output is increased at a slower rate. The submaximal power output levels and their associated heart rates can be used with either the single- or multi-stage models to estimate aerobic fitness.

Calculation Example, Male (k = 61). Assume a man's exercise heart rate is 135 beats·min^{-1} at Stage III of the Ross submaximal treadmill protocol. The power output for Stage III is 24.4 ml·kg^{-1}·min^{-1}. If the man's age is 35, the single-stage (k = 61) estimated $\dot{V}O_2$ Max (Formula 8.9) would be

$$\dot{V}O_2\text{ Max} = 24.4 \times \left(\frac{220 - 35 - 61}{135 - 61}\right) = 24.4 \times \left(\frac{124}{74}\right) = 40.9\text{ ml}\cdot\text{kg}^{-1}\cdot\text{min}^{-1}$$

Calculation Example, Female (k = 73). Assume a 28-year old woman's exercise heart rate is 145 beats·min^{-1} after 6 minutes of cycle ergometer exercise at 600 kpm/min ($\dot{V}O_2$ = 1500 ml·min^{-1} or 1.5 L·min^{-1}). Single-stage (k = 73) estimated $\dot{V}O_2$ Max (Formula 8.9) would be

$$\dot{V}O_2\text{ Max} = 1.5 \times \left(\frac{220 - 28 - 73}{145 - 73}\right) = 1.5 \times \left(\frac{119}{72}\right) = 2.48\text{ L}\cdot\text{min}^{-1}$$

Since cycle ergometer power output typically expresses $\dot{V}O_2$ in L·min^{-1}, Formula 8.1 must be used to determine aerobic fitness. Assume the women's weight is 123 pounds, or 55.9 kg. Her $\dot{V}O_2$ Max per kilogram of body weight is

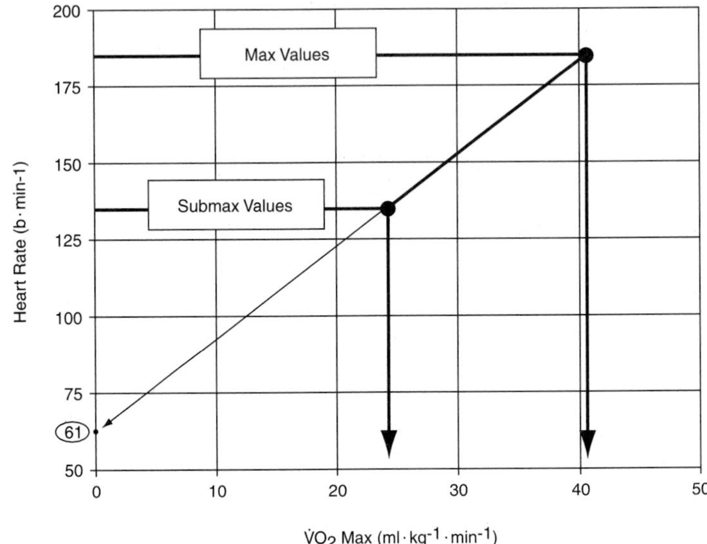

Figure 8.14
A graphic illustration of the theory supporting the single-stage $\dot{V}O_2$ Max estimation model. The model was developed with subjects who were tested at submaximal and maximal levels. These two points from the line used to estimate $\dot{V}O_2$ Max from submaximal heart rate and power output. (Source: CSI Software Company, Houston, TX. Reprinted by permission.)

$$\dot{V}O_2\ (\text{ml}\cdot\text{kg}^{-1}\cdot\text{min}^{-1}) = \left(\frac{2.48 \times 1000}{55.9}\right) = \left(\frac{2480}{55.9}\right) = 44.4\ \text{ml}\cdot\text{kg}^{-1}\cdot\text{min}^{-1}$$

The single-stage model uses just one submaximal level to estimate $\dot{V}O_2$ Max. How can this be? We have always been taught that two points are needed to draw a straight line. This is the logic of the multi-stage model. Figure 8.14 shows the theoretical logic of the single-stage model. This is illustrated with data from the man's calculation example.

Åstrand and Rhyming did have two data points when they developed their nomogram (Åstrand & Ryhming 1954), which is the single-stage model. They tested their subjects at two levels, one submaximal power output, and then at $\dot{V}O_2$ Max. The male and female constants of 61 and 73 appear to be resting heart-rate values, but this is not the case. The constants are the intercepts of the line formed from the submaximal and maximal parameters. The constants represent heart rate value for a $\dot{V}O_2$ of 0. The values of 61 and 73 are average values of all males and females tested.

Aerobic Fitness Field Tests

Field tests are useful for testing large numbers of subjects. The field tests available to estimate aerobic fitness include distance-run/walk tests and submaximal walking and run tests. Provided in this section are the adult run/walk tests made popular by Cooper (Cooper 1968; Cooper 1970) and generalized 1-mile-run test (Cureton et al. 1995). The Rockport walk and BYU jog tests are submaximal tests that use heart-rate response to movement time as a means of assessing aerobic capacity. All these tests have published regression equations to estimate aerobic fitness from performance.

Maximal Tests—Distance Runs

Running performance has been shown to be highly related to $\dot{V}O_2$ Max. When performed properly, running tests provide valid assessments of aerobic fitness, but are not as accurate as the regression equations derived for treadmill protocols in which the speed and elevation are strictly regulated. The most common run tests involve jogging and/or walking distances ranging from 1 to 1.5 miles, or running as far as possible in 12 minutes. It is important to remember that **distance-run tests** are maximal exercise tests with all the attendant risks. Unsupervised maximum distance-run tests are not appropriate for older people at higher risk of ischemic heart disease.

Cooper Distance-Run Tests. Dr. Kenneth Cooper was one of the first to popularize distance-run/walk tests. The goal of his research (Cooper 1968) was to provide a field test to assess the aerobic fitness of United States Air Force personnel. His sample consisted of 115 men who ranged considerably in age (17–52 years), weight (114–270 pounds), and aerobic fitness (28–60 ml·kg^{-1}·min^{-1}). The subjects first completed the distance-run/walk test of the miles covered in 12 minutes. On the next day the subject completed a maximal treadmill test in which $\dot{V}O_2$ Max was measured by indirect calorimetery. Cooper found a very high correlation ($r = 0.90$) between distance covered in 12 minutes and measured $\dot{V}O_2$ Max. He published a regression equation with a function to estimate distance traveled in miles (D) from $\dot{V}O_2$ Max (ml·kg^{-1}·min^{-1}). The formula is

Cooper's 12-Minute Run/Walk Model ***(8.10)***

$$\text{Distance (miles)} = 0.3138 + (0.0278 \times \dot{V}O_2 \text{ Max ml·kg}^{-1}\text{·min}^{-1})$$

Table 8.5 provides distance-run/walk performance levels developed with Formula 8.10. Provided is the distance in miles covered in 12 minutes and the equivalent elapsed time for a 1.5-mile distance. The 1.5-mile run/walk has become a popular adult field test of aerobic fitness. The 1.5-mile distance was estimated by computing the movement rate (miles per min) of the 12-minute test and calculating the equivalent rate for a 1.5-mile distance (min per 1.5 miles).

Generalized 1-Mile-Run/Walk Test. Cureton and associates (1995) published a comprehensive study relating 1-mile-run/walk performance with $\dot{V}O_2$ Max. Their variable sample consisted of over 750 males and females who ranged in age from 8 to 25 years. The goal of the study was to develop a generalized regression equation that provided valid estimates of aerobic fitness for youth and adults of both sexes. This classic study provides an excellent example of a concurrent validation study.

These researchers found that the relationship between 1-mile-run time and $\dot{V}O_2$ Max was not linear and that sex, age, and body mass index (BMI) accounted for aerobic fitness variance. The multiple correlation of the generalized equation was 0.72 and the standard error of estimate was 4.8 ml·kg^{-1}·min^{-1}. The generalized 1-mile-run/walk formula is

Cuerton's 1-Mile-Run/Walk Generalized Equation ***(8.11)***

$$\dot{V}O_2 \text{ Max (ml·kg}^{-1}\text{·min}^{-1}) = 108.94 - (8.41 \times T) + (0.34 \times T^2) + (0.21 \times \text{Age} \times G) - (0.84 \times \text{BMI})$$

where T is mile-run/walk time in minutes, and G is gender coded: female = 0, male = 1.

Table 8.5 Walk/run Performance Levels Estimated from $\dot{V}O_2$ Max from the Cooper (1968) Equation

$\dot{V}O_2$ Max ($ml \cdot kg^{-1} \cdot min^{-1}$)	Miles in 12 minutes	Miles per Minute	1.5-Mile Time (min:sec)
60	1.98	0.165	9:05
58	1.93	0.161	9:21
56	1.87	0.156	10:37
54	1.81	0.151	10:55
52	1.76	0.147	10:14
50	1.70	0.142	10:34
48	1.65	0.137	10:55
46	1.59	0.133	11:18
44	1.54	0.128	12:43
42	1.48	0.123	12:09
40	1.43	0.119	12:37
40	1.43	0.119	12:37
38	1.37	0.114	13:08
36	1.31	0.110	13:42
34	1.26	0.105	14:18
32	1.20	0.100	14:57
30	1.15	0.096	15:41
28	1.09	0.091	16:29
26	1.04	0.086	17:22

The equation is complex and difficult to use without the use of a computer. Table 8.6 provides $\dot{V}O_2$ Max estimates for select values. The equation is illustrated in the computer calculation section provided in the appendix of this text. Provided next are sample calculations for a male and female to illustrate the application of the equation.

Computation Example, Female. Assume the following data on a woman: mile time, 9 minutes 20 seconds (9.33 minutes); age, 17 years; and BMI, 19.8. The estimated aerobic fitness levels (Formula 8.11) is:

$$\dot{V}O_2 \text{ Max } (ml \cdot kg^{-1} \cdot min^{-1}) = 108.94 - (8.41 \times 9.33) + (0.34 \times 9.33 \times 9.33) + (0.21 \times 17 \times 0) - (0.84 \times 19.8)$$

$$= 108.94 - 78.46 + 29.60 + 0 - 16.63 = 43.45 \text{ ml} \cdot kg^{-1} \cdot min^{-1}$$

Computation Example, Female. Assume the following data on a man: mile time, 8 minutes 45 seconds (8.75 minutes); age, 16 years; and BMI 20.1. The estimated aerobic fitness levels (Formula 8.11) is:

$$\dot{V}O_2 \text{ Max } (ml \cdot kg^{-1} \cdot min^{-1}) = 108.94 - (8.41 \times 8.75) + (0.34 \times 8.75 \times 8.75) + (0.21 \times 16 \times 1) - (0.84 \times 20.1)$$

$$= 108.94 - 73.59 + 26.03 + 3.36 - 16.88 = 47.86 \text{ ml} \cdot kg^{-1} \cdot min^{-1}$$

One limitation of the generalized equation is that it becomes inaccurate for very slow mile-run/walk times. The equation should not be used if the run/walk time is more than 12 minutes.

Table 8.6 One-Mile Run/Walk $\dot{V}O_2$ Max ($ml \cdot kg^{-1} \cdot min^{-1}$) Estimated for Males and Females of Different Ages and BMI Levels

Mile-Run/ Walk Time (min)	Male BMI Level				Female BMI Level			
	15	20	25	30	15	20	25	30
Age 10 Years								
6	60	56	52	48	58	54	50	46
8	53	49	44	40	51	47	42	38
10	46	42	38	34	44	40	36	32
12	46	42	38	34	44	40	36	32
Age 15 Years								
6	61	57	53	49	58	54	50	56
8	54	50	46	41	51	47	42	38
10	49	45	41	37	46	42	38	34
12	48	43	39	35	44	40	36	32
Age 20 Years								
6	62	58	54	50	58	54	50	46
8	55	51	47	42	51	47	42	38
10	50	46	42	38	46	42	38	34
12	49	44	40	36	44	40	36	32

Distance-Run Test Procedures. The general steps to follow when administering distance-run tests are:

1. Select the appropriate distance-run/walk test.
2. The subject may walk, jog, or use a combination of both to achieve the best score. Ideally, the runner should be reasonably exhausted at the end of the test.
3. It is a good idea to let subjects practice their walking/jogging pace prior to taking the test. Traveling too fast will lead to exhaustion prior to completing the distance and traveling too slow will not fully tax maximal aerobic capacity.
4. Convert the distance-run performance to $\dot{V}O_2$ Max to evaluate aerobic fitness.

Safety Consideration. Remember, a timed distance-run test should be considered a maximal test. It has all the attendant risks of a maximal test, with the added risk of being unsupervised. Maximal distance-run tests are suitable only for young people in good condition without significant cardiovascular disease risk factors.

Submaximal Walking and Jogging Tests

A limitation of laboratory tests is the need for a cycle ergometer or treadmill to regulate power output. Walking and jogging on level ground is another method of regulating power output. The walking and jogging tests described next allow the person to travel at a self-determined pace. $\dot{V}O_2$ Max is estimated from movement time and from heart-rate response to the exercise.

The Rockport Walk Test. The Rockport Walk Test (Kline et al. 1987) provides a means of estimating $\dot{V}O_2$ Max from heart-rate response to walking speed. A track and heart-rate monitoring equipment are all that are needed to administer the test. The Rockport test involves walking as fast as possible for 1 mile and then measuring the exercise heart rate immediately after the walk. In the original study, heart rate was monitored electronically. Several inexpensive electronic heart-rate monitors are now commercially available and recommended. The test is suitable for both men and women.

The data needed to estimate $\dot{V}O_2$ Max include the following:

1. Weight measured in pounds.
2. Mile walk time measured to 1/100th of a second. Note, a walk time of 15 minutes and 30 seconds would be 15.5.
3. Exercise heart rate (beats·min^{-1}) measured immediately at the conclusion of the walk.
4. Age measured to the last year.
5. Gender coded, female = 0, and male = 1.

Multiple regression equations were developed to estimate $\dot{V}O_2$ Max (ml·kg^{-1}·min^{-1}) from these variables. A general equation (R = 0.88, SEE = 5 ml·kg^{-1}·min^{-1}) was developed for males and females. The formula is

Rockport Walk Test **(8.12)**

$$\dot{V}O_2 \text{ Max (ml·kg}^{-1}\text{·min}^{-1}) = 132.85 - (0.39 \times \text{Age}) - (0.08 \times W) - (3.26 \times T) - (0.16 \times HR) + (6.32 \times G)$$

where W is body weight in pounds, T is mile-run time in minutes, HR is exercise heart rate, and G is gender, female = 0 and male = 1.

The general procedures for the Rockport Walk Test are:

1. Do not use the equation with individuals who are taking medications that affect heart rate (e.g., hypertension medications). Inaccurate heart-rate measurements substantially alter test accuracy.
2. Practice walking the mile at a brisk, constant pace.
3. The subject must walk fast enough to get their heart rate above 120 beats/min. If the person's walk pace does not bring their heart rate to this level, the test is not appropriate—their fitness level is too high.

Calculation Example. Assume the following data for a man: age, 27 years; weight, 165 pounds; mile walk time, 15 minutes and 45 seconds (15.75 min); and exercise heart rate, 144 beats·min^{-1}. Using Formula 8.12, $\dot{V}O_2$ Max (ml·kg^{-1}·min^{-1}) is:

$$\dot{V}O_2 \text{ Max (ml·kg}^{-1}\text{·min}^{-1}) = 132.85 - (0.39 \times 27) - (0.08 \times 165) - (3.26 \times 15.75) - (0.16 \times 144) + (6.32 \times 1)$$

$$= 132.85 - 10.53 - 13.20 - 51.34 - 23.04 + 6.32 = 41.06 \text{ ml·kg}^{-1}\text{·min}^{-1}$$

With the exception of sex, all regression coefficients have a negative sign, showing that the individuals with the highest VO_2 Max would be those who are younger, have less body weight, and combine a low mile walk time with a low heart rate. Appendix B illustrates the application of the Rockport fomulas.

BYU Jog Test. A major limitation of the Rockport Walk Test is that highly fit individuals cannot walk fast enough to elevate their heart rate above 45% of VO_2 Max ($\approx$ 120 beats·min^{-1}). Researchers at Brigham Young University (BYU) developed a similar test that replaces walking with jogging (George et al. 1993). The test protocol requires the subject to jog at a steady pace for 1 mile. Exercise heart rate is measured immediately after the run. The recommended test procedures include the following:

1. Do not allow subjects who are taking medications that affect their heart rate to take the test. Inaccurate heart-rate measurements substantially affect test accuracy.
2. The subject first takes a 2- to 3-minute warm-up jog.
3. The goal is to jog the 1 mile at a steady and suitable pace. Many subjects tend to run at an "all-out" rate. However, this test is a submaximal one. To ensure that it is a submaximal effort, run time and exercise heart limits are set. These limits are:

- Jogging pace, $\geq$8 minutes for males and $\geq$9 minutes for females.
- Exercise heart rate, $\leq$180 beats/min.

4. The variables needed for this test are:

- Weight measured in kilograms.
- Mile jog time measured in minutes.
- Exercise heart rate (beats/min) measured immediately after the walk.
- Gender, with female = 0 and male = 1.

The researcher developed a regression formula (R = 0.87, SEE = 3.0 ml·kg^{-1}·min^{-1}) that can be used with men and women. The formula is

BYU Jog Test **(8.13)**

$$VO_2 \text{ Max (ml/kg/min)} = 100.500 - (0.164 \times W) - (1.438 \times T) - (0.193 \times HR) + (8.344 \times G)$$

where W is body weight kilograms, T is mile-run time in minutes, HR is exercise heart rate, and G is gender, female = 0 and male = 1.

Calculation Example. Assume the following data obtained on a woman: weight, 165 pounds (75 kg); mile walk time, 6 minutes and 20 seconds (6.33 min); and exercise heart rate, 164 beats·min^{-1}. Applying these data to Formula 8.13, VO_2 Max (ml·kg^{-1}·min^{-1}) is

$$VO_2 \text{ Max (ml·kg}^{-1}\text{·min}^{-1}) = 100.50 - (0.16 \times 75) - (1.44 \times 6.33) - (0.19 \times 164) (8.344 \times 0)$$

$$= 100.50 - 12.00 - 9.12 - 31.16 + 0 = 48.2 \text{ ml·kg}^{-1}\text{·min}^{-1}$$

The BYU Jog Test was developed from a homogeneous sample of young, fit college students. The test will not likely be acceptable for less fit subjects. For those subjects, the Rockport test would likely be more appropriate. Appendix B illustrates the application of the BYU Jog Test formula.

Nonexercise Aerobic Fitness Tests

$\dot{V}O_2$ Max can be estimated without testing individuals (Jackson et al. 1990). Aerobic fitness can be estimated with reasonable accuracy from the individual's age, sex, body composition, and self-report level of aerobic exercise. Metabolically determined $\dot{V}O_2$ Max is the test used to evaluate employees and astronauts at the NASA/Johnson Space Center (Houston, TX). This has provided a very large database of men and women with a measured $\dot{V}O_2$ Max. Prior to being tested, each employee rated their physical activity (see Figure 8.15) during the previous month. Multiple regression was used to estimate $\dot{V}O_2$ Max from exercise rating in combination with age, sex, and a body composition parameter consisting of either percent body fat or body mass index (BMI). Chapter 9 gives the methods used to measure and compute percent body fat and BMI.

CODE FOR PHYSICAL ACTIVITY

Use the appropriate number (0 to 7) which best describes your general ACTIVITY LEVEL for the PREVIOUS MONTH.

DO NOT PARTICIPATE REGULARLY IN PROGRAMMED RECREATION SPORT OR HEAVY PHYSICAL ACTIVITY.

0 - Avoid walking or exertion, e.g., always use elevator, drive whenever possible instead of walking.
1 - Walk for pleasure, routinely use stairs, occasionally exercise sufficiently to cause heavy breathing or perspiration.

PARTICIPATED REGULARLY IN RECREATION OR WORK REQUIRING MODEST PHYSICAL ACTIVITY, SUCH AS GOLF, HORSEBACK RIDING, CALISTHENICS, GYMNASTICS, TABLE TENNIS, BOWLING, WEIGHT LIFTING, YARD WORK.

2 - 10 to 60 minutes per week.
3 - Over one hour per week.

PARTICIPATE REGULARLY IN HEAVY PHYSICAL EXERCISE SUCH AS RUNNING OR JOGGING, SWIMMING, CYCLING, ROWING, SKIPPING ROPE, RUNNING IN PLACE OR ENGAGING IN VIGOROUS AEROBIC ACTIVITY TYPE EXERCISE SUCH AS TENNIS, BASKETBALL OR HANDBALL.

4 - Run less than one mile per week or spend less than 30 minutes per week in comparable physical activity.
5 - Run 1 to 5 miles per week or spend 30 to 60 minutes per week in comparable physical activity.
6 - Run 5 to 10 miles per week or spend 1 to 3 hours per week in comparable physical activity.
7 - Run over 10 miles per week or spend over 3 hours per week in comparable physical activity.

Figure 8.15 Scale for rating level of physical activity. The directions are to select one value that best represents the level of physical activity for the previous month. (The scale developed for use in the Cardio-pulmonary Laboratory, NASA/Johnson Space Center, Houston, Texas.) (Source: Jackson and Ross, R. M. *Understanding Exercise for Health and Fitness,* 1997. Reprinted by permission.)

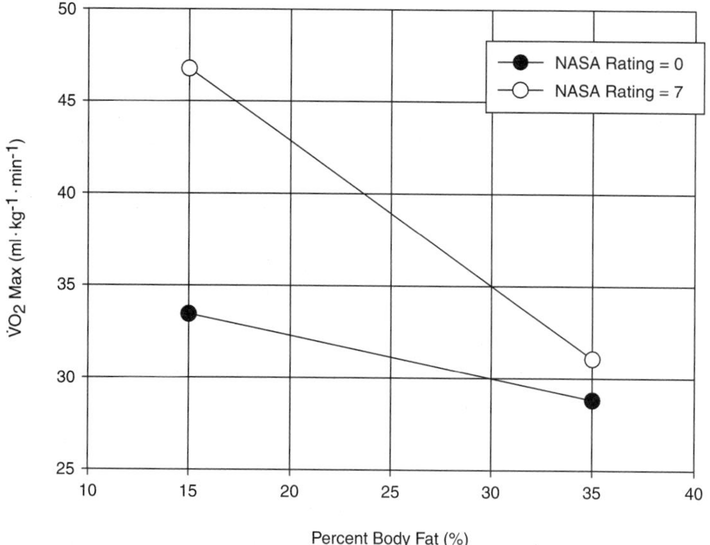

Figure 8.16
Graphic illustration of the interaction of self-report level of physical activity and percent body fat. Provided are $\dot{V}O_2$ Max estimates for men age 45 years. When percent body fat is high, there is very little difference between active and sedentary individuals. When percent fat is low, there is a substantial difference between active and sedentary individuals. (Source: CSI Software Company, Houston, TX. Reprinted by permission.)

The original research (Jackson et al. 1990) provided two equations that could be used for males and females. The difference in the equations was the body composition variable. The most accurate equation ($R = 0.81$, $SEE = 5.3$ ml·kg^{-1}·min^{-1}) used skinfold-determined percent body fat (Jackson & Pollock 1978; Jackson, Pollock, & Ward 1980). The equation that used BMI was slightly less accurate ($R = 0.78$, $SEE = 5.7$ ml·kg^{-1}·min^{-1}), but more feasible for mass testing.

A limitation of these early equations was that the sample size of the women was considerably smaller than that of the men. We recently published additional studies from this database (Jackson et al. 1995; Jackson et al. 1996) in which the goal was to examine the influence of aging on $\dot{V}O_2$ Max. In this research we used a very stringent definition of $\dot{V}O_2$ Max and had a much larger sample of women. With the larger sample of women, it became possible to develop gender-specific equations. In these aging studies we discover what is termed "an interaction" of self-report physical activity and percent body fat. Figure 8.16 illustrates this interaction. Shown are the $\dot{V}O_2$ Max estimates for 45-year-old men with activity ratings of 0 and 7 at 15% and 35% body fat levels. The difference in $\dot{V}O_2$ Max between activity rating of 0 and 7 at 35% fat is only 2 ml·kg^{-1}·min^{-1}, but at 15% fat the difference is 14 ml·kg^{-1}·min^{-1}.

What is the reason for this interaction? We believe that this activity and percent fat interaction[6] describes one's level of habitual physical activity. The profile of a person with a low percent body fat and high SR-PA is someone who exercises regularly and expends sufficient calories to control weight. Those who exercise regularly tend to be lean. In contrast, one who has a high percent body fat and high activity rating is likely to be someone who has just started an exercise program. The activity percent body fat interaction tends to provide a better indication of one's activity level.

[6]The interaction term is obtained by multiplying the activity rating and percent body fat terms.

Table 8.7 Descriptive Statistics of the Men and Women Used to Develop the University of Houston Nonexercise Equations

Variable	Men (n = 1477)		Women (n = 409)	
	Mean	SD	Mean	SD
Age (yrs)	45.9	7.8	39.4	9.6
Percent body fat (%)	20.6	6.0	26.2	7.8
BMI (Wt/Ht^2)	25.5	3.1	23.8	4.0
Self-report physical activity (rating)	4.1	2.1	4.0	2.3
$\dot{V}O_2$ Max (ml·kg^{-1}·min^{-1})	38.4	8.0	31.6	8.3

Nonexercise Equations

This aging research (Jackson et al. 1995; Jackson et al. 1996) resulted in the publication of separate percent body fat equations for males and females. We have used these same databases to develop separate male and female BMI equations. Table 8.7 gives the descriptive statistics of the samples used to develop these equations. Provided next are the male and female equations for the percent body fat and BMI models. The regression coefficients show that those with the highest aerobic capacity are those who are younger, more aerobically active, and leaner. Appendix B provides examples of these calculations with a database computer program. Tables 8.8 and 8.9 provide estimates for men and women of various ages, levels of body composition, and activity ratings.

Percent Body Fat Nonexercise Equations. Provided next are the male and female nonexercise formulas that use percent body fat. A calculation example is provided to illustrate the application of the formula.

Men—University of Houston Percent Fat Nonexercise
(R = 0.79, SEE = 4.9 ml·kg^{-1}·min^{-1}) ***(8.14)***

$$\dot{V}O_2 \text{ Max (ml·kg}^{-1}\text{·min}^{-1}) = 47.820 - (0.259 \times \text{Age}) - (0.216 \times \%\text{fat}) + (3.275 \times \text{AR}) - (0.082 \times \%\text{fat} \times \text{AR})$$

Women—University of Houston Percent Fat Nonexercise
(R = 0.85, SEE = 4.4 ml·kg^{-1}·min^{-1}) ***(8.15)***

$$\dot{V}O_2 \text{ Max (ml·kg}^{-1}\text{·min}^{-1}) = 45.628 - (0.265 \times \text{Age}) - (0.309 \times \%\text{fat}) + (2.175 \times \text{AR}) - (0.044 \times \%\text{fat} \times \text{AR})$$

where AR is activity code (0 to 7), and %fat is percent body fat.

Calculation Example, Percent Body Fat Model. Assume we have the following data on a man: age, 28 years; percent body fat, 27.4%; and activity rating of 3. Using Formula 8.14, nonexercise $\dot{V}O_2$ Max is:

$$\dot{V}O_2 \text{ Max (ml·kg}^{-1}\text{·min}^{-1}) = 47.820 - (0.259 \times 28) - (0.216 \times 27.4) + (3.275 \times 3) - (0.082 \times 27.4 \times 3)$$

$$= 47.820 - 7.252 - 5.918 + 9.825 - 6.740 = 37.7 \text{ ml·kg}^{-1}\text{·min}^{-1}$$

Table 8.8 $\dot{V}O_2$ Max ($ml \cdot kg^{-1} \cdot min^{-1}$) Estimates for Selected Age, Body Composition, and Activity Levels for Men

Self-Report Rating	Percent Body Fat Level				BMI Level			
	15%	20%	25%	30%	23	26	29	32
Age 20 Years								
7	53.7	49.8	45.8	41.9	55.5	52.5	49.5	46.5
5	49.6	46.5	43.4	40.3	51.3	48.9	46.5	44.0
3	45.6	43.2	40.9	38.6	47.1	45.3	43.4	41.6
1	41.5	40.0	38.5	37.0	42.9	41.7	40.4	39.1
Age 30 Years								
7	51.2	47.2	43.3	39.3	51.9	48.9	45.9	42.9
5	47.1	43.9	40.8	37.7	47.7	45.3	42.9	40.4
3	43.0	40.7	38.4	36.0	43.5	41.7	39.8	38.0
1	38.9	37.4	35.9	34.4	39.3	38.0	36.8	35.5
Age 40 Years								
7	48.6	44.6	40.7	36.7	48.3	45.3	42.3	39.3
5	44.5	41.4	38.2	35.1	44.1	41.7	39.2	36.8
3	40.4	38.1	35.8	33.5	39.9	38.0	36.2	34.3
1	36.3	34.8	33.3	31.8	35.7	34.4	33.1	31.9
Age 50 Years								
7	46.0	42.0	38.1	34.1	44.7	41.7	38.7	35.7
5	41.9	38.8	35.6	32.5	40.5	38.1	35.6	33.2
3	37.8	35.5	33.2	30.9	36.3	34.4	32.6	30.7
1	33.7	32.2	30.7	29.3	32.1	30.8	29.5	28.2
Age 60 Years								
7	43.4	39.5	35.5	31.6	41.1	38.1	35.1	32.0
5	39.3	36.2	33.1	29.9	36.9	34.4	32.0	29.6
3	35.2	32.9	30.6	28.3	32.7	30.8	28.9	27.1
1	31.1	29.7	28.2	26.7	28.5	27.2	25.9	24.6

BMI Nonexercise Equations. Provided next are the male and female BMI nonexercise formulas. A calculation example is provided to illustrate the application of the formula.

Men—University of Houston BMI Nonexercise
($R = 0.74$, $SEE = 5.4\ ml \cdot kg^{-1} \cdot min^{-1}$) *(8.16)*

$$\dot{V}O_2 \text{ Max (ml/kg/min)} = 55.688 - (0.362 \times \text{Age}) - (0.331 \times \text{BMI}) + (4.310 \times \text{AR}) - (0.096 \times \text{BMI} \times \text{AR})$$

Women—University of Houston BMI Nonexercise
($R = 0.82$, $SEE = 4.7\ ml \cdot kg^{-1} \cdot min^{-1}$) *(8.17)*

$$\dot{V}O_2 \text{ Max } (ml \cdot kg^{-1} \cdot min^{-1}) = 44.310 - (0.326 \times \text{Age}) - (0.227 \times \text{BMI}) + (4.471 \times \text{AR}) - (0.135 \times \text{BMI} \times \text{AR})$$

where AR is activity code (0 to 7), and BMI is body mass index.

Table 8.9 $\dot{V}O_2$ Max ($ml \cdot kg^{-1} \cdot min^{-1}$) Estimates for Selected Age, Body Composition, and Activity Levels for Women

Self-Report Rating	Percent Body Fat Level				BMI Level			
	20%	25%	30%	35%	19	23	27	31
Age 20 Years								
7	43.2	40.1	37.0	34.0	46.8	42.1	37.4	32.8
5	40.6	38.0	35.3	32.7	43.0	39.4	35.8	32.2
3	38.0	35.8	33.6	31.4	39.2	36.7	34.1	31.6
1	35.4	33.7	31.9	30.1	35.4	33.9	32.5	31.0
Age 30 Years								
7	40.6	37.5	34.4	31.3	43.6	38.9	34.2	29.5
5	38.0	35.3	32.7	30.0	39.7	36.1	32.5	28.9
3	35.4	33.2	31.0	28.8	35.9	33.4	30.9	28.4
1	32.8	31.0	29.3	27.5	32.1	30.7	29.2	27.8
Age 40 Years								
7	37.9	34.8	31.7	28.7	40.3	35.6	30.9	26.2
5	35.3	32.7	30.0	27.4	36.5	32.9	29.3	25.7
3	32.7	30.5	28.3	26.1	32.7	30.1	27.6	25.1
1	30.1	28.4	26.6	24.8	28.9	27.4	26.0	24.5
Age 50 Years								
7	35.3	32.2	29.1	26.0	37.0	32.4	27.7	23.0
5	32.7	30.0	27.4	24.7	33.2	29.6	26.0	22.4
3	30.1	27.9	25.7	23.5	29.4	26.9	24.4	21.8
1	27.5	25.7	24.0	22.2	25.6	24.2	22.7	21.3
Age 60 Years								
7	32.6	29.5	26.4	23.4	33.8	29.1	24.4	19.7
5	30.0	27.4	24.7	22.1	30.0	26.4	22.8	19.1
3	27.4	25.2	23.0	20.8	26.2	23.6	21.1	18.6
1	24.8	23.1	21.3	19.5	22.3	20.9	19.4	18.0

Calculation Example, BMI Model. Assume we have the following data on a woman: age, 32 years; BMI of 21.3; and activity rating of 7. Using Formula 8.17, nonexercise $\dot{V}O_2$ Max is:

$$\dot{V}O_2 \text{ Max } (ml \cdot kg^{-1} \cdot min^{-1}) = 44.310 - (0.326 \times 32) - (0.227 \times 21.3) + (4.471 \times 7) - (0.135 \times 21.3 \times 7)$$

$$= 44.310 - 10.432 - 4.835 + 31.297 - 20.128 = 40.2 \ ml \cdot kg^{-1} \cdot min^{-1}$$

Accuracy of Nonexercise Formulas

The nonexercise tests are especially feasible for mass testing. Since heart rate is not a factor of the nonexercise test, it can be validly used with individuals taking heart-rate-altering medication. With the ease of test administration, one may question the accuracy of them. Figures 8.17 through 8.19 present scattergrams between measured $\dot{V}O_2$ Max and estimated from the maximal treadmill time (Foster et al. 1984) and the two nonexercise models (Jackson et al. 1990). A random sample of 600 men and women from the databases (Jackson et al. 1995; Jackson et al. 1996) were used to develop these scattergrams.

The figures show that maximum treadmill time is the most accurate test, but the two nonexercise models provide excellent estimates. An examination of the scattergrams for the two nonexercise models shows that the models are least accurate for highly fit subjects. Table 8.10 provides the standard errors for these three prediction models. Provided are the error estimates for the total sample and contrasted by fitness groups. The total groups were split into groups, highly fit and the remaining men and women. The highly fit groups were defined by a measured $\dot{V}O_2$ Max ≥ 45 and ≥ 50 $ml \cdot kg^{-1} \cdot min^{-1}$ for the women and men, respectively. Only about 5% of men and women would be expected to be above these points.

The maximum treadmill time prediction errors were the lowest over all levels of aerobic fitness, but all prediction models showed a similar trend. All were least accurate with highly fit subjects. The nonexercise models would not be suitable for highly fit subjects. An examination of the two nonexercise scattergrams shows that at this high level, the nonexercise models underestimate true $\dot{V}O_2$ Max.

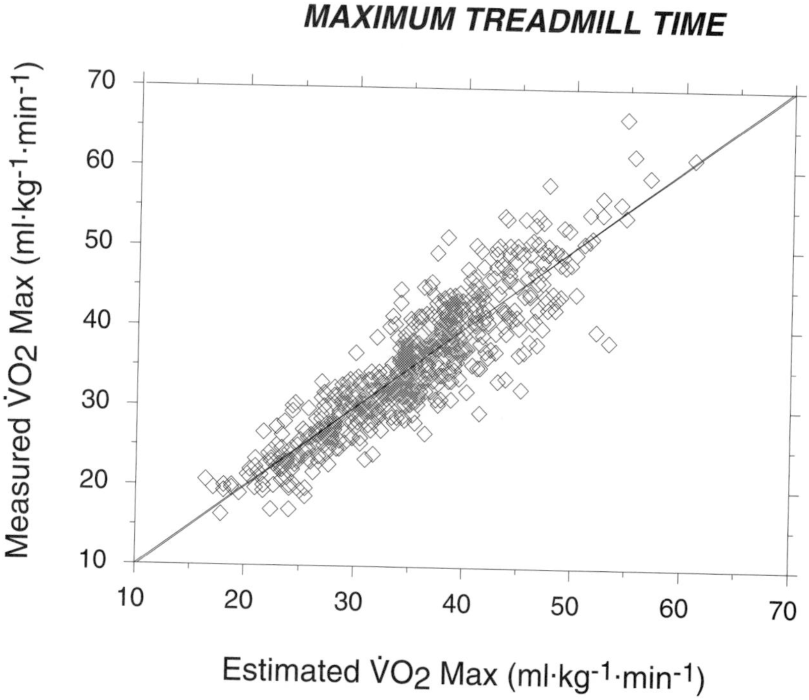

MAXIMUM TREADMILL TIME

Measured $\dot{V}O_2$ Max ($ml \cdot kg^{-1} \cdot min^{-1}$)

Estimated $\dot{V}O_2$ Max ($ml \cdot kg^{-1} \cdot min^{-1}$)

Figure 8.17
Scattergram between measured $\dot{V}O_2$ Max and estimated from maximum treadmill time (Foster et al. 1984). The line of identity is provided for reference. (Source: CSI Software Company, Houston, TX. Reprinted by permission.)

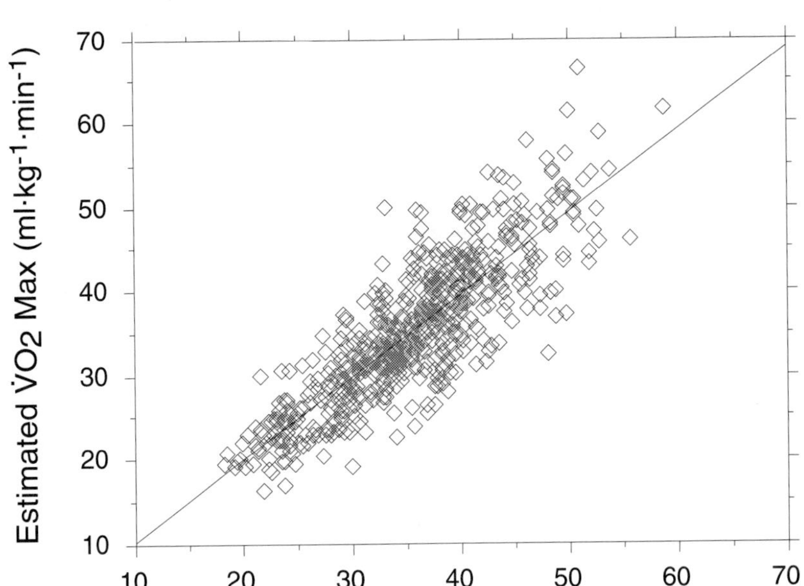

Figure 8.18
Scattergram between measured $\dot{V}O_2$ Max and estimated from nonexercise percent body fat model. The line of identity is provided for reference. (Source: CSI Software Company, Houston, TX. Reprinted by permission.)

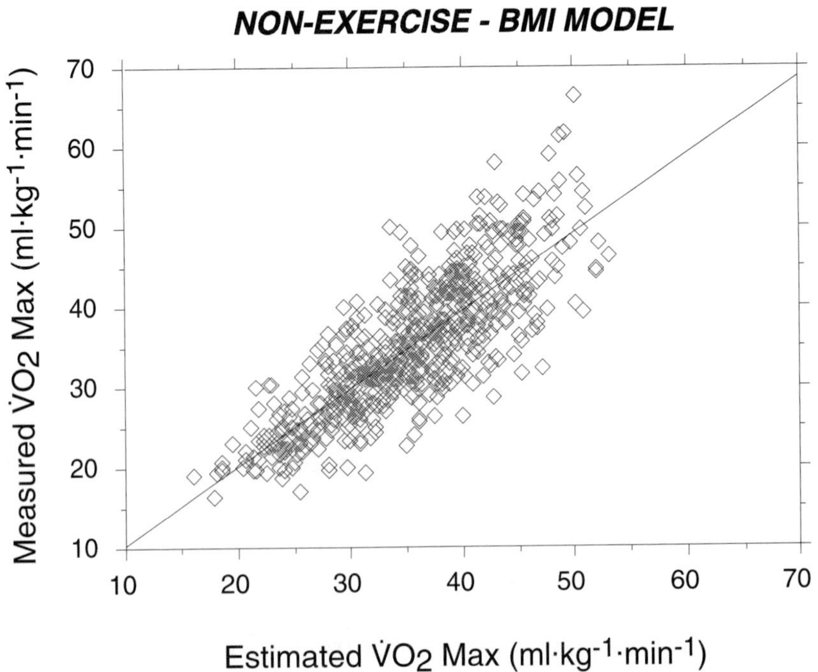

Figure 8.19
Scattergram between measured $\dot{V}O_2$ Max and estimated from nonexercise body mass index model. The line of identity is provided for reference. (Source: CSI Software Company, Houston, TX. Reprinted by permission.)

Table 8.10 A Comparison of the Accuracy* of the Nonexercise Equations with Maximum Treadmill Time for the Total Sample and Split into Aerobic Fitness Groups

	Women			Men		
Prediction Model	**All**	**<45**	**≥45**	**All**	**<50**	**≥50**
Max treadmill time	3.8	3.4	6.6	3.9	3.7	5.9
% Fat nonexercise model	4.4	4.0	7.6	4.9	4.5	7.6
BMI nonexercise model	4.7	4.3	8.2	5.4	4.9	9.1

*Standard errors of estimate ($ml \cdot kg^{-1} \cdot min^{-1}$)

The standard error of measurement for the direct measurement of $\dot{V}O_2$ Max is about 1 $ml \cdot kg^{-1} \cdot min^{-1}$. The reported standard error for estimating $\dot{V}O_2$ Max from maximal treadmill time is 3–4 $ml \cdot kg^{-1} \cdot min^{-1}$, while the standard error for estimating $\dot{V}O_2$ Max from the nonexercise prediction models is between 4.5 and 5.5 ml/kg/min. These data are clear. If accuracy is of concern, a max test with indirect calorimetery must be used. While the nonexercise tests are more practical, there is a cost. They are less accurate, especially for highly fit subjects.

Summary

Aerobic fitness is a major component of adult fitness tests and important for health promotion. Many universities, YMCAs, private corporations, and commercial organizations provide adult health-related fitness programs. Individuals with significant cardiovascular risk factors need a stress test prior to starting an exercise program. A stress test is a medical test designed to diagnose heart disease from the exercise EKG and cardiovascular responses to exercise. In contrast, a fitness evaluation evaluates aerobic fitness.

There are many different methods to evaluate aerobic fitness. Table 8.11 summarizes these methods. $\dot{V}O_2$ Max may be measured by either maximal or submaximal tests. The most valid method is a maximal test where $\dot{V}O_2$ Max is measured directly from expired gases. Typically, this method is reserved for research purposes. A second maximal method is to estimate $\dot{V}O_2$ Max from treadmill time with regression equations. Distance-run/walk tests are accurate field tests that are most appropriate for evaluating youth aerobic fitness. Submaximal tests are more realistic for mass use. $\dot{V}O_2$ Max is estimated from submaximal power output and exercise heart-rate response to the exercise level. Single- and multi-stage models are available for estimating $\dot{V}O_2$ Max. A second type of submaximal test that is more practical for field testing involves measuring exercise heart rate immediately after a 1-mile walk or jog. The final method does not require exercise testing. The nonexercise $\dot{V}O_2$ Max method involves estimating aerobic fitness from age, self-report physical activity, and body composition measured by percent body fat or BMI. The maximal treadmill test is the most accurate, with a standard error of 3–4 ml/kg/min, while the standard error of the submaximal and nonexercise models is between 4.5 and 5.5 ml/kg/min.

Table 8.11 A Comparison of the Methods Used to Estimate $\dot{V}O_2$ Max

Method	Advantage	Limitation	Comments and Cautions
Maximal Tests			
Indirect calorimetry	Most accurate	Maximal test; expensive equipment & trained personnel needed	High-risk subjects need medical monitoring
Maximal treadmill time	Highly accurate	Maximal test; expensive equipment & trained personnel needed	High-risk subjects need medical monitoring
Distance-run tests	Feasible for mass testing	Maximal test; subject motivation affects results	High-risk subjects need medical monitoring
Submaximal Tests			
Single-stage	Submaximal effort	Expensive equipment; heart-rate variability; estimate max heart rate	Not suitable for individuals on drugs that alter heart rate
Multi-stage	Submaximal effort	Expensive equipment; heart-rate variability; estimate max heart rate; difficult to measure multiple stages	Not suitable for individuals on drugs that alter heart rate
Walk or Jog Tests			
Rockport Walk Test	Submaximal effort; just need a heart-rate monitor	Too easy for highly fit	Not suitable for individuals on drugs that alter heart rate
BYU Jog Test	Submaximal effort; just need a heart-rate monitor	Too difficult for low fit	Not suitable for individuals on drugs that alter heart rate; developed on young, fit adults
Nonexercise Methods			
Percent fat model	Just need to test %Fat; not affected by drugs	Subjective rating of activity; no cardiac function	Not appropriate for highly fit men and women
BMI model	Just need height/weight; not affected by drugs; can be all self-report	Subjective rating of activity; no cardiac function	Not appropriate for highly fit men and women

Formative Evaluation of Objectives

Objective 1 Identify the role of aerobic fitness in health.

1. What is the relationship between aerobic fitness and health?
2. How aerobically fit does one need to be in order to enjoy health benefits?

Objective 2 Differentiate between a stress test and fitness evaluation.

1. What is the major difference between a stress test and fitness evaluation?
2. What types of individuals should have a stress test prior to starting an exercise program?

Objective 3 Define the methods used to measure $\dot{V}O_2$ Max from (a) maximal tests; (b) submaximal tests; (c) walking and running field tests; and (d) nonexercise models.

1. What is $\dot{V}O_2$ Max for the following treadmill time and protocols?
   a. 10 minutes for (1) Bruce; (2) Balke?
   b. 18 minutes for (1) Bruce; (2) Balke?
   c. Would you expect someone to last 25 minutes on the Bruce or Balke? Why or why not?
2. Calculate $\dot{V}O_2$ Max from the following:
   a. Female with a maximal heart rate of 187, and submaximal values of 6 METs and heart rate of 145 beats/min.
   b. Male, age 37 years. Submaximal power output on a bike of 900 kmp/min and heart rate of 140 beats/min.
   c. A 28-year-old person had the following submaximal treadmill data: max heart rate, 175 beats/min; 3.4 mph and 9% grade after 3 minutes of exercise; and exercise heart rate of 146 beats/min.
3. What procedures would you need to follow to estimate $\dot{V}O_2$ Max with the multi-stage model?
4. What is the similarity between submaximal test methods and the Rockport Walk Test and the BYU Jog Test?
5. What variables compose the nonexercise models? Explain why these variables can be expected to be related to $\dot{V}O_2$ Max.

Objective 4 Define the levels of aerobic fitness needed for health promotion and physically demanding exercise.

1. What are the variables used to establish normative $\dot{V}O_2$ Max standards, and what is the reason these variables are used?
2. What is the basis for health-related aerobic fitness standards?

Objective 5 Identify maximal and submaximal treadmill protocols.

1. Define the speeds and elevations for the Balke and Bruce treadmill protocols.
2. Define the speeds and elevations for the Ross and Bruce submaximal treadmill protocols.

Objective 6 Identify cycle ergometer submaximal protocols.

1. List the power output loads you would follow to test a typical woman.
2. List the power output loads you would follow to test a typical man.
3. What would be the power output differences for (a) single-stage model and (b) multi-stage model?

Additional Learning Activities

A true understanding of $\dot{V}O_2$ Max is best obtained by measuring it.

1. Find a partner and measure your $\dot{V}O_2$ Max by (1) multi-stage model; (2) single-stage model; (3) the Rockport Walk Test; (4) the BYU Jog Test. If your college or university has metabolic equipment, try this method and compare the results you get from maximal treadmill time with those from submaximal models.
2. It may be difficult to complete some $\dot{V}O_2$ Max tests, but this is not true for the nonexercise method. Evaluate your aerobic fitness with the nonexercise models.
3. Maximum distance-run tests can be used to evaluate aerobic fitness. Conduct a validation study with the nonexercise models. Have a group of students complete the 1.5-mile-walk/run test and estimate their $\dot{V}O_2$ Max with a nonexercise model. What is the correlation between the two aerobic fitness measures?
4. Develop a computer program to complete the calculations presented in this chapter. Provided at the end of the chapter are equations that can be used to make these calculations on spreadsheet or database programs.

Bibliography

ACSM. (1990). The recommended quantity and quality of exercise for developing and maintaining cardiorespiratory and muscular fitness in healthy adults. *Medicine and Science in Sports and Exercise, 22,* 265–274.

ACSM. 1991. *Guidelines for exercise testing and prescription.* 3d ed. Vol. 4. Philadelphia: Lea & Febiger.

Åstrand, P. and K. Rodahl. 1970. *Textbook of work physiology.* New York: McGraw-Hill.

Åstrand, P. O. and K. Rodahl. 1986. *Textbook of work physiology.* 3d ed. New York: McGraw-Hill.

Åstrand, P. O. and I. Ryhming. 1954. A nomogram for calculation of aerobic capacity (physical fitness) from pulse rate during submaximal work. *Journal of Applied Physiology* 7:218–221.

Balke, B. 1963. A simple field test for assessment of physical fitness. *Civil Aeromedical Research Institute Report:* 63–66.

Blair, S. N. et al. 1989. Physical fitness and all-cause mortality: A prospective study of healthy men and women. *Journal of the American Medical Association* 262:2395–2401.

Blair, S. N. et al. 1995. Changes in physical fitness and all-cause mortality: A prospective study of healthy and unhealthy men. *Journal of the American Medical Association* 273(14):1093–1098.

Borg, G. 1977. Physical work and effort. *Proceedings of the First International Symposium.* Wenner-Gren Center, Stockholm, Sweden. Oxford, England: Pergamon Press.

Brouha, L. 1943. The step tests: A simple method of measuring physical fitness for muscular work in young men. *Research Quarterly* 14:31–36.

Bruce, R. A., F. Kusumi, and D. Hosmer. 1973. Maximal oxygen intake and nomographic assessment of functional aerobic impairment in cardiovascular disease. *American Heart Journal* 85:546–562.

Buskirk, E. R. and J. L. Hodgson. 1987. Age and aerobic power: The rate of change in men and women. *Federation Proceedings* 46:1824–1829.

Consolazio, L. J., R. F. Johnson, and L. J. Pecora. 1963. *Physiological measurements of metabolic functions in man.* New York: McGraw-Hill.

Cooper, K. H. 1968. A means of assessing maximal oxygen intake. *Journal of the American Medical Association* 203:201–204.

Cooper, K. H. 1970. *The new aerobics.* New York: Bantam Books.

Cureton, K. J. et al. 1995. A generalized equation for prediction of VO_2 Peak from 1-mile run/walk performance. *Medicine and Science in Sports and Exercise* 27(3):445–451.

Foster, C. et al. 1984. Generalized equations for predicting functional capacity from treadmill performance. *American Heart Journal* 107:1229–1234.

Franks, B. D. and E. T. Howley. 1989. *Fitness facts: The healthy living handbook.* Champaign, IL: Human Kinetics.

George, J. D. et al. 1993. VO_2 Max estimation from a submaximal 1-mile track jog for fit college-age individuals. *Medicine and Science in Sports and Exercise* 25:401–406.

Gettman, L. R. 1993. Chapter 19. Fitness testing. In *Resource manual for guidelines for exercise testing and prescription.* Philadelphia: Lea & Febiger.

Golding, L. A., C. R. Meyers, and W. E. Sinning. 1989. *The Y's way to physical fitness.* 3d ed. Chicago: National Board of YMCA.

Hagberg, J. M. et al. 1985. A hemodynamic comparison of young and older endurance athletes during exercise. *Journal of Applied Physiology* 58:2041–2046.

Holloszy, J. O. 1983. Exercise, health, and aging: A need for more information. *Medicine and Science in Sports and Exercise* 15:1–5.

Jackson, A. S. et al. 1990. Prediction of functional aerobic capacity without exercise testing. *Medicine and Science in Sports and Exercise* 22:863–870.

Jackson, A. S. et al. 1995. Changes in aerobic power of men ages 25–70 years. *Medicine and Science in Sports and Exercise* 27:113–120.

Jackson, A. S. and M. L. Pollock. 1978. Generalized equations for predicting body density of men. *British Journal of Nutrition* 40:497–504.

Jackson, A. S., M. L. Pollock, and A. Ward. 1980. Generalized equations for predicting body density of women. *Medicine and Science in Sports and Exercise* 12:175–182.

Jackson, A. S. and R. M. Ross. 1997. *Understanding exercise for health and fitness.* 3d ed. Dubuque, IA: Kendall/Hunt.

Jackson, A. S. et al. 1996. Changes in aerobic power of women, ages 20 to 64 years. *Medicine and Science in Sports and Exercise* 28:884–891.

Jones, N. L. and E. J. M. Campbell. 1982. *Clinical exercise testing.* Philadelphia: W. B. Saunders.

Kline, G. M. et al. 1987. Estimation of VO_2 Max from a one-mile track walk, gender, age and body weight. *Medicine and Science in Sports and Exercise* 19:253–259.

Mahar, M., A. Jackson, and R. L. Ross. 1985. Predictive accuracy of single and double stage sub max treadmill work for estimating aerobic capacity. *Medicine and Science in Sports and Exercise* 17: 206–207.

Mitchell, J. H. and G. Blomqvist. 1971. Maximal oxygen uptake. *The New England Journal of Medicine* 284:1018–1022.

Mitchell, J. H., B. J. Sproule, and C. B. Chapman. 1958. The physiological meaning of the maximal oxygen intake test. *Journal of Clinical Investigation* 37:538–547.

Nagel, F. J., B. Balke, and J. P. Naughton. 1965. Gradational step tests for assessing work capacity. *Journal of Applied Physiology* 20:745–748.

Noakes, T. D. 1988. Implications of exercise testing for prediction of athletic performance: A contemporary perspective. *Medicine and Science in Sports and Exercise* 20:319–330.

Pollock, M. L. et al. 1976. A comparative analysis of four protocols for maximal treadmill stress testing. *American Heart Journal* 92:39–42.

Pollock, M. L. et al. 1987. Effect of age and training on aerobic capacity and body composition of master athletes. *Journal of Applied Physiology* 62:725–731.

Pollock, M. L., A. S. Jackson, and C. Foster. 1986. The use of the perception scale for exercise prescription. In Borg, G. and D. Ottoson (Eds.). *The perception of exertion in physical work. Proceedings of an International Symposium.* Stockholm: Wiener-Glenn.

Pollock, M. L., D. H. Schmidt, and A. S. Jackson. 1980. Measurement of cardiorespiratory fitness and body composition in the clinical setting. *Comprehensive Therapy* 6:12–27.

Pollock, M. L., J. H. Wilmore, and S. M. Fox, III. 1984. *Exercise in health and disease.* Philadelphia: W. B. Saunders.

Rogers, M. A. et al. 1990. Decline in $\dot{V}O_2$ Max in master athletes and sedentary men. *Journal of Applied Physiology* 68:2195–2199.

Ross, R. M. 1989. *Interpreting exercise tests: Clinical interpretation of cardiopulmonary exercise (CPX) tests.* CSI Software: Houston.

Ross, R. M. and A. S. Jackson. 1986. Development and validation of total work equations for estimating the energy cost of walking. *Journal of Cardiopulmonary Rehabilitation* 6:182–192.

Ross, R. M. and A. S. Jackson. 1990. *Exercise concepts, calculations, and computer applications.* Carmel, IN: Benchmark Press.

Rowell, L. B., H. L. Taylor, and Y. Wang. 1964. Limitations to prediction of maximal oxygen intake. *Journal of Applied Physiology* 19:919–927.

Sloan, A. W. 1959. A modified Harvard step test for women. *Journal of Applied Physiology* 14:235–241.

U.S. Public Health Service. 1990. *Healthy people 2000: National health promotion and disease prevention objectives.* Washington, DC: U.S. Department of Health and Human Services.

U.S. Public Health Service. 1996. *Physical activity and health: A report of the surgeon general.* Washington, DC: U.S. Department of Health and Human Services.

CHAPTER

Evaluating Body Composition

Contents

Key Words

anorexia nervosa
bioelectrical impedance analysis (BIA)
body composition
body density
body mass index (BMI)
circumferences
desired weight
fat weight
fat-free weight
generalized equations
hydrostatic weighing
multicomponent model
obesity
overweight
percent body fat
plethysmograph
residual lung volume
two-component model

Objectives

With the growing body of literature supporting the value of regular physical activity for health and fitness, the evaluation of body composition has become an important aspect of both youth and adult fitness. Additionally, suitable body composition levels are important for athletic performance. The purposes of this chapter are to: (1) provide an understanding of public health problems associated with body composition; (2) outline the methods used to evaluate body composition; and (3) evaluate the validity of common field methods.

After reading Chapter 9, you should be able to:

1. Identify the public health problems associated with body composition.
2. Identify the methods used to measure body composition of youth and adults.
3. Identify the limitations of the two-component percent body fat model when applied to children, the elderly, and ethnic groups.
4. Calculate percent body fat of youth and adults from skinfold equations.
5. Evaluate body composition of youths and adults.
6. Calculate weight goals for selected levels of desired percent body fat.
7. Evaluate the accuracy of the various methods used to measure body composition.

Introduction

Health-related fitness and athletic training programs are designed to control body weight and body composition. This is accomplished through regular exercise and proper nutrition. Suitable levels of **body composition** are also important for athletic competition. Excess body fat lowers aerobic fitness and reduces the ability to perform many activities that require jumping and moving quickly. However, being too thin is not desirable either. Suitable body composition is important for general health and appearance and for maximizing athletic performance. For these reasons, accurate measurements of body composition are needed to develop sound preventive health programs and athletic programs. There is a growing body of medical research documenting that undesirable levels of body composition are associated with public health problems. While obesity-related public health problems tend to be adult health problems, adulthood obesity is linked to one's body composition as a youth.

Public Health Risks

The relationship between weight and mortality is J-shaped (Lew & Garfinkel 1979). This means that being significantly under or over ideal weight can have serious health consequences. Figure 9.1 illustrates this relationship. A certain degree of musculature and body fat not only provides protection from injury and thermal stress, but also enhances good health. Although much of the high mortality associated with being too thin is due to underlying diseases such as cancer, even when this is taken into consideration, being too thin is still not healthy. Excessive weight loss caused by severe diet restriction can be a health hazard and should be avoided. Eating disorders associated with being too thin are a serious health problem.

Cardiovascular Diseases

Being overweight is associated with many medical problems, such as hypertension, diabetes, and heart disease. These illnesses lead to increased morbidity and reduced longevity. About one-third of Americans are overweight to the extent that they suffer from serious health problems (Lew & Garfinkel 1979). Between the ages of 25 and 50 years, an average American gains about 50 pounds of body weight—about 2

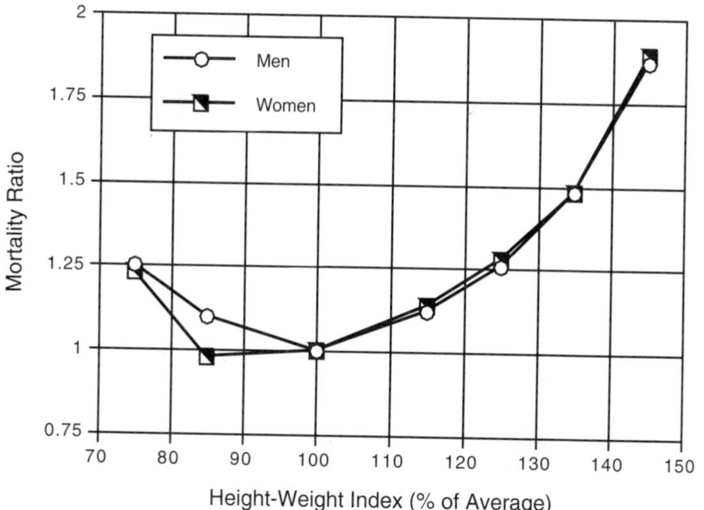

Figure 9.1
All-cause mortality ratio for various percentages of average weight. For both men and women, when compared to average weight, the underweight and overweight individuals had the higher mortality ratios. Graph made from published data (Lew & Garfinkel 1979). (Graph from Jackson & Ross 1997. Used with permission.)

pounds per year. Almost all of this weight gain is body fat. The success rate for the treatment of adulthood obesity is only 25%, lower than the cure rate for most cancers. Overweight people are more likely to lead a sedentary life, and if they decide to start an exercise program, are less likely to be successful (Dishman 1988). Early intervention with proper diet, exercise, and education are key factors for maintaining an ideal weight.

Many overweight people become diabetic during adulthood. Adult-onset diabetes is a disease primarily of the obese, and a major cardiovascular disease risk factor. All obese people are not diabetic, but a subgroup of the obese are particularly at risk. Adults who have "apple shaped" bodies are particularly prone to develop diabetes mellitus. The "apple shape" is due to the accumulation of body fat around the abdomen. This pattern of fat accumulation has more serious health consequences than general adiposity. Just as being overweight can cause diabetes, losing weight can reverse the condition. Often, when people with diabetes lose weight, they are no longer diabetic. This adult form of diabetes is a true "lifestyle" disease.

Overweight people are more likely to be diabetic, hypertensive, and have higher cholesterol levels. Since these are major, independent risk factors in cardiovascular disease, some believe that the increased incidence of cardiovascular disease associated with being overweight is due just to these risk factors. This is not true. Being overweight puts you at a higher risk of heart disease and stroke (Hubert et al. 1983). Figure 9.2 graphically shows that being overweight increases the risk of cardiovascular disease. These researchers also discovered that changes in weight affected risk. Overweight people who lost weight reduced their risk of cardiovascular disease (Figure 9.3).

Breast Cancer

Breast cancer is the most common cancer among women. And it is second only to lung cancer as a cause of death from cancer among women. The causes of breast cancer are very complex, but recent research showed that weight gain is associated with the risk of breast cancer.

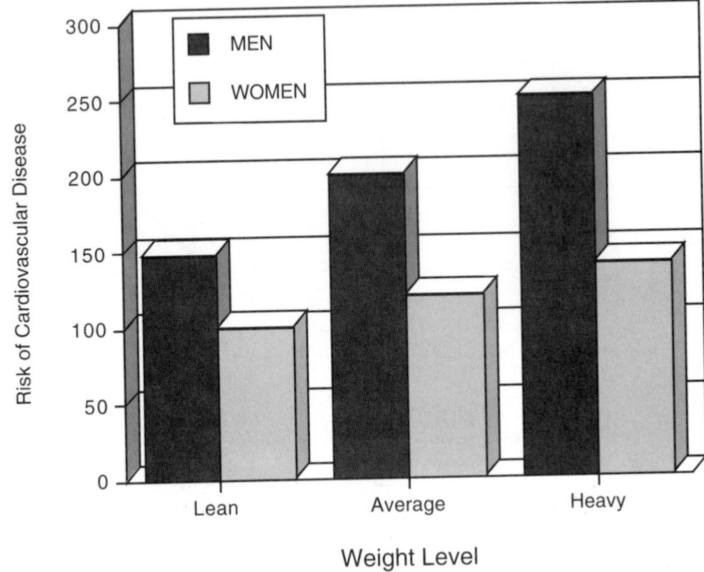

Figure 9.2
The 26-year incidence of cardiovascular disease (per 100,000) based upon weight for a given height for the men and women in the Framingham heart study. The subjects were nonsmokers who were under 50 years of age, and had normal cholesterol and blood pressure levels. Graph made from published data (Hubert et al. 1983). (Graph from Jackson & Ross 1977. Used with permission.)

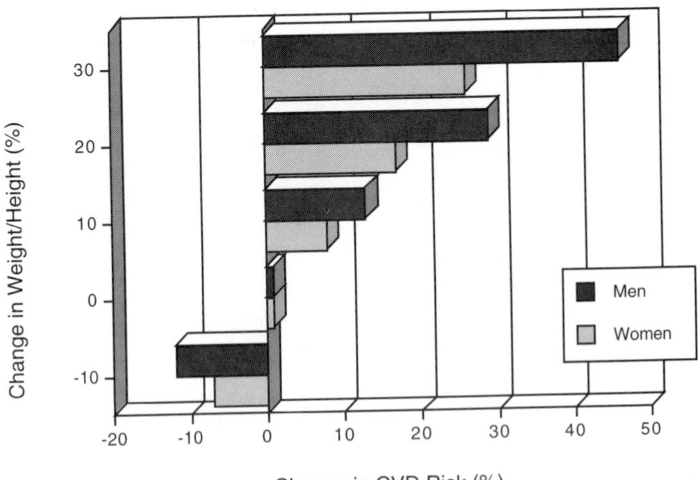

Figure 9.3
Losing weight decreases the risk of cardiovascular disease (CVD), while gaining weight increases the risk. This provides evidence that the relationship between obesity and cardiovascular disease may be causal. Graph developed from published data (Hubert et al. 1983). (Graph from Jackson & Ross 1997. Used with permission.)

Medical researchers (Huang 1997) studied over 95,000 U.S. female nurses aged 30 to 55 years who were followed for 16 years. They discovered that weight gain after the age of 18 years was unrelated to breast cancer incidence before menopause, but was associated with the incidence after menopause. Postmenopausal weight gain increased both the risk of breast cancer incidence and the mortality. About 16% of the breast cancers were attributed to excessive weight gain (≥ 44 pounds). While the medical complexities of breast cancer go well beyond the intent of this text, this important public health study does highlight the importance of body composition and weight control on women's health. Breast cancer is one of the most dreaded diseases of women. Avoiding excessive weight gain during adult life appears to be an important factor in reducing the risk of this cancer.

Eating Disorders

While medical problems associated with body composition are most often related to being overweight, being seriously underweight also is associated with health problems, namely eating disorders. Anorexia nervosa and bulimia nervosa are eating disorders that are on the rise and correspond to societal pressure for women to be thin. It is estimated that about 90% of individuals with eating disorders are women (Foreyt et al., in press). Anorexia nervosa most often begins in early to late adolescence, with the greatest risk for onset between the ages of 14 and 18 years. The average age of onset for bulimia is 17 to 19 years. It is estimated that about 1% of young women are anorexic. The prevalence of bulimia nervosa is approximately 1–3%, but it has been estimated that 4–19% of young women engage in significant levels of bulimic behavior (Foreyt et al., in press).

The causes of anorexia nervosa and bulimia nervosa are complex and not well understood. In American society, beauty is often associated with thinness. Advertisements in the mass media constantly reinforce this notion. The intelligent application of body composition assessment and education can help people establish desirable, intelligent weight goals. The healthy body weight for a well-muscled woman is often higher than what is the social norm. Percent body fat evaluation offers a sound method of establishing a person's desirable weight. Body composition methods and standards, and methods of determining one's desired weight (Formula 9.15), are fully presented in this chapter. Chapter 14 discusses eating disorder scales.

Sources of Adulthood Obesity

The prevalence of obesity is going up for both children and adults (Kuczmarski 1994; Troiano 1995). The scientific reason for weight gain is that the person consumes more calories than he or she expends (Ross & Jackson 1990). While the principle of caloric balance is well understood, it is not clear why some persons gain while others do not. The difference may be due to genetic, environmental, and psychological influences.

The medical problems associated with obesity usually occur in adulthood, but the success of adult weight-reduction programs is poor (Panel 1993; Skender 1996). Medical researchers (Whitaker 1997) studied medical records of parents and children in an effort to determine the factors that lead to obesity in young adulthood (age 21–29 years).[1] The factors considered were the person's obesity status in childhood and their parents' obesity status. Figure 9.4 summarizes the results of this study.

[1]Obesity is defined as a body mass index (Formula 9.8) at or above the 85th percentile for the person's age and sex.

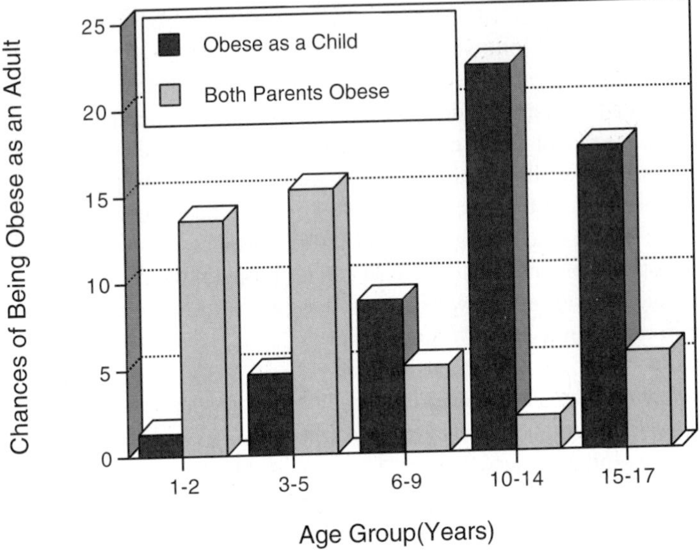

Figure 9.4
Odds ratios for obesity in young adulthood according to the subject's obesity status in childhood and their parents' obesity status. Graph made from published data (Whitaker 1997).

Before the age of 5 years, the primary predictor of obesity in young adulthood is the obesity of their parents. If both parents are obese, the child's chances of being obese in adulthood are 14 to 15 times higher than for a child with nonobese parents. From the ages of 6 to 9 years, both childhood and parental obesity are related to adulthood obesity. For ages 10 to 17 years, the obesity status of the child becomes a dramatic determinate of adulthood obesity. A 10- to 17- year-old obese child is about 20 times more likely to be obese as an adult.

The association between parental obesity and adulthood obesity is likely due to both genetic and environmental factors within families. The high risk of adulthood obesity associated with adolescent obesity is much more likely to be due to environmental factors. These data signal the need for sound adolescent weight-control programs. The methods for evaluating body composition presented in this chapter can be useful to identify youth at risk of becoming obese adults.

Body Density and Percent Body Fat

In simple terms, body weight consists of fat weight and fat-free weight.[2] **Percent body fat** is simply the proportion of total weight that is fat weight. Percent body fat is measured from **body density,** the ratio of body weight and body volume. The underwater weighing method is the most common way to measure body volume. A newer, less common method is performed with a "body box," or body plethysmograph.

[2] Many use the term "lean body mass" or "lean body weight" rather than *fat-free weight.* Lean body weight has a density less than 1.100 g/cc because it contains from 2–3% essential lipid. Lohman (1992) maintains that fat-free weight is the appropriate term.

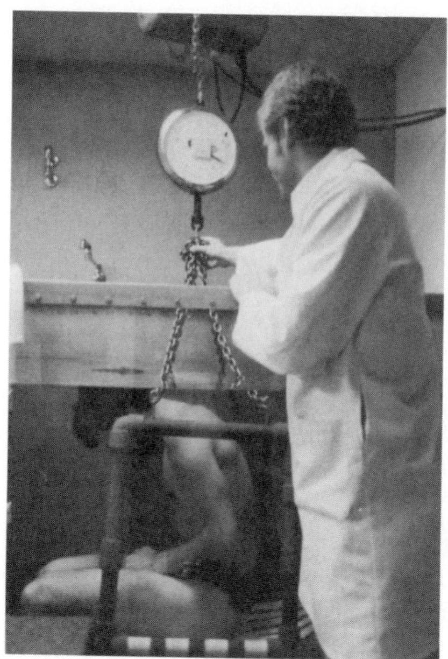

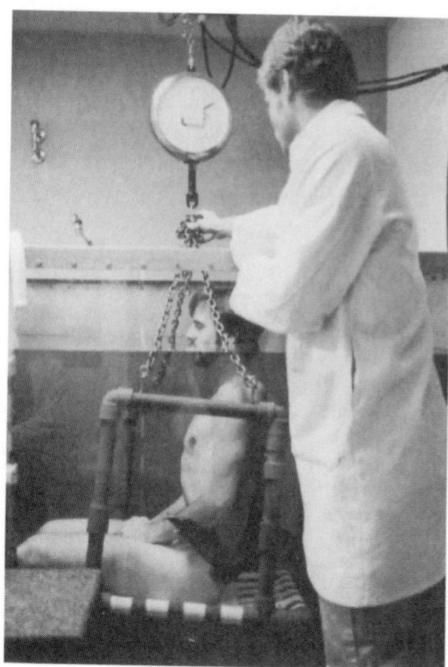

Figure 9.5
Method of determining body density by underwater weighing. (Photos courtesy of Dr. M. L. Pollock. University of Florida.)

Although the terms *overweight* and *obesity* are often used interchangeable, there are important differences between them. **Overweight** is weight that exceeds the "normal" weight defined for an individual on the basis of sex, height, and frame size. It is based on norms compiled by insurance companies. **Obesity** is the excessive accumulation of fat weight and is expressed as percent body fat.

Measuring Body Density by Underwater Weighing

The **hydrostatic** (or underwater) **weighing** method (see Figure 9.5) is the most common laboratory method used to measure body composition. Numerous laboratories located at universities and medical centers have the equipment for underwater weighing determinations. The measurement objective of the hydrostatic weighing is to measure body volume, which is then used with body weight to calculate body density. Percent fat is calculated from body density.

Underwater Weighing. The underwater weighing method is based on the Archimedes principle for measuring the density of an object. When an object, in this case a person, is submerged under water, the difference between the weight in air and under water equals the weight of water displaced. The weight of water displaced divided by the density of water is the volume of water displaced or the volume of the object (i.e., the person). The objective of underwater weighing is to measure body volume. Body density is the ratio of weight in air and body volume. Dry land weight, underwater weight, residual lung volume, and water density are needed to calculate body density. The basic steps needed to measure hydrostatically determined body density are summarized next.

Determining Underwater Weight. Body density is typically measured in the laboratory in a specially constructed tank (see Figure 9.5), but it can be measured in a swimming pool if there is no turbulence. The subject sits on a specially devised chair that is attached to a scale, leans forward, and submerges the head while performing a maximal expiration. Since many subjects are too buoyant, it may be difficult to submerge them. In these instances, a scuba weight belt is placed on the subject's lap. Figure 9.5 shows that the subject is typically sitting on a chair. Both the weight of the chair and the scuba weight belt must be subtracted from the obtained weight to calculate true underwater weight.

Underwater weight is measured to the nearest 0.01 kg with a calibrated scale. The Chatillon 15-kilogram scale shown is commonly used; however, electronic scales that use load cells are also commercially available. A minimum of seven to ten trails should be administered. The average of the three trials with the highest weights, and within 0.025 kg, is used. It has been shown that underwater weight will systematically increase. The person must practice to reach true underwater weight, which is typically reached after three to five trials. The underwater weight is greatly dependent on the amount of air in the lungs when submerged. The subject must be weighed while breath holding after a complete expiration.

Determining Land Weight. Body weight can be easily and accurately determined by weighing. However, it is important to be weighed under standard conditions because total body water, which is a major determinant of body weight, can vary considerably from day to day. The body is composed of approximately 60% water. That is, a 70 kg individuals has over 40 kg of body water. Heavy exercise may result in a water loss as high as 2 to 3 kg per hour.

Determining Air in the Body. The volume of the body that is air can introduce the largest source of error in the underwater weighing method. This is primarily because the density of air and other gases in the body are so close to zero that even a small error in volume measurement makes a significant change in total body density. The major potential sources of measurement error are (1) the volume of air left in the lungs after expiration (residual volume) and (2) air elsewhere, particularly in the gastrointestinal tract. The most common method used to measure the body's air component is to measure **residual lung volume** and add a value of 100 ml to residual volume to account for air in the gastrointestinal tract. Air bubbles in the hair, bathing caps, bathing suits, and on the body also can introduce errors. The methods used to estimate residual volume are based on dilution or wash-out techniques. Wilmore (1969) describes these methods in detail.

Residual lung volume is often difficult to measure and some have suggested it be estimated. The suggested prediction methods (Going 1996) are estimating it (1) with a regression equation using age, height, and sex, or (2) as a constant fraction of vital capacity (0.24 in males and 0.28 in females). Research (Morrow 1986) has shown that these prediction methods are not suitable and can introduce considerable measurement error.

The most accurate way of measuring the volume of air in the body is by use of a "body box," or body **plethysmograph** (Figure 9.6). This technique uses the principle of compressibility of gases, Boyle's law. While in a box, the individual breathes in and out against a closed diaphragm. The movement causes compression of the gas in the body, leading to small changes in volume and pressure in the box. These are then measured and used to calculate the volume of air in the individual's body. The major advantage of the body box is that it measures the total air component consisting of residual lung volume and gastrointestinal air.

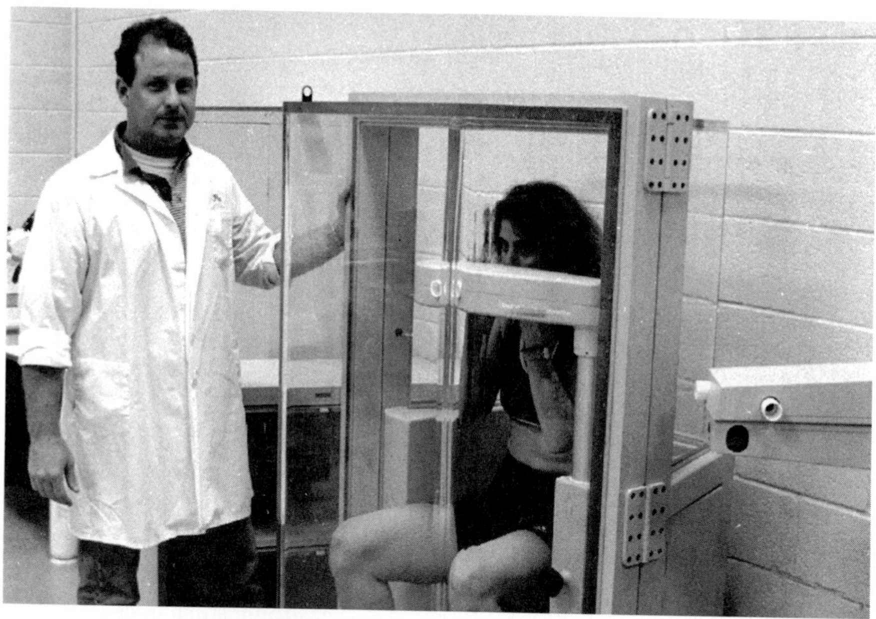

Figure 9.6
The "body box," or body plethysmograph, is the most accurate method of measuring the body's air component.

Determining the Density of Water. The density of water is a function of its temperature and can be calculated by

Density of Water (9.1)

$$Dw = 1.005932 - (0.0003394 \times TW)$$

where Dw is water density and TW is the temperature of water measured in centigrade.

Computing Body Volume. The values needed to calculate body volume (BV) are body weight on land (Wt), body weight in water (Ww), the density of water (Dw), and the body's air component (Ba) (e.g., residual lung volume + 100 ml). Body volume (BV) is calculated by

Body Volume (9.2)

$$BV = \left(\frac{Wt - Ww}{Dw}\right) - Ba$$

Computing Body Density. The values need to compute body density are body volume (BV) and body weight on land (Wt).

Body Density (9.3)

$$BD = \left(\frac{Wt}{BV}\right)$$

Calculation Example, Underwater Body Density. Assume the following values were obtained on an individual.

Table 9.1 Effects of Component Errors on Underwater-Determined Siri Percent Body Fat*

Underwater Weight Variable	Actual Value	Error Conditions 1	2	3
Air component (L)	1.2	1.3	1.6	2.2
% fat	15.0	14.3	12.2	8.0
Underwater weight (kg)	3.36	3.38	3.41	3.46
%fat	15.0	14.9	14.6	14.3
Body weight (kg)	70.0	70.1	70.5	71.0
%fat	15.0	15.1	15.3	15.5
Water temp (°C)	36.0	36.1	36.5	37.0
%fat	15.0	15.1	15.1	15.2

*Constructed from published data in Going 1996; Pollock & Wilmore 1984.

- Body weight (Wt), 70.15 kg
- Underwater weight (Ww), 3.36 kg
- Body's air component (Ba), 1.2 L (RV = 1.1, gastrointestinal tract 100 ml, or 0.1L)
- Density of water (Dw), 0.995678 (30°C)

Equation 9.2 is used to measure body volume (BV), and Formula 9.3 determines body density (BD). The calculations are

Computing Body Volume

$$BV = \left(\frac{70.15 - 3.36}{0.995678}\right) - 1.2 = 65.88$$

Computing Body Density (g/cc)

$$BD = \left(\frac{70.15}{65.88}\right) = 1.065$$

Accuracy of Underwater Weighing Method. The underwater weighing method is considered the "gold standard" of measuring body density. While many believe that measuring underwater is the biggest source of inaccuracy, this is not the case. The air component is the most error prone variable. Table 9.1 provides the potential errors associated with realistic measurement errors of the variables used to measure underwater percent body fat. Provided is the degree that actual percent body fat would vary for three different error conditions. Typically the measurement error of underwater weight is less than 0.1 kg. Body weight and water temperature can be measured very accurately. Residual lung volume can be difficult to measure, and the air in the gastrointestinal tract is estimated at 100 ml (0.1 L). Air component errors of ±0.1 L translate to percent body fat errors of ±0.7% fat, but air component errors of ±1 L result in huge percent body fat errors of ±8.0% fat. Estimating residual volume from age, height, and sex yields air component errors in this magnitude (Morrow 1986). If the underwater weighing method is to be used, the air component must be measured accurately.

Plethysmography. Body volume can also be measured in a "body box," or body **plethysmograph** (see Figure 9.6). At the time this chapter was being written, one commercial body box was available and we were conducting research at the University of Houston to develop the methodology. This technique is based on Boyle's law, which is "the pressure of a gas varies inversely with its volume." Since the air volume of the box can be determined, adding the person changes the pressure and makes it possible to measure the new volume in the box.

While Boyle's law is well known and accepted, the technology is just now being developed. Validation studies are needed to determine the accuracy of this method. The major potential advantage of the body box over underwater weighing is ease in testing. It can be very difficult to measure the underwater body weight of someone who is not comfortable in the water.

Converting Body Density to Percent Body Fat

Variation in body density can be due to air, fat weight, and fat-free weight. The density of air is zero, and the density of fat weight (tissue) is about 0.90 g/cc. The density of fat-free weight varies from about 1.0 g/cc to as high as 3.0 g/cc, with an average assumed to be 1.10 g/cc. Fat-free weight consists of muscle, blood, bone, and organs. The two-component models for computing percent body fat from body density are based on the assumption that the density of fat tissue is 0.90 g/cc and of fat-free weight 1.10 g/cc. Researchers are starting to question this assumption when computing the percent body fat of youth, the elderly, and ethnic groups. This has led to the development of multi-component models.

Two-Component Models. The first equations developed for converting body density to percent body fat were published by Siri (1961) and Brŏzek et al. (1963). The equations provide nearly identical percent body fat values throughout the human range of body fatness. The formulas are and are based on the **two-component model,** that assumes that the density of fat tissue is 0.9 g/cc and the density of fat-free weight is 1.10 g/cc.

Siri Percent Body Fat *(9.4)*

$$\text{fat} = \left(\frac{495}{\text{BD}}\right) - 450$$

Brozek Percent Body Fat *(9.5)*

$$\%\text{fat} = \left(\frac{457}{\text{BD}}\right) - 414$$

There is growing evidence that the Siri and Brŏzek equations may not be accurate when applied to some ethnic groups. The ethnic differences in body density are believed to be due to fat-free weight differences associated with bone mineral content (Sinning 1996; VanLoan 1996). Cross-sectional data (Vickery 1988) show that the mean body density of black men (1.075 g/cc) is significantly higher than white men (1.065 g/cc). It was also found that the mean of the sum of seven skinfolds is not different, suggesting that "the difference in the relationship of skinfolds to body density in African-American and white men is due to variation in the composition of "fat-free weight."

Sinning (1996) suggests that the high mineral content of bone in African-Americans results in a fat-free density higher than the value of 1.1 g/cm assumed by the Brŏzek and Siri equations and recommends an equation published by Schutte and associates (Schutte et al. 1984) be used to convert body density to percent body fat for black males. The formula is

Schutte formula for African-Americans **(9.6)**

$$\%\text{fat} = \left(\frac{437.4}{\text{BD}}\right) - 392.8$$

Figure 9.7 compares the Siri, Brŏzek, and Schutte equations for computing percent body fat from body density. The Siri and Brŏzek equations yield almost identical estimates through the body density range. The Schutte equation gives higher percent body fat estimates than the Brŏzek and Siri equations through the range, with the largest differences under 25%. Sinning (1996) maintains that the Schutte equation is especially appropriate for lean black athletes.

Calculation Example, Determining Percent Body Fat from Body Density. Given next is percent body fat computed with the two-component models for a body density of 1.065 g/cc. Provided are estimates with the Siri (Formula 9.4), Brŏzek (Formula 9.5), and Schutte (Formula 9.6) equations.

Siri Percent Body Fat

$$\%\text{fat} = \left(\frac{495}{1.065}\right) - 450 = 14.8\%$$

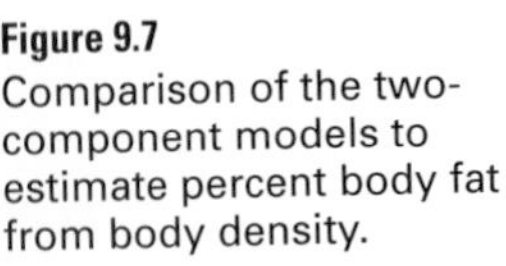

Figure 9.7
Comparison of the two-component models to estimate percent body fat from body density.

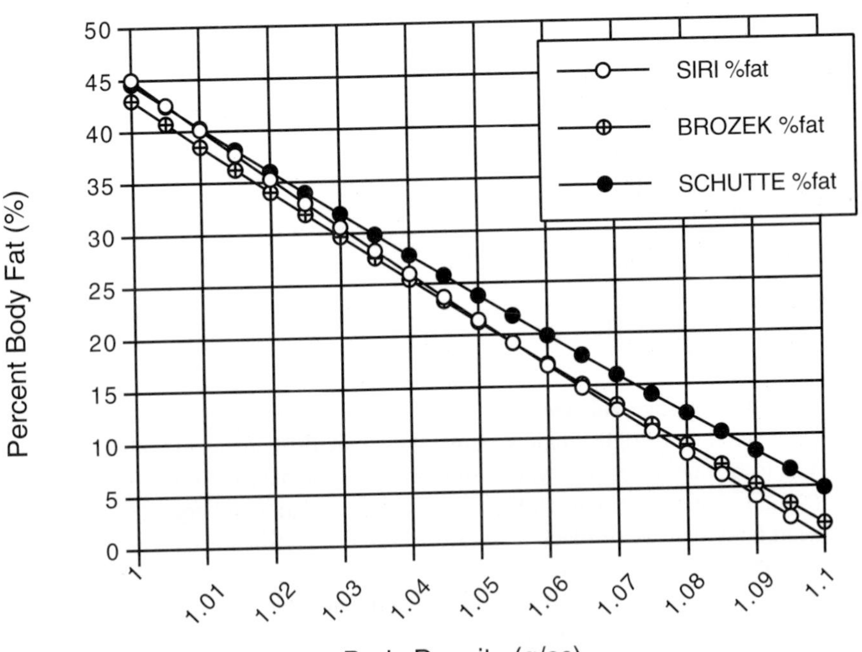

Brŏzek Percent Body Fat

$$\%\text{fat} = \left(\frac{457}{1.065}\right) - 414 = 15.1\%$$

Schutte Formula for African-Americans

$$\text{Schutte: } \%\text{fat} = \left(\frac{437.4}{1.065}\right) - 392.8 = 17.9\%$$

Multicomponent Model. The Siri, Brŏzek, and Schutte methods of estimating percent body fat from body density are considered by many to be the "gold standard" for assessing body composition. Each is based on the two-component model that assumes the density of fat tissue to be 0.9 g/cc and the density of fat-free weight to be 1.10 g/cc. This is likely true for adults between the ages of 20 and 50 years. Lohman (1992) argues convincingly that the two-component model has serious limitations when measuring the body composition of the elderly, children, and possibly ethnic groups, because the total body water and bone mineral content of these extreme groups vary from the values of the 20- to 50-year-old subjects.

During childhood and the elderly years, the body is changing more dramatically. Changes in body water and bone mineral content alter the density of the fat-free component. As these values increase over reference values, there is a linear increase in percent body fat errors obtained with the two-component method. Lohman (1992) provides an excellent discussion on the effect of bone mineral differences on the accuracy of percent body fat determinations. Changes in the body's bone mineral content alters the density of fat-free weight. The two major sources of differences among individuals in bone mineral content can be traced to genetics and environmental conditions. Some inherit a higher bone mineral content than others. Due to life-style, some will develop a higher mineral content. For example, it has been shown that the bone diameter of the playing arm of tennis players is larger than their other arm.

Osteoporosis is a major source of bone loss in the elderly, especially for women. This disease is characterized by a decrease in bone density that results in an increase in bone porosity and leads to weak, fragile bones that break easily. The reasons for osteoporosis are not known, but the lack of sufficient calcium in the diet and lack of physical activity are believed to be important determinants, leading many scientists to believe that diet and strenuous exercise can help maintain skeletal integrity and reduce the risk of osteoporosis (Ross & Jackson 1990). The extent that bone mineral loss in the elderly limits the accuracy of the two-component model is a topic of current study.

Since differences in water and bone mineral content affect body density, the equations for converting body density of adults to percent body fat cannot be validly used with children. The development of multicomponent formulas for use with children and youth is described in a series of reports (Boileau et al. 1985; Lohman 1992; Lohman 1986; Lohman et al. 1984). The **multicomponent model** includes not only body density (BD) but also water (w) and mineral (m) content. A mulitcomponent formula (Lohman 1992) that can be used for children or adults of any age and any ethnicity is

Multicomponent Percent Fat Model **(9.7)**

$$\%\text{Fat} = \left(\frac{2.749}{\text{BD}}\right) - (0.727 \times \text{w}) - (1.146 \times \text{m}) - 2.053$$

With the development of dual energy radiography, technology is becoming available to estimate bone mineral content and bone density. This presents the possibility of developing a multicomponent model that adjusts for water and bone mineral content variance in fat-free weight. A detailed discussion of this topic is beyond the scope of this text, and the interested reader is directed to the work of Lohman (1992) and Heymsfield and associates (1996). The multicomponent model is typically used in body composition laboratories found in medical settings.

Anthropometric Assessment of Body Composition

Due to the need for highly trained technicians and expensive laboratory equipment, hydrostatically determined body composition is rarely used in field settings. The most common alternative is to use some form of anthropometric method. This includes weight-height ratios, body circumferences, and skinfold measurements.

Body Mass Index

Body mass index (BMI) is the weight-height ratio often used in field settings. It is the measure of body composition typically used in large-scale public health studies, but it also is an alternative item on the FITNESSGRAM® Youth Fitness battery (Chapter 10). BMI is computed by

Body Mass Index **(9.8)**

$$\text{BMI} = \left(\frac{\text{Weight}}{\text{Height} \times \text{Height}}\right)$$

where weight is in kilograms and height is in meters.

While BMI is correlated with hydrostatically determined percent body fat, the correlations are lower than found with skinfold measurements and waist circumference (Table 9.2). The limitation of the BMI can be traced to the numerator of the formula, body weight. Body weight is affected not only by fat mass but also by fat-free mass, consisting of muscle, organs, and skeletal mass. BMI is not used to determine degree of obesity; rather it defines overweight. Table 9.3 gives the BMI criterion used to define overweight for the *Healthy People 2000* project (U.S. Public Health Service 1990) outlined in Chapter 1. The criterion for overweight varies for males and females of different ages.

Calculation Example; Computing BMI. Assume a person's weight is 142 pounds (64.61 kg) and their height is 5 feet 4 inches, or 64 inches (1.63 meters). The person's BMI (Formula 9.8) is 24.3 kg/m^2.

$$\text{BMI} = \left(\frac{64.61}{1.63 \times 1.63}\right) = \frac{64.61}{2.6569} = 24.3$$

Estimating Percent Body Fat from BMI

Medical researchers (Gallagher 1996) have published a generalized formula for estimating percent body fat from BMI. They studied over 700 black and white men and women who ranged in age from 20 to 94 years. The multicomponent model was used to measure percent body fat. They found that age, BMI, and gender (Female = 0, Male = 1) is significantly related to percent fat, but ethnicity is not. The formula is

Gallagher et al. Formula (R = 0.819, SEE = 5.68 %fat) ***(9.9)***

$$\%\text{fat} = (1.45 \times \text{BMI}) + (0.12 \times \text{Age}) - (11.61 \times \text{Gender}) - 10.02$$

Calculation Example, Estimating Percent Body Fat from BMI. Assume a man (age 45 years) and woman (age 37 years), each with a BMI of 24.3 kg/m^2. Using Formula 9.9, their estimated percent body fat values are

Table 9.2 Linear Correlations between Body Density and Anthropometric Variables for Adults*

Variables	Men (n = 402)	Women (n = 283)
General Characteristics		
Height	0.03	0.06
Weight	0.63	0.63
Body mass index	0.69	0.70
Skinfolds		
Chest	0.85	0.64
Axilla	0.82	0.73
Triceps	0.79	0.77
Subscapula	0.77	0.67
Abdomen	0.83	0.75
Suprailium	0.76	0.76
Thigh	0.78	0.74
Sum of seven	0.88	0.83
Circumferences		
Waist	0.80	0.71
Gluteal	0.69	0.74
Thigh	0.64	0.68
Biceps	0.51	0.63
Forearm	0.35	0.41

*Contructed from published data in Jackson & Pollock 1978; Jackson, Pollock & Ward 1980.

Table 9.3 BMI Criterion Used to Define Overweight for the *Healthy People 2000* Public Health Program

	Body Mass Index Level	
Age Group	**Males**	**Females**
12–14	≥24.3	≥24.8
15–17	≥25.8	≥25.7
18–19	≥23.4	≥25.7
≥20	≥27.8	≥27.3

Man: BMI = 24.3, Age 45 years

$$\%fat = (1.46 \times 24.3) + (0.12 \times 45) - (11.61 \times 1) - 10.02$$

$$= 35.48 + 5.40 - 11.61 - 10.02 = 19.25\%$$

Woman: BMI = 24.3, Age 37 years

$$\%fat = (1.46 \times 24.3) + (0.12 \times 37) - (11.61 \times 0) - 10.02$$

$$= 35.48 + 4.44 - 0 - 10.02 = 29.90\%$$

Body Circumferences

Body **circumferences** have also been used to assess body composition. The approaches followed include estimating body density from combinations of body circumference measurements, and using the ratio of waist and hip circumference measurements.

Body circumferences are correlated with hydrostatically determined body density. The circumferences that tend to be most highly correlated are in the abdominal and hip regions. In 1981, the United States Navy changed from using height and weight standards to percent body fat estimated from body circumferences (Hodgdon & Beckett 1984a; Hodgdon & Beckett 1984b). The variables used for the Navy equations are height, abdomen circumference, hip circumference, and neck circumference (Hodgdon & Beckett 1984c). Tran and associates (1989, 1988) published generalized equations for estimating hydrostatically determined body density from various combinations of circumference measurements. The subjects used varied considerably in age and body composition. Table 9.4 gives the generalized equations developed on the general population. The procedures for measuring body circumferences are given in other sources (Behnke & Wilmore 1974; Hodgdon & Beckett 1984c).

Waist-Hip Ratio (WHR)

Medical research has shown that people with central, visceral types of obesity are particularly at risk for developing cardiovascular disease, stroke and noninsulin dependent diabetes mellitus. This central visceral obesity is measured by the waist-hip ratio. The measurements used in the waist-hip ratio equation are:

- Waist circumference (waist-C) is measured at the waist horizontally at the umbilicus.
- Hip circumference (hip-C) is measured at the largest horizontal circumference around the buttocks.

Table 9.4 Generalized Regression Equations for Predicting Body Density of Men and Women from Body Circumference Measurements*

	Regression Equation	R	SEE g/cc
Males	$BD = 1.21142 + (0.00085 \times V_1) - (0.00050 \times V_2) - (0.00061 \times V_3) - (0.00138 \times V_4)$	0.84	0.0090
Females	$BD = 1.168297 - (0.002824 \times V_4) + (0.000012 \times V_1)^2 - (0.000733 \times V_3) + (0.000510 \times V_5) - (0.000216 \times V_6)$	0.89	0.009

Key: V_1 = weight (kg); V_2 = iliac circumference (cm); V_3 = hip circumference (cm); V_4 = abdominal circumference (cm); V_5 = height (cm); V_6 = age (years).

Table 9.5 Degree of Health Risk Estimated from the Body Mass Index and Waist-Hip Ratio

BMI	Waist-Hip Ratio—Males			Waist-Hip Ratio—Females		
	<0.85	0.85–1.0	≥1.0	≤0.70	0.70–0.85	>0.85
20 to <25	Very low	Low	Moderate	Very low	Low	Moderate
25 to <30	Low	Moderate	High	Low	Moderate	High
30 to <35	Moderate	High	Very high	Moderate	High	Very high
35 to <40	High	Very high	Very high	High	Very high	Very high
≥40	Very high	Very high	Very high	Very high	Very high	Very high

Waist-Hip Ratio (WHR) *(9.10)*

$$WHR = \left(\frac{\text{Waist} - C}{\text{Hip} - C}\right)$$

The development of central, visceral obesity is believed to be caused by an alteration in the body's metabolic system. Several of these endocrine abnormalities are associated with insulin resistance that is believed to be the cause of the increased disease risk. While the BMI has been used to identify overweight individuals, Bray (1993) proposed that both BMI and WHR be used to define health risk. Table 9.5 gives health-risk estimates.

Skinfolds

Skinfold measurements are highly correlated with hydrostatically determined body density. Skinfold measurements involve measuring a double thickness of subcutaneous fat with a specially designed caliper (Figure 9.8). Several acceptable calipers are available for measuring skinfold fat. A skinfold caliper that conforms to specifications established by the committee of the Food and Nutrition Board of the National Research Council of the United States should be used. The Lange, Harpenden, and Lafayette calipers meet these criteria.[3] The Harpenden caliper gives measurements about 1 to 4 mm lower than the Lange and Lafayette calipers (Lohman 1982).

Skinfold Sites. Many are concerned about the accuracy of skinfolds. Accuracy is ensured by using a suitable caliper and having a trained technician measure skinfold fat at the proper locations. Improper site selection is probably the most common reason for error in measuring skinfold fat. The skinfold sites and methods are listed here. All measurements are taken on the right side of the body. Figures 9.9 through 9.16 illustrate the measurement methods and site location.

[3]The Lange caliper is manufactured by Cambridge Scientific Industries, Cambridge, MD. The Harpenden caliper is manufactured by British Indicators LTD., St. Albans, Herts, England, and distributed in the United States by Quinton Equipment, Seattle, WA. Lafayette Instrument Company, Lafayette, IN, manufactures the Lafayette caliper.

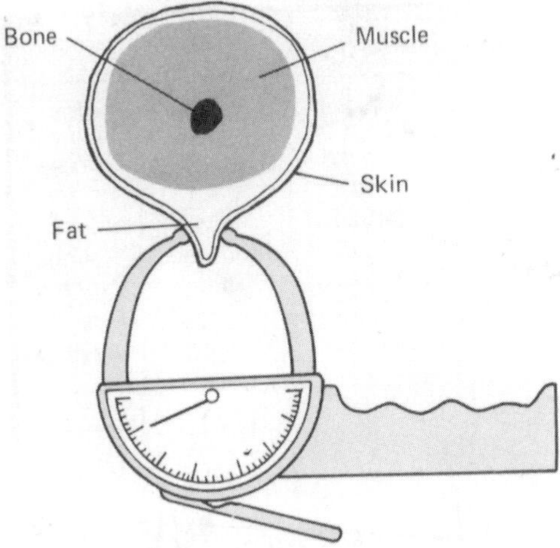

Figure 9.8
Measurement of skinfold fat.

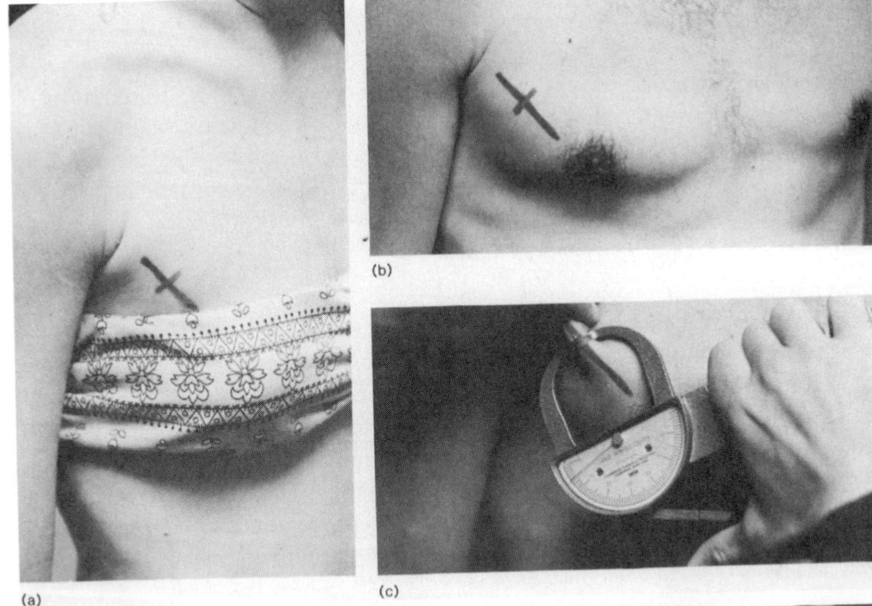

Figure 9.9
(a) and (b) Skinfold test sites for men and women;
(c) placement of calipers for chest skinfold test. (Photos courtesy of Pollock, M. L., D. H. Schmidt, & A. S. Jackson, *Measurement of Cardiorespiratory Fitness and Body Composition in the Clinical Setting, Comprehensive Therapy,* Vol. 6(9), pgs. 12–27, 1980. Published with permission of the Laux Company, Inc., Harvard, MA)

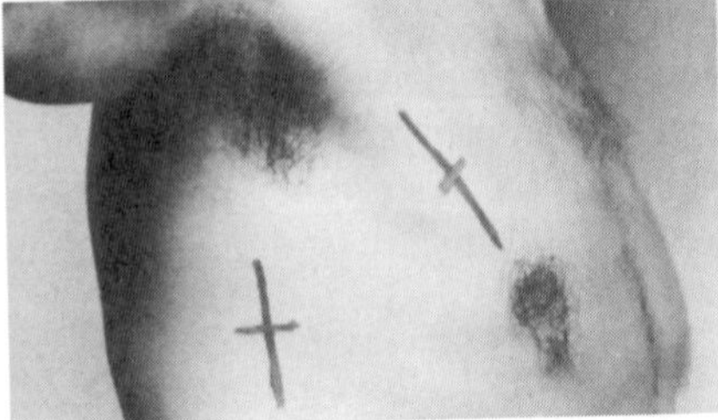

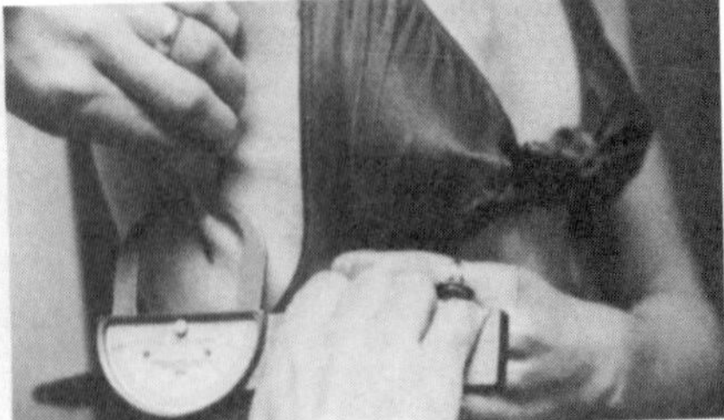

Figure 9.10
Test site and placement of calipers for axilla skinfold. The axilla skinfold site is shown in relation to the man's chest site. (Photos courtesy of Polock, M. L., D. H. Schmidt, & A. S. Jackson, *Measurement of Cardiorespiratory Fitness and Body Composition in the Clinical Setting, Comprehensive Therapy,* Vol. 6(9), pgs. 12–27, 1980. Published with permission of the Laux Company, Inc., Harvard, MA)

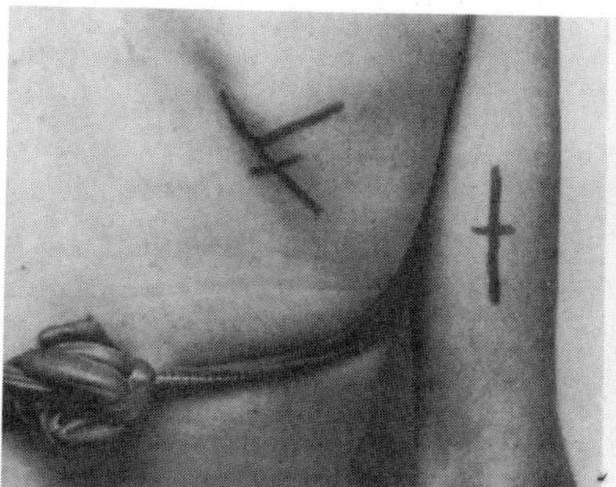

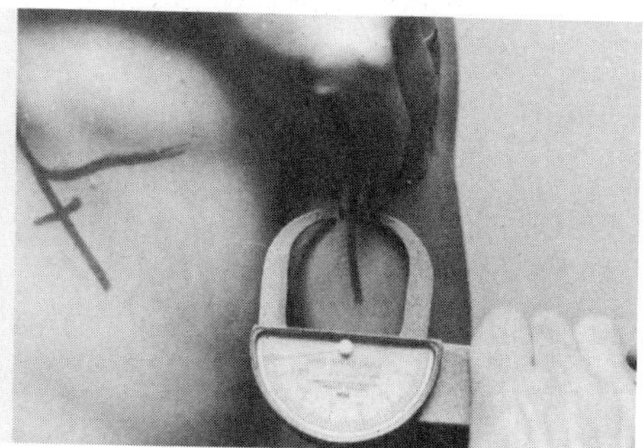

Figure 9.11
Test site and placement of calipers for triceps skinfold. The triceps skinfold site is shown in relation to the subscapular skinfold site. (Photos courtesy of Pollock, M. L., D. H. Schmidt, & A. S. Jackson, *Measurement of Cardiorespiratory Fitness and Body Composition in the Clinical Setting, Comprehensive Therapy,* Vol. 6(9), pgs. 12–27, 1980. Published with permission of the Laux Company, Inc., Harvard, MA)

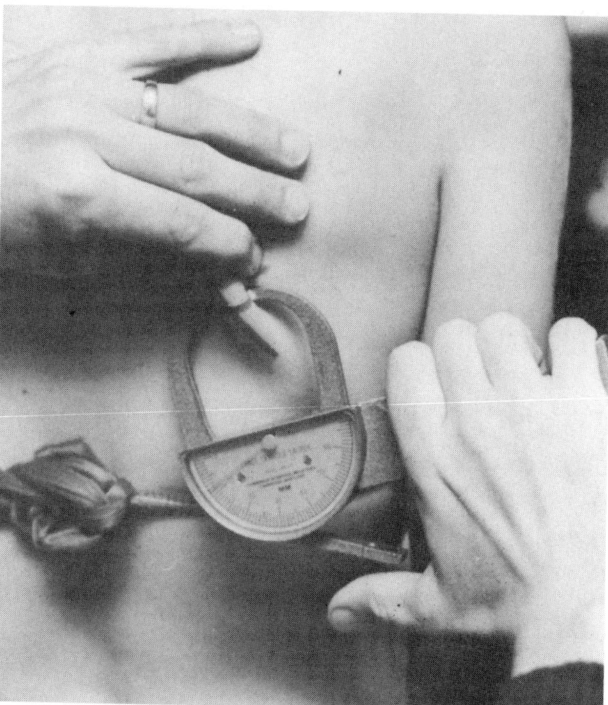

Figure 9.12
Placement of calipers for subscapular skinfold. The proper site location is shown in Figure 9.11. (Photos courtesy of Pollock, M. L., D. H. Schmidt, & A. S. Jackson, *Measurement of Cardiorespiratory Fitness and Body Composition in the Clinical Setting, Comprehensive Therapy,* Vol. 6(9), pgs. 12–27, 1980. Published with permission of the Laux Company, Inc., Harvard, MA)

1. **Chest:** a diagonal fold taken half the distance between the anterior axillary line and nipple for men and one-third of the distance from the anterior axillary line to the nipple for women (Figure 9.9).
2. **Axially:** a vertical fold on the midaxillary line at the level of the xiphoid process of the sternum (Figure 9.10).
3. **Triceps:** a vertical fold on the posterior midline of the upper arm (over the triceps muscle), halfway between the acromion and olecranon porcesses; the elbow should be extended and relaxed (Figure 9.11).
4. **Subscapula:** a fold taken on a diagonal line coming from the vertebral border to 1–2 cm from the inferior angle of the scapula (Figure 9.12).

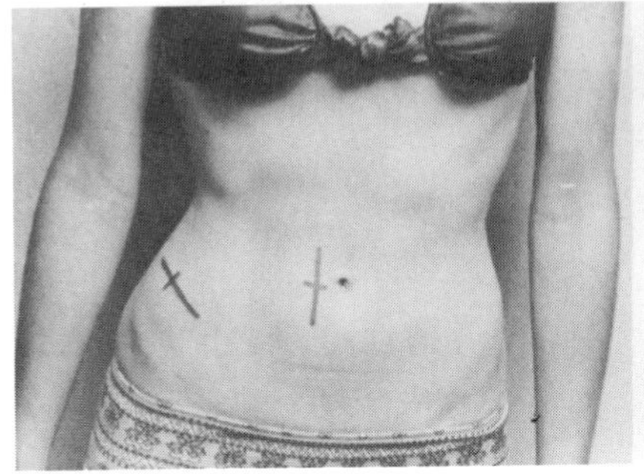

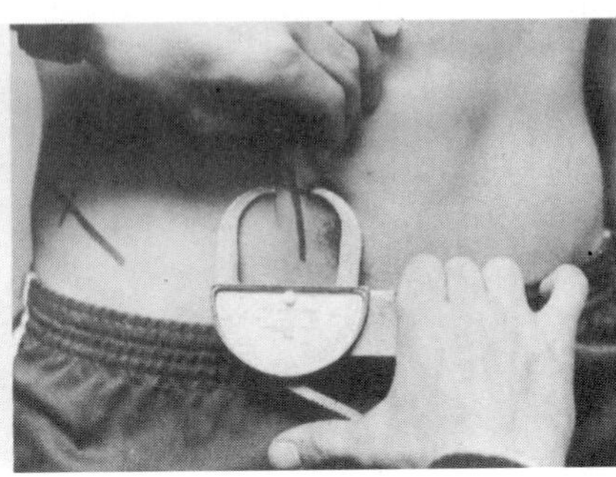

Figure 9.13 Test site and placement of calipers for abdominal skinfold. The abdominal site is shown in relation to the suprailium site. (Photos courtesy of Pollock, M. L., D. H. Schmidt, & A. S. Jackson, *Measurement of Cardiorespiratory Fitness and Body Composition in the Clinical Setting, Comprehensive Therapy,* Vol. 6(9), pgs. 12–27, 1980. Published with permission of the Laux Company, Inc., Harvard, MA)

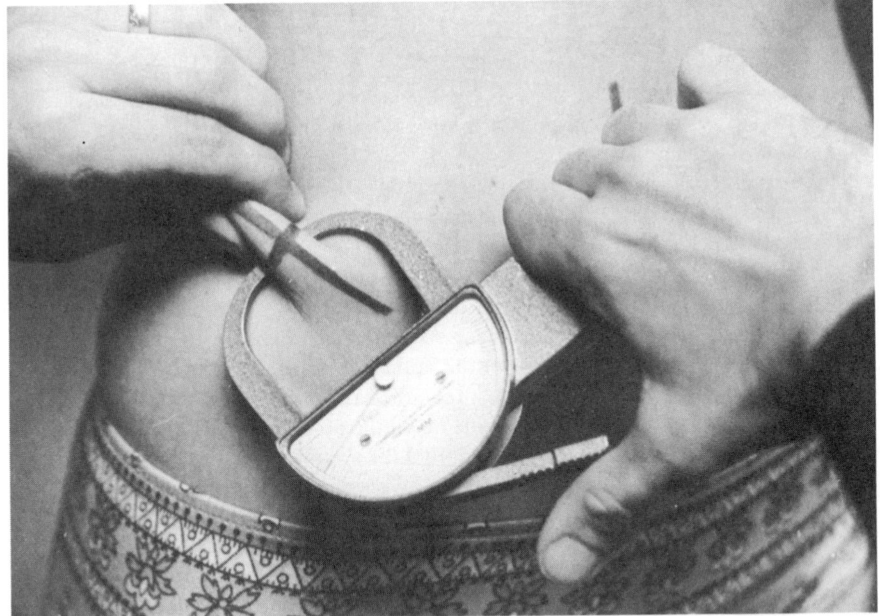

Figure 9.14 Caliper placement for suprailium skinfold. The proper site location is shown in (Photos courtesy of Pollock, M. L., D. H. Schmidt, & A. S. Jackson, *Measurement of Cardiorespiratory Fitness and Body Composition in the Clinical Setting, Comprehensive Therapy,* Vol. 6(9), pgs. 12–27, 1980. Published with permission of the Laux Company, Inc., Harvard, MA)

5. **Abdomen:** a vertical fold taken at a lateral distance of approximately 2 cm from the umbilicus (Figure 9.13).
6. **Suprailium:** a diagonal fold above the crest of the ilium at the spot where an imaginary line would come down from the anterior axillary line (Figure 9.14).
7. **Thigh:** a vertical fold on the anterior aspect of the thigh midway between hip and knee joints (Figure 9.15).
8. **Medial calf:** The right leg is placed on a bench with the knee flexed at 90°. The level of the greatest calf girth is marked on the medial border. A vertical skinfold is raised on the medial side of the right calf 1 cm above the mark, and the fold is measured at the maximal girth (see Figure 9.16).

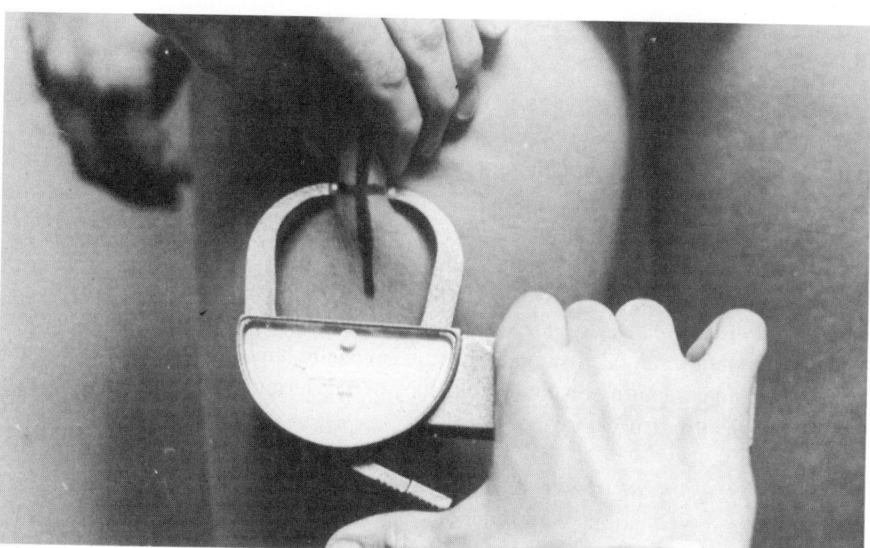

Figure 9.15
Caliper placement for thigh skinfold. (Photos courtesy of Pollock, M. L., D. H. Schmidt, & A. S. Jackson, *Measurement of Cardiorespiratory Fitness and Body Composition in the Clinical Setting, Comprehensive Therapy,* Vol. 6(9), pgs. 12–27, 1980. Published with permission of the Laux Company, Inc., Harvard, MA)

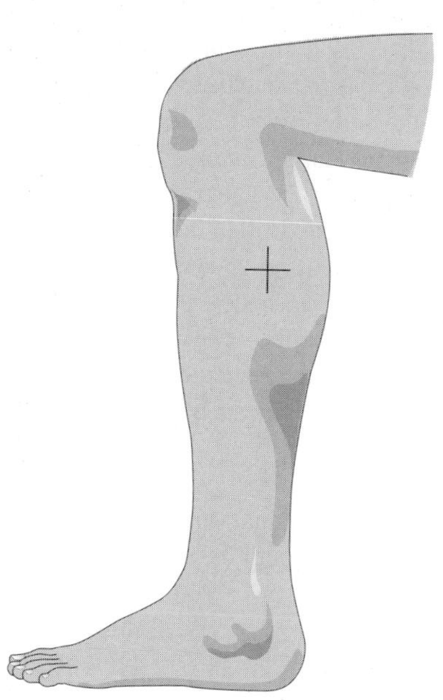

Figure 9.16 Test site and placement of calipers for medial calf.

Skinfold Test Methods.

When taking a skinfold measurement, the left hand pinches and pulls the skin, and the caliper is held in the right hand. Grasp the skinfold firmly by the thumb and index finger. The caliper is perpendicular to the fold at approximately 1 cm (0.25 in) from the thumb and forefinger. Then release the caliper grip so that full tension is exerted on the skinfold. Use the pads at the tip of thumb and finger to grasp the skinfold. (Testers may need to trim their nails.) Read the dial to the nearest 0.5 mm approximately one to two seconds after the grip has been released. A minimum of two measurements should be taken. If they vary by more than 1 mm, a third should be taken.

If consecutive fat measurements become smaller and smaller, the fat is being compressed; this occurs mainly with "fleshy" people. The tester should go on to the next site and return to the trouble spot after finishing the other measurements; the final value will be the average of the two that seem to best represent the skinfold fat site. Typically, the tester should complete a measurement at one site before moving to another. It is better to make measurements when the skin is dry, because when the skin is moist or wet the tester may grasp extra skin (fat) and get larger values. Measurements should not be taken immediately after exercise or when a subject is overheated because the shift of body fluid to the skin will increase skinfold size. Practice is necessary to grasp the same size of skinfold consistently at the same location every time. Consistency can be ensured by having several technicians take the same measurements and comparing results. Proficiency in measuring skinfolds may take practice sessions with up to 50 to 100 subjects.

Skinfold Assessment of Percent Body Fat of Adults. Many people have published regression equations with functions to predict hydrostatically measured body density from various combinations of anthropometric variables. More than one hundred equations appear in the literature. The results of these studies are provided in Table 9.6.

Early researchers developed equations for relatively homogeneous populations, termed population-specific equations. The more recent trend is to use what are termed **generalized equations,** equations that can be validly used with heterogeneous samples. Population- specific equations were developed on relatively small, homogeneous samples, and their application is limited to that sample. The generalized equations were developed on large heterogeneous samples using models that accounted for the nonlinear relationship between skinfold fat and body density. Age was found to be an important variable for generalized equations (Durnin & Wormsley 1974; Jackson & Pollock 1978; Jackson et al. 1980). The main advantage of the generalized approach is that one equation replaces several without a loss in prediction accuracy. A detailed discussion of population-specific and generalized equations can be found in other sources (Cureton 1984; Jackson 1984; Lohman 1982).

Generalized Skinfold Equations. Separate skinfold equations are needed for men and women. Men and women differ in both storage and essential fat content (Figure 9.17). Table 9.7 gives the descriptive statistics for the variables used to develop generalized equations for men and women. When all seven skinfolds were summed, the mean of the men's and women's distribution were nearly the same, but men and women differed considerably at the various sites. The women's means for the limb skinfold, triceps, and thigh were substantially higher than the men's values, while the men's means on the remaining five sites, mainly in the region of the trunk, tended to be higher.

Multiple regression models were used to develop generalized skinfold equations for men (Jackson & Pollock 1978) and women (Jackson et al. 1980). Figure 9.18 gives the scattergram between the sum of seven skinfolds and hydrostatically measured body density. The male and female bivariate distribution is similar, except the distribution of women is "shifted" downward. For the same sum of seven skinfold values, women tend to have a lower body density. This is due to their higher percent body

Table 9.6 Means and Standard Deviations of Hydrostatically Determined Body Density and Concurrent Validity of Regression Equations for Males and Females

Source	Sample		Body Density		Regression Analysis	
	Age	n	Mean	SD	R	SE
Males						
Brozek and Keys (1951)	20.3	133	1.077	0.014	0.88	0.007
Brozek and Keys (1951)	45–55	122	1.055	0.012	0.74	0.009
Durnin and Wormsley (1974)	17–19	24	1.066	0.016	*	0.007
Durnin and Wormsley (1974)	20–29	92	1.064	0.016	*	0.008
Durnin and Wormsley (1974)	30–39	34	1.046	0.012	*	0.009
Durnin and Wormsley (1974)	40–49	35	1.043	0.015	*	0.008
Durnin and Wormsley (1974)	50–68	24	1.036	0.018	*	0.009
Forsyth and Sinning (1973)	19–29	50	1.072	0.010	0.84	0.006
Haisman (1970)	22–26	55	1.070	0.010	0.78	0.006
Jackson and Pollock (1978)	18–61	308	1.059	0.018	0.92	0.007
Katch and McArdle (1973)	19.3	53	1.065	0.014	0.89	0.007
Katch and Michael (1973)	17.0	40	1.076	0.013	0.89	0.006
Pascale et al. (1956)	22.1	88	1.068	0.012	0.86	0.006
Pollock et al. (1976)	18–22	95	1.068	0.014	0.87	0.007
Pollock et al. (1976)	40–55	84	1.043	0.013	0.84	0.007
Sloan (1967)	18–26	50	1.075	0.015	0.85	0.008
Wilmore and Behnke (1969)	16–36	133	1.066	0.013	0.87	0.006
Wright and Wilmore (1974)	27.8	297	1.061	0.014	0.86	0.007
Females						
Durnin and Rahaman (1967)	18–29	45	1.044	0.014	0.78	0.010
Durnin and Wormsley (1974)	16–19	29	1.040	0.017	*	0.009
Durnin and Wormsley (1974)	20–29	100	1.034	0.021	*	0.011
Durnin and Wormsley (1974)	30–39	58	1.025	0.020	*	0.013
Durnin and Wormsley (1974)	40–49	48	1.020	0.016	*	0.011
Durnin and Wormsley (1974)	50–68	37	1.013	0.016	*	0.008
Jackson et al. (1980)	18–55	249	1.044	0.016	0.87	0.008
Katch and McArdle (1973)	20.3	69	1.039	0.015	0.84	0.009
Katch and Michael (1968)	19–23	64	1.049	0.011	0.70	0.008
Pollock et al. (1975)	18–22	83	1.043	0.014	0.84	0.008
Pollock et al. (1975)	33–50	60	1.032	0.015	0.89	0.007
Sinning (1978)	17–23	44	1.064	0.010	0.81	0.006
Sloan et al. (1962)	20.2	50	1.047	0.012	0.74	0.008
Wilmore and Behnke (1970)	21.4	128	1.041	0.010	0.76	0.007
Young (1964)	53.0	62	1.020	0.014	0.84	0.008
Young et al. (1962)	17–27	94	1.034	0.009	0.69	0.007

*Correlation not reported.

fat, which is due largely to the women's higher level of essential fat. Table 9.8 gives generalized skinfold equations for the sum of seven skinfolds for men and women. A quadratic component is used to adjust for the nonlinearity, and age is an independent variable to account for aging.

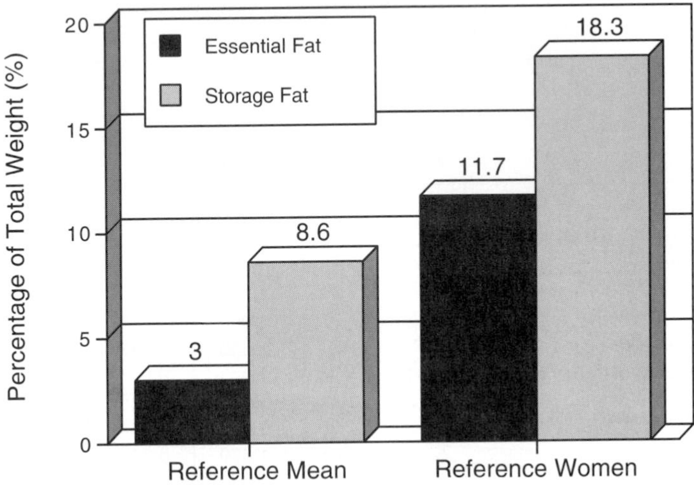

Figure 9.17
Not only do women have a higher percentage of their weight in storage fat, but also in essential fat consisting of lipids of the bone marrow, central nervous system, mammary glands, and other organs. Graph made from published data (Lohman 1992) of the fat distribution in reference to man and woman with the following characteristics: reference man, body weight 70 kg, 14.7% body fat; reference woman, body weight 56.8 kg. 26.9% body fat.

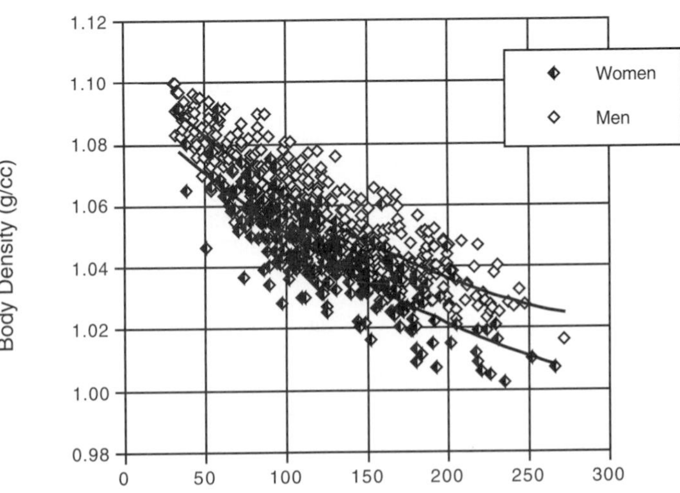

Figure 9.18
The nonlinear relationship between the sum of seven skinfolds of men and women and body density measured by the underwater weighing method. For the same level of skinfold fat, women have a lower body density. This is due to the difference in essential fat that is measured by the underwater weighing method, but not the skinfold method. (Graph developed from published data: Jackson & Pollock 1978; Jackson, Pollock & Ward 1980).

Table 9.7 Descriptive Statistics of Samples Used to Develop Generalized Body Density Equations for Men and Women

Variables	Men (n=402)		Women (n=283)	
	Mean	SD	Mean	SD
General Characteristics				
Age (yr)	32.8	11.0	31.8	11.5
Height (cm)	179.0	6.4	168.6	5.8
Weight (kg)	78.2	11.7	57.5	7.4
Body mass index*	24.4	3.2	20.2	2.2
Laboratory determined				
Body Density (g/cc)	1.058	0.018	1.044	0.016
Percent fat (%)	17.9	8.0	24.4	7.2
Lean weight (kg)	63.5	7.3	43.1	4.2
Fat weight (kg)	14.6	7.9	14.3	5.7
Skinfolds (mm)				
Chest	15.2	8.0	12.6	4.8
Axilla	17.3	8.7	13.0	6.1
Triceps	14.2	6.1	18.2	5.9
Subscapula	16.0	7.0	14.2	6.4
Abdomen	25.1	10.8	24.2	9.6
Suprailium	16.2	8.9	14.0	7.1
Thigh	18.9	7.7	29.5	8.0
Sum of Skinfolds (mm)				
All seven	122.9	52.0	125.6	42.0
Chest, abdomen, thigh (Σ3) (men)	59.2	24.5		
Triceps, suprailium, thigh (Σ3) (women)		61.6	19.0	

Table 9.8 Generalized Regression Equations for Predicting Body Density of Men and Women from the Sum of Skinfold Fat and Age

	Regression Equation	R	g/cc	% fat
Males	$BD = 1.11200000 - (0.00043499 \times V_1) + (0.00000055 \times V_1)^2 - 0.00028826 \times V_2)$	0.90	.008	3.4
Females	$BD = 1.0970 - (0.0004697 \times V_1) + (0.00000562 \times V_1)^2 - (0.00012828 \times V_2)$	0.85	0.008	3.8

Key: V^l = sum of seven skinfolds; V^2 = age in years.

It was discovered that equations that use the sum of three skinfolds (Σ3) were highly correlated (R = 0.97) with the sum of seven skinfolds (Jackson & Pollock 1978; Jackson et al. 1980). This showed that the sum of three skinfolds could be used without the loss of accuracy. The sum of three equations has become the standard. To enhance testing, different sites are used for men and women. The female and male sites and equations are

Females: $\Sigma 3$ = Triceps, Suprailium, and Thigh (R = 9.84, SEE = 0.009) **(9.11)**

$$BD = 1.099421 - (0.0009928 \times \Sigma 3) + 0.00000023 \times \Sigma 3^2) - (0.0001382 \times \text{Age})$$

Males: $\Sigma 3$ = Chest, Abdomen, and Thigh (R = 0.91, SEE = 0.008) **(9.12)**

$$BD = 1.10938 - (0.0008267 \times \Sigma 3) + 0.0000016 \times \Sigma 3^2) - (0.0002574 \times \text{Age})$$

Calculation Example, Estimating Percent Body Fat from Sum of Skinfold. Assume the following measurements for a man and a woman.

- Woman: age 29 years; skinfolds: triceps = 18 mm, suprailium = 14 mm, thigh = 30 mm; $\Sigma 3$ = 62 mm. Using Formula 9.11 to estimate body density and the Siri equation (Formula 9.4), percent body fat is 24.5%.

$$BD = 1.099994921 - (0.0009929 \times 62) + [0.0000023 \times (62 \times 62)] - (0.0001392 \times 29)$$
$$= 1.099994921 - 0.0615598 + 0.0088412 - 0.0040368 = 1.0431$$

$$\%\text{fat} = \left(\frac{495}{1.0431}\right) - 450 = 24.5\%$$

- Man: age 40 years, skinfolds: chest = 15 mm, abdomen = 26 mm, thigh = 20 mm; $\Sigma 3$ = 61 mm. Using Formula 9.12 to estimate body density and the Siri equation (Formula 9.4), percent body fat is 19.9%.

$$BD = 1.10938 - (0.0008267 \times 61) + (0.0000016 \times (61 \times 61) - (0.0002574 \times 40)$$
$$= 1.10938 - 0.0504287 + 0.0059536 - 0.010296 = 1.0533$$

$$\%\text{fat} = \left(\frac{495}{1.0533}\right) - 450 = 19.95\%$$

Tables 9.9 and 9.10 provide percent body fat estimates from the quadratic sum of three skinfolds and age. The YMCA Adult Fitness test (Golding et al. 1989) includes a similar table for a different combination of skinfolds. To use these tables, first select the appropriate skinfold sites and measure them following the recommended measurement procedures. Using the sum of three skinfolds and age, find the percentage that is closest to the subject's age and sum of skinfolds. For example, if the sum of the triceps, suprailium, and thigh skinfolds for a 29-year-old woman is 62 millimeters, the closest age category is 30 years and the closest sum of skinfolds is 61 millimeters. Her estimated percent body fat would be approximately 24.2%, as compared to the calculated value of 24.5%. The generalized equations can be difficult to use without computational help. This can be easily done with a PC and common spreadsheets and relational database computer programs.

The multiple correlations and standard errors of measurement for the generalized equations are well within the range reported for population-specific equations.

Table 9.9 Estimates of Percentage of Fat for Men; Sum of Chest, Abdomen, and Thigh Skinfolds

Sum of Skinfolds (mm)	Age in Years							
	20	25	30	35	40	45	50	55
16	3.5	4.1	4.6	5.2	5.7	6.2	6.8	7.3
19	4.5	5.0	5.6	6.1	6.7	7.2	7.7	8.3
22	5.5	6.0	6.5	7.1	7.6	8.2	8.7	9.3
25	6.4	6.9	7.5	8.0	8.6	9.1	9.7	10.2
28	7.3	7.9	8.4	9.0	9.5	10.1	10.6	11.2
31	8.3	8.8	9.4	9.9	10.5	11.0	11.6	12.1
34	9.2	9.7	10.3	10.8	11.4	12.0	12.5	13.1
37	10.1	10.7	11.2	11.8	12.3	12.9	13.4	14.0
40	11.0	11.6	12.1	12.7	13.2	13.8	14.4	14.9
43	11.9	12.5	13.0	13.6	14.1	14.7	15.3	15.8
46	12.8	13.4	13.9	14.5	15.0	15.6	16.2	16.7
49	13.7	14.2	14.8	15.4	15.9	16.5	17.1	17.6
52	14.5	15.1	15.7	16.2	16.8	17.4	17.9	18.5
55	15.4	16.0	16.5	17.1	17.7	18.2	18.8	19.4
58	16.2	16.8	17.4	18.0	18.5	19.1	19.7	20.2
61	17.1	17.7	18.2	18.8	19.4	19.9	20.5	21.1
64	17.9	18.5	19.1	19.6	20.2	20.8	21.4	21.9
67	18.7	19.3	19.9	20.5	21.0	21.6	22.2	22.8
70	19.5	20.1	20.7	21.3	21.9	22.4	23.0	23.6
73	20.3	20.9	21.5	22.1	22.7	23.2	23.8	24.4
76	21.1	21.7	22.3	22.9	23.5	24.0	24.6	25.2
79	21.9	22.5	23.1	23.7	24.2	24.8	25.4	26.0
82	22.7	23.3	23.9	24.4	25.0	25.6	26.2	26.8
85	23.4	24.0	24.6	25.2	25.8	26.4	27.0	27.6
88	24.2	24.8	25.4	26.0	26.5	27.1	27.7	28.3
91	24.9	25.5	26.1	26.7	27.3	27.9	28.5	29.1
94	25.7	26.2	26.8	27.4	28.0	28.6	29.2	29.8
97	26.4	27.0	27.6	28.2	28.7	29.3	29.9	30.5
100	27.1	27.7	28.3	28.9	29.5	30.1	30.7	31.3
103	27.8	28.4	29.0	29.6	30.2	30.8	31.4	32.0
106	28.5	29.1	29.6	30.2	30.8	31.4	32.1	32.7
109	29.1	29.7	30.3	30.9	31.5	32.1	32.7	33.3
112	29.8	30.4	31.0	31.6	32.2	32.8	33.4	34.0
115	30.4	31.0	31.6	32.2	32.8	33.5	34.1	34.7

These findings show that a generalized equation can be used to replace several different population-specific equations and are valid for adults varying greatly in age and body fatness. Still, an important caution should be raised when using the generalized equations. They were developed on men and women ranging from 18 to 61 years of age and using the two-component model that does not consider body water and mineral content. These equations should not be applied to children and may lose accuracy with the elderly (Lohman 1992). They may also lose accuracy with extremely obese individuals.

Table 9.10 Estimates of Percentage of Fat for Women; Sum of Triceps, Suprailium, and Thigh Skinfolds

Sum of Skinfolds (mm)	Age in Years							
	20	25	30	35	40	45	50	55
22	9.8	10.1	10.4	10.7	11.0	11.3	11.6	11.9
25	11.0	11.3	11.6	11.9	12.2	12.5	12.8	13.1
28	12.1	12.4	12.7	13.0	13.3	13.6	13.9	14.2
31	13.2	13.5	13.8	14.1	14.4	14.7	15.0	15.3
34	14.3	14.6	14.9	15.2	15.5	15.8	16.1	16.4
37	15.4	15.7	16.0	16.3	16.6	16.9	17.2	17.5
40	16.5	16.8	17.1	17.4	17.7	18.0	18.3	18.6
43	17.5	17.8	18.1	18.4	18.8	19.1	19.4	19.7
46	18.6	18.9	19.2	19.5	19.8	20.1	20.4	20.7
49	19.6	19.9	20.2	20.5	20.8	21.2	21.5	21.8
52	20.6	20.9	21.2	21.6	21.9	22.2	22.5	22.8
55	21.6	21.9	22.3	22.6	22.9	23.2	23.5	23.8
58	22.6	22.9	23.2	23.6	23.9	24.2	24.5	24.8
61	23.6	23.9	24.2	24.5	24.9	25.2	25.5	25.8
64	24.6	24.9	25.2	25.5	25.8	26.1	26.5	26.8
67	25.5	25.8	26.1	26.5	26.8	27.1	27.4	27.7
70	26.4	26.7	27.1	27.4	27.7	28.0	28.4	28.7
73	27.3	27.7	28.0	28.3	28.6	29.0	29.3	29.6
76	28.2	28.6	28.9	29.2	29.5	29.9	30.2	30.5
79	29.1	29.5	29.8	30.1	30.4	30.7	31.1	31.4
82	30.0	30.3	30.6	31.0	31.3	31.6	31.9	32.3
85	30.8	31.2	31.5	31.8	32.2	32.5	32.8	33.1
88	31.7	32.0	32.3	32.7	33.0	33.3	33.6	34.0
91	32.5	32.8	33.2	33.5	33.8	34.1	34.5	34.8
94	33.3	33.6	34.0	34.3	34.6	35.0	35.3	35.6
97	34.1	34.4	34.7	35.1	35.4	35.7	36.1	36.4
100	34.9	35.2	35.5	35.9	36.2	36.5	36.8	37.2
103	35.6	35.9	36.3	36.6	36.9	37.3	37.6	37.9
106	36.3	36.7	37.0	37.3	37.7	38.0	38.3	38.7
109	37.1	37.4	37.7	38.1	38.4	38.7	39.1	39.4
112	37.8	38.1	38.4	38.8	39.1	39.4	39.8	40.1
115	38.4	38.8	39.1	39.4	39.8	40.1	40.5	40.8

Evaluating Body Composition of Adults

It is important to assess both body weight and percent body fat because they provide two related pieces of information about a person's body composition. Body weight is easy to measure, and once someone has an understanding of a desirable body weight for his or her frame, weight can be used to monitor changes in body composition. The shortcoming of using only body weight is that the fat-free weight component, frame size, and muscle development are not accurately considered. Two individuals of the same height, sex, and age may weigh the same but have different levels of fat-free weight and body fat.

Percent Body Fat Standards

What is a desirable percent body fat standard for adults? Being seriously overweight clearly increases one's risk of heart disease, hypertension, and diabetes, and results in a lower life expectancy. Still, too many Americans, especially young women, are

Table 9.11 Ranges of Percent Body Fat for Male and Female Athletes

Sport	Percent Fat Range	
	Men	**Women**
Baseball/softball	8–14	12–18
Basketball	6–12	10–16
Cycling	5–11	8–15
Football	6–18	
Golf	10–16	12–20
Gymnastics	5–12	8–16
Ice/field hockey	8–16	12–18
Racquetball	6–14	10–18
Rowing	6–14	8–16
Rugby	6–16	
Skating	5–12	8–16
Skiing	7–15	10–18
Swimming	6–12	10–18
Tennis	6–14	10–20
Track—running events	5–12	8–15
Track—field events	8–18	12–20
Triathlon	5–12	8–15
Volleyball	7–15	10–18

*From published data in Wilmore & Costill 1994.

overly concerned about being thin. Being underweight, too, can result in serious health problems. Athletes generally have a lower percent body fat than the total population. The percent body fat level depends on the athlete's sex and event performed. Table 9.11 presents data published by Wilmore and Costill (1994) of percent body fat ranges of elite athletic groups. Highly trained endurance athletes (e.g., distance runners) will normally have very low levels of body fat. The average percent body fat of world-class distance runners is very low, averaging about 5% for men and ranging from 12% to 15% for women. This is an unrealistically low level for most who are not exercising to the level of these athletes. Most world-class runners run from 10 to 15 miles each day of the week. At this mileage, they expend over 1000 kilocalories a day just from exercise.

Because of the errors associated with measuring body composition, it is not possible to define exact percent body fat standards. Lohman (1992) summarizes the problems of evaluating body composition of adults.

> In adults, with aging, the fat distribution may change. Now, we cannot easily sort out the influences of changes in fat distribution with changes in density of fat-free body associated with bone mineral loss or body fatness prediction with age. For example, using the Jackson-Pollock equations on 30- and 50-year-old females with the sum of three skinfolds (triceps, abdomen, suprailium) equal to 60 mm, we obtain a percent fat of 25.7% for the 18- to 22-year-old and 27% for the 55-year old with the same skinfold. Is this change associated primarily with a change in fat distribution or with a change in the density of the fat-free body? All the Durnin and Womersley (1974) equations, as well as the Jackson and Pollock equations (1978, 1980), are based on the two-component model and assume constant density of the fat-free body with aging. (p. 45)

Table 9.12 Standards for Evaluating Body Composition of Adults

Body Composition Standard	Age Group In Years			
	Under 30	30–39	40–49	Over 49
Men				
High	>28%	>29%	>30%	>31%
Moderately high	22–28%	23–29%	24–30%	25–31%
Optimal range	11–21%	12–22%	13–23%	14–24%
Low	6–10%	7–11%	8–12%	9–13%
Very low	≥5%	≥6%	≥7%	≥8%
Women				
High	>32%	>33%	>34%	>35%
Moderately high	26–32%	27–33%	28–34%	29–35%
Optimal range	15–25%	16–26%	17–27%	18–28%
Low	12–14%	13–15%	14–16%	15–17%
Very low	≥11%	≥12%	≥13%	≥14%

Table 9.13 Standards for the Interpretation of Adults Percent Body Fat Standards

High	Percent fat at this level indicates the person is seriously overweight to a degree that this can have adverse health consequences. The person should be encouraged to lose weight through diet and exercise. Maintaining weight at this level for a long period of time places the person at risk of hypertension, heart disease, and diabetes. A long-term weight loss and exercise program should be initiated.
Moderately High	It is likely that the person is significantly overweight, but the level could be high due in part to measurement inaccuracies. It would be wise to carefully monitor people in this category and encourage them not to gain additional weight. People in this category may want to have their body composition assessed by the underwater weighing method.
Optimal Range	It would be highly desirable to maintain body composition at this level.
Low	This is an acceptable body composition level, but there is no reason to seek a lower percent body fat level. Loss of additional body weight could have health consequences.
Very Low	Percent fat level at this range should be reached only by high-level endurance athletes who are in training. Being this thin may carry its own additional mortality. Individuals, especially females, this low are at risk of having an eating disorder such as anorexia nervosa.

Table 9.12 gives standards for evaluating body composition of adults considering these limitations. These standards were developed from major published normative databases that consider both sex and age characteristics. The interpretation of the standards is furnished in Table 9.13. These standards not only consider the problems

associated with obesity, but also the problem of being underweight. The relation between weight and all-cause mortality is J- shaped; the highest and lowest death rates are associated with being too light as well as being too heavy (Lew & Garfinkel 1979). This was shown at the beginning of this chapter. It has also been shown that failing to gain weight is associated with a shorter life expectancy, compared to individuals who are at the optimal weight range for their age, sex, and height (Paffenbarger et al. 1986). It is likely that the J-shaped weight and mortality rates found in epidemiological studies can be traced partly to wasting diseases such as cancer, but there is morbidity associated with the diet restrictions and/or high levels of exercise. For example, anorexia nervosa is characterized by excessive diet and exercise, resulting in extreme weight loss. This often is a problem of some young women and, for too many, it is a fatal disease.

Defining Weight-Reduction Goals

It is possible for two individuals of the same height and body weight to differ substantially in percent body fat, which is why we use it as the standard for evaluating body composition. If percent body fat (%fat) and body weight are known, it becomes possible to calculate **fat weight** and **fat-free weight.** Once these are known, it becomes possible to estimate a sound weight goal. For many adults, the goal is weight reduction. If percent body fat is known, an estimate of a realistic goal can be easily obtained. The weight-reduction goal is the estimated body weight for a desired percent body fat level. It is estimated from fat-free weight and desired percent fat level. The formulas for making these calculations are

Fat Weight *(9.13)*

$$\text{Fat Weight} = \left[\text{Weight} \times \left(\frac{\%\text{fat}}{100}\right)\right]$$

Fat-Free Weight *(9.14)*

$$\text{Fat-Free Weight} = (\text{Weight} - \text{Fat Weight})$$

Determine Weight Goal *(9.15)*

$$\text{Weight Goal} = \frac{\text{Fat} - \text{Free Weight}}{\left[1 - \left(\frac{\text{Desired }\%\text{Fat}}{100}\right)\right]}$$

Calculation Example. The formula can be easily illustrated. Assume the body composition characteristics of a man are the following: weight, 187 pounds, and percent body fat, 26.3%. We must first calculate fat weight (Formula 9.13) and fat-free weight (Formula 9.14).

$$\text{Fat Weight} = \left[187 \times \left(\frac{26.3}{100}\right)\right] = 49.2 \text{ pounds}$$

$$\text{Fat-Free Weight} = 187 - 49.2 = 137.8 \text{ pounds}$$

The weight goal for 20%fat (Formula 9.15) would be

$$\text{Desired Weight (20\%fat)} = \frac{137.8}{\left[1 - \left(\frac{20}{100}\right)\right]} = \frac{137.8}{0.80} = 172.25 \text{ pounds}$$

The weight goal provides an estimate of what the person's weight would be if his/her fat-free weight component remained the same but the body fat changed to the desired goal. Sedentary adults who start an exercise program tend to increase muscle mass and lose fat weight. This results in a decrease in percent fat but sometimes without the projected weight loss. When a program uses only diet, both fat and fat-free weight are lost, often leaving percent fat relatively unchanged or even slightly increased, while total weight is reduced. It is important to monitor both body weight and percent body fat during an adult weight-reduction program to be sure that the participant's body composition is being altered in the desired direction.

Skinfold Assessments of Percent Body Fat of Children and Youth

Data provided in Figure 9.19 graphically shows that the body composition of American youth is changing in an unfavorable direction: children are fatter than they were 20 years ago. The changing activity pattern and nutrition of today's youth is likely responsible, and this is a concern of public health officials. As documented in Chapter 1, a reduction in the prevalence of overweight children is an objective of the *Healthy People 2000* program (U.S. Public Health Service 1990). Body composition tests are included in health-related youth fitness tests provided in Chapter 10.

Several investigations (Table 9.14) have used the two-component model to estimate body density of children from anthropometric variables. Children vary considerably in growth and developmental characteristics during their school years. In

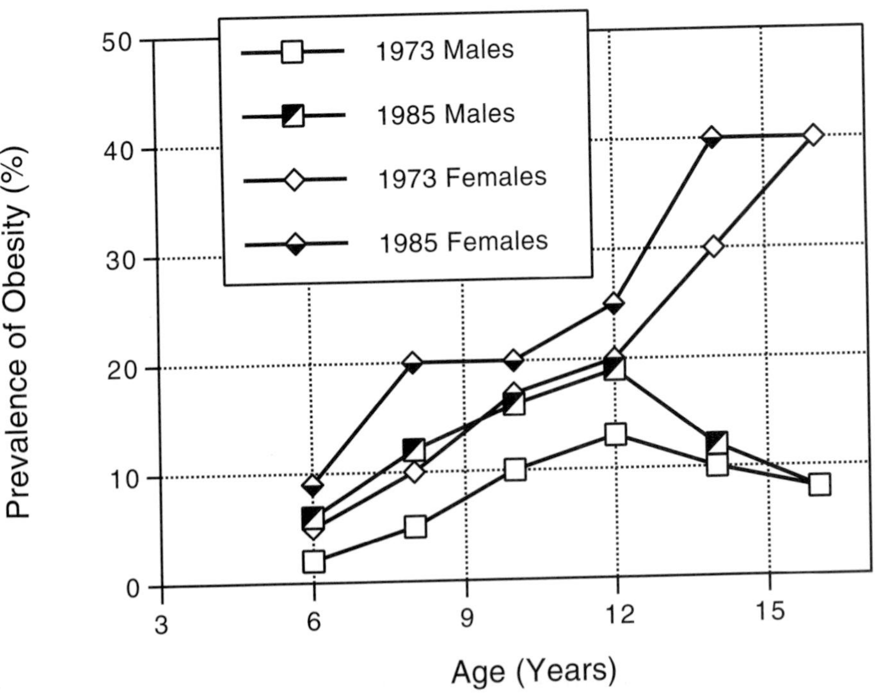

Figure 9.19 Prevalance of obesity based on 25% fat for males and 31% fat for females in 1973 (NHES 1973) and 1985 (NCYFS 1985). Graph developed from published data. (Lohman 1992).

comparison to adults, children have a higher water and lower bone mineral content, and these values change during their developmental years. Figure 9.20 shows this age-dependent decrease in body water for boys and girls. Chemical maturity is not reached until late adolescence. Due to chemical immaturity, the two-component model overestimates the percent body fat of children (Lohman 1992).

Many laboratories have the capacity to conduct underwater weighting studies, but very few have the capacity to measure body water and mineral content. Lohman (1992) developed several skinfold equations for estimating the percent body fat of youth. These equations use the sum of two different skinfold combinations: (1) sum of triceps and calf skinfolds and (2) sum of triceps and subscapula skinfolds. The sex-specific triceps and calf skinfold equations were developed with the multicomponent model and are recommended for use with children and youth of any age or ethnicity. These formulas are

Percent Body Fat Equation for Children and Youth—Males *(9.16)*

$$\%\text{fat} = [(0.735 \times \text{Triceps} + \text{Calf})] + 1.0$$

Percent Body Fat Equation for Children and Youth—Females *(9.17)*

$$\%\text{fat} = [(0.610 \times \text{Triceps} + \text{Calf}) + 5.0]$$

Calculation Example, Estimating Percent Body Fat of Youth. Assume that the sums of triceps and calf skinfolds for a boy and girl are both 20 mm. Formula 9.16 is used to estimate percent body fat for the boy, and Formula 9.17 is used for the girl. The percent body fat estimates are 15.7% and 17.2% for the boy and girl, respectively.

Table 9.14 Means and Standard Deviations of Hydrostatically Determined Body Density and Concurrent Validity of Regression Equations for Youth

Source	Sample		Body Density		Regression Analysis	
	Age	n	Mean	SD	R	SE
Males						
Cureton et al. (1975)	8–11	49	1.053	.013	.77	.008
Durnin and Rahaman (1967)	12–15	48	1.063	.012	.76	.008
Harsha et al. (1978)	6–16	79	1.046	.018	.84	.010
Harsha et al. (1978)	6–16	49	1.055	.020	.90	.009
Parizkova (1961)	9–12	57	*	*	.92	.011
Females						
Durnin and Rahaman (1967)	13–16	38	1.045	.011	.78	.008
Harsha et al. (1978)	6–16	52	1.033	.016	.85	.008
Harsha et al. (1978)	6–16	39	1.041	.019	.90	.008
Parizkova (1961)	9–12	56	*	*	.81	.012
Parizkova (1961)	13–16	62	*	*	.82	.010

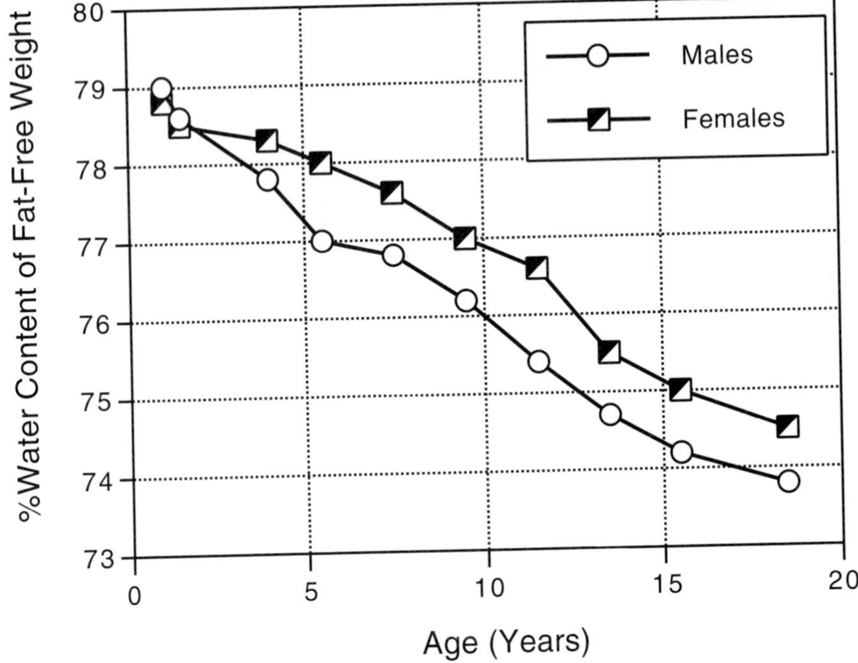

Figure 9.20 The percentage of body water content of fat-free weight of children declines with age. Not correcting for these differences in body water results in an overestimate of a child's true percent body fat. Graph made from published data. (Lohman 1992)

Table 9.15 Sum of Triceps and Calf Skinfolds, Estimated Percent Body Fat, and Standard for Evaluating Body Composition of Children and Youth*

Standard	Males		Females	
	ΣTriceps and Calf	%Fat	ΣTriceps and Calf	%Fat
Very low	≤5	≤4.7%	≤11	≤12%
Low	6–10	5.2–9.0%	12–16	12.1–15.0%
Optimal	11–25	9.1–20.0%	17–32	15.1–25.0%
Moderately high	26–32	20.1–25.0%	33–40	25.1–29.9%
High	33–40	25.1–31.0%	41–50	30–36.0%
Very high	>40	>31.0%	>50	>36.0%

*Constructed from data published by Lohman 1992.

Boy $\Sigma 3 = 20$

$\%\text{fat} = (0.735 \times 20) + 1.0 = 15.7\%$

Girl $\Sigma 3 = 20$

$\%\text{fat} = (0.610 \times 20) + 5.0 = 17.2\%$

Table 9.15 gives the standard suggested by Lohman (1992) to evaluate the body composition of children and youth. Provided are the sum of triceps and calf skinfolds and the equivalent percent body fat values. These standards are consistent with the adult standards previously presented.

Bioelectrical Impedance Method

A somewhat new technique for measuring body composition is **bioelectrical impedance analysis (BIA).** It is based on the principle that the electrical resistance of the body to a mild electric current is related to total body water. Total body water and fat-free weight are highly related. The BIA method is simple and requires only the placement of four electrodes, two on the subject's ankle and two on the wrist. A current is transmitted into the subject, and the resistance in ohms is read directly into a microcomputer that calculates body composition.

In the early stages of BIA technology, the accuracy of BIA was a major concern. One study showed that this method was no more accurate than the weight-height ratio of body mass index (Jackson et al. 1988). Recent research (Lohman 1992) showed that with suitable equations, BIA estimates of percent body fat have an accuracy similar to skinfold estimates, except for the obese and very lean. Equations developed on the general population tend to underestimate percent body fat of the obese and overestimate the percent body fat of very lean subjects. More research is needed to develop generalized BIA equations.

Comparison of Body Composition Methods

Table 9.16 provides an evaluation and comparison of the methods available to assess body composition. If accuracy is a major concern, the underwater weighing method with measured residual lung volume is the method of choice for measuring body density. The disadvantage of this method is that it is expensive and requires specialized equipment and trained testers. In addition, many do not enjoy the underwater weighing experience, and it is impossible to measure underwater weight accurately if the subject has a fear of water and cannot sit still fully submerged after an expiration. Using predicted residual lung volume rather than measuring it makes the underwater weighing method much less accurate. The "body box," or body plethysmograph has the potential to overcome the problems associated with underwater weighing, but the method needs more validation research. With increased interest in assessing the body composition of children, the elderly, and various ethnic groups, more researchers will move to the multicomponent model.

A common problem associated with skinfold measurements is the measurement error among testers. With properly trained testers, percent body fat estimated from skinfolds can be reliably measured. Using three testers who varied in experience, but practiced together, the reliability was found to exceed 0.99 for the sum of seven and three skinfolds. The standard error of measurement was about 1% body fat (Jackson, Pollock & Gettman 1978). In a more comprehensive study (Jackson et al. 1978), both day-to-day and tester-to-tester measurement error of the skinfold, BIA, and hydrostatic estimates of percent body fat were examined. Table 9.17 lists these results. All reliability estimates were high, with standard errors of measurement about 1% body fat. The skinfold method is likely the most feasible option for general use and offers several advantages over the other field methods.

1. **Accuracy and reproducibility.** When testers are properly trained, it is reliable, and results are reproducible from day to day and tester to tester.
2. **Simplicity and cost.** The skinfold method is simple to perform, not embarrassing, easy to teach to others, and the equipment required is not expensive. While the BIA method may have similar accuracy, the equipment is much more expensive. The BMI method is most practical but less accurate.

Table 9.16 Comparison of Methods Available to Evaluate Body Composition of Humans

Method	Strengths	Limitations	Accuracy—%Fat
Multicomponent	Most accurate; can be used for all age groups	Need expensive equipment; very few labs have the capacity to measure body water and mineral content; must measure residual lung volume	1 %fat, >3% if residual volume is not measured
Two component (Siri & Brŏzek %fat equations)	Accurate with mature adults; many labs have the capacity	Need expensive equipment; cannot be used with children and elderly; must measure residual lung volume	1 %fat, >3% if residual volume is not measured
Skinfolds Generalized equations	Inexpensive; feasible for mass testing; appropriate for most adults (ages 20–50)	Tester errors measuring skinfolds; does not measure essential fat; developed with two-components model	3.5–4%fat
Skinfolds— Population specific equations	Inexpensive; feasible for mass testing	Does not measure essential fat; developed with two-component model; suitable for limited populations (e.g., young adult males)	3.5–4.0%fat for the limited population
Lohman's children's equations	Inexpensive; feasible for mass testing; based on multicomponent model	Tester errors measuring skinfolds; does not measure essential fat	3.6–3.9%fat
Bioelectric impedance	Feasible for mass testing; just need to attach four electrodes; potential method of measuring body water	Validated on two-component model; standard equations are not readily available; lacks accuracy with very lean and obese; expensive equipment; tester errors	3.5–4.5%fat
Body circumferences	Very inexpensive; feasible for mass testing	Tester errors measuring circumferences; does not measure essential fat; developed on two-component model; not very popular	3.7–4.5%fat
Body mass index (BMI)	Most feasible for mass testing (just need height and weight); large normative databases available; overweight standards are defined	Does not differentiate between fat and fat-free weight; does not estimate %fat; least accurate	≥4.5%fat
Waist-hip ratio	Feasible for mass testing; measures body fat that appears to increase the risk of diabetes and cardiovascular diseases	Does not provide an estimate of percent body fat	Not known

3. **Fat deposits.** Recent work (Larsson et al. 1984) suggests that not only is total body fat related to health, but the location of the deposits is also important. Fat around the abdomen seems to be a greater risk factor to longevity than total body fat. Only anthropometric data can evaluate fat deposition. The waist-hip ratio provides the best measure of this body fat.

Table 9.17 Reliability Estimates and Standard Errors of Measurement (%Fat) for Hydrostatically Determined Percent Body Fat, and Estimated Percent Body Fat from the Sum of Skinfolds, and Bioelectric Impedance*

Variable	Males (n = 24)		Females (n = 44)	
	R_{xx}	SEM	R_{xx}	SEM
Measured percent body fat	.97	1.1	.97	1.2
Skinfold estimated percent body fat	.98	1.0	.99	0.9
BIA estimated percent body fat	.96	1.4	.97	1.5

*From Jackson et al. 1988

4. **Education.** Individuals can gain better understanding of the concept of excess body fat by actually measuring body fat. They may then use subjective assessments such as "pinch an inch" to gauge their progress.
5. **Measuring fat.** Gaining body fat results in the accumulation of subcutaneous fat, which is the fat that can be pinched. Thus, even if there is an error in estimating percent body fat, a reduction in the sum of skinfolds means a reduction in fat.

Summary

Overweight is the excessive body weight for an individual's height, while obesity is the excessive accumulation of body fat. Both have a negative influence on health. Cardiovascular diseases, diabetes, and breast cancer are associated with the excessive accumulation of body fat. In contrast, being too lean can suggest the presence of an eating disorder. The sources of adulthood obesity are both genetic and the level of one's body composition as a youth. While the body mass index (BMI) is often used to measure body composition from height and weight, its limitation is that it does not differentiate between fat and fat-free weight. Body density is the ratio of body volume and dry land weight. The most valid method of measuring body density is by underwater weighing. Once density is known, standard equations are available to convert body density to percent body fat. These calculations are based on the assumption that the density of fat weight is 0.90 g/cc and that of lean weight 1.10 g/cc. These density constants may vary somewhat among individuals, which introduces biological errors in calculating percent body fat, especially for children, the elderly, and various ethnic groups. The multicomponent model, which uses total body water and bone mineral content, corrects for these biological errors. The major source of measurement error of the underwater weighing method is the failure to measure residual lung volume. The most common field methods are skinfolds, bioelectrical impedance analysis (BIA), circumferences, and BMI. These methods are less accurate but more realistic for mass testing. Skinfolds are likely the most common field method used to estimate percent body fat, but with the development of more generalized equations, the BIA methods will become an attractive alternative. Body mass index is suitable for defining overweight in populations of individuals, but lacks the accuracy to assess an individual's body composition.

Formative Evaluation of Objectives

Objective 1 Identify the public health problems associated with body composition.

1. Identify the medical problems associated with high levels of percent body fat.
2. Are there problems with being too lean?

Objective 2 Identify the methods used to measure body composition of youth and adults.

1. Outline the steps you would follow to measure percent body fat by the hydrostatic weighing method.
2. Outline the steps you would follow to measure percent body fat using the generalized skinfold equations.
3. Are the generalized skinfold equations suitable for children?
4. How do you estimate the percent body fat of children?

Objective 3 Identify the limitations of the two-component model for computing percent body fat when applied to children and elderly.

1. What is the limitation of the two-component model for computing percent body fat?
2. How does the multicomponent model adjust for the limitation?

Objective 4 Calculate percent body fat of youths and adults from skinfold equations.

1. A 42-year-old woman has a sum of seven skinfolds of 130 mm. What is her body density and percent body fat? What would these values be if she had a sum of three skinfolds of 64 mm?
2. A 38-year-old man has the following skinfold values: sum of seven of 142 mm and sum of three of 65 mm. What would be his estimated body density and percent body fat?
3. What is the percent body fat for a 15-year-old boy with a sum of 25 for calf and triceps skinfold?
4. Evaluate the body composition of a 12-year-old girl with a sum of 32 for calf and triceps skinfolds.

Objective 5 Be able to evaluate body composition of youths and adults.

1. What is the percent body fat level used to define level of obesity in children?
2. Why are adult body composition standards adjusted for age?
3. Is there a danger in having a percent body fat that is too low?

Objective 6 Calculate weight goals for selected levels of desired percent body fat.

1. Assume a 165-pound woman's percent body fat is 35%. What would her weight be if she was 23%? How about 28%?
2. Assume a football player's body weight is 245 pounds and his measured percent body fat is 23%. If a coach would like the player's body composition to be between 10% and 15%, what would his weight range be?

Objective 7 Evaluate the accuracy of the various methods used to measure body composition.

1. What is the major source of measurement error for measuring percent body fat by the hydrostatic weighing method?
2. The standard error of prediction for estimating percent body fat from skinfolds ranges from about 3.5 to 4.0% body fat. What does this mean?
3. What is the limitation of using BMI to evaluate percent body fat?

Additional Learning Activities

1. Measure the skinfold thickness on several individuals. The secret to obtaining accurate percent body fat estimates from the generalized skinfold equations is to measure skinfold thickness correctly. Work with a partner and compare your results. Follow the instructions and pictures provided in this chapter.
2. Have your body composition determined by the underwater weighing method. This is the most valid method of measuring body composition. Be certain your residual lung volume is measured.
3. Many commercial fitness centers use electronic machines to estimate the percent body fat of members; a common method is the BIA method. Go to a center to have your body composition measured, and if you have also had it done by the hydrostatic method, compare the results. Ask the person taking the measurements to explain to you how the machine works and how accurate the equations are.
4. If you have a microcomputer and the software, use a database program and develop a system for calculating percent body fat for the generalized equations. You will be surprised how easy and powerful database programs are. Examples are provided in the Computer Calculations section of the appendix.

Bibliography

Behnke, A. R. and J. H. Wilmore. 1974. *Evaluation and regulation of body build and composition.* Englewood Cliffs, NJ: Prentice-Hall.

Boileau, R. A., T. G. Lohman, and M. H. Slaughter. 1985. Exercise and body composition in children and youth. *Scandinavian Journal of Sport Sciences* 7:17–27.

Bray, G. A. 1993. Fat distribution and body weight. *Obesity Research* 1:203–205.

Brŏzek, J. and A. Keys. 1951. The evaluation of leanness-fatness in man: Norms and intercorrelations. *British Journal of Nutrition* 5:194–206.

Brŏzek, J., F. Grande, and J. T. Anderson. 1963. Densitometric analysis of body composition: Revision of some quantitive assumptions. *Annals of New York Academy of Science* 110:113–140.

Cureton, K. J. 1984. A reaction to the manuscript by Jackson. *Medicine and Science in Sport and Exercise* 16:621–622.

Cureton, K. J., R. A. Boileau, and T. G. Lohman. 1975. A comparison of densitometric, Potassium-40, and skinfold estimates of body composition in prepubescent boys. *Human Biology* 47:321–336.

Dishman, R. K. ed. 1988. *Exercise adherence: Its impact on public health.* Champaign, IL: Human Kinetics.

Durnin, J. V. G. A. and R. Passmore. 1967. *Energy, work and leisure.* London: Heinemann Educational Books.

Durnin, J. V. G. A. and J. Wormsley. 1974. Body fat assessed from total body density and its estimation from skinfold thickness: Measurements on 481 men and women aged from 16 to 72 years. *British Journal of Nutrition* 32:77–92.

Forsyth, H. L. and W. E. Sinning. 1973. The anthropemetric estimation of body density and lean body weight of male athletes. *Medicine and Science in Sports* 5:174–180.

Foreyt, J. P. et al. In press. Anorexia nervosa and bulimia nervosa.

Gallagher, D. et al. 1996. How useful is body mass index for comparison of body fatness across age, sex, and ethnic groups. *American Journal of Epidemiology* 143(3):228–239.

Golding, L. A., C. R. Meyers, and W. E. Sinning. 1989. *The Y's way to physical fitness* 3rd ed. Chicago: National Board of YMCA.

Haisman, M. F. 1970. The assessment of body fat content in young men from measurements of body density and skinfold thickness. *Human Biology* 42:679–688.

Harsha, D. W., R. R. Fredrichs, and G. S. Berenson. 1978. Densitometry and anthropometry of black and white children. *Human Biology* 50:261–280.

Heymsfield, S. B., Wang, Z, Withers, R. T. 1996. Chapter 7. Multicomponent molecular level models of body composition analysis. In Roche, A. F., S. B. Heymsfield, T. G. Lohman, (eds). *Human body composition.* Champaign, IL: Human Kinetics.

Going, S. B. 1996. Chapter 1. Densitometry. In Roche, A. F., S. B. Heymsfield, and T. G. Lohman (Eds). *Human body composition.* Champaign, IL: Human Kinetics.

Hodgdon, J. A. and M. B. Beckett. 1984a. *Prediction of percent body fat for U.S. Navy men from body circumferences and height.* Report No. 8411, Naval Health Research Center, San Diego, CA.

Hodgdon, J. A. and M. B. Beckett. 1984b. *Prediction of percent body fat for U.S. Navy women from body circumferences and height.* Report No. 8429, Naval Health Research Center, San Diego, CA.

Hodgdon, J. A. and M. B. Beckett. 1984c. *Technique for measuring body circumferences and skinfold thickness.* Report No. 84 39, Naval Health Research Center, San Diego, CA.

Huang, Z. et al. 1997. Dual effects of weight and weight gain on breast cancer risk. *Journal of the American Medical Association* 278(17):1407–1411.

Hubert, H. B. et al. 1983. Obesity as an independent risk factor for cardiovascular diseases: A 26-year follow-up of participants in the Framingham heart study. *Circulation* 67:968–977.

Jackson, A. S. 1984. Research progress in research design and analysis of data procedures for predicting body density. *Medicine and Science in Sports and Exercise* 16:616–620.

Jackson, A. S. and M. L. Pollock. 1978. Generalized equations for predicting body density of men. *British Journal of Nutrition* 40:497–504.

Jackson, A. S., M. L. Pollock, and L. R. Gettman. 1978. Intertester reliability of selected skinfold and circumference measurements and percent fat estimates. *Research Quarterly* 49:546–551.

Jackson, A. S., M. L. Pollock, and A. Ward. 1980. Generalized equations for predicting body density of women. *Medicine and Science in Sports and Exercise* 12:175–182.

Jackson, A. S. et al. 1988. Reliability and validity of bioelectrical impedance in determining body composition. *Journal of Applied Physiology* 64:529–534.

Katch, F. I. and W. D. McArdle. 1973. Prediction of body density from simple anthropometric measurements in college age women and men. *Human Biology* 45:445–454.

Katch, F. I. and E. D. Michael. 1968. Prediction of body density from skinfold and girth measurements of college females. *Journal of Applied Physiology* 25:92–94.

Katch, F. I. and E. D. Michael. 1969. Densitometric validation of six skinfold formulas to predict body density and percent fat of 17-year-old boys. *Research Quarterly* 40:712–716.

Kuczmarski, R. J. et al. 1994. Increasing prevalence of overweight among US adults: The National Health and Nutrition Examination Surveys, 1960 to 1991. *Journal of the American Medical Association* 272:205–211.

Larsson, B. et al. 1984. Abdominal adipose tissue distribution, obesity, and risk of cardiovascular disease and death: 13-year follow-up of participants in the study of men born in 1913. *British Medical Journal* 288:1401–1404.

Lew, E. A. and L. Garfinkel. 1979. Variations in mortality by weight among 750,000 men and women. *Journal of Chronic Diseases* 32:181–225.

Lohman, T. G. 1981. Skinfolds and body density and their relation to body fatness: A review. *Human Biology* 53:181–225.

Lohman, T. G. 1982. Body composition methodology in sport medicine. *Physician and Sports Medicine* 10:46–58.

Lohman, T. G. 1986. Application of body composition techniques and constants for children and youth. *Exercise and Sports Sciences Review* 14:325–357.

Lohman, T. G. 1992. *Advances in body composition assessment.* Champaign IL: Human Kinetics.

Lohman, T. G. et al. 1984. Bone mineral measurements and their relation to body density relationship in children, youth and adults. *Human Biology* 56:667–679.

Morrow, J. R. et al. 1986. Accuracy of measured and predicted residual lung volume on body density measurement. *Medicine and Science in Sport and Exercise* 18:647–652.

NCYFS. 1985. *Summary of findings from National Children and Youth Fitness Study.* Washington, DC: Department of Health and Human Services.

NHES. 1973. *Sample design and estimation procedures for a national health examination survey of children* (National Center for Health Statistics Publication No. HRA 74 1005). Rockville, MD: Health Resources Administration.

Paffenbarger, R. J. et al. 1986. Physical activity, all cause mortality, and longevity of college alumni. *New England Journal of Medicine* 314:605–613.

Panel NIH Technology Assessment Conference. 1993. Methods for voluntary weight loss and control. *Annals of Internal Medicine* 199:764–770.

Parizkova, J. 1961. Total body fat and skinfold thickness in children. *Metabolism* 10:794–807.

Pascale, L. et al. 1956. Correlations between thickness of skinfolds and body density in 88 soldiers. *Human Biology* 28:165–176.

Pollock, M. L. 1975. Prediction of body density in young and middle-aged women. *Journal of Applied Physiology* 38:745–749.

Pollock, M. L., T. Hickman, and Z. Kendrick. 1976. Prediction of body density in young and middle-aged men. *Journal of Applied Physiology* 40:300–304.

Pollock, M. L., J. H. Wilmore, and S. M. Fox III. 1984. *Exercise in health and disease.* Philadelphia: W. B. Saunders.

Ross, R. M. and A. S. Jackson. 1990. *Exercise concepts, calculations, and computer applications.* Carmel, IN: Benchmark Press.

Schutte, J. E. et al. 1984. Density of lean body mass is greater in blacks than in whites. *Journal of Applied Physiology: Respiratory, Environmental and Exercise Physiology* 56:1647–1649.

Sinning, W. E. 1996. Chapter 13. Body composition in athletes. In Roche, A. F., S. B. Heymsfield, and T. G. Lohman, (Eds.). *Human Body Composition.* Champaign, IL: Human Kinetics.

Sinning, W. E. 1978. Anthropometric estimation of body density, fat, and lean body weight in women gymnasts. *Medicine and Science in Sports* 10:234–249.

Siri, W. E. 1961. Body composition from fluid space and density. In Brŏzek, J. and A. Hanschel (Eds.). In *Techniques for measuring body composition.* Washington, DC: National Academy of Science.

Skender, M. L. et al. 1996. Comparison of 2-year weight loss trends in behavioral treatments of obesity: Diet, exercise, and combination interventions. *Journal of the American Dietetic Association* 96:342–346.

Slaughter, M. H. et al. 1988. Skinfold equations for estimating of body fatness in children and youth. *Human Biology* 60:709–723.

Sloan, A. W., J. J. Burt, and C. S. Blyth. 1962. Estimation of body fat in young women. *Journal of Applied Physiology* 17:967–970.

Troiano, R. P. et al. 1995. Overweight prevalence and trends for children and adolescents: The National Health and Nutrition Examination Surveys, 1963 to 1991. *Archives of Pediatric and Adolescent Medicine* 149:1085–1091.

Tran, Z. and A. Weltman. 1989. Generalized equation for predicting body density of women from girth measurements. *Medicine and Science in Sports and Exercise* 21:101–104.

Tran, Z. V., A. Weltman, and R. L. Seip. 1988. Predicting body composition of men from girth measurements. *Human Biology* 60:167–176.

USDHHS (U.S. Department of Health and Human Services). 1988. *The Surgeon General's report on nutrition and health* (p. 727). U.S. Department of Health and Human Services, Public Health Service, Washington, DC.

_______. 1990. *Healthy people 2000: National health promotion and disease prevention objectives.* Washington, DC: U.S. Department of Health and Human Services.

VanLoan, M. D. 1996. Chapter 11. Total body composition—Birth to old age. In Roche, A. F., S. B. Heymsfield and T. G. Lohman (Eds.). *Human body composition.* Champaign, IL: Human Kinetics.

Vickery, S. R., K. J. Cureton and M. A Collins. 1988. Prediction of body density from skinfolds in black and white young men. *Human Biology* 60:135–149.

Whitaker, R. C. et al. 1997. Predicting obesity in young adulthood from childhood and parental obesity. *The New England Journal of Medicine* 337(13):869–873.

Wilmore, J. H. 1969. A simplified method for determination of residual lung volumes. *Journal of Applied Physiology* 27:96–100.

Wilmore, J. H. and A. R. Behnke. 1969. An anthropometric estimation of body's density and lean body weight in young men. *Journal of Applied Physiology* 27:25–31.

Wilmore, J. H. and D. L. Costill. 1994. *Physiology of sport and exercise.* Champaign, IL.: Human Kinetics.

Young, C. M. 1964. Prediction of specific gravity and body fatness in older women. *Journal of American Dietetic Association* 45:333–338.

Young, C. M., M. Martin, and W. R. Tensuan. 1962. Predicting specific gravity and body fatness in young women. *Journal of American Dietetic Association* 40:102–107.

CHAPTER

Evaluating Youth Fitness

Contents

Key Words

AAHPERD Youth Fitness Test (YFT)
AAHPERD HRFT
aerobic fitness (circulatory-respiratory endurance)
body composition
Chrysler Fund-AAU test
distance-run tests
flexibility
health-related physical fitness
motor fitness
muscular endurance
muscular strength
President's Challenge test
Prudential FITNESSGRAM®
skinfold fat
speed
Texas Youth Fitness Test (FYT)

Objectives

One important goal of school physical education programs is to develop physical fitness. The two methods used to evaluate youth fitness are motor fitness tests and health-related fitness tests. Here we describe the historical shift in youth fitness testing. The first youth fitness tests were motor fitness tests that placed emphasis on athletic excellence. The athletic fitness orientation has been replaced with health-related tests that reflect a public health concern. The public health information in Chapter 1 provides the academic foundation for the move from an athletic orientation to one with emphasis on health promotion. Presently, there are three national youth fitness tests: (1) Prudential FITNESSGRAM®; (2) Chrysler Fund-AAU; and (3) President's Challenge. These three programs are described, compared, and evaluated. After reading Chapter 10, you should be able to:

1. Identify the general tests that compose a motor fitness battery.
2. Identify the general tests that compose a health-related battery.
3. Differentiate between motor fitness and health-related fitness batteries.
4. Identify and evaluate the national health-related fitness batteries.
5. Understand how to administer the Prudential FITNESSGRAM® test battery to evaluate youth fitness.

Introduction

The concern for positive health extends to all ages. Periodic fitness testing emphasizes an active life-style to achieve and maintain low amounts of fat, high levels of aerobic fitness, and sufficient muscular strength, muscular endurance, and flexibility in the lower trunk and posterior thigh areas for healthy low-back function (AAHPERD 1980; AAHPERD 1984). In the past, physical fitness has been defined in broad terms, and tests have measured either an aspect of physiological function or selected aspects of motor performance. This type of test has been termed motor fitness and includes not only strength and endurance components, but also factors of speed, power, and agility (Clarke 1971). Motor fitness tests represent more potential for athletic excellence than fitness for health promotion. As the concept of physical fitness moved away from athletic participation toward health, the components changed to include cardiorespiratory function, body composition (leanness/fatness), strength, endurance, and low-back flexibility, traits shown by medical and exercise scientists to promote health and reduce the risk of disease.

In the text both motor fitness and health-related batteries are discussed. A review of these tests and health-related fitness programs provides you with an understanding of the essential difference between motor fitness and health-related fitness and of the programs available for use in the public schools.

Historical View of Youth Fitness Testing

Americans have always valued physical fitness. Sometimes a specific event has stimulated interest in promoting youth physical fitness. For example, early interest in physical fitness can be traced to the number of men who failed physical examinations for induction into the military during World War II. Even though most of the medical examination failures were not related to physical fitness, they still heightened the concern for youth fitness. In the middle 1950s, the publication of the Kraus and Hirschland study (1954) showed European children scored higher than American children on the Kraus-Weber minimum muscular fitness test. While the Kraus-Weber test was not a true fitness test, it was the motivating force behind our first national youth fitness test, the AAHPERD Youth Fitness Test (1958). The most recent event motivating an emphasis on youth fitness is the growing body of medical research relating physical activity and obesity to health and degenerative diseases. This is discussed in Chapter 1. These historical events led to the development of youth fitness programs. In many educational settings, a physical fitness test battery is the program's major, and often only, component.

What Is Physical Fitness

In order to measure something, it must first be defined. While there has always been a general acceptance of the value of physical fitness, it is difficult to find a precise definition of physical fitness. This can be seen in one of the initial definitions of physical fitness advanced by the President's Council on Physical Fitness and Sports (Clarke 1971). Physical fitness was defined as:

> the ability to carry out daily tasks with vigor and alertness, without undue fatigue, and with ample energy to enjoy leisure time pursuits and to meet unforeseen emergencies. Thus, physical fitness is the ability to last, to bear up, to withstand stress, and to persevere under difficult circumstances where an unfit person would quit. It is the opposite to becoming fatigued from ordinary efforts, to lacking energy to enter zestfully into life's activities, and to becoming exhausted from unexpected, demanding physical exertion.
>
> The definition given implies that physical fitness is more than 'not being sick' or merely 'being well.' It is different from immunity to disease. It is a positive quality, extending on a scale from death to abundant life. All living individuals, thus, have some degree of physical fitness, which is minimal in the severely ill and maximal in the highly trained athlete; it varies considerably in different people and in the same person from time to time.

This broad definition of physical fitness did not give test makers much direction. What has provided operational definitions of physical fitness has been the tests used to evaluate this elusive construct. The initial youth fitness tests placed an emphasis on athletic excellence, while the most current youth fitness tests focus on health. Provided next is a brief overview of this historical movement.

Motor Fitness

The initial physical fitness tests were what Clarke (1971) termed **motor fitness.** Six components composed motor fitness. Table 10.1 gives the motor fitness components and items commonly included on youth fitness tests to measure each component. The **AAHPERD Youth Fitness Test (YFT)** was the first national fitness test and was used extensively in the public schools. The original AAHPERD YFT was published in 1958 and revised in 1975 and 1976. The initial items of the AAHPERD YFT were:

1. 50-yard dash
2. Pull-ups (boys) and flexed-arm hang (girls)
3. Sit-ups (straight leg)
4. Shuttle run
5. Standing broad jump
6. Softball throw for distance
7. 600-yard run/walk

The AAHPERD YFT was developed by a group of physical educators who met and selected tests based on logic; it was not developed through test validation research.

Table 10.1 Motor Fitness Components and Common Youth Fitness Test Items.

Component	Common Test Item
Muscular strength	Pull-ups Flexed-arm hangs Push-ups
Muscular endurance	Bent-knee sit-up
Circulatory-respiratory endurance	600-yard run
Muscular power	Standing long jump
Agility	Shuttle run test
Speed	50-yard dash

The running, jumping, and throwing test items were included in the original battery to encourage athletic excellence. This has led some to refer to these types of tests as "athletic fitness" rather than "motor" or "physical fitness."

Health-Related Physical Fitness

The development of **health-related physical fitness** tests represented a major shift away from an athletic emphasis to promoting health. These tests were developed in response to both the growing dissatisfaction with traditional motor fitness batteries and the growing body of evidence supporting the value of regular, vigorous exercise for health promotion. In 1975 a group of exercise physiologists and measurement specialists met at Indiana University to discuss the growing medical evidence supporting the role of fitness and physical activity on health. This meeting led to the development of the term "health-related fitness" and the publication of a position paper on the role of fitness in health (Jackson 1976). The position paper defined health-related fitness; criteria for test selection; and health-related fitness components. These are provided next.

> *Definition.* Physical fitness testing, and programs for development of fitness, should emphasize the relationship between health and physical activity. Physical fitness is a multifaceted continuum that is affected by physical activity. . . .
>
> *Criteria for Test Selection.* Since physical fitness can be operationally defined by the tests used for its evaluation, specific criteria were needed for choosing the tests. The criteria selected were as follows:
>
> 1. A physical fitness test should measure an area which extends from severely limited dysfunction to high levels of functional capacity.
> 2. It should measure capacities that can be improved with appropriate physical activity.
> 3. It should accurately reflect an individual's physical fitness status as well as changes in functional capacity by corresponding test scores and changes in these scores.
>
> *Health-Related Components.* The areas of physiological function which are related to positive health, are a national concern, and appear to meet the above criteria are:
>
> 1. Cardiorespiratory function
> 2. Body composition (leanness/fatness)
> 3. Abdominal and low back/hamstring musculoskeletal function.

Table 10.2 provides a historical summary of health-related fitness tests. These tests are the basis of the current youth fitness tests presented at the end of this chapter. Listed are the test items and comments relating to each test.

Table 10.2 Health-Related Fitness Tests That Led to the Development of Contemporary Tests

Test	Test Items	Comments
Texas Youth Fitness Test (1973)	***Physical Fitness Components*** 1. Pull-ups, dips, and flexed-arm hang 2. Bent-leg sit-ups (2 min). 3. 1.5 mile- and 12-minute run/walk for distance (grades 7–12); 9-minute run/walk for time, 1-mile run/walk for time (grades 4 to 6). ***Motor Ability Components*** 1. 50-yard timed sprint 2. Shuttle run 3. Standing long jump	1. Split test items into physical fitness and motor ability (athletic) components 2. First test to use distance-run tests longer than 600 yards 3. Provided award for just the fitness components 4. Was a motivating influence on developing the health-related movement
South Carolina Test (Pate 1978)	1. Cardiorespiratory function: 1-mile run/walk or 9-minute run for distance 2. Body composition: the sum of triceps and abdominal skinfolds 3. Abdominal and low-back musculoskeletal function: bent-knee sit ups in 1 minute, and sit-and-reach	1. Followed guidelines of the health-related position paper 2. Used criterion-referenced standards
Manitoba Physical Performance Test (1977)	1. Cardiovascular endurance: 800-meter run (ages 5–9); 1600-meter run (ages 10–12); 2400-meter run (ages 13–60) 2. Flexibility: sit-and-reach 3. Muscular endurance: 1-minute speed bent-knee sit-ups and flexed-arm hang 4. Body composition: percentage fat estimated from biceps, triceps, subscapular, and suprailium skinfolds	1. Developed by the Manitoba (Canada) Department of Education (1977) for boys and girls ages 5 to 19 2. Broadened the geographic scope of the health-related fitness movement
AAHPERD HRFT (1980, 1984)	1. Cardiorespiratory function: 1-mile run/walk or 9-minute run for all students. The Texas 1.5-mile- or 12-minute-run/walk tests are optional for students 13 years or older 2. Body composition (leanness/fatness): sum of triceps and subscapular skinfolds or triceps skinfold if only one site is used 3. Abdominal and low-back/hamstring musculoskeletal function. Modified, timed (60 sec), bent-knee sit-ups and sit-and-reach tests	1. Developed by a joint committee representing the Measurement and Evaluation, Physical Fitness, and Research Councils of AAHPERD 2. First national health-related fitness test, but did not develop into a popular test 3. Included not only test items and norms, but also information on the general principles of exercise prescription
Fit Youth Today (1986)	1. 20-minute steady state run 2. Bent-knee curl-up 3. Sit-and-reach 4. Body composition percent body fat estimated from the sum of triceps and medical calf skinfolds	1. Used criterion-referenced norms 2. Endorsed by the ACSM 3. The FYT curriculum emphasized student understanding of key health-related fitness concepts
Physical Best	1. 1-mile run/walk 2. Body composition by skinfolds and optional body mass index 3. Sit-and-reach 4. Bent-knee sit-ups 5. Pull-ups	1. National test program with good educational component and award system 2. Did not prove to be successful and merged with the FITNESSGRAM® in January, 1994

Common Health-Related Fitness Test Items

The move from a motor or athletic fitness emphasis has resulted in a common group of health-related fitness test items. They include distance runs, body composition, pull-ups, flexed-arm hangs, sit-ups, and low-back flexibility. Included in this section are the test procedures for these common fitness tests. Chapter 9 gives the methods used to measure body composition in children and youth, but the special considerations for measuring children are restated in this section.

The current trend in national health-related fitness tests is to use criterion-referenced, rather than norm-referenced, standards. The purpose of criterion-referenced norms is to define the level of fitness needed for health promotion. The "roots" of criterion-referenced standards come from normative standards. Also provided with these tests are the national norms published by the National Children and Youth Fitness Studies (NCYFS) I and II. These norms are a representative sample of children in the United States (Ross 1985; Ross 1987).

Distance-Run Tests

All health-related youth fitness test batteries include **distance-run tests** to measure **aerobic fitness.** The AAHPERD YFT (1976) included the 600-yard run as a test of endurance. However, exercise physiologists maintain that 600 yards is more anaerobic than aerobic (Balke 1963). The distance-run tests of health-related batteries are 1 mile or longer. Provided next is the evidence supporting the validity of distance-run tests, test methods, and normative data.

Validity of Distance-Run Tests. Cooper (1968), whose study intensified efforts to establish the concurrent validity of distance runs, reported a correlation of 0.90 between $\dot{V}O_2$ Max and the distance covered during a 12-minute run/walk. Factor analysis studies have shown that distance runs normally measure two factors: (1) **speed,** represented in distances less than 440 yards; and (2) endurance, represented in longer distances 1 mile or longer (Burke 1976; Disch et al. 1975; Jackson & Coleman 1976). Intermediate distances (from 600 to 800 yards) have been found to measure both speed and endurance.

Distance-run tests have been shown to have moderate to high correlations with $\dot{V}O_2$ Max when the runs are 1 mile or longer and 9 minutes or more in duration. The concurrent validity coefficients for running tests involving youth are listed in Table 10.3. Prior to 1973, the longer distance runs were not considered acceptable tests for public school children, but now they are. As an additional guide for evaluating distance-run tests, the sample characteristics, distance-run test means, and standard deviations of samples of school-aged children are listed in Table 10.4.

Distance-Run Test Methods. Distance-run tests can be scored in two ways: the elapsed time to cover a distance (e.g., 1 mile); and the distance traveled in a specified time, usually 9 or 12 minutes. The 1-mile run has become the most popular distance-run test. A second unique test, the 20-minute steady state run, is also described.

Test. Maximal Distance-Run Test

Objective. To measure maximal aerobic fitness or $\dot{V}O_2$ Max (see Chapter 8).

Validity and Reliability. The 1-mile and 9-minute runs are valid field tests of cardiorespiratory function and performance because they are related to $\dot{V}O_2$ Max, along

Table 10.3 Means and Standard Deviations of above $\dot{V}O_2$ Max and Concurrent Validity of Distance-Run Tests with Children and Youth

Source	Sample	Run	$\dot{V}O_2$ Max (ml/kg/min)		
			Mean	SD	r_{xy}
Cureton et al. (1995)	450 males, ages 8–25	1 mile	50.1	4.7	.68
	263 males, ages 8–25	1 mile	45.0	3.6	.64
Cureton et al. (1977)	140 boys, age 10	1 mile	48.0	6.7	.66
	56 girls, age 10	1 mile	45.5	5.9	.66
Doolittle and Bigbee (1968)	9 boys, grade 9	12 minutes	*	*	.90
Gutin et al. (1976)	15 boys and girls, age 11	1800 yards	47.5	5.8	.76
		1200 yards			.81
Gutin et al. (1976)	33 girls, age 11–12	1120 yards	37.0	5.9	.70
Jackson and Coleman (1976)	22 boys, grades 1–6	9 minutes	44.5	4.6	.82
		12 minutes			.82
	25 girls, grades 1–6	9 minutes	40.6	4.1	.71
		12 minutes			.71
Krahenbuhl et al. (1977)	20 boys, age 8	0.75 miles	47.6	7.1	.64
		1 mile			.71
	18 girls, age 8	0.75 miles	42.9	5.7	.22
		1 mile			.26
Muksud and Coutts (1971)	17 boys, age 11–14	12 minutes	47.4	4.0	.65
Vodak and Wilmore (1975)	69 boys, age 9–12	6 minutes	53.6	5.6	.50

* Value not published.

Table 10.4 Descriptive Statistics for Distance-Run Tests

Source	Sample	Run	Mean	Std Dev
Cooper et al. (1975)	778 boys and girls, grades 9–12	12-minute run/walk	2235*	475
			2640**	563
	437 boys and girls, grades 9–12	12-minute run/walk	2358*	510
			2340**	545
Doolittle et al. (1969)	100 girls, grades 9–10	12-minute run/walk	2202	***
	45 girls, grade 9	12-minute run/walk	2296	***
Gutin et al. (1976)	15 boys and girls, ages 10–12	12-minute run/walk	2320	400
Jackson and Coleman (1976)	25 boys, grades 1–6	12-minute run/walk	2560	314
	25 girls, grades 1–6	12-minute run/walk	2255	284
Maksud and Coutts (1971)	44 boys, ages 13–14	12-minute run/walk	2381	270
Texas Test (1973)	662 girls, grades 4–6	9-minute run/walk	1536	277
	556 boys, grades 4–6	9-minute run/walk	1778	355
	375 girls, grades 4–6	1-mile run/walk	10:09	1:54
	312 boys, grades 4–6	1-mile run/walk	8:54	1:59
	1397 girls, grades 7–12	12-minute run/walk	1862	357
	1234 boys, grades 7–12	12-minute run/walk	2543	428
	471 girls, grades 4–6	1.5-mile run/walk	16:11	2:36
	745 boys, grades 4–6	1.5-mile run/walk	11:29	1:44

*Pretest **Posttest ***Value not given

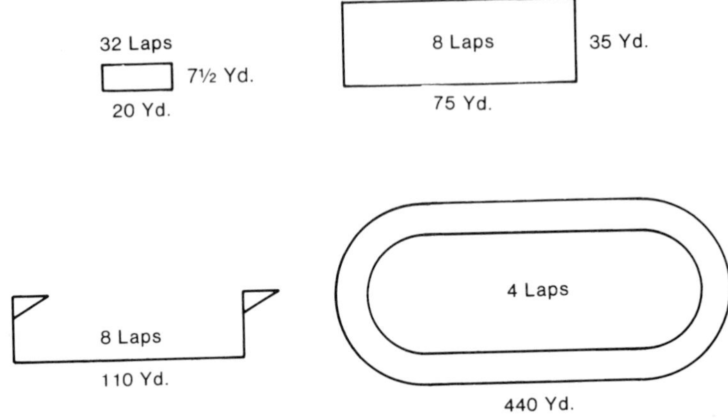

Figure 10.1 Test courses for administering the distance-run tests.

with other physiological parameters of cardiorespiratory function, and provide an index of the participant's ability to run distances. Also, the proposed runs give essentially the same information as those of longer distance. The 1.5-mile and 12-minute run alternatives are offered mainly because of their current widespread use. Distance runs have acceptable reliability when administered carefully to properly prepared students. The test user should note that other factors (body fatness, running efficiency, maturity, motivation) also affect distance-run time.

Equipment. The two distance-run tests can be administered on a 440-yard or 400-meter track, or on any other flat measured area (the 110-yard or 100-meter straightaway, other outside fields, an indoor-court area). Sample test courses are shown in Figure 10.1.

Procedures. Instruct students to run the distance as fast as possible. This should begin on the signal "Ready, Start!" As they cross the finish line, call out elapsed time to the participants (or their partners). Walking is allowed, but the objective is to cover the distance in the shortest possible time.

Scoring. The elapsed-time tests are scored to the nearest second; the distance-covered tests are scored in yards.

Norms. Tables 10.5 and 10.6 provide the NCYPS youth distance-run norms for males and females (Ross et al. 1987). The distance run for children ages 6 and 7 was 0.5 miles (Table 10.5), while the 1-mile run/walk was used for ages 8 to 18 years (Table 10.6).

Test. 20-Minute Steady State Run (FYT 1986)

Objective. To duplicate aerobic exercise level recommended by ACSM for fitness (ACSM 1990).

Validity and Reliability. The test has face validity in that it duplicates the level of aerobic exercise recommended to develop aerobic fitness.

Table 10.5 The 0.5-Mile NCYFS Distance-Run Norms for Boys and Girls (Min:Sec)

Percentile	Boys		Girls	
	Age 6	Age 7	Age 6	Age 7
90	4:27	4:11	4:46	4:32
75	4:52	4:33	5:13	4:54
50	5:23	5:00	5:44	5:25
25	5:58	5:35	6:14	6:01
10	6:40	6:20	6:51	6:38

Table 10.6 The 1-Mile NCYFS Distance-Run Norms for Boys and Girls (Min:Sec)

Age	Males, Percentile					Females, Percentile				
	P10	P25	P50	P75	P90	P10	P25	P50	P75	P90
8	14:05	12:14	10:39	9:29	8:46	14:48	12:59	11:32	10:23	9:39
9	13:37	11:44	10:10	9:00	8:10	14:31	12:45	11:13	9:50	9:08
10	12:27	11:00	9:52	8:48	8:13	14:20	12:52	11:14	10:09	9:09
11	12:07	10:32	9:03	8:02	7:25	14:35	12:54	11:15	9:59	8:45
12	11:48	10:13	9:03	8:02	7:25	14:07	12:33	10:58	9:52	8:34
13	10:39	9:06	8:04	7:14	6:48	13:45	12:17	10:52	9:30	8:27
14	10:34	9:10	7:51	7:08	6:27	13:13	11:49	10:32	9:16	8:11
15	10:13	8:30	7:30	6:52	6:23	14:07	12:18	10:46	9:28	8:23
16	9:36	8:18	7:27	6:39	6:13	13:42	12:10	10:34	9:25	8:28
17	10:43	8:37	7:31	6:40	6:08	13:46	12:03	13:34	9:26	8:20
18	10:50	8:34	7:35	6:42	6:10	15:18	12:14	10:51	9:31	8:22

Equipment. Same test course used for traditional distance-run tests.

Procedures. The 20-minute steady state run should not be administered to an untrained group. The test should be administered at the end of an aerobic fitness conditioning program of suitable length. Students must learn to pace themselves. The test involves simply running for 20 minutes on a level surface and then measuring the distance covered.

Scoring. The distance in miles covered in 20 minutes.

Norms. Table 10.7 provides the criterion-referenced norms suitable for health promotion.

Comment. The value of the 20-minute steady state run is that it duplicates the type of aerobic exercise recommended for health promotion. The test provides a sound educational example. The test communicates to students the goal of an aerobic exercise program.

Table 10.7 Criterion-Referenced Standards in Miles Traveled for Males and Females for the Texas FYT 20-Minute Steady State Run

Grade Level	Males	Females
4	1.8	1.6
5	2.0	1.8
6	2.2	2.0
7–12	2.4	2.2

Table 10.8 NCYFS Norms for Sum of Triceps and Calf Skinfolds for Boys and Girls (mm)

Percentile	Boys				Girls			
	6	7	8	9	6	7	8	9
90	12	12	12	12	15	15	15	16
75	14	14	14	15	18	18	19	20
50	16	17	18	21	21	22	24	26
25	20	22	24	28	27	28	33	35
10	27	32	37	40	33	37	43	45

Body Composition

Statistics show that the prevalence of overweight of youth is a major public health problem. Not only is the prevalence of youth obesity going up (Kuczmarski 1994), obese children become obese adults (Whitaker 1997). The inclusion of the skinfold test in youth fitness batteries has been controversial. Many parents and physical education teachers do not feel that skinfolds should be used to test youth. Extreme care and sensitivity needs to be practiced when measuring **skinfold fat** of school-aged children. While the testing procedures are fully outlined in Chapter 9, we would like to emphasize the following issues when testing children.

1. The triceps, subscapula, and calf are the recommended sites for children. We recommend the use of triceps and calf skinfold because clothing does not need to be removed. Measuring the subscapular skinfold of a female requires raising the shirt in back for access to the skinfold site. This can be embarrassing for some students.
2. It is best to have a female teacher test female students.
3. Skinfold measurements should always be measured in a private setting.
4. If the student or parent objects to the skinfold test, the BMI may be used.

Chapter 9 provides a detailed discussion of the validity of skinfold measurements for evaluating body composition of youth. Skinfold regression equations for estimating percent body fat from the sum of calf and triceps skinfolds are provided in Chapter 9. Lohman (1992) provides equations for the sum of triceps and subscapula sites. Table 10.8 provides the NCYFS norms for ages 6 to 9 for the sum of triceps and calf skinfolds. Table 10.9 provides the NCYFS sum of triceps and subscapular skinfolds for ages 10 to 18.

Table 10.9 NCYFS Norms for Sum of Triceps and Subscapular Skinfolds for Boys and Girls (mm)

Age	Males, Percentile					Females, Percentile				
	P10	P25	P50	P75	P90	P10	P25	P50	P75	P90
10	35	24	17	14	12	26	27	20	16	13
11	36	25	18	14	12	40	30	21	17	14
12	38	24	17	14	12	40	29	22	18	15
13	34	23	17	13	11	43	31	24	19	15
14	33	22	17	13	12	40	33	26	20	17
15	32	22	17	14	12	43	34	28	23	19
16	30	22	17	14	12	42	33	26	22	19
17	30	22	17	14	13	42	36	28	23	20
18	30	24	18	15	23	42	34	27	22	19

Common Endurance and Flexibility Test Items

Sit-up, pull-up, flexed-arm hang, and sit-and-reach tests are items common to health-related fitness batteries. Provided next are test procedures and normative standards for these tests.

Pull-Up Test. The pull-up test has been a test commonly used with males, but it also has been used with females. The NCYFS obtained pull-up normative test data on both boys and girls. The test procedures and NCYFS pull-up norms are provided next.

Equipment. A horizontal bar positioned at a height that allows the student to hang without touching the ground.

Procedure. The bar should be adjusted to a height that allows the student to hang free from the floor. From the hanging position with an overhand grip (palms forward), the body is pulled upward until the chin rests over the bar and then lowered until the arms are straight. This movement should be repeated to exhaustion. The student is not allowed to kick, jerk, or use a "kip" movement. The Chrysler Fund-AAU test allows the student to use either handhold, palms forward or backward.

Scoring. The student's score is the number of correctly executed chins. Table 10.10 provides the NCYFS norms for males and females, ages 10 to 18.

Flexed-Arm Hang Test. Table 10.10 shows that the pull-up test is a difficult test for girls. Many girls cannot complete one pull-up. The flexed-arm hang test is an easier test and was the test used in the AAHPERD YFT (1976). Provided in this section are the test methods and AAHPERD normative standards.

Equipment. A horizontal bar positioned at a height that allows the student to hang without touching the ground, and a stopwatch.

Procedure. The student uses the overhand grasp (palms forward). With the assistance of two spotters, one in front and one behind, the pupil raises the body off the

Table 10.10 NCYFS Norms for Pull-ups for Boys and Girls (Number Completed)

Age	Males, Percentile					Females, Percentile				
	P10	P25	P50	P75	P90	P10	P25	P50	P75	P90
10	0	0	1	4	8	0	0	0	1	3
11	0	0	2	5	8	0	0	0	1	3
12	0	0	3	5	8	0	0	0	1	3
13	0	1	4	7	10	0	0	0	1	2
14	0	2	5	8	12	0	0	0	1	2
15	1	4	7	10	14	0	0	0	1	2
16	2	6	9	12	14	0	0	0	1	2
17	2	5	9	12	15	0	0	0	1	2
18	3	6	10	13	16	0	0	0	1	2

Table 10.11 Percentile Rank Norms for Girls on the AAHPER Flexed-Arm Hang Test (in Sec)

Percentile	Age in Years							
	9–10	11	12	13	14	15	16	17+
95	42	39	33	34	35	36	31	34
75	18	20	18	16	21	18	15	17
50	9	10	9	8	9	9	7	8
25	3	3	3	3	3	4	3	3
5	0	0	0	0	0	0	0	0

floor to a position where the chin is above the bar, the elbows are flexed, and the chest is close to the bar. Start the stopwatch when the student reaches the hanging position. Stop the watch when (1) the student's chin touches the bar; (2) the student's head tilts backward to keep the chin above the bar; or (3) the student's chin falls below the level of the bar. The Chrysler-AAU test allows the student to use either handhold, palms forward or backward.

Scoring. The score is the number of seconds measured to the nearest second that the student maintained the hanging position. Selected AAHPERD norms are listed in Table 10.11.

Bent-Knee Sit-Ups. A sit-up test is a common test in youth fitness batteries. The test procedures and NCYFS norms are provided next.

Objective. To evaluate abdominal muscular strength and endurance.

Validity and Reliability. You can improve the validity and reliability of the test by giving students sufficient instruction and practice in the correct sit-up procedure before testing. The validity of the sit-up test has been determined logically. Studies show that abdominal muscles are being used in the performance of a sit-up. The re-

Table 10.12 NCYFS Norms for 1-Minute Bent-Knee Sit-Ups for Boys and Girls (Number Completed)

Age	Males, Percentile					Females, Percentile				
	P10	P25	P50	P75	P90	P10	P25	P50	P75	P90
6	9	14	19	24	28	6	14	18	23	28
7	12	18	23	28	32	11	16	21	27	33
8	15	20	26	30	35	13	19	25	29	34
9	16	23	28	33	39	15	21	26	31	36
10	22	28	34	40	47	20	25	31	37	43
11	22	30	36	41	48	20	26	32	37	42
12	25	32	38	44	50	21	28	33	40	46
13	28	32	40	46	52	21	27	33	40	46
14	30	35	41	47	52	23	29	35	41	47
15	31	36	42	48	53	24	30	35	40	45
16	32	38	43	49	55	23	30	35	40	49
17	31	37	43	50	56	24	30	36	40	47
18	31	36	43	50	54	24	30	35	40	47

liability of the test has been satisfactory, with test-retest reliability coefficients ranging from 0.68 to 0.94.

Equipment. Use mats or other comfortable surfaces for the students. A stopwatch, or watch or clock with a sweep second hand, can be used for timing.

Procedure. To start, the student lies on the back with knees flexed and feet on the floor, heels 12 to 18 inches from the buttocks. Arms are crossed on the chest, with hands on opposite shoulders. The feet should be held down by a partner to keep them on the testing surface. The student, by tightening his or her abdominal muscles, curls to the sitting position, touching elbows to thighs. Arms must remain on the chest, as should the chin. To complete the sit-up, the student returns to the down position until the midback touches the testing surface.

The timer gives the signal "Ready, Start!" The student starts on the word "Go" and must stop on the word "Stop." The student should know before the test begins that resting between sit-ups is allowed but that the objective is to perform as many correctly executed sit-ups as possible in a 60-second period.

Scoring. Record the number of correctly executed sit-ups completed in 60 seconds. Table 10.12 provides the NCYFS norms for the sit-up test.

Sit-and-Reach. The sit-and-reach test was not commonly used with motor or athletic fitness test batteries, but is an item of most health-related fitness tests. Provided next are the test procedures and NCYFS norms.

Objective. To evaluate the flexibility of the lower back and posterior thighs.

Validity and Reliability. You can improve the validity and reliability of the test by giving students sufficient instruction and warm-up. Warm-up should include slow,

Table 10.13 NCYFS Norms for Sit-and-Reach for Boys and Girls (Inches)

Age	Males, Percentile					Females, Percentile				
	P10	P25	P50	P75	P90	P10	P25	P50	P75	P90
6	10.5	12.0	13.5	15.0	16.0	11.5	12.5	14.0	15.5	16.5
7	10.0	11.5	13.5	15.0	16.0	11.5	13.0	14.5	16.0	17.0
8	9.5	11.5	13.5	14.5	16.0	11.0	12.5	14.0	17.0	16.0
9	9.5	11.0	13.0	14.5	15.5	11.0	12.5	14.0	16.0	17.0
10	10.0	11.5	13.5	14.5	16.0	10.5	13.0	14.5	16.5	17.5
11	9.5	11.5	13.0	15.0	16.5	11.5	13.0	15.0	16.5	18.0
12	8.5	11.0	13.0	15.0	16.0	12.0	14.0	15.5	17.0	19.0
13	9.0	11.0	13.0	15.0	16.5	12.0	14.0	16.0	18.0	20.0
14	9.0	11.0	13.5	15.5	17.5	12.5	15.0	17.0	18.5	19.5
15	9.5	12.0	14.0	16.5	18.0	13.5	15.5	17.0	19.0	20.0
16	10.0	13.0	15.0	17.0	19.0	14.0	16.0	17.5	19.0	20.5
17	10.5	13.0	15.5	17.5	19.5	13.5	15.5	18.0	19.0	20.5
18	10.0	13.0	15.0	17.5	19.5	13.0	15.5	17.5	19.0	20.5

sustained, static stretching of the lower back and posterior thighs. The test has been validated against several other flexibility tests. The validity coefficients have ranged between 0.80 and 0.90. The test also has logical validity in that a student must have good flexibility in the lower back, hips, and posterior thighs to score well. Reliability coefficients for this test have been high, ranging above 0.70.

Equipment. The test apparatus has a specially constructed box (12″ × 12″ × 2″) with a measuring scale. The test can be scored in inches or centimeters. When scored in inches, the measuring scale is 12 inches at the level of the feet. When scored in centimeters, the scale is 23 centimeters at the level of the feet.

Procedure. To start, have the student remove his or her shoes and sit at the test apparatus with knees fully extended and feet shoulder-width apart. The feet should be flat against the end board. To perform the test, the student extends the arms forward, with hands placed on top of each other. The pupil reaches directly forward, palms down, along the measuring scale four times, and holds the position of maximum reach on the fourth trial. This position must be held for 1 second.

Scoring. The score is the farthest point reached, measured to the nearest inch or centimeter, on the fourth trial. The administrator should remain close to the scale and note the most distant line touched by the fingertips of both hands. If the hands reach unevenly, administer the test again.

Norms. Table 10.13 provides the NCYFS youth sit-and-reach norms for the test scored in inches.

Other Considerations. Repeat the test trial if (1) the student's hands reach out unevenly or (2) the knees are flexed during the trial. You can prevent the knees from flexing by keeping your hand, or a monitor's hand, lightly on the knees. To prevent

Table 10.14 National Youth Fitness Test Batteries Contrasted by Fitness Component and Test Item

Fitness Component	President's Challenge	Chrysler Fund-AAU	Prudential FITNESSGRAM®
Aerobic Fitness	1-mile run Endurance shuttle run	1-mile run	1-mile run The PACER
Body Composition	None	None	Skinfolds or body mass index
Strength and Endurance Components			
Abdominal	Sit-ups	Sit-ups	Curl-up
Upper Body	Pull-ups Flexed-arm hang	Pull-ups Flexed-arm hang Isometric push-up	Push-up Pull-ups Flexed-arm hang Modified pull-up
Trunk and Lower Body	None	Isometric leg squat	Trunk lift
Flexibility	Sit-and-reach V-sit	V-sit	Back saver sit-and-reach Shoulder stretch
Motor Fitness Components	Shuttle run	Shuttle run 50–100 yard run Standing long jump	None

the apparatus from sliding away from the student, place it against a wall or a similar immovable object.

National Health-Related Youth Fitness Tests

In the early stages of development, youth fitness programs consisted of just a test battery. The public school fitness programs consisted of just testing students. The **Texas Youth Fitness Test (FYT)** and **AAHPERD Health-Related Fitness Test (HRFT)** programs changed this by developing educational programs that integrated a health and fitness curriculum with testing. In 1993, there were four national youth fitness tests for use in the public schools. These were: (1) AAHPERD's Physical Best; (2) Prudential FITNESSGRAM[1]; (3) **President's Challenge**[2]; and (4) **Chrysler Fund-AAU**[3].

The test items of AAHPERD's Physical Best and the Prudential FITNESSGRAM® were nearly identical. In January 1994, AAHPERD adopted the popular Prudential FITNESSGRAM® in an effort to help create a single youth fitness program for all of the nation's schools. Provided next is a comparison of these tests and standards. The final section is a comprehensive review of the Prudential FITNESSGRAM®. This popular test has a solid public health foundation and has been administered to millions of youth.

Comparison of Test Items

Table 10.14 lists the fitness components and items of the three national tests. All three programs use the 1-mile run/walk to evaluate aerobic fitness. The pull-up and flexed-

[1]The Prudential FITNESSGRAM, Cooper Institute for Aerobic Research, 12330 Preston Road, Dallas, TX 75230. (214) 701-8001.

[2]For information on this test write to President's Challenge, Poplars Research Center, 400 East 7th Street, Bloomington, IN 47405.

[3]The Chrysler Fund-Amateur Athletic Union Physical Fitness Program, 400 E. 7th Street, Poplars Room 711, Bloomington, IN 47405. Phone 1 800 258-5497.

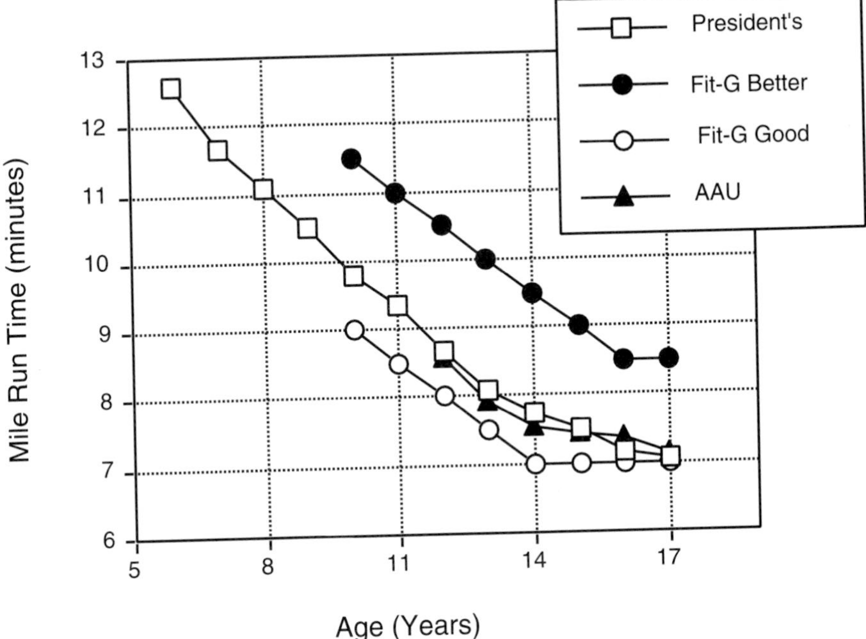

Figure 10.2
National youth fitness test mile-run criterion-referenced standards for boys. The Prudential FITNESSGRAM® provides two standards, "Good" and "Better." The "Good" standard represents the level of aerobic fitness needed for health promotion. (Source: CSI Software Company, Houston, TX. Reprinted by permission.)

arm hang are common to all batteries. Two of the programs include the same bent-knee sit-up test to evaluate abdominal strength and endurance, while the Prudential FITNESSGRAM® changed to the curl-up test that places less strain on the back.

A major difference among the programs is the inclusion of body composition and use of motor fitness items. The President's Challenge and Chrysler Fund-AAU batteries do not include body composition items, but do include one motor fitness test item. The Prudential FITNESSGRAM® program does not have a motor fitness item, but includes body composition items.

Comparison of Criterion-Referenced Standards

All programs provide criterion standards for evaluating health-related fitness levels. It is not possible to compare performance standards across the four batteries because each includes different test items. The 1-mile run/walk is an important health-related item of all four tests. Figures 10.2 and 10.3 graphically compare the criterion-referenced standard of each test for the 1-mile run/walk for boys and girls. While the President's Challenge and Chrysler Fund-AAU batteries include just one criterion-referenced standard, The Prudential FITNESSGRAM® test includes two standards. "Good" is the minimal standard, while "better" would be considered more desirable. The boy's Prudential FITNESSGRAM® "good" standard is considerably less demanding than either the President's Challenge and Chrysler Fund-AAU standards, while the "better" standard is similar to the standards of the President's Challenge and Chrysler Fund-AAU. The Prudential FITNESSGRAM® "better" and President's Challenge standards for girls are similar, while the Chrysler Fund-AAU girl's standard is much more demanding. The girl's Prudential FITNESSGRAM® "good" standard is the least demanding of all standards.

Which standard is the most appropriate? The Prudential FITNESSGRAM® "good" criterion-referenced standard most closely represents a minimal health-related

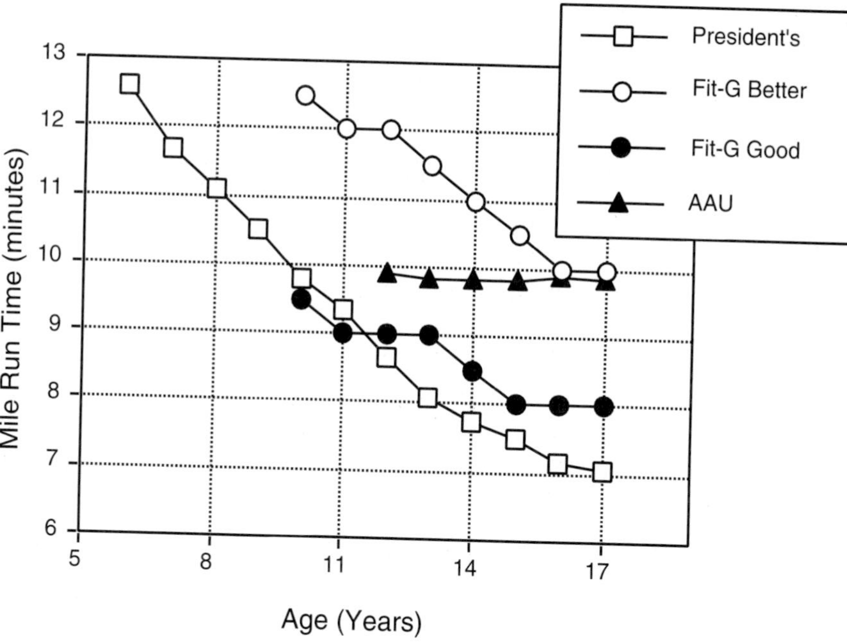

Figure 10.3
National youth fitness test mile run criterion-referenced standards for girls. The Prudential FITNESSGRAM® provides two standards, "Good" and "Better." The "Good" standard represents the level of aerobic fitness needed for health promotion. (Source: CSI Software Company, Houston, TX. Reprinted by permission.)

criterion-referenced standard. Cureton and Warren (1990) give a detailed discussion of the process followed to develop the Prudential FITNESSGRAM® "good" standard. They make convincing arguments based on scientific evidence that the President's Challenge and Chrysler Fund-AAU standards exceed the aerobic fitness level needed for health promotion. Blair and associates (1989) showed that once a moderate level of aerobic fitness was reached, becoming more aerobically fit did not enhance health. The Prudential FITNESSGRAM®'s "good" youth aerobic-fitness standards are consistent with the adult health-promotion standards provided in Chapter 8. "Better" in the Prudential FITNESSGRAM® and the Chrysler Fund-AAU and President's criterion standards are more demanding mainly because they were derived largely from normative data rather than health-promotion standards.

Prudential FITNESSGRAM®

The most comprehensive and academically sound health-related fitness program is the **Prudential FITNESSGRAM®**. This program was developed by a team of professionals working with personnel from the Institute for Aerobics Research of the Cooper Clinic (1992). The program is sponsored by the Prudential Insurance Company of America and has been consistently revised in light of new scientific evidence.

This popular test is a comprehensive youth fitness program that includes an excellent health-related fitness test with sound criterion-referenced standards and well-developed educational materials, as well as having the best computerized reporting system. The program is designed not only to enhance physical fitness, but also to develop affective, cognitive, and behavioral components that enhance participation in regular physical activity.

Criterion-Referenced Standards

The goal of the criterion-referenced standard is to define a level of fitness suitable for health promotion. The Prudential FITNESSGRAM® program provides standards for "upper and lower" limits of healthy fitness. Figure 10.4 provides an example of the computer output used to score the test and shows the "healthy fitness zone." The computer scoring system is an important aspect of the Prudential FITNESSGRAM®. It clearly communicates a student's fitness status. The lower level ("good") reflects a "minimally acceptable level of health," and the upper standard ("better") represents a level designed to motivate students and provide them a fitness challenge.

With proper exercise, all students should be able to achieve the "good" level. The "Health Fitness Level" was developed with the use of best available public health and exercise physiology data. Cureton and Warren (1990) provide an excellent discussion of the methods used to develop the aerobic capacity healthy fitness zone. Tables 10.15 and 10.16 show the "good" and "better" levels for the recommended tests for boys and girls, respectively.

Test Items

Next is a brief presentation of the test items of the Prudential FITNESSGRAM®. The tests measure three components: (1) aerobic capacity; (2) **muscular strength, muscular endurance,** and **flexibility;** and (3) body composition. There are five recommended tests and several tests that can be substituted. The default items of the computer software are:

1. 1-mile run/walk
2. Percent body fat from sum of triceps and calf skinfolds
3. Curl-ups
4. Trunk lift
5. Push-ups

Aerobic Capacity. Aerobic capacity may be evaluated in two ways. The recommended test is the 1-mile run/walk, while the pacer test is a recommended alternative test.

Test. 1-Mile Run/Walk

Description. The 1-mile-run/walk test can be used for all students, but performance standards have purposefully not been established for students in grades K–3. The goal for these young children is to complete the 1-mile distance at a comfortable pace.

Test Procedures. Follow the standard distance-run procedures previously presented in this chapter.

Scoring. Tables 10.15 and 10.16 list standards for the healthy fitness zone for the 1-mile run/walk.

The Pacer test is an optional test that is strongly recommended for participants in grades K–3. This Progressive Aerobic Cardiovascular Endurance Run (PACER) is a 10-meter shuttle run that becomes progressively more demanding. The pace is regulated with a tape recording. A time of 9 seconds is allowed to run the 20 meters during the first minute, and each minute the pace increases by reducing the 20-meter run time requirement by about a half second. This requires the student to increase exercise intensity at a systematic rate, which is the same physiological principle used to regulate the power output of treadmill and cycle ergometer tests (see Chapter 8).

The**Prudential** **FITNESS**GRAM®

COMMITTED TO HEALTH RELATED FITNESS

Jane Jogger
FITNESSGRAM Jr. High
FITNESSGRAM Test District

Instructor: Bridgman Gregg
Grade: 04 ***Period:*** 09 ***Age*** 09

Test Date	Height	Weight
MO - YR	FT - IN	LBS
10.92	5.00	101
05.93	5.01	106

AEROBIC CAPACITY

HEALTHY FITNESS ZONE — ***Current*** ***Past***

One Mile Walk/Run

Needs Improvement	Good	Better		min:sec	
10:00		07:30		9:01	9:12

Max VO₂ *Indicates ability to use oxygen. Expressed as ml of oxygen per kg body weight per minute. Healthy Fitness Zone = 35+ for girls & 42+ for boys.*

ml/kg	
47	47

MUSCLE STRENGTH, ENDURANCE & FLEXIBILITY

HEALTHY FITNESS ZONE

Curl-up (Abdominal)

Needs Improvement	Good	Better		# performed	
21		40		12	05

Push-up (Upper Body)

Needs Improvement	Good	Better		# performed	
12		25		27	20

Trunk Lift (Trunk Extension)

Needs Improvement	Good	Better		inches	
9		12		10	10

The test of flexibility is optional. If given, it is scored pass or fail and is performed on the right and left.
Test given: Back Saver Sit and Reach

Right P
Left P

BODY COMPOSITION

HEALTHY FITNESS ZONE

Percent Body Fat

Needs Improvement	Good	Better		% fat	
25.0		10.0		27.0	31.1

You can improve your abdominal strength with curl-ups 2 to 4 times a week. Remember your knees are bent and no one holds your feet.

Your upper body strength was very good. Try to maintain your fitness by doing strengthening activities at least 2 or 3 times each week.

To improve your body composition, Jane, extend the length of vigorous activity each day and follow a balanced nutritional program, eating more fruits and vegetables and fewer fats and sugars. Improving body composition may also help improve your other fitness scores.

Your aerobic capacity is in the Healthy Fitness Zone. Maintain your fitness by doing 20-30 minutes of vigorous activity at least 3 or 4 times each week.

To parent or guardian: *The Prudential FITNESSGRAM is a valuable tool in assessing a young person's fitness level. The area of the bar highlighted in yellow indicates the "healthy fitness zone." All children should strive to maintain levels of fitness within the "healthy fitness zone" or above. By maintaining a healthy fitness level for these areas of fitness your child may have a reduced risk for developing heart disease, obesity or low back pain. Some children may have personal interests that require higher levels of fitness (e.g. athletes).*

Recommended activities for improving fitness are based on each individual's test performance. Ask your child to demonstrate each test item for you. Some teachers may stop the test when performance equals the upper limit of the "healthy fitness zone" rather than requiring a maximal effort.

Developing good exercise habits is important to maintaining lifelong health. You can help your son or daughter develop these habits by encouraging regular participation in physical activitiy.

Developed by
The Cooper Institute
for Aerobics Research
Dallas, Texas

Sponsored by
The Prudential
Insurance Company
of America

Figure 10.4 Computer output for the Prudential FITNESSGRAM Health-related youth fitness program. The program is used by over 3 million students. (Courtesy of the Institute of Aerobic Research, Dallas, Texas.)

Table 10.15 The Health-Related Criterion-Referenced Standards for the Prudential FITNESSGRAM® for Boys

Age	1-Mile Run (min:sec)		Percent Fat		Curl-Ups (Number)		Trunk Lift (Inches)		Push-Ups (Number)	
	Good	Better	Good	Better	Good	Better	Good	Better	Good	Better
5			25	10	2	10	6	12	3	8
6	No time—		25	10	2	10	6	12	3	8
7	completion of		25	10	4	14	6	12	4	10
8	the run only		25	10	6	20	6	12	5	13
9			25	10	9	24	9	12	6	15
10	11:30	9:00	25	10	12	24	9	12	7	20
11	11:00	8:30	25	10	15	28	9	12	8	20
12	10:30	8:00	25	10	18	36	9	12	10	20
13	10:00	7:30	25	10	21	40	9	12	12	25
14	9:30	7:00	25	10	24	45	9	12	14	30
15	9:00	7:00	25	10	24	47	9	12	16	35
16	8:30	7:00	25	10	24	47	9	12	18	35
17	8:30	7:00	25	10	24	47	9	12	18	35
>17	8:30	7:00	25	10	24	47	9	12	18	35

Table 10.16 The Health-Related Criterion-Referenced Standards for the Prudential FITNESSGRAM® for Girls

Age	1-Mile Run (min:sec)		Percent Fat		Curl-Ups (Number)		Trunk Lift (Inches)		Push-Ups (Number)	
	Good	Better	Good	Better	Good	Better	Good	Better	Good	Better
5			32	17	2	10	6	12	3	8
6	No time—		32	17	2	10	6	12	3	8
7	Completion of		32	17	4	14	6	12	4	10
8	the run only		32	17	6	20	6	12	5	13
9			32	17	9	22	6	12	6	15
10	12:30	9:30	32	17	12	26	9	12	7	15
11	12:00	9:00	32	17	15	29	9	12	7	15
12	12:00	9:00	32	17	18	32	9	12	7	15
13	11:30	9:00	32	17	18	32	9	12	7	15
14	11:00	8:30	32	17	18	32	9	12	7	15
15	10:30	8:00	32	17	18	32	9	12	7	15
16	10:00	8:00	32	17	18	32	9	12	7	15
17	10:00	8:00	32	17	18	32	9	12	7	15
>17	10:00	8:00	32	17	18	32	9	12	7	15

Body Composition. **Body composition** can be measured by percent body fat estimated from the sum of triceps and calf skinfolds and body mass index. The equations developed by Lohman (1992) are used to estimate percent body fat. Chapter 9 gives the equations and test methods. Tables 10.15 and 10.16 lists the healthy fitness zone percent body fat standards. The body mass index (BMI) is an optional body composition test.

Muscle Strength, Endurance, and Flexibility. The Prudential FITNESSGRAM® includes common strength, endurance, and flexibility test items, with the exception that more care has been taken to standardize test procedures. This has been done by standardizing the cadence.

Test. Curl-Up

Description. This test replaces the sit-up test common to most motor and health-related test batteries. A completed curl is the initial phase of the sit-up and involves raising the head and shoulders off the mat. Music is provided to control the rate of exercise at 20 curl-ups per minute. The test is to maintain the exercise rate as long as possible or complete a maximum of 75 curl-ups.

Procedures. The cadence of the test is regulated with a tape recorder. The cadence is 1 curl-up every 3 seconds until a maximum of 75 is reached. A cardboard strip is used to regulate the curl-up. A 30″ × 3″ strip is used for children in grades K–4 and a 30″ × 4.5″ strip is used for older children. The student being tested lies in a supine position on a mat with the knees bent at about 140°. The arms are straight and parallel to the trunk with the palms resting on the mat. The cardboard strip is placed under the knees with the fingers touching the nearest edge. A completed repetition involves curling up so that the fingers slide to the other side of the strip. Another student should stand on the strip to prevent movement.

Scoring. The number of curl-ups completed at a rate of 1 repetition every 3 seconds. The student is stopped when 75 curl-ups are completed. Tables 10.15 and 10.16 provide the healthy fitness zone standards for the curl-up test.

Test. Trunk Lift

Description. The trunk-lift test measures the student's trunk extensor strength and flexibility. The test requires the student to lift their upper body to a maximum of 12 inches off the floor using the back muscles.

Procedures. The student starts the test lying face down on a mat with their hands under their thighs. The test involves lifting the upper body up to a maximum height of 12 inches. The student holds the position until the height of the lift can be measured with a ruler. The height is measured from the floor to the chin.

Scoring. Each student is given two trials. Their score is the height their chin is held off the floor. Their score is the highest reading measured to the nearest inch. Students are encouraged not to exceed 12 inches because excessive arching can cause compression of the discs in the back. Tables 10.15 and 10.16 provide the healthy fitness zone standards for the trunk-lift test.

Test. Push-Ups

Description. The test involves completing as many push-ups as possible at a set cadence of 1 push-up every 3 seconds.

Procedures. Students work in pairs, one taking the test while the other counts the number of completed push-ups. The test taker starts face down with hands under the shoulders and body straight. From this position, the student pushes their body up, while keeping the body straight, until the arms are straight. From this position, the student lowers their body, while keeping the body straight, until the arms bent to a 90° angle and the upper arms are parallel to the floor. Then, the student pushes up to the straight-arm position. This is repeated at a cadence of 20 repetitions per minute, 1 push-up every 3 seconds. The test is continued until the student cannot maintain the pace or demonstrates poor form.

Scoring. The number of push-ups completed at a rate of 1 repetition every 3 seconds. Tables 10.15 and 10.16 provide the healthy fitness zone standards for the push-up test.

Award Program

The Prudential FITNESSGRAM® award program is designed not only for recognition but for motivation. The philosophy of the program comes from three important concepts: (1) fitness is for a lifetime; (2) fitness is for everyone; and (3) fitness is fun and enjoyable. The program refers to its system as a "recognition" program rather than an "award" program because "awards often are perceived to be something that is 'given' rather than 'earned' and because awards may be perceived as something only a select few can receive" (1992, p. 55).

The Prudential FITNESSGRAM® recognition system is based on four sources of research evidence. First, to be effective, recognition must be based on achievement of goals that are challenging yet attainable. Second, if a recognition system is not based on goals that seem attainable, children and youth will not be motivated to try. Third, intrinsic motivation for any behavior, including exercise and physical fitness behaviors, must be based on continuous feedback of progress. Awards that are perceived as controlling rather than informative do not build intrinsic motivation. Finally, awards that are given to those with exceptionally high scores on fitness tests will often go to those who have the gift of exceptional heredity, early maturity, and to those already receiving many awards for their physical accomplishments.

The Prudential FITNESSGRAM® recognition system has several levels.

1. "It's Your Move." This is for students in grades K–6. To get this recognition award, students must perform the Prudential FITNESSGRAM® assessment and complete physical activities at home, at school, and with the community.
2. Behavior Recognition, "Get Fit" and "Fit for Life." These incentive programs are designed to recognize participants for any of the following activities: (1) completion of exercise log; (2) achievement of specific goals; and (3) fulfillment of contractual agreement.
3. Performance Recognition, "I'm Fit." The Prudential FITNESSGRAM® uses criterion-referenced standards that represent a level of fitness that offers a degree of protection against disease that results from sedentary living. Performance is judged by two general categories: needs improvement, and health fitness zone that ranges from "good" to "better." The FITNESSGRAM® computer printout (see Figure 10.4) shows this system. This incentive program recognizes participants in two ways: (1) achievement of health fitness zone on

five of six test items or on four of five test items; and (2) improvement in their performance on at least two test items.

Educational Program

The Prudential FITNESSGRAM® offers a sound educational program that integrates testing and a computer-generated student evaluation system with cognitive teaching materials. Figure 10.4 shows the Prudential FITNESSGRAM® computer output. The Prudential FITNESSGRAM® program adopted the educational materials developed for the AAHPERD Physical Best program. These teaching materials provide teachers with sound information designed to integrate exercise with important exercise physiology and exercise epidemiology concepts. The Prudential FITNESSGRAM® provides teachers with the capacity to teach American youth the value of exercise for health promotion. These materials and approach are consistent with the goals of *Healthy People 2000* provided in Chapter 1. Many medical scientists now view physical education as an important public health program.

Future Trends

The philosophy and performance standards of the Prudential FITNESSGRAM® are most consistent with the public health view articulated in the *Healthy People 2000* goals (1990). These are outlined in Chapter 1. The leadership in youth fitness testing reflected in the Prudential FITNESSGRAM® program is due to their advisory board and the capacity to initiate needed changes. The Prudential FITNESSGRAM® includes leading exercise epidemiologists, exercise physiologists, measurement specialists, psychologists, educators, and computer technologists. This group provides an important scientific thrust, and the program is located at a leading exercise research organization, the Cooper Institute for Aerobics Research. This close relationship gives the Prudential FITNESSGRAM® the capacity to put current scientific research into practice. Since AAHPERD dropped its Physical Best test, the Prudential FITNESSGRAM® has become the nation's youth health-related fitness program.

Summary

The evaluation of youth fitness has evolved from an emphasis on motor fitness to health-related fitness. Motor fitness tests include tests not only of strength and endurance but of speed, power, and agility. Motor fitness tests reflect an athletic orientation and endorse the philosophy of awarding the athletically gifted. With the growing body of medical evidence supporting the role of exercise, weight control, and aerobic fitness in health, the trend in youth fitness testing has shifted away from this athletic orientation to one of health promotion. The components of health-related batteries are aerobic fitness, body composition, muscular strength and endurance, and flexibility. There are three national health-related fitness batteries available. Compared to motor fitness tests, these national health-related tests have been expanded to include not only testing but educational materials that integrate the cognitive and affective components with the physiological aspects of health-related fitness. The Prudential FITNESSGRAM® is a true health-related program, while the President's Challenge and Chrysler Fund-AAU tests include motor fitness test items. The philosophy of fitness test award programs is moving from one that rewards only a high level of performance to one that encourages regular exercise designed to achieve fitness levels suitable for health promotion. Criterion-referenced standards are being refined to define the level of fitness needed for health.

Formative Evaluation of Objectives

Objective 1 Identify the general tests that compose a motor fitness battery.

1. The most popular motor fitness test is the AAHPERD YFT. List the tests that compose this battery.
2. What is the general nature of motor fitness test items?

Objective 2 Identify the general tests that compose a health-related battery.

1. What is the general nature of health-related fitness test items?
2. What are the test items of the four national health-related fitness test batteries?

Objective 3 Differentiate between motor fitness and health-related fitness batteries.

1. Motor fitness and health-related fitness batteries evolved from different philosophies of fitness. Explain these philosophies.
2. Health-related fitness tests can be used to teach students the value of exercise for health promotion. For what can motor fitness tests be used?
3. What is the major difference between the test items included on motor fitness batteries and health-related fitness batteries?

Objective 4 Identify and evaluate the national health-related fitness batteries.

1. List and describe the four national health-related youth fitness test batteries.
2. What is their difference in philosophy concerning performance standards and awards?

Objective 5 Understand how to administer the Prudential FITNESSGRAM® test battery to evaluate youth fitness.

1. Describe the test items of the Prudential FITNESSGRAM®.
2. Describe how you would evaluate the fitness of a person who has been tested with the Prudential FITNESSGRAM®.

Additional Learning Activities

1. Gain experience in youth fitness testing. Go to the public schools and help a teacher administer fitness tests.
2. Learn how to take skinfold measurements accurately. With one or more of your classmates, take triceps, subscapular, and calf skinfolds on a group of students. Compare your results with your classmates. If your scores do not agree, figure out what you are doing differently. Check the procedures and pictures in Chapter 9 to standardize your testing methods. Repeat the procedure and check your results again.
3. Order a health-related youth fitness test package. You will be surprised by how comprehensive they are.

Bibliography

AAHPER. 1976. *Youth fitness test manual.* Washington, DC.

AAHPERD. 1980. *Health related physical fitness manual.* Washington, DC.

AAHPERD. 1989. *Physical best: Instructor's guide.* Reston, VA.

AAHPERD. 1984. *Technical manual: Health related physical fitness.* Washington, DC.

AAU. 1992. *Chrysler fund-AAU physical fitness program 1992–93 testing packet.* Bloomington, IN.

ACSM. 1990. The recommended quantity and quality of exercise for developing and maintaining cardiorespiratory and muscular fitness in healthy adults. *Medicine and Science in Sports and Exercise* 22:265–274.

American Health and Fitness Foundation. 1986. *FYT program manual.* Austin, TX.

Balke, B. 1963. A simple field test for assessment of physical fitness. *Civil Aeromedical Research Institute Report:*63–66.

Blair, S. N. et al. 1989. Physical fitness and all-cause mortality: A prospective study of healthy men and women. *Journal of the American Medical Association* 262:2395–2401.

Burke, E. 1976. Validity of selected laboratory and field tests of physical working capacity. *Research Quarterly* 47:95–104.

Clarke, H. H. Ed. 1971. Basic understanding of physical fitness. In *Physical fitness research digest.* Washington, DC: President's Council on Physical Fitness and Sport.

Cooper, K. H. 1968. A means of assessing maximal oxygen intake. *Journal of the American Medical Association* 203:201–204.

Cureton, K. J. 1977. Determinants of distance running performance in children: Analysis of a path model. *Research Quarterly* 48:270–279.

Cureton, K. J. and G. L. Warren. 1990. Criterion-referenced standards for youth health-related fitness tests: A tutorial. *Research Quarterly for Exercise and Sport* 61:7–19.

Disch, J., R. Frankiewicz, and A. S. Jackson. 1975. Construct validation of distance run tests. *Research Quarterly* 46:169–176.

Doolittle, R. L. and R. Bigbee. 1968. The twelve-minute run-walk: A test of cardiorespiratory fitness of adolescent boys. *Research Quarterly* 39:491–495.

Gutin, B. et al. 1976. Relationship among submaximal heart rate, aerobic power, and running performance in children. *Research Quarterly* 47:536–539.

Jackson, A. S. et al. 1976. A position paper on physical fitness. Position paper of a joint committee representing the Measurement and Evaluation, Physical Fitness, and Research councils of the AAHPER. Washington, DC: AAHPER.

Jackson, A. S. and A. E. Coleman. 1976. Validation of distance run tests for elementary school children. *Research Quarterly* 47:86–94.

Krahenbuhl, G. et al. 1977. Field estimation of $\dot{V}O_2$ Max in children eight years of age. *Medicine and Science in Sports* 9:37–40.

Kraus, H. and R. P. Hirschland. 1954. Minimum muscular fitness test in school children. *Research Quarterly* 25:177–188.

Kuczmarski, R. J. et al. 1994. Increasing prevalence of overweight among US adults: The National Health and Nutrition Examination Surveys, 1960 to 1991. *Journal of the American Medical Association* 272:205–211.

Lohman, T. G. 1992. *Advances in body composition assessment.* Champaign, IL: Human Kinetics.

Maksud, M. G. and K. Coutts. 1971. Application of the Cooper twelve-minute run-walk test to young males. *Research Quarterly* 42:54–59.

Manitoba Department of Education. 1977. *Manitoba physical fitness performance test manual and fitness objectives.* Manitoba, Canada.

Pate, R. R. Ed. 1978. *South Carolina physical fitness test manual.* Columbia, SC: Governor's Council on Physical Fitness.

Prudential FITNESSGRAM *Test administration manual.* 1992. Dallas: The Cooper Institute for Aerobic Research.

Ross, J. et al. 1985. New standards for fitness measurement. *Journal of Physical Education Recreation and Dance* 56(1):62–66.

Ross, J. et al. 1987. New health-related fitness norms. *Journal of Physical Education Recreation and Dance* 58(9):66–71.

Ross, R. M. and A. S. Jackson. 1990. *Exercise concepts, calculations, and computer applications.* Carmel, IN: Benchmark Press.

Texas Governor's Commission on Physical Fitness. 1973. *Physical fitness-motor ability test.* Austin, TX.

U.S. Public Health Service. 1990. *Healthy people 2000: National health promotion and disease prevention objectives.* Washington, DC: U.S. Department of Health and Human Services.

Vodak, P. and J. H. Wilmore. 1975. Validity of the 6-minute jog-walk and 600-yard run-walk in estimating endurance capacity in boys, 9–12 Years of Age. *Research Quarterly* 46:230–234.

Whitaker, R. C. et al. 1997. Predicting obesity in young adulthood from childhood and parental obesity. *The New England Journal of Medicine* 337(13):869–873.

CHAPTER

Evaluating Elderly Aging and Adult Fitness

Contents

Key Words

cross-sectional method
functional adult fitness
longitudinal method
physically dependent
physically elite
physically fit
physically frail
physically independent

Objectives

With the aging of the American population, adult fitness is becoming an important priority. Public health research clearly documents that a sedentary life-style is a risk of all-cause mortality and many degenerative diseases. Not only is fitness an important determinate of health, it is also a key factor of "quality of life." An adequate level of fitness is needed for independent living for the elderly. Many elderly individuals do not have the level of fitness needed to live independently. As our elderly population grows, this will become more of a problem. The low fitness exhibited by many elderly Americans is due not just to aging but also to life-style. This chapter will help you understand the role of aging and life-style on fitness and health. The methods used to evaluate adult fitness are presented.

After reading Chapter 11 you should be able to:

1. Identify the methods used to study the decline in fitness associated with aging.
2. Understand the general age-related decline in health-related fitness.
3. Identify the types of tests used to evaluate adult fitness.
4. Identify the types of tests used to evaluate functional adult fitness.
5. Identify the computer programs available to use in adult fitness programs.

Aging and Fitness

By the year 2000, the American population will grow to 270 million, and the population as a whole will be older. In 1975, the median age for Americans was 29 years. In the year 2000, it will increase to 36 years (i.e., 50% of Americans will be 36 years or older). In 1950, only 8% of Americans were over age 65. By the year 2000, this will grow to 13% of the total American population, 35 million people. The period of greatest increase in the number of people 65 and older, of both sexes, will be from 2010 to 2020, when the "baby boomers" reach retirement age.

The segment labeled the "oldest old" is expanding rapidly. In 1890 only 3% of U.S. population was older than 80 years. This grew to 12.3% in 1988. The most dramatic increases in the number of people over 80 are projected to occur between 1990 and 2000. The number is expected to total 4.6 million by the year 2000 (U.S. Public Health Service 1990). One of the fastest growing age categories is the centenarians, those over 100 years of age. It is estimated that there are now 25,000 Americans who are over 100 years. It is projected that this number will grow to 100,000 by the year 2000 (Spirduso 1995).

Older Americans have more health problems and are more inactive. Over 40% of people over age 65 report no leisure-time physical activity. Less than one-third participate in regular moderate physical activity, such as walking and gardening, and less than 10% engage routinely in vigorous physical activity. In the National Health Interview Survey (Kovar 1986), nearly 40% of men and women over age 65 reported activity-dependent limitations. Data from the National Institute on Aging found that many adults over age 65 cannot perform common physical tasks (Cornoni-Huntley et al. 1986). Over half could not do heavy housework, and up to one-third could not walk a half-mile. Although some of this disability is due to chronic health problems such as arthritis, emphysema, and cardiovascular disease, it is also believed to be due, in part, to low levels of physical fitness.

Research Methods

To understand the effect of aging on fitness, a discussion of the research methods used to study aging is helpful. The two methods used to study the rate at which fitness declines with age are cross-sectional and longitudinal. A brief discussion of each follows.

Cross-Sectional Method. The **cross-sectional method** is used more than the longitudinal method because cross-sectional data are more readily available. All that is needed is a large sample of subjects who were tested once and vary greatly in age. For example, the Y's Way to Fitness test has a large normative database (n ≈ 20,000) of men and women who vary from age 18 to over age 65 (Golding, Meyers & Sinning 1989). This would be suitable for a cross-sectional study.

There are two general ways to examine the cross-sectional change in fitness with age. The first method is quite simply to plot a measure of central tendency (i.e., mean or median) with age. This provides a "graphic picture" of the general trend. A second method is to define the rate of decline. Regression is the statistical technique used to define the rate of decline. Typically, simple linear regression is used, but if the relationship is not linear, a nonlinear equation can be used. These statistical methods are presented in Chapter 2. The basic formula for a simple linear model is

Cross-Sectional Aging Equation **(11.1)**

$$Y = bX + a$$

where Y is the fitness variable, b is the regression weight, X is age, and a is the intercept of the simple linear regression equation. The regression weight (b) defines the cross-sectional, age-related rate of decline.

Figure 11.1 illustrates this method. Provided are data to define the cross-sectional rate at which $\dot{V}O_2$ Max declines with the age of women. The bivariate plot and the simple regression line define the change in the X variable, age, associated with the Y variable, measured $\dot{V}O_2$ Max ($ml \cdot kg^{-1} \cdot min^{1}$). These data come from a study (Jackson et al. 1996) designed to define the rate at which aerobic fitness of women declines with age. While regression equations are often used to predict one variable from another (e.g., estimate $\dot{V}O_2$ Max from mile-run time), the purpose of the regression

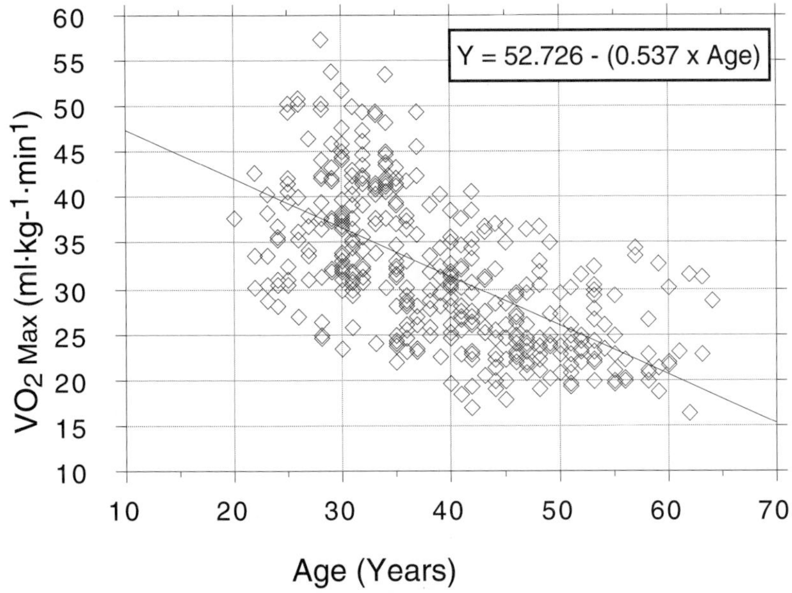

Figure 11.1
A bivariate plot showing the cross-sectional rate at which aerobic fitness of women declines with age. The graph was made from data from over 400 women, who were each tested just once. The graph was made from published data (Jackson et al. 1996). (Source: CSI Software Company, Houston, TX. Reprinted by permission.)

analysis in a cross-sectional aging study is to define the age-$\dot{V}O_2$ Max slope, or the rate at which aerobic fitness declines with age. The slope, in this context, is the regression weight (b). Figure 11.1 shows that the regression slope is -0.537. Based on these data the cross-sectional rate that the aerobic fitness of women declines with age was defined as 0.537 $ml \cdot kg^{-1} min^{-1} \cdot year^{-1}$.

While cross-sectional methods are often used to define the aging rate, the method suffers from at least two major problems. First, the sample is not completely representative of the total population. It is well known that mortality rates are related to age. As we age, our chances for survival decrease. The older subjects of cross-sectional samples tend to be the healthiest subjects of the sample. The least healthy do not live to the oldest age group. This is especially true for aerobic fitness, where low fitness levels increase the risk for all-cause mortality (Blair et al. 1989). A second problem is that cross-sectional slopes define the general trend, not the true aging effect. For example, it is well-known that life-style affects the rate at which aerobic fitness declines with age (Buskirk & Hodgson 1987; Jackson et al. 1995; Jackson et al. 1996). Cross-sectional methods can assess only age differences, not age changes (Spirduso 1995).

Longitudinal Method. The **Longitudinal method** is the other method used to examine the age-related change of fitness. This method is less used because two measures are needed over two periods of time. The objective is to evaluate age changes. The basic formula is

Longitudinal Aging Equation ***(11.2)***

$$\text{Rate of Decline} = \left(\frac{T1 - T2}{\text{Age } 2 - \text{Age } 1}\right)$$

where T2 is the variable measured at Age 2 and T1 is the variable measured at Age 1. This can easily be shown with published data (Jackson et al. 1996). The aerobic fitness of NASA female employees was measured on two occasions. The mean ages and levels of aerobic fitness were: T1, Age 1 = 44.1 years, $\dot{V}O_2$ Max = 30.1 ml/kg/min; and T2, Age 2 = 47.9 years, $\dot{V}O_2$ Max = 27.8 ml/kg/min. Using Formula 11.2, the longitudinal rate was defined as -0.34 ml/kg/min/year.

While the longitudinal method provides the actual rate at which the person declined with age, the method also has limitations. First, two measures at two different points in time are needed. This tends to be expensive and sometimes impossible to achieve. Second, while a longitudinal change reflects the actual change of the individual, the change is not likely the "true" aging rate. A summary of longitudinal aerobic fitness studies shows that age-related longitudinal changes in aerobic fitness ranged from no change to declines of nearly 1.5 ml/kg/min/year (Buskirk & Hodgson 1987). This large difference can be traced to both aging and life-style.

Defining the Age Decline of Fitness

Cross-sectional and longitudinal research clearly show that adult fitness declines with age. Provided next is a brief discussion of the trends associated with aerobic fitness, body composition, and strength. In the discussion of the YMCA adult fitness tests, additional cross-sectional changes are provided.

Aerobic Fitness. It is well established that the aerobic fitness of men and women declines with age. The Fick equation (McArdle, Katch, & Katch 1991; Taylor,

Buskirk & Henschel 1955; Taylor et al. 1963) provides the physiological logic for the aging effect associated with aerobic fitness. The Fick equation defines VO_2 Max as the product of three variables:

- ***Maximal heart rate.*** The rate that oxygenated blood is ejected from the heart per minute.
- ***Stroke volume.*** The volume of oxygenated blood that is ejected with each heart beat.
- ***Arterial-venous oxygen difference.*** The difference in the oxygen concentration between arterial blood (when it leaves the heart) and venous blood (when the blood returns to the heart). The arterial-venous oxygen difference represents the volume of oxygen extracted by the body to produce energy.

It is well established that maximum heart rate declines with age. If stroke volume and the arterial-venous components were unaffected, the decline in exercise heart rate would represent the age-related decline in aerobic fitness. Exercise habits have been shown to increase stroke volume and enhance the body's capacity to extract oxygen from the blood (Hagberg et al. 1985). The cross-sectional estimates of the age-related decline in aerobic fitness are consistently reported to be in the range of 0.4–0.5 $ml{\cdot}kg^{-1}min^{-1}{\cdot}year^{-1}$. In contrast, the longitudinal estimates are variable, ranging from 0.04 to 1.43 $ml{\cdot}kg^{-1}min^{-1}{\cdot}year^{-1}$ (Buskirk & Hodgson 1987). The results of two large studies (Jackson et al. 1995; Jackson et al. 1996) conducted with NASA/Johnson Space Center employees showed that the difference in results found with cross-sectional and longitudinal studies is largely due to life-style.

As men and women age, they not only put on fat weight and lose fat-free weight but also become less active. The NASA studies showed that about 50% of the cross-sectional decline in aerobic fitness associated with age was due to changes in percent body fat and exercise habits. Figure 11.2 shows the results of the study. Provided is the cross-sectional decline in VO_2 Max for men and women. The average rate of decline was 0.46 $ml{\cdot}kg^{-1}min^{-1}{\cdot}year^{-1}$ and 0.54 $ml{\cdot}kg^{-1}min^{-1}{\cdot}year^{-1}$, for men and women respectively. However, when percent body fat and self-report level of physical activity were statistically controlled, the rate of decline was cut nearly in half to 0.26 $ml{\cdot}kg^{-1}min^{-1}{\cdot}year^{-1}$. This means that if individuals do not change their percent body fat and exercise habits, the rate of decline can be expected to be 0.26 $ml{\cdot}kg^{-1}min^{-1}{\cdot}year^{-1}$.

A cross-sectional rate of decline in aerobic fitness of 0.26 $ml{\cdot}kg^{-1}min^{-1}{\cdot}year^{-1}$ does have support from longitudinal research. Kasch and associates (1985, 1990) compared 25-year longitudinal changes of physically active and inactive men. The rate of decline in aerobic power of their active men was 0.25 $ml{\cdot}kg^{-1}min^{-1}{\cdot}year^{-1}$, nearly identical to the NASA data. In contrast, the aerobic fitness of inactive men declined at a rate of 0.77 $ml{\cdot}kg^{-1}min^{-1}{\cdot}year^{-1}$. Over the 25 years, the active subjects lost an average of 7.5 pounds of weight, while the inactive subjects gained about 7 pounds. At the start of the study, the percent body fat levels of the men were similar, but at the conclusion of the 25-year study, the body fat levels were 17% and 26% for the active and inactive men, respectively. The inactive men became less active and increased their percent body fat, and their aerobic fitness declined at a steeper rate.

The NASA aging studies (Jackson et al. 1995; Jackson et al. 1996) also included longitudinal data. While the average aerobic fitness of the men did not change between tests, the women's aerobic fitness declined at a rate of 0.6 $ml{\cdot}kg^{-1}min^{-1}{\cdot}year^{-1}$.

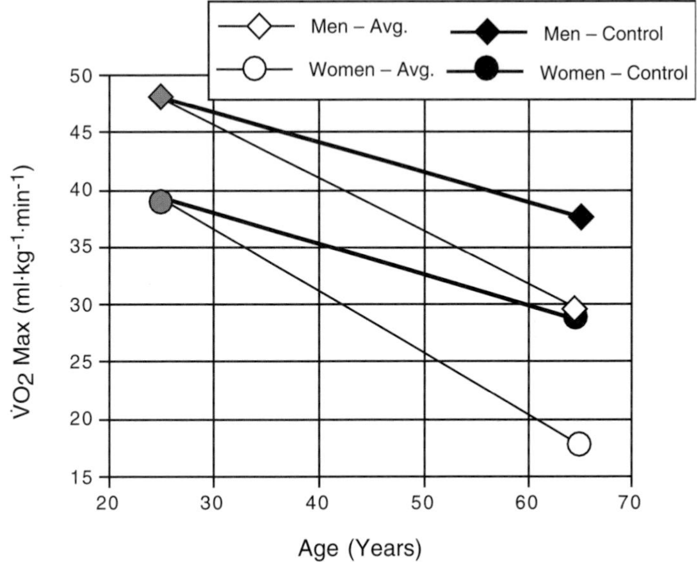

Figure 11.2
The average (Avg) and controlled (Control) decline in aerobic fitness from age 25 to 65 years. The controlled rate of decline is the rate of decline if activities, habits, and percent body fat remained unchanged. (Graph made from published data (Jackson et al., 1995; 1996). (Source: CSI Software Company, Houston, TX. Reprinted by permission.)

The primary reason the men did not show a longitudinal decline was that many had enrolled in a health-related fitness program and increased their fitness. Closer analysis showed that life-style dramatically influenced the rate at which aerobic fitness longitudinally changed. Figure 11.3 graphically illustrates this. Those men and women who decreased their exercise level and increased their percent body fat showed the steepest yearly decrease in aerobic fitness. In contrast, those men and women who increased their exercise level and decreased their percent body fat actually increased their $\dot{V}O_2$ Max between the two tests.

These data show that the change in aerobic fitness over time varies considerably, and is due not only to aging but to life-style. Figure 11.4 illustrates the change in aerobic fitness as it relates to aging. The average aerobic fitness of the NASA men (Jackson et al. 1995) at age 30 was 45 ml·kg^{-1}·min^{-1}, and represents men who were moderately active (30–60 minutes of aerobic exercise per week), and somewhat lean (15–20%fat). Figure 11.4 shows the theoretical decline from the average fitness level for a 30-year old man of 45 ml·kg^{-1}·min^{-1} to projected levels at age 70 for three different life-styles. If men maintained a physically active life-style (i.e., aerobically exercise 3 or more hours per week) and remained lean ($\approx$ 15%fat), their projected aerobic power at age 70 would be 42 ml·kg^{-1}·min^{-1}, only 3 ml·kg^{-1}·min^{-1} below the average 30-year old man. This would be just a 7% decline in aerobic capacity. The figure also shows the projected change from average for men who became sedentary and increased their percent body fat to about 30%. The estimated aerobic power at age 70 for these sedentary men would be in the low 20s, representing a loss of nearly 50% of their aerobic power. Many of these men are at risk of losing their capacity to function independently. The third example represents men at about 20% fat who remained moderately active by exercising aerobically for 30 to 60 minutes a week. A 70-year old man with this

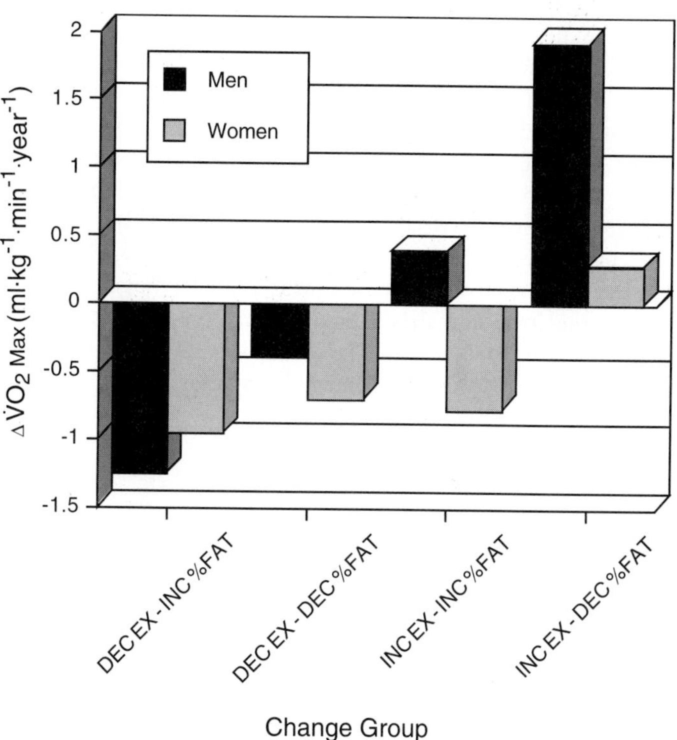

Figure 11.3
Longitudinal changes in aerobic fitness of men and women who changed their life-style. The rate at which aerobic fitness declines is directly related with changes in life-style.* (Graph made from published data (Jackson et al., 1995; 1996). (Source: CSI Software Company, Houston, TX. Reprinted by permission.)
*(DECEX-INC%FAT = decreased exercise and increased % fat)

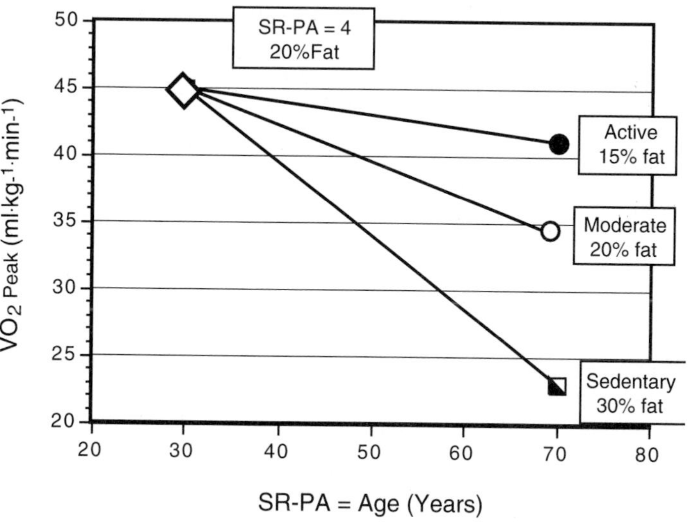

Figure 11.4
Projected changes in aerobic fitness from age 30 to 70 years for different exercise and body composition conditions. (Source: CSI Software Company, Houston, TX. Reprinted by permission.)

profile would be expected to have an aerobic capacity of 34 $ml \cdot kg^{-1} \cdot min^{-1}$, a 40-year decline of less than 25% in their aerobic fitness, about half the decline projected for the sedentary man.

The importance of aerobic fitness has been demonstrated by Blair and associates who showed that low levels of aerobic fitness increase the risk of mortality (Blair et al. 1989; Blair et al. 1995). For many elderly, living an active life-style is more important than longevity (Larson & Bruce 1987). A goal of aging is not just living longer and dying later, but also what Shephard (1986) terms a "quality-adjusted lifespan." For many elderly this is the level of aerobic fitness needed to function independently. The cross-sectional and longitudinal data show that life-style, exercise, and body composition are major determinates of this. The levels of aerobic fitness defined by the American Medical Association for independent living are

- Severe impairment—15 $ml \cdot kg^{-1} \cdot min^{-1}$
- Moderate impairment—20 $ml \cdot kg^{-1} \cdot min^{-1}$

Body Composition. The weight and percent body fat of American adults increase with age. Figure 11.5 shows the average change in body mass index (BMI) of American men and women for different age groups (Frisancho 1990). These data are a representative sample of American men and women and show that the BMI of both men and women increase steadily to about age 45 years. At that point, the BMI of men levels off, while the women's continues to increase and levels off about 10 years later.

Figure 11.6 gives the cross-sectional trend for age and percent body fat. These data came from the medical database at the Cooper Clinic in Dallas (Pollock & Wilmore 1990). These cross-sectional data show that percent body fat of both men and women systematically increases from the early 20s to the 50s, where there is a tendency to level off. The increase for women is at a steeper rate than for men. This systematic increase in percent body fat is likely due to increases in fat weight and decreases in fat-free weight. After age 30, a general decrease in fat-free mass and muscle mass has been observed (Wilmore & Costill 1994). How much of the decrease in fat-free mass is due to aging and how much is due to exercise habits is difficult to determine. However, research published on master runners does suggest that some loss of fat-free mass is due to aging. Pollock and associates (Pollock et al. 1987) reported that the master runners who average running over 22 miles a week still showed a loss of fat-free weight at a rate of about 0.25 pounds per year.

Longitudinal research shows that life-style is a major determinate of changes on body composition. Research (Skender 1996) from the Behavioral Medicine Research Center at Baylor College of Medicine (Houston, TX) provides a comprehensive view of the longitudinal effect of weight changes associated with diet and exercise. In a two-year experimental study, Baylor scientists compared the weight loss of three groups: (1) diet only; (2) exercise only; and (3) diet and exercise. The 127 men and women who participated in the study were at least 30 pounds overweight when they started. Figure 11.7 gives the results of the study. During the first three months, the exercise group lost very little, while the two diet groups showed dramatic weight losses. Between 3 and 12 months the diet-only group leveled off,

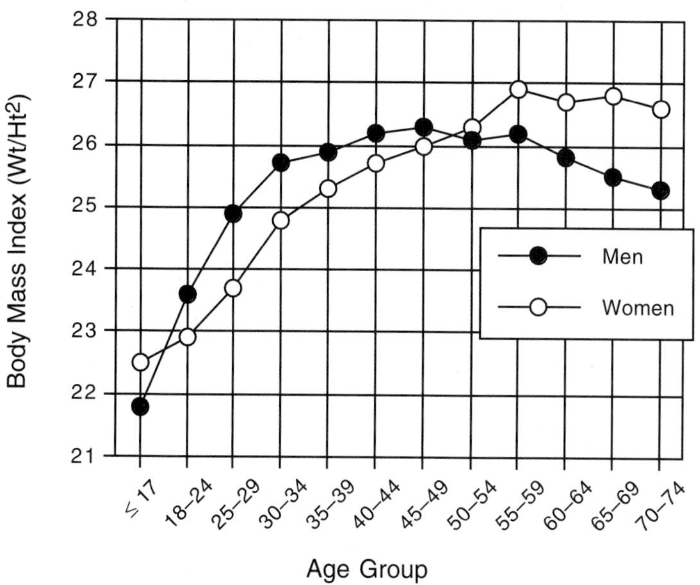

Figure 11.5
Average cross-sectional change in body mass index of American men and women. Graph made from NHANES data published by Frisancho, 1990. (Source: CSI Software Company, Houston, TX. Reprinted by permission.)

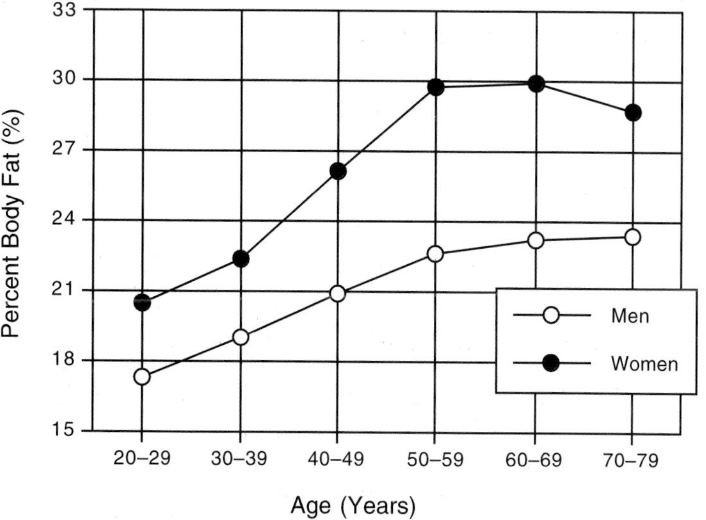

Figure 11.6
Average cross-sectional change in percent body fat of men and women. Graph made from published data from the Cooper Clinic Coronary Risk Profile Charts, Dallas Texas (Pollock & Wilmore 1990). (Source: CSI Software Company, Houston, TX. Reprinted by permission.)

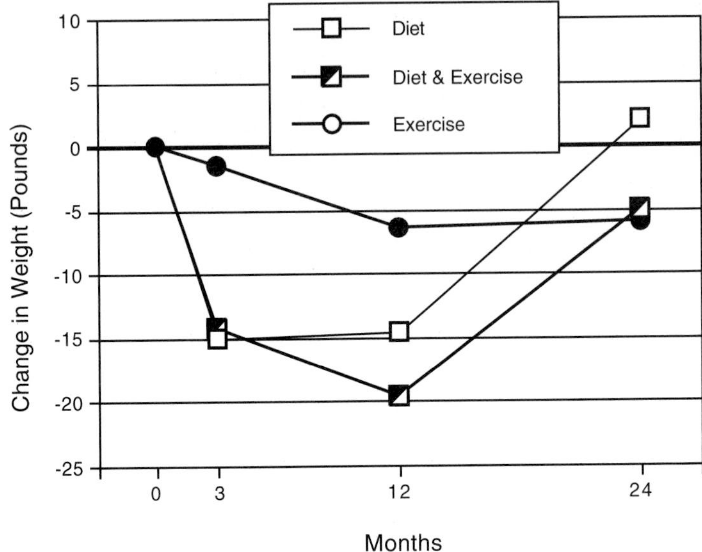

Figure 11.7
Longitudinal 2-year changes in body weight associated with diet and exercise programs. Life-style greatly influences weight change and body composition. (Graph made from published data (Skender 1996). (Source: Jackson and Ross, *Understanding Exercise for Health and Fitness,* 1997. Reprinted by permission.)

and then during the next 12 months gained all their weight back and even exceeded their start point. The exercise-only group progressively lost weight over the first 12 months and maintained the weight loss for the next 12 months. The diet-and-exercise group lost the most weight during the first 12 months, but their weight rebounded in the final 12 months to the level reached by the exercise-only group. These data not only demonstrate importance of exercise on weight control, but also the influence life-style has on the age-related changes in body composition. Aging is responsible for part of adult changes in body composition, but life-style plays a major role.

Muscular Strength. In youth, muscular strength increases with age. The maximum strength of men and women generally is reached between the ages of 20 and 30 years. After this age, there tends to be a gradual decrease in strength (McArdle, Katch & Katch 1991; Montoye 1977). Figure 11.8 shows this general trend.

While a general age-related decrease in strength has consistently been shown with the general adult population, those who work at jobs that require strength above the levels essential for sedentary life-style do not show a decline in strength with age (Blakley 1994; Petrofsky 1975). Figure 11.9 shows the cross-sectional strength trends of over 12,000 construction workers. Included are data on over 900 men age 50 and older (Blakley 1994). The strength tests are the isometric tests presented in Chapter 7. The graphs show very little change in grip, arm, and back strength. The mean differences between the strongest age group and workers in the 60–70-year group were quite small. These data suggest that physically demanding jobs provide a training effect that helps workers maintain strength as they age. These data suggest that much

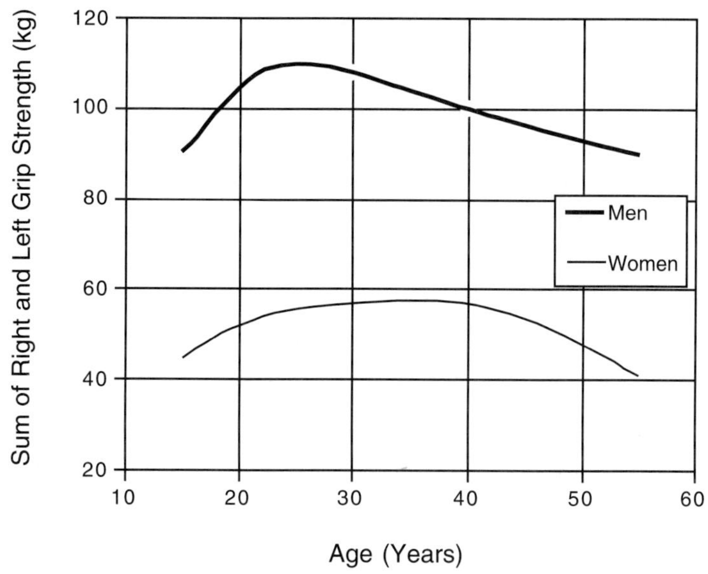

Figure 11.8
Cross-sectional age-related change in grip strength of men and women. Strength levels increase in youth, reaching peak strength in the 30s and 40s and then systematically declines. (Smoothed graphs made from published data) (Montoye 1977). (Source: CSI Software Company, Houston, TX. Reprinted by permission.)

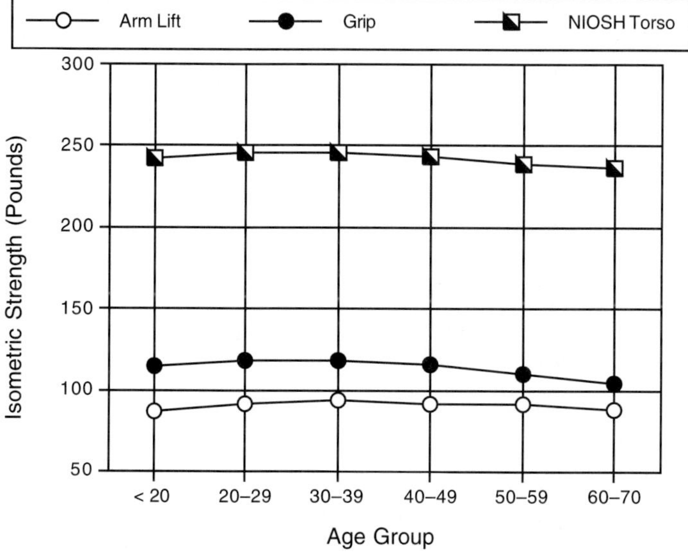

Figure 11.9
Cross-sectional change in isometric strength of construction workers. (Graph made from published data) (Blakley, Quinones, Crawford & Jago 1994). (Source: CSI Software Company, Houston, TX. Reprinted by permission.)

of the age-related decline in strength found in the general population is due to environment, that is to the lack of activities that overload the major muscle groups.

While the general trend for adults is to lose strength as they age, research shows that strength training can increase strength substantially in adults at any age. Strength development programs for the elderly are gaining in popularity. Muscular strength is related to function mobility of the elderly. Leg strength is important in maintaining balance, walking, and in preventing falls of the elderly (Spirduso 1995). Strength training studies show that the elderly can have the same rate of strength gain as the young, but they start and end at lower levels. The strength training results achieved with the elderly are summarized in another source (Spirduso 1995). With the aging of the American population, the need to maintain strength while we age is becoming more recognized.

Evaluating Adult Fitness

This section presents adult fitness tests. The first is the test developed by the YMCA, which is the central component of the YMCA's adult fitness program. It is likely the most popular adult fitness test. The second test is the United States Army Physical Fitness Test (APFT). While the APFT is not used with civilians, it does illustrate a philosophy on adult physical fitness.

Y's Way to Fitness

The Y's Way to Fitness program is one of the most comprehensive, popular adult fitness programs (Golding, Meyers & Sinning 1989). It is more than just a fitness test; it is a complete adult fitness program. Leading exercise science and medical professionals helped develop the program. In addition to test procedures and norms, the test includes: basic exercise physiology; program administration recommendations; medical guidelines; and fitness programming. Provided next are the Y's adult fitness tests and normative standards. The included tests tend to be standard adult health-related fitness tests that have been shown to be both reliable and valid. The norms are extensive. They were developed on data from over 20,000 men and women of various ages. The cross-sectional age-related changes in fitness are also provided.

Aerobic Fitness. Either a cycle ergometer or step test can be used to evaluate aerobic fitness. The cycle ergometer test is a submaximal test consisting of several workloads. This test is discussed in Chapter 8. The Y's $\dot{V}O_2$ Max norms are given in Table 11.1. Figure 11.10 shows the cross-sectional decline in aerobic fitness with age. These data show the familiar linear decline in fitness with age. The average rate of decline was about 0.47 $ml \cdot kg^{-1} \cdot min^{-1} \cdot year^{-1}$ for men and about 0.43 $ml \cdot kg^{-1} \cdot min^{-1} year^{-1}$ for women. The Y's 3-minute step test is provided next.

Test. Y's 3-Minute Step Test

Purpose. To measure exercise heart rate after 3 minutes of exercise. The step test is provided to replace the cycle test in environments where a cycle ergometer test is not suitable.

Equipment. The test equipment needed are: a 12-inch-high sturdy bench; a metronome set at 96 beats per minute; a timer to measure the 3-minute test period and recovery heart rate; and a stethoscope to count recovery heart rate.

Test Procedures. The step test is first demonstrated to the subject. The step rate is 24 steps per minute. The metronome is set at 96 beats per minute, four

Table 11.1 YMCA Adult Norms for $\dot{V}O_2$ Max ($ml \cdot kg^{-1} \cdot min^{-1}$)*

Age	95th	75th	50th	25th	5th
Men					
18–25	71	53	45	35	29
26–35	64	50	41	34	26
36–45	60	44	37	30	21
46–55	54	40	34	28	22
56–65	49	37	31	25	18
over 65	42	33	26	21	17
Women					
18–25	67	48	40	32	22
26–35	59	46	37	30	22
36–45	53	39	32	26	19
46–55	48	35	29	24	18
56–65	43	32	26	21	15
over 65	39	28	23	18	15

*Adapted from Golding, L. A. et al., *Y's Way to Physical Fitness,* 1989.

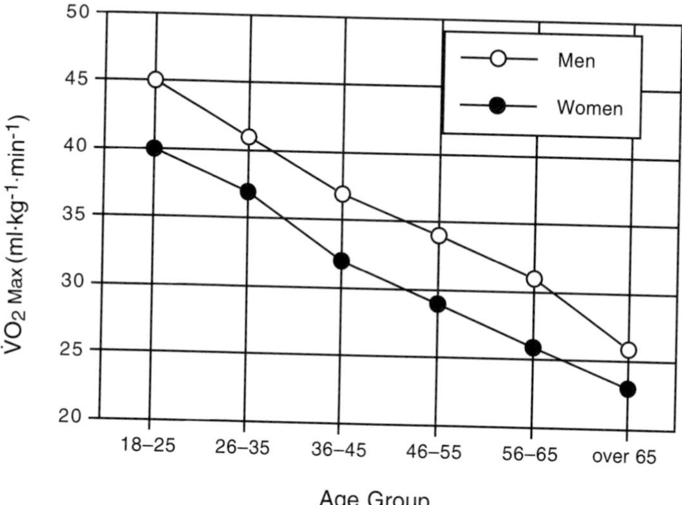

Figure 11.10 Cross-sectional change in aerobic fitness of men and women. (Graph made from Y's Way to Fitness normative data) (Golding, Meyers & Sinning 1989). (Source: CSI Software Company, Houston, TX. Reprinted by permission.)

clicks per step—that is, up, up, down, down (4 × 24 = 96). The subject faces the bench and steps in place to pick up the beat of the metronome. Once the subject has the pace, the test can begin. When the subject starts the first step, the timer is started. The subject continues bench stepping at 24 steps per minute for 3 minutes. At the end of the last step, the subject sits down immediately. The test administrator places the stethoscope on the

Table 11.2 YMCA Norms for the 3-Minute Step Test (Heart Rate Beats per Minute)*

Age	95th	75th	50th	25th	5th
			Men		
18–25	72	88	102	118	137
26–35	76	88	103	119	140
36–45	74	94	108	120	142
46–55	81	96	113	124	145
56–65	74	97	109	122	136
over 65	74	95	109	122	140
			Women		
18–25	79	97	112	128	149
26–35	80	97	116	129	148
36–45	80	101	114	130	146
46–55	88	102	118	127	147
56–65	83	103	116	129	148
over 65	83	100	120	129	149

*Adapted from Golding, L. A. et al., *Y's Way to Physical Fitness,* 1989.

person's chest, picks up the heart rhythm and counts the heart rate for 1 minute. The count begins on a beat, counting that beat as "zero one."

Score. The subject's score is the 1-minute postexercise heart rate. Table 11.2 provides normative data to evaluate performance.

Body Composition. Body composition is evaluated from the sum of skinfold fat. The YMCA test uses the same sites for men and women. Either the sum of three (Σ3) or sum of four (Σ4) skinfold measurements may be used. The recommended sites are

Σ3

1. Abdomen
2. Ilium
3. Triceps

Σ4

1. Abdomen
2. Ilium
3. Triceps
4. Thigh

The methods used to measure skinfold fat are fully presented in Chapter 9. Published data (Jackson & Pollock 1978; Jackson, Pollock & Ward 1980) were used to develop sex-specific regression equations to estimate percent body fat from the sum of skinfolds. The *Y Way to Fitness* test manual provides "look-up" tables to expedite the calculations. Table 11.3 gives the Y's percent body fat normative standards. Figure 11.11 shows the age-related change in percent body fat for the YMCA database. Percent body fat for both men and women increases with age, then levels off and declines slightly.

Table 11.3 YMCA Adult Norms for Percent Body Fat (%fat)*

Age	95th	75th	50th	25th	5th
Men					
18–25	6	10	15	22	30
26–35	10	15	20	25	32
36–45	12	18	23	27	32
46–55	14	20	24	29	34
56–65	17	21	25	29	34
over 65	17	21	24	28	33
Women					
18–25	15	20	25	29	37
26–35	15	21	25	31	39
36–45	17	23	28	33	41
46–55	19	25	30	36	42
56–65	20	26	32	36	42
over 65	17	25	31	36	40

*Adapted from Golding, L. A. et al., *Y's Way to Physical Fitness,* 1989.

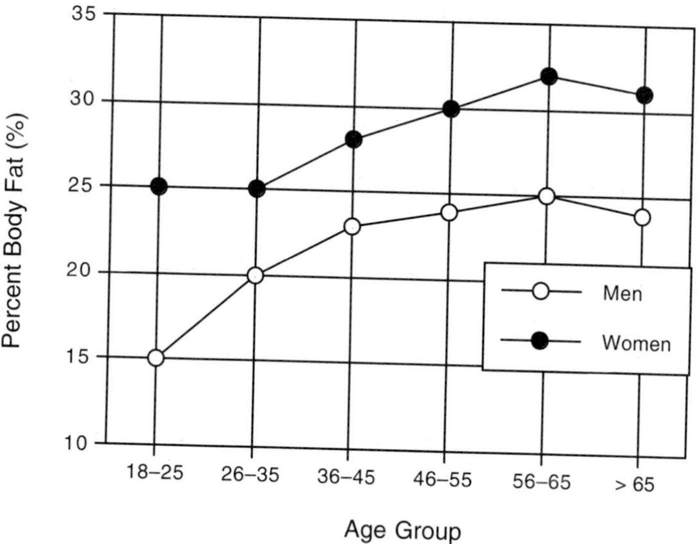

Figure 11.11
Cross-sectional change in percent body fat of men and women. (Graph made from Y's Way to Fitness normative data) (Golding, Meyers & Sinning 1989). (Source: CSI Software Company, Houston, TX. Reprinted by permission.)

Muscular Strength. The bench press is used to measure strength and endurance. Rather than using a 1-RM test, an absolute endurance test is used. Absolute endurance is measured by using the same load for everyone. A 35-pound weight is used with women and an 80-pound barbell for men. The Y's bench-press test is not a maximum

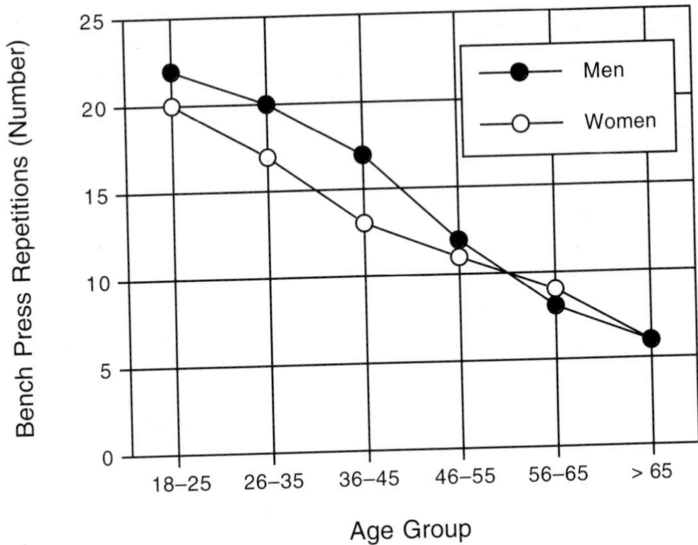

Figure 11.12 Cross-sectional change in bench press strength of men and women. (Graph made from Y's Way to Fitness normative data) (Golding, Meyers & Sinning 1989). (Source: CSI Software Company, Houston, TX. Reprinted by permission.)

strength test; it is an absolute endurance test. The correlation between absolute endurance and maximum strength is high, ranging from 0.75 to 0.97 (deVries 1994). Figure 11.12 gives the cross-sectional decline in bench-press performance of men and women tested with the Y's Way to Fitness test (Golding, Meyers & Sinning 1989). These data show that bench-press absolute endurance of men and women declines with age at a linear rate.

Test. Bench Press

Purpose. To measure muscular strength and absolute muscular endurance.

Equipment. The equipment needed are: 35-pound barbell for women and 80-pound barbell for men; a metronome set at 60 beats per minute; and a bench that is commonly used for the bench-press exercise.

Test Procedures. The subject assumes a supine position on the bench with the knees bent and feet on the floor. Hand the barbell to the subject in the "down" position. From this position, the subject presses the barbell upward to extend the elbows fully and then returns to the "down" position. The rhythm is kept by the metronome, with each click representing a movement up or down. The subject exercises at a rate of 30 repetitions per minute ($2 \times 30 = 60$). The subject is encouraged to breathe regularly and not strain during the test, so as to avoid the Valsalva maneuver.

Score. The subject's score is the number of repetitions completed to exhaustion. Table 11.4 provides bench-press norms for age and sex.

Muscular Endurance. A 1-minute sit-up test is used to measure muscular endurance. Figure 11.13 shows the cross-sectional change in the muscular endurance

Table 11.4 YMCA Norms for the Bench-Press Test (Number of Repetitions)*

Age	95th	75th	50th	25th	5th
			Men		
18–25	42	30	22	13	8
26–35	40	26	20	12	2
36–45	34	24	17	10	2
46–55	28	20	12	6	1
56–65	24	14	8	4	0
over 65	20	10	6	2	0
			Women		
18–25	42	28	20	12	2
26–35	40	25	17	9	1
36–45	32	21	13	8	1
46–55	30	20	11	5	0
56–65	30	16	9	3	0
over 65	22	12	6	2	0

*Adapted from Golding, L. A., et al., *Y's Way to Physical Fitness,* 1989.

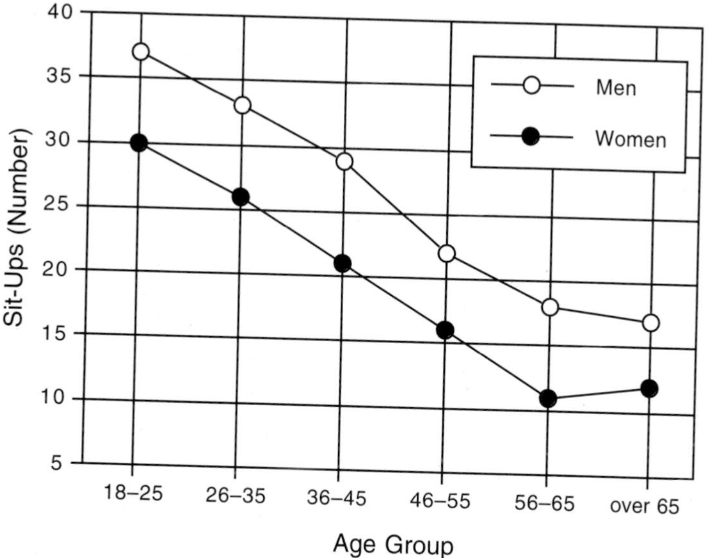

Figure 11.13
Cross-sectional change in sit-up performance of men and women. (Graph made from published Y's Way to Fitness normative data) (Golding, Meyers & Sinning (1989). (Source: CSI Software Company, Houston, TX. Reprinted by permission.)

sit-ups test. The sit-up ability of males and females shows a systematic decrease from youth to about age 60, where it levels off. Aging and sit-up performance has not been a topic of research in aging research, so it has not been determined how much of the loss is due to aging and how much is due to the lack of training.

Table 11.5 YMCA Norms for the Sit-Up Test (Number of Repetitions)*

Age	95th	75th	50th	25th	5th
Men					
18–25	54	45	37	30	24
26–35	50	41	33	28	12
36–45	46	36	29	22	9
46–55	41	29	22	17	8
56–65	37	26	18	12	4
over 65	33	22	17	10	4
Women					
18–25	48	37	30	24	10
26–35	42	33	26	20	2
36–45	38	27	21	14	2
46–55	30	22	16	9	1
56–65	29	18	11	6	1
over 65	26	18	12	4	0

*Adapted from Golding, L. A. et al., *Y's Way to Physical Fitness,* 1989.

Test. 1-Minute Timed Sit-Ups

Purpose. To measure muscular endurance of the abdominal muscles.

Equipment. The equipment needed are a stopwatch and a soft mat.

Test Procedures. The subject assumes a supine position on the mat with the knees bent at about a 90° angle. In this position the heels are about 18 inches from the buttocks. The fingers are next to the ears. A partner holds the ankles for support. On the command "Go," the subject does as many sit-ups as possible in 1 minute. In the "up position," the elbows should alternately touch the opposite knee. In the "down position," the shoulders must touch the mat, but the head does not need to touch the mat.

Score. The subject's score is the number of correct sit-ups completed in 1 minute. Table 11.5 provides normative data to evaluate performance.

Flexibility. Trunk flexibility is a common component of both youth and adult fitness tests. Trunk flexibility is believed to be important for the prevention of low-back problems, but the link has not been clearly defined (Plowman 1992). Figure 11.14 shows the cross-sectional change in flexibility found in the Y's Way to Fitness normative database (Golding, Meyers & Sinning 1989). These data show that women are more flexible than men over all age groups. This sex difference is consistent with youth fitness results (Cooper Institute 1992). With age, both men and women lose flexibility. The rate of loss for men is greater than that of women.

Test. Trunk Flexion

Purpose. To measure trunk flexion.

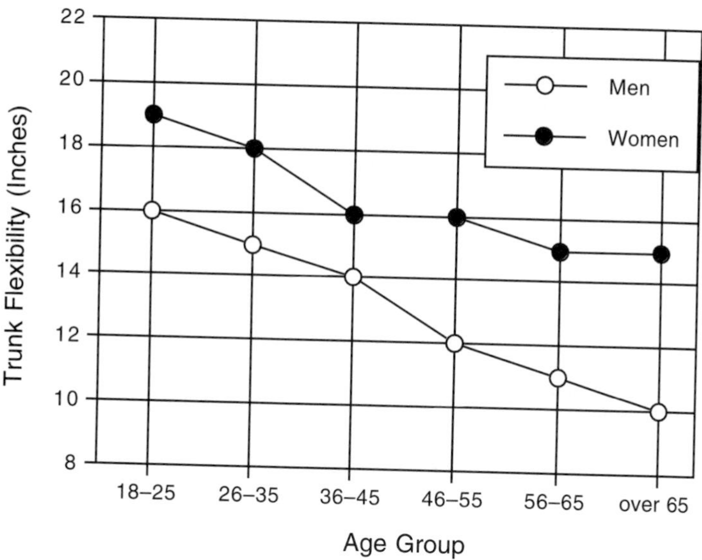

Figure 11.14
Cross-sectional change in flexibility of men and women. (Graph made from published normative data) (Golding, Meyers & Sinning 1989). (Source: CSI Software Company, Houston, TX. Reprinted by permission.)

Equipment. While commercial equipment is available for this test, measurement can also be done with just a yardstick. The yardstick is taped to the floor at the 15-inch mark of the yardstick. The 15-inch mark is where the feet are placed.

Test Procedures. The subject sits on the floor straddling the yardstick with the 0 mark toward their body. The legs are extended and the feet are at the 15-inch tape. The feet are about 10–12 inches apart. The participant slowly reaches forward with both hands as far as possible on the yardstick and holds the position momentarily. The subject is encouraged to exhale and drop their head between their arms. The fingertips together are in contact with the yardstick.

Score. The best of three trials measured to the nearest 0.25 of an inch is the subject's score. Norms for men and women of selected age groups are provided in Table 11.6.

U.S. Army Fitness Test

The United States Army requires soldiers to maintain a level of physical fitness. The Army Physical Fitness Test (APFT) consists of three items designed to assess muscular endurance and cardiorespiratory endurance. The test items are: push-ups, sit-ups, and the 2-mile run. The fitness program provides alternate tests for soldiers who cannot take the APFT for medical reasons. Soldiers over age 40 must be cleared through a cardiovascular screening program before taking the APFT.

APFT Test Items. Provided next is a brief description of the three-item APFT. A complete discussion of the APFT is provided in the U.S. Army physical fitness manual (FM 21-20).

Table 11.6 YMCA Norms for the Flexibility Test (Distance Reached in Inches)*

Age	95th	75th	50th	25th	5th
Men					
18–25	22	18	16	12	9
26–35	22	18	15	12	7
36–45	21	17	14	11	5
46–55	20	16	12	9	4
56–65	19	15	11	7	3
over 65	18	13	10	7	3
Women					
18–25	25	21	19	16	12
26–35	24	20	18	15	11
36–45	23	19	16	13	9
46–55	22	18	16	13	8
56–65	21	18	15	12	7
over 65	21	18	15	11	6

*Adapted from Golding, L. A. et al., *Y's Way to Physical Fitness*, 1989. Source: CSI Software Company, Houston, TX. Reprinted by permission.

Push-Up Test. The push-up test is the number of correct push-ups that can be completed in 2 minutes. At the start of the test, the soldier assumes the front-leaning rest position in which, when viewed from the side, the body should form a generally straight line from the shoulders to the ankles. On the command "Go," the soldier begins the push-up by bending the elbows and lowering the entire body as a single unit until the upper arms are at least parallel to the ground. The soldier may rest in the front-leaning rest position, but cannot rest on the ground. The soldier completes as many push-ups as possible in 2 minutes at their own cadence.

Sit-Up Test. The objective of the sit-up test is to do as many sit-ups as possible within a 2-minute test period. The starting position is lying on the back with the knees bent at a 90° angle. Another person holds the soldier's ankles with just their hands. The fingers are interlocked behind the head, and the backs of the hands must be touching the ground. At the command "Go," the upper body is raised forward to, or beyond, the vertical position; that is, the base of the neck is beyond the base of the spine. After reaching the vertical position, the upper body is lowered to the ground until the bottom of the shoulder blades touches the ground. The head, hands, arms, and elbows are not required to touch the ground. The test is terminated if the soldier stops and rests in the down (starting) position. The person maintains their own cadence.

2-Mile Run Test. The 2-mile run test is used to measure aerobic fitness. The soldiers are instructed to complete the run without any physical help—for example, by being pulled, pushed, or carried. Walking is permitted, but discouraged. The goal is to complete the 2-mile distance as fast as possible.

Table 11.7 Level of Performance Required to Pass the Army Physical Fitness Test (APFT) for Men and Women, Contrasted by Age Groups

Age Group	Push-Ups (Number)		Sit-Ups (Number)		2-Mile Run (min:sec)	
	Men	Women	Men	Women	Men	Women
17–21	42	18	52	50	15:54	18:54
22–26	40	16	47	45	16:36	19:36
27–31	38	15	42	40	17:18	21:00
32–36	33	14	38	35	18:00	22:36
37–41	32	13	33	30	18:42	23:36
42–46	26	12	29	27	19:06	24:00
47–51	22	10	27	24	19:36	24:30
≥ 52	15	9	26	22	20:00	25:00

Taken from *FM 21-20 Physical Fitness Training,* Headquarters, Department of the Army, 1992.

Table 11.8 Army Physical Fitness Test (APFT) Alternate Test Standards (min:sec) by Event, Sex, and Age

Age Group	800-Yd Swim		6.2-Mile Bike		2.5-Mile Walk	
	Men	Women	Men	Women	Men	Women
17–21	20:00	21:00	24:00	25:00	34:00	37:00
22–26	20:30	21:30	24:30	25:30	34:30	37:30
27–31	21:00	22:00	25:00	26:00	35:00	38:00
32–36	21:30	22:30	25:30	26:30	35:30	38:30
37–41	22:00	23:00	26:00	27:00	36:00	39:00
42–46	22:30	23:30	27:00	28:00	36:30	39:30
47–51	23:00	24:00	28:00	30:00	37:00	40:00
≥ 52	24:00	25:00	30:00	32:00	37:30	40:30

APFT Performance Standards. Age-adjusted performance standards are provided for men and women. Test performance is converted to a score scale that ranges from 0 to 100. While the top score is 100 points, a score of 60 is required to pass a test. The 0 to 100 point score scale is adjusted to account for sex and age differences. The scoring standards are comprehensive and can be found in the test manual (U.S. Army FM 21-20). Provided in Table 11.7 are levels of performance required to pass the APFT for the selected age groups.

Alternate APFT Events. The APFT alternate events are provided for soldiers who, for medical reasons, cannot take the three-item test. The alternate tests are timed endurance tests. Table 11.8 provides the alternate test standards by event, sex, and age. The alternate aerobic events are:

- 800-yard swim test
- 6.2-mile stationary cycle ergometer test with a resistance setting of 2 kiloponds (see Chapter 8)

- 6.2-mile bicycle test on a conventional bicycle using one speed
- 2.5-mile walk test

U.S. Army Body Composition. Although not part of the APFT, the body composition of soldiers is evaluated. Soldiers who do not meet weight standards for their height or whose appearance suggests that they have excessive body fat are required to have their body composition measured. Age and sex standards are used to evaluate a soldier's percent body fat. Those who do not meet the standards are placed on a formal, supervised weight-loss program that includes diet and exercise components. Provided next are the United States Army percent body fat standards (U.S. Army 1992) for men and women adjusted for age.

Age	**Percent Body Fat Standard**	
	Men	Women
17–20	20%	30%
21–27	22%	32%
28–39	24%	34%
≥40	26%	36%

Evaluating Functional Adult Fitness

While the YMCA and U.S. Army tests are similar to youth fitness tests, the "graying of America" has led to a new concept of adult fitness testing, functional adult fitness tests. The need for **functional adult fitness** testing and exercise training programs for the elderly can be traced to the increasing number of older Americans and escalating health care costs. The U.S. House of Representatives Select Committee on Aging estimated in 1992 that the annual cost of physical frailty was $54–80 billion and would likely be over $132 billion by the year 2030. There is good evidence to suggest that increasing the functional fitness of the elderly can reduce these costs (Rikli 1997; Spirduso 1995).

Functional adult fitness tests are designed to measure basic fitness components such as strength, endurance, and motor ability (Rikli 1997). Spirduso (1995) identified five hierarchical categories of the functional ability of the elderly.

1. ***Physically Dependent.*** The **physically dependent** are individuals who cannot execute basic activities of daily living, such as dressing and bathing. These individuals require full-time help.
2. ***Physically Frail.*** The **physically frail** are individuals who can meet their basic needs, but cannot perform many activities of daily living, such as preparing meals or shopping.
3. ***Physically Independent.*** The **physically independent** are fully independent individuals who are quite sedentary. They are likely borderline frail and close to losing their capacity to function independently.
4. ***Physically Fit.*** The physically fit are individuals who exercise regularly and are typically well above average in functional ability. They likely engage regularly in strenuous activities such as jogging, rowing, tennis, and other forms of aerobic exercise.

Table 11.9 The Fitness Components and Test Items of Functional Adult Fitness Components

Fitness Component	AAHPERD Test	LifeSpan Test	Groningen Test
Aerobic fitness	880-yard walk	6-minute walk, or 2-min step-in-place	Walking endurance
Upper body strength	Arm curl	Arm curl	Grip strength
Lower body strength	None	Chair stand	None
Upper body flexibility	None	Scratch test	Shoulder flexibility
Lower body flexibility	Sit-and-reach	Chair sit-and-reach	Sit-and-reach
Agility and/or balance	Agility/dynamic balance	8-foot Up-and-Go	Balance test
Body composition	Ponderal index	Body mass index	None
Fine motor abilities	"Soda pop" coordination test	None	Manual dexterity reaction time

5. ***Physically Elite.*** The physically elite are a very small proportion of men and women who train regularly and compete in master athletic events. These are master athletes who are very fit (see Pollock et al. 1987 for an example of master athletes).

The primary target group of functional fitness tests are the individuals in the physically independent group. The test items of functional adult fitness tests reflect the person's ability to perform common activities of daily living, such as rising from a chair, walking, stair climbing, lifting, reaching, and bending (Rikli 1997). Provided next are three adult functional fitness tests. The first is the AAHPERD test, the second is a test of the LifeSpan Project, and the final test is the Groningen test developed in The Netherlands. Table 11.9 provides a comparison of the fitness components and test items of these three functional fitness tests.

AAHPERD Test

The American Alliance for Health, Physical Education, Recreation and Dance (AAHPERD) test (Osness 1996) was developed by a committee appointed by AAHPERD's Council on Aging and Adult Development. The definition used to define functional fitness by the AAHPERD Committee was "the physical capacity of the individual to meet ordinary and unexpected demands of daily life safely and effectively." The general purposes of the AAHPERD functional fitness test are:

- Assess the individual's current condition to be able to determine the appropriate exercise prescription that will reduce risk and enhance physiological and psychological change.
- Be able to quantify change that may have taken place during an exercise program.

Provided next is a basic description of each test. Table 11.10 provides the normative data for men and women of various age groups. The sample sizes used to develop these statistics ranged from 11 to over 300 individuals for each age group. These norms were used to develop three functional fitness levels: below average, average, and above average. The test methods and evaluation standards are fully presented in the test manual (Osness 1996).

Table 11.10 Means and Standard Deviations for the AAHPERD Functional Fitness Test Contrasted by Gender and Age Groups

Gender	Test Statistic	Age Group 60–64	65–69	70–74	75–79	80–84	85–90
Ponderal Index (Ratio of height in inches by cube root of weight in pounds)							
Men	Mean	11.92	11.89	12.03	11.93	11.61	11.88
Men	SD	0.44	0.48	0.64	0.64	0.55	0.68
Women	Mean	11.69	11.82	11.83	11.92	11.64	12.01
Women	SD	0.80	0.81	0.77	0.69	0.95	0.80
Flexibility—Men (Inches)							
Men	Mean	19.9	19.8	17.9	18.5	18.4	16.2
Women	SD	5.0	5.0	6.1	5.6	3.9	2.8
Women	Mean	23.2	23.6	22.6	22.9	20.9	19.5
Women	SD	5.0	6.2	5.7	6.3	5.9	6.2
Agility/Balance—Men (Elapsed time, sec)							
Men	Mean	25.4	26.5	28.2	31.7	32.6	33.6
Men	SD	6.1	8.0	13.1	8.3	9.2	16.5
Women	Mean	25.0	27.4	29.0	34.0	37.1	42.2
Women	SD	5.4	6.2	7.0	10.6	15.1	15.7
Coordination—Men (Elapsed time, sec)							
Men	Mean	11.7	12.5	13.0	13.4	14.2	13.6
Men	SD	2.7	2.3	3.5	2.4	3.1	3.4
Women	Mean	12.1	12.6	12.9	13.6	14.5	15.7
Women	SD	3.2	3.4	3.7	4.6	3.8	3.3
Strength/Endurance—Men (Repetitions)							
Men	Mean	23.7	21.5	21.1	20.1	20.5	17.8
Men	SD	5.5	6.9	5.8	4.1	2.6	5.1
Women	Mean	21.8	21.2	20.8	17.7	17.6	16.2
Women	SD	6.2	6.7	6.1	5.2	4.9	4.8
880-Yard Walk—Men (Minutes)							
Men	Mean	7.1	7.8	8.3	9.7	8.1	9.5
Men	SD	1.3	1.5	1.3	3.7	1.4	1.4
Women	Mean	8.4	9.0	9.1	10.0	10.7	10.4
Women	SD	1.6	2.1	2.4	1.9	2.3	2.1

From Osness, W. H et al. *Functional Fitness Assessment for Adults Over 60 Years.* Dubuque: Kendall/Hunt, 1996, pp. 28–33.

Body Composition Component

Test. Ponderal Index

Procedure. The ponderal index is a height-weight ratio. The manual provides a nomogram to make this calculation. Unlike the more commonly used body mass index (see Chapter 9), a low ponderal index reflects a high body weight for a given height, that is, high level of body fatness.

Lower Body Flexibility Component

Test. Trunk/Leg Flexibility

Procedure. The test equipment is similar to that used for the Y's Way to Fitness. A yardstick is taped to the floor with a line at the 25-inch mark (the YMCA test uses the 15-inch mark). The subject sits with the legs flat on the floor and heels at the 25-inch line. The feet are spread about 12 inches. The test requires the subject to reach forward keeping both hands together. The object is to reach the furthest point possible on the yardstick. The person is first given two warm-up trials, followed by two trials for score.

Scoring. The person's score is the best score of the two trials. The test is scored to the nearest 0.5 inch.

Agility and/or Balance Component

Test. Agility/Dynamic Balance

Procedure. The test station consists of a chair with arms and two cones that are located 6 feet to the side of the chair and 5 feet behind the chair. On command, the subject stands, moves to the right, goes around the cone, returns to the chair, sits down, lifts the feet off the ground, and without hesitating, immediately stands and repeats the move (with the exception of going around the left cone), and then returns to the chair. This is the first circuit. The entire circuit is then immediately repeated. The test consists of the two circuits. After a 30-second rest, the second trial (consisting of two circuits) is administered. A warm-up trial is administered first to be certain the subject understands the test.

Scoring. The time for each trial (two circuits) is measured to the nearest 0.1 second. The subject's score is the time for the best trial.

Fine Motor Abilities Component

Test. "Soda Pop" Coordination Test

Procedure. The test is administered with the person sitting on a chair facing a table. The general tasks involve lifting an unopened (12 oz) soda can, turning the can, and placing it on a target taped on the table. The test target is made from masking tape. A 30-inch strip is placed on the table, with 6 crosses (numbered 1 to 6) placed across the 30-inch strip. The crosses are 5 inches apart. The test starts with a soda can on every other cross, that is, numbers 1, 3, and 5. On a starting command, the subject lifts the first can, turns it over and places it on the next cross (i.e., number 2), moves can two from cross 3 to cross 4, and moves the third can from cross 5 to cross 6. Once the third can is placed, the subject immediately returns the cans to the original spot, that is, from cross 6 to 5, 4 to 3, and 2 to 1. This completes the first trip. Without hesitation, the same six moves are repeated. The test trial involves lifting, turning, and moving the cans a total of 12 times.

Scoring. The subject is given two practice trials, followed by two trials for score. The trial is scored to the nearest 0.1 seconds required to complete the 12 moves. The best score of the two trials is the subject's score.

Upper Body Strength Component

Test. Strength/Endurance

Procedure. The test is an absolute endurance test where the subject repeatedly lifts a weight with their arm. A 4-pound weight is used with women and a 8-pound weight with men. If 4- and 8-pound dumbbells are not available, it is recommended that 0.5 gallon plastic milk bottles filled with sand to the proper weight be used. The subject sits in a chair with their back straight against the chair and the nondominant hand at rest in their lap. The dominant arm is hanging to the side. Using their dominant arm, the test involves repeatedly lifting the weight through the biceps' full range of motion for 30 seconds.

Scoring. The subject's score is the number of repetitions completed in 30 seconds.

Aerobic Fitness Component

Test. 880-Yard Walk

Procedure. A suitable test course is needed. The test involves walking as fast as possible for 880 yards. Running is not allowed. Care needs to be taken to screen for orthopedic and cardiovascular conditions (Osness 1996, p. 20), including the following:

- Significant orthopedic problems that may be aggravated by prolonged continuous walking (8–10 min)
- History of cardiac problems (i.e., recent heart attack, frequent arrhythmia, valvular defects) that can be negatively influenced by exertion
- Lightheadedness upon activity
- History of uncontrolled hypertension (high blood pressure)

Scoring. One trial is given, with time recorded in minutes and seconds. The test is scored to the nearest second.

LifeSpan Project

The LifeSpan assessment battery is an ongoing, funded project to develop a fitness test that assesses the major physical parameters that support functional mobility and physical independence of older adults. At the time this chapter was being written the data collection phase of the project was well under way. This major testing project includes a national scientific review panel consisting of leading professionals in medicine, exercise science, and gerontology. It is likely that the LifeSpan Project adult functional fitness test will become the "yardstick" by which all other tests are compared.

Functional fitness defined in the LifeSpan project is "the physical capacity and ability to perform normal everyday activities safely and effectively." A major goal of the LifeSpan is to develop national fitness standards for older adults. The test is designed to provide fitness and allied health professionals with an assessment tool to:

1. Identify those individuals who are at risk of losing function.
2. Provide information that can be used to prescribe appropriate rehabilitative or preventive activities.
3. Provide outcome data for evaluating program effectiveness.

LifeSpan Test Selection Criteria. The LifeSpan test battery includes seven tests that measure six fitness components. Twelve criteria were established to use as guidelines for test development. These criteria are:

1. Represent major functional fitness components, i.e., the key physical parameters associated with independent active living.
2. Have acceptable test-retest reliability of > 0.80.
3. Have acceptable validity with documentation to support at least two of the following: content validity, criterion validity, and/or construct validity.
4. Reflect the usual age-related changes in functional status.
5. Be able to detect physical changes due to training/exercise.
6. Be able to assess across wide ranges of functional ability, from the borderline frail to the high fit. The goal was to avoid "ceiling" and "floor" effects so that all, or most all, participants could receive a score. No one "fails" the test.
7. Be easy to administer and score by paraprofessionals and volunteer technicians who often assist in administering the test.
8. Require minimum equipment and space so it can be administered in typical senior centers and other similar settings.
9. Be capable of being administered in the home setting.
10. Be safe to perform without medical release, with exceptions only for extreme conditions.
11. Be socially acceptable and meaningful.
12. Be reasonably quick to administer. Individual testing time requirement: no more than 30–45 minutes; group testing time: be able to assess approximately 24 people in 90 minutes, using 7 volunteer assistants.

LifeSpan Test Items. The functional fitness test includes seven tests that have six fitness components. A 6-minute walk for distance is the recommended test for cardiovascular endurance, but a 2-minute step-in-place test is an alternative cardiovascular test. While the test items of the LifeSpan project are similar to those of the AAHPERD functional fitness test, there are at least two important differences (Rikli 1997). First, the LifeSpan battery includes a lower body strength item, while the AAHPERD test does not. Lower body strength and endurance is a predictor of disability and is associated with the risk of falling, a major health hazard of the elderly. Second, the 880-yard AAHPERD walk test is too long for many adults. Many community-residing adults over age 75 years have difficulty walking even one-quarter of a mile. The test items of the LifeSpan Project includes a 6-minute walk test and an alternative 2-minute stepping test.

Provided next is a brief description of the test items of the LifeSpan Project. If you would like to administer the test, you are encouraged to obtain the test booklet that provides the complete test procedures. By the time this book that you are reading is published, it is likely that the LifeSpan test and its extensive normative database will be available.

Lower Body Strength Component

Test. Chair Stand

Test Procedures. The test begins with the participant seated in the middle of the chair, back straight, and feet approximately shoulder-width apart and flat on the floor. One foot is positioned slightly in front of the other to help maintain balance. The arms are crossed and held against the chest. The purpose of the test is to stand up and sit down as many times as possible in 30 seconds. Following a demonstration by the tester, a practice trial of one or two repetitions is given.

Scoring. The score is the total number of stands executed correctly within 30 seconds.

Upper Body Strength Component

Test. Arm Curl

Test Procedures. The participant is seated on a chair, back straight and feet flat on the floor, and with the dominant side of the body close to the edge. The purpose of the test is to complete as many arm curls as possible in 30 seconds. A 5-pound dumbbell is used with women and an 8-pound weight with men. The test begins with the arm in the down position beside the chair, perpendicular to the floor. At the signal "Go," the participant lifts the weight through a full range of motion, and then returns to starting position. Following a demonstration by the tester, a practice trial of two to three repetitions is given to check for proper form.

Scoring. The score is the total number of curls executed within 30 seconds.

Lower Body Flexibility Component

Test. Chair Sit-and-Reach Test

Test Procedures. While in a sitting position with one foot extended and the other foot flat on the floor, the test involves bending forward and reaching down the extended leg in an attempt to touch the toes. One hand is on top of the other hand. The person's preferred leg is extended. The preferred leg is the one that produces the better score. Following a demonstration by the tester, the participant is asked to determine the preferred leg and is then given two practice (stretching) trials.

Scoring. Using an 18-inch ruler, the scorer records the number of inches (to the nearest 0.5 inch) that the person is short of reaching the toe (minus score) or that the person reaches beyond the toe (plus score). The middle of the toe at the end of the shoe represents a zero score. The person is given two trials for score, and the best score is used.

Caution. The tester should be aware of people who have balance problems sitting on the edge of the chair. Care should be taken that the chair does not tip forward when the person sits on the front edge.

Body Composition Component

Test. Body Mass Index

Purpose. Assess body composition

Test Procedures. Body mass index is the ratio of body weight and height. This is fully presented in Chapter 9.

Agility and/or Balance Component

Test. 8-Foot Up-and-Go

Test Procedures. The test begins with the participant fully seated in the chair (erect posture), hands on thighs, and feet flat on the floor (one foot slightly in front of the other). The chair is positioned against a wall or in some other way secured so that it does not move during the testing. On the signal "Go," the person gets up from the chair, walks as quickly as possible around a cone, and returns to the chair. The cone is 8 feet in front of the chair. The participant is encouraged to walk as quickly as possible. Following a demonstration, the participant should walk through the test one time for practice. The subject is given two trials for score.

Scoring. The score is the elapsed time (nearest 0.1 second) from the signal "Go" until the subject returns to a seated position on the chair. The best score of the two trials is used to evaluate performance.

Upper Body Flexibility Component

Test. Scratch Test

Test Procedures. In a standing position, the participant places the preferred hand over the same shoulder and reaches as far as possible down the middle of the back, palm down and fingers extended (elbow will be pointed up). The hand of the other arm is placed behind the back, palm up, reaching up as far as possible in an attempt to touch (or overlap) the extended middle fingers of both hands. Following a demonstration by the tester, the participant is asked to determine their preferred hand, which is defined as the hand that results in the better score.

Scoring. The person's score is the distance of overlap, or distance between the tips of the middle fingers. The distance is measured with a ruler to the nearest 0.5 inch.

Aerobic Fitness Component

Tests. 6-Minute Walk Test and 2-Minute Step-in-Place

Test Procedures. The test station consists of a rectangle 20 yards long and 5 yards wide. A complete trip around the rectangle is 50 yards. The 50-yard course is marked by ten 5-yard segments. The test involves walking as fast as possible for 6 minutes.

Scoring. The score is the total number of yards walked in 6 minutes measured to the nearest 10-yard indicator.

Precautions. The test should be discontinued if at any time participants show signs of dizziness, pain, nausea, or undue fatigue.

Alternate Test. 2-Minute Step-in-Place Test

Table 11.11 Means, Standard Deviations, Stability Reliability, and Concurrent Validity Coefficients of the Groningen Fitness Test for the Elderly*

	Men				Women			
Test	**Mean**	**SD**	r_{xx}	r_{xy}	**Mean**	**SD**	r_{xx}	r_{xy}
Walking (# of 16.67-m int.)	44.1	18.4	0.94	0.49	34.2	17.5	0.95	0.72
Grip strength (kg)	43.0	8.6	0.94	**	26.7	5.6	0.91	**
Hip flexibility (cm)	21.9	5.9	0.98	0.74	29.6	8.8	0.96	0.63
Shoulder flexibility(°)	47.9	50.5	0.88	0.51	50.5	6.9	0.86	0.54
Balance (time)	73.8	12.2	0.87	0.80	71.6	13.7	0.85	0.15
Manual dexterity (sec)	51.9	12.9	0.92	0.67	48.6	9.0	0.88	0.46
Reaction time (msec)	245	57	0.83	0.52	262	62	0.87	0.75

*Data from Van Heuvelen 1998.

**Assumed face validity.

Test Procedures. The purpose of the test is to complete as many steps as possible in 2 minutes. The proper knee-stepping height is at a level even with the midway point between the middle of kneecap and top of the iliac crest. This tends to be a height of 10 to 12 inches. The test booklet provides procedures for monitoring the stepping height. A practice test should be given prior to the test day so that participants can experiment with pacing. Participants should be verbally encouraged to do their best, but not pushed to the point of overexertion or beyond what they feel is safe.

Scoring. The score is the total number of steps taken within 2 minutes. Only full steps are to be counted. A full step is each time the knee reaches the minimum height. To assist with pacing, subjects should be told when 1 minute has passed and when there are 30 seconds to go.

Groningen Fitness Test for the Elderly

The Groningen test (Lemmink 1996; VanHeuvelen 1998) was developed in The Netherlands and is being used in longitudinal research designed to study the health-related fitness of older people. The test measures the quality of life. The test consists of seven items that were found to be reliable and valid. The items were correlated with laboratory items to establish concurrent validity. Table 11.11 provides a summary of the test statistics. Provided are the means, standard deviations, stability reliability coefficients, and concurrent validity coefficients. The subjects tested included over 600 men and women who ranged in age from 57 to 91 years. Each of the test items was found to negatively correlate with age, showing that performance decreases with age. Provided next is an abridged description of the test items (VanHeuvelen 1998). You are encouraged to contact the authors for a complete copy of the test.

Aerobic Fitness Component

Test. Walking Endurance

Test Description. This test is administered on a rectangular course divided into three 16.7-meter (≈ 18 yards) intervals. The test starts by having the subject walk at a pace of 4 kilometers per hour (2.5 miles per hour). Every 3 minutes, walking speed is increased by 1 kilometer per hour (0.625 miles per hour). The top speed is 7 kilometers per hour (≈ 4.4 miles per hour). The objective is to keep up the effort as long as possible. The score is the number of 16.7-meter intervals completed.

Upper Body Strength Component

Test. Grip Strength

Test Description. Grip strength is measured on a hand dynamometer (see Chapter 7) with the preferred hand, arm held at the side. The subject is given three trials and the best of the three trials is used for the subject's score.

Lower Body Flexibility Component

Test. Hip Flexibility

Test Description. The test is the common sit-and-reach test. The subject is given three trials, and the best of the three trials is used for the subject's score.

Upper Body Flexibility Component

Test. Shoulder Flexibility

Test Description. The subject holds both handles of a cord. One handle is fixed, and the other is a sliding handle. The subject passes the cord over the head from the front of the body to behind the body. The arms are kept straight and as close together as possible. The shaft of the sliding handle combined with the length of the arm is used to determine the score. The subject is given three trials, and the best of the three trials is used for the subject's score.

Agility and/or Balance Component

Test. Balance

Test Description. The subject stands on a platform that can tilt sideways. For 30 seconds the subject attempts to keep the platform in equilibrium, that is, so that the base does not touch the floor. The total time in equilibrium is the score. The subject is given three trials, and the best of the three trials is used for the subject's score.

Fine Motor Abilities Component

Tests. Manual Dexterity and Reaction Time

Test Description—Manual Dexterity. The manual dexterity task requires the subject to replace 40 blocks from a full board to an empty board as quickly as possible. The subject uses their preferred hand. The score is the time taken to complete the task.

Test Description—Reaction Time. This is a standard simple reaction time test (Rudisill & Jackson 1992). A visual stimulus is present to the subject, who responds by pushing a button as quickly as possible. The reaction time is the elapsed time between signal and reaction. The subject's score is the median of fifteen trials.

Adult Fitness Computer Applications

The use of microcomputer technology in adult fitness and the health promotion industry has grown at an accelerated pace. This trend was started in the late 1960s by Dr. Kenneth Cooper when the Institute for Aerobics Research developed a computer system for the quantification of exercise with aerobics points (Cooper 1970). This computer system was designed to develop a database for studying the effects of exercise on health. This database was used to document that low aerobic fitness is a risk factor of all-cause mortality (Blair et al. 1989; Blair et al. 1995).

When the Tenneco Corporation of Houston, Texas, developed their employee health and fitness program, a computerized system was developed to quantify exercise by caloric expenditure (Baun & Baun 1985). The Tenneco system was especially important because it signaled that the trend in the corporate fitness industry was a commitment to computerization. Tenneco's development of its own customized computer software was a very expensive venture. Now, more affordable commercial software is available for evaluating adult fitness.

Provided next is a brief discussion of commercial software available for adult fitness programs. There are many different types of programs with adult fitness applications, such as health risk appraisals, nutritional analyses, fitness assessments, exercise prescription, and quantification of energy expenditure (i.e., exercise logging). We have limited the presentation to just fitness assessment, exercise prescription, and monitoring energy expenditure.

Assessing Fitness—General Fitness Assessment (GFA)

Evaluation of fitness is an essential component of an individualized exercise program. Figure 11.15 is the three-page computerized report of a sample fitness evaluation. The report includes all the major components of fitness, an individualized interpretation of the person's fitness, and training parameters for developing physical fitness. The bar graph is a display of the person's fitness in comparison to others of a similar age and same sex. Below the bar graph is a complete listing of the person's data, that is, actual. The value next to the score is the average score for a person of a similar age and the same sex, that is, norm. The next two pages of the report provide the person with an

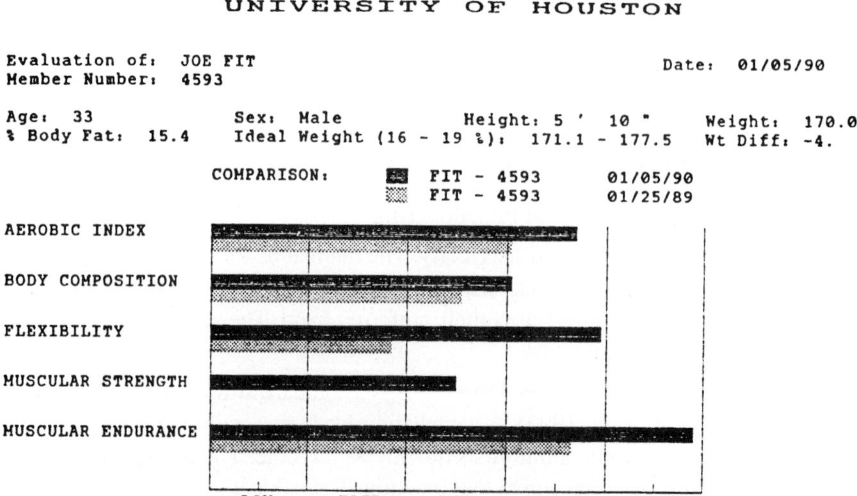

Figure 11.15
Sample printout of a General Fitness Assessment showing the person's fitness level, an interpretation of their fitness, and training parameters for improving fitness. (Source: CSI Software Company, Houston, TX. Reprinted by permission.)

Member Name: **Date:** 3/21/97

INTERPRETATION

The General Fitness Assessment (GFA) evaluates the key elements of fitness; Aerobic Capacity, Body Composition, Flexibility, Muscular Strength and Endurance. If you are fit your body functions well. You work, play and exercise with minimal risk of injury or fatigue. You have the energy you need. You are trim and you reduce the risk of serious health problems including cardiovascular disease, the leading cause of death. In short, you look good, and are taking good care of yourself. Let's review some of your specific results.

AEROBIC CAPACITY

Adequate Aerobic Capacity is the heart of good fitness. Aerobic exercise conditions your cardiovascular system (heart, muscles and lungs), consumes calories (reducing body fat) and protects you from cardiovascular disease. Maximum aerobic capacity or the maximum amount of oxygen you can consume per minute is also known as $\dot{V}O_2max$. It is much like maximum horsepower for an automobile. Your $\dot{V}O_2max$ is 35.3 ml/kg/min. Normal for you is 31. Your aerobic index is AVERAGE.

Aerobic exercise consists of activities such as walking, jogging, swimming, running, stairclimbing, cycling and aerobic dance. In order to exercise at a sufficient intensity to improve your fitness but not too strenuously, so as not to cause injury and burnout, follow your heart rate. Your training heart rate should be approximately 144 to 156 beats per minute. These are the heart rates at 65% to 74% of your $\dot{V}O_2max$. At the present level of fitness this will burn approximately 430 to 490 calories per hour.

BODY COMPOSITION

Proper body composition is important in order to look good, feel good and also reduce your risk of heart disease. It is determined by assessing body weight and the relative proportion of fat-free weight and body fat. Body composition is affected by both diet and exercise.

Your weight is 137 lbs. and your percent body fat is 20.8%. This represents 28 pounds of fat. Normal percent body fat range for a person of your age and sex is 23 to 32. In order to achieve this goal you should loose about 0 pounds of fat while maintaining the same fat-free weight.

Your fat-free weight, consisting primarily of muscle, bone and vital organs is 108 pounds. The ideal weight range for you, based upon normal body fat is 130 to 142 pounds.

Figure 11.15 *(continued)* General Fitness Assessment

Based upon these results your Body Composition category is GOOD. As you change your body weight, periodically check your percent body fat to make sure you are maintaining adequate muscle mass.

MUSCULAR FLEXIBILITY

Flexibility refers to the ability of the muscles, tendons and ligaments around a joint to provide support while allowing movement throughout the full range of motion. In order to prevent injury, it is important that a joint has sufficient range of motion and is strong enough to withstand the stress and strain of exercise. Your flexibility measurements are FAIR. Stretch after warming up to increase or maintain flexibility.

MUSCULAR STRENGTH

Your muscular strength score compared to other Females in your age group is FAIR. Muscular Strength is the maximum force that a muscle group can exert under various conditions. Resistance training using relatively low repetitions and higher intensity will maximize strength gains. Be sure to adequately warm up before resistance training.

MUSCULAR ENDURANCE

Muscular endurance allows you to work or exercise for a long period of time without fatigue. Generally, a lower intensity, higher repetition, muscle resistance program will produce optimal improvements. Your muscular endurance assessment is AVERAGE.

SUMMARY

Megan, your overall fitness score is 48.4, which is AVERAGE.

TRAINING PARAMETERS

Train at least 30 minutes per session and 4 sessions per week.

Watts	95 to 110	$\dot{V}O_2$ ml	1430 to 1650
KPM	560 to 670	$\dot{V}O_2$ ml/kg/min	23 to 26.5
KCal/hour	430 to 490	METs	6.6 to 7.6
Walk/Jog(min/mile)	11.4 to 9.9	Heart Rate	144 to 156

Sample printout of a General Fitness Assessment showing the person's fitness level, an interpretation of their fitness, and training parameters for improving fitness. (Source: CSI Software Company, Houston, TX. Reprinted by permission.)

individualized interpretation of their fitness and scientifically sound training suggestions. The final section of the report is training parameters. The training parameters for all forms of aerobic exercise are standard output of the GFA. The training parameters come from the person's $\dot{V}O_2$ Max, and parameters are provided for all forms of exercise.

The field of personal training has become a new career option for graduates of programs in physical education and exercise science. A major responsibility of a personal trainer is to design an individualized exercise program. Commercial software like this can be valuable to the personal trainer. Once a client's fitness data are in the computer and the fitness profile developed, the CSI software has the capacity to develop a sound individualized exercise program, as illustrated in Figure 11.16. Using the training parameters from the fitness evaluation, the computer can generate a weekly workout sheet consisting of:

- Warm-up and cool-down activities.
- Appropriate aerobic exercise.
- Strength development activities.

Strength training may be prescribed by sets and reps of certain weights. Aerobic intensity can be prescribed by units such as miles traveled or by percentage of $\dot{V}O_2$ Max, training heart rate zone (THRZ), or RPE. These values can then be used by you to document a well-balanced exercise program as well as to determine energy expended by calories expended and aerobic minutes.

Monitoring Aerobic Exercise—Exercise Logging

Paffenbarger's classic studies (Paffenbarger et al. 1986; Paffenbarger et al. 1984) have shown that exercise caloric expenditure is related to health. Logging exercise caloric expenditure by hand is difficult and cumbersome; the computer simplifies the task.

Trainee:

Trainer: I.M. Fit

WarmUP:
Side Stretches - Stretch slowly (5 minutes)
Warm-up All Muscle Groups
STEP 4-6 PLTFRM-Easy does it

Cool:
Cool Down - 5 minutes

EXERCISES	DESCRIPTION	3/21/97 SAT	3/22/97 SUN	3/23/97 MON	3/24/97 TUE	3/25/97 WED	3/26/97 THU	3/27/97 FRI
Aerobics	45 min 70-85% THRZ			*		*		*
Cycling (Road)	60 min 10 Miles Hard	*	*					
Step Aerobics	55 min 70-85% THRZ				*		*	
Walk/Jog/Run	25 min 2 Miles		*		*		*	
Strength Training	15 reps 45 lbs			*		*		*

Figure 11.16
Sample computer-generated individualized training program. The symbol * indicates the exercise to be done on the given day. (Source: CSI Software Company, Houston, TX. Reprinted by permission).

Figure 11.17
Sample output from the Exerlog program. After receiving information, the program provides instantaneous feedback in kilocalories, the number of minutes that exercise was done at a suitable intensity (aerobic minutes) and aerobic points, which are numerical descriptions of exercise intensity and duration. (Source: CSI Software Company, Houston, TX. Reprinted by permission.)

Page 1

	MOST RECENT	(LOSS) or GAIN
BODY WEIGHT	124.0	0

AVERAGE MILE (MIN)	8.7	BEST MILE (MIN)	7.7

DATE: 05/05/89 MEMBER # 2222A

FREDA A FITNESS
2345 FRED STREET
HOUSTON, TX 77001-1111

MESSAGE:
BE A PART OF IT! JOIN OUR SUMMER SOFTBALL TEAM. SEE PATTI IN ATHLETICS.

THIS MONTH'S ACTIVITIES

DATE	ACTIVITY	UNITS	DURATION	AEROBIC POINTS	CALORIES	AEROBIC MINUTES
04/05/89	WALK/JOG/RUN	5.8 MI	45:00	33.5	566	43.0
04/06/89	TREADMILL		45:00	32.7	554	41.0
04/06/89	STAIRMASTER		55:00	55.2	560	50.0
04/06/89	SWIMMING	1.2 MI	45:00	25.1	354	35.0
04/07/89	CYCLING (ROAD)	25.0 MI	120:00	23.5	985	100.0
04/08/89	CYCLE ERGOMETER		55:00	55.2	560	50.0
04/09/89	AEROBIC DANCE		55:00	11.0	411	35.0
04/09/89	PROG RESISTANCE		30:00	6.0	189	10.0
04/10/89	SUPER CIRCUIT		25:00	6.5	187	10.0
04/10/89	TENNIS DOUBLES	3.0 SET	75:00	1.2	391	30.0
04/11/89	WALK/JOG/RUN	3.0 MI	30:00	14.0	295	
04/11/89	SCHWINN AIRDYNE		45:00	17.5	458	30.0
04/12/89	WALK/JOG/RUN	6.2 MI	48:00	36.2	610	48.0

TOTALS

ACTIVITY	PREVIOUS TOTAL	THIS MONTH'S TOTAL	CUMULATIVE YEAR'S TOTAL
WALK/JOG/RUN (MI)	38.30	15.00	53.30
STAIRMASTER (HRS)	4.00	0.92	4.92
CYCLE ERGOMETER (HRS)	3.82	0.92	4.74
SWIMMING (MI)	3.30	1.20	4.50
CYCLING (ROAD) (MI)	127.00	25.00	152.00
TOTAL CALORIES (1.7 lbs)	46194	6120	52314
TOTAL AEROBIC MINUTES	2993	482	3475
TOTAL AEROBIC POINTS	1507	317	1825

AEROBIC POINTS: ONE POINT EQUALS APPROXIMATELY 7.0 ML/KG/MIN OF OXYGEN UPTAKE ABOVE RESTING. TRY TO OBTAIN AT LEAST 30 POINTS PER WEEK.
AEROBIC MINUTES: THE NUMBER OF MINUTES YOUR HEART IS PERFORMING IN ITS TRAINING ZONE. TRY TO OBTAIN AT LEAST 60 PER WEEK.
CALORIES: 3500 CALORIES REPRESENTS THE ENERGY DERIVED FROM LOSING APPROXIMATELY 1 LB. OF WEIGHT. CSI 1987

In addition, it provides instantaneous feedback of various key aspects of exercise, such as energy expenditure and training intensity. With a computer logging program, body weight, activities done, calories, and aerobic minutes of exercise can be tracked. The CSI Exerlog program is very user friendly and can calculate the energy expenditure for many different exercise modes. Figure 11.17 shows the example of an exercise logging computer report.

Summary

The American population is aging. In 1975, the median age for Americans was 29 years; by the year 2000 the median age will be 36 years. Not only is the average age increasing, the number of the "oldest old" is increasing. Public health research documents the importance of maintaining a level of fitness as an adult. Cross-sectional and longitudinal research has documented that fitness decreases with age. What is less clear is how much of the decline in fitness is due to aging and how much is due to life-style. There is ample research to show that suitable amounts of exercise slow the age-related decline in these important components. Adult fitness is assessed in two general ways. The first involves tests that are similar to those used to assess youth fitness. The YMCA's adult fitness program is a popular, scientifically sound test with normative standards. The YMCA test includes the same fitness components measured in youth fitness tests, such as aerobic fitness, body composition, flexibility, and muscular strength and endurance. The second general method of assessing adult fitness is functional fitness. The relatively new functional fitness tests are designed for older adults, men and women over age 60 years, and are designed to assess the person's capacity to function independently. The fitness components are similar to the components measured by the YMCA test, but the test items consist of functional living tasks, such as walking for 6 minutes. Functional fitness is important not only to the individual but to American society. Older individuals do not want to be dependent on others and the health care costs of being functionally dependent are much higher.

Formative Evaluation of Objectives

Objective 1 Identify the methods used to study the decline in fitness associated with aging.

1. How is the rate at which fitness declines with age determined with a cross-sectional research study?
2. How is the rate at which fitness declines with age determined with a longitudinal research study?
3. What are the limitations of the cross-sectional and longitudinal methods?

Objective 2 Understand the general age-related decline in health-related fitness.

1. Describe the expected change in fitness associated with aging.
2. What is the influence of life-style on the decline in fitness with aging?

Objective 3 Identify the types of tests used to evaluate adult fitness.

1. What are the tests of the Y's Way to Fitness battery?
2. How do the adult fitness test items compare to youth fitness test items?

Objective 4 Identify the types of tests used to evaluate functional adult fitness.

1. What is the general philosophy of functional fitness tests?
2. Describe the general nature of adult functional fitness tests.

Objective 5 Identify the computer programs available to use in adult fitness programs.

1. What types of computer programs are available for adult fitness evaluation?
2. Describe how an exercise specialist or personal trainer could use computer programs to individualize an adult fitness program.

Additional Learning Activities

1. Visit a YMCA and gain an understanding of the Y's Way to Fitness program. If you have the opportunity, become involved in the testing phase of the program. It is the leading adult health-related fitness test.
2. There are many different adult fitness programs—at corporations, hospitals, or even at your college or university. Volunteer to work in the program. You learn through experience, and the experience can help you find a job.
3. Investigate fitness programs for the elderly. These can be found in community centers or retirement homes. You may be surprised to find that they are becoming very popular. Volunteer to work in this setting. This experience could become very valuable in the future.
4. If you can find the opportunity, work with someone to administer a functional adult fitness test. With the "graying of America," testing the elderly could lead to a job opportunity.
5. Visit an adult fitness facility and examine their computer applications.

Bibliography

Baun, W. B. and M. Baun. 1985. A corporate health and fitness program: Motivation and management by computers. *JOPERD* 55:43–45.

Blair, S. N. et al. 1989. Physical fitness and all-cause mortality: A prospective study of healthy men and women. *Journal of the American Medical Association* 262:2395–2401.

Blair, S. N. et al. 1995. Changes in physical fitness and all-cause mortality: A prospective study of healthy and unhealthy men. *Journal of the American Medical Association* 273(14):1093–1098.

Blakely, B. R. et al. 1994. The validity of isometric strength tests. *Personnel Psychology* 37:247–274.

Buskirk, E. R. and J. L. Hodgson. 1987. Age and aerobic power: The rate of change in men and women. *Federation Proceedings* 46:1824–1829.

Cooper Institute for Aerobics Research. 1992. *The Prudential FITNESSGRAM test administration manual.* Dallas: The Cooper Institute for Aerobic Research.

Cooper, K. H. 1970. *The new aerobics.* New York: Bantam Books.

Cornoni-Huntley, et al. 1986. *Populations for epidemiologic studies of the elderly: Resource data book.* Government Printing Office, NIH Pub. No. 86–2443.

deVries, H. A. and T. J. Housh. 1994. *Physiology of exercise for physical education, athletics and exercise science.* 5th ed. Dubuque, IA: Wm. C. Brown.

Frisancho, A. R. 1990. *Anthropometric standards for assessment of growth and nutritional status.* Ann Arbor, MI: University of Michigan Press.

Golding, L. A., C. R. Meyers, and W. E. Sinning. 1989. *The Y's way to physical fitness.* 3d ed. Chicago: National Board of YMCA.

Hagberg, J. M. et al. 1985. A hemodynamic comparison of young and older endurance athletes during exercise. *Journal of Applied Physiology* 58(6):2041–2046.

Jackson, A. S. et al. 1995. Changes in aerobic power of men ages 25–70 years. *Medicine and Science in Sports and Exercise* 27:113–120.

Jackson, A. S. and M. L. Pollock. 1978. Generalized equations for predicting body density of men. *British Journal of Nutrition* 40:497–504.

Jackson, A. S., M. L. Pollock, and A. Ward. 1980. Generalized equations for predicting body density of women. *Medicine and Science in Sports and Exercise* 12:175–182.

Jackson, A. S. et al. 1996. Changes in aerobic power of women, ages 20 to 64 years. *Medicine and Science in Sports and Exercise* 28:884–891.

Kasch, F. W. et al. 1990. The effect of physical activity and inactivity on aerobic power in older men (a longitudinal study). *The Physician and Sportsmedicine* 18:73–81.

Kasch, F. W., J. P. Wallace, and S. P. VanCamp. 1985. Effects of 18 years of endurance exercise on the physical work capacity of older men. *Journal of Cardiopulmonary Rehabilitation* 5:308–312.

Kovar, M. G. 1986. National Center for Health Statistics, *Aging in the eighties, preliminary data from the supplement on aging to the national health interview survey, United States, January-June 1984. Advanced data from vital and health statistics.* No. 115. DHHS Pub. No. 86–1250. Public Health Service, Hyattsville, MD.

Larson, E. B. and R. A. Bruce. 1987. Health benefits of exercise in an aging society. *Archives of Internal Medicine* 147:353–356.

Lemmink, K. 1996. The Gronigen Fitness Test for the Elderly, Development of a Measurement Instrument. Ph.D Dissertation, Department of Human Movement Sciences, University of Groningen, Groningen, The Netherlands.

McArdle, W. D., F. I. Katch, and V. L. Katch. 1991. *Exercise physiology: Energy, nutrition, and human performance.* 3d ed. Philadelphia: Lea & Febiger.

Montoye, H. J. and Lamphiear, D. E. 1977. Grip and arm strength in males and females, age 10 to 69. *Research Quarterly* 48:109–120.

Osness, W. H. et al. 1996. *Functional fitness assessment for adults over 60 years: A field based assessment.* 2d ed. Dubuque: Kendall/Hunt.

Paffenbarger, R. J. et al. 1986. Physical activity, all cause mortality, and longevity of college alumni. *New England Journal of Medicine* 314:605–613.

Paffenbarger, R. S., Jr. et al. 1984. A natural history of athleticism and cardiovascular health. *Journal of American Medical Association* 252:491–495.

Petrofsky, J. S. and A. R. Lind. 1975. Aging, isometric strength and endurance and cardiovascular responses to static effort. *Journal of Applied Physiology* 38:91–95.

Plowman, S. A. 1992. Chapter 8. Physical activity, physical fitness, and low back pain. In Holloszy, J. O. (Ed.). *Exercise and sport sciences reviews.* Baltimore: Williams & Wilkins.

Pollock, M. L. et al. 1987. Effect of age and training on aerobic capacity and body composition of master athletes. *Journal of Applied Physiology* 62(2):725–731.

Pollock, M. L. and J. H. Wilmore. 1990. *Exercise in health and disease.* 2d ed. Philadelphia: W. B. Saunders.

Rikli, R. E. and C. J. Jones. 1997. Assessing physical performance in independent older adults: Issues and guidelines. *Journal of Aging and Physical Activity* 5:244–261.

Rudisill, M. E. and A. S. Jackson. 1992. *Theory and application of motor learning.* Onalaska, TX: MacJR Publishing.

U.S. Public Health Service. 1990. *Healthy people 2000: National health promotion and disease prevention objectives.* DHHS Publication No. (PHS) 91–50212. Washington DC: Department of Health and Human Services.

Shephard, R. J. 1986. Physical training for the elderly. *Clinical Sports Medicine* 5:515–533.

Skender, M. L. et al. 1996. Comparison of 2-year weight loss trends in behavioral treatments of obesity: Diet, exercise, and combination interventions. *Journal of the American Dietetic Association* 96:342–346.

Spirduso, W. W. 1995. *Physical dimensions of aging.* Champaign, IL: Human Kinetics.

Taylor, H. L., E. Buskirk, and A. Henschel. 1955. Maximal oxygen intake as an objective measure of cardiorespiratory performance. *Journal of Applied Physiology* 8:73–80.

Taylor, H. L. et al. 1963. The standardization and interpretation of submaximal and maximal tests of working capacity. *Pediatrics* Part 2:703–710.

U.S. Army. 1992. *FM 21–20 physical fitness training.* Washington DC: Department of the Army.

VanHeuvelen, M. et al. 1998. Physical fitness related to age and physical activity in older persons. *Medicine and Science in Sports and Exercise* 30(3):434–441.

Wilmore, J. H. and D. L. Costill. 1994. *Physiology of sport and exercise.* Champaign, IL: Human Kinetics.

12

CHAPTER

Evaluating Skill Achievement

Contents

Key Words

accuracy tests
objective evaluation
rating scales
skill tests
subjective evaluation
wall valley tests

Objectives

The achievement of sport skills can be measured by three general means: skill tests, rating skills, and performance itself. Skill tests are an objective, often-used means of evaluating a variety of psychomotor objectives. These tests can be standardized or developed individually. Rating scales are instruments that standardize and define a performance that will be subjectively evaluated by a teacher. Finally, in some instances the performance itself can be used to evaluate achievement.

After reading Chapter 12, you should be able to:

1. Identify the four general types of sport skill tests.
2. Evaluate the four general types of sport skill tests using the criteria of reliability, validity, and feasibility for mass testing.
3. Evaluate the weaknesses and strengths of rating scales.
4. Identify motor skills that are best evaluated by performance.
5. Outline methods that could be used to develop reliable, valid, and feasible measurement procedures for evaluating motor skill achievement.

Introduction

A universal goal of physical education programs is to produce permanent, measurable changes in student psychomotor behavior, in skills ranging from touch football to modern dance, from volleyball to scuba diving. For the achievement of psychomotor objectives to be evaluated, the measurement procedures—tests, rating scales, or other instruments—must parallel the instructional objectives. Today the trend is away from standardized evaluation methods, whose objectives often vary from instructional ones (see Authentic Assessment section, Chapter 5). Instead, it is the teacher—the person who has developed the instructional objectives—who must develop the procedures for evaluating them.

Sport skill tests are an objective method for evaluating motor skill achievement. Several of these tests are outlined in the chapter. From them, you should be able to develop your own reliable, valid skill tests.

Rating scales are a subjective but systematic method for evaluating those skills that do not lend themselves to objective evaluation. The subjectivity of the method presents numerous problems, but there are procedures for constructing reliable, valid scales discussed in the text.

Finally, for certain skills (e.g., golf, bowling, archery) performance can provide an objective score for skill evaluation. The advantages and limitations of performance-derived evaluation are presented here as well.

Sport skill testing is seldom conducted outside of physical education programs and athletic programs. For individuals not likely to conduct sport skill testing, this chapter still has value. Most people are going to have measurement situations where they have to develop their own tests and procedures. In this chapter you will encounter a variety of measurement situations, often with measurement problems, and you will see how tests were developed for these situations. The problem solving/test development procedures that were followed in developing sport skill tests are the same procedures used in developing fitness tests, pre-employment screening tests, and other physical performance tests.

Sport Skill Tests

Skill tests require an environment similar to the game environment and standardized procedures for administration. The validity of skill tests is judged to some extent on the consistency between testing and performing environments. This does not mean you must recreate exactly the playing environment; it does mean that the movements and the activity must correspond to those of the actual sport. For example, you can use repeated volleying of a tennis ball against a wall to measure achievement in the skill of the tennis ground stroke; however, the student must be using the correct form.

The virtue of skill tests is a subject of ongoing debate. Many skill tests offer an objective, reliable, and valid method for evaluating motor skill objectives, while others do not. Do not use a skill test that does not meet your evaluation needs or the important criteria of reliability, validity, and feasibility for mass testing. Also, be sure to adopt tests that were developed on students of the same sex, age, and experience level as your students. You can also modify an existing test to meet your needs. Strand and Wilson (1993) describe many skill tests that might be adopted or modified for use in your testing program. Chapters in books by Barrow, McGee, and Tritscher (1989), Hastad and Lacy (1994), and Miller (1994) may be helpful in identifying sport skill tests.

Although skill tests are most useful for the evaluation of learning, they can also be used for (1) placement, (2) diagnosis, (3) prediction, (4) comparative evaluation, and (5) motivation. The tests used to evaluate achievement can be placed into four groups: (1) accuracy tests, (2) wall volley tests, (3) total bodily movement tests, and (4) throws, kicks, or strokes for power or distance. A few tests have aspects of several groups and so are combination tests. Provided next are sample tests that illustrate each general group of skill tests.

Accuracy Tests

Accuracy tests involve throwing, striking, or kicking an object toward a target for accuracy. Basketball free throws, and badminton or tennis or volleyball serves at a target, are common accuracy tests.

The basic disadvantage of accuracy tests is that the target scoring system (5-4-3-2-1-0 or 3-2-1-0) does not allow discrimination among skill levels. For example, it would be meaningless to use a single tennis serve as an index of serving skill if the score could range from only 0 to 3. This lack of variability reduces reliability. Two general procedures, however, can improve the reliability of accuracy tests. The first increases the variability of the target. A target with a range from 0 to 1 (hit or miss) is less reliable than a target whose range is from 0 to 2 or 0 to 5. Given 10 serves, the range of scores for a target scored 0 or 1 would be from 0 to 10; on a target scored 0 to 3 the range would be from 0 to 30, a more precise measure. The second procedure increases the number of trials. Obviously twenty trials yield more reliable results than do five or ten. Ideally, then, fifteen to thirty trials should be administered for most accuracy tests. Of course, too many trials can make a test unfeasible for mass testing.

Wall Volley Tests

Wall volley tests require the student to repeatedly stroke, pass, throw, or kick an object at a wall over a specified period of time with the number of successful trials the unit of measurement, or for a specified number of successful trials with time as the unit of measurement. For example, using correct form, how many seconds does it take an individual to pass a basketball against a wall 10 times.

In general, wall volley tests tend to be reliable, but because the testing and playing environments can differ considerably, validity poses a problem. Does repeatedly passing a ball against a wall truly measure a student's basketball passing skill? Because the wall volley test environment differs from the game environment, it is especially important that students be allowed to practice the test. Then too, wall volleying can be a useful way to practice a skill, allowing the student both practice in the skill and greater familiarity with the testing environment.

Notice in the example of the basketball passing test that the number of passes against the wall was set (10) and the score was the amount of time it took to complete the 10 passes. An alternative procedure and scoring system for wall volley tests is to count the number of hits on the wall in a set length of time, usually 15 to 60 seconds. The advantage of the alternative procedure is that only one timer is needed and several students may take the test at the same time if sufficient wall space is available. The student's partner counts the number of hits and watches for correct form.

Tests of Total Bodily Movement

These tests require the subject to run a standardized test course using movements characteristic of the sport. An example is a basketball dribbling test.

Basketball Control Dribble Test (AAHPERD 1984)

Objective: To measure skill in handling the ball that a player is moving.

Equipment: Standard inflated basketballs, a stopwatch, and six obstacles arranged as shown in Figure 12.1.

Procedure: The player stands on his or her nondominant hand side of Cone A with a ball in hand. At the signal "Go," the player begins dribbling with the nondominant hand to the nondominant hand side of Cone B and continues to dribble through the course using the preferred hand, changing hands when desired until he or she crosses the finish line. The ball may be dribbled with either hand, but legal dribbles must be used. Each player is allowed three trials.

Scoring: The score in seconds and tenths of seconds is the time required to dribble the entire course. The last two trials are timed and recorded; and the sum of the two is the player's score on the test.

Other considerations: In general these tests are reliable. Their value, and thus validity, is determined by the extent to which they relate to the objectives being taught. Allow students to practice on the test course. They will learn how to travel it more efficiently with each practice or trial. These types of tests, like most skill tests, can also be used as skill practice.

Throws, Kicks, or Strokes for Power or Distance

These tests, among the more common types of skill tests, measure the student's ability to throw, kick, or strike an object forcefully. Obvious examples are the softball throw for distance, the football punt for distance, and the golf drive for distance.

Normally such tests are reliable because the distance the object travels can be accurately measured. Attention must be paid, however, to each test's relevance to the instructional objectives. Certainly many variations of this test could be used.

Combination Tests

These tests are a combination of several of the four groupings just mentioned, usually speed and accuracy. An example is a basketball speed shooting test and basketball passing test.

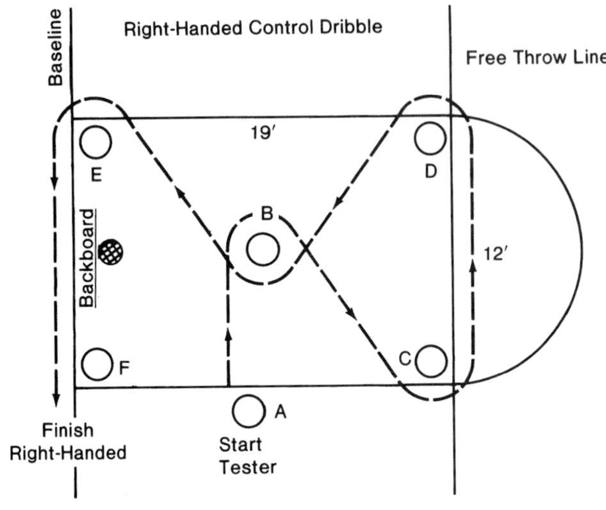

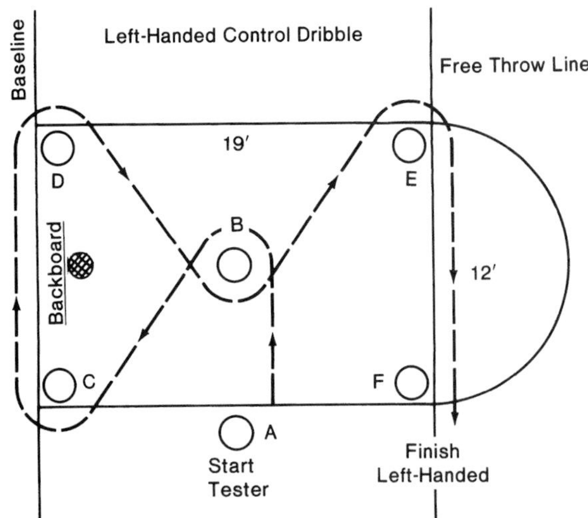

Figure 12.1
AAHPERD Basketball Control Dribble Test as an example of a total bodily movement test. (Reprinted by permission of the American Alliance for Health, Physical Education, Recreation and Dance, Reston, VA 22091.)

Speed Spot Shooting (AAHPERD 1984)

Objective: To measure skill in rapidly shooting from specified positions.

Equipment: Standard inflated basketball, standard goal, stopwatch, marking tape.

Procedure: Grades 5 and 6 shoot from 9 feet; grades 7, 8, and 9 shoot from 12 feet; grades 10, 11, 12, and college shoot from 15 feet (Figure 12-2). Three 60-second trials are administered, with the first trial considered practice and the last two scored. During each trial a student must shoot at least once from each of the five spots (A-E) and may shoot a maximum of four lay-up shots, but not two in succession.

Scoring: Two points are awarded for each shot made, and one point is awarded for each unsuccessful shot that hits the rim. The final score is the total of the last two trial points.

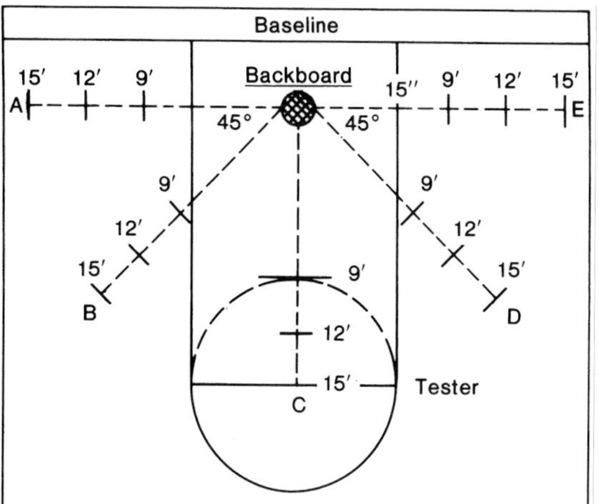

Figure 12.2
Speed Spot Shooting Test.
(Source: AAHPERD, 1984. *Basketball Skills Test Manual for Boys and Girls,* Reston, VA 22091.)

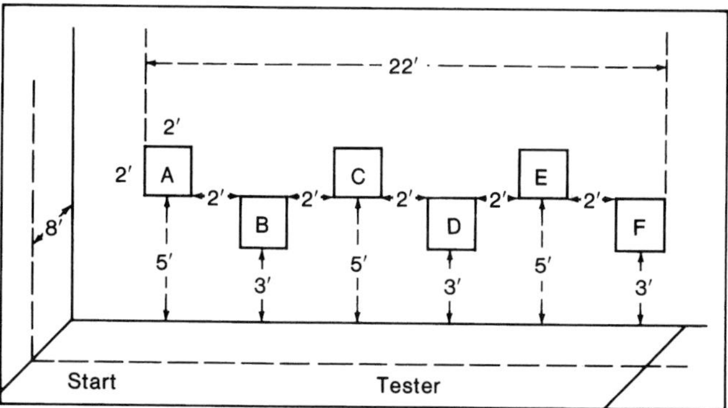

Figure 12.3
Basketball Passing Test.
(From Johnson, B. L. and J. K. Nelson. 1979. *Practical Measurements for Evaluation in Physical Education.* Minneapolis, MN: Burgess Publishing Co. and AAHPERD, *Basketball Skills Test Manual for Boys and Girls,* 1984.)

Passing (AAHPERD 1984)

Objective: To measure skill in passing and recovering the ball while moving.

Equipment: Standard inflated basketball, stopwatch, smooth wall surface, marking tape.

Procedure: Six squares are marked on the wall, and a restraining line is marked on the floor 8 feet from the wall (Figure 12.3). Three 30-second trials are administered, with the first trial considered practice and the last two timed. The player, holding a ball, stands behind the restraining line and faces target A. On the command "Go," the player chest-passes at target A, recovers the rebound, and moves opposite target B. From behind the restraining line the player chest-passes at target B. This pattern continues until target F, where two chest-passes are executed. Then the player moves to the left, passes at target E, and continues to move left passing at each target in turn.

Scoring: Each pass that hits the desired target counts two points. Each pass hitting the wall but missing the target counts one point. The sum of the last two trial points is the final score.

Rating Scales

Rating scales are useful for evaluating qualities that cannot be measured objectively, or at least not easily and efficiently. This section focuses on procedures for constructing and using rating scales; particularly to evaluate skill achievement.

Subjective or Objective Evaluation?

Most of the measurement techniques discussed to this point have had good objectivity for the simple reason that most of the measurements conducted in physical education are objective rather than subjective. With **objective evaluation,** the test has a clearly defined scoring system, so the scorer does not affect the final score. Examples of objective tests are a mile run measured with a stopwatch, a standing long jump measured with a tape, a 1-minute sit-up measured in number of executions, or a basketball free throw test. If a student makes seven free throws out of ten shots, two scorers would have little difficulty arriving at the same score. Remember, objectivity is the degree of agreement between two or more competent scorers. With subjective evaluation, a qualified person or persons judge(s) the quality of a performance and assign(s) a score, so the scorer can and does affect the final score. A subjective evaluation may be based on a defined scoring system, as in the scoring of gymnastics events in competition, or the evaluation may be just the impressions of each scorer. In the latter case, agreement between the scorers would probably not be high and objectivity would be low. Rating scales are designed to help objectify subjective evaluation by defining the scoring system, just as a tape measure defines the system of scoring the distance a person jumps.

Some people do not think highly of subjective evaluations, but it must be remembered that **subjective evaluations** are often used to determine the validity of objective tests. Judges' ratings are among the most widely used criteria for validating skill tests for team sports. Although it is true that anything that exists can be measured, the system for measuring it may not be an objective test. Certainly, wherever feasible, objective evaluation should be used. But many important instructional objectives cannot be measured objectively. In fact, objective skill tests are not even available for gymnastics, folk dancing, fencing, and teamwork. For a number of the more complex team sports, it would be almost impossible to develop a test or test battery to validly measure total playing ability for two reasons:

1. The difficulty of identifying or measuring in a short period of time all the skill components that make up a given sport, and
2. The difficulty of objectively measuring the interaction among the skill components of a given sport, making the sum of the measurable components less than descriptive of the whole sport.

Subjective evaluation may also be more efficient than objective testing. Certain subjective scoring can be carried out while the students are practicing or competing, making it unnecessary to set aside special testing periods. Also, the number of trials required in certain tests for objective evaluation can make those tests unfeasible for mass testing. For example, assume that a teacher wants to evaluate student skills in serving and passing a volleyball for a class of sixty. The two recommended objective tests (AAHPER 1969) would require a total of 600 serves and 1200 passes to reliably evaluate these skills. Certainly a more efficient use of time would be to develop a rating scale and evaluate the students while they play the game.

Problems with Subjective Evaluation

Subjective evaluation must be not only valid, reliable, and efficient, but also as objective as possible. We can satisfy these four criteria if the procedure is well planned.

The first stage in the planning process is the determination of which skills are going to be evaluated and how much each skill is going to affect the final score. Consider, for example, a teacher who, at the end of a volleyball unit, has not planned what to evaluate or how to weigh what has been evaluated. This teacher may have neglected not only to observe the same skills in each student, but also to weigh each equally in the final score. Serving skill may account for 35% of one student's final score and only 20% of another's.

The second stage in the planning process is the formulation of performance standards. Suppose that a teacher, having decided which skills to evaluate and their weight, begins to evaluate the students' serves without formulating performance standards. If the teacher expected well-placed, hard-to-return services and the first few students do not serve well, the teacher may unconsciously lower his or her standards, applying different criteria to the next students. These sliding standards would give two students of equal ability different scores.

The third stage in the planning process is a system for immediate recorded scoring. Even when a teacher knows what to evaluate, the weight of each evaluation, and the performance standards, unless the scores are recorded immediately, the evaluation will probably be neither reliable nor valid. Scores are too easily interchanged if the teacher tries to remember the score of each student and record it later.

In a sense, a rating scale reflects the careful planning procedure required to give reliability, validity, and objectivity to subjective evaluation. The scale lists the traits to be evaluated, reflects the teacher-determined importance of each trait, describes the performance standards, and provides a format for immediate recorded scoring.

Constructing a Rating Scale

The process of constructing a rating scale is threefold: (1) determining the purpose of the subjective evaluation, (2) identifying the basic components of the trait being evaluated, and (3) selecting the levels of ability for each component.

Purpose. The purpose of a rating scale determines the degree to which subjective evaluations must discriminate among ability groups. The more they must discriminate, the greater the number of classifications of ability. If, for example, posture is subjectively evaluated, only two classifications (acceptable-unacceptable) or three classifications (excellent-average-poor) may be needed. For grading purposes, three to five classifications are usually adequate; occasionally seven to ten are used in competition.

Basic Components. The trait being rated is almost always evaluated in parts or components, which must themselves be identified. The importance of each component and subcomponent must be defined so that points reflecting their relative value can be assigned. In Table 12.1, for example, three components are identified and three subcomponents are listed under each. These components and subcomponents reflect the instructional objectives of the activity.

Levels of Ability. The third step in the process is to decide how many levels of ability should be assigned to each component. Two levels—pass-fail—are usually considered too crude an evaluation procedure. When three levels of ability are sufficient,

Table 12.1 Sample Volleyball Rating Scale

Each of the three components of volleyball-playing ability has a point value of 15, and is scored on a 5-4-3-2-1 basis:

5 points—Exceptional ability, near perfect for the age and sex of the participant.
4 points—Above average ability, not perfect but quite skillful for the age and sex of the participant.
3 points—Average ability, typical for the age and sex of the participant.
2 points—Below average ability, characterized by more mistakes than is typical performance for the age and sex of the participant.
1 point—Inferior ability, far below typical performance for the age and sex of the participant.

For each subheading, circle the appropriate score.

I. Serve					
A. Height above net	5	4	3	2	1
B. Accuracy of placement	5	4	3	2	1
C. Difficulty of return	5	4	3	2	1
II. Setting or Spiking—choose one					
A. Setting					
1. Height above net	5	4	3	2	1
2. Accuracy of placement	5	4	3	2	1
3. Coordination with spiker	5	4	3	2	1
B. Spiking					
1. Accuracy of placement	5	4	3	2	1
2. Difficulty of return	5	4	3	2	1
3. Coordination with setter	5	4	3	2	1
III. General team play					
A. Hustle	5	4	3	2	1
B. Alertness—saves and play of difficult shots	5	4	3	2	1
C. Teamwork	5	4	3	2	1
Total Score ________					

a student can be rated above average, average, or below average on each subcomponent. A five-level scoring system is probably the most common: Each student is rated superior, above average, average, below average, or inferior on each subcomponent. Systems beyond five levels require that the teacher be knowledgeable enough about the characteristics being evaluated to identify small differences in ability or status. If a teacher creates more ability levels than he or she can identify, the reliability of the evaluations will be low. Remember that reliability and objectivity are improved when the rating scale lists exactly what is looked for in each subcomponent.

Using the Scale

No rating scale, however well prepared, works unless it is used. You should have a copy of the scale for each subject and record the ratings on it immediately after the evaluation. There are also several ways to improve the effectiveness of a rating scale:

increasing the number of qualified raters, retesting on several occasions, allowing sufficient time for both the test and the evaluation, preparing the students, and developing your own scale where possible.

Number of Raters. The reliability and validity of subjective evaluations increase as the number of raters increases, as predicted by the Spearman-Brown prophecy formula and the validity prediction formula (Chapters 3 and 4), provided of course that the raters are qualified. One well-qualified rater is preferable to several poorly qualified raters. When there are several raters, objectivity improves if they decide before the rating what they are looking for and what standards to use. For example, assume there are four judges in a gymnastics meet—two college coaches and two high school coaches—and that each rates performers on a 10-point system. The college coaches may expect more of the performers than do the high school coaches. Thus, if the participants are junior high boys, the judges must decide whether a perfect score indicates perfect performance, or the best that can be expected of this age group.

Number of Trials. Rating each student on several occasions within a short period—three days, for example—and using the average of the ratings as a score usually improves the score's reliability and validity. The justification and advantages of rating each person several times are the same as the reasons for using multiple trials on a physical performance test. By rating each person on several different days, we minimize the chances of a student receiving a poor rating because of an off day, or a high score due to luck.

If you are able to rate a student on several different occasions, do not look at the student's previous ratings, which are likely to influence your evaluation. For example, if you know that a student was rated below average on the first performance, there is little chance that you will rate the student above average on a subsequent performance, even if the student deserves it. This preconceived idea of ability is a problem common to all forms of subjectivity evaluation.

Testing Time. Allow enough time to rate an individual completely and to record the ratings immediately. It is better to rate only ten people each hour and to do a good job than to try to rate thirty people in an hour and to obtain invalid ratings.

Student Preparation. As with objective tests, the students should know what is expected of them and what you will be looking for when you evaluate them. Let the students know that you plan to evaluate them in the near future so that they can prepare themselves if they want to. This makes the evaluation a type of formative evaluation and communicates to the students their weaknesses. Finally, students should be informed that they are being evaluated the day that ratings are made.

Teacher-Prepared Scales. We believe that teachers should construct their own rating scales. The objectives of the course, the manner in which it is taught, the types of students, and their prior experiences are all variables that affect what is evaluated and how. Only a teacher-made rating scale can meet the evaluation needs of a specific situation. In preparing your own scales, you can look to others, like those shown in Tables 12.2 and 12.3 for help.

Table 12.2 Badminton Rating Scale

The four areas of badminton-playing ability may all be rated during competition. However, the first two areas may be rated in a noncompetitive situation, if so desired, by asking the student to demonstrate the various serves and strokes.

Each subarea is scored on a 3-2-1 basis:

3 points—Above average ability, considerably more skillful than the performance typical of the student's age and sex.
2 points—Average ability, typical performance for age and sex.
1 point—Below average ability, far inferior to typical performance for age and sex.

For each subarea, circle the appropriate score.

I. Serve

A. Position of shuttlecock upon contact—racket head strikes shuttlecock below waist level.	3 2 1
B. Position of racket at end of serve—if short serve, racket head does not rise above chest; if long serve, racket head stops between shoulders and top of head at end of serve.	3 2 1
C. Placement of serve—well placed relative to type of serve and position of opponent.	3 2 1
D. Height of serve relative to type of serve—short serve is low over net; drive serve is low over net and deep; clear serve is high and deep.	3 2 1

II. Strokes—consider placement and quality of each stroke

A. Clear—high and deep.	3 2 1
B. Smash—hit from position above head and in front of body; path of bird is down.	3 2 1
C. Drive—sharp and low over net; hit from position about shoulder height; can be deep or midcourt, but not short.	3 2 1
D. Drop—hit from position waist-to shoulder-height; low over net; a hairpin-type shot.	3 2 1

III. Strategy

A. Places shots all over court.	3 2 1
B. Executes a variety of shots at the most opportune moments.	3 2 1
C. Takes advantage of opponent's weaknesses (for example, poor backhand, strength problem in back court, poor net play).	3 2 1
D. Uses own best shots.	3 2 1

IV. Footwork and Position

A. Near center court position, so flexible to play any type of shot.	3 2 1
B. Has control of body at all times during play.	3 2 1
C. Body is in correct position when making each shot (usually determined by the feet).	3 2 1
D. Racket is shoulder-to-head-height and ready for use (wrist cocked) at all times; eyes are on the shuttlecock at all times.	3 2 1

Total Score _______

Suggested by Bill Landin, Indiana University

Table 12.3 Swimming Rating Scale for Elementary Backstroke

The arm stroke, leg kick, complete stroke, and stroke efficiency are rated on a three-point scale. Complete stroke and stroke efficiency are double-weighted so as to be twice as influential as arm stroke and leg kick in the total rating.

Circle the appropriate score for each area.

A. Arm Stroke

3 points—Arms do not break water or rise above top of head; elbows are kept at sides and fingers move up midline of body; stroke is powerful and smoothly coordinated.

2 points—Arms do not break water or rise above top of head; elbows are usually kept at sides and fingers move up midline to body; stroke is reasonably powerful and reasonably well-coordinated.

1 point —Arms break water and/or rise above top of head; elbows are not kept at sides and fingers do not move up midline of body; stroke is not powerful and/or poorly coordinated.

B. Leg Kick

3 points—Legs drop at knees for whip kick; toes are outside of heels as feet spread; kick is powerful and smoothly coordinated.

2 points—Legs drop at knees for whip kick but some flexation occurs at hips; toes are not outside of heels as feet spread, causing knees to spread; kick is reasonably powerful and reasonably well-coordinated.

1 point —Legs do not drop at knees for whip kick, but are brought toward stomach by flexing at the hips; knees spread too wide; no power in kick; kick is poorly coordinated.

C. Complete Stroke

6 points—Arms and legs are coordinated during stroke; arms are at sides, trunk and legs straight, and toes pointed during glide position.

4 points—Minor deviations from the standard for 6 points occur.

2 points—Arms and legs are not coordinated during stroke; glide position is poor with reference to arm-trunk-leg-toe position.

D. Stroke Efficiency

6 points—Long distance is covered in glide; body is relaxed in water; swims in straight line; hips on surface.

4 points—Average distance is covered in glide; body is relaxed in water; does not swim in straight line; hips slightly below surface.

2 points—Little distance is covered in glide; body is not relaxed in water; does not swim in straight line; hips are well below surface (swimmer is sitting in water rather than lying on top of it).

Total Score ____________

The Performance

For many motor skills, performance is a reliable means of evaluating instructional objectives. It is important to remember that in this context the performance environment is also the evaluation environment. The instructional objectives and the performance may thus be identical, and logical validity more readily assured. For example, a tumbling objective might be to execute a forward roll; when the student does so, the objective has been evaluated.

When performance is evaluated, it is usually in terms of achievement, but it could be in terms of developmental or biomechanical instructional objectives. Among the skills where performance can serve as a means of evaluation are the following:

Archery. Archery achievement is validly determined by measuring the student's accuracy in shooting a standardized target from a specified distance.

Bowling. The bowling average achieved under standardized conditions is an objective measure of bowling skill. Subjectively evaluating bowling form would certainly be possible.

Golf. If the school has access to a golf course, the student's score on several rounds can serve as an objective index of golf skill. This criterion is well accepted by touring professionals.

Swimming. The number of breaststrokes required to swim 25 yards is an objective measure of breaststroke ability. Stroke mechanics and/or form are commonly evaluated.

Procedures for Evaluating Skill Achievement

We recognize that teachers are not researchers. The procedures below for the development of skill test batteries represent the application of scientific test construction principles to the public school teacher's situation. They also represent several years' work. Do not expect high-quality evaluation of psychomotor objectives to be instantly performed.

1. *Define what is to be measured.* This is one of the most important steps in the test construction process: If it is not carried out correctly, subsequent procedures will also be incorrect. Use your instructional objectives as the source of what is to be measured. These objectives describe the skills that should be achieved during an instructional phase, so they also define what needs to be measured.
2. *Select a measuring instrument.* Choose tests or rating scales that measure the achievement of the instructional objectives. In most instances the process of matching objectives and measuring instruments is based on logic. Remember that the skill learned during instruction must also be the skill used during the test. That is, individual differences in scores on a basketball dribble test must be due to individual differences in dribbling skill, not to unrelated factors.

   In selecting a measuring instrument, you can choose from among published skill tests, construct a rating scale, or use the performance itself. It may be necessary to alter an instrument to fit your instructional objectives. In constructing a skill test battery, skill tests and rating scales can be used together to evaluate the different motor skill components of an activity. For example, you can use a serving test to evaluate the achievement of volleyball serving skill and a rating scale to evaluate spiking skill. When it is impossible to evaluate all the skills you have taught, as it usually is, select those that are most important.
3. *Pretest the instrument.* Before you administer a test or rating scale to a class, try it out on a group of five to fifteen students. No matter how explicit test instructions appear, you will truly understand the test and its procedures only after you have administered it. Several important questions must be answered:

Does the test seem to be valid? Does it measure the stated instructional objective? Does it seem to be reliable? Are the directions clear? What is the best way to standardize its administration? How long does it take to test one student? If the test is too long, you may have to set up several test stations and recruit and train additional testing personnel. At this point you should also develop standardized procedures for administering the test.

4. *Revise the test and testing procedures.* On the basis of your findings from the pretest, you may want to devise, delete, or add tests to the battery. If the changes are numerous, you should administer the revised test to another small group.

5. *Administer the instrument.* At the end of the instructional phase, administer the selected test to the class.

6. *Evaluate the administered test.* After you administer the battery, examine the reliability, validity, and feasibility of each test.
   a. *Reliability.* Because testing procedures and the variability of the group can affect reliability, it is important that you estimate each test's reliability for your testing procedures and students. If a test lacks reliability, it may be necessary to use additional trials, to alter your testing procedures, or to search for a better test.
   b. *Validity.* Once you have determined reliability, you must determine validity. In most instances, you can do so logically. If the test obviously measures an instructional objective, you can assume logical validity. For example, a test that requires a student to swim 25 yards in as few strokes as possible using the sidestroke is a valid test of sidestroke skill. If validity cannot be determined logically, you could compare the scores achieved by the best and poorest students in the class. If the achieved scores do not confirm your observations, the test is suspect. Or, you could compare the test scores with tournament standings. If the tests are valid, the two sets of scores should be related.
   c. *Feasibility.* Tests can be both reliable and valid, yet simply impractical for mass testing. If you cannot revise the testing procedures to make them applicable for mass testing, you must select or develop a new battery.

7. *Revise the final battery.* The final battery should consist of reliable, valid instruments that measure important instructional objectives. A battery normally consists of from three to five individual tests. Two criteria for compiling the final battery are (1) that the selected tests be reliable, valid, and feasible for mass testing, and (2) that the correlation among the final items be low. If the correlation between two tests in the final battery is high, one should be eliminated.

8. *Develop standards.* Once you have finalized the content of the battery, you must develop norm-referenced or criterion-referenced standards. T-score and percentile norms (see Chapters 2 and 5) are especially useful. T-score norms have the advantage of allowing you to sum the test items and calculate a total score for the entire battery. Criterion-referenced standards based on research finds or personal beliefs are useful because they are a minimum proficiency standard. Many published tests provide national norms; however, you should try to develop your own norms because testing procedures and climatic conditions vary.

Sample Sport Skill Tests

AAHPERD Sport Skill Test Series

The Research Council of the AAHPERD (formerly the AAHPER) published several sport skill tests in the late 1960s that were developed from the combined efforts of researchers, city directors of physical education, and public school teachers. The manuals list administration procedures as well as percentile norms for boys and girls ages 10 to 18. They are available at nominal cost from the AAHPERD.

The following criteria were used in developing the tests:

Validity. Each test should measure the student's ability to perform a skill basic to the sport.

Reliability. Accuracy tests should have reliability above .70; the other tests should have reliability above .80.

Test environment. Preference was given to tests that were also a method of practicing the skill.

Scoring. Preference was given to tests that could be scored objectively.

Degree of difficulty. Each test should differentiate among the various skill levels at each grade level.

Variability. The distribution of scores for each age level should be normal.

The report of a committee that evaluated the 1960s AAHPER series concluded that the procedures for the test items are vague (Morris 1977); that the items should be studied in typical physical education situations and the results reported; that a task analysis of the sport skills should be conducted if logical validity is to be used for the selection and retention of items; that some of the items fail to meet the criterion of reliability; and that, although the test items are supposed to measure skill achievement, some of them actually predict potential achievement. This last is of special concern, in that many of the tests include basic ability items (speed, jumping, agility) that predict, rather than indicate, skill ability.

The Measurement and Evaluation Council of the AAHPERD formed a task force in 1979 to revise and expand the AAHPER sport skill test series. The basketball and softball skills tests were revised and a tennis test was added to the series. Presently, volleyball and soccer skills committees are at work.

The AAHPERD sport skills tests presently available are not without merit. A brief discussion of each test battery follows, for your reference. Individuals planning to use these tests should obtain the test manuals from AAHPERD in order to have the complete administrative procedures, norms, and recommended drills.

Basketball. The basketball battery consists of four tests recommended for boys and girls, with minor changes for sex differences (AAHPERD 1984). The basketball battery is presently being revised and neither the 1984 or a new test manual is available.

Speed Spot Shooting. This test was presented earlier in the chapter (see page 390).

Passing. This test was presented earlier in the chapter (see pages 391).

Control Dribble. This test was presented earlier in the chapter (see pages 389 and 390).

Defensive Movement. The purpose of this test is to measure basic defensive movement. A course of six cones is set up on the free throw lane of the

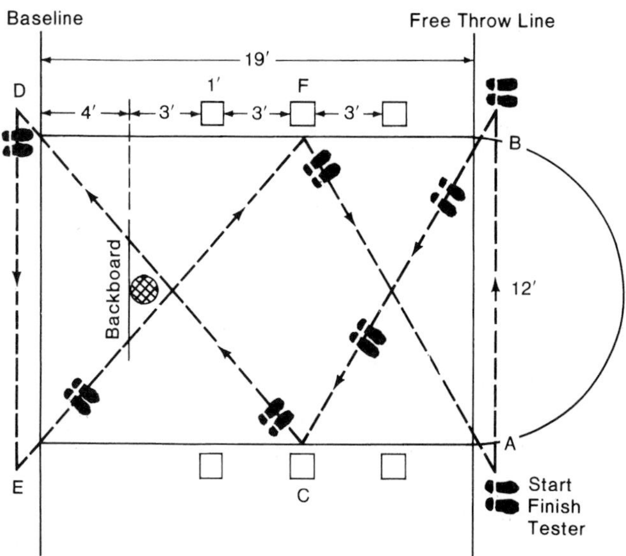

Figure 12.4
AAHPERD Basketball Defensive Movement Test. (Reprinted by permission of the American Alliance for Health, Physical Education, Recreation and Dance, Reston, VA 22091.)

court (see Figure 12.4). Three timed trials of side-stepping (slide-step) through the course are administered. The final score is the sum of the last two trial times.

In a factor analysis study of basketball skill tests, 21 items were administered to 70 male subjects (Hopkins 1977). Four factors were identified: (1) shooting, (2) passing, (3) jumping, and (4) moving with or without the ball. A similar study (Gaunt 1979), using 20 variables administered to 167 female subjects, also identified four factors: (1) lay-up shooting, (2) passing, (3) explosive leg strength, and (4) dribbling. These findings influenced the selection of tests in this battery.

Softball. The softball battery (AAHPERD 1991) consists of four tests recommended for boys and girls grades 5 through college.

Batting. The softball outfield is marked off into three power zones (for grades 5–8: 120 feet, 180 feet, and more than 180 feet from home plate) and into three placement areas (left, center, and right field), so there are nine scoring areas. Hit balls that come to rest in the farthest center field scoring area receive the most points. Fewer points are given for hits to right or left field and hits not reaching the farthest scoring area. The test consists of two practice trials and six test trials of hitting a ball off of a batting tee for distance and accuracy. The sum of the six test trials is the batter's score.

Fielding Ground Balls. A tester throws a ball on a smooth field and the student tries to field the ball cleanly. Two practice and six test trials are administered. Each test trial is scored based on how cleanly the ball is fielded and where the ball is fielded. The score is the sum of the points for the six test trials. The directions are specific as to dimensions and marking of the test area, ball velocity and placement, and assignment of points.

Overhand Throwing. The test involves throwing a softball for distance and accuracy. Players have 3 to 4 minutes of short-throw warm-up and then have two trials to throw the softball as far and as straight as possible down a throwing line. The trial scored is the ground distance the ball went before hitting the ground minus the number of feet the ball landed away from the throwing line. The better of the two trials is a player's score. This score is very reliable and more economical than the mean of two trial scores.

Base Running. This test involves running the first two bases for time. One reduced-speed practice trial and two test trials are administered. A trial score is the time it takes to run from home plate to first base to second base. The score is the better of the two trials for the same reason given for the overhand throwing test.

Tennis. The tennis battery (AAHPERD 1989) consists of two tests and an optional test recommended for boys and girls grades 9 through college. The committee who developed this battery found that tennis is not taught at the junior high school level as much as previously believed. They found three test items that had acceptable reliability, validity, and administrative efficiency.

Ground Stroke: Forehand and Backhand Drive. The test measures the ability to hit ground strokes with both accuracy and power. The score for each trial is based on placement and power. The placement score is where the ball lands in a target area, with deep shots on the court receiving more points than shots near the net. The power for each shot landing in the target area is how deep on the court the second bounce lands. Placement scores are 0 to 4 and power scores are 1 to 3.

Serving. The test measures serving accuracy and power. As with the ground stroke test, the tennis court is marked with scoring areas and power zones. Students are permitted about 5 minutes of warm-up prior to being tested. Sixteen services are scored for placement and power. Accuracy of each serve is scored 0 to 2, and power for each serve landing in the tennis court is scored 1 to 2 depending on how deep the second bounce of the serve lands. The score for the test is the sum of the points for the sixteen trials.

Volley Test (optional). The test measures the ability to volley the ball accurately from a position near the net. The court is divided into seven areas, which are scored 1 to 4 points. The tester hits ten balls to the forehand side and ten balls to the backhand side of the student. The student hits each ball over the net, aiming at the target areas. The first four balls hit from each side are considered practice. The score on the test is the sum of the points for the twelve trials.

Other Sport Skill Tests

Following are numerous other sport skill tests as examples of the types of tests that have been used in the past. If these tests meet your needs, use them. However, we hope that many physical education teachers will use these tests as examples to construct their own sport skill tests.

Badminton

Sebolt Short Service Test (Sebolt 1968)

Objective: To measure the achievement of the badminton short service.

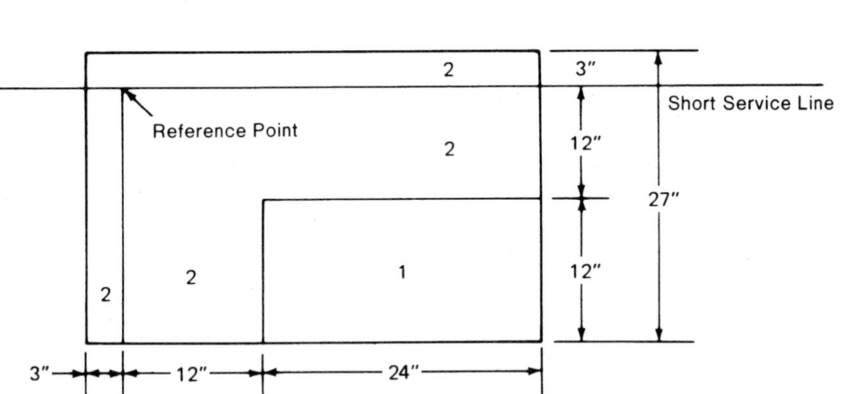

Figure 12.5
Scoring zones for the Sebolt Short Service Test.
(Reprinted by permission of Don Sebolt, Virginia Polytechnic Institute, Blacksburg, VA.)

Validity and reliability: Because the ability to serve the shuttlecock close to the net and into the front middle corner of the opponent's service court is an important badminton skill, logical validity is assumed. With college students, the correlation between performance on a ladder tournament and the service test was .61. The intraclass reliability for the students was estimated at .72 and .79.

Equipment:. The test is administered on a standard court, with scoring zones as shown in Figure 12.5. A string is stretched 16 inches directly above and parallel to the net. A badminton racket and ample supply of new indoor shuttlecocks are needed.

Procedure: Each student is given a 5-minute warm-up period on a practice court before being tested. The test consists of twenty legal serves from the right service court. The bird must be served between the net and the string into the target area. Shuttlecocks served above the string are scored 0. If the shuttlecock hits the string, another serve is allowed. Shuttlecocks that hit the net are scored in the same manner as birds that clear the net.

Scoring: A scorer is needed for each test station. The student's score is the sum of the twenty serves. The scoring zones are shown in Figure 12.5. A shuttlecock that hits on the line is awarded the higher value.

Other considerations: An objective of the short serve is to serve the shuttlecock near the net and have it land near or on the short service line. The 3-inch band outside the service court, an important feature of the test, encourages the student to serve for the line. In the game situation, a shuttlecock landing just outside the service court should be hit because the player cannot be certain if the bird is in or short. If several test stations are available, the test is feasible for mass use.

Golf

Green Golf Test (Green, East & Hensley 1987)

Objective: To measure the five basic skill components of golf: putting, chipping, pitching, using middle-distance irons, and driving.

Validity and reliability: A group of 146 subjects were administered each item of the test battery on each of two days near the end of a beginning-level golf class. Reliability coefficients were at least .70, except for the pitch shot for females and the short putt for both males and females.

A group of 66 subjects completing a beginning-level golf class at the college level were used to validate the test. Multiple regression was used to estimate validity with the score on 36 holes of golf the criterion measure and the predictor variables the golf battery items. Validity was .72 for a two-item test battery of middle-distance shot and pitch shot, increasing to .77 for a four-item test battery of middle-distance shot, pitch shot, long-putt, and chip shot.

Items:

Middle-distance shot. The test was four trials of hitting a ball at a target 140 yards away (males) or 110 yards away (females). The score was the sum of the perpendicular distance in yards each ball came to rest from the target.

Pitch shot. Six trials from 40 yards away from the flagstick were used. A seven through nine iron, pitching wedge, or sand wedge was used for the test. The score for the test was the sum of the distance in feet each of the six pitch shots were from the flagstick.

Long putt. This test was putting from six proportionately spaced positions around the cup. All positions were 25 feet from the cup. The score was the sum of the distance in inches that each putt stopped from the cup.

Chip shot. Six trials from 35 feet away from the flagstick were used. The score for the test was the sum of the distance in feet each of the chip shots stopped from the flagstick.

Gymnastics

Gymnastics Skills Test for College Women (Ellenbrand 1973)

The 16-item battery consists of the following events: balance beam (5 items), floor exercise (4 items), uneven parallel bars (5 items), and vaulting (2 items). The items were selected using the following criteria: contribution to the category in which they were placed, extent to which they were considered basic skills (as opposed to a variation of some skill), progression within the category, and similarity to a gymnastics performance.

Objective: To measure achievement of gymnastics skills.

Validity and reliability: Concurrent validity was estimated by correlating the scores of three judges of varied experience (an experienced gymnastics teacher, a college teacher with limited gymnastics teaching experience, a student majoring in physical education with a single basic course in gymnastics) with the ratings of two experienced gymnastics judges. The correlations were balance beam, .93; floor exercise, .97; uneven parallel bars, .99; vaulting, .88; and total test, .97. The intercorrelations among the four events ranged from .44 to .70, low enough to warrant the inclusion of all four. The reliability for each event and for the total test was investigated again using the three judges of varied experience. In addition the test was administered on a second day by one teacher. The intraclass reliability estimates were as follows:

Event	Among Teachers	Between Days
Balance beam	.99	.98
Floor exercise	.97	.99
Uneven parallel bars	.99	.94
Vaulting	.97	.99
Total tests	.98	.99

Procedure: The skills for each item were ordered from simple to difficult. The difficulty ratings were logically assigned. The student selects one skill under each item that demonstrates her achievement in that area. She should have an opportunity to practice. Deduct points for falls, but give students the opportunity to repeat stunts.

We present here the test items and difficulty ratings for the floor exercises only (see Table 12.4). For the floor exercise event, skills are performed on the length of mats provided. A return trip can be used if necessary. Connecting skills can be added if needed for preparation of a selected skill (e.g., a round-off to prepare for a back handspring). However, extra steps and runs should be avoided because they detract from the execution rating.

Other considerations: This test is designed to evaluate the instructional objectives of gymnastics for college women only; it should not be used for other students. However, the same logic could be applied to develop a test for any gymnastics or tumbling class.

Racquetball

Racquetball Battery (Poteat 1983)[1]

Objective: To measure basic racquetball playing ability of beginning players.

Validity and reliability: Twelve collegiate and professional racquetball instructors evaluated the skills test battery as to its logical validity and all agreed that the test battery items measured skills necessary for beginning racquetball players. Further, correlations between test items and expert ratings of the skill involved in the test item varied from .62 to .76.

Stability reliability coefficients for the items varied from .75 to .84. Internal consistency reliability coefficients varied from .85 to .91.

Equipment: A regulation racquetball court with official markings is necessary. Also, a racquetball racquet, stopwatch, measuring tape, and four racquetballs and marking tape are needed.

Procedures: The original battery consisted of forehand and backhand passing shot, service placement, forehand and backhand wall play, and wall volley

[1]Reprinted by permission of Charles Poteat.

Table 12.4 Floor Exercise Items from Ellenbrand Gymnastics Test

Test Item: Tumbling Skills (Rolls)

Difficulty		*Skills*	*Difficulty*		*Skills*
0.5	a.	Forward roll to stand	4.5	i.	Back extension
0.5	b.	Backward roll to knees	5.0	j.	Dive forward roll (layout)
1.0	c.	Back roll to stand	6.0	k.	Back tuck somersault (aerial)
2.0	d.	Pike forward or back roll	6.5	l.	Back pike somersault
2.0	e.	Straddle roll (forward or back)	6.5	m.	Forward tuck somersault
3.0	f.	Dive forward roll (pike)	7.0	n.	Back layout somersault
4.0	g.	Handstand forward roll	8.0	o.	Somersault with a twist
4.0	h.	Back roll to headstand			

Test Item: Tumbling Skills (Springs)

Difficulty		*Skills*	*Difficulty*		*Skills*
1.0	a.	Handstand snap-down	5.0	h.	Back handspring
2.0	b.	Round-off	5.0	i.	Front handspring on one hand or with a change of legs
2.5	c.	Neck spring (kip)			
3.0	d.	Head spring	5.5	j.	Series of front handsprings
3.5	e.	Front handspring to squat	6.0	k.	Series of back handsprings
4.0	f.	Front handspring arch to stand	6.5	l.	Back handspring to kip (cradle)
4.5	g.	Front handspring walk-out	6.5	m.	Back handspring with twist

Test Item: Acrobatic Skills

Difficulty		*Skills*	*Difficulty*		*Skills*
1.0	a.	Mule kick (three-quarter handstand)	4.0	i.	Dive cartwheel
1.0	b.	Bridge (back arch position)	4.0	j.	Tinsica
2.0	c.	Handstand	4.5	k.	Dive walk-over
2.0	d.	Cartwheel	5.0	l.	Handstand with half turn or straddle-down to a sit
2.5	e.	Backbend from standing			
3.0	f.	Front limber	5.0	m.	One-handed walk-overs
3.0	g.	One-handed cartwheel	6.0	n.	Butterfly (side aerial)
4.0	h.	Walk-overs (forward and back)	7.0	o.	Aerial cartwheel or walk-over

Test Item: Dance Skills

Difficulty		*Skills*
1.0	a.	Half turn (one foot), run, leap
2.0	b.	Half turn, step, hitch kick forward, step, leap
3.0	c.	Half turn, slide, tour jeté, hitch kick
4.0	d.	Full turn (one foot), step, leap, step, leap
5.0	e.	Full turn, tour jeté, cabriole (beat kick forward)
6.0	f.	One and one-half turns, step, leap, step, leap with a change of legs

Scoring: The score is the product of the skill difficulty and the execution rating. The following scale is used for the execution rating:

3 points: Correct performance; proper mechanics; execution in good form; balance, control, and amplitude in movements.

2 points: Average performance; errors evident in either mechanics or form; some lack of balance, control, or amplitude in movement.

1 point: Poor performance; errors in both mechanics and form; little balance, control, or amplitude in movements.

0 points: Improper or no performance; incorrect mechanics or complete lack of form; no display of balance, control, or amplitude in movements.

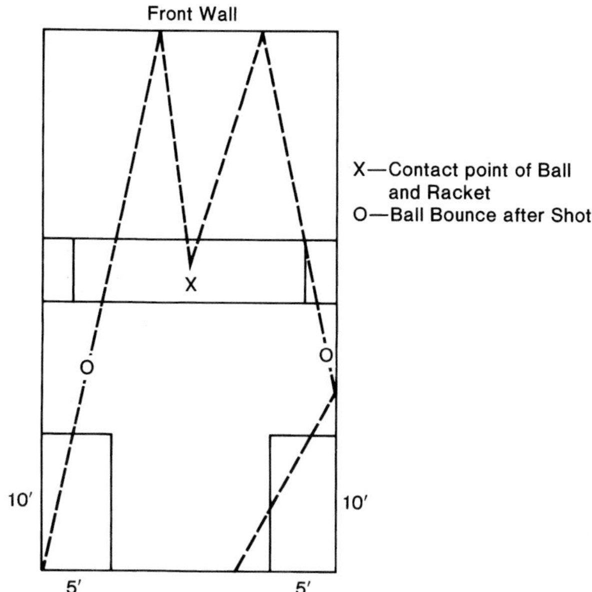

Figure 12.6
Court markings for the service placement and examples of good serves.
(Reprinted by permission of Charles Poteat, Lincoln Memorial University, Harrogate, TN.)

tests. Because of high correlations between comparable passing and wall play items, the author suggests dropping the passing shot item but changing the wall play item so it has the same target area and scoring procedure as the passing shot and service placement items. The three suggested test items in their original form are presented here.

1. *Service placement.* The court markings for this test item are shown in Figure 12.6. The student stands in the center of the service area, bounces the ball, and hits it to the front wall so that it will rebound and hit in or pass through the 10 × 5 foot target area. The ball is served to the student's backhand. The student is allowed 10 attempts per trial and 2 trials. No points are awarded if the ball is an illegal serve or contacts the front wall higher than 5 feet above the floor. One point is awarded if the ball bounces in the target area or passes through the target area. The ball may contact the side wall if the above criteria are met. Each successful serve is awarded one point. The maximum total is 20.
2. *Back wall play.* The court markings for this test item are shown in Figure 12.7. The student stands about 5 feet from the back wall and 20 feet from the side wall. He or she throws the ball to the back wall so that it bounces to the side wall, and then bounces on the floor. The player then returns the ball to the front wall so that the ball does not contact the side wall on the way to the front wall. The ball must contact the front wall at a height of five feet or less above the floor. The student is allowed 2 trials of 10 attempts per trial with the forehand stroke, and 2 trials of 10 attempts per trial with the backhand stroke. No points are awarded if the above criteria are not met. The score is recorded as the total number of successful attempts for both trials.
3. *Wall volley.* The student, holding two balls, begins the test from the service line 15 feet from the front wall. The student drops one of the balls and hits it to the front wall, then continues to rally the ball for 30 seconds. The ball may bounce any number of times on the return to the subject or the ball may be volleyed. The subject may not cross the service line to contact the ball, but may cross the line to

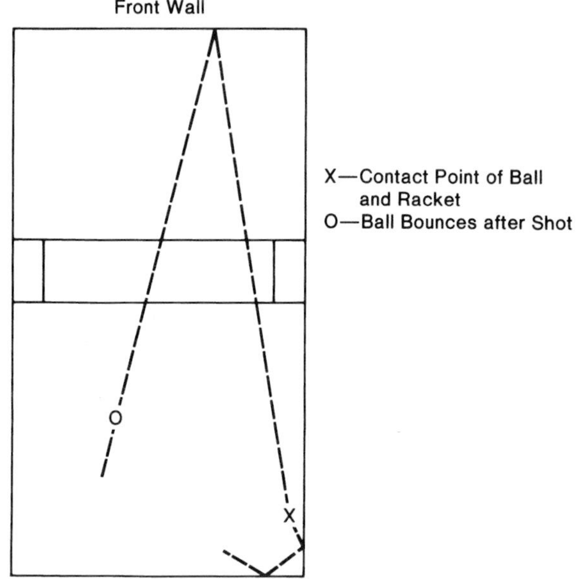

Figure 12.7
Court markings for the back wall play and examples of good attempts. (Reprinted by permission of Charles Poteat, Lincoln Memorial University, Harrogate, TN.)

retrieve a ball. Any stroke may be used to rally the ball. If the ball passes the player, he or she may put the second ball in play. Additional balls may be obtained from the test administrator. Two 30-second trials are given. One point is awarded for each legal hit to the front wall. The total score is the total number of successful attempts.

Other considerations: Poteat (1983) provides T-scores for scores on each test and percentile ranks for sum of the T-scores. He states that all items in his test battery have sufficient range to discriminate among students with varying ability. The test battery takes 15–18 minutes to administer to each student. If a single item is administered, it probably should be a wall volley (Hensley, East & Stillwell 1979). Their wall volley test and most tests of this type allow the student to use either a forehand or backhand stroke. Karpman and Isaacs (1979) maintain there should be one of each.

Dowd (1990) hypothesized that beginning-level racquetball skill of college students is represented by serve, kill shot, and passing/defense shots. For males, Dowd found a volley component represented by the long wall volley and a drive serve component represented by the short-drive serve. However, for females, Dowd found a volley component represented by the long wall volley, a placement component represented by the forehand overhead ceiling shot, and a kill component represented by the forehand kill shot set up with a toss and hit.

Soccer

Soccer Battery (Yeagley 1972)

Objective: To measure basic soccer skills of beginning players.

Validity and reliability: The validity of each of the four test items was examined with two different criteria: (1) the ratings of four judges on the soccer juggling skill and (2) the composite standard score of the four tests. The concurrent validity coefficients were as follows:

	Judges' Ratings	Composite Standard Score
1. Dribble	−.66	−.80
2. Wall volley	.54	.81
3. Juggling	.69	.74
4. Heading	.38	.61

A multiple correlation of .76 was reported between the criterion (the judges' ratings) and the dribble and juggling tests. The addition of the wall volley and heading tests increased the multiple correlation to only .78; thus, we recommend that dribble and juggling be used if a short form is wanted. With a sample of male physical education majors who were beginning soccer players, the following internal-consistency coefficients were reported: dribble, .91; wall volley, .90; juggling, .95; and heading, .64.

Equipment: The test was designed to be administered in a standard gym with the basketball floor markings used to outline the various test stations. Nine soccer balls inflated to 10 pounds and stopwatches accurate to a tenth of a second are needed. Two assistants are needed for each test.

Procedures: The four tests are as follows:

1. *Dribble.* The course for the dribble test is on half a basketball court, as shown in Figure 12.8. On the signal "Go," the student dribbles around the obstacles following the course. The test is scored by the time measured to the nearest second from the signal until the student dribbles the ball across the finish line between the four line markings and brings the ball to a halt using only the feet. It is legal to touch, knock down, or move any obstacle with the ball or the feet so long as the course outline is followed. Two trials are given, and the best time is used.
2. *Wall volley.* The test course for the wall volley consists of an unobstructed wall 8 × 24 feet, and a restraining line 15 feet from the wall (Figure 12.8). On the signal "Go," the student begins kicking the ball from behind the restraining line and continues kicking the rebounded ball to the kickboard area as many times as possible in 30 seconds. Any type of kick and any legal trapping method is permissible; however, to score a legal volley, the nonkicking foot must be behind the restraining line. Additional balls should be available in case the student loses control of the volleyed ball. The score is the number of legal volleys during the 30-second period. Two trials are given, and the best score is used.
3. *Juggling.* This test also uses half a basketball court as the testing area. The student starts at any point in the area, holding one soccer ball. On the signal "Go," the subject bounces the ball to the floor and then tries to juggle or tap the ball into the air with his or her other body parts as many times as possible in 30 seconds. All parts of the body excluding the arms and hands can be used to continue juggling the ball. (The primary parts used for juggling are the feet, thighs, and head; but the shoulders, chest, and other parts are also legal.) The ball is allowed to bounce on the floor any number of times between touches, although it does not have to bounce at all. It is to the student's advantage to keep the ball in the air for a series of rapidly controlled juggles. The student's score is the number of legal juggles completed in the 30-second period. Juggles outside the half court boundary are not counted. Each time the student controls the ball with the hands or arms, 1 point is deducted. Two trials are given, and the best score is used.
4. *Heading.* The course for the heading test is also shown in Figure 12.8. The student stands at any point in the heading area, which is the far half of the center circle.

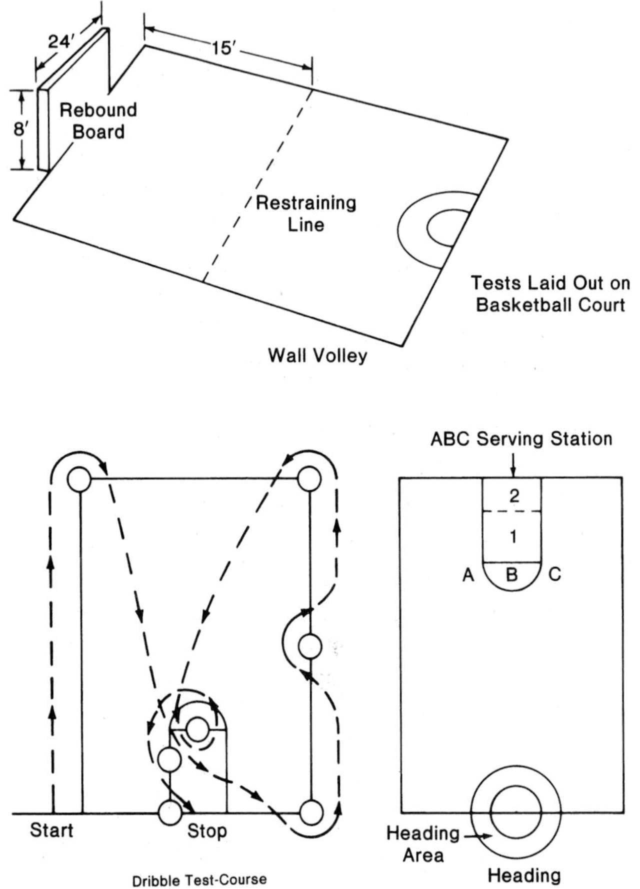

Figure 12.8
Test course for the Yeagley Soccer Battery Test.
(Reprinted by permission of J. L. Yeagley, Indiana University, Bloomington, IN.)

The center line of the basketball court is the restraining line, behind which one foot must be placed when the ball is headed. The ball is thrown by the tester from the three spots designed in the figure. The throw should be soft, ideally at the same arc on each trial, and no higher than 15 feet. A total of three tosses are administered from spots A and C, four tosses from B. The student being tested can refuse a poorly tossed ball. The student tries to head the tossed ball in the specified scoring zone. Ten trials are administered, and the total points of these trials constitute the subject's score. Balls landing on the line receive the higher value.

Other considerations: One advantage of this battery is that it can be administered in a gym. This not only controls for environmental conditions, but also allows the teacher to proceed with skill testing, even in bad weather. A test of total soccer skill ability is not available. Yeagley reported that the juggling test is used as an instructional technique for developing ball sensitivity "touch," very important in performing basic soccer skills. The juggling test was selected by the American Professional Soccer League for a national youth soccer skill test. Coaches and teachers in European countries have used ball juggling as the primary test item in national youth soccer skill contests for the past several years.

If four testing stations are available (two basketball courts), the test could be administered to a class of thirty students during a 50-minute class period.

The reliability of the heading test is somewhat low. For a total of twenty trials the estimated reliability is .78.

Red Cross Swimming Skills. The American Red Cross has identified basic swimming skills for various swimming classification groups. The skills are subjectively rated on a pass-fail basis. The ratings can be used for the formative evaluation of swimming achievement.

A. Beginner skills

1. Water adjustment skills
2. Hold breath—10 sec.
3. Rhythmic breathing—10 times
4. Prone float and recovery
5. Prone glide
6. Back glide and recovery
7. Survival float

B. Advanced beginner skills

1. Bobbing—deep water
2. Rhythmic breathing to side
3. Survival float—2 min.
4. Crawl stroke
5. Elementary backstroke
6. Survival stroke
7. Treading water—30–45 sec.

Summary

The achievement of psychomotor objectives is a universal goal of physical education programs. We can measure the achievement of psychomotor skills with three general procedures: skill tests, rating scales, and the performance itself.

Skill tests require the creation of an environment similar to the game environment and the standardization of procedures for administration. The validity of skill tests can be judged in part by the extent to which the testing environment duplicates the playing environment. There are four general types of skill tests:

1. Accuracy tests. Accuracy tests require the subject to throw, strike, or kick an object at a target for accuracy. Examples are the basketball free throw, the badminton short serve, and the volleyball serve.
2. Wall volley tests. Wall volley tests require the subject to repeatedly stroke, pass, throw, or kick an object at a wall. The score may be the number of successful volleys completed during a specified time period or the time required to execute a specified number of volleys.
3. Tests of total bodily movement. These tests require the subject to run a standardized test course using movements typical of the sport. Dribbling a basketball through an obstacle course is one example.
4. Throws, kicks, or strokes for power or distance. These tests require the subject to throw, kick, or strike an object (a football, a shuttlecock, etc.) for distance.

Rating scales are a device for evaluating skill achievement subjectively. They are used for evaluating qualities that cannot be efficiently measured by objective means. In a sense these scales add a measure of objectivity to subjective measurements and can yield reliable, valid measurements of skill achievement if they are properly constructed and used.

For some motor skills, the performance itself is a reliable, valid method of evaluating achievement. This type of evaluation tends to be content-valid because the performance environment is also the evaluation environment. Archery, bowling, golf, and swimming are skills that can be evaluated by performance.

The steps in the development of reliable, valid procedures for evaluating skill objectives are as follows:

1. Define what is to be measured.
2. Select a measuring instrument.
3. Pretest the instrument.
4. Revise the test and testing procedures.
5. Administer the instrument.
6. Evaluate the administered test.
7. Revise the final battery.
8. Develop norms.

Formative Evaluation of Objectives

Objective 1 Identify the four general types of sport skill tests.

1. Skill tests involve creating an environment similar to the game situation and standardizing testing procedures. Numerous skill tests have been published for a variety of sport skills. Skill tests can be categorized under one of four general groups. Summarize the characteristics of each group.
   a. Accuracy tests
   b. Wall volley tests
   c. Tests of total bodily movement
   d. Throws, kicks, or strokes for power or distance

Objective 2 Evaluate the four general types of sport skill tests using the criteria of reliability, validity, and feasibility for mass testing.

1. In order for a test to be valid it must first be reliable. However, a test may be both reliable and valid but still not be feasible for mass use. In order to evaluate the achievement of motor skill objectives, the teacher must select skill tests that meet acceptable levels of reliability and validity and that can be administered in the public school. Each of the four general categories of skill tests has inherent weaknesses and strengths. Identify the basic weakness associated with each category and summarize the actions you could take to improve its effectiveness.
   a. Accuracy tests
   b. Wall volley tests
   c. Tests of total bodily movement
   d. Throws, kicks, or strokes for power or distance

Objective 3 Evaluate the weaknesses and strengths of rating scales.

1. In many evaluation situations it is neither feasible nor possible to measure motor skill achievement with an objective sport skill test. In these situations a rating scale is used. A rating scale is a subjective measurement procedure.

Differentiate between the terms *objective* and *subjective* as applied to the evaluation of motor skill achievement.

2. List the weaknesses and strengths of rating scales.
3. Like all forms of measuring instruments, rating scales must be reliable. Certain procedures in the development and use of rating scales help guard against measurement error and ensure objectivity. Outline the procedures you should follow when constructing and using this type of measurement instrument.

Objective 4 Identify motor skills that are best evaluated by performance.

1. For many motor skills the actual performance may be used to evaluate skill achievement. List the basic advantage of using performance as a criterion for skill evaluation.
2. The text offers several illustrations in which skill achievement can be evaluated by performance. Identify an additional motor skill that could be evaluated in this way. Using your example, outline the specific procedures you would follow to evaluate achievement in the skill.

Objective 5 Outline methods that could be used to develop reliable, valid, and feasible measurement procedures for evaluating motor skill achievement.

1. The text lists systematic procedures for evaluating skill achievement. Briefly outline these procedures.

Additional Learning Activities

1. Many studies published in research journals have attempted to develop sport skill tests. Select three or four articles and review them. Pay close attention to the methods used to establish the reliability and validity of the tests and the procedures used to develop the battery. Would you use the tests for your physical education class?
2. Often a published skill test does not fit the specific needs of a teacher, who must either revise the published tests or develop a new one. Select a sport skill and develop a test to evaluate it. You might alter an existing test, develop an alternate scoring system, or develop a new test. Administer the test to a group of students and calculate its reliability. Is your test feasible for mass use? Do the most highly skilled students achieve the best test scores?
3. A test can be valid for one group of students but not for another. Select a published sport skill test and determine the concurrent validity of the test with a group of students. In order to accomplish this you must select a criterion measure. (You may want to review Chapter 3 before you begin.)
4. Select a skill that cannot be evaluated with an objective skill test and construct a rating scale for it. With a classmate, independently rate the performance of a group of students and then calculate the correlation between your two ratings. How reliable were your ratings? Remember that reliability can be improved by properly training raters.

5. For some skills, performance provides an objective score for evaluating their achievement. Using a skill such as archery, bowling, or golf, estimate the stability reliability of the performance scores. Remember that for stability reliability you must have the performance scores of the same group of students for two different days.

Bibliography

AAHPERD. 1984. *Basketball skills test manual for boys and girls.* Reston, VA.

AAHPERD. 1989. *Tennis skills test manual for boys and girls.* Larry Hensley (Ed.). Reston, VA.

AAHPERD. 1991. *Softball skills test manual for boys and girls.* Roberta Rikli (Ed.). Reston, VA.

Barrow, H. M., R. McGee, and K. A. Tritscher. 1989. *Practical measurement in physical education and sport.* 4th ed. Philadelphia: Lea & Febiger.

Dowd, D. A. 1990. A factor analysis of selected beginning-level racquetball skill tests. Ed.D. dissertation, University of Georgia, Athens, GA.

Ellenbrand, D. A. 1973. Gymnastics skills tests for college women. Master's thesis, Indiana University, Bloomington, IN.

Gaunt, S. 1979. Factor structure of basketball playing ability. P.E.D. dissertation, Indiana University, Bloomington, IN.

Green, K. N., W. B. East, and L. D. Hensley. 1987. A golf skill test battery for college males and females. *Research Quarterly for Exercise and Sport* 58:72–76.

Hastad, D. N. and A. C. Lacy. 1994. *Measurement and evaluation in physical education and exercise science.* 2d ed. Scottsdale, AZ: Gorsuch Scarisbrick.

Hensley, L., W. East, and J. Stillwell. 1979. A racquetball skills test. *Research Quarterly* 50:114–118.

Hopkins, D. R. 1977. Factor analysis of selected basketball skill tests. *Research Quarterly* 48:535–540.

Karpman, M. and L. Isaacs. 1979. An improved racquetball skills test. *Research Quarterly* 50:526–527.

Miller, D. K. 1994. *Measurement by the physical educator: Why and how.* 2d ed. Dubuque, IA: Brown & Benchmark.

Morris, H. H. 1977. A critique of the AAHPER skill test series. Paper presented to the Measurement and Evaluation Council, AAHPER National Convention, Seattle, WA.

Poteat, C. 1983. A skill test battery to measure overall racquetball playing ability. Ed.D. dissertation, University of Georgia, Athens, GA.

Sebolt, D. R. 1968. Badminton skill tests. Unpublished paper, Virginia Polytechnic Institute and State University.

Strand, B. N. and R. Wilson. 1993. *Assessing sport skills.* Champaign, IL: Human Kinetics.

Yeagley, J. 1972. Soccer skills test. Unpublished paper, Indiana University, Bloomington, IN.

PART FOUR 4

Cognitive and Affective Testing

CHAPTER

Evaluating Knowledge

Contents

Key Words

completion item
discrimination index
discrimination test
essay test
item
item analysis
item difficulty
knowledge test
mastery test
matching item
multiple-choice item
objective test
short-answer item
taxonomy
true-false item

Objectives

The process of evaluating knowledge is threefold: (1) constructing a knowledge test based on the cognitive objectives of the unit, (2) administering it, and (3) analyzing it. Before the actual construction, the type of test and the test items must be selected to be sure that the content is correct and the items themselves are well constructed. In addition, it is important to administer and score the test so that all people have the same opportunity to do well, and so that the scores themselves are valid. Finally, it is vital to analyze the test to determine the quality of each item and the test as a whole. This analysis indicates not only quality of the test, but also how it might be revised. Questionnaires are commonly used in many situations in our disciplines. Constructing a questionnaire is similar to constructing a knowledge test. Before attempting to construct and use a questionnaire, a person must know the basic procedures to follow.

After reading Chapter 13 you should be able to:

1. Differentiate among various types of knowledge tests.
2. Define the levels of knowledge most applicable to physical education and adult fitness.
3. Outline the basic procedures used for constructing, administering, and scoring a knowledge test.
4. Evaluate knowledge test items.
5. Analyze knowledge tests in terms of test reliability and item analysis.
6. Discuss the uses of questionnaires and how to construct them.

Introduction

Knowledge is one of the objectives of most physical education programs. Teachers want their students to know the rules, etiquette, terminology, procedures, and strategy of various sports and physical activities. Students should understand the role of exercise on health and physical fitness and how to stay fit. Many health-related fitness programs have knowledge objectives. The extent to which these objectives are met can best and sometimes exclusively be determined with a knowledge test.

Knowledge is often retained longer than physical skill and fitness. Obviously people lose a degree of skill and fitness as they stop participating in sports, but they can continue to enjoy sports as spectators if they have acquired sufficient knowledge. Then, too, as health-related physical fitness programs become more popular, greater emphasis is being placed on the cognitive aspects of physical fitness and health (see Chapter 1). Knowledge, then, is a wanted objective of physical education programs and adult fitness programs and should be one of the first areas of attention in any measurement procedure.

Knowledge is also an objective in adult fitness programs and rehabilitation programs. The instructor or clinician wants the program participants to know why fitness is important, how to develop and maintain fitness, the importance of good diet, why stress management is important, the adverse effects of smoking, and why they received an injury and how not to become reinjured. To determine if program participants have this knowledge as they enter the program or are obtaining this knowledge as a result of handouts and verbal presentations during the program, a knowledge questionnaire (test) must be administered. This knowledge questionnaire is scored not to grade each participant, but to determine what information needs to be provided to program participants.

Table 13.1 Bloom's Taxonomy of Educational Objectives

1.00	Knowledge 1.10 Knowledge of specifics 1.20 Knowledge of ways and means of dealing with specifics 1.30 Knowledge of the universals and abstractions in a field
2.00	Comprehension 2.10 Translation 2.20 Interpretation 2.30 Extrapolation
3.00	Application
4.00	Analysis 4.10 Analysis of elements 4.20 Analysis of relationships 4.30 Analysis of organizational principles
5.00	Synthesis 5.10 Production of a unique communication 5.20 Production of a plan for operations 5.30 Derivation of a set of abstract relations
6.00	Evaluation 6.10 Judgments in terms of internal evidence 6.20 Judgments in terms of external evidence

Levels of Knowledge

There are different levels or degrees of knowledge. This is apparent whenever a group of people is tested: Their understanding of a given topic can range from superficial to thorough.

Bloom's **taxonomy** of educational objectives (1956) proposes six levels of behavior arranged in ascending order of complexity: knowledge, comprehension, application, analysis, synthesis, and evaluation. Each level corresponds to a level of knowledge. Bloom then divides the levels of behavior and provides illustrative questions for each subdivision. Table 13.1 lists Bloom's six levels and their subdivisions. Because the two highest levels are quite complex and usually exceed the educational objectives of a typical physical education activity course, adult fitness program, or rehabilitation program, only the first four levels of knowledge in the taxonomy are presented, defined, and illustrated with a test question in Table 13.2. The educational objectives of most courses and programs do exceed Bloom's first level because teachers, exercise specialists, and clinicians, want students and participants to acquire more than a superficial knowledge of the topics covered.

Although the majority of questions on many physical education knowledge tests require the students only to remember facts, some questions should draw on higher levels of knowledge. And certainly, as the class becomes more advanced, the number of knowledge questions should be smaller, and the number of questions from the higher levels of the taxonomy should be larger.

Types of Knowledge Tests

Knowledge tests are either essay or objective tests and either mastery or discrimination tests. Each question on a knowledge test, whether stated as a question or not, is called an **item.** Teachers, exercise specialists, and clinicians must choose the type of test they want before they can begin to construct it.

Table 13.2 The First Four Levels of Bloom's Taxonomy

Level	Definition	Sample Question for Golf Test
I. Knowledge	Recall of ideas, terms, facts, etc.	What is a slice?
II. Comprehension	The use of translation, interpretation, or extrapolation to understand certain ideas, terms, facts, etc.	What causes a slice?
III. Application	The use of general ideas, rules of procedure, or generalized methods in particular and concrete situations.	The following scores were recorded by four golfers on 9 holes. In what order should the golfers tee off on the 8th tee?
IV. Analysis	The separation of a phenomenon into its constituents so that its nature, composition, and organizational principles may be determined.	A golf ball is located on a hill above the cup, and the shot will be made downhill onto a very fast green. The ball is best played with what kind of grip and stroke, and off what part of the club face?

Player	1	2	3	4	5	6	7	8	9	Total
A	3	6	3	4	3	4	7	3	6	39
B	4	5	4	4	4	5	4	3	4	37
C	6	6	5	3	3	3	3	3	3	35
D	3	3	4	4	2	4	5	7	3	35

Essay versus Objective

An **essay test** is any test on which people answer each item with whatever information they choose and write their answers in sentences. The answer to an essay item may be short or long, depending on how much the person knows and how full an answer the item requires. **Objective tests**—true-false, multiple choice, matching, and the like—have potential answers provided with each test item. After reading an item, a person selects one of the provided answers. For example, T or F on a true-false item.

The question of which test to use—essay or objective—raises both philosophical and economic issues. Some educators believe that objective tests encourage students to memorize facts rather than integrate facts together into a total understanding. These people use essay tests on the theory that the students must have a total understanding to answer essay questions. Other educators maintain that essay tests allow students to write everything they know about the subject, while objective tests determine if they know only what has been asked. Students frequently complain after objective tests that the teacher did not ask any of the things they knew. We can think of the items on an objective test as a sample from an infinite number of items that could have been used.

Economically, objective tests are time-consuming to construct but quick to score, while essay tests are the reverse. It does not take long to construct three to five general essay-type items, but it takes considerable time to properly read and score each one. Whenever tests are to be used with many people, either in one testing session or over numerous sessions, objective tests are more economical than essays in terms of total time involvement. Once the objective test is developed, it is easy to use and score. This is probably the major reason why objective tests are used more than essay tests.

Mastery versus Discrimination

A **mastery test**—a kind of formative evaluation with criterion-referenced standards—is used to determine whether the students or program participants have mastered the material. Items on the test pertain to information everyone is expected to know. Many of these items are easy, and often the entire class or group answers them correctly. However, the performance standards for mastery tests tend to be high. Bloom and his associates (1971, 1981) recommend that the criterion for passing a knowledge test be 80% to 90% correct answers. A mastery test is graded pass-fail or proficient-nonproficient. It is commonly used in physical education and adult fitness programs.

The purpose of a **discrimination test**—a form of summative evaluation with norm-referenced standards—is to differentiate among students in terms of knowledge. Each test item is written to discriminate among ability groups. Thus, discrimination tests include a larger number of difficult items than do mastery tests. They often do not elicit basic information because it does not discriminate sufficiently. As a result of using a discrimination-type test, a few excellent students will have high scores on the test while the rest of the students will have lower scores. Discrimination tests are seldom used outside of education.

Mastery tests tend to include items from the knowledge, comprehension, and application levels of Bloom's taxonomy (1956); discrimination tests tend to include items from the higher levels. Because discrimination tests are more difficult than mastery tests, their performance standards must be lower. The test mean and standard deviation need to be considered when developing the grading scale (see Chapters 2 and 5).

The decision about which test to use—mastery or discrimination—should depend on how the test scores will be used. For a formative evaluation of student or participant achievement, a mastery test should be used. For a summative evaluation of student or participant achievement, a discrimination test should be used. Formative evaluation is on a pass-fail basis; summative evaluation allows the teacher to identify individual differences in achievement by assigning letter grades.

Some teachers have mistakenly used mastery tests to make summative evaluations. The reliability of letter grades based on scores of mastery tests is almost always low because most of the items are too easy to discriminate well. To achieve high reliability, test items must discriminate sufficiently so that the students' scores are spread out. Later in the chapter we will show that the larger the standard deviation, the higher the Kuder-Richardson reliability. Low reliability means, in turn, that the standard error of measurement (see Chapter 3) is similar in value to the standard deviation for the test.

An example should clarify these points. Assume a mastery test is administered in a first aid class and letter grades are assigned based on the test scores. Suppose that the grading standard for a 100-point test is A: 93–100, B: 87–92, C: 78–86, D: 70–77, and F: below 69. If the standard deviation is 8 and the reliability of the test is .44, the standard error of measurement for the test is 6. Thus, the probability is .68 that a student who scored 88 will score between 82 and 94 (88 ± 6) if retested. Notice that 82 is a C and 94 is an A; the assigned grade is not reliable. If formative standards are used and a score of 80 or above is considered passing, the large standard error of measurement poses no problem because the student passes whether the score is 82 or 94. This is not to suggest that large standard errors are desirable or will not cause problems for other scores. For the person with a score close to the pass-fail cutoff score, the size of the standard error may be quite critical.

Table 13.3 Sample Table of Specifications for a Basketball Test

	Type of Test Items		
Subject Topic	*Knowledge*	*Comprehension*	*Application*
Rules	15%	5%	0%
Player duties	20%	10%	0%
Offensive plays	10%	10%	10%
Defenses	5%	5%	0%
Strategy	0%	0%	10%

Similarly, assume that the instructional objectives for a physical education unit pertain to knowledge of the rules of a sport. The best policy in this situation is probably to use a mastery test for formative evaluation. If a student can correctly answer 80% of the items on the test, the teacher can assume that the student has enough knowledge to play the sport. The mastery test is designed essentially to measure knowledge of basic rules. Similar thinking would apply in an adult fitness program.

Of course, mere knowledge of the rules is not sufficient for playing a sport. The rules must be applied and several different rules may have to be considered to resolve a situation. To interpret rules, the higher levels of the cognitive domain must be used. The teacher might use a discrimination test for summative evaluation of the students' ability to apply, analyze, and synthesize the rules in a game situation. Although students may know all the basic rules, they are likely to differ in their ability to understand, apply, and interpret them.

Construction

Whenever possible, the teacher, exercise specialist, or clinician should develop his or her own knowledge tests. A major advantage of instructor-made tests is that they tend to cover the material stressed in the unit in terminology the people understand. Thus, instructor-made tests tend to have logical validity (see Chapter 4). Another person's test not only may omit important material and include irrelevant material, but also may confuse people with the use of unfamiliar terminology.

Procedure

Typically, there are four general procedural steps to follow in constructing a good knowledge test:

Step 1. Construct a table of specifications.

Step 2. Decide the nature of the test.

Step 3. Construct the test items.

Step 4. Determine the test format and administrative details.

A table of specifications is an outline for the test construction. It lists the areas and levels of knowledge to be tested, as shown in Table 13.3. By adhering to a table of specifications, the test developer ensures that all the material on it is covered and that the correct weight is given to each area.

In deciding which type of test to give, consider the advantages and disadvantages of essay and objective tests, and then, if an objective test is chosen, of true-false, multiple-choice, or other types of items. There is no reason why a test must be composed of a single type of item, although all items of the same type should be grouped together. Tests that include both true-false and multiple-choice items, or some objective and some essay items, are not uncommon.

The third step is writing the test items. Begin this task well in advance of the testing session. It is important to allow enough time to develop items that are carefully conceptualized and constructed. In fact, after constructing the items, the constructor should read them, correct them, and then put them aside for at least a day before reading them again. A fresh look may pinpoint other errors and ambiguities.

Finally the test format is chosen. One important consideration is the directions, which should appear at the top of the test. The directions must clearly indicate how to take the test, what is the policy for guessing, whether a question may have more than one correct answer, and so on. Another consideration is the presentation of the items. They should be typed neatly with enough space to make them easy to read. When several items pertain to information supplied on the test (e.g., a diagram), the information and the items should be on the same page. Examples of good test format are presented later in the chapter.

Types of Test Items

True-False. A **true-false item** consists of a short, factual statement. If the statement appears to be true, the person marks True or T; otherwise the person marks False, or F. This type of item is quite popular.

The advantages of true-false items are as follows:

1. The rapidity with which people can answer these items makes it possible to include many items on the test.
2. It is easier and quicker to construct true-false items than other types of objective items.
3. Test items can be scored quickly.
4. Factual information is easily tested.
5. Standardized answer sheets can be used.

The disadvantages are these:

1. Probably only the first level of Bloom's taxonomy (1956), knowledge, can be tested by a true-false test.
2. People have a 50% chance of guessing the correct answer.
3. It is easy for a person to cheat by glancing at another person's paper.
4. This type of item can encourage memorization rather than understanding of facts.
5. This type of item is often ambiguous, in that the test taker and the test maker may not interpret an item in the same way.
6. True-false items often test trivial information.
7. To ensure reliability, a true-false test requires more items than does a multiple-choice test.

Construction Procedures: Many people believe that true-false test items are easy to construct. Unfortunately this is not entirely the case. Although they are easier to construct than some other types of objective items, true-false items must be constructed with care, using the following rules:

1. Keep the statement short. If it is long, the test taker may have to read it several times, which means that fewer items can be asked.
2. Use only a single concept in any one statement. This way, if a person answers incorrectly, you can identify the concept he or she does not know.
3. Keep the vocabulary simple.
4. Do not reproduce statements exactly from the text unless your objective is for the student to identify the passage.
5. Whenever possible, state the items positively rather than negatively.
6. Avoid using words like "always," "never," "all," and "none." Absolute statements are almost always false, and many people know this.
7. Do not allow more than 60% of the items to have the same answer. People expect approximately half the items to be true, which influences their thinking as they take a test.
8. Avoid long strings of items with the same answers.
9. Avoid patterns in the answers like true, false, true, false, and so on.
10. Do not give clues in one item to the answer of another. For example, don't let the statement in item 1 help answer item 14.
11. Avoid interdependent items. They put the person who misses the first item in double jeopardy.

Examples of Poor True-False Items:

1. T(F) In soccer, the hands cannot touch the ball except when the ball is thrown in or when the player is the goalie.
   Explanation. The key word "legally" has been omitted. Also, two questions are being asked: (1) Can the hands be used to throw the ball in? (2) Can the goalie touch the ball with his or her hands?
2. T(F) Never go swimming just after you have eaten.
   Explanation. An absolute like "never" should not be used. A better item would be "It is not recommended that a person go swimming immediately after eating."
3. T(F) Physical fitness is important because a sound body and a sound mind usually go hand in hand, and, further, the physically fit person does not tire as easily as the unfit person and, thus, is usually more productive, but the fit person does not necessarily live longer than the less fit person.
   Explanation. The statement is too long and includes multiple concepts.
4. T(F) A timed run may be used to test aerobic capacity.
   Explanation. The statement is ambiguous because the distance of the timed run isn't stated.

Multiple Choice. A **multiple-choice item** is composed of a short complete or incomplete question or statement followed by three to five potential answers. The first part of the item, the question or statement, is called the "stem"; the answers are called "responses." After reading the stem, the person selects the correct response. Complete stems are preferred over incomplete stems. Multiple-choice items are the most popular type of item with professional test makers, and are commonly used by all people who construct knowledge tests.

Among the advantages of this type of item are the following:

1. Because people can answer each multiple-choice item quickly, many items can be included in the test.
2. Test items can be scored quickly.
3. All levels of knowledge in Bloom's taxonomy can be tested with multiple-choice items.
4. The chances of a person guessing correctly are less than for true-false items, and decrease as the number of responses (plausible answers) increases.
5. Standardized answer sheets can be used.

Among the disadvantages of multiple-choice items are these:

1. Fewer items can be asked than with true-false items.
2. Considerable time is needed to think of enough plausible responses to each item.
3. There is a certain danger of cheating on multiple-choice items.
4. To some degree, multiple-choice items encourage memorization of facts without regard to their implications. This is more of a problem with items at the lower end of Bloom's taxonomy, and is generally less of a problem than it is with true-false items.
5. People are unable to demonstrate the extent of their knowledge; they can respond only to the items as constructed. Of course this is a legitimate criticism of all objective test questions.

Constructive Procedures: Multiple-choice items are not easy to construct. The development of items with good stems and responses takes time, and it can be difficult to think of enough responses for an item. It is not uncommon to spend 15–30 minutes constructing a single item. However, if the following few rules are followed, you should end up with an acceptable test.

1. Keep both stems and responses short and explicit.
2. Make all responses approximately the same length. Beginning test constructors have a tendency to include more information in the correct responses than in the incorrect responses, a fact the test takers quickly pick up.
3. Use apparently acceptable answers for all responses. There is no excuse for writing obviously incorrect or sloppy responses.
4. If possible, use five responses for each item. This keeps the guess factors acceptably low (.20), and it is usually hard to think of more. It is desirable that all multiple-choice items on a test have the same number of responses.
5. If the stem is an incomplete sentence or question, make each response complete the stem.
6. Do not give away the correct answer with English usage. If the stem is singular, all responses should be singular. Words beginning with a vowel must be preceded by "an."
7. Do not give away the answer to one item in the content of another.

8. Do not allow the answer to one item to depend on the answer to another. If people answer the first incorrectly, they will answer the second incorrectly as well.
9. Do not construct the stem in such a way that you solicit a person's opinion. For example, do not begin questions with "What should be done?" or "What would you do?"
10. If the items are numbered, use letters (a,b,c,d,e) to enumerate the responses. People tend to confuse response numbers with item numbers if the responses are numbered, particularly when standardized answer sheets are used.
11. Try to use each letter as the correct answer approximately the same number of times in the test. If the constructor is not careful, (c) may be the correct response more often than any other, which could help people guess the correct answer.
12. State the stem in positive rather than negative terms.

Examples of Poor Multiple-Choice Items:

1. What should you do if the right front wheel of your car goes off the pavement as you are driving?
   a. Brake sharply.
   b. Cut the front wheels sharply to the left.
   c. Brake sharply and cut the wheels sharply to the left.
   d. Brake sharply and turn the wheels gradually to the left.
   *e. Brake gradually, maintaining control of the car by driving along the shoulder of the road if necessary. Then pull gently back onto the pavement when speed is reduced.

   Explanation. (1) the stem asks for the person's opinion; (2) it is understood, but should be stated in the stem, that the right front wheel went off the right side of the pavement; (3) the longest response is the correct answer.
2. A multiple-choice item is a
   *a. very popular and commonly used type of item.
   b. alternative to a true-false item.
   c. important type of knowledge test item.
   d. very easy type of item to construct.
   e. limited application type of item.

   Explanation. Responses b and c can be eliminated because the stem ends in "a" and they both begin with vowels. The best solution is to end the stem at "is" and to add "a" or "an" to each response.
3. Which of the following does *not* serve on an IEP committee?
   *a. Child
   b. Parent
   c. Adapted physical education teacher
   d. Principal
   e. None of the above

   Explanation. It looks like the test constructor could not think of five different responses, so response e was inserted. Does the e response indicate none of the above do not serve on an IEP committee, which means that all of them do serve? Or does the e response indicate that none of the responses above are the correct response? The double negative certainly causes problems in interpreting and answering the item.

Table 13.4 A Sample Matching Test

Volleyball

For each item on the left-hand side of the page, find an answer on the right-hand side. Place the letter of the correct answer in the space provided at the left side of each item. Each answer can be used only once.

	Items	
____	1. The official height of the net in feet	a. 6
____	2. The number of players on an official team	b. 8
____	3. The number of points needed to win a game	c. 12
____	4. Loss of the serve	d. 15
____	5. Loss of a point	e. 18
____	6. Illegal play	f. 21
		g. Net serve that goes over
		h. More than 3 hits by receiving team
		i. Reaching over the net to spike the ball
		j. Stepping on a side boundary line
		k. Serving team carries the ball

Golf

In items 7–10, determine which of the four clubs listed on the right is best suited for the shot described on the left. Each answer can be used more than once.

	Items	
____	7. Tee shot on a 90-yard hole	l. Three-wood
____	8. 100-yard approach to the green	m. Two-iron
____	9. Fairway shot 140 yards from the green	n. Five-iron
____	10. 200-yard shot from the rough	o. Nine-iron

4. Pick the incorrect statement from the following:
   a. Only the serving team can score in volleyball.
   *b. In badminton, a person cannot score unless he or she has the serve.
   c. In tennis, a set has not been won if the score is 40–30.
   d. In tennis, volleyball, and badminton, a net serve is served again.
   e. In tennis and badminton, a player cannot reach over the net to contact the ball or shuttlecock.

   Explanation. (1) When an incorrect response is to be identified, try to state all responses positively so as not to confuse the students. (2) In response e, it would be preferable to say "it is illegal for a player to reach. . . ." (3) Change the stem to "Pick the *false* statement . . .," so the person evaluates each response as true or false and is looking for the false response.

Matching. In a **matching-item** test, a number of short questions or statements are listed on the left side of the page and the answers are listed in order on the right. Matching items are a logical extension of multiple-choice items in that both provide the person with several answers from which to choose. Matching items are used less often than true-false or multiple-choice items, but they are very helpful in situations in which the same answers can be used with several test items. A sample matching test is shown in Table 13.4.

Among the advantages of matching items are the following:

1. You can save space by giving the same potential answers for several questions.
2. The odds of guessing the right answer are theoretically quite low because there are so many answers to choose from. In actuality, people will probably be able to detect that no more than five to eight answers apply to any given question.
3. These items are quicker to construct than multiple-choice questions.

The disadvantages of matching items are these:

1. Matching items usually test only factual information (the lowest level in Bloom's taxonomy).
2. Matching items are not particularly versatile, and a multiple-choice item often serves just as well.
3. Standardized answer sheets usually cannot be used with these items.

Construction Procedures: To develop a fair test, carefully plan the format and directions using the following rules:

1. State the items and potential answers clearly; neither should be more than two lines long.
2. Number the items and identify the potential answers with letters.
3. Allow a space at the left of each item for the correct answer.
4. Keep all items and answers on the same page.
5. Make all items similar in content. It is preferable to construct several sets of matching items rather than to mix content.
6. Arrange potential answers in logical groupings—all numerical answers together, all dates together, and so on. This saves people the time necessary to scan all the answers before responding.
7. Provide more answers than items to prevent people from deducing answers by elimination.
8. In the directions, tell the people whether an answer can be used more than once.
9. Have several potential answers for each item.

Completion. In a **completion item,** one word or several words are omitted from a sentence, and a person is asked to supply the missing information. This type of item has limited usefulness and application, and is less satisfactory than a multiple-choice item. In fact, many textbooks don't discuss this type of item in detail. Unless completion items are stated carefully, students may be uncertain what information the teacher wants. For example, consider the following item:

Three playing combinations in racquetball are ____________, ____________, and ____________.

Some people will answer singles, doubles, and cutthroat, while others, thinking about doubles play, will respond side-by-side, front-and-back, and rotation. The acceptable answers to the item "$.02 and $.03 are ______?" must include "$.05," "5," "a nickel," "5 pennies," and "money." Obviously true-false or multiple-choice items could do the job with less ambiguity.

Short Answer and Essay. **Short-answer items** and **essay items** are appropriate when the teacher wants to determine the student's depth of knowledge and their capacity to assemble and organize facts. For each item, students answer with whatever facts and in whatever manner they think appropriate.

The advantages of essay items are the following:

1. Students are free to answer essay items in the way that seems best to them.
2. These items allow students to demonstrate the depth of their knowledge.
3. These items encourage students to relate all the material to a total concept rather than just learn the facts.
4. The items are easy and quick to construct.
5. All levels of Bloom's taxonomy can be tested with essay items.

Their disadvantages are these:

1. Essay items are time-consuming to grade.
2. The objectivity of test scores is often low.
3. The reliability of test scores is often low.
4. Essay items require some skill in self-expression; if this skill is not an instructional objective, the item lacks validity.
5. Penmanship and neatness affect grades, which again lowers the item's validity.
6. The halo effect; students expected to do well on the test tend to be scored higher than they may deserve.

Construction Procedures: Most teachers can construct reasonably good short-answer or essay items. However, if an item is hastily constructed, the students may not respond in the manner wanted. The biggest disadvantage of this type of item may be its grading. Teachers must key an item carefully to identify the characteristics wanted in the answer and to determine how partial credit points are assigned. Without an answer sheet, the reliability of scores is often low. For example, if a test item is worth 20 points and 5 specific facts should be mentioned in the answer, each fact is worth 4 points. If only 3 of the 5 facts are included, the student receives 12 points. Thus, if the teacher should grade the item again, the student is likely again to receive 12 points. Research that required an instructor to grade a set of essay tests twice has found the test-retest reliability is usually low. The objectivity of essay test grades has also been investigated by assigning two qualified teachers to grade a set of essays independently. The objectivity has seldom been high.

If the following rules for constructing short-answer and essay items are followed, the items should be satisfactory:

1. State the item as clearly and concisely as possible.
2. Note on the test the approximate time students should spend on each item.

3. Note on the test the point value for each item.
4. Carefully key the test before administration. This is the only way to identify ambiguous items.

Sample Tests

Ideally teachers should construct their own knowledge tests. Those constructed by others often do not have the terminology or material emphasis needed for every teacher and class. If, for example, two teachers do not use the same technique, the correct answer to a question about that technique will not be the same for both instructors. The content and emphasis of a knowledge test also are influenced considerably by the age, sex, and ability level of the students. Knowledge tests can quickly become outdated as ideas, techniques, and rules change.

There are several sources of knowledge tests. Some have been published in research journals, and most books and manuals about specific sports and skills include sample knowledge tests. McGee and Farrow (1987) published a book of test questions for fifteen different activities. Unpublished knowledge tests (theses, dissertations, tests constructed by teachers in your school system) are also available.

Several sample knowledge test items are included here.

Badminton

Part I. True-False. If the answer is true, put a plus (+) to the left of the item number. If the answer is false, put a minus (−) to the left of the item number. Please respond to each item.

_____1. In singles play it is poor tactics to return your opponent's drop with another drop unless your opponent is completely out of position in the back court.

_____2. Proper position of the feet is more important in the execution of strokes made from a point near the rear boundary line than from a point near the net.

_____3. Players A-1 and A-2, a two-person team, are trailing in their game 5-3. They have just broken the serve of Team B, so A-1 will start the serve in the right service court for Team A.

Part II. Multiple-Choice. To the left of the item number, put the letter of the answer that is most correct. Please respond to each item.

_____4. During the execution of a stroke, the arm is straightened
a. at no particular time.
b. just prior to contact between racket and bird.
c. at the moment of contact between racket and bird.
d. just after contact is made between racket and bird.

_____5. If your opponent is in the back left-hand corner of his or her court when you play the bird, what number in the diagram on the next page represents your best target?
a. 1
b. 2
c. 3
d. 4

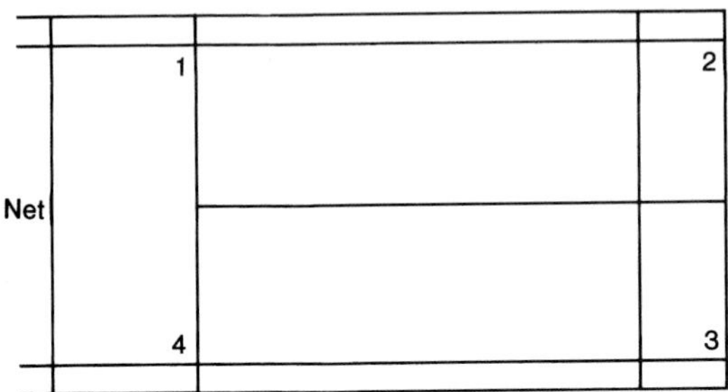

Part III. Identification. Give the official names of the lines of the court that are numbered in the diagram, placing the name next to the number.

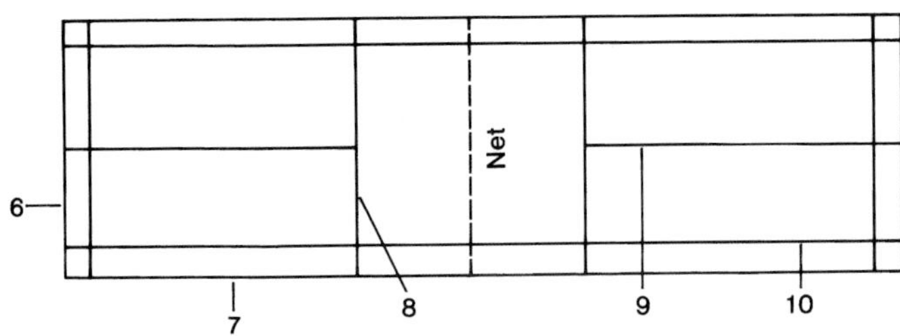

Volleyball

Read the instructions that precede each section of the test before you answer any of the items in that section.

Part I. True-False. If the statement is true, blacken the a on the answer sheet. If the statement is false, blacken b on the answer sheet for that numbered statement.

1. To start the game, Team A serves. Team B's first server will be the player who started the game as the right forward.
2. If the spiker is left-handed, the "ideal" set-up will be on his or her right side.
3. The blocker's jump is begun just before the spiker's jump.

Part II. Matching. Read each numbered statement and choose the best answer from the five responses. Then, on the answer sheet, blacken the letter of the correct response for that numbered statement. Use the same five responses for items 4 through 7.

a. Point for Team A
b. Point for Team B
c. Loss of serve
d. Legal, play continues
e. Reserve or serve over

4. While Team B is serving, a player on Team A tries to play the ball, but it bounces off his or her shoulder and a teammate successfully spikes the ball over the net where it strikes the floor inbounds.
5. During the return of B's serve, a player on Team A spikes the ball, which lands inbounds on B's side of the net.
6. Team A serves. Team B sets the ball for its spiker, while Team A sets up a two-person block. During the spike-block play, Spiker B lands over the center line; however, one of A's blockers' hands goes over the net.
7. Team B serves. Team A sets the ball for the spiker, while Team B sets up a two-person block. Player A spikes the ball into Blocker B's hands and the ball bounds over Team A's end line.

Fitness Concepts

Please do not write on this exam.

1. As a result of regular cardiovascular training, resting heart rate
   A. increases.
   B. decreases.
   C. does not change (resting heart rate is unaffected).
   D. changes cannot be predicted.
2. Decreases in lean body mass are
   A. frequently seen in diets below 1200 calories.
   B. rarely seen during periods of starvation.
   C. uncommon in near-fasting diets.
   D. common among smokers.
3. The overload principle states that
   A. muscles have to be taxed beyond their regular accustomed loads to increase their physical capacity.
   B. the resistance placed on the muscles must be of a magnitude significant enough to cause physiological adaptation.
   C. the load placed on the muscle(s) must be systematically and progressively increased over a period of time.
   D. All are correct choices.
4. The leading cause of death in the United States is
   A. cancer.
   B. cardiovascular heart disease.
   C. coronary heart disease.
   D. hypertension.
5. Which of the following is NOT a component of a successful weight loss program, weight maintenance, and achievement of recommended body composition?
   A. a lifetime exercise program
   B. a diet low in fat and refined carbohydrates
   C. a diet high in complex carbohydrates and fiber foods
   D. a diet high in protein and low in carbohydrates
6. To develop muscular strength, it is recommended that an individual should work between _____ repetitions.
   A. 3 and 8
   B. 9 and 15
   C. 15 and 20
   D. 20 and 30

Administration and Scoring

Administration Procedures

A test setting should be quiet, well lighted, properly heated, odor-free, spacious, and comfortable. The failure to furnish a comfortable and distraction-free testing site places people at a disadvantage. Physical education teachers often are not careful about the testing atmosphere and setting: The practice of instructing students to lie on the gym floor to take a test while other students participate in another part of the gym leaves much to be desired.

The teacher must also consider test security. During a test, students should all face the same direction. They should be sitting close enough to allow the teacher to see everyone, but far enough apart to preclude cheating and whispering. In a classroom, you may assign a student to every other seat or, better still, to every other seat of every other row. Encourage students to keep their eyes on their own papers and their papers covered. Sometimes alternate test forms, with the same items arranged on each form in a different order, are used. Also a procedure for collecting the papers is essential. If students stand around the teacher waiting to turn in their tests, they can exchange answers while they wait; and, students still taking the test can exchange answers while the teacher is busy collecting other students' tests.

If you plan to use the same test with several classes, you must ensure that students who have taken the test do not give the test items and answers to those yet to take it. If only two consecutive classes are to take the test, security poses no problem. However, if even as much as an hour elapses between the two administrations, the test's contents will probably be known to the second class. The best approach, then, is to use several forms of the test. Of course each form must test the same material. A common procedure with multiple-choice tests is to construct parallel items. For example, all forms of the test include an item dealing with aerobic capacity. With true-false tests, a common procedure is to reword some of the items on the second form so that the answer changes.

Scoring Procedures

On an essay test, remove the person's name from the test paper to increase the validity and objectivity of scoring, and score each student's answer to a single item before going on to the next item. This procedure, and the use of a key, increases the likelihood that the same standards will be applied to all answers. Reliability suffers when an essay test is scored in a hurry. This is one reason why essay tests take so much time to score.

The scoring of true-false and multiple-choice items, although usually less time-consuming than essay questions, can be tedious if it is done by referring alternately to the answer key and each person's answers. Standardized answer sheets can speed up the scoring of true-false and multiple-choice tests. These answer sheets can be constructed by the teacher or test administrator or purchased commercially. A sample of a commercial, standardized answer sheet is shown in Figure 13.1. These standardized answer sheets have the advantage of being machine-scorable, thus eliminating the time needed to score the tests by hand. Machines to score tests vary from the large and expensive ones used by scoring services and universities to the small and inexpensive desktop model used by individual schools or programs. In addition, the use of standardized answer sheets makes it possible to reuse test booklets.

A layover answer key—a standardized answer sheet on which the correct answers are cut or punched out—is used to score standardized tests by hand. To use a layover answer key, first scan the person's answer sheet to make sure there are no multiple responses to any of the test items. Then the layover answer key is placed on top of the answer sheet, and the number of visible pencil marks is the person's score. A 50-question true-false or multiple-choice test can be scored in 20 to 30 seconds using a layover answer sheet.

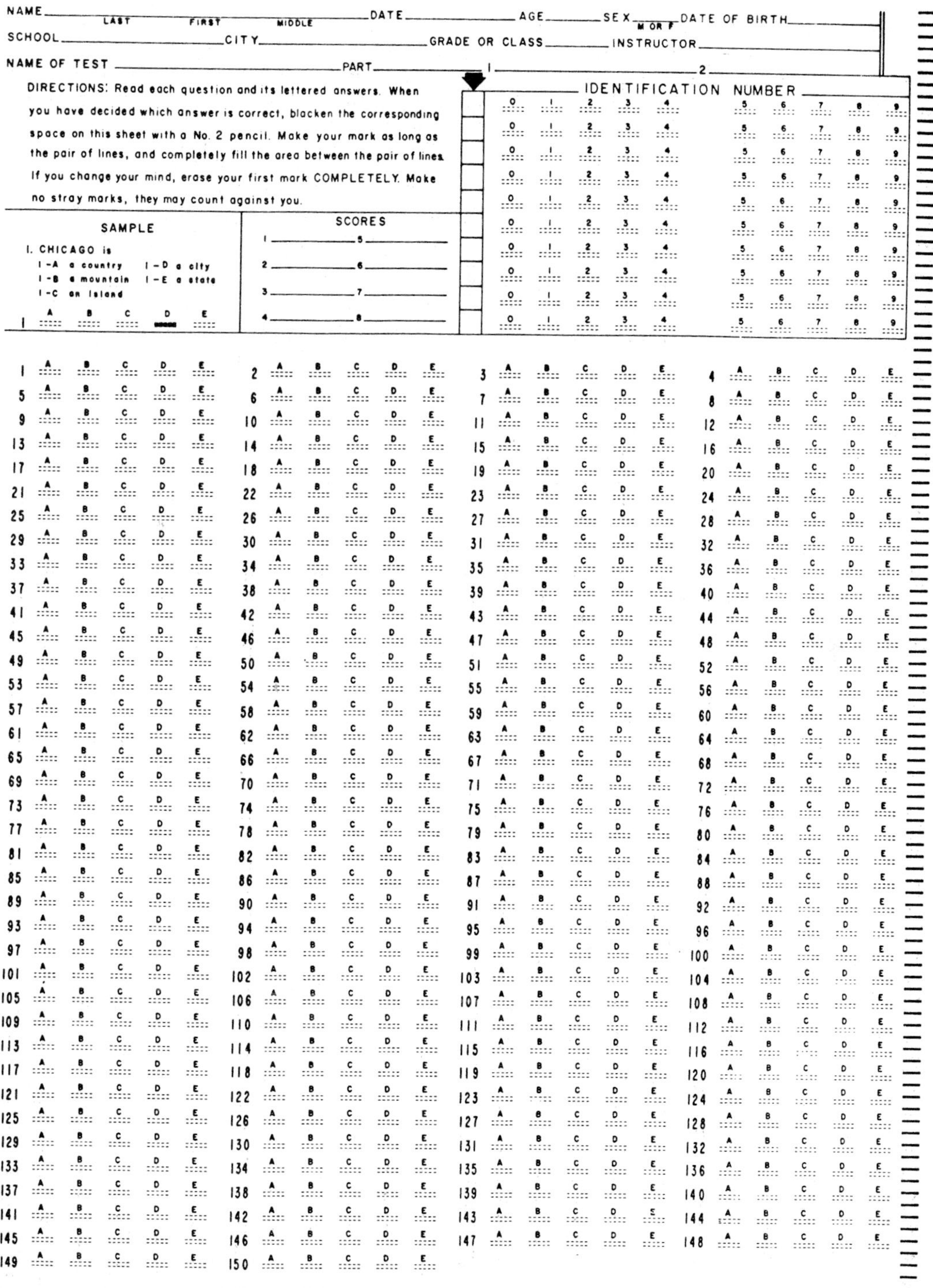

NAME ______ LAST FIRST MIDDLE ______ DATE ______ AGE ______ SEX ______ M OR F DATE OF BIRTH ______

SCHOOL ______ CITY ______ GRADE OR CLASS ______ INSTRUCTOR ______

NAME OF TEST ______ PART ______ 1 ______ 2 ______

DIRECTIONS: Read each question and its lettered answers. When you have decided which answer is correct, blacken the corresponding space on this sheet with a No. 2 pencil. Make your mark as long as the pair of lines, and completely fill the area between the pair of lines. If you change your mind, erase your first mark COMPLETELY. Make no stray marks, they may count against you.

IDENTIFICATION NUMBER

0	1	2	3	4	5	6	7	8	9
0	1	2	3	4	5	6	7	8	9
0	1	2	3	4	5	6	7	8	9
0	1	2	3	4	5	6	7	8	9
0	1	2	3	4	5	6	7	8	9
0	1	2	3	4	5	6	7	8	9
0	1	2	3	4	5	6	7	8	9
0	1	2	3	4	5	6	7	8	9
0	1	2	3	4	5	6	7	8	9
0	1	2	3	4	5	6	7	8	9

SAMPLE

I. CHICAGO is
I-A a country I-D a city
I-B a mountain I-E a state
I-C an island

I A B C D E

SCORES

1 ______ 5 ______
2 ______ 6 ______
3 ______ 7 ______
4 ______ 8 ______

1 A B C D E	2 A B C D E	3 A B C D E	4 A B C D E
5 A B C D E	6 A B C D E	7 A B C D E	8 A B C D E
9 A B C D E	10 A B C D E	11 A B C D E	12 A B C D E
13 A B C D E	14 A B C D E	15 A B C D E	16 A B C D E
17 A B C D E	18 A B C D E	19 A B C D E	20 A B C D E
21 A B C D E	22 A B C D E	23 A B C D E	24 A B C D E
25 A B C D E	26 A B C D E	27 A B C D E	28 A B C D E
29 A B C D E	30 A B C D E	31 A B C D E	32 A B C D E
33 A B C D E	34 A B C D E	35 A B C D E	36 A B C D E
37 A B C D E	38 A B C D E	39 A B C D E	40 A B C D E
41 A B C D E	42 A B C D E	43 A B C D E	44 A B C D E
45 A B C D E	46 A B C D E	47 A B C D E	48 A B C D E
49 A B C D E	50 A B C D E	51 A B C D E	52 A B C D E
53 A B C D E	54 A B C D E	55 A B C D E	56 A B C D E
57 A B C D E	58 A B C D E	59 A B C D E	60 A B C D E
61 A B C D E	62 A B C D E	63 A B C D E	64 A B C D E
65 A B C D E	66 A B C D E	67 A B C D E	68 A B C D E
69 A B C D E	70 A B C D E	71 A B C D E	72 A B C D E
73 A B C D E	74 A B C D E	75 A B C D E	76 A B C D E
77 A B C D E	78 A B C D E	79 A B C D E	80 A B C D E
81 A B C D E	82 A B C D E	83 A B C D E	84 A B C D E
85 A B C D E	86 A B C D E	87 A B C D E	88 A B C D E
89 A B C D E	90 A B C D E	91 A B C D E	92 A B C D E
93 A B C D E	94 A B C D E	95 A B C D E	96 A B C D E
97 A B C D E	98 A B C D E	99 A B C D E	100 A B C D E
101 A B C D E	102 A B C D E	103 A B C D E	104 A B C D E
105 A B C D E	106 A B C D E	107 A B C D E	108 A B C D E
109 A B C D E	110 A B C D E	111 A B C D E	112 A B C D E
113 A B C D E	114 A B C D E	115 A B C D E	116 A B C D E
117 A B C D E	118 A B C D E	119 A B C D E	120 A B C D E
121 A B C D E	122 A B C D E	123 A B C D E	124 A B C D E
125 A B C D E	126 A B C D E	127 A B C D E	128 A B C D E
129 A B C D E	130 A B C D E	131 A B C D E	132 A B C D E
133 A B C D E	134 A B C D E	135 A B C D E	136 A B C D E
137 A B C D E	138 A B C D E	139 A B C D E	140 A B C D E
141 A B C D E	142 A B C D E	143 A B C D E	144 A B C D E
145 A B C D E	146 A B C D E	147 A B C D E	148 A B C D E
149 A B C D E	150 A B C D E		

Figure 13.1 Standardized commercial answer sheet.

To score commercial answer sheets by machine, the person must use a pencil to mark the answer sheets. Many colleges and school districts offer free scoring services to their personnel. The answer key and answer sheets are fed into a machine that scores the tests and stamps a score on each answer sheet.

Analysis and Revision

Most objective tests are used more than once. After the test has been administered and scored, it should be examined to determine the merits of the test and of each item, and to identify those items that should be revised or deleted before the test is used again. The failure to analyze a knowledge test after its first administration lowers the reliability and validity of the test scores.

After administering and scoring a test, the following characteristics should be examined:

1. Overall difficulty
2. Variability in test scores
3. Reliability
4. The difficulty of each item
5. The discrimination, or validity, of each item
6. Quality of each response in a multiple-choice item

Analyzing the Test

Difficulty and Variability. The overall difficulty of a test is determined by calculating the mean performance for the group tested. The higher the mean, the easier the test. The variability in test scores is determined by calculating the standard deviation. The larger the standard deviation, the more reliable the test, and the more the test discriminates among ability groups.

Reliability. The reliability of a knowledge test is usually estimated using either the Kuder-Richardson or coefficient alpha method. As indicated in Chapter 3, coefficient alpha is the same as an intraclass reliability coefficient. The administration of the test twice on different days to estimate stability reliability as discussed in Chapter 3 is inappropriate because persons would be expected to do better the second day due to a carryover of knowledge and an exchange of information about the test.

The Kuder-Richardson Formulas 20 and 21 are typically used to estimate the reliability of a knowledge test. Nunnally and Bernstein (1994) state that with dichotomous items (items scored as either right or wrong) Formula 20's reliability coefficient is the same as coefficient alpha. (In Chapter 3 we illustrated coefficient alpha.) Formula 20 (commonly used in computer programs) is time-consuming to use because the percentage of the class answering each item correctly must be determined. On the assumption that all test items are equally difficult, Formula 20 can be simplified to Formula 21. Although Formula 21 is commonly used, it underestimates the reliability coefficient when test items vary in difficulty, which they usually do. Formula 21 should be considered an estimate of the minimum test reliability. The Kuder-Richardson Formula 21 is as follows:

Table 13.5 Kuder-Richardson Formula Scores

	Item										
Person	**1**	**2**	**3**	**4**	**5**	**6**	**7**	**8**	**9**	**10**	**X**
A	1	1	1	1	0	1	1	1	1	1	9
B	1	0	0	0	0	1	1	0	1	1	5
C	0	1	0	0	0	0	1	1	0	1	4
D	1	1	0	0	0	1	0	1	1	1	6
E	1	1	0	0	0	1	1	1	1	1	7

$\overline{X} = 6.2$
$s^2 = 2.96$

$$r_{21} = \frac{k(s^2) - \overline{X}(k - \overline{X})}{(k - 1)(s^2)} \qquad (13.1)$$

where k is the number of test questions, s^2 is the test's standard deviation squared, and $\overline{X}$ is the test mean.

Problem 13.1. Use the information in Table 13.5 to calculate the Kuder-Richardson Formula 21 reliability coefficient of the test.

Solution. Where k is 10, s^2 is 2.96, and $\overline{X}$ is 6.2, the reliability coefficient using Formula 21 is .23:

$$r = \frac{(10)(2.96) - (6.2)(10 - 6.2)}{(10 - 1)(2.96)} = \frac{2.96 - (6.2)(3.8)}{(9)(2.96)}$$

$$= \frac{29.6 - 23.56}{26.64} = \frac{6.04}{26.64} = .23$$

Formula 20 yields a correlation coefficient of .63, which as suggested is a higher value than the .23 yielded by Formula 21.

The Kuder-Richardson Formula 20 is as follows:

$$r_{20} = \left(\frac{k}{k - 1}\right)\left(\frac{(s_x)^2 - \Sigma pq}{(s_x)^2}\right) \qquad (13.2)$$

where k is the number of test items, $(s_x)^2$ is the variance of the test scores $[\Sigma X^2/n - (\Sigma X)^2/n^2]$, *p* is the percentage answering an item correctly, *q* is 1 − p, and Σpq is the sum of the *pq* products for all *k* items.

Problem 13.2. Determine the Kuder-Richardson Formula 21 reliability of the test presented in Table 13.5.

Solution. Using the figures in Table 13.5, we can calculate the following p, q, and pq for the ten items:

Item	1	2	3	4	5	6	7	8	9	10
p	.8	.8	.2	.2	.0	.8	.8	.8	.8	1.0
q	.2	.2	.8	.8	1.0	.2	.2	.2	.2	.0
pq	.16	.16	.16	.16	.00	.16	.16	.16	.16	.00

Where k is 10, $(s_x)^2$ is 2.96, and Σpq is 1.28, r is .63:

$$r = \left(\frac{10}{10 - 1}\right)\left(\frac{2.96 - 1.28}{2.96}\right) = \left(\frac{10}{9}\right)\left(\frac{1.68}{2.96}\right) = \frac{16.8}{26.64} = .63$$

Remember that—all other factors being equal—the larger the standard deviation, the higher the reliability coefficient. If in Problem 13.1 the scores had been 9, 8, 7, 5, and 4; $\overline{X}$ was 6.6; and s^2 was 3.44, the reliability coefficient r using Formula 21 would have been .39. Thus, high reliability is harder to obtain with homogeneous groups than it is with heterogeneous ones.

As noted above, coefficient alpha is the same as Kuder-Richardson Formula 20 with dichotomous items. If the items have more than two possible answers (like answers A, B, C, D, E on a knowledge test or scores 1 to 5 on an attitude scale), Kuder-Richardson formulas are not appropriate but coefficient alpha can be utilized. Coefficient alpha is commonly provided when computer analysis of a knowledge test is conducted.

Item Analysis

The last two relevant characteristics of a test—the difficulty and validity of the items and the efficiency of responses—can be determined by an item analysis, a procedure that is important but tedious to do by hand. This analysis should be conducted whenever a test is used the first time.

For the results of an item analysis to be reliable and valid, a large number of people (over 100) must have taken the test. There are several reasons why a large number is essential, one being that all ability levels are apt to be represented. Also, some estimates of correlation coefficients are used in the item analysis procedure, and coefficients based on small groups are often uncommonly high or low and thus untrustworthy.

The first step in an item analysis is to identify a top and bottom group from the total test scores. We will use the top and bottom 27% of the scores. Use only the tests of people in these ranges in the analysis. The next step is to make a chart on which to record the answer each person in the top and bottom groups chose for each item. Figure 13.2 shows a sample chart using the test papers of the top and bottom 16 students in a class of 60. You can see that 12 students in the top group and 5 students in the bottom group answered item 1 correctly. By using only the top and bottom 27% of the test papers in the analysis, we minimize the work of constructing the chart and can also determine how well each item discriminates between the best and worst students. With the information in the chart, it is possible to determine the difficulty and validity of each test item, and whether all responses functioned.

Item Difficulty. Because each person answers each item correctly or incorrectly, we can calculate the percentage of people who chose the right answer. This percentage, called the **item difficulty** (D), is large when the test item is easy, and small when it is hard. We use the following formula to determine item difficulty:

ITEM	CORRECT ANSWER		RESPONSE a	b	c	d	e	OMIT
1	b	top		卌 卌 //	///	/		
		bottom	//	卌	卌	//	//	
2	e	top	//	//	/	///	卌 ///	
		bottom	//	///	//	卌	////	
3	c	top			卌 卌 卌 /			
		bottom		///	卌 卌 ///			
4	a	top	卌	卌 ///	///			
		bottom	卌 卌	//	////			

Figure 13.2
Chart showing answers selected by top and bottom groups in a class of students taking a given test.

$$D = \frac{\text{number right in top group} + \text{number right in bottom group}}{\text{number in top group} + \text{number in bottom group}} \qquad (13.3)$$

Problem 13.3. Determine the difficulty of item 1 in Figure 13.2.

Solution. Where the number right in the top group is 12, the number right in the bottom group is 5, and the number of students in each of the groups is 16, the item difficulty, D, is .53, or 53% of the students answered the question correctly.

$$D = \frac{12 + 5}{16 + 16} = \frac{17}{32} = .53$$

Discrimination Index. Item validity, or item discrimination, indicates how well a test item discriminates between those who performed well on the test and those who did poorly. If, as is wanted, an item is answered correctly by more of the better performers than the worse performers, it discriminates positively; if more of the worse performers answer the item correctly than do the better performers, the item is a poor one and discriminates negatively. The first time a test is used, it is not uncommon to find that a few items discriminate negatively. These items should be revised or rejected before the test is used again.

The **discrimination index** (r) is essentially a correlation coefficient between scores on one item and scores on the whole test. Thus its value ranges from +1 to −1; +1 corresponds to the best possible positive discrimination. The calculation of the correlation between scores on each item and on the total test is too time-consuming, but we can estimate it, using the top and bottom 27% of the class, with the following formula:

$$r = \frac{\text{number right in top group} - \text{number right in bottom group}}{\text{number in each group}} \qquad (13.4)$$

Problem 13.4. Determine the discrimination index of Item 1 in Figure 13.2.

Solution. Where the number right in the top group is 12, the number right in the bottom group is 5, and the number of students in each group is 16, the discrimination, or validity, index r is .44:

$$r = \frac{12 - 5}{16} = \frac{7}{16} = .44$$

The discrimination index is quite easy to compute with a calculator; it can be tedious if done by hand.

It is apparent from the discrimination index formula that a positive value is obtained when more people in the top group than in the bottom group answer an item correctly; a zero value is obtained when the same number of people in both groups answer correctly.

We assume in determining item validity that the total test score is a valid measure of knowledge. Therefore, total test validity must be determined, usually by examining the logical validity, before the item analysis. Item validity has no meaning if the total test is not valid. Also, as noted earlier, all other factors being equal, the larger the standard deviation, the more reliable the test. The more a test discriminates, the larger the standard deviation tends to be.

It is worth noting as well that the difficulty of a test item affects the maximum attainable discrimination index. If, for example, the difficulty of an item is .50, a discrimination index of 1.0 is obtained if all people in the top group and none in the bottom group answer the item correctly. If, however, the difficulty of a test item is .60, the best possible discrimination (.80) is obtained when 100% of the top group and 20% of the bottom group respond to the item correctly. The maximum possible discrimination if item difficulty is .40 is also .80. As item difficulties go up or down from .50, the maximum possible discrimination index decreases. For this reason teachers who want to develop discrimination tests, rather than mastery tests, try to write as many test items whose difficulty is approximately .50 as possible—a difficult task.

Response Quality. Ideally, at least some of the people whose test papers are analyzed should select each response of a multiple-choice item. The instructor can use the chart developed to do the item analysis to determine whether all responses were indeed selected. Figure 13.2 shows that all responses were selected in Item 1, but only responses b and c were selected for item 3. Thus item 3 might as well have been a true-false item.

Item Analysis by a Computer. The **item analysis** just presented is time-consuming to do by hand. The computer can be used to complete an item analysis. When standardized answer sheets are used, the process is quite easy. As noted previously, many schools offer machine scoring. As each answer sheet is scored, the machine can record the student's name, test score, and response to each item. This information for the entire group is then submitted to the computer for item analysis. Computer analysis is more complete than the item analysis undertaken by hand because all the students' scores are used; the top group becomes the upper 50% of those tested. At many colleges, universities, and public school districts, the item analysis service is free.

A sample of the data from a microcomputer printout of an item analysis appears in Table 13.6. The test was administered to 52 people and was composed of

Table 13.6 Sample Item Analysis Printout

Student ID	Student Name	Raw Score	% Right	Percentile Rank
1234	AC	8	53	22
2562	BZ	9	60	42
2981	CC	13	87	87
3324	DF	12	80	75
•	•	•	•	•
•	•	•	•	•
•	•	•	•	•
2617	GJ	5	33	3

No. of Respondents	= 52	Mean Score	= 9.9	High Score	= 14
No. of Items	= 15	Median Score	= 9.0	Low Score	= 2
		Stand. Dev.	= 2.52		

Item Analysis

Question		*Upper Quarter*	*Lower Quarter*	*Total Count*	*Total %*	*Discrim. Index*	*Diff. Factor*
1	A	0	0	1	2	0.0	0.8
	B*	13	8	42	81	0.4	
	C	0	0	1	2	0.0	
	D	0	3	4	8	−0.2	
	E	0	2	4	8	−0.2	
2	A	1	4	11	21	−0.2	0.6
	B*	12	5	29	56	0.5	
	C	0	0	1	2	0.0	
	D	0	2	3	6	−0.2	
	E	0	2	8	15	−0.2	
3	A	0	0	0	0	0.0	0.4
	B*	11	1	22	42	0.8	
	C	2	12	29	56	−0.8	
	D	0	0	0	0	0.0	
	E	0	0	1	2	0.0	
4	A*	13	10	45	87	0.2	0.9
	B	0	2	2	4	−0.2	
	C	0	1	2	4	−0.0	
	D	0	0	1	2	0.0	
	E	0	0	2	4	0.0	
5	A	0	1	1	2	−0.0	0.9
	B	0	2	3	6	−0.2	
	C*	13	8	45	87	0.4	
	D	0	1	2	4	−0.0	
	E	0	1	1	2	−0.0	
6	A	0	2	2	4	−0.2	0.7
	B	0	0	3	6	0.0	
	C*	10	5	34	65	0.4	
	D	2	4	7	13	−0.2	
	E	1	2	6	12	−0.0	

* = correct answer

Table 13.6 Sample Item Analysis Printout—*Continued*

Item Analysis

Question		*Upper Quarter*	*Lower Quarter*	*Total Count*	*Total %*	*Discrim. Index*	*Diff. Factor*
7	A	0	1	2	4	−0.0	0.9
	B	0	0	0	0	0.0	
	C*	13	9	46	88	0.3	
	D	0	0	0	0	0.0	
	E	0	3	4	8	−0.2	
8	A*	7	3	19	37	0.3	0.4
	B	0	2	6	12	−0.2	
	C	4	8	20	38	−0.3	
	D	2	0	7	13	0.2	
	E	0	0	0	0	0.0	
9	A	0	0	0	0	0.0	0.7
	B*	12	11	37	71	0.0	
	C	0	0	0	0	0.0	
	D	1	1	6	12	0.0	
	E	0	1	9	17	−0.0	
10	A*	6	0	7	13	0.5	0.1
	B	6	10	36	69	−0.3	
	C	1	0	3	6	0.0	
	D	0	3	4	8	−0.2	
	E	0	0	2	4	0.0	
11	A	2	3	8	15	−0.0	0.5
	B*	9	4	26	50	0.4	
	C	1	1	6	12	0.0	
	D	1	2	4	8	−0.0	
	E	0	3	8	15	−0.2	
12	A	0	8	11	21	−0.6	0.8
	B	0	0	1	2	0.0	
	C*	13	5	39	75	0.6	
	D	0	0	0	0	0.0	
	E	0	0	1	2	0.0	
13	A	0	2	3	6	−0.2	0.8
	B	0	3	6	12	−0.2	
	C	0	1	1	2	−0.0	
	D	0	1	2	4	−0.0	
	E*	13	6	40	77	0.5	
14	A	0	0	0	0	0.0	0.7
	B	0	8	14	27	−0.6	
	C*	13	5	37	71	0.6	
	D	0	0	0	0	0.0	
	E	0	0	1	2	0.0	
15	A	0	0	0	0	0.0	0.9
	B*	12	11	45	87	0.0	
	C	0	1	3	6	−0.0	
	D	1	1	4	8	0.0	
	E	0	0	0	0	0.0	

Total in Upper Quarter = 13　　Number of Respondents = 52
Total in Lower Quarter = 13　　Number of Test Items = 15

* = correct answer

15 multiple-choice items. Notice much useful information accompanies the analysis. Having the raw score, percent of items correctly answered, and percentile rank for each person plus the mean, median, and standard deviation for the test provided can save the instructor a lot of calculations.

In the term analysis section of the printout, the correct answer for each item is starred (*). Because all calculations are done so quickly by the computer, frequencies and percentages are reported for each answer to each item. For item 6, of the 13 people in the upper quarter of the group in terms of total test score, 10 people selected answer C, 2 people selected answer D, and 1 person selected answer E. Similar information is reported for the 13 people in the lower quarter of the group in terms of total test score. Under the total count heading the number of people in the total group (n = 52) who selected each answer is reported. Thirty-four people selected answer C, the correct answer, which is 65% of the total group. A discrimination index is reported for each answer to each item based on the discrimination index formula used when calculating by hand and the frequencies under upper and lower quarter. For item 6, answer C, the discrimination index reported to one decimal place is .4 [(10 −5)/13]. The difficulty factor reported to one decimal place is based on the total count and total percent for the correct answer. For item 6, the difficulty factor is .7. Item 6 is a good item since all five answers functioned (see under total count heading) and the item discrimination and difficulty factor are acceptable. Notice that a negative item discrimination is desirable for the incorrect answers since it indicates that more of the lower quarter than upper quarter people selected the answer. Item 6 also fulfills this standard with the exception of answer B, which was not selected by any of the people in the upper and lower quarters. In looking over the item analysis, item 3 was very difficult (.4) with fabulous discrimination (.8), but it was basically a true-false item with answers B and C selected. Although item 5 was easy (difficulty = .9), it discriminated well (.4) and all answers functioned. Item 4 was not as good as item 5 due to low discrimination (.2). Item 8 was not good due to low difficulty factor (.4) and two answers with similar positive discrimination indexes. Item 10 is too hard. The reliability of the test is not provided, but it can be quickly calculated from the information on the computer printout using either the Kuder-Richardson 20 or 21 Formulas.

Problem 13.5. Determine the reliability of the knowledge test using the information in Table 13.6.

Solution. Where K is 15, s is 2.52 so $s^2 = 6.35$, and $\overline{X}$ is 9.9, the reliability coefficient using Kuder-Richardson Formula 21 is .50:

$$r = \frac{(15)(6.35) - (9.9)(15 - 9.9)}{(15 - 1)(6.35)} = \frac{95.25 - 50.49}{88.9} = \frac{44.76}{88.9} = .50$$

Solution. Using the figures in Table 13.6, we can calculate the following p, q, and pq for the 15 items, with p = Total % for the correct answer to an item and q = (1 − p):

Item	**1**	**2**	**3**	**4**	**5**	**6**	**7**	**8**	**9**	**10**	**11**	**12**	**13**	**14**	**15**
p	.81	.56	.42	.87	.87	.65	.88	.37	.71	.13	.50	.75	.77	.71	.87
q	.19	.44	.58	.13	.13	.35	.12	.63	.29	.87	.50	.25	.23	.29	.13
pq	.15	.25	.24	.11	.11	.23	.11	.23	.21	.11	.25	.19	.18	.21	.11

Table 13.7 Standards for Evaluating a Discrimination Type Multiple-Choice Test

1. The total test
   a. The validity of the test is acceptable.
   b. The reliability of the test is acceptable.
   c. The mean performance of the class approximates that wanted by the teacher.
   d. At least 90% of the class finished the test (not applicable to speed tests).
2. Each test item
   a. Difficulty: No more than 5% of the test items have difficulty indexes above .90, and no more than 5% are below .10.
   b. Discrimination:
      (1) More than 25% of the test items have discrimination indexes above .40.
      (2) More than 25% of the test items have discrimination indexes between .21 and .39.
      (3) More than 15% of the test items have discrimination indexes between .0 and .20.
      (4) Less than 5% of the test items have zero or negative discrimination indexes.
   c. Responses: On each test item, each response was selected by at least 5% of the students whose test papers were used in the item analysis.

Where K is 15, s^2 is 6.35, and $\Sigma pq = 2.69$, the reliability coefficient using Kuder-Richardson Formula 20 is .62:

$$r = \left(\frac{15}{15 - 1}\right)\left(\frac{6.35 - 2.69}{6.35}\right) = \left(\frac{15}{14}\right)\left(\frac{3.66}{6.35}\right) = \frac{54.9}{88.9} = .62$$

Revising the Test

After calculating the difficulty of and discrimination index for each item, the overall quality of the test and of each item must be determined so the test can be revised as necessary. A set of standards for evaluating discrimination type multiple-choice tests appears in Table 13.7.

Using these standards, we can evaluate the four items in Figure 13.2:

Item 1. D is .53; r is .44. All responses functioned; a good item.

Item 2. D is .38; r is .25. All responses functioned; an acceptable but difficult item.

Item 3. D is .91; r is .19. Only two responses functioned; essentially an easy true-false item. Revision might improve the responses. If left as is, it should be changed to a true-false item.

Item 4. D is .47; r is −.31. Three responses functioned. Revise or reject the item. Either the item itself or response b misled many of the top group. If this problem is corrected by revision, most students will probably answer correctly because ten of the bottom group did so this time. However, because it is unlikely that the item will ever discriminate and because two responses do not function, the item probably should be rejected.

Questionnaires

The construction of questionnaires follows procedures and strategies very similar to those for knowledge tests. Questionnaires are commonly utilized by teachers, exercise specialists, therapists, and researchers to quickly and economically collect information from a group. Often the group is widely dispersed, so the questionnaire is sent and returned by mail. Information such as beliefs, practices, attitudes, knowledge, and so forth are commonly obtained by the use of a questionnaire. Student evaluation of instructor and course, participant evaluation of an exercise program, participant recall of exercise adherence or barriers to exercise, people's attitudes toward exercise, smoking, or drugs, and people's knowledge about the benefits of exercise and tension reduction are all examples of the use of a questionnaire. Several attitude questionnaires, rating scales, and inventories are presented in Chapter 14. Presented in Table 13.8 is a questionnaire that was sent to public school physical education teachers to determine their attitudes toward physical fitness testing.

Many things influence the success of obtaining information with a questionnaire. Of concern here is getting people to complete and return the questionnaire, particularly if it is mailed to them. A few things that influence the success of a questionnaire are cover letters, timing, appearance, form, length, and content. A letter from you and maybe some influential person on the front of the questionnaire will improve the return rate. Sending or giving the questionnaire to people when they have time to complete it will improve the returns. Sending a questionnaire to people two weeks before Christmas would be a mistake. A questionnaire should be typed, on good paper, with a neat and professional appearance to improve the return rate. The form of the questionnaire in regard to people understanding the directions and easily or quickly responding to the questions influences the return rate. If the questionnaire looks short, people are more likely to return it than if it looks long. Using small type and both sides of the paper makes a questionnaire look short. If the content of the questionnaire is of interest to the people completing it and you are willing to share your results with them, the return rate may be fairly good. If the content of the questionnaire is threatening or too personal, this may hurt the return rate. For example, the question, "Please check the illegal drugs listed below that you regularly use" is threatening. Questions concerning a person's exact age or income are too personal and are better asked in intervals. For example, "Is your age 1. 18–25, 2. 26–40, 3. 41–60, or 4. 61–85?"

In Table 13.8, responses to each item are identified with numbers rather than letters. Usually the volume of data (5000 scores if 100 people each respond to a 50-item questionnaire) requires that the computer be used for the analysis of questionnaire data. The computer always can analyze numbers, whereas letters (a, b, etc.) for the responses to each item may cause problems. Also in Table 13.8, the last seven items are used to obtain demographic information. Generally it is best to place demographic items at the end of the questionnaire. Notice that for demographic items 2 and 4, exact values were not needed and/or the people responding would not know exact values or would not provide exact values; so the responses to these items were in nonoverlapping intervals.

The minimum data analysis for a questionnaire is frequency counts for the responses to each item. For example, in Table 13.8 the number of yes and the number of no responses to item 1 is determined. Often each of the demographic items is crosstabulated with each of the nondemographic items to see if different classifications of the people (in terms of a demographic item) responded differently to a nondemographic item. For example, does gender (demographic item 5) influence response to administration of the Youth Fitness Test (nondemographic item 2) in Table 13.8. The outcome of this crosstabulation is as follows:

Table 13.8 Example Questionnaire

The AAHPERD Fitness Tests Opinionnaire

The American Alliance for Health, Physical Education, Recreation and Dance (AAHPERD) presently distributes the Youth Fitness Test (used by the President's Council on Physical Fitness and Sport), which was introduced in 1957 and the Health-Related Physical Fitness Test, which was introduced in 1980. AAHPERD must decide whether to continue to distribute the two tests, combine the two tests into one test, or discontinue one test. Numerous groups and committees have given AAHPERD their recommendations. However, public school physical education teachers have had very limited input on this important issue. This is your opportunity to make your views known. What AAHPERD does will influence what fitness tests are available to you in the future.

Endorsed by: American Alliance for Health, Physical Education, Recreation and Dance
State Consultant for Physical Education, Georgia Department of Education

This opinionnaire should take less than 15 minutes to complete. Please complete each questionnaire and return it today in the stamped self-addressed envelope.

1. Are you aware of the Youth Fitness Test (due to college classes, reading, workshops, etc.)? (circle number)
   1. Yes
   2. No
2. Have you administered the Youth Fitness Test within the last three years? (circle number)
   1. Yes
   2. No
3. Does your school or school system require that you administer the Youth Fitness Test on a regular basis? (circle number)
   1. Yes
   2. No
4. If you were given the choice, would you administer the Youth Fitness Test on a regular basis? (circle number)
   1. Yes
   2. No
5. Are you aware of the Health-Related Physical Fitness Test (due to college classes, reading, workshops, etc.)? (circle number)
   1. Yes
   2. No
6. Have you administered the Health-Related Physical Fitness Test within the last three years? (circle number)
   1. Yes
   2. No
7. Does your school or school system require that you administer the Health-Related Physical Fitness Test on a regular basis? (circle number)
   1. Yes
   2. No
8. If you were given the choice, would you administer the Health-Related Physical Fitness Test on a regular basis? (circle number)
   1. Yes
   2. No

Table 13.8 Example Questionnaire—*Continued*

9. What should AAHPERD do with the two fitness tests they presently distribute? (circle a number)
   1. Combine the two tests into one test of 9 items from which teachers could choose what items to administer.
   2. Discontinue the Health-Related Physical Fitness Test and continue the Youth Fitness Test.
   3. Discontinue the Youth Fitness Test and continue the Health-Related Physical Fitness Test.
   4. Continue to distribute both tests so teachers have a choice of tests.

Finally, we would like to ask a few questions to help us interpret the results and to give you a chance to make comments and suggestions.

1. Is your school located in a rural or urban area? (circle number)
   1. Rural
   2. Urban
2. What is the student population of your school? (circle number)
   1. 0–100
   2. 101–500
   3. 501–1,000
   4. 1,001–1,500
   5. Over 1,500
3. What is your school called? (circle number)
   1. Elementary School
   2. Middle School/Junior High School
   3. Senior High School
   4. Other (specify grade levels) ________________
4. What is your age? (circle number)
   1. 20–29 years
   2. 30–39 years
   3. 40–49 years
   4. 50–59 years
   5. 60 years or older
5. What is your gender? (circle number)
   1. Female
   2. Male
6. What is the highest degree you hold? (circle number)
   1. Bachelors
   2. Masters
   3. Specialist
   4. Doctorate
7. Are you usually (presently or the majority of the time) a member of the Georgia Association for HPERD (GAHPERD) and/or the American Alliance for HPERD (AAHPERD)? (circle number)
   1. No, neither organization
   2. Yes, GAHPERD
   3. Yes, AAHPERD
   4. Yes, both organizations

		Item 2	
		Yes	No
Gender	Female	25	35
	Male	78	12

The number in each cell (square) is a frequency for a combination of the two items; so we see that 25 females responded Yes to item 2, whereas 78 males responded Yes. Gender influenced response to item 2 since most males responded Yes but less than one-half of the females responded Yes. If each of the seven demographic items were crosstabulated with each of the eight nondemographic items, there would be 56 crosstabulations, which is too many to do by hand. All packages of statistical computer programs have a crosstabulation program.

A more comprehensive discussion of questionnaire construction and use is not possible in the space provided in this book. The interested reader should consult any of a number of good texts on the subject such as Weisberg and Bowen (1977) and Sudman and Bradburn (1982) or research books with a chapter on the subject, such as Baumgartner and Strong (1998).

Summary

Knowledge testing should be a component of most measurement programs. Before trying to construct a knowledge test, you must be aware of the types of knowledge tests and items, the advantages and disadvantages of each, and the construction process.

Certain techniques are necessary in administering a knowledge test, and their use can help you obtain reliable, valid scores. It is also important to be aware of the different techniques that can be used in grading a knowledge test after it is administered.

You should understand the importance of analyzing a knowledge test after it has been administered and should master the techniques used in item analysis. Improving the quality of knowledge tests through item analysis should be every teacher's goal.

Finally, the value and many uses of questionnaires must be recognized. Valid information can be obtained easily and quickly using questionnaires, provided they are correctly constructed and analyzed.

Formative Evaluation of Objectives

Objective 1 Differentiate among various types of knowledge tests.

1. Knowledge tests can be classified as either essay or objective tests. Differentiate between these two basic test types.
2. Knowledge tests can also be classified as either mastery or discrimination tests. Differentiate between these two categories in terms of the difficulty and the objectives of the tests.

Objective 2 Define the levels of knowledge most applicable to physical education and adult fitness.

1. The taxonomy for educational objectives lists six classes, or levels, of knowledge. Ranging from low to high, the levels are knowledge, comprehension, application, analysis, synthesis, and evaluation. Define the first four of these levels and write a test item for each.

Objective 3 Outline the basic procedures for constructing, administering, and scoring a knowledge test.

1. Listed below are basic steps that a teacher can follow in constructing a knowledge test. Summarize the major decisions made at each step.
   a. Construct a table of specifications.
   b. Decide what type of test to give.
   c. Construct the test items.
   d. Determine the test format and administrative details.
2. The teachers must consider the basic problems and procedures of test administration.
   a. What types of considerations should be given to the testing environment and test security?
   b. Is it advantageous to have alternate forms of the same test on hand?
3. Differentiate between the procedures used to score an essay test and those for an objective test.
4. Listed in the text are basic rules that professional test makers follow in constructing various types of test items. Briefly summarize these basic procedures, being sure to list the key points.

Objective 4 Evaluate knowledge test items.

1. In constructing a test, you can choose from several types of items. Each type has its advantages and disadvantages, as discussed in the text. Briefly summarize these advantages and disadvantages for each type of item listed below.
   a. true-false
   b. multiple-choice
   c. matching
   d. completion
   e. short answer and essay
2. What is wrong with the following multiple-choice item?
   a. The score of a student on a multiple-choice test is the number of correct answers minus some fraction of the number wrong. On a 50-item, 5-response test, a student had 30 items correct and omitted 5. The student's score should be (1) 26; (2) 27; (3) 28; (4) 29; (5) 30.
3. What is wrong with the following two multiple-choice items that were together on an archery test?
   a. What is the term that designates a bow made of several pieces of wood and/or other materials? (1) Self-bow; (2) Laminated bow; (3) Multiple bow; (4) Chrysal bow.
   b. Which of the following is the smoothest shooting wood for a self-bow? (1) Birch; (2) Lemonwood; (3) Hickory; (4) Yew.

Objective 5 Analyze knowledge tests in terms of test reliability and item analysis.

1. Test reliability is useful for evaluating knowledge tests. Assume that a 50-item multiple-choice test was administered to 225 students. Calculate the test reliability from the following.
   a. A test mean of 37 and a standard deviation of 3.5.

2. It is difficult to write a reliable knowledge test on the first try. A test's quality will improve if an item analysis is conducted after the first administration and the test is revised accordingly. An item analysis consists of item difficulty and item discrimination.
   a. Define term difficulty and interpret the following item difficulties: (1) .68 and (2) .21.
   b. Define term discrimination and interpret the following discrimination indices: (1) .45, (2) .15, (3) .03, and (4) −.67.
3. Outline the basic procedures involved in an item analysis.

Objective 6 Discuss the uses of questionnaires and how to construct them.

1. What are at least five uses of questionnaires in your area of interest?
2. What are at least six desirable characteristics of a questionnaire?

Additional Learning Activities

1. Several of the books referenced in the text offer complete discussions of knowledge test construction and analysis. Read some of them to increase your familiarity with the subject.
2. Construct a knowledge test composed of some true-false and some multiple-choice items. Administer the test and do an item analysis.
3. As noted in the text, an item analysis can be obtained by using a standardized answer sheet and a test-scoring service on campus. Determine the type of standardized answer sheet to use and the procedures to follow in using your school's service.

Bibliography

Baumgartner, T. A. and C. H. Strong. 1998. *Conducting and reading research in health and human performance.* 2d ed. Dubuque, IA: McGraw-Hill.

Bloom, B. S. Ed. 1956. *Taxonomy of educational objectives: Cognitive domain.* New York: McKay.

Bloom, B. S. et al. 1971. *Handbook on formative and summative evaluation of student learning.* New York: McGraw-Hill.

Bloom, B. S. et al. 1981. *Evaluation to improve learning.* New York: McGraw-Hill.

McGee, R. and A. Farrow. 1987. *Test questions for physical education activities.* Champaign, IL: Human Kinetics.

Nunnally, J. C. and I. H. Bernstein. 1994. *Psychometric theory.* 3d ed. New York: McGraw-Hill.

Sudman, S. and N. Bradburn. 1982. *Asking questions: A practical guide to questionnaire design.* San Francisco: Jossey-Bass.

Weisberg, H. F. and B. D. Bowen. 1977. *An introduction to survey research and data analysis.* San Francisco: W. H. Freeman and Co.

CHAPTER 14

Exercise Psychological Measurement

Contents

Key Words

activity factor
affective domain
anorexia nervosa
attitude scale
binge-eating
body image
bulimia nervosa
eating disorders
evaluation factor
potency factor
psychophysical
psychological state measure
psychological trait measure
rating of perceived exertion (RPE)
semantic differential scales

Objectives

Measuring psychological dimensions is of interest to physical education teachers, exercise specialists, sport psychologists, and researchers. However, psychological dimensions are difficult to measure in a reliable and valid manner. As discussed in Chapter 1, regular vigorous exercise has a positive influence on cardiovascular health and longevity, but many who start exercise programs will quit. Affective behavior interests, attitudes, appreciations, values, and emotional sets or biases are not only difficult to measure, but also difficult to teach (Krathwohl et al. 1964). As Ebel (1972) has noted:

> Feelings . . . cannot be passed along from teacher to learner in the way information is transmitted. Nor can the learner acquire them by pursuing them directly as he might acquire understanding by study. Feelings are almost always the consequences of something—of success, of failure, of duty done or duty ignored, of danger encountered or danger escaped.

While physical educators have always valued affective objectives, we have not developed affective instruments that can be used by teachers in school settings. While the affective instruments useful to physical education teachers lack availability, the instruments available in sport psychology are growing at an accelerated rate. There are so many sport psychology scales that it becomes difficult to select representative examples. Ostrow (1996) published a book that evaluates over 300 sport psychological instruments and places them into one of sixteen different categories. His system is presented to aid the interested reader in selecting exercise psychology measures. The primary purpose of this chapter is to describe the process by which exercise psychology instruments are developed. We pay special focus to exercise-related psychological instruments. These include psychological instruments designed to measure: self-motivation toward exercise; exercise and self-esteem; psychophysical perceived exertion; and eating disorders.

After reading chapter 14 you should be able to:

1. Evaluate the validity of physical education attitude scales.
2. Outline the procedures used to develop semantic differential scales.
3. Describe the nature of the Self-Motivation Inventory (SMI).
4. Describe the nature of instruments designed to relate exercise and self-esteem.
5. Describe the nature of eating disorder scales.
6. Evaluate the validity and value of the psychophysical rating of perceived exertion scales (RPE).
7. Describe the general categories of sport psychology scales.

Measuring Attitudes

Much of the physical education research in the **affective domain** has focused on attitudes (see Figure 14.1) and their measurement. "Attitudes concern feelings about particular social objects—physical objects, types of people, particular persons, social institutions, government policies" (Nunnally 1978). Attitudes are generally measured with scales that require a student to agree or disagree with a series of statements, worded both positively and negatively. Several types of scales are used to determine a respondent's degree of affect. The most common offer two alternatives, Disagree-Agree, or five alternatives: Strongly Disagree, Disagree, Undecided, Agree, Strongly Agree. A 7-step scale can be created by adding Very Strongly Disagree and Very Strongly Agree to the 5-step scale.

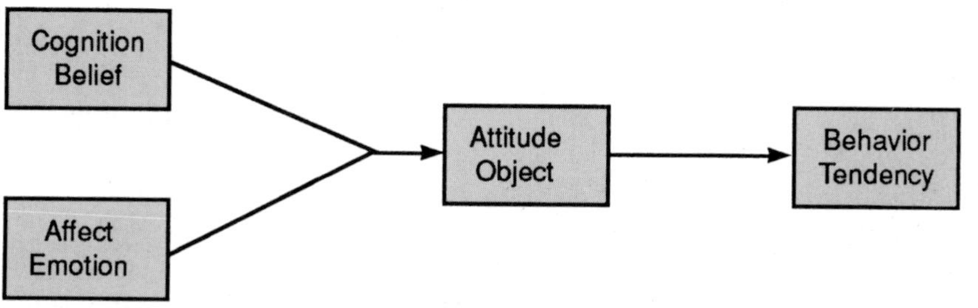

Figure 14.1
Attitudes are a function of beliefs and emotion. An attitude scale is used to measure a person's feelings toward the object. The true validity of the attitude scale is determined by the individual's behavior. Many have a positive attitude toward physical fitness but lead a sedentary life-style.

Nunnally (1978) recommends the use of a graphic scale demarcated with numbers, like that shown below, to clearly convey degrees of feeling. A graphic scale also allows greater flexibility in selecting the number of steps offered.

Completely disagree _1_:_2_:_3_:_4_:_5_:_6_:_7_: Completely agree

An attitude scale lists various statements that elicit one's feelings about the attitude object. The individual's attitude is determined by adding the scores of the statements. In scoring them, the positive statement scores are simply added as they appear; the point values for the negative statements, however, must be reversed by subtracting the score from the total number of levels plus 1. Using a 7-step scale like the one shown here, the marked score of a negative statement is subtracted from 8. For example, assume that a student marks a "2" next to the following statement: "If for any reason a few subjects must be dropped from the school program, physical education should be one of the subjects dropped." Notice that this is a negative statement in terms of an attitude toward physical education and that by scoring it with a low number the student is actually showing a positive attitude toward physical education. In contrast, assume that a student marks a 2 next to the following statement: "Participation in physical education activities establishes a more wholesome outlook on life." Because the statement is positive, a score of 2 on the 7-step scale indicates a negative attitude.

Most psychological instruments use positive and negative statements. Negatively worded states must be reverse scored in order to reflect the intended response. This is accomplished by subtracting the recorded score from a value of one point higher than the highest possible response value. This would be the value "8" for the illustrated graphic scale. The formula is

Reverse Scoring an Item **(14.1)**

$$\text{Final Value} = [(1 + \text{Highest Scale Value}) - \text{Recorded Value}]$$

Calculation example. To illustrate, assume the 7-step scale was used, and a student marked the score of "2" for a negative statement. Since the student tended to disagree with the negative worded statement, reverse scoring results in a value reflecting a positive response. The calculation would be

$$\text{Final Value} = [(1 + 7) - 2] = 5$$

The process is cumbersome to complete by hand, but easily accomplished with the computer. The computer calculation section in appendix B provides reverse scoring examples for the psychological instruments provided in this chapter.

Validity of Attitude Scales

An attitude scale is a self-report measure and suffers from the weaknesses typical of this type of instrument. Its principal limitation is that it reflects only what individuals know and are willing to relate about their attitudes. Students who like a teacher tend to respond more favorably than their true attitudes warrant, and often favorable responses on a self-report scale are accompanied by contrary behavior. For example, students may express a favorable attitude toward physical activity and fitness, yet be inactive and unfit.

Because it is unrealistic to establish an attitude scale's concurrent validity with actual behavior, most scales claim face validity. This involves defining the content area to be measured and devising attitude statements that logically relate to it. Usually an individual's attitude toward the content area is represented by the total score on the scale. Unfortunately this has created a serious problem of validity on physical education attitude scales. If you sum all the scores on the scale, it is essential that all statements measure the same general attitude.

Several physical education teachers and exercise specialists have published attitude scales. The targeted objects have included physical education (Adams 1963; Carr 1945; Edington 1968; Kappes 1954; Kneer 1971; Mercer 1971; O'Bryan & O'Bryan 1979; Penmon 1971; Seaman 1970; Wear 1951, 1955); athletic competition (Harris 1968; Lakie 1964; McCue 1953; McGee 1956; Scott 1953); creative dance (Allison 1976); and sportsmanship (Johnson 1969). These published scales report high reliability estimates (≥0.85), but their validity has not been established. In addition, the scales have not proved to be valuable to the public school physical education teacher, exercise specialist, or researcher.

Attitude Toward Physical Activity (ATPA)

The attitude scale developed by Kenyon (1968b) is especially important and an excellent example of measurement procedures. The publication of the ATPA scales marked a departure from using physical education as the attitude object. Rather, Kenyon's scales were designed to measure the reasons why individuals exercised. He recognized that exercise motives were multidimensional, that there were different reasons for people being physically active. The methods used to develop the six scales of the ATPA provide an excellent example of the use of construct validity.

Kenyon (1968b) demonstrated that attitude must be considered multidimensional. That is, there are several different types of attitudes toward an object and the composite score must be split into several scores to validly measure each dimension. For example, assume that a scale measures two factors in a subject's attitude toward physical education: (1) the value of physical education for social development, and (2) the value of physical education for health and fitness. By simply summing all the scores, two individuals with very different attitudes might receive the same total score. Yet, one may highly value physical education for social development; the other may consider it valueless for social development but important for health and fitness. Thus, the total score is not a valid representation of the true feelings of either person.

The ATPA scale for men consists of 59 items, and the parallel scale for women consists of 54 items. Following is a description of the six dimensions. The complete instrument with instructions is provided in other sources (Baumgartner & Jackson 1982; Kenyon 1968c; Safrit 1981). The six dimensions measured by the ATPA and sample statements are given next. Examples of positive (+) and negative (−) statements were selected.

Dimension 1. Physical Activity as a Social Experience. Physical education teachers and exercise specialists maintain that physical activity meets certain social needs. Individuals who score high on this factor would value physical activities "whose primary purpose is to provide a medium for social intercourse, that is, to meet new people and to perpetuate existing relationships." The internal consistency reliability estimates for this scale are about .70. Examples of items used to measure physical activity as a social experience are:

(+) The best way to become more socially desirable is to participate in group physical activities.

(−) Of all the kinds of physical activities, I don't particularly care for those requiring a lot of socializing.

Dimension 2. Physical Activity for Health and Fitness. The importance of physical activity for maintaining health and fitness is generally recognized. Individuals who score high on this factor would value physical activity for its "contribution to the improvement of one's health and fitness." The internal consistency reliability estimates are about 0.79. Examples of items used to measure physical activity for health and fitness are:

(+) Physical education programs should stress vigorous exercise since it contributes most to physical fitness.

(−) Of all physical activities, those whose purpose is primarily to develop physical fitness would not be my first choice.

Dimension 3. Physical Activity as the Pursuit of Vertigo. The pursuit of vertigo is the search for excitement: "those physical experiences providing, at some risk to the participant, an element of thrill through the medium of speed, acceleration, sudden change of direction, exposure to dangerous situations, with the participant usually remaining in control." The internal consistency reliability estimates ranges are 0.88 for men and 0.87 for women. Examples of items used to measure pursuit of vertigo are:

(+) Among the best physical activities are those which represent a personal challenge, such as skiing, mountain climbing, or heavy-weather sailing.

(−) I would prefer quiet activities like swimming or golf rather than activities such as water skiing or sailboat racing.

Dimension 4. Physical Activity as an Aesthetic Experience. Many people believe that forms of physical activity have a certain beauty or artistry. People who score high on this factor perceive the aestheticism of physical activity. The internal consistency reliability estimates were 0.82 and 0.87 for men and women, respectively. Examples of items used to measure physical activity as an aesthetic experience are:

(+) The most important value of physical activity is the beauty found in skilled movement.

(−) I am not particularly interested in those physical activities whose sole purpose is to depict human motion as something beautiful.

Table 14.1 Semantic Differential Scales Illustrated*

Physical Fitness		
(E) pleasant	___:___:___:___:___:___:___	unpleasant
(A) relaxed	___:___:___:___:___:___:___	tense
(A) passive	___:___:___:___:___:___:___	active
(E) unsuccessful	___:___:___:___:___:___:___	successful
(P) delicate	___:___:___:___:___:___:___	rugged
(A) fast	___:___:___:___:___:___:___	slow
(E) good	___:___:___:___:___:___:___	bad
(P) weak	___:___:___:___:___:___:___	strong
(A) lazy	___:___:___:___:___:___:___	busy
(P) heavy	___:___:___:___:___:___:___	light
(E) unfair	___:___:___:___:___:___:___	fair

*Note: Any concept may be used. The concept "Physical Fitness" is illustrated.

Dimension 5. Physical Activity as a Catharsis. Many believe that physical activity can provide a release from the frustrations of daily living. The validity of this factor has not been fully established. A negative relationship was reported between catharsis scores and preference for "physical activity for recreation and relaxation." The internal consistency reliability estimates were 0.77 and 0.79 for men and women, respectively. Examples of items used to measure physical activity as a catharsis are:

(+) Practically the only way to relieve frustrations and pent-up emotions is through some form of physical activity.

(−) There are better ways of relieving the pressures of today's living than having to engage in or watch physical activity.

Dimension 6. Physical Activity as an Ascetic Experience. Individuals who score high on this scale value the type of dedication involved in championship-level performance. Such activity demands long, strenuous, often painful training and competition, forcing a deferment of many of the gratifications of general physical activity. The internal consistency reliability estimates were 0.81 for men and ranged from 0.74 to 0.78 for women. Examples of items used to measure physical activity as an aesthetic experience are:

(+) I would gladly put up with the necessary hard training for the chance to try out for the U.S. Women's Olympic Team.

(−) A sport is sometimes spoiled if allowed to become too highly organized and keenly competitive.

Semantic Differential Scales

A flexible device for measuring attitudes is the **semantic differential scale,** which asks the subject to respond to bipolar adjectives to measure attitude (Osgood et al. 1957; Snider & Osgood 1969). An example is shown in Table 14.1. The approach is flexible in that many different attitude objects can be measured without revising the scale. In Table 14.1, for example, the object "physical fitness" could be replaced with others such as "Intramural Football," "Physical Education Class," "Interschool Athletics," or some other concept.

Table 14.2 Bipolar Adjective Pairs for the Evaluation, Potency, and Activity Factors of Semantic Differential Scales

Evaluative Factor	Potency Factor	Activity Factor
good-bad	deep-shallow	excitable-calm
new-old	heavy-light	stable-unstable
health-unhealthy	strong-weak	happy-sad
beautiful-ugly	full-empty	hot-cold
fresh-stale	light-dark	fast-slow
valuable-worthless	smooth-rough	tense-relaxed
pleasant-unpleasant	dominant-submissive	active-passive
fair-unfair	hard-soft	changeable-stable
successful-unsuccessful	thick-thin	lazy-busy
honest-dishonest	rugged-delicate	dynamic-static

When originally developed, the object being measured was stated in global, neutral terms such as "Intramural Football." A limitation of stating the attitude object in global terms is that the scale lacks the sensitivity to make strong behavior predictions. There is a major trend in sports psychology to move from the measurement of general to more specific traits (Ajzen & Fishbein 1980). This can be easily accomplished with semantic differential scales by including the intended behavior with the attitude statement. For example, the general attitude object "Intramural Football" could be replaced with the more specific phrase "My participation this year in the football intramural program."

Semantic Dimensions. The process of developing semantic differential scales involves first defining the object to be evaluated and then selecting the bipolar adjective pairs. Numerous studies using various concepts have concluded that three major factors are measured by the semantic differential technique: evaluation, potency, and activity. Table 14.2 provides the bipolar adjective pairs that measure these three dimensions.

The **evaluation factor** is the most common factor. It involves the degree of "goodness" the subject attributes to the object being measured. For most instances, evaluation is the only factor of interest. The most common adjective pair is "good-bad". The **potency factor** involves the strength of the concept being rated. Common potency factors are "hard-soft" and "strong-weak". The **activity factor** is measured by adjective pairs that describe action, like "fast-slow." These factors and adjective pairs provide a flexible method for evaluating attitudes toward an object.

Construction of Semantic Differential Scales. The first step in constructing a semantic differential scale is the selection of concepts relevant to the general attitude being evaluated. The second step is the selection of appropriate adjective pairs. Two criteria determine the pairs: how well they represent the factor, and their relevance to the concept in question.

Certain adjective pairs have proved valid for measuring the evaluation, potency, and activity factors. Because a minimum of three adjective pairs is suggested to measure a factor reliably, at least nine adjective pairs are needed to measure all three factors. Finally, the adjective pairs must be at the reading comprehension level of the students being evaluated and must relate logically to the concept in question.

The letters E, P, and A in Table 14.1 identify the factor measured by the adjective pair. These letters would not appear on the instrument itself. The various adjective pairs are randomly ordered to prevent those relating to a single factor from being clustered. It is also essential that both negative and positive adjectives appear in each column.

Scoring and Interpretation. The respondent places a mark at that point between the two adjectives that best reflects his or her feeling about the concept. There are several ways to score semantic scales, but the one we find the easiest is to develop a key, with the lowest point value assigned to the first space on the left side and the highest assigned to the last space on the right side. The scoring system would be

unsuccessful __1__:__2__:__3__:__4__:__5__:__6__:__7__ successful

pleasant __1__:__2__:__3__:__4__:__5__:__6__:__7__ unpleasant

Since the adjectives "successful" and "pleasant" are the positive ends of the scale, the pleasant-unpleasant scale scoring is reversed by subtracting "8" for the obtained score (i.e., $8 - 1 = 7$). The student's score on a factor is the sum for all bipolar adjectives that measure that factor. Thus, if all three factors are measured, each scale yields three scores. The reverse scoring and summing of scale scores can be easily completed by computer.

Because this data can be analyzed statistically, it is possible to develop norms from them. The semantic differential scale was designed to measure an individual's feelings about a given concept. Nunnally (1978) reports that the evaluation factor serves as a definition of attitude, so that responses to this factor's adjective pairs are excellent measures of verbalized attitudes. Often, just the evaluation factor is used. The potency and activity factors tend to be partly evaluative, but they also tend to reveal the respondent's interpretation of the concept's physical characteristics. Assume, for example, that two groups of students are administered a semantic differential scale for the concept "physical education class." One group is enrolled in a 12-week basic course in archery; the other, in a basic body-conditioning course that involves distance running and weight training. Although both groups might rate the physical education class "good" on the evaluation factor, their responses are likely to differ on the potency and activity factors. The archery students are apt to respond to the potency adjectives "delicate" and "weak." Students in the conditioning class are more likely to rate their class "strong" and "hard," and the activity adjectives "active," "fast," and "busy." Thus, all three factors would be useful to determine how the students feel about the concept.

Sample Semantic Differential Scale

The Children's Attitude Toward Physical Activity Inventory (CATPA-I) is a fine example of the use of semantic differential scales to measure attitude. The instrument was developed by Simon and Smoll (1974) and adapted by Schutz and associates (1985) to measure Kenyon's dimensions of physical activity. The general design of the CATPA-I is shown in Figures 14.2 and 14.3. The normative information of the scale is provided in other sources (Schutz et al. 1985).

Physical activity for social growth
Taking part in physical activities that give you a chance to meet new people.

Physical activity to continue social relations
Taking part in physical activities that give you a chance to be with your friends.

Physical activity for health and fitness
Taking part in physical activities to make your health better and to get your body in better condition.

Physical activity as a thrill but involving some risk
Taking part in physical activities that could be dangerous because you move very fast and must change direction quickly.

Physical activity as the beauty in movement
Taking part in physical activities that have beautiful and graceful movements.

Physical activity for the release of tension
Taking part in physical activities to reduce stress or to get away from problems you might have.

Physical activity as long and hard training
Taking part in physical activities that have long and hard practices. To spend time in practice you need to give up other things you like to do.

Figure 14.2
Children's Attitude Toward Physical Activity Inventory (CATPA-I) inventory subdomain descriptions. (Schultz et al. 1985).

How Do You Feel about the Idea Below?

Physical Activity for Social Growth
Taking Part in Physical Activities that Give You a Chance to Meet New People

Always Think about the Idea in the Box

If You Do Not Understand This Idea, Mark This Box ☐ and Go to the Next Page.

1. Good						Bad
2. Of No Use						Useful
3. Not Pleasant						Pleasant
4. Nice						Awful
5. Happy						Sad

Figure 14.3
Scale format for the Children's Attitude Toward Physical Activity Inventory (CATPA-I), grades 7 through 11.

Psychological Determinants of Physical Activity

As shown in Chapter 1, sedentary life-style and obesity are risk factors of many chronic diseases and mortality. These data are the basis for the development of adult and youth health-related fitness programs. So compelling are these data that in 1985, the Centers for Disease Control established objectives that call for 60% of 18- to 65-year-olds to be regular participants in vigorous exercise by 1990. Unfortunately, this objective was not met. It is estimated that only 20% of Americans exercise regularly and intensely enough to meet current ACSM guidelines for developing fitness or for health promotion. The typical dropout rate from supervised exercise programs remains at 50% (Dishman 1990). Of major companies that provide employee fitness programs, only 20-40% of eligible employees will participate, but of these only 33-50% will exercise on a regular basis at a vigorous intensity—a small fraction of those eligible to participate.

The reasons individuals adhere to exercise programs are complex and not fully understood. Past and present personal attributes, environmental factors, and physical activity characteristics are determinants of the exercise habits of adults. Some of the determinants of exercise behavior reported by Dishman (1990) are briefly summarized next.

- *Smoking behavior.* Smokers are more likely to drop out of exercise programs and less likely to utilize worksite exercise facilities than nonsmokers.
- *Occupational level.* Blue-collar workers are more likely to drop out of exercise programs and less likely to utilize worksite exercise facilities than white-collar workers.
- *Body composition.* The overweight are less likely to stay with a fitness program. Even in easy walking programs, 60–70% of obese individuals drop out.
- *Exercise history.* Past exercise participation is the best predictor of physical activity. At NASA, we discovered that self-report level of physical activity and $\dot{V}O_2$ Max were factors related to exercise compliance (Wier & Jackson 1989).
- *Self-motivation.* The personality trait of self-motivation (Dishman 1980) is related to exercise behavior. The self-motivated individual often leaves a supervised program, but continues a personal exercise program.
- *Level of knowledge.* Knowledge and belief in the health benefits of physical activity motivate individuals to initiate exercise programs and return following relapse.
- *Positive affect.* Feelings of enjoyment and well-being are strong motives of regular participation of physical activity.
- *Perceived exercise capacity.* Specific efficacy beliefs about the ability to exercise tend to increase exercise compliance in medically supervised rehabilitation and free-living exercise programs.

Provided in this section are psychological instruments used to assess the motives of exercise. The Self-Motivation Inventory (SMI) (Dishman 1981) is provided in its entirety. The SMI correlates with exercise behavior and identifies those most likely to drop out of an exercise program. We have incorporated the SMI into the University of Houston required personal health-related fitness course and have developed norms for college students (Jackson & Ross 1997). The second section reviews Sonstroem's Physical Estimation and Attraction Scales (PEAS). The PEAS is important because it is the first exercise-specific instrument to evaluate the importance of the physical self as a motivator of exercise behavior (Fox 1997; Sonstroem 1997).

Self-Motivation Inventory (SMI)

Self-motivation is a personality trait that is related to exercise behavior. A psychological trait is a construct that tends to be stable. A psychological trait minimizes the role of situational and environmental influences. This means that someone who scores high on the SMI will likely be self-motivated in many different situations. Being a stable psychological construct, it provides a means of predicting future behavior. In this sense, it is like a basic physical ability described in Chapter 7. Dishman (1990) describes the self-motivation trait as:

> It is believed that self-motivation reflects willpower or self-regulatory skills such as effective goal setting, self-monitoring of progress, and self-reinforcement. These factors are believed to be important for maintaining physical activity and intentions to change behavior. Successful endurance athletes have consistently scored high on self-motivation, and self-motivation has discriminated between adherents and dropouts across a wide variety of settings, including athletic conditioning, adult fitness, preventive medicine, cardiac rehabilitation, commercial spas, corporate fitness, and free-living activity in college students. (p. 83)

Dishman and Ickes (1981) developed the Self-Motivation Inventory (SMI) to measure the self-motivation trait. The psychological trait measure is a 40-item scale, which consists of 20 positively keyed and 20 negatively keyed statements. Using a sample of over 400 undergraduate men and women, the internal consistency reliability was estimated to be 0.91. Stability reliability has been found to be high, exceeding 0.86 (Dishman & Ickes 1981).

Dishman and Ickes' initial analysis produced ten different factors, suggesting that self-motivation consisted of ten different dimensions. This suggests that one would need ten different scores to adequately measure self-motivation. Merkle (1997) examined the construct validity of the SMI with over 1600 college students enrolled in a required health-related fitness course. Her factor analysis of the 40-item SMI produced eight factors that were similar to those found in the initial analysis. Further analysis showed that six of the eight factors were highly correlated, demonstrating that self-motivation construct consisted of six related dimensions. The six correlated factors were consistent with Dishman's interpretation of self-motivation. The six factors and a sample item are:

Commitment—I'm not very good at committing myself to do things.

Lethargy—I don't like to overextend myself.

Drive—Sometimes I push myself harder than I should.

Persistence—I can persevere at stressful tasks even when they are physically tiring or painful.

Reliability—I'm not very reliable.

Discipline—I'm good at keeping promises, especially ones I make to myself.

Finding that the six self-motivation factors were correlated supports the practice of using a single SMI score, which is the sum of the items represented by the six factors. This reduced the SMI from the original 40 items to 35 items. The revised SMI is provided next.

Scale. Self-Motivation Inventory (35-item)

Purpose. Measure the personality trait of self-motivation, which has been shown to be a consistent predictor of exercise adherence.

Reliability. The internal consistency reliability of the original and revised forms was 0.91 and 0.88, respectively. The 40-item scale was found to be stable, and the test-retest reliability was 0.92. The time between test administrations was one month.

Table 14.3 Percentile Rank Norms for the Self-Motivation Inventory

Percentile	SMI Level	Women	Men
90	High	150	149
75	Above average	140	140
50	Average	129	127
25	Below average	116	113
10	Low	103	101

Source: Jackson, A. S. and R. M. Ross, *Understanding Exercise for Health and Fitness,* 1997. Reprinted by permission.

Validity. The factor analyses support the construct validity of the SMI. The predictive validity of the scale was examined by determining if the scale predicted the likelihood that female college students would quit the physically demanding college crew team. Scores between dropouts and those who adhered were compared at three points in time: the first 10 days; 8 weeks; and 32 weeks, when the final team cuts were made. The analysis showed that the mean SMI of the dropouts were significantly lower than that of the adherents at each of the points in time (Dishman 1980). The SMI was found to predict adherence to a medically supervised cardiovascular and muscular endurance training program (Dishman 1980). The predictors of exercise adherence were percent body fat, body weight, and SMI. The SMI was the only psychological instrument that was found to predict exercise adherence. Using the three predictors, it was possible to correctly classify 80%. The profile of dropouts was high body fat, high body weight, low SMI. With college students, the SMI is significantly correlated with self-report exercise habits, but not body composition (Merkle 1997).

Scoring. Scoring: the point values for each response are: (1) extremely uncharacteristic of me; (2) somewhat uncharacteristic of me; (3) neither characteristic nor uncharacteristic of me; (4) somewhat characteristic of me; (5) extremely characteristic of me. Items negatively keyed are scored 6 − X, where X is the assigned value (1 to 5). SMI score is the sum of all items. A microcomputer program for scoring the SMI is shown in the Computer Calculations section provided as an appendix of this book.

Norms. Table 14.3 provides percentile rank norms for men and women. The norms were developed on over 1600 University of Houston College students who completed the required personal fitness course (Jackson 1997).

35-Item SMI Instructions and Items. Read each of the following statements. Respond to each statement using the scantron. Mark the letter that best describes how characteristic the statement is when applied to you. The choices are:

A: Extremely Uncharacteristic of Me

B: Somewhat Uncharacteristic of Me

C: Neither Characteristic nor Uncharacteristic of Me

D: Somewhat Characteristic of Me

E: Extremely Characteristic of Me

Be sure to answer every question. Be honest and complete in your responses.

1. I'm not very good at committing myself to do things.
2. Whenever I get bored with projects I start, I drop them to do something else.
3. I can persevere at stressful tasks even when they are physically tiring or painful.
4. If something gets too much of an effort to do I am likely to just forget it.
5. I'm really concerned about developing and maintaining self-discipline.
6. I'm good at keeping promises, especially ones I make to myself.
7. When I take on a difficult job I make a point of sticking with it until it is completed.
8. I'm willing to work for the things I want as long as it's not a big hassle.
9. I have a lot of self-motivation.
10. I'm good at making decisions and standing by them.
11. I generally take the path of least resistance.
12. I get discouraged easily.
13. If I tell someone that I will do something, you can depend on it being done.
14. I don't like to overextend myself.
15. I'm basically lazy.
16. I have a hard driving aggressive personality.
17. I work harder than most of my friends.
18. I can persist in spite of pain or discomfort.
19. I like to set goals and work toward them.
20. Sometimes I push myself harder than I should.
21. I seldom if ever let myself down.
22. I'm not very reliable.
23. I like to take on jobs that challenge me.
24. I change my mind about things quite easily.
25. I have a lot of willpower.
26. I'm not likely to put myself out if I don't have to.
27. Things just don't matter much to me.
28. I avoid stressful situations.
29. I often work to the point of exhaustion.
30. I never force myself to do things I don't feel like doing.
31. It takes a lot to get me going.
32. Whenever I reach a goal, I set a higher one.
33. I can persist in spite of failure.
34. I have a strong desire to achieve.
35. I don't have much self-discipline.

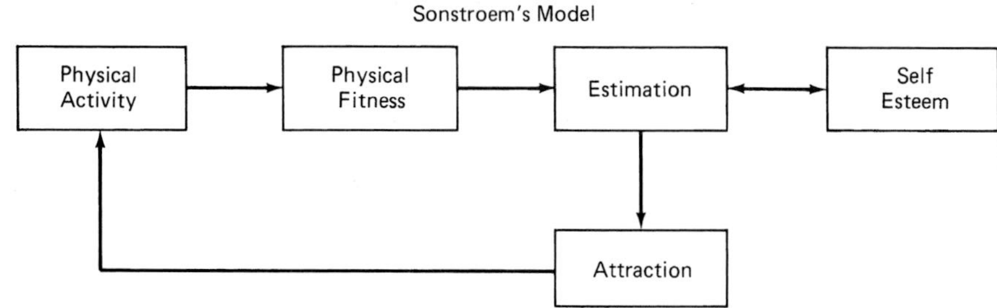

Figure 14.4 Sonstroem's 1975 psychological model for physical activity. (Source: Sonstroem, R. J. 1974. Attitude testing examining certain psychological correlates of physical activity. *Research Quarterly* 45: 93–103.)

Exercise and Self-Esteem Instruments

There is a growing interest in the study of exercise and self-esteem (Sonstroem 1997). This interest stems from growing importance of the physical self as a motivator of exercise behavior and a contributor to mental health and well-being (Fox 1997). These scales are state instruments, or scales that reflect change from one situation to the next. How one feels in one situation or environment is not predictive of others. When the situation changes, so does the psychological state. Some of the more common exercise-related psychological state measures (Fox 1997) are

Perceived competence—A statement of personal ability that generalizes across a domain, such as sport or exercise.

Perceived ability—A more specific statement of competence restricted to a limited set of behaviors, such as playing soccer or other sports.

Body image—The mental representation an individual has of their body.

Self-efficacy—A statement of expectancy about one's ability to accomplish a specific task.

Physical Estimation and Attraction Scales (PEAS)

Sonstroem (1974) is credited with developing the first social psychological scale designed to measure the components of the physical self as a motivator of physical activity. His global scale, Physical Estimation and Attraction Scale (PEAS), provided the theoretical basis for many of the newer state instruments.

The Physical Estimation and Attraction Scales (PEAS) developed by Sonstroem (1974) were incorporated into a model (see Figure 14.4) explaining the psychological benefit of physical activity and motivation to participate in physical activity (Sonstroem 1978). The 33 Estimation items measure self-perceptions of (attitudes toward) one's own physical abilities. Estimation is conceived to be a component of general self-esteem. The 54 Attraction items assess interest in or attraction to vigorous physical activity. Of the 100 items, 2 pertain to the social aspects of physical activity, and 11 neutral items (not scored) are included to hide the nature of the scale. Examples of Estimation and Attraction items are presented below. The entire PEAS may be obtained from Baumgartner and Jackson (1982), Safrit (1981), or by writing to Dr. Sonstroem at the University of Rhode Island.

The Estimation items ask students to affirm or deny their own physical characteristics, fitness, athletic ability, or potential in motor performance. Examples of items include the following:

I am stronger than a good many of my friends.

It is difficult for me to catch a thrown ball.

I am in better physical condition than most boys my age.

Even with practice I doubt that I could learn to do a handstand well.

The Attraction items ask students to affirm or deny their personal interests or likes for certain forms of physical activity. Sample items are as follows:

Sports provide me with a welcome escape from present-day life.

I love to run.

Playing tennis appeals to me more than golfing does.

I enjoy the discipline of long and strenuous physical training.

Reliability and Validity of PEAS. Reliability and validity research had been conducted with boys in grades 8 through 12. Internal consistency reliability estimates of 0.87 and 0.89 and stability reliability estimates of 0.92 and 0.94 have been reported for the estimation and attraction scales, respectively (Sonstroem 1974, 1976).

Construct validity research has supported the two scales (Sonstroem 1974). Both estimation and attraction were found to be correlated with height, weight, and athletic experience and unrelated to intelligence quotient (Sonstroem 1974). Sonstroem (1976) found the scales to be relatively free of response distortion. Dishman (1980) identified a tendency for subjects to "fake bad" on the attraction scale under instructions to do so.

Repeated research has shown that self-perceptions of physical ability (Estimation scores) correlate well with actual physical fitness scores and with measures of self-esteem, as Sonstroem's model hypothesizes (Dishman 1978; Fox, Corbin & Couldry 1985; Sonstroem 1978). Estimation scores have been significantly related to mental health scales of the Tennessee Self-Concept Scale (Sonstroem 1976). Physical fitness seems to bear no direct association with self-esteem, which suggests that what people think about their fitness and bodies is more related to positive mental adjustment than their actual fitness level. Estimation scores have been shown to increase following exercise experiences (Dishman & Gettman 1981; Kowal, Patton & Vogel 1978). Attraction scores have been found to be related to self-reports of participation in sport-type activities (Neale et al. 1969; Sonstroem 1978; Sonstroem & Kampper 1980). Sonstroem and Kampper (1980) administered the PEAS to boys in grades 7 and 8 at the beginning of a school year. They found that Attraction, first, and Estimation, second, predicted those boys who would subsequently try out for the touch football and soccer teams. Scores, however, failed to predict staying with a team for the entire season. The PEAS has not been found to predict exercise adherence.

Evolving Research Applications. Sonstroem and Morgan (1989) have proposed a model that explains how exercise program experiences influence self-esteem by means of such variables as physical self-efficacy and physical competence. They suggest that physical competence can be assessed by the Estimation scale. The current trend is to develop specific self-efficacy and perceived competence scale.

To illustrate, Garcia and King (Garcia 1991) developed an exercise self-efficacy scale. Self-efficacy is based on Bandura's social psychological theory (Bandura 1977) and is the belief that one can execute a specific behavior demanded to achieve a specific outcome. The Garcia-King instrument consisted of 16 items in which the respondent rated their confidence that they could exercise under 16 different conditions.

The confidence rating ranges from 0% (I cannot do it at all) to 100% (I am certain that I can do it). The individual's score is the average of the 16 responses. Some examples of the conditions specific to exercise used by Garcia and King are:

I could exercise when tired.

I could exercise during bad weather.

I could exercise when I have a lot of work to do.

I could exercise when I have no one to exercise with.

The current research trend is to develop theory-based multidimensional and situation-specific self-perception scales. For example, Fox and Corbin (1989) developed a physical self-perception profile consisting of four dimensions of physical self-worth. The dimensions were: perceived sport competence; physical condition; attractive body; and strength.

Eating Disorders

Eating disorders[1] are extremely complex problems and have been historically documented. Cases of self-inflicted starvation and weight loss were noted as early as the fourth century when it was recorded that pale, thin, fasting women died of the regimen (Foryet, In press). Biological, family, and cultural factors are associated with eating disorders. Eating disorders are much more prevalent among young women than men. It is estimated that about 90% of individuals with eating disorders are women (Foryet, In press). The incidence of these disorders appears to be on the rise and corresponds to societal pressure for women to be thin.

Nature of Eating Disorders

The common eating disorders are anorexia nervosa, bulimia nervosa, and binge-eating. **Binge-eating** is a less well defined eating disorder and often judged to be a behavioral trait of bulimia nervosa. The causes of anorexia nervosa and bulimia nervosa are complex and not well understood. In American society, women associate thinness with beauty. Advertisements in the mass media constantly reinforce this notion. Anorexics and bulimics tend to judge their self-worth in terms of shape and weight. Table 14.4 summarizes the recognized characteristics used to diagnose anorexia nervosa (APA 1994; Foryet, In press).

The central characteristic of **anorexia nervosa** is "drive for thinness." Persons with anorexia strive to lose weight beyond the point of social desirability, attractiveness, and good health. Individuals with this disorder are highly motivated to adhere to socially derived notions of beauty and femininity, which in our society has become thinness (Foryet, In press). Mass advertising with female models constantly reinforces this notion. Anorexia nervosa begins in early to late adolescence, with the greatest risk for onset between the ages of 14 and 18 years. It is estimated that about 1% of young women are anorexic. Anorexia nervosa has potentially lethal consequences. This disorder has a 20% mortality rate, the highest of any psychological disorder.

The essential characteristic of **bulimia nervosa** is an excessive intake of food, usually high in calories, in a relatively short period. Although this varies considerably, as many as 30,000 calories may be consumed during a binge. This binge eating

---

[1]This section was written with the assistance of John Foreyt, Ph.D., and Carlos Poston II, Ph.D., from the Nutrition Research Center, Baylor College of Medicine, Houston, Texas.

Table 14.4 The Recognized Characteristics Used to Diagnose Anorexia Nervosa (APA 1994; Foryet, In press).

Anorexia Nervosa	Bulimia Nervosa
Refusal to maintain body weight at or above a minimally normal weight for one's age and height.	Recurrent episodes of binge eating that includes eating a large amount of food within a discrete period of time (e.g., 2-hour period); and a sense of lack of control over eating.
Denial of the seriousness of their current low weight.	Recurrent inappropriate compensatory behavior designed to prevent weight gain. These may include self-induced vomiting, misuses of laxatives, fasting, or excessive exercise.
Intense fear of gaining weight or becoming fat, though underweight.	The binge eating and inappropriate compensatory behaviors occur regularly, at least twice a week, for an extended time period, e.g., three months.
Amenorrhea, or the absences of at least three consecutive menstrual cycles in postmenarcheal females.	The bulimic's self-evaluation is unduly influenced by body shape and weight.

is accompanied by recurrent methods to prevent weight gain, such as vomiting or using laxatives. The average age of onset for bulimia is 17–19 years. The prevalence of bulimia nervosa is approximately 1–3%. It has been estimated that 4–19% of young women engage in significant levels of bulimic behavior. The bulimic needs psychological counseling to develop self-esteem and overcome serious concerns about **body image.** Unlike the anorexic, the bulimic may not experience serious weight loss; many maintain a normal weight.

Eating Disorder Scales

Psychological inventories are used to help identify those at risk of developing eating disorders. While these paper and pencil tests provide useful information, the diagnosis of eating disorders can be made only by professionals after intensive evaluation. The first instruments used to assess anorexic behavior were behavioral rating scales (Slade 1973). The Eating Attitudes Test (EAT) was the first objective self-report measure of anorexia nervosa (Garner 1979). A more recent scale is the Eating Disorder Inventory (Garner 1984).

Eating Disorder Inventory (EDI). The EDI is the most comprehensive eating disorder scale (Garner 1984). The scale was constructed to assess both psychological and behavioral traits associated with both anorexia nervosa and bulimia nervosa. The 64-item scale consists of eight subscales. Table 14.5 provides a summary of the scales. The EDI is a comprehensive scale used to help diagnose eating disorders. The scale was developed by psychological professionals and was not intended to be used by nonprofessionals. The EDI illustrates the complexities of an eating disorder.

Eating Attitudes Test (EAT). The most popular scale is the Eating Attitudes Test or EAT. The original EAT consisted of 40 items that the subject rated on a Likert scale that ranged from never to always. Further research (Garner 1982) with a large sample

Table 14.5 A Description of the Eating Disorder Inventory (EDI) Scales and the Reliability of Each Scale.

Scale	Scale Description
Drive for thinness (r_{xx} = 0.92)	Excessive concern with dieting, preoccupation with weight and entrenchment in an extreme pursuit of thinness
Bulimia (r_{xx} = 0.90)	The tendency toward episodes of uncontrollable overeating, binge eating, and recurrent methods to prevent weight gain such as self-induced vomiting.
Body dissatisfaction (r_{xx} = 0.92)	The belief that parts of the body are too large, e.g., hips, thighs, buttocks.
Ineffectiveness (r_{xx} = 0.85)	A feeling of general inadequacy, insecurity, worthlessness, and not being in control of one's life.
Perfectionism (r_{xx} = 0.88)	Excessive personal expectations for superior achievement.
Interpersonal distrust (r_{xx} = 0.81)	A sense of alienation and general reluctance to form close relationships.
Interoceptive awareness (r_{xx} = 0.85)	The lack of confidence in recognizing and accurately identifying emotions and sensations of hunger or satiety.
Maturity fears (r_{xx} = 0.96)	A wish to retreat to the security of the preadolescent years because of the overwhelming demands of adulthood.

From: Garner 1984; Rhea 1995.

of female anorexia nervosa patients produced a 26-item form of the EAT. The correlation between the 26- and 40-item tests was very high, 0.97. The 26-item scale was found to measure three general factors. Table 14.6 gives the three factors and sample items. Women with eating disorders were found to differ significantly from controls on the 26-item scale.

A possible limitation of the EAT is that it was developed as a screening test for detecting previously undiagnosed cases of anorexia nervosa in populations at high risk for the disorder (Garner 1979; Garner 1982). Koslowsky and associates (Koslowsky 1992) examined the validity of the 26-item EAT with a sample of over 800 young, female Israeli soldiers. Over 90% of the women were 18 or 19 years of age, an age group at risk for eating disorders. Since military service in Israel is mandatory, this sample was representative of the total Israeli female population of this age group. Their analysis showed that the scale measured four different factors. Table 14.6 gives these factors and sample test items.

The Israeli Army study demonstrated that the EAT is a reliable instrument for the general population. While research (Garner 1979; Koslowsky 1992) shows that the EAT consists of several factors, the first factor, dieting, was the predominant, most important factor. Additional analyses showed that the other factors tended to be correlated with the dieting factor.

Table 14.6 Factors and Sample Items of the Eating Attitudes Test (EAT) from Two Studies

Factor	Sample Items
26-Item EAT Study (Garner et al. 1982)	
Dieting (R_{xx} = 0.90)	I eat diet foods. I am preoccupied with the thought of having fat on my body.
Bulimia and food preoccupation (R_{xx} = 0.86)	I have an impulse to vomit after meals. I have gone on eating binges where I feel that I may not be able to stop.
Oral control (R_{xx} = 0.84)	I cut my food into small pieces. I feel that others pressure me to eat.
Israeli Army Study (Koslowsky et al. 1992)	
Dieting (R_{xx} = 0.90)	I engage in dieting behavior. I am preoccupied with the thought of having fat on my body.
Oral control (R_{xx} = 0.74)	I enjoy eating new and rich foods. Other people think I am too thin.
Awareness of food content (R_{xx} = 0.76)	I avoid foods with sugar in them. I eat diet foods.
Food preoccupation (R_{xx} = 0.56)	I feel that food controls my life. I give too much time and thought to food.

College Student EAT Screening Version. Both the 40- and 26-item versions of the EAT were developed by psychological professionals to use for identifying individuals at risk for eating disorders and help in the diagnosis of eating disorders. Eating disorders is a topic of the University of Houston personal fitness course required of all students (Jackson 1997). One objective of the course is to help students be aware of eating disorders and help determine if they may be at risk. The 26-item EAT (Garner 1982) was administered to over 2300 students who were enrolled in the course. These data were factor analyzed (Suminski et al. 1998) and the analysis produced the same four factors found in the Israeli Army study (Koslowsky 1992). The goal of this analysis was to develop a shortened version of the EAT that measured just the principle factor, dieting. This analysis produced a 10-item screening version of the scale.

Scale. 10-Item EAT

Purpose. The purpose of the scale is to provide students with a general assessment of the EAT dieting factor.

Reliability. Using a sample of 2327 male and female college students, the internal consistency reliability was found to be 0.95.

Validity. The scale has construct validity for the EAT dieting factor. The factor has been shown to discriminate between eating-disordered females and controls (Garner 1979) and correlate with body image (r = 0.40) and the number of diets in the past year (r = 0.55) (Koslowsky 1992).

Scoring. The scoring method is a 5-response Likert scale. The scoring method was established to facilitate machine scoring on scantron score sheets. The

Table 14.7 Normative Eating Disorder Standards Developed on University of Houston Students*

Percentile	Risk Level	Women	Men
90	High	41	42
75	Above average	33	31
50	Average	23	18
25	Below average	16	13
10	Low	12	11

*Source: Jackson, A. S. and R. M. Ross, *Understanding Exercise for Health and Fitness,* 1997. Reprinted by permission.

choices and point values are: A, Always (5); B, Usually (4); C, Sometimes (3); D, Rarely (2); E, Never (1). The subject's score is the sum of their responses on the 19 items.

Norms. Table 14.7 provides normative data of the eating disorder scale administered to over 2000 University of Houston college students (Jackson 1997). A high score on this scale represents a tendency to exhibit a risk of eating disorder behaviors. It does not mean the person has an eating disorder, only that the score is high in relation to the ways in which other college students responded on the scale. Female students were found to score significantly higher on the scale than male students.

10-Item EAT Instructions and Items

Eating Behavior. Please read each item below. Most of the statements relate to food or eating, although other types of statements have been included. Place a mark on your scantron for each of the numbered statements using the letter description that best applies to you. The choices are:

A: Always

B: Usually

C: Sometimes

D: Rarely

E: Never

1. I vomit after I have eaten.
2. I feel extremely guilty after eating.
3. I am preoccupied with a desire to be thinner.
4. I am preoccupied with the thought of having fat on my body.
5. I eat diet foods.
6. I feel that food controls my life.
7. I give too much time and thought to food.
8. I engage in dieting behavior.
9. I like my stomach to be empty.
10. I have the impulse to vomit after meals.

A Note of Caution. It is important to understand that the diagnosis of an eating disorder can be confirmed only through a comprehensive assessment by a competent professional. The purpose of the 10-item scale is to provide students with normative data to compare their status with other college students. Most colleges and universities have psychological services available to students who want more comprehensive information. The students are confidentially given their 10-item EAT score and use the normative information to interpret their score. Students are also given information about the services provided at the university counseling center to seek additional help if concerned.

Psychophysical Ratings

Individuals are able to perceive and rate strain during physical exercise. The **rating of perceived exertion (RPE)** is a valid and simple method for determining exercise intensity. The RPE is a **psychophysical** scale that was developed by the Swedish psychologist Gunnar Borg (1962, 1978, 1982) and is used extensively for exercise testing and exercise prescription (Borg, In press). It is Borg's opinion (1982) that perceived exertion is the single best indicator of the degree of physical strain because the overall perception rating integrates many sources of information elicited from the peripheral working muscles and joints, central cardiovascular and respiratory functions, and central nervous system. "All these signals, perceptions and experiences are integrated into a configuration of a 'Gestalt' perceived exertion" (Borg 1982).

Borg has published two RPE scales. The first is a category scale with values ranging from 6 to 20, which assumes a linear relation between exercise heart rate and RPE rating (Borg 1962). The second scale was developed to be consistent with the nonlinearity of psychophysical ratings (Borg 1972, 1982).

Borg's Linear RPE Scale

Borg's linear RPE scale was the first developed to measure perceived exertion of aerobic exercise. The Borg RPE scale increases linearly with exercise heart rate. The scale values range from 6 to 20. This was proposed to denote heart rates ranging from 60 to 200 beats/min. For example, a rating of 15 was meant to correspond with a heart rate of 150 beats/min. Borg did not intend that the heart rate-RPE rating be taken literally, because many factors can affect exercise heart rate. Age, exercise mode, environment (e.g., heat, humidity), anxiety, and drugs (e.g., beta-blocker drugs that are used to control high blood pressure) all can affect exercise heart rate. The influence of aging on RPE is illustrated in Figure 14.5 . The scale has been shown to correlate between 0.80 and 0.90 with heart rate, $\dot{V}O_2$, and lactic acid accumulation (Borg 1982).

The RPE scale (Figure 14.6) is very popular and very easy to use. Research by Pollock, Jackson, and Foster (1986) shows that the scale provides an excellent estimate of exercise intensity and can be used to prescribe exercise and to regulate exercise testing. RPE values of 12 and 13 represent exercise intensities at about 60% of heart rate reserve[2] and $\dot{V}O_2$ Max. Ratings of 16 and 17 correspond to about 90% of heart rate reserve and 85% of $\dot{V}O_2$ Max. Values $\geq$ 18 are considered to be an indication that the person has reached their maximum. These ranges have been valid for both leg and arm exercise and for subjects on beta-blocker drugs that lowered $\dot{V}O_2$ Max and maximal heart rate (Pollock, Jackson & Foster 1986). The instructions used for the RPE scale during exercise testing follow:

[2]Percent Heart Rate Reserve = [X × (Max HR − Rest HR)] + Rest HR, where X is the desired percentage and HR is heart rate (Pollock, Wilmore & Fox 1984).

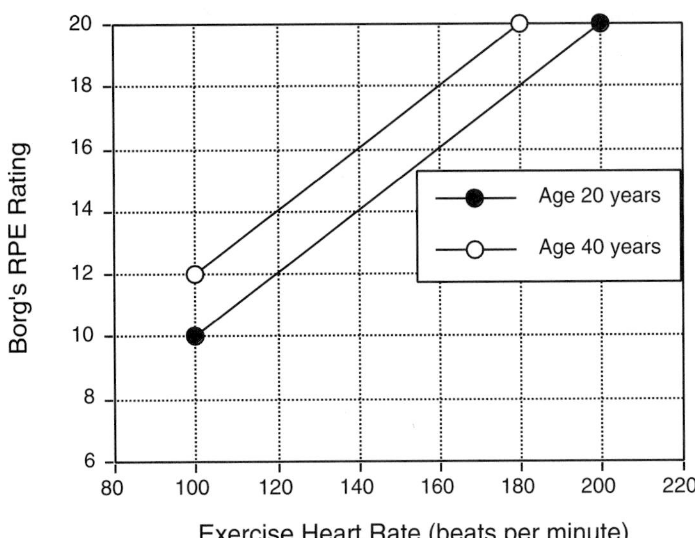

Figure 14.5
Graph shows the linear change in the heart rate and Rating of Perceived Exertion (RPE) ratings. The RPE scale was initially used to duplicate exercise heart rate (i.e., HR = RPE × 10), but maximum heart rate decreases with age. RPE ratings for older individuals can be expected to be associated with lower exercise heart rates than younger individuals. RPE ratings ≥ 18 are typically an indication that the person has reached their maximum. The RPE scale has become a standard for most exercise testing laboratories. (Source: CSI Software Company, Houston, TX. Reprinted by permission.)

Figure 14.6
The 15-grade category scale for rating perceived exertion (RPE scale). (Source: Dr. G. Borg, Dept. of Psychology, University of Stockholm, Stockholm, Sweden.)

6
7 Very, very light
8
9 Very light
10
11 Fairly light
12
13 Somewhat hard
14
15 Hard
16
17 Very hard
18
19 Very, very hard
20

Instructions—15-grade RPE Scale.

You are now going to take part in a graded exercise test. You will be walking or running on the treadmill while we are measuring various physiological functions. We also want you to try to estimate how hard you feel the work is; that is, we want you to rate the degree of perceived exertion you feel. By perceived exertion we mean the total amount of exertion and physical fatigue. Don't concern yourself with any one factor such as leg pain, shortness of breath, or work grade, but try to concentrate on your total, inner feeling of exertion. Try to estimate as honestly and objectively as possible. Don't underestimate the degree of exertion you feel, but don't overestimate it either. Just try to estimate as accurately as possible.3

[3]Instructions developed by William Morgan, Ed.D., University of Wisconsin, Madison, WI. Published with permission.

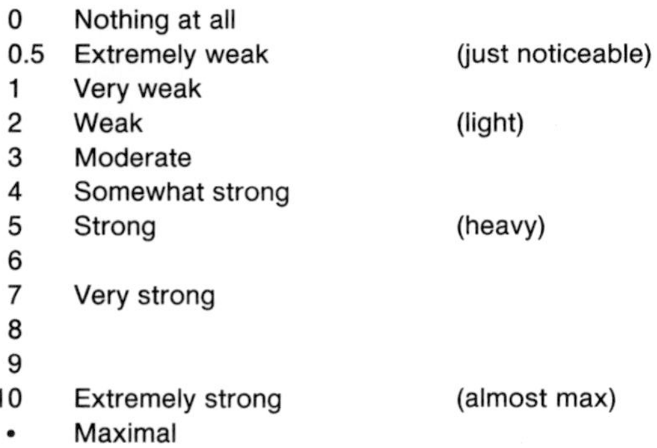

Figure 14.7
Borg's category scale with ratio properties (CR-10). (Source: Dr. G. Borg, Dept. of Psychology, University of Stockholm, Stockholm, Sweden.)

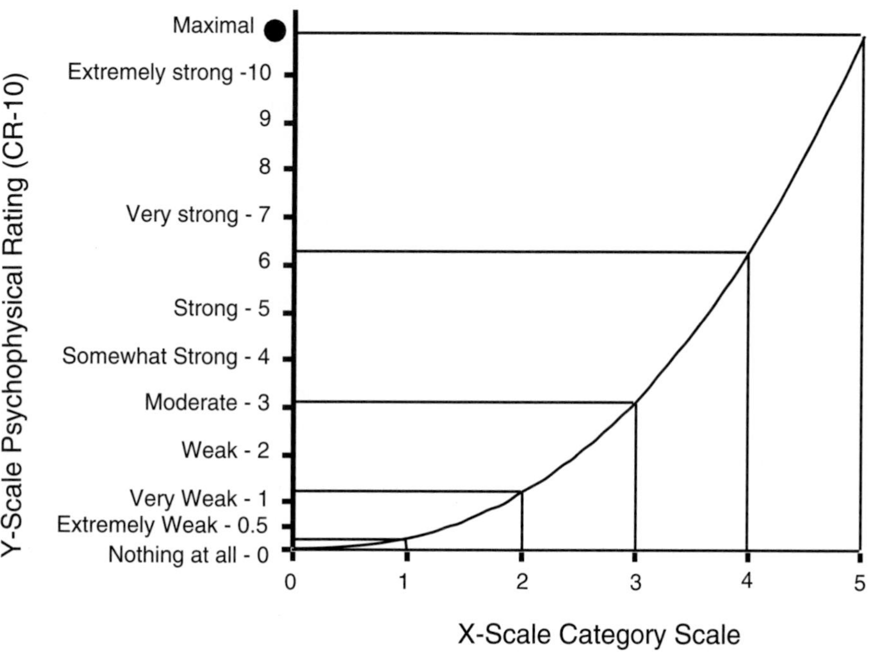

Figure 14.8
The theoretical basis of Borg's CR-10 scale. A linear increase in the physical stimulus produces a ratio increase in the perception of the stimulus. (Source: CSI Software Company, Houston, TX. Reprinted by permission.)

Borg's Category Scale with Ratio Properties

The assumption of Borg's linear RPE scale is that the perception of physical exertion changes at a linear rate. Figure 14.5 shows this. Changes in exercise heart rate (X variable) are assumed to produce a linear change in RPE (Y variable). Stevens' classic **psychophysical** work (Stevens 1957; Stevens 1975) showed that sensory perception often does change at a linear rate, rather than nonlinearly. Stevens' work provides the theoretical and mathematical basis for Borg's ingenious Category (C)–Ratio (R) scale, or CR-10 scale (Borg 1972; Borg 1982). Figure 14.7 gives Borg's CR-10 scale.

The CR-10 scale is one that uses an accelerating power function to model the physical stimulus with its psychophysical perception. Figure 14.8 shows the theoretical basis of category scale with ratio properties. The X-axis, physical stimulus, is a category scale, while the Y-axis is the psychophysical scale with ratio properties. As the physical stimulus (e.g., the person's exercise intensity) increases from low to maximum, the psychophysical perception rating increases at an accelerated rate. Note the

CR-10 change for a 1-unit change on the category scale (X). A change from 1 to 2 produces a CR-10 change from about 0.2 to 1.2, but changes from 2 to 3 and 3 to 4 produce CR-10 changes from 1.2 to 3.1, and 3.1 to 6.3, respectively. Mathematically this accelerated curve is called a power function.

The instructions[4] for the ratio RPE scale are:

Instructions—CR-10 Scale

> We would like you to estimate the exertion you feel by using this scale. The scale starts with 0 "Nothing at all" and goes on to 10, "Extremely strong" that is "Almost max." For most people this corresponds to the hardest physical exercise they have ever done, as for example the exertion you feel when you run as fast as you can for several minutes till you are completely exhausted, or when you are lifting or carrying something which is so heavy that you nearly can't make it. Maybe it is possible to imagine exertion or pain that is even stronger, and that is why the maximum value is somewhat over 10. If you feel the exertion or pain to be stronger than "Extremely strong" (almost max) you can use a number that is over 10, for example 11, 13 or an even higher number.
>
> If the exertion is "Very weak" you should answer with the number 1. If it is only "Moderate" you say 3 and so on. Feel free to use any number you wish on the scale, as well as half values, as, for example, 1.5 or decimals such as 0.8, 1.7 or 2.3. It is important that you give the answer that you yourself feel to be right and not that which you think you ought to give. Answer as honestly as possible and try neither to overestimate nor underestimate the degree of exertion that you feel.

The feature of the ratio RPE scale is that numbers anchor verbal expressions that are simple and understandable. The expressions are placed in a position on the ratio scale where they belong according to their quantitative meaning. A simple range of 0 to 10 is used to anchor the verbal expressions. It is permissible to use fractional ratings (e.g., 2.5 or 3.8) and values above 10. The CR-10 scale has been shown to correlate highly with both blood lactate and muscle lactate level, which are the biochemical markers of cardiorespiratory and muscle fatigue (Borg 1982). The CR-10 scale has been shown to be useful for evaluating individual's capacity to perform common industrial tasks, such as lifting heavy objects (Chin 1995; Hidalgo et al. 1997; Jackson et al. 1997; Karwowski 1996; Resnik 1995). Psychophysically defined demanding lift loads increase the risk of back injury (Snook, Campanelli & Hart 1978; Snook & Ciriello 1991; Waters et al. 1993). The scale is used as a basis for helping individuals define safe lifting weights for their physical capacity (Jackson et al. 1997).

Borg provides convincing evidence that the CR-10 scale is useful for describing aerobic and anaerobic levels of exercise intensity (Borg, 1998). Ergonomic research (Chin 1995; Hidalgo et al. 1997; Jackson et al. 1997; Karwowski 1996; Resnik 1995) shows the CR-10 scale is extremely useful for rating the difficulty of industrial lifting tasks. Figure 14.9 graphically shows the accelerated increase in psychophysical perception (ratio) associated with the linear increase in lift weight (category). Shown are the curves produced by stronger and weaker subjects. These curves show that while lift weight increases at a linear rate, the perception of lift difficulty increases at an accelerated rate. As expected, the CR-10 rating for a common lift load (e.g., 60 pounds) of the weaker subjects is higher than the stronger subject (CR-10 rating of

---

[4]Personal communication with Dr. Gunnar Borg, Department of Psychology, University of Stockholm, Stockholm, Sweden, November 1985.

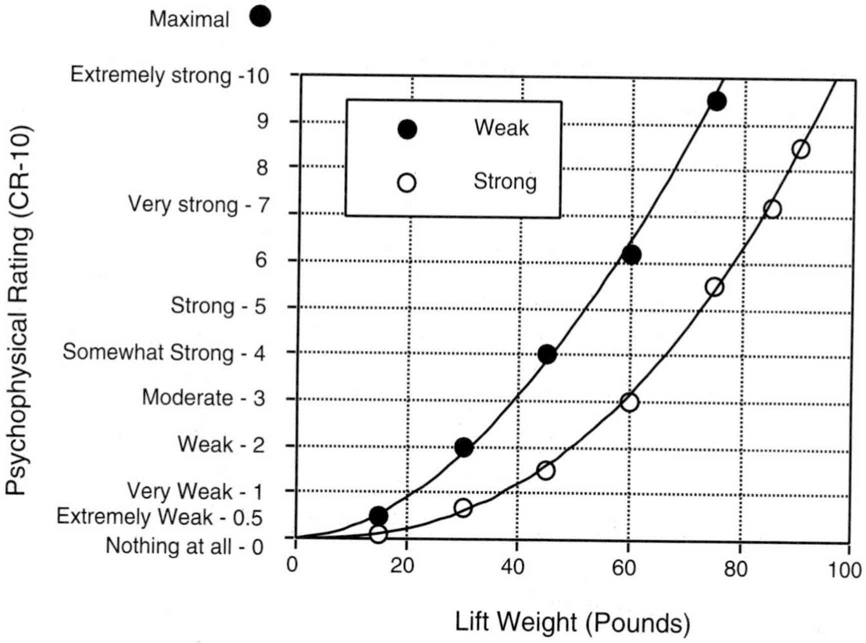

Figure 14.9
Graphic representation of the nonlinear relationship between changes in lift weight and psychophysical rating of lift difficulty. The lift task was lifting boxes that varied with weight from floor to knuckle height. The psychophysical rating is the subject's CR-10 rating of lift difficulty. The stronger group were those who were able to lift at least 95 pounds, and the weaker group were individuals wit a maximum lift of 75 pounds. (Graph made from published data Jackson 1997) (Source: CSI Software Company, Houston, TX. Reprinted by permission.)

6.1 vs. 3.0), but both groups produce accelerated curves. When both the weak and strong subjects approach their maximum, the psychophysical rating increases at an accelerated rate.

Uses of Psychophysical

Psychophysical ratings are used for many different purposes. Some of the more common uses include the following.

Exercise Testing. The RPE scale is used to judge exercise intensity when administering a graded exercise test on a treadmill or cycle ergometer. The objective of an exercise test is to slowly and systematically increase the exercise intensity from submaximal levels to maximal. Often, percent of maximal heart rate is used to quantify exercise intensity. But in most instances maximal heart rate is not known and must be estimated from age (Max HR $= 220 -$ age). However, there tend to be errors in this estimate of as much as ± 10 to 15 beats per minute. Additionally, many adults take medication for common health problems, such as hypertension. Often these drugs lower resting and exercise heart rate, but do not affect RPE. The RPE ratings are used to determine when a subject is reaching his or her maximal tolerance (≥ 18 on the 6–20 RPE scale and > 7.0 on the CR-10 scale).

Exercise Prescription. Percentage of $\dot{V}O_2$ Max is the most valid method of prescribing exercise, but this is typically not known. Therefore, percentage of maximal heart rate reserve is recommended. A difficulty with this method is that maximal heart rate must be known, and some individuals are taking medications that affect heart rate. It has been found that RPE ratings (see Figure 14.10) are an excellent method of selecting the proper intensity for exercise and can be used to supplement heart rate estimates (Pollock, Jackson & Foster 1986).

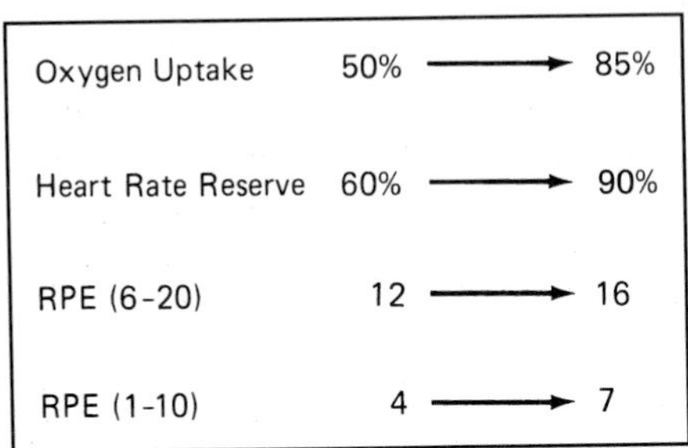

Figure 14.10 Recommended training zone for exercise prescription. (Adapted from Pollock, Wilmore and Fox 1984.)

Quantification of Energy Expenditure. Many adult fitness programs seek to quantify energy expended through exercise, which is often expressed in kilocalories. This can be done very accurately with aerobic exercise modes such as walking, jogging, or cycling because external work can be quantified (see Chapter 10). There are other popular aerobic exercise modes, such as aerobic dancing or playing tennis, where external work cannot be quantified. Individuals vary in the intensity to which they exercise. Many fitness centers use commercial computer software to quantify exercise by caloric expenditure. Chapter 1 illustrates this software. This software uses psychophysical ratings to estimate exercise intensity when external work cannot be measured. To illustrate, more calories would be expended when playing tennis at an RPE rating of 7, Very strong, as compared to a rating of 3, Moderate. This method is illustrated in another source (Jackson & Ross 1997).

Rating Work Difficulty. Psychophysical methods are used to define the difficulty of industrial jobs, such as lifting. Psychophysical criteria are one kind used to define acceptable workloads for industrial populations (NIOSH 1981; Waters et al. 1993). Acceptable workloads are defined as those one can perform without undue strain.

Injury Prevention. Demanding lift loads increase the risk of back injury. Epidemiological data (Snook, Campanelli and Hart 1978) estimate that about 67% of industrial back injuries could be eliminated if workers lifted loads psychophysically judged to be acceptable. Using this logic, the CR-10 scale is used as a basis for helping individuals define safe lifting weights for their level of fitness (Chin 1995; Hidalgo et al. 1997; Jackson et al. 1997; Karwowski 1996; Resnik 1995).

Sport Psychology Instruments

The psychology of exercise and sport is a developing academic discipline, dependent on having reliable and valid instruments. Initially, general psychological scales (e.g., Spielberger's Trait and State Anxiety Scale) were used in sport psychology, but the more recent trend has been to develop sport- and exercise-specific scales. The sport-specific scales have their roots in the more general psychological scales. The publication of these specific scales reflects the evolution of sport psychology as a discipline independent of the general area of psychology.

Ostrow (Ostrow 1996) published a comprehensive summary of psychological scales, questionnaires, and inventories in the area of sport and exercise sciences. Included are 314 instruments listed in 20 different categories. The instruments were found through computer literature searches of more than 45 journals and conference proceedings over a 30-year period. Once Ostrow completed a summary of the instrument, it was forwarded to the principal test author for review. The author updated and revised the summary, which was then used to develop the final copy. The summary contains the following information on each of the instruments:

1. Source—Bibliographical listing
2. Purpose of the instrument
3. A general description of the instrument
4. The methodology used to construct the instrument
5. The reported reliability estimates for populations studied
6. The method used to validate the instrument
7. Normative data on the populations tested
8. Who to contact to obtain the instrument, including e-mail address when available
9. References when the scale has been used

Ostrow's directory is a valuable resource for anyone attempting to find a psychological instrument for use in sport and exercise science settings. Listed next are the 20 categories used by Ostrow (Ostrow 1996) to place the 314 instruments. Following each category is Ostrow's description of each general category and the number of instruments reviewed.

Achievement Orientation. Number of instruments reviewed, 18. Instruments measure achievement orientations of sport participants in terms of competitiveness, the desire to win, striving for goals, task versus ego orientation, motives to approach/avoid success and to avoid failure, and perceptions of motivational climate and effort.

Aggression. Number of instruments reviewed, 7. Instruments measure the aggressive tendencies of sport participants in terms of instrumental and reactive aggression, physical and nonphysical aggression, and perceptions among players and spectators of the legitimacy of aggressive behavior.

Anxiety. Number of instruments reviewed, 31. Instruments measure anxiousness among sport participants in terms of cognitive and somatic trait and state anxiety, worry cognitions, and concerns regarding concentration disruption, social evaluation, and fear of injury. Coping strategies for dealing with anxiety are examined. Athlete burnout and sources of stress experienced by youth sport participants, officials, coaches, and cheerleaders are also assessed.

Attention. Number of instruments reviewed, 5. Four of the 5 instruments are sport-specific versions of Nideffer's test of attention and interpersonal style, which is based on a two-dimensional conceptual framework of attention, containing broad/narrow and internal/external components. The remaining instrument examines attention among elite rifle shooters from a multidimensional perspective.

Attitudes toward Exercise and Physical Activity. Number of instruments reviewed, 17. Instruments measure attitudes of children, college students, physical education teachers, and other groups toward the values of participating in exercise and related physical activities. Enjoyment of physical activity, attraction to being physically active, pathological attitudes toward exercise, and the attitudinal beliefs among nonexercisers are also evaluated.

Attitudes/Values toward Sport. Number of instruments reviewed, 29. Instruments measure the attitudes of sport participants towards the values of sport participation, professional versus play orientations expressed during sport participation, sportsmanship attitudes, and the values youth sport coaches hold regarding the potential outcomes of competitions for children. Tests assess children's beliefs about the purposes of sport, perceptions of coaching behaviors, attitudes toward sport officials, and the values of professional sport to the community as perceived by spectators. Also includes role expectancies for female versus male participation in sport, and attitudes toward female involvement in sport and perceived and experienced role conflict among female athletes.

Attributions. Number of instruments reviewed, 9. Instruments measure the explanations sport participants give for their successes and failures in sport and related physical activities.

Body Image. Number of instruments reviewed, 17. Instruments measure the attitudes of individuals toward their body appearance and structure, and confidence in movement. Tests assessing individual difference in body esteem and body satisfaction are also prominent. One scale determines the extent to which people become anxious when others observe or evaluate their physiques.

Cognitive Strategies. Number of instruments reviewed, 13. Instruments measure the cognitive skill that athletes employ prior to and during sport competition. These strategies include self-talk, coping with anxiety, imagery, association/dissociation, and concentration. Instruments also assess thoughts during running, coping strategies that athletes employ to adjust to pain, task-irrelevant cognitions, and thoughts that occur following mistakes during athletic competition.

Cohesion. Number of instruments reviewed, 7. Instruments measure attraction to the group, interpersonal interactions, group integration, and team unity across sport team members and coach.

Confidence—Exercise. Number of instruments reviewed, 18. Instruments measure perceptions of movement competence, physical fitness capacities, and the physical self-concept. The strength of perceived self-efficacy in relation to exercise participation and one's confidence in overcoming barriers toward exercising are also assessed.

Confidence—Sport. Number of instruments reviewed, 19. Instruments measure perceptions of sport performance competence and perceptions of competence in the coaching role. The strength of perceived self-efficacy in relation to sport performance, and perceptions of self-acceptance within the sport domain are also evaluated.

Imagery. Number of instruments reviewed, 5. Instruments measure individual differences in visual imagery of movement, the imagery of kinesthetic sensations, and in imagery utilization.

Leadership. Number of instruments reviewed, 4. Instruments measure the perceptions/preferences of athletes for specific leader behaviors from the coach, the coach's perceptions of his or her own leader behavior, and satisfaction with various aspects of leadership in sport. Tests also assess the leadership tendencies of soccer players and the leadership qualities of athletic administrators.

Life Adjustment. Number of instruments reviewed, 5. Instruments measure life events and stressors, such as injury, that are experienced by athletes and that necessitate adjustment.

Locus of Control. Number of instruments reviewed, 6. Instruments measure individuals' perceptions of internal and/or external factors that control their reinforcements in relation to exercise, behavior, sport performance, injury rehabilitation, and career choice.

Miscellaneous. Number of instruments reviewed, 21. Instruments measure a variety of psychological constructs, including the affective responses of athletes to experiencing injury, the athletic identity, attitudes toward sport psychological services, psychological factors related to spectator attendance and allegiance to sport teams, sportsmanship attitudes, officials' role satisfaction, and athletes' superstitious beliefs.

Motivation—Exercise. Number of instruments reviewed, 37. Instruments measure reasons for adherence to exercise and injury rehabilitation programs, commitment to exercise and running, perceived benefits/barriers to exercise participation, and the motives/incentives that individuals express for participating in running and other forms of exercise. Also reviewed are perceived exertion, feeling states that stem from exercising, negative addiction to exercise/running, and stages of exercise behavior change.

Motivation—Sport. Number of instruments reviewed, 20. Instruments measure the motives individuals express for participating in sport, the degree of satisfaction derived from sport participation, and the reasons that inhibit people from engaging in sport. Tests also assess spectator motivation, sport commitment, flow states in sport, and perceptions of psychological momentum.

Multidimensional. Number of instruments reviewed, 26. Instruments measure multiple personality traits, attitudes, motives, beliefs, or psychological skills evident among individuals participating in sport or exercise.

Uses of Psychological Scales

Psychological scales are readily available and easy to administer and score. This enhances their use, but also presents a potential danger. Psychological instruments, especially personality inventories, can be threatening and potentially harmful when administered and interpreted by the untrained or naive. The legitimacy of using psychological instruments can be clarified by asking two simple questions.

1. Do you have a need and right to secure such data?
2. Are you capable of validity interpreting and using the test results in a way that will help the person being tested?

It is difficult to conceive of any valid purpose for the use of psychological scales such as personality inventories and behavior rating scales by public school physical education teachers and exercise specialists, but other psychological inventories have legitimate educational and research purposes. Some specific examples follow.

Achievement of class objectives. A common objective of physical education programs is the development of a positive feeling toward class activities and physical activity in general. Semantic differential scales would be especially useful to evaluate this.

Administrative planning, curriculum development, and evaluation of teaching methods. Again, semantic differential scales could provide data that could be used to evaluate the effectiveness of instruction units and methods of instruction. Children may improve their physical fitness, but they could develop negative feelings toward physical activity in general. Psychological scales could be used for these purposes.

Individual diagnosis and remediation. The identification of children with a low self-concept, self-esteem, or body image could be very important. Altering a child's attitude in a positive direction could enhance his or her mental health.

Screening. Psychological scales can be used to identify individuals at risk for eating disorders. Care must be taken to help interested individuals find professional services.

Research. A current problem in physical education and exercise science is a lack of understanding of the psychological motives of sports participation and exercise adherence. Although medical research has clearly established that lack of exercise and obesity are major cardiovascular disease risk factors (see Chapter 1), we still do not know why some people are physically active and others are not. This will be a major area of research in the future. Trait instruments, such as the SMI, can be useful to identify those at risk of dropping from exercise programs. State instruments will likely be useful for creating favorable environments that will enhance exercise behavior.

Summary

Most of the published physical education attitude scales were developed on the assumption that a single factor was being measured. Scales that gauge attitudes toward physical education report high reliability, but their construct validity of what factors are measured is yet to be determined. The Kenyon and Sonstroem scales are multidimensional instruments that have established construct validity. Semantic differential scales that use bipolar adjectives to measure feelings about concepts are a flexible technique for measuring attitude. Many adults who start exercise programs will quit. It has been shown that adherence to exercise is related to self-motivation as measured by the SMI. There is a growing group of researchers who are examining the influence of exercise on self-esteem. These state instruments have their roots in Sonstroem's global scale, Physical Estimation and Attraction Scale (PEAS). The Estimation items ask students to affirm or deny their own physical characteristics, fitness, athletic ability, or potential in motor performance , and the Attraction items ask students to affirm or deny their personal interests or likes for certain forms of physical activity. Eating disorders is a growing, serious problem. The prevalence of eating disorders, anorexia nervosa and bulimia nervosa, is highest among young women between the ages of about 14 and 19 years. The incidence of these disorders appears to be on the rise and corresponds to societal pressure for women to be thin. The psychophysical RPE scales have been shown to be useful for determining exercise intensity. Borg has developed two scales, either of which can be used for exercise testing; exercise prescription; quantification of energy expenditure; rating work difficulty; and injury prevention. The area of exercise and sport psychology is expanding rapidly. Ostrow (1996) has developed a comprehensive system to categorize and evaluate exercise psychological instruments.

Formative Evaluation of Objectives

Objective 1 Evaluate the validity of physical education attitude scales.

1. Attitude scales are self-report instruments designed to measure attitudes by the way one responds to statements. In terms of validity, what is the basic weakness of this type of measurement?
2. Kenyon's attitude scale offers a valid method of measuring attitudes toward physical activity. The scale measures six different types, or dimensions, of attitudes. Identify and briefly describe each.

Objective 2 Outline the procedures used to develop semantic differential scales.

1. Semantic differential scales provide a flexible method for evaluating attitudes. Research indicates that three basic factors are measured with these scales: evaluation, potency, and activity. Define these concepts and list three adjective pairs that measure each of them.
2. Outline the process you would follow to develop semantic differential scales.
3. Outline the procedure for scoring semantic differential scales that would calculate a score for each of the three factors.
4. What are the concepts being measured by the Children's Attitude Toward Physical Activity Inventory? What semantic dimensions are being used with the CATPA-I?

Objective 3 Describe the nature of the Self-Motivation Inventory (SMI).

1. What does the SMI predict?
2. How might one use the SMI?

Objective 4 Describe the nature of instruments designed to relate exercise and self-esteem.

1. The Physical Estimation and Attraction Scales were developed to explain motivation toward physical activity. Identify and briefly describe each scale.
2. Why are scales related to exercise self-esteem state instruments?

Objective 5 Describe the nature of eating disorder scales.

1. What are the most common types of eating disorders?
2. What is the nature of eating disorder instruments?
3. What is the EAT?

Objective 6 Evaluate the validity and value of the psychophysical rating of perceived exertion scales.

1. What are the similarities and differences between the two Borg RPE scales?
2. How can the RPE scales be used?
3. In order to improve aerobic fitness, one should exercise at what level on the RPE scales?

Additional Learning Activities

1. Several studies have sought to determine the correlation between attitude and physical fitness. Review the articles published in the Research Quarterly to determine whether a positive attitude is associated with a high level of physical fitness. How was attitude measured? How was physical fitness measured?
2. Select either the CATPA-I or the PEAS and administer it to a group of students. Can you develop a microcomputer or SPSS program to score the scale?
3. Select a concept (e.g., physical fitness, athletics, aerobic dance) of particular interest to you and develop semantic differential scales to measure attitude toward the concept. Administer the scales to various groups and determine whether the groups' means differ. You might use male and female physical education majors as your groups. You may want to consult a basic statistics text to determine whether the means between the groups are significantly different.
4. Administer the CATPA-I to a group of children. Be sure to read the proper instructions (Schutz et al. 1985) and administer either the scale for 3rd graders or the scale for older children.
5. What are the reasons adults do not continue exercise programs? Conduct a review of the exercise science literature to answer this question. A good place to start is to conduct a computer search for research published by R. K. Dishman.
6. Learn how to use either of the Borg RPE scales. This can be accomplished several ways. If you take a maximal exercise test, relate the submaximal ratings with percent of heart rate reserve, or $\dot{V}O_2$ Max. A second method is to exercise at an exercise intensity that will produce an aerobic training effect and rate this intensity by either the 6 to 20 or 1 to 10 scale.
7. Take the EAT and evaluate your risk for an eating disorder. If you want more information, go to the counseling center at your university.

Bibliography

Adams, R. S. 1963. Two scales for measuring attitude toward physical education. *Research Quarterly* 34:91–94.

Ajzen, I. and M. Fishbein. 1980. *Understanding attitudes and predicting social behavior.* Englewood Cliffs, NJ: Prentice-Hall.

Allison, P. R. 1976. An instrument to measure creative dance attitude of grade five children. Ph.D. Dissertation, University of Alabama, Tuscaloosa, AL.

APA. 1994. *Diagnostic and statistical manual of mental disorders.* 4th ed. Washington, DC: American Psychiatric Association.

Bandura, A. 1977. Self-efficacy: Toward a unifying theory of behavioral change. *Psychological Review* 84(2):191–215.

Baumgartner, T. A. and A. S. Jackson. 1982. *Measurement for evaluation in physical education.* 2d ed. Dubuque, IA: Wm. C. Brown.

———. 1995. *Measurement for evaluation in physical education and exercise science.* 5th ed. Dubuque, IA: Wm. C. Brown.

Borg, B. 1972. A ratio scaling method for interindividual comparisons. University of Stockholm 12: Reports from the Institute of Applied Psychology.

Borg, G. 1962. *Physical performance and perceived exertion.* Lund, Sweden: Gleerup.

Borg, G. 1977. *Physical work and effort.* Wenner-Gren Center, Stockholm, Sweden: Pergamon Press (Oxford).

Borg, G. 1978. Subjective effort in relation to physical performance and working capacity. In *Psychology: From research to practice.* New York: Plenum Publishing.

Borg, G. 1982. Psychophysical bases of perceived exertion. *Medicine and Science in Sports and Exercise* 14:371–81.

Borg, G. 1982. A category scale with ratio properties for intermodal and interindividual comparisons. In Geissler, H. G. and P. Petzold (Eds.). *Psychophysical judgment and the process of perception.* Berlin: VEB Deutscher Verlag der Wissenschaften.

Borg, G. 1998. *Borg's perceived exertion and pain scaling method.* Champaign, IL: Human Kinetics.

Carr, M. G. 1945. The relationship between success in physical education and selected attitudes expressed in high school freshmen girls. *Research Quarterly* 16:176–91.

Chin, A., R. R. Bishu, and S. Halbeck. 1995. Psychophysical measures of exertion. Are they muscle group dependent. *Proceedings of the Human Factors Society,* 39, 694–698.

Dishman, R. K. 1978. Aerobic power, estimation of physical ability, and attraction to physical activity. *Research Quarterly* 49:285–92.

———. 1980. The influence of response distortion in assessing self-perceptions of physical ability and attitude toward physical activity. *Research Quarterly for Exercise and Sport* 51:286–98.

———. 1984. Chapter 29. Motivation and exercise adherence. In Silva, J. and R. Weinberg (Eds.). *Psychology foundation of sport.* Champaign, IL: Human Kinetics.

———. 1988. *Exercise adherence: Its impact on public health.* Champaign, IL: Human Kinetics.

———. 1990. Chapter 7. Determinants of participation in physical activity. In Bouchard, C. et al. (Eds.). *Exercise, fitness, and health: A consensus of current knowledge* (pp. 75–102). Human Kinetics: Champaign.

Dishman, R. K. and L. R. Gettman. 1981. Psychological vigor and self-perceptions of increased strength. *Medicine and Science in Sports and Exercise* 15:118.

Dishman, R. K. and W. Ickes. 1981. Self-motivation and adherence to therapeutic exercise. *Journal of Behavioral Medicine* 4:421–36.

Dishman, R. K., W. Ickes, and W. P. Morgan. 1980. Self-motivation and adherence to habitual physical activity. *Journal of Applied Social Psychology* 10:115–32.

Ebel, R. L. 1972. What are schools for? *Phi Delta Kappan* 54:3–7.

Edington, C. W. 1968. Development of an attitude scale to measure attitudes of high school freshmen boys toward physical education. *Research Quarterly* 39:505–12.

Foreyt, J. P. et al. In press. *Anorexia nervosa and bulimia nervosa.*

Fox, K. R., C. R. Corbin, and W. H. Couldry. 1985. Female physical estimation and attraction to physical activity. *Journal of Sport Psychology* 7:125–36.

Fox, K. R. Ed. 1997. *The physical self: From motivation to well-being.* Champaign: Human Kinetics.

Garcia, A. W. and A. C. King. 1991. Predicting long-term adherence to aerobic exercise: A comparison of two models. *Journal of Sport and Exercise Psychology* 13:394–410.

Garner, D. M. 1984. *The eating disorder inventory manual.* Odessa, FL: Psychological Assessment Resources.

Garner, D. M. and Garfinkel, P. E. 1979. The eating attitudes test: An index of the symptoms of anorexia nervosa. *Psychological Medicine* 10:273–279.

Garner, D. M. et al. 1982. The Eating Attitudes Test: Psychometric features and clinical correlates. *Psychological Medicine* 12:871–878.

Harris, B. 1968. Attitudes of students toward women's athletic competition. *Research Quarterly* 39:278–84.

Hidalgo, J. et al. 1997. A comprehensive lifting model: Beyond the NIOSH lifting equation. *Ergonomics* 40(9):916–927.

Jackson, A. S. et al. 1997. Role of physical work capacity and load weight on psychophysical lift ratings. *International Journal of Industrial Ergonomics* 20:181–190.

Jackson, A. S. and H. Osborn. 1983. Validity of isometric strength tests for predicting performance in underground coal mining tasks. Houston, TX: Employment Services, Shell Oil Company.

Jackson, A. S., M. L. Pollock, and A. Ward. 1980. Generalized equations for predicting body density of women. *Medicine and Science in Sports* 12:175–82.

Jackson, A. S. and R. M. Ross. 1997. *Understanding exercise for health and fitness.* 3d ed. Dubuque, IA: Kendall/Hunt.

Johnson, M. L. 1969. Construction of sportsmanship attitude scales. *Research Quarterly* 40:312–16.

Kappes, E. E. 1954. Inventory to determine attitudes of college women toward physical education and student services of the physical education department. *Research Quarterly* 25:429–38.

Karwowski, W. and N. Brokaw. 1992. Implications of the proposed revisions in a draft of the revised NIOSH lifting guide (1991) for job redesign: A field study. *Proceedings of the Human Factors Society 36th Annual Meeting* 36:659–663.

Koslowsky, M. et al. 1992. The factor structure and criterion validity of the short form of the Eating Attitudes Test. *Journal of Personality Assessment* 58(1):27–35.

Kenyon, G. S. 1968a. A conceptual model for characterizing physical activity. *Research Quarterly* 39:96–105.

———. 1968b. Six scales for assessing attitude toward physical activity. *Research Quarterly* 39:566–74.

———. 1968c. Values held for physical activity by selected urban secondary school students in Canada, Australia, England, and the United States. Washington, DC: U.S. Office of Education.

Kneer, M. E. 1971. Kneer attitude inventory and diagnostic statements. In *A practical approach to measurement in physical education.* Philadelphia, PA: Lea & Febiger.

Kowal, D. M., J. F. Patton, and J. A. Vogel. 1978. Psychological states and aerobic fitness of male and female recruits before and after basic training. *Aviation, Space, and Environmental Medicine* 49:603–6.

Krathwohl, D. R. 1964. *Taxonomy of education objectives handbook II. The affective domain.* New York: McKay.

Lakie, W. L. 1964. Expressed attitudes of various groups of athletes toward athletic competition. *Research Quarterly* 35:497–503.

McCue, B. F. 1953. Constructing an instrument for evaluating attitudes toward intensive competition in team games. *Research Quarterly* 24:205–10.

McGee, R. 1956. Comparison of attitudes toward intensive competition for high school girls. *Research Quarterly* 27:60–73.

Mercer, E. L. 1971. Mercer attitude scale. In *A practical approach to measurement in physical education.* Philadelphia, PA: Lea & Febiger.

Merkle, L. A. 1997. Factor analysis of the self-motivation inventory. Doctoral Dissertation, Department of Health and Human Performance, University of Houston, Houston, TX.

Neale, D. C. 1969. Physical fitness, self-esteem and attitudes toward physical activity. *Research Quarterly* 40:743–49.

NIOSH. 1981. *Work practices guide for manual lifting.* Washington, DC: U.S. Department of Health and Human Services.

Nunnally, J. C. 1978. *Psychometric theory.* New York: McGraw-Hill.

O'Bryan, M. H. and K. G. O'Bryan. 1979. Attitudes of males toward selected aspects of physical education. *Research Quarterly* 40:343–82.

Osgood, C. 1957. *The measurement of meaning.* Urbana, IL: University of Illinois Press.

Ostrow, A. C. 1996. *Directory of psychological tests in the sport and exercise sciences.* 2d ed. Morgantown, WV: Fitness Information Technology.

Penmon, M. M. 1971. Penmon physical education attitude inventory for inner-city junior high school girls. In *A practical approach to measurement in physical education.* Philadelphia, PA: Lea & Febiger.

Pollock, M. L., A. S. Jackson, and C. Foster. 1986. The use of the perception scale for exercise prescription. In *The perception of exertion in physical work* (pp. 161–176). Wenner-Gren Center, Stockholm, Sweden.

Pollock, M. L., J. H. Wilmore, and S. M. Fox III. 1984. *Exercise in health and disease.* Philadelphia, PA: W. B. Saunders.

Resnik, M. L. 1995. The generalizability of psychophysical ratings in predicting the perception of lift difficulty. *Proceedings of the Human Factors Society,* 39, 679–682.

Rhea, D. J. 1995. Risk factors for the development of eating disorders in ethnically diverse high school athlete and non-athlete urban populations. Doctoral Dissertation, Department of Health and Human Performance, University of Houston, Houston, TX.

Riddle, P. K. 1980. Attitudes, beliefs, behavioral intentions, and behaviors of men and women toward regular jogging. *Research Quarterly for Exercise and Sport* 51:663–74.

Safrit, M. J. 1981. *Evaluation in physical education.* Englewood Cliffs, NJ: Prentice-Hall.

Safrit, M. M., T. M. Wood, and R. K. Dishman. 1985. The factorial validity of the physical estimation and attraction scales for adults. *Journal of Sport Psychology* 7:166–90.

Schutz, R. W. et al. 1985. Inventories and norms for children's attitudes toward physical activity. *Research Quarterly for Exercise and Sport* 56:256–65.

Scott, P. M. 1953. Attitudes toward athletic competition in elementary school. *Research Quarterly* 24:353–61.

Seaman, J. A. 1970. Attitudes of physically handicapped children toward physical education. *Research Quarterly* 41:439–45.

Simon, J. A. and F. L. Smoll. 1974. An instrument for assessing children's attitudes toward physical education. *Research Quarterly* 45:407–15.

Slade, P. D. 1973. A short anorexic behavior scale. *British Journal of Psychiatry* 122:83–85.

Snider, J. G. and C. E. Osgood. 1969. *Semantic differential technique: A sourcebook.* Chicago, IL: Aldine.

Snook, S. H., R. A. Campanelli, and J. W. Hart. 1978. A study of three preventive approaches to low back injury. *Journal of Occupational Medicine* 20:478–481.

Snook, S. H. and V. M. Ciriello. 1991. The design of manual handling tasks: Revised tables of maximum acceptable weights and forces. *Ergonomics* 34:1197–1213.

Sonstroem, R. J. 1974. Attitude testing examining certain psychological correlates of physical activity. *Research Quarterly* 45:39, 103.

———. 1976. The validity of self-perceptions regarding physical and athletic ability. *Medicine and Science in Sports* 8:126–32.

———. 1978. Physical estimation and attraction scales: Rationale and research. *Medicine and Science in Sports* 10:97–102.

———. 1988. *Psychological models in exercise adherence: Its impact on public health.* Champaign, IL: Human Kinetics.

———. 1997. Chapter 1. The physical self-system: A mediator of exercise and self-esteem. In Fox, K. R. (Ed.), *The physical self: From motivation to well-being.* Champaign, IL: Human Kinetics.

Sonstroem, R. J. and K. P. Kampper. 1980. Prediction of athletic participation in middle school males. *Research Quarterly for Exercise and Sport* 51:685–94.

Sonstroem, R. J. and W. P. Morgan. 1989. Exercise and self-esteem: Rationale and model. *Medicine and Science in Sports and Exercise* 21:329–37.

Stevens, S. S. 1975. *Psychophysics: Introduction to its perceptual, neural, and social prospects.* New York: Wiley.

Stevens, S. S. and E. Galanter. 1957. Ratio scales and category scales for a dozen perceptual continua. *Journal of Experimental Psychology* 54:377–411.

Suminski, R. R. et al. 1998. Construct validation of a 10-item eating attitudes screening test for college students. In review.

Van Schoyck, R. S. and A. F. Grasha. 1981. Attentional style variations and athletic ability: The advantage of a sport-specific test. *Journal of Sport Psychology* 3:149–165.

Waters, T. R. et al. 1993. Revised NIOSH equation for the design and evaluation of manual lifting tasks. *Ergonomics* 7:749–766.

Wear, C. L. 1951. The evaluation of attitude toward physical activity as an activity course. *Research Quarterly* 22:114–26.

———. 1955. Construction of equivalent forms of an attitude scale. *Research Quarterly* 26:113–19.

Wier, L. T. and A. S. Jackson. 1989. Factors affecting compliance in the NASA/JSC fitness program. *Sports Medicine* 8:9–14.

Appendix A
SPSS Package of Programs

Presented here are some instructions on using the SPSS 8.0 for Windows Student Version. The appendix is written referencing the manuals for the standard version of SPSS 8.0 for Windows. The standard version and student version of SPSS do things in the same manner.

A few comments about the rapid change in SPSS versions and the inclusion of SPSS in this edition of our book are necessary. When the book was being revised most people were using SPSS version 6.1 (SPSS 6.1.) and SPSS version 7.5 (SPSS 7.5) was just starting to be used. The book was revised based on SPSS 6.1. A year later SPSS 6.1 and SPSS 7.5 were being used by many people and SPSS version 8.0 (SPSS 8.0) was just starting to be used. SPSS 6.1 and SPSS 7.5 differ considerably in regard to terms and windows since SPSS 6.1 operates on Windows 3.1 and SPSS 7.5 operates on Windows 95. SPSS 8.0 also operates on Windows 95 so it is very similar to SPSS 7.5. Since SPSS 8.0 for Windows Student Version is being distributed with the book, this appendix was revised from SPSS 6.1 to SPSS 8.0 procedures shortly before the book was published. If there are mistakes in this appendix, please accept our apologies.

If you have access to a standard version of SPSS you will probably not use the student version distributed with the book. No matter what version of SPSS you are using, most of the information in this appendix, particularly the SPSS 8.0 for Windows Statistical Procedures section applies to all versions. Users of SPSS 6.1 will find more differences than users of SPSS 7.5 between the procedures presented in this appendix and the procedures for the version being used.

SPSS 8.0 for Windows Basics

Click with the left button of the mouse unless otherwise indicated.

1. Getting in to SPSS
   A. Probably you must save your data on floppy disk. So, insert a floppy disk in the disk drive now.
   B. Click on **Start** and then **Programs.** Click on SPSS 8.0 Student Version for Windows.
   C. This opens the **Untitled-SPSS Data Editor** window.

2. Entering the data
   A. Click on the **SPSS Data Editor** window title bar to make it the active window if it is not already highlighted. Then define all variable names before entering the data.
   B. To define a variable name, double click on the dimmed title *var* at the top of the column you want to name. This opens the **Define Variable** dialog box.
   C. Enter a variable name in the **Variable Name:** text box. [NOTE] The following rules apply to valid variable names and file names: 1) one word, 2) maximum 8 characters, 3) no special characters (!,*,?, -, etc). You may backspace to correct typos. Then, click on **OK.** [NOTE] The first column you have not named is labeled **var00001.**
   D. After defining all variable names, put the cursor on the first empty cell (square) in the first column and click once. Type a score which is displayed in the space below the **SPSS Data Editor** menu. Each time you press **Enter,** the value appears with two decimal places in the cell, and the cursor will move down. If you press **Tab** rather than **Enter** the cursor will move to the right.
   E. If a person has no score for a variable (score is missing), enter it as a blank (enter no score and press **Enter** or **Tab**). The missing score is represented by a period (.).
   F. After entering all the data for a column or row, select the first cell in the next column (the next defined variable) or row (next person) by using the mouse to click on the cell or using the arrow keys on the keyboard or using the arrow keys on the right and bottom margin of the **SPSS Data Editor** to move to the cell.
   G. Do step D and E until all data are entered.

3. Saving the data
   A. After the last score is entered, click on **File** in the **SPSS Data Editor** menu and then click on **Save**. This opens the **Save Data As** dialog box. Enter a name for the data file (see rules in 2-C) in the **File name:** text box. Select **a:** drive in the **Save in:** dialog box.
   B. At the **Save as type:** make sure the file type is **SPSS (*.sav).** Now click on **Save.**
   C. [NOTE] The untitled window title will be changed to the drive and file name which you entered in 3-A. The **SPSS Data Editor** window is still displayed. If this does not happen, save the data again.

4. Editing the data
   A. You can change data values which are incorrect, so the data entered should be still displayed on the screen.
   B. Where there are mistakes, click on the incorrect score or use the arrow keys to move to the incorrect score, type in the correct value and press the enter key. After all editing, save the data again by clicking on **File** in the **SPSS Data Editor** menu and then click on **Save.** Make sure the **SPSS Data Editor,** and not an **Output** or **Syntax** window, is active because **Save** will save the active window. The data is saved (watch that light on the disk drive come on and off) and the **SPSS Data Editor** window is still displayed.

C. If you type in a score twice you may want to delete it rather than change it. If you leave out a score you may want to insert it. This may require deleting or inserting a row of data. To delete a row, click on the row to be deleted, the entire row will be highlighted, from the **SPSS Data Editor** menu click on **Edit** and then **Clear.** To insert a row (case) click on the row where you want to insert a row. Click on **Data** in the **SPSS Data Editor** menu, click on **Insert Case,** the row you clicked on and all rows below it will be moved down, enter the data. [NOTE] See the SPSS Base 8.0 User's Guide, pp. 45-66 for more details.

5. Analyzing the data
   A. After doing steps 2-4, click on **Statistics** in the **SPSS Data Editor** menu. And then, click on the statistical procedures which you want to use. [NOTE] For specific procedures, see the SPSS 8.0 for Windows Statistical Procedures later in this appendix.
   B. The results of the analysis are displayed on the screen. After this you can print the output if desired or do another analysis on the same data or enter another set of scores and analyze it or retrieve another set of scores on disk and analyze it.
6. Printing output of the analysis
   A. To print the contents of the output of the analysis, make sure the **SPSS Viewer** (called **SPSS Output Navigator** in SPSS 7.5) is the active window. If it is not the active window, click on **Window** in the menu bar and then **Output-SPSS Viewer.** The content of the active window is displayed on the right hand side of the screen (content pane). Use the arrow keys to move around the screen or move through the output objects on the left hand side of the screen (outline pane).
   B. The following two print options are available. The option **All Visible Output** is to print the entire file. This option prints all output including hidden items, and is the default for printing. The option **Selection** is to print just selected parts of the file. Highlight the part of the file to be printed by clicking on the output icon in the outline pane. Now print the highlighted contents. SPSS tends to produce many partially full pages of printout. To decrease the number of printed pages, use the **Selection** print option.
   C. From the **SPSS Viewer** menus click on **File** and then on **Print. . . .** This opens the print dialog box.
   D. The name of the file is shown in the dialog box. The printer name is also displayed. Click on the print option desired. By default, one copy is printed. If you want multiple copies, enter the number of copies you want to print. To print the contents, click on **OK.**
   E. If you want to print the content of the **SPSS Data Editor** window, do step B to D after activating the **SPSS Data Editor** window.
7. Getting out of SPSS
   A. To end an SPSS session, click of File under the **SPSS Data Editor** or the **SPSS Viewer** menu and then, click on **Exit SPSS** in the drop down menu.
   B. [NOTE] SPSS will ask whether you want to save the contents of the **Output** and **SPSS Data Editor** windows. If you want to save them, click on **Yes.** If not, click on **No.** Only if you want to keep the contents

on disk and you have not previously saved the contents do you need to click on **Yes.**

8. Retrieving data saved on disk (Data entered using **SPSS for Windows**)
   A. To open a saved data file, from the **SPSS Data Editor** menu click on **File.** This opens the **Open File** dialog box.
   B. Click on the drive **a:** or the drive to use from the **Look in:** dialog box and then click on **SPSS (*.sav)** in the **Files of type** list. You can click on a file from the list to use it or you can type in a filename. Then click on **Open.**
   C. The retrieved data file is displayed on the screen.
9. Importing and exporting data
   A. Importing data is using data not entered using SPSS (e.g. a word processing program).
   B. Exporting data is using data entered using SPSS in some other program (e.g. Excel).
   C. A file format must be selected when importing or exporting data. The file format can be either fixed field or free field. With fixed field the scores must be kept in specified columns and decimal points do not have to be entered whereas with free field the scores only have to be separated by one blank space and decimal points must be entered.
   D. [NOTE] For more detailed procedures on importing and exporting data, see the references below. Chapter 1 (pp. 105-114) of the SPSS 8.0 for Windows Brief Guide has the basic information.

Reference

SPSS Inc.(1998). *SPSS Base 8.0 User's Guide.* Chicago: SPSS Inc.
SPSS Inc. (1998). *SPSS 8.0 for Windows Brief Guide.* Chicago: SPSS Inc.

SPSS 8.0 for Windows Statistical Procedures

Click on Statistics under the **SPSS Data Editor** menu and all of the sub-headings are displayed. Click on one of the sub-headings of Statistics and all of procedures under the sub-heading are displayed.

SPSS has a **Help** feature which can be clicked on from the **SPSS for Windows** menu or any procedure menu. **Help** is excellent for learning about a statistical procedure or what to do in a procedure. To quit **Help,** click on **Cancel.**

1. Frequencies
   A. Click on **Statistics** under the **SPSS Data Editor** menu. Click on **Summarize.** Click on **Frequencies.** . . . This opens the **Frequencies** dialog box.
   B. Click on one or more variables from the left variable box. The variable(s) is highlighted. Click on the arrow button and the variable(s) will show in the Variables box. By default, frequency tables are displayed with the data listed in ascending order (small to large). If small score is a good score, the data should be displayed in descending order. Click on **Format,** click on **Descending** (value), and then click on **Continue** when through.
   C. To get optional descriptive and summary statistics, click on **Statistics. . .** in the **Frequencies** dialog box. Click on the statistics desired. Click on **Continue** when through.

D. To get optional bar charts or histograms, click on **Charts . . .** in the dialog box. Click on the charts or histograms desired in the dialog box. Then click on **Continue** when through.
E. Click on **OK** when ready to analyze the data.

2. Descriptives
   A. To get descriptive statistics, click on **Statistics** under the **SPSS Data Editor** menu. Click on **Summarize.** Click on **Descriptives. . . .** This opens the **Descriptives** dialog box.
   B. Click on one or more variables from the left variable box. The variable(s) is highlighted. Click on the arrow button and the variable(s) will show in the Variables box. By default, mean, standard deviation, minimum score, and maximum score will be displayed.
   C. If you want to get additional statistics, click on **Options. . .** under the Descriptive dialog box. This opens the **Descriptives:Options** dialog box.
   D. Click on one or more options from the box. Click on **Continue** when through.
   E. Click on **OK** when ready to analyze the data.

3. One-Sample T Test
   A. Click on **Statistics** under the **SPSS Data Editor** menu. Click on **Compare Means.** Then click on **One-Samples T Test. . . .**
   B. Click on one or more variables from the left variable box to use in the analysis. The variable(s) is highlighted. Click on the arrow button to put the variables in the **Test Variable(s)** box. Click on the value in **Test Value** and enter a number which is the value of the mean against which the variable is tested (the hypothesized population mean).
   C. By default, the confidence interval is 95%. If you want to change this value, click on **Options** in the dialog box then type the numeric value for the confidence interval. Click on **Continue** when through.
   D. Click on **OK** when ready to analyze the data.

4. Independent-Samples T Test (2 independent groups)
   A. Click on **Statistics** under the **SPSS Data Editor** menu. Click on **Compare Means.** Click on **Independent-Samples T Test . . . .**
   B. Click on one or more variables from the left variable box to use in the analysis. The variable(s) is highlighted. Click on the arrow button to put the variable(s) in the **Test Variable(s)** box.
   C. Click on a variable to form the two groups and then click on the arrow button for **Grouping Variable.**
   D. Then you must define a value of the grouping variable for each groups. To define groups, click on **Define Groups. . . .** Enter a value of the **Grouping Variable** which identifies (is the code for) **Group 1.** Click on **Group 2** and enter a value for **Group 2** for the grouping variable. Click on **Continue** when through.
   E. By default, the confidence interval is 95% (alpha = .05). See 3-C to change it.
   F. Click on **OK** when ready to analyze the data.

5. Paired-Samples T Test (dependent groups and repeated measures)
   A. Click on **Statistics** under the **SPSS Data Editor** menu. Click on **Compare Means.** Click on **Paired-Samples T Test. . . .**
   B. Click on (highlight) one of the variables from the left variable box and click on the arrow button. It appears as **Variable 1** under **Current Selections.** Click on another variable from the left variable box and click on the arrow button to move the pair to the **Paired Variables:** dialog box. Other pairs can be entered.
   C. To change the confidence interval, do step 3-C.
   D. Click on **OK** when ready to analyze the data.
6. One-Way ANOVA
   A. Click on **Statistics** under the **SPSS Data Editor** menu. Click on **Compare Means.** Click on **One-Way ANOVA. . . .**
   B. Click on (highlight) one or more variables from the left variable box to test (analyze). Click on the arrow button to put the variable(s) in the **Dependent List:** box.
   C. Click on a variable for forming groups and click on the arrow button to put it in the **Factor** box.
   D. Click on **Options . . . ,** click on **Descriptive** and any other options desired. When through click on **Continue.**
   E. If you want post hoc tests, click on **Post Hoc. . .** and click on one of the 18 tests. When through, click on **Continue.**
   F. Click on **OK** when ready to analyze the data.
7. Correlation
   A. Click on **Statistics** under the **SPSS Data Editor** menu. Click on **Correlate.** Click on **Bivariate. . . .**
   B. Click on (highlight) two or more variables from the left variable box in the **Bivariate Correlations** dialog box. Click on the arrow button and the variable(s) will show in the **Variables** box.
   C. Click on one or more of the correlation coefficients in the box (usually Pearson).
   D. If you want a significance test, click on the type of significance test: **One-tailed** or **Two-tailed** (usually two-tailed).
   E. Click on **OK** when ready to analyze the data.
8. Linear Regression
   A. Click on **Statistics** under the **SPSS Data Editor** menu. Click on **Regression.** Click on **Linear . . . .**
   B. Click on (highlight) a variable from the left variable box for the dependent score (the Y-score). Click on the arrow button to put the variable in the **Dependent** box. Click on (highlight) a variable(s) from the left variable box for the independent variable (the X-score(s)). Click on the arrow button to put the variable(s) in the **Independent** box.
   C. Click on one of the regression models (usually **Enter**).
   D. Click on **OK** when ready to analyze the data.
9. Reliability Analysis
   A. This analysis is in the SPSS standard version but not in the SPSS student version. See SPSS Professional Statistics CHAPTER 6.

B. Click on **Statistics** under the **SPSS Data Editor** menu. Click on **Scale.** Click on **Reliability Analysis. . . .**

C. Click on (highlight) a variable from the left variable box and then click on the arrow button to put it in the **Items:** box. Do this for at least two variables. These are the repeated measure like trials or days.

D. The **Model:** box should have **Alpha** in it. If it does not, click on the down arrow in **Model:** and click on **Alpha.**

E. Click on **Statistics. . .** in the **Reliability Analysis** dialog box if interested in additional information. You might click on **Item** under **Descriptives for** and **F Test** under **ANOVA Table.** Click on **Continue** when through.

F. Click on **OK** when ready to analyze the data.

10. Percentiles

A. In the SPSS 8.0 for Windows Brief Guide, see page 132.

B. Analyze the data using the **Frequencies** procedure making sure that the scores are listed from worst to best (ascending order if large score is good). If frequency tables are not desired, click on **Display Frequency Tables** to eliminate that option.

C. After getting into **Frequencies,** click on **Statistics. . .** in the **Frequencies** dialog box, and then on **Percentile(s): .**

D. The percentiles desired must be indicated by typing a number between 0 and 100 into the **percentile** box and then clicking on Add. Do this for each percentile desired. After indicating the percentiles desired, click on **Continue** to get out of **Statistics.**
Example: if the percentiles 5th, 10th, 15th, . . . , 100th are desired

Percentile Box	***Add***
5	click
10	click
.	.
.	.
.	.

E. The default for **Cut Points,** which is an alternative to typing in percentiles, is **10 equal groups** yielding the 10th, 20th, etc. percentiles.

F. Click on **OK** when ready to analyze the data.

11. Standard Scores (Z-scores)

A. See the SPSS 8.0 for Windows Brief Guide page 132 for more information.

B. A z-score for each variable analyzed is calculated assuming large score is good no matter whether the data is listed in ascending or descending order. If small score is good, the sign of the z-score is reversed (e.g. −2.0 should be 2.0).

C. Analyze the data using the **Descriptives** procedure.

D. Click on **Save standardized values as variables** in the **Descriptives** dialog box. Click on **OK** when ready to analyze the data. The z-scores are calculated, and added to the file containing the original data. A message does appear in the output that this occurred. The names of the z-scores will be the names of the original data with a z in front of them (e.g. for the original variable CAT the z-score is ZCAT). Z-score can be seen by displaying the data file on the screen and printing it if desired. The data file must be saved again for the z-scores to be saved with the data. In most cases, saving the z-scores is not necessary. If saving the z-scores, it might be good to save them as a new file so the original data file is retained as one file, and the original data with z-scores are another file. When saving the z-scores use **Save As.**

E. Sum of the z-scores can be obtained by using the Transformation procedure (presented in this document) and writing the formula for obtaining the sum of the z-scores allowing for the fact that some z-scores have the wrong sign (z-scores for scores when small score is good will have the wrong sign. For example, if the original data were X1, X2, and X3 the z-scores are ZX1, ZX2, and ZX3, ZSUM is the name used for the sum of the z-scores.

ZSUM = ZX1 + ZX2 − ZX3 (for X3, small score is good)

12. Transformation
    A. See chapter 9 and 12 in the SPSS 8.0 for Windows Brief Guide.
    B. Many things can be done with transformations such as change the values of variables, grouping variables, creating new variables, etc. Here we discuss creating new variables.
    C. Click on **Transform** and then **Compute. . . .** In the **Compute Variable** dialog box the name of the variable to be computed is typed in the **Target Variable:** box and the numeric expression or equation for calculating the target variable is typed in the **Numeric Expression:** box. Click on **OK** when ready to do the analysis. The computed variable is displayed on the screen and saved with the original data.
    D. Examples: There are 3 scores named X1, X2 and X3 on each person and for all three scores large score is good.
        (1) The sum (to be named SUMX) of the 3 scores is desired.
            Target Variable: SUMX
            Numerical Expression: X1 + X2 + X3
        (2) The data have already been analyzed calculating z-scores for each score (see Standard Score in this document). These z-scores are named ZX1, ZX2, and ZX3. The sum of the z-scores (to be named ZSUM) is desired.
            Target Variable: ZSUM
            Numerical Expression: ZX1 + ZX2 + ZX3

    NOTE: The target variable is added to the file containing the original data (and z-scores in the case of ZSUM). The data file must be saved again for the target variable to be saved with the rest of the file (see 11-D for save procedures).

13. Histogram
    A. See pages130–131 in the SPSS 8.0 for Windows Brief Guide.
    B. Click on **Graphs,** and then on **Histogram . . . .**
    C. In the **Histogram** dialog box, click on (highlight) a variable from the left variable box and then click on the arrow button so the variable is listed

under the **Variable:** box. Note a variable can be removed from the **Variable:** box by clicking on it and then on the arrow button.

D. If the default format for histogram is acceptable, click on **OK** to obtain the graph. The histogram is displayed in the **SPSS Viewer (SPSS Output Navigator** in SPSS 7.5). If you want to display the normal curve with the histogram, click on **Display normal curve** before clicking on **OK.** A normal curve will be superimposed over the histogram.

E. [NOTE] Double click on a graph in the **SPSS Viewer** to bring it in the **SPSS Chart Editor.** Double clicking on a graph created from interactive graphics activates the chart manager. The **SPSS Chart Editor** on the chart manager can be used to edit the chart. See chapters 6 through 8 and appendices A and B in the SPSS 8.0 for Windows Brief Guide for more details.

F. By default the histogram has bars showing the data divided into around 10 evenly spaced intervals. Usually 10-20 intervals are used with continuous data putting 2-5 different scores in an interval (e.g. 15-17 is interval size = 3). The base intervals of the histogram in the **SPSS Chart Editor** can be changed. See chapter 36 in the SPSS Base 8.0 User's Guide for details.

14. Line Chart (similar to frequency polygon)
    A. In the SPSS Base 8.0 User's Guide see pages 391-424.
    B. Click on **Graphs** and then on **Line. . . .**
    C. In the **Line Charts** dialog box click on **Simple** line chart and **Summaries for groups of cases.** Then click on **Define,** click on (highlight) the variable from the left variable box to use, click on the arrow button to put the highlighted variable in the **Category Axis:** box, and click on **N of cases.** Click on **OK** when ready to obtain the graph. The line chart is displayed in the **SPSS Viewer** (see Histogram for details on editing the chart).
    D. By default the line chart has the data divided into around 15 intervals for the X-axis. Usually 10-20 labels (intervals) are used with continuous data putting 2-5 different score values in an interval (e.g., 15-17 is interval size = 3). The labels (intervals) for the X-axis can be altered. See chapter 36 in the SPSS Base 8.0 User's Guide for details.

15. Scatterplot
    A. See pages 155-161 in the SPSS 8.0 for Windows Brief Guide.
    B. Click on **Graphs,** then **Scatter . . . ,** and then **Simple** in the **Scatterplot** dialog box.
    C. Now click on **Define.** Click on (highlight) a variable from the left variable box and then click on the arrow button to put it in the **X Axis:** box. Do the same thing for a second variable to put it in the **Y Axis:** box.
    D. Click on **OK** when ready to obtain the graph.
    E. The scatterplot is displayed in the **SPSS Viewer** (see Histogram for details on editing the charts).

Appendix B Computer Calculations

This section provides major equations used in the book. These equations are written to be compatible for use with database and spreadsheet microcomputer programs. They were used and checked for accuracy on a microcomputer database program. You will need to examine your program documentation to make the equations compatible with the program you have. The microcomputer mathematical operands are addition +; subtraction −; multiplication *; and division /.

1.0 Some Common Conversions

Weight in pounds (WTLB) and kilograms (WTKG). Height in inches (HTIN), centimeters (HTCM), and in meters (HTM). Body Mass Index (BMI).

WTKG = WTLB/2.2

WTLB = WTKG * 2.2

HTCM = HTIN * 2.54

HTIN = HTCM/2.54

HTM = HTCM/100

BMI = (WTKG/(HTM * HTM))

1.1 Calculation Examples

Subject	WTLB	WTKG	HTIN	HTCM	HTM	BMI
Jim	208	94.54	70	177.8	1.778	29.91
Jane	164	74.54	64	162.6	1.625	28.21
Bob	168	76.36	72	182.9	1.828	22.83
Mary	124	56.36	66	167.6	1.676	20.05

2.0 $\dot{V}O_2$ Calculations

2.1 Common Calculations

$\dot{V}O_2$ calculations when expressed as ml/kg/min, $\dot{V}O_2$ ml/min, and METs. The basic equations are

VO2KG = (VO2ML/WTKG) * 1000

METS = VO2KG/3.5

2.1.1 Calculation Examples

Subject	VO2ML	VO2KG	METS
Jim	2400	25.384	7.25
Jane	2354	31.578	9.02
Bob	3679	48.177	13.76
Mary	3258	57.803	16.51

2.2 Power Output

Power output (PO) calculations (ACSM 1991; Ross & Jackson 1990) cycle ergometer from kilopond meters per minute (KPM) to $\dot{V}O_2$ (ml/min).

PO = (2 * KPM) + 300

Treadmill from walking speed in miles per hour (MPH) and treadmill elevation (%) (GRADE) to $\dot{V}O_2$ (ml/kg/min)

Total Work Method (Ross & Jackson 1986; Ross & Jackson 1990)

POTW = ((262.5 + (21 * GRADE)) * (MPH/60))

ACSM Method (ACSM 1991)

POACSM = (((0.1 * 26.8 * MPH) + 3.5) + ((26.8 * MPH * 1.8) * (GRADE/100)))

2.2.1 Calculation Examples

Subject	KPM	PO	Grade	MPH	POACSM	POTW
Jim	300	900	3	3.4	17.5	18.4
Jane	450	1200	4	3.5	19.6	20.2
Bob	1200	2700	10	3.8	32.0	29.9
Mary	900	2100	12	3.7	34.8	31.7

2.3 Maximal Treadmill Time

$\dot{V}O_2$ Max (ml/kg/min) from maximal treadmill time in minutes (BKT or BRT) and cardiac health status (CHS) where 0 represents individuals with angina pectoris, previous heart attack, or heart bypass surgery, and 1 represents healthy individuals.

Balke Protocol (Pollock et al. 1976)

BKVO2 = 14.99 + (1.444 * BKT)

Bruce Protocol (Foster et al. 1984)

BRVO2 = 13.30 − (0.03 * BRT) + (0.297 * (BRT*BRT)) − (0.0077 * (BRT*BRT*BRT)) + (4.2 * CHS)

2.3.1 Calculation Examples

Subject	BKT	BRT	CHS	BKVO2	BRVO2
Jim	7	6	0	25.1	22.1
Jane	12	9	0	32.3	31.5
Bob	23	12	1	48.2	46.6
Mary	28	16	1	55.4	61.5

2.4 Maximal Distance Run Test

Cueton's 1-mile test uses: mile time (T), age (in years) (AGE); body mass index (BMI), and gender (G) coded 0 for female and 1 for male. The equation is

Mile VO_2/Max Equation

$$\dot{V}O_2\ \text{Max} = 108.94 - (8.41 \times T) + (0.34 \times T^2) + (0.21 \times \text{Age} \times G) - (0.84 \times \text{BMI})$$

2.4.1 Calculation Example

Subject	MILE TIME (T)	AGE	BMI	GENDER (G)	VO2MAX
Joe	9.33	17	19.8	0	43.4
Jane	10.22	16	20.1	1	45.0
Tom	8.65	15	18.2	0	46.3
Mary	10.25	18	22.3	1	43.5

3.0 Submaximal Models

3.1 Single-Stage Model

The single-stage model (Åstrand & Ryhming 1954; Ross & Jackson 1990) uses age (AGE), one submaximal power output (POTW), and exercise heart rate (HR). The term SEX represents a 0 for women and 1 for men.

Single-Stage Equation

VO2KG = (POTW * ((220 − AGE − 73 − (SEX * 10))/(HR − 73 − (SEX * 10))))

3.1.1 Calculation Examples

Subject	POTW	AGE	SEX	HR	VO2KG
Jim	18.44	52	0	145	24.3
Jane	20.21	55	1	148	25.5
Bob	29.92	43	1	135	54.1
Mary	31.73	32	0	130	64.0

3.2 Multi-Stage Model

The multi-stage model (Golding et al. 1989; Ross & Jackson 1990) uses age, two submaximal power output values (low level = PO1, high level = PO2), and two exercise heart rates (low level = HR1, high level = HR2). We have split the equation into two parts. The first step is to compute the power output exercise heart rate slope (SLOPE) (i.e., the unit increase in power output per beat increase in heart rate). The second equation estimates the above $\dot{V}O_2$ Max (VO2KG) by using the slope to estimate. The above $\dot{V}O_2$ unit of measurement is dependent upon the method used to compute power output.

Multi-Stage Equations

SLOPE = ((PO2 − PO1) / (HR2 − HR1))

VO2KG = PO2 + (SLOPE * (220 − AGE − HR2))

3.2.1 Calculation Examples

Subject	AGE	PO2	PO1	HR2	HR1	SLOPE	VO2KG
Jim	52	18.4	14.9	142	125	0.2058	23.8
Jane	55	22.0	18.4	149	130	0.1894	25.0
Bob	43	29.2	22.0	138	122	0.4500	46.7
Mary	32	29.2	22.0	135	118	0.4235	51.6

3.3 Rockport Walk Test

The variables needed are age (AGE), weight in pounds (WTLB), mile walk time in minutes (WMILE), and exercise heart rate (HR) measured after walk. The term SEX represents a 0 for women and 1 for men.

Rockport Equation

VO2KG = 139.168 − (0.388 * AGE) − (0.077 * WTLB) − (3.265 * WMILE) − (0.156 * HR) + (SEX * 6.318)

3.3.1 Calculation Examples

Subject	WTLB	SEX	WMILE	HR	VO2KG
Jim	208	1	18.20	162	18.3
Jane	164	0	17.60	174	26.9
Bob	168	1	12.10	122	57.3
Mary	124	0	12.30	118	58.6

3.4 BYU Jog Test

The variables needed are weight in kilograms (WTKG), mile jog time in minutes (JMILE), and exercise heart rate (HR) measured after the jog. The term SEX represents a 0 for women and 1 for men.

BYU Equation

VO2KG = 100.5 − (0.164*WTKG) − (1.438 * JMILE) − (0.193 * HR) + (SEX * 8.344)

3.4.1 Calculation Examples

Subject	WTKG	SEX	JMILE	HR	VO2KG
Jim	94.54	1	14.20	162	33.3
Jane	74.54	0	15.80	174	40.3
Bob	76.36	1	8.65	122	60.3
Mary	56.36	0	9.20	118	55.3

3.5 Nonexercise Models

The variables used for the nonexercise models include age (AGE), self-report exercise level (EX, score from Figure 8.15), percent body fat (%fat) or BMI.

3.5.1 Percent Fat Equations

Men—University of Houston Percent Body Fat Nonexercise

VO2MAX = 47.820 − (0.259 × AGE) − (0.216 × %fat) + (3.275 × AR) − (0.082 × %fat × AR)

Women—University of Houston Percent Body Fat Nonexercise

VO2MAX = 45.628 − (0.265 × AGE) − (0.309 × %fat) + (2.175 × AR) − (0.044 × %fat × AR)

3.5.2 BMI Equations

Men—University of Houston BMI Nonexercise

VO2MAX = 55.688 − (0.362 × AGE) − (0.331 × BMI) + (4.310 × AR) − (0.096 × BMI × AR)

Women—University of Houston BMI Nonexercise

VO2MAX = 44.310 − (0.326 × AGE) − (0.227 × BMI) + (4.471 × AR) − (0.135 × BMI × AR)

3.5.3 Calculation Examples—Men Nonexercise

Subject	AGE	%FAT	BMI	AR	VO2 %FAT	VO2BMI
Joe	35	14.8	22.1	7	50.0	51.0
John	40	25.2	28.6	2	34.5	34.9
Mike	42	19.3	24.3	5	41.3	42.3
Tom	25	15.6	23.4	6	50.0	51.3

3.5.4 Calculation Examples—Women Nonexercise

Subject	AGE	%FAT	BMI	AR	VO2 %FAT	VO2BMI
Debbie	29	19.8	23.4	7	41.0	38.7
Jane	25	25.3	22.1	5	36.5	38.6
Mary	36	28.4	28.6	4	31.0	28.5
Dina	41	29.6	24.3	3	28.2	29.0

4.0 Body Composition

This section provides equations for estimating percent body fat from skinfolds for children and adults and computing a weight goal for a desired percent body fat level. The weight goal method is only suitable for adults. These equations were written to be compatible for use with database and spreadsheet microcomputer programs. They were used and checked for accuracy on a microcomputer database program. You will need to examine your program documentation to make the equations compatible with the program you have.

4.1 Estimating Percent of Children (Lohman 1992)

The only values needed to estimate the percent body fat (%FAT) of children are the sum of the triceps and calf skinfolds (SUM). Separate equations are needed for boys and girls. The equations are

Boys

%FAT = (0.735*SUM) + 1.0

Girls

%FAT = (0.610*SUM) + 5.0

4.1.1 Calculation Example Boys

Student	Triceps	Calf	SUM	%Fat
Jimmy	4	3	7	6.1
Tommy	10	11	21	16.4
Tony	15	11	26	20.1
Chris	20	14	34	26.0

4.1.2 Calculation Example Girls

Student	Triceps	Calf	SUM	%Fat
Mary	4	3	7	9.3
Judy	10	11	21	17.8
Debra	15	11	26	20.9
Sue	25	20	45	32.5

4.2 Estimating Percent of Adults (Jackson & Pollock 1978; Jackson et al. 1980)

The generalized equations for adults use age in combination with the sum of seven skinfolds (Σ7) or the sum of three skinfolds (Σ3). The sum of three for males includes chest, abdomen, and thigh skinfolds. The sum of three for women includes triceps, suprailium, and thigh skinfolds. The Siri equation was used to convert body density to percent body fat. The equations are

Men

BDM7 = 1.11200000 − (.00043499*Σ7) + (.00000055* (Σ7*Σ7)) − (.00028826*AGE)

BDM3 = 1.10938000 − (.0008267*Σ3) + (.00000016(*Σ3*Σ3)) − (.0002574*AGE).

Women

BD = 1.0970 − (.0004697*Σ7) + (.00000056*(Σ7*Σ7)) − (.00012828*AGE)

$$BD = 1.099421 - (.0009929*\Sigma 3) + (.00000023*(\Sigma 3*\Sigma 3)) - (.0001392*AGE)$$

Siri Equation

$$SIRI\ \%FAT = ((495/BD) - 450)$$

4.2.1 Calculation Example—Men

Subject	Σ7	Σ3	Age	Σ7-BD	Σ3-BD	Σ7-%Fat	Σ3-Fat
John	85	42	25	1.07179	1.06851	11.8	13.3
Mike	95	46	30	1.06699	1.06397	13.9	15.2
Tom	150	65	35	1.04904	1.04731	21.9	22.6
Paul	191	78	42	1.03687	1.03506	27.4	28.2

4.2.2 Calculation Example—Women

Subject	Σ7	Σ3	Age	Σ7-BD	Σ3-BD	Σ7-%Fat	Σ3-Fat
Jane	85	42.0	25	1.05791	1.05464	17.9	19.4
Judy	95	46.0	30	1.05358	1.05006	19.8	21.4
Kim	134	56.0	35	1.03963	1.03967	26.1	26.1
Dina	149	62.0	42	1.03406	1.03290	28.7	29.2

4.3 Computing Weight Goal

The weight goal is a method of computing the person's weight for a desired percent fat level. This should only be used with adults. You must know the person's current percent body fat (%FAT) and body weight (WT). From this information, fat-free weight (FFWT) is computed and used to compute what the person's body weight would be (GOAL) for a desired percent body fat level (D %FAT). The equations are

$$FFWT = WT - (WT* (\%FAT/100))$$

$$GOAL = FFWT / (1 - (D\ \%FAT/100)).$$

4.3.1 Calculation Example Weight Goal

Subject	WT	%Fat	D %Fat	FFWT	GOAL
Jim	278	38.2	20	171.8	214.8
Jane	165	34.2	25	108.6	144.8
Bob	176	22.5	20	136.4	170.5
Mary	132	26.7	22	96.8	124.0

Glossary

A

AAHPERD HRFT One of the first health-related fitness tests sponsored by AAHPERD 444

AAHPERD YFT A youth fitness test developed by a group of physical educators who met and selected tests on the basis of logic 323

Absolute Endurance Test An endurance test that uses a weight load constant for all subjects tested 214

Accuracy Test A test in which the student projects an object at a target for a score 388

ACSM The American College of Sports Medicine, which is a leading exercise science professional organization 14, 247

Activity Factor A semantic differential factor that involves motion; measured by adjective pairs such as fast-slow and excitable-calm 455

Aerobic Fitness Physical working capacity of VO_2 Max 241, 326

Affective Domain A system used to categorize affective behavior to help teachers formulate affective objectives 450

Agility The ability to change the direction of the body or body parts rapidly 225

Analysis of Variance A statistical technique for dividing total test variance into parts 89, 99

Anorexia Nervosa Excessive diet and exercise resulting in extreme weight loss 464

Attitude A feeling about a particular object, such as a physical object, a certain type of person, or a social institution 450

Authentic Assessment Evaluating students in a real-life or authentic setting 151

B

Balance The ability to maintain body position 231

Basic Physical Ability A trait, more general than a psychomotor skill, that provides the foundation for the successful execution of many different psychomotor skills; also called *psychomotor ability* 182

Bell-Shaped Curve See *normal curve* 46

Bioelectrical Impedance Method (BIA) A technique for measuring body composition based on the principle that the electrical resistance of the body to a mild electric current is related to total body water. 313

Body Cathexis Scale A self-report scale used to measure body image 465

Body Composition The classification of the body into fat weight and lean body weight 280

Body Density A value used to calculate percentage body fat; calculated with the underwater weighing method, it is determined by the following formula 284:

$$\text{Body density} = \frac{\text{weight}}{\text{volume}}$$

Body Image The attitude one has toward the body and the manner in which one's own body is perceived 465

Body Mass Index (BMI) The ratio of weight and height and defined as BMI = Weight/Height^2, where weight is in kilograms and height is in meters 292

Bulimia Nervosa Excessive intake of food accompanied by methods to prevent weight gain, such as vomiting or using laxatives 465

C

Cardiorespiratory Function The ability to continue work; depends on efficient respiratory (lungs) and cardiovascular (heart and blood vessels) systems 223

Cardiovascular Disease The leading cause of death of Americans. The most common are heart disease and strokes 16

Central Tendency The tendency of scores to be concentrated at certain points; measures of central tendency that include the mode, median, and mean 47

Chrysler Fund-AAU A youth physical fitness test that includes both motor fitness and health-related fitness test items. The test is administered at Indiana University (IU) 335

Circulatory-Respiratory Endurance A component of motor fitness characterized by moderate contractions of large muscle groups over long periods of time 223

Classification Index A mathematical formula used to combine age, height, and weight to predict excellence in the ability to perform a wide variety of motor tasks 181

Closed Kinetic Chain When the end segment or joint meets with external resistance that prevents or restrains free movement 200

Coefficient of Determination The amount of variability in one measure explained by the other measure 76

Completion Item A knowledge test item that asks students to complete or fill in the blanks in the item 427

Concurrent Validity The degree to which scores on a test correlate with scores on an accepted standard 124

Construct Validity The degree to which a test measures some part of a whole skill or an abstract trait 126

Continuous Scores Scores with the potential for an infinite number of values 40

Coronary Heart Disease A major form of cardiovascular disease that affects coronary arteries, the arteries that deliver oxygen and nutrients to the heart muscle (myocardium). A build up of plaque restricts the blood flow through the coronary arteries 17

Correlation A mathematical technique for determining the relationship between two sets of scores 78

Correlation Coefficient A value between −1.0 and 1.0 that indicates the degree of relationship between two sets of measures 75

Criterion-Referenced Standard A standard that explicitly defines the task to be achieved 6

Criterion Score An individual's recorded score; the score used to represent a person's ability 106, 130

Criterion Variable See *dependent variable* 78

Cross-Validation If the prediction formula and standard error seem acceptable, the prediction formula should be proven on a second group of individuals similar to the first 81

Curvilinear Relationship A relationship between two measures that is best described by a curved line 77

Cycle Ergometer A machine that regulates the work performed while cycling; workload can be accurately altered by increasing or decreasing the resistance on the ergometer 250

D

Decision Validity An indication of the validity of a criterion-referenced test using logic 130

Dependent Variable The Y variable of a regression equation and is often called the criterion variable 78

Desired Weight A body weight determined for a specified percent body fat 309

Discrete Scores Scores with the potential for a limited number of specific values 40

Discrimination Index A value indicating how well a knowledge test item differentiates between the high- and low-scoring students 437

Discrimination Test A test designed to identify different ability groups based on test scores 420

Distance-Run Tests Running tests used to evaluate cardiorespiratory function; normally of 1 mile or longer in distance, or 9 minutes or more in duration 261, 326

Domain-Referenced Validity An indication of the validity of a criterion-referenced test expressed as a numeric value 130

Dynamic Balance The ability to maintain equilibrium while moving from one point to another 230

E

Essay Test A test that asks students to respond to questions in writing 419, 428

Evaluation A decision-making process that involves (1) the collection of suitable data (measurement); (2) a judgment of the value of these data against a standard; and (3) a decision based on these data and standards xiii, 4

Evaluation Factor A semantic differential factor that involves a degree of "goodness"; measured by adjective pairs such as good-bad and beautiful-ugly 455

F

False Negative Stress Test The stress test fails to identify coronary heart disease in patients who have heart disease 247

False Positive Stress Test The stress test results indicate coronary artery disease in patients who do not have heart disease 247

Fat Weight In measuring a person's body, the weight in pounds that is body fat 309

Fat-Free Weight See *lean body weight* 309

Final Grade The grade assigned at the end of a unit or grading period 147

Flexibility The range of motion about a joint 229, 338

Formative Evaluation The process of judging achievement at the formative stages of instruction to determine the degree of mastery and to pinpoint that part of the task yet to be mastered; often used as a form of student feedback 5

Frequency Polygon A graph of a frequency distribution with scores along the horizontal axis and frequencies along the vertical axis 46

G

General Motor Ability The theory that individuals who are highly skilled on one motor task will be highly skilled on other motor tasks 181

Generalized Equations Equations that can be validly used with heterogeneous samples 300

H

Health-Related Physical Fitness A scientific body of knowledge that links the positive effects of regular, vigorous exercise with the prevention of degenerative disease 4, 324

Hydrostatic Weighing The underwater weighing method used to determine body volume, which is then used with dry land body weight to calculate body density 285

I

Independent Variable The X variable of a regression equation and often called the predictor variable 78

Individual with Disability An individual requiring special program or testing considerations due to limited ability to perform certain activities 173

Instructional Objectives Objectives that make clear to both students and teacher what is to be accomplished, including: (1) the task to be learned; (2) the conditions under which the task will be performed; and (3) the criterion-referenced standard that will be used to evaluate the achievement xiii

Internal-Consistency Reliability Coefficient The degree to which an individual's scores are unchanged within a day 99

Interval Scores Scores that have a common unit of measure between consecutive scores but not a true zero point 40

Intraclass Correlation Coefficient A correlation coefficient that estimates test reliability; derived with analysis of variance 100

Isokinetic Strength Strength that is measured by recording the force exerted through the entire range of motion 214

Isometric Strength Strength that is measured by recording the force exerted against an immovable object 202

Isotonic Strength Strength that involves moving an object through a defined range of motion; often measured with a 1-RM test, which is the maximum weight that can be lifted during one repetition 211

Item A question or statement on a knowledge test; one of the tests in a battery of tests 418

Item Analysis An item-by-item analysis of a knowledge test to identify valid questions 438

Item Difficulty The difficulty of a knowledge test item; the percentage of a group that correctly answers an item 436

K

Kappa Coefficient An indication of the reliability of a criterion-referenced test; one of two commonly used 117

Kiloponds (kp) The unit of measurement used to quantify resistance on a bicycle ergometer; kp represents the unit of resistance in kilograms 250

Kinesthesis The ability to perceive the body's position in space and the relationship of its parts 232

Knowledge Test A paper-and-pencil test that measures knowledge 418

L

Lean Body Weight The weight of the body with the fat tissue removed; also called *fat-free weight* 284

Leptokurtic Curve More sharply peaked than a normal curve 46

Line of Best Fit See *regression line* 72

Linear Relationship A relationship between two measures that is best described by a straight line 77

Logical Validity A validity technique based on the subjectively established fact that the test measures the wanted attribute 123

M

Mass Testability The degree to which a large number of students can be tested in a short period of time 168

Mastery Test A test that determines how well students have mastered the material 420

Matching Item A knowledge test item that asks students to match columns of questions and answers 426

Maximal Exercise Test The objective is to increase systematically exercise intensity until the subject reaches exhaustion 252

Maximal Oxygen Uptake ($\dot{V}O_2$ Max) The amount of oxygen one utilizes during exhausting work; the criterion for validating field tests of cardiorespiratory function 252

Maximal Stress Test A diagnostic medical test that systematically increases exercise to determine physical working capacity and changes in exercise blood pressure and the exercise EKG. This is an initial screening test for cardiovascular disease 253

Mean A measure of central tendency, or average; obtained by dividing the sum of the scores by the number of scores 50

Measurement The collection of information on which a decision is based 4

Median A measure of central tendency, or average; the score below which 50% of a group scored 48

MET A unit used to quantify oxygen consumption. A MET equals a $\dot{V}O_2$ of 3.5 $ml \cdot kg^{-1} min^{-1}$ and is the oxygen uptake at rest 242

Mode A measure of central tendency, or average; the most frequent score for a group of people 48

Motor Educability The ability to learn motor skills easily and well 181

Motor Fitness A category of the psychomotor domain that is defined by the component's strength, power, and endurance 323

Motor Skill The level of proficiency achieved on a specific motor task; also called *psychomotor skill* 181

Multicomponent Model The method used to measure percent body fat from the underwater weighing method. The model assumes that the density of fat is 0.9 $g \cdot cc^{-1}$ but also uses total body water and bone density to adjust density estimate of the fat-free weight component 291

Multiple-Choice Item A knowledge test item that asks students to select an answer from three or more provided answers 423

Multiple Correlation The correlation between a criterion and two or more predictors that have been mathematically combined to maximize the correlation between the criterion and predictors 81

Multiple Prediction The prediction of the value of one measure based on the performance of two or more other measures; also called *multiple regression* 81

Multi-Stage Exercise Test A method used to estimate $\dot{V}O_2$ Max from two or more submaximal workloads and heart rates 256

Muscular Endurance The ability to persist in physical activity or to resist muscular fatigue 338

Muscular Power Traditionally, the maximum force released in the shortest possible time; more appropriately, the rate at which work can be performed by involved muscle groups 216

Muscular Strength The maximum force a muscle group can exert during a brief period of time 198, 338

N

Natural Breaks A grading technique that assigns grades by breaks in the distribution of scores 142

Negatively Skewed Curve Long, low tail on the left, indicating few students received low scores 46

Nominal Scores Scores that cannot be ordered from best to worst 40

Normal Curve A symmetrical curve centered around a point that is the mean score; also called *bell-shaped curve* 68

Norm-Referenced Standard A standard that judges a performance in relation to the performance of other members of a well-defined group 6

Norms Performance standards based on the scores of a group of people 7

O

Obesity The excessive accumulation of fat weight 285

Objective A test where two or more people score the same test and assign similar scores 4

Objective Evaluation A test in which the student's performance yields a score without a value judgment by the scorer (see *subjective measure*); also a test that asks students to respond to questions by selecting one of two or more provided answers 392

Objective Tests True–false, multiple choice, matching, and the like 419

Objectivity The degree to which multiple scorers agree on the magnitude of scores 96

Open Kinetic Chain When the limb segment is free in space 200

Ordinal Scores Scores that can be ordered from best to worst but that do not have a common unit of measure 40

Overweight That weight that exceeds the "normal" weight based on gender, height, and frame size 285

Oxygen Uptake The amount of oxygen one uses for a given level of exercise 242

P

Percent Body Fat That proportion of total weight that is fat weight 284

Percentile A score that has a specified percentage of scores below it fixed 56

Percentile Rank A score value that indicates the percentage of scores below a given score 54

Physical Best The health-related fitness test sponsored by AAHPERD. In January 1994, the test was discontinued when AAHPERD decided to endorse the Prudential FITNESSGRAM® health-related fitness test 177, 325

Platykurtic Curve Less sharply peaked curve 46

Plethysmograph A device, or "body box," used for measuring the volume of air in the body 286

Positively Skewed Curve The tail of the curve is on the right 46

Posttest Procedures The analysis and recording of test scores 172

Potency Factor A semantic differential factor that involves the strength of the concept; measured by adjective pairs such as strong-weak and smooth-rough 455

Power The rate at which work is performed; calculated with the following formula: 216

$$\text{Power} = \frac{\text{work}}{\text{time}}$$

Power Output The rate of work used to define exercise intensity. The power output for a cycle ergometer is increased by placing more resistance on the flywheel and increasing the cycle peddling rate. The power output for treadmill exercise is increased by increasing treadmill speed and increasing the grade 249

Prediction The estimating of the value of one measure based on the value of one or more other measures; see also *multiple regression* 78

Predictive Validity The degree to which one measure can predict performance on a second measure 125

Predictor Variable See *independent variable* 78

President's Challenge A test battery with slight modifications of the AAHPERD YFT and consisting of five tests 335

Pretest Planning The procedures that must be followed before a test is administered; includes knowing the test, developing test procedures and directions, and preparing the students and the testing facility 170

Prevalence Refers to the disease rate within a defined group of people (cohort). It is the percentage of individuals within the group affected 10

Program Evaluation Determination of the extent to which a program achieves the standards and objectives set forth for it 156

Proportion of Agreement Coefficient An indication of the reliability of a criterion referenced test; one of two commonly used 116

Prudential FITNESSGRAM® The leading American health-related fitness test. The test was developed at the Cooper Institute for Aerobics Research, Dallas, TX 337

Psychomotor Ability See *basic physical ability* 182

Psychomotor Skill See *motor skill* 181

Psychophysical A term used to describe scientific methods used to integrate psychological and physical parameters. An example of a psychophysical test is Borg's RPE scale 469

R

Range A measure of the variability or heterogeneity in a set of scores; the difference between the largest and smallest scores 51

Rank Order Straightforward, norm-referenced method of grading 143

Rank Order Correlation Coefficient *Rho* or *Spearman's rho;* calculated when the scores for the two sets of scores are ranks 76

Rank-Order Grading A grading technique that assigns grades after ordering the scores 143

Rating of Perceived Exertion Scale (RPE) A scale developed by Dr. G. Borg of Stockholm, Sweden that is used to rate the intensity of exercise 253, 463

Rating Scale A set of standards or a checklist for measuring performance subjectively 392

Ratio Scores Scores that have a common unit of measure between consecutive scores and a true zero point 40

Regression Line Often termed the "line of best fit" and is the line that is defined by predicting the dependent variable from the independent variable 72, 78

Reliability The degree of consistency with which a test measures what it measures 96

Residual Lung Volume The amount of air remaining in the lungs after a full expiration. This measurement is used when estimating body density by the underwater weighing method 286

S

Semantic Differential Scales A method of measuring attitude by having someone react toward an object or concept by responding to bipolar adjective pairs 454

Short-Answer Item A knowledge test item that requires the student to write a short answer to the item 428

Simple Frequency Distribution An ordered listing of a set of scores, complete with the frequency of each score 43

Simple Prediction (Regression) The prediction of the value of one measure, the dependent variable, using another measure, the independent variable 78

Single-Stage Exercise Test A method used to estimate $\dot{V}O_2$ Max from one submaximal workload and heart rate 258

Skewed Curve A curve that is not symmetrical; see *normal curve* 68

Skill Test A test that measures physical skill, not fitness 388

Skinfold Calipers An instrument used to measure the thickness of subcutaneous fat tissue 295

Skinfold Fat The subcutaneous fat tissue that lies just below the skin 330

Speed The ability to move rapidly 222, 326

Stability Reliability Coefficient The degree to which an individual's scores are unchanged from day to day 98

Standard Deviation A measure of the variability, or spread, of a set of scores around the mean 51

Standard Error of the Mean A value indicating the amount of variation to expect in the mean if subjects were tested again 83

Standard Error of Measurement The amount of error expected in a measured score 80, 113

Standard Error of Prediction A value indicating the amount of error to expect in a predicted score 79

Standard Score A test score calculated using the test mean and standard deviation; usually expressed as a *z* or *T* 60

Static Balance The ability to maintain total body equilibrium while standing in one spot 230

Subjective A test lacking a standardized scoring system, which introduces a source of measurement error 4

Subjective Evaluation A test in which the scorer must make a value judgment before assigning the performer a score 392

Submaximal Exercise Test A test used to evaluate cardiorespiratory function by measuring one's ability to perform work at submaximal workloads and then predicting $\dot{V}O_2$ Max from submaximal heart rate 255

Summative Evaluation The process of judging achievement at the end of instruction 5

T

T-Scores Used to combine different tests together; usually rounded off to the nearest whole number and rarely negative 61

t-Test An inferential statistical test used to determine if two means are equal in value 83

Taxonomy A classification for parts of a system; the educational taxonomies for the cognitive, affective, and psychomotor domains are used to formulate educational objectives 418

Teacher's Standards A grading technique that compares students' scores to a standard developed by the teacher 143

Test-Retest Method The procedure used to correlate the scores of a test administered on each of two days; used to establish stability reliability 98

Texas Youth Fitness Test A motor fitness test, split into physical fitness components and motor ability components 335

True–False Item A knowledge test item that asks students to answer either *True* or *False* 422

Two-Component Model The method used to measure percent body fat from the underwater weighing method. The model assumes that the density of fat is $0.9\ g{\cdot}cc^{-1}$ and the fat-free weight is $1.0\ g{\cdot}cc^{-1}$ 289

U

Underwater Weighing Determining a person's body weight in water; one method used to determine body density. See also *hydrostatic weighing* 285

Useful Score A test score that can be used immediately or inserted into a formula with little effort 169

V

Validity The degree to which a test measures what it is supposed to measure 122

Variability The degree of heterogeneity in a set of scores; measures include the range and the standard deviation 51

Variance The square of the standard deviation 54

$\dot{V}O_2$ Max See *maximal oxygen uptake* 241

W

Wall Volley Tests Skill tests that require the student to repeatedly volley a ball against a wall 388

Z

z-Score A standard score with mean 0 and standard deviation 61

Name Index

Subject Index